The Palgrave Handbook of African Social Ethics

Editors
Nimi Wariboko
Boston University
Boston, MA, USA

Toyin Falola
Department of History
University of Texas
Austin, TX, USA

ISBN 978-3-030-36492-2   ISBN 978-3-030-36490-8 (eBook)
https://doi.org/10.1007/978-3-030-36490-8

© The Editor(s) (if applicable) and The Author(s) 2020
This work is subject to copyright. All rights are solely and exclusively licensed by the Publisher, whether the whole or part of the material is concerned, specifically the rights of translation, reprinting, reuse of illustrations, recitation, broadcasting, reproduction on microfilms or in any other physical way, and transmission or information storage and retrieval, electronic adaptation, computer software, or by similar or dissimilar methodology now known or hereafter developed.
The use of general descriptive names, registered names, trademarks, service marks, etc. in this publication does not imply, even in the absence of a specific statement, that such names are exempt from the relevant protective laws and regulations and therefore free for general use.
The publisher, the authors and the editors are safe to assume that the advice and information in this book are believed to be true and accurate at the date of publication. Neither the publisher nor the authors or the editors give a warranty, expressed or implied, with respect to the material contained herein or for any errors or omissions that may have been made. The publisher remains neutral with regard to jurisdictional claims in published maps and institutional affiliations.

Cover illustration: ManuelVelasco / Getty Images

This Palgrave Macmillan imprint is published by the registered company Springer Nature Switzerland AG.
The registered company address is: Gewerbestrasse 11, 6330 Cham, Switzerland

Nimi Wariboko • Toyin Falola
Editors

The Palgrave Handbook of African Social Ethics

palgrave
macmillan

Acknowledgments

This handbook would not have been possible without the contributions of the authors of the various chapters. They gladly joined us to make the dream of a handbook on African social ethics come true. Special thanks to Dr. Adeshina Afolayan of the University of Ibadan. He not only contributed a chapter but played an active role in recruiting contributors for us, and in the final phases of the project generously helped us to put the manuscripts in the format our publishers wanted. We also thank Philip Getz, Amy Invernizzi, and their team at Palgrave Macmillan for their infinite patience and for providing the platform to publish this handbook.

Nimi Wariboko
Toyin Falola

CONTENTS

1   Introduction   1
    Nimi Wariboko and Toyin Falola

Part I   Family and Community (Eros as in Belonging, Togetherness)   9

2   Ethics of Family, Community and Childrearing   11
    Victor Ojakorotu and Nelson Goldpin Obah-Akpowoghaha

3   Power Dynamics in Nuclear and Extended Families: A Feminist Foucauldian Analysis   27
    Olayinka Oyeleye

4   Abuses of Children (Labor and Witchcraft Accusations)   51
    Samson O. Ijaola

5   *Praying for Husbands!* Single Women Negotiating Faith and Patriarchy in Contemporary Kenya   69
    Damaris Parsitau

6   The Meaning of Human Person in the African Context   93
    David Nderitu

7   Personhood in Africa   103
    George Kotei Neequaye

8   African Communal Ethics   129
    Polycarp Ikuenobe

9 Between Community and My Mother: A Theory of Agonistic Communitarianism 147
Nimi Wariboko

Part II   Polity (Violence, Power, Figures) 165

10 Pluralism and African Conflict: Towards a Yoruba Theory of African Political Ethics of Neighbourliness 167
Olufemi Ronald Badru

11 Religion and Politics in Africa: An Assessment of Kwame Nkrumah's Legacy for Ghana 185
Ebenezer Obiri Addo

12 Ethics of Superpowers and Civil Wars in Africa 203
Comfort Olajumoke (Jumoke) Verissimo

13 When the Ancestors Wage War: Mystical Movements and the Ethics of War and Warfare 217
Georgette Mulunda Ledgister

14 State and Society in Africa: A Comparative Perspective 231
Olufemi Vaughan

15 Political Ethics of Kwame Nkrumah 247
Ebenezer Obiri Addo

16 Political Ethics of Léopold Sédar Senghor 257
Aliou Cissé Niang

17 The Political Ethics of Frantz Fanon 283
Chika C. Mba

Part III   Economy (Energies of Exchange, Market) 297

18 Spirit/Religion and Ethics in African Economies 299
J. Kwabena Asamoah-Gyadu

19 Corruption, Nepotism, and Anti-Bureaucratic Behaviors 317
Bola Dauda

20	The Bretton Woods Institutions and Economic Development in Africa Sunday Olaoluwa Dada	339
21	The Ethics of State Capture: Dangote and the Nigerian State Saheedat Adetayo	371

Part IV	Culture (Creativity, and Forms of Organizing Creativity, Muses)	389
22	Religion, Media and Ethics in Africa Anthony Okeregbe	391
23	Ethical Benchmarks in Life and Art of Fela Anikulapo-Kuti Sanya Osha	409
24	Ethical Thought of Kwasi Wiredu and Kwame Gyekye II George Kotei Neequaye	423
25	Ethical Thought of Paulin Hountondji George Kotei Neequaye	437
26	Strangers and Patriots: Anthony Kwame Appiah and the Ethics of Identity Adeshina Afolayan	453
27	Ritual Archives Toyin Falola	473

Part V	Religion (Comprehensive Worldview)	499
28	The Role of Religious Practitioners in Sustaining Social Morality Obaji Agbiji and Emem O. Agbiji	501
29	Religion and Social Justice in Africa Patrick Kofi Amissah	525
30	*The Spirit Names the Child*: Pentecostal Names and Trans-ethics Abimbola A. Adelakun	543

31	African Environmental Ethics Oluwatoyin Vincent Adepoju	569
32	Ethical Thought of Archbishop Desmond Tutu: Ubuntu and Tutu's Moral Modeling as Transformation and Renewal Sheila A. Otieno	589
33	"Reminders of What Once Was": The Ethics of Mercy Amba Oduyoye Oluwatomisin Oredein	605

Index   623

Notes on Contributors

Ebenezer Obiri Addo teaches Africana studies at Seton Hall University, South Orange, NJ, USA. He specializes in African religious tradition, politics, literatures, and cultures. His subfield is African diasporan studies. He is the author of *Kwame Nkrumah: A Case Study of Religion and Politics in Ghana* (1997) and co-author of *A Teacher's Guide to Chinua Achebe's Things Fall Apart* (2008).

Abimbola A. Adelakun is an assistant professor in the African/African Diaspora Department, the University of Texas, Austin, Texas, USA. Her areas of research are theater/performance, Pentecostalism/Pentecostal culture, spirituality/religious creativity, Yoruba studies, and black popular culture.

Oluwatoyin Vincent Adepoju is the founder and director of Compcros, Comparative Cognitive Processes and Systems, a research and publication system exploring diverse approaches to knowledge. His focus is on intersections of the visual and verbal arts, philosophy, and spirituality.

Saheedat Adetayo is a doctoral student in Philosophy at the University of Ibadan, Nigeria. Her areas of research include development studies, African philosophy, social and political philosophy, and feminist philosophy.

Adeshina Afolayan teaches philosophy at the University of Ibadan, Nigeria. His areas of specialization include philosophy of politics, cultural studies, and African philosophy. He is the co-editor of *Palgrave Handbook of African Philosophy* (2017), co-editor of *Pentecostalism and Politics in Africa* (2018), and the author of *Philosophy and National Development in Nigeria* (2018).

Emem O. Agbiji is a research fellow at the Research Institute for Theology and Religion, University of South Africa (UNISA), South Africa. Her research is on pastoral care, health, and development. She is the co-director of World Arise Initiative, Oklahoma, USA, and has authored academic articles.

Obaji Agbiji is a research fellow at the Research Institute for Theology and Religion, University of South Africa (UNISA), South Africa, and a Leadership and Management consultant in New Jersey, USA. He researches and writes on religion, development, leadership, ecology, and ethics.

Patrick Kofi Amissah is an honorary research fellow at the School of History, Archaeology and Religion, Cardiff University, UK. His research interests include biblical studies, contextual social justice, political theology, and pastoral care and counseling.

J. Kwabena Asamoah-Gyadu is Professor of Contemporary African Christianity and Pentecostal/Charismatic Theology at the Trinity Theological Seminary, Legon, Ghana. He has written widely on themes ranging from religion in Africa to the intersections in contemporary Pentecostalism and modern media on the continent. Asamoah-Gyadu is a fellow of the Ghana Academy of Arts and Sciences.

Olufemi Ronald Badru teaches philosophy and politics at the Lead City University, Ibadan, Nigeria. He works within political, moral, and legal philosophy. His recent publication is "An African Philosophical Account of Just War Theory," *Ethical Perspectives*, vol. 26, no. 2 (2019): 153–181.

Sunday Olaoluwa Dada teaches philosophy at the Department of Philosophy, Ekiti State University, Ado-Ekiti, Nigeria. His areas of research interest include development studies, African philosophy, and cultural studies. His publications have appeared in reputable local and international journals.

Bola Dauda is a retired scholar whose works have been translated into Spanish, French, and Chinese. His areas of specialization include the politics of representation, nation-building, bureaucracy-democracy relations, ethics, and governance. He is the co-author of *Decolonizing Nigeria 1945–1960* (2017).

Toyin Falola is the Jacob and Frances Sanger Mossiker Chair in the Humanities and distinguished teaching professor at the University of Texas, Austin, USA. His research interests include African history, African American studies, and Nollywood. Among his many books are *Music, Performance and African Identities* (2012), *Yoruba Fiction, Orature and Culture* (2011), *Facts, Fictions, and African Creative Imaginations* (co-edited, 2010), and *Cultural Identity and Nationalism* (2009)

Samson O. Ijaola teaches in the Department of Philosophy and Religious Studies, Samuel Adegboyega University, Ogwa, Edo State, Nigeria. His scholarly works have appeared in national and international edited volumes and peer-reviewed journals. His research areas include Christian studies, philosophy of religion, science and religion, gender studies, peace and conflict studies, and African studies. He is also the editor of *SAU Journal of Humanities*.

Polycarp Ikuenobe teaches philosophy at Kent State University, Kent, Ohio, USA. His areas of specialization include social and political philosophy and African philosophy. He is the author of *Philosophical Perspectives of Communalism and Morality in African Traditions* (2006).

Georgette Mulunda Ledgister teaches African Christianity at Agnes Scott College in Atlanta, Georgia, USA. Her areas of specialization include social ethics, comparative religions, conflict transformation, and gender studies. She provides conflict response training to corporations, civic organizations, and faith-based institutions.

Chika C. Mba is a research fellow at the Institute of African Studies, University of Ghana, Legon, Ghana. His areas of specialization include global justice, African philosophy, Frantz Fanon, and postcolonial theory.

David Nderitu teaches philosophy at Egerton University, Kenya. His areas of specialization include bioethics, African philosophy, and ancient philosophy. Nderitu is a Ph.D. candidate at Moi University, Kenya.

George Kotei Neequaye teaches African philosophy, Christian ethics, ethics and leadership, mother-tongue hermeneutics, and liturgics at the Trinity Theological Seminary, Legon-Ghana. He is a contributor to the book *Rethinking the Great Commission: Emerging African Perspectives* (2018).

Aliou Cissé Niang is Associate Professor of New Testament at Union Theological Seminary in New York, USA. Niang is the author of *Faith and Freedom in Galatia and Senegal* (2009); co-author of *Text, Image, and Christians in the Graeco-Roman World* (2012); "Catholic Epistles," *Anselm Companion to the New Testament* (2014); "Catholic Epistles," *Anselm Companion to the Bible* (2014); "Space and Human Agency in the Making of the Story of Gershom through a Senegalese Christian Lens," *Forum-Journal of Biblical Literature* (2015); "Islandedness, Translation, and Creolization," in *Islands, Islanders, and Bible: RumInations* (2015); "Christianity in Senegal" in Lamport and Jenkins, *Encyclopedia of Christianity in the Global South* (2018); and "Diola Religion" in Lamport and Jenkins, *Encyclopedia of Christianity in the Global South* (2018).

Nelson Goldpin Obah-Akpowoghaha is a postdoctoral fellow at North-West University, South Africa. His areas of specialization include peace and conflict studies, African politics, comparative politics, and political theory.

Victor Ojakorotu is Professor of Politics and International Relations and the Deputy School Director of Government Studies, North-West University, South Africa. He is a versatile scholar in international relations with numerous books and articles to his credit.

Anthony Okeregbe teaches philosophy at the University of Lagos, Nigeria. His areas of specialization include philosophy of religion and existential inquiries into African lifeworlds. He is the co-editor of *A Study in African Socio-Political Philosophy* (2012).

Oluwatomisin Oredein is Assistant Professor of Black Religious Traditions and Constructive Theology and Ethics at Brite Divinity School, Fort Worth, TX, USA. Her work engages articulations of African feminist and womanist theologies and ethics.

Sanya Osha teaches philosophy at the Tshwane University of Technology, Pretoria, South Africa.

Sheila A. Otieno is a Ph.D. candidate at Boston University's School of Theology, specializing in Social Ethics. Her research centers around personhood, community dynamics, and aspects of belonging on the African continent based on the cultural transfers of African religiosity into social life.

Olayinka Oyeleye is a doctoral candidate in the Department of Philosophy, University of Ibadan, Nigeria. Her research areas include ethics, feminist philosophy, and gender studies, among others. Some of her works include "Feminism(s) and Oppression: Rethinking Gender from a Yoruba Perspective" (*Handbook of African Philosophy*) and "Ìwà l'ewà: Toward a Yorùbá Feminist Ethics" (*Yorùbá Studies Review*)

Damaris Parsitau teaches religion and gender at Egerton University, Kenya. Her areas of specialization include religion, women's bodies and sexualities, religion, gender, and sexual citizenship, and African Pentecostalism. She has authored many articles, book chapters, and monographs.

Olufemi Vaughan is the Alfred Sargent Lee & Mary Ames Lee Professor of African Studies at Amherst College, USA. He is the author and editor of many books and scholarly articles, including *Religion and the Making of Nigeria* (2016) and *Nigerian Chiefs: Traditional Power in Modern Politics, 1890s–1990s* (2000).

Comfort Olajumoke (Jumoke) Verissimo is studying for a Ph.D. in English at the University of Alberta, Canada. Her research is on trauma and/as grievance in the Nigeria-Biafra War literature. Her latest work is a novel, *A Small Silence* (2019).

Nimi Wariboko is the Walter G. Muelder Professor of Social Ethics at Boston University, USA.

CHAPTER 1

Introduction

Nimi Wariboko and Toyin Falola

The *Handbook of African Social Ethics* (HASE) fills a gap in the study of Africa. There is currently no single companion or handbook on African Social Ethics. There are, however, companions and handbooks on African philosophy, which have limited entries on social ethics. There are one or two books (especially on religion) that come closest to the kind of transdisciplinary engagement in Africa's ethics and society that HASE undertakes. But they are not texts on ethics or philosophy as they are often narrowly focused on religious examination of the issues facing the continent and on certain subjects that contain materials close to what the HASE provides.

The key benefits of HASE over such books or companions are (a) HASE pays special attention to issues pertaining to ethics more generally rather than aided by a religious lens; (b) HASE represents a broader scope of scholarship, attending to the more intersectional and interdisciplinary aspects of African ethos and the moral aspects of African society; (c) HASE includes a wider range of scholars (i.e. not only those in religious studies) who articulate the wide gamut of moral sources available within African cultural experiences and how societies appropriate them for ethical use; and (d) HASE makes allowances for alternative moral sources available right from precolonial time and in substitutive epistemologies, permitting an expansive (and additional) spectrum of previously unconsidered systems of knowledge.

Specifically, this handbook is designed with three basic audiences in mind. First, for mainstream academic African and Africana social ethicists and philosophers in Africa and the African Diaspora who are interested in the direction their discipline needs to take in the twenty-first century. Second, it is meant for

N. Wariboko (✉)
Boston University, Boston, MA, USA

T. Falola
Department of History, University of Texas, Austin, TX, USA

© The Author(s) 2020
N. Wariboko, T. Falola (eds.), *The Palgrave Handbook of African Social Ethics*, https://doi.org/10.1007/978-3-030-36490-8_1

the students of African social ethics who urgently need to know how to link academic discourses of ethics to the lived experiences of Africans and to the promotion of human flourishing on the continent. HASE is also meant for the general researchers in African history and development who are interested in the social-ethical dimensions of the debate on how Africa can truly harness its indigenous ethos and global civilizational patterns in order to make significant sociopolitical progress in the twenty-first century.

We are painfully aware that this Handbook is not as comprehensive as we wanted when we embarked on it many years ago. We wanted to generate many more chapters than what we have here, so we could cover almost all possible areas of African social ethics. We engaged the scholars to produce the relevant chapters, but as this kind of projects often goes, a number of our colleagues did not deliver their chapters even after extending the deadline for submission of chapters multiple times. Yet this Handbook provides excellent perspectives and insightful chapters on social ethics in Africa.

Indeed, it contains a robust collection of leading-edge discourses on African social ethics and ethical practices that speak to students, scholars, and educated citizens in the twenty-first century. It focuses on how social ethics as a stand-alone discipline or as a subdiscipline under philosophy hits the ground; that is, how the ethical thoughts of Africans are forged within the context of everyday life and how in turn ethical and philosophical thoughts inform day-to-day living. The goal is to offer bold, incisive, and fresh interpretations of the ethical life and thought in Africa in a style and presentation accessible to the average reader. Designed and published in the formats of print and e-book and as a perpetual online living reference work, *The Handbook of African Social Ethics* creates a cutting-edge moment for cumulating, updating, and extending studies of African social ethics beyond the present and into the future.

The typical handbook on ethics tells the story of ethics as theoretical debates, elucidations, or discursive practices. This Handbook tells the story of African ethics as a dynamic and open social reality that bears the marks of changes, ruptures, contradictions, and passages of time. This is to say that ethics is understood as a historical phenomenon, and it is best examined as a historical movement, the dynamics of ethos of a people, rather than as a theoretical construct. It is ethics as lived, experienced in everyday life, and not ethics as argued in academic tomes.

If we want to focus on ethics as lived, as experienced historical-social existence, how do we organize the discussions or contents of this Handbook? The short answer is that the organizational patterns of life should condition or determine the categories of discourses or entries in a handbook or companion on African social ethics. This is what we have exactly done in this Handbook.

Unfortunately, this is not the usual approach. The typical approach of handbooks of ethics is to divide their chapters or entries according to the subdisciplines in the field of ethics, regions, periods, intellectual developments, or key thinkers. HASE, however, takes a different approach: it is configured around the five major spheres of life—family, polity, economy, creativity, and dominion (religion). Our approach, centered on life, does not necessarily reject the regnant approach; it only offers a different organizational principle, which is robust enough to incorporate the categories of the regnant method. The concerns, advantages, and sensibilities of the regnant organizational form are embedded in our discourses and configured to yield their insights under the rubrics of the spheres of life. Each chapter approaches ethics as a process that unlocks the power of truth, justice, and harmony embodied in the forms of human sociality or exemplified in the five spheres of life.

Our effort to privilege spheres of life in a sense pays homage to the traditional African conception of ethics as ethos (social practices and discursive practices) that enhances life; promotes harmony between all spheres, dimensions, and forms of life; and encourages human flourishing. This Handbook seeks to demonstrate how Africans have been able to integrate the powers or forces of life that *stand behind* and *stand with* the five spheres of life to create viable civilizations. No civilization or large historical organization of social existence exists without the viable integrations of the forces, energies with their institutional patterns.

The contents of *The Handbook of African Social Ethics* are organized to pay a great deal of attention to the "spiritual and moral energies" behind human flourishing and civilizations in Africa. The five basic spheres of life (family, polity, economy, creativity, and dominion [religion]) are often correlated with five powers—five forms of spiritual energies that invite and even capture people's loyalties (these powers or energies *eros/familial piety*, *mars/violence*, the *muses/forces of creativity*, *mammon/economy*, and *dominion*/worldview, comprehensive moral vision, religion).[1] These powers not only enable people to move beyond the boundaries and capabilities left to them by their ancestors but also, sometimes, anchor them to antiquated practices, institutions, and beliefs.

"Humans are sexual, political, economic, cultural, and religious creatures. Each one of these dimensions of life involves a certain potentiality and needs an institutional matrix to house, guide and channel its energies."[2] They are organized into *spheres* of life. Eros relates to the family sphere, muses to the arts and mass media, mars (violence) to the political, mammon to economy, and religion to the whole society. Religion defines what is right, good, and fitting in the other spheres and in human relationship with God, gods, or spirits. These spiritual energies not only guide current practices, they are implicated in the human drive toward transcendence and the future.

The Handbook of African Social Ethics aspires to convey a critical sense of African ethics as a longing and practice of human flourishing, the fluid, delicate interactions between the moral and spiritual energies that claim the loyalties of Africans, and the various creative institutional matrices they have created to guide the five powers to engender greater possibilities of excellence (actualization of their potentialities) for better levels of human flourishing in everyday existence.

Overall, this Handbook presents the ethical practices, institutions, and thoughts in Africa as transdisciplinary subject matters that are critical in the interpretation and understanding of contemporary African societies. Thus, we hope that the readership of *Handbook of Africa Social Ethics* will not be confined to students of philosophy and social ethics alone but will include the wider readerships in the humanities and social sciences—and even beyond.

The implicit view of ethics in the chapters that constitute this book is expansive. Here, ethics points us to ends beyond the existing forms of human sociality. It insists that an existing order can find those ends beyond itself only when its agents rise beyond themselves. Thus, HASE offers analytical insights not for only Africans to engage their inherited moral systems and emergent ethos but also offers resources that can nudge some of them to resist existing orders that absolutize themselves and to forge and strain toward a new window of "elsewhere" and "else-when."

> This idea of window points us toward both what is present and what is absent in an extant order. In ethics we are trying to paint a portrait of our community and/or the subject of our focus. The portrait becomes a space (e.g. a "rectangle") through which the community or the subject is seen. But it also provides the lens, perspective to see what is absent in the community. Like all windows, an "ethical-window" marks the boundary between what is currently obtained (what is inside the house) and what is outside, what we can strive for in the open, unconfined space. Through this window we are trying to see what is outside of ourselves, outside of our current existing order, but it is not always totally transparent; we see through an inherited (though continually reworked) mental representation. We are trying to see the world, the cosmos outside, through our particular *throwness* into the world.[3]

This Handbook is in large part an attempt to provide a window on creativity and an avenue to show how the creative principles at work in African communities and the larger cosmos are harnessed for human flourishing. The expansive view of ethics as exemplified in HASE relates the inner life of social institutions to the invisible rhythms and creative force that sustain and move the universe as grasped by Africans in their everydayness.

Since we are committed to providing an expansive view of social ethics in Africa, the chapters here are not calibrated to either argue that African ethic is communitarian or individualistic. Collectively, they tend to strike a delicate balance between these two extremes, presenting a general view of the themes under discussion. Often in books on African social ethics, scholars present the view that the ethic worth promoting in Africa is communalism (communitarianism); some of them going as far as to argue it is the only authentic African indigenous ethic, or it was only this ethic that existed in precolonial Africa. This is not a correct position. African ethic was not monolithic or static over the ages before colonialism. Historian Moses Ochonu aptly makes this point in a recent book. He argues that too much epistemic visibility has been given to the "incorrect notion of precolonial Africa as a site of subsistent communalism, an undifferentiated societal continuum supposedly unspoiled by the twin capitalist evils of the profit motive and private wealth accumulation…. Evidence…

indicates that a communitarian ethos underpinned and mediated the entrepreneurial pursuits of precolonial Africans."[4]

Philosopher Kwame Gyekye could not be any clearer on this point than what he has declared about Akan social thought. He maintains that communality and individuality coexist in Akan ethos, illustrating it with indigenous art motif of the two-headed crocodile with one stomach. Gyekye argues that:

> The symbol of the crossed crocodiles with two heads and a common stomach has great significance for Akan social thought. While it suggests the rational underpinnings of the concept of communalism, it does not do so to the detriment of individuality. The concept of communalism, as it is understood in Akan thought, therefore does not overlook individual rights, interests, desires, and responsibilities, nor does it imply the absorption of the individual will into the "communal will," or seek to eliminate individual responsibility and accountability. Akan social thought attempts to establish a delicate balance between concepts of communality and individuality.[5]

What Gyekye argues here applies, by and large, to most African communities. There is now a mix of communitarianism and individualism, cooperation, and conflict—two systems or ethos in interaction in modern Africa. The coexistence of the two systems has implication for how social ethicists evaluate African community leaders. In our opinion, good leaders are those who prepare their "communities to allow their members to develop their potentialities in the pursuit of ever-greater common good. How well a community does this will depend on how it allows individuals to develop their unique traits, capabilities, and potentialities and on how well these individual endowments are related to each other in the pursuit of the common good. A [good] community is the one that is adept at combining these two opposite tendencies or processes: a movement toward uniqueness counterbalanced by movement toward union."[6] Ultimately, the overarching perspective that emerges from this Handbook is that African social ethic is a set of social practices that are geared toward the creation of possibilities for community and participation by all its members so that their potentialities can be drawn out for the common good.

The 32 chapters (excluding this introductory chapter) of this Handbook are distributed into five sections, corresponding to the five spheres of life. There are eight chapters in (a) family and Community sphere; (b) eight chapters in the sphere of polity (violence, power, and figures); (c) four chapters in the economic sphere (energies of exchange and market); (d) six chapters in the sphere of culture (creativity, forms of organizing creativity, muses); and (e) six chapters in the sphere of religion (comprehensive worldview). Collectively, they offer us an insightful examination of the ethos of present-day sub-Saharan Africa.

> Ethos concerns the operational morality of a people, their deepest presuppositions, the inner guidance system of their society that defines the mutual responsiveness of citizens to one another, that conditions the kind of relationships

deemed appropriate between leadership and institutions, and evokes the necessary loyalty of citizens to leaders and systems. It is ethos that shows what is the "fitting" thing to do in a situation and the "proper" expectations, roles, and functions in any given environment. What is the "proper" thing to do by institutions or leaders requires what anthropologist Clifford Geertz calls "thick descriptions." Those morally formed in a particular society have the "thick descriptions" of any interactions at their fingertips. They orient their behaviors, legitimize their actions, and condition their spiritual energies.[7]

These 32 chapters interrogate the current state and future possibilities of contemporary ethos of African communities, offering a window into social practices that ground normative behaviors and in turn gives us a comprehensive survey of the ground norms that anchor social practices. The lessons contained in this book are significant for understanding how citizens, leaders, policymakers, and scholars might go about generating restructuring, remoralizing, and renewing African communities for socioeconomic development.

Notes

1. See also Nimi Wariboko, *The Principle of Excellence: A Framework for Social Ethics* (Lanham, Lexington Books, 2009), 35–36; Max Stackhouse, "Introduction" in *God and Globalization: Volume 1: Religion and the Powers of the Common Life*, ed. Max Stackhouse with Peter Paris (Harrisburg, PA: Trinity Press International, 2000), 35.
2. Max Stackhouse, "Introduction" in *God and Globalization: Volume 2: The Spirit and the Modern Authorities*, ed. Max Stackhouse with Don S. Browning (Harrisburg, PA: Trinity Press International, 2001), 5. In another place, he wrote:

   [P]eople carve out spheres of social activity, clusters of institutions that house, guide, and constrain, and in certain ways, permit, even encourage, these powers to operate. Each sphere is regulated by customary or legislated rules, and each is defined by its own specification of ends and means, as these accord with the nature of the activity and its place in the whole society or culture. Each sphere develops methods of fulfilling its own standards, ways to mark accomplished goals, definitions of excellence, and standards of success. (See Max Stackhouse, *God and Globalization*, vol. 1, 39)

3. Nimi Wariboko, *Methods of Ethical Analysis: Between Theology, History and Literature* (Eugene, Or.: Wipf & Stock, 2013), 21–22.
4. Moses E. Ochonu, "Introduction: Toward African Entrepreneurship and Business History" in Moses E. Ochonu (ed.) *Entrepreneurship in Africa: A History Approach* (Bloomington, IN: Indiana University Press, 2018), pp. 1–27; quotation from p. 16.
5. Kwame Gyekye, *An Essay on African Philosophical Thought: The Akan Conceptual Scheme* (Cambridge: Cambridge University Press, 1987), 160–61.
6. Wariboko, *Principle of Excellence*, 8.
7. Nimi Wariboko, *Ethics and Society in Nigeria: Identity, History, Political Theory* (Rochester: University of Rochester Press, 2019), 131.

Bibliography

Gyekye, Kwame. 1987. *An Essay on African Philosophical Thought: The Akan Conceptual Scheme*. Cambridge: Cambridge University Press.

Ochonu, Moses E. 2018. Introduction: Toward African Entrepreneurship and Business History. In *Entrepreneurship in Africa: A History Approach*, ed. Moses E. Ochonu, 1–27. Bloomington: Indiana University Press.

Stackhouse, Max. 2000. Introduction. In *God and Globalization: Volume 1: Religion and the Powers of the Common Life*, ed. Max Stackhouse with Peter Paris, 1–52. Harrisburg: Trinity Press International.

———. 2001. Introduction. In *God and Globalization: Volume 2: The Spirit and the Modern Authorities*, ed. Max Stackhouse with Don S. Browning, 1–36. Harrisburg: Trinity Press International.

Wariboko, Nimi. 2009. *The Principle of Excellence: A Framework for Social Ethics*. Lanham: Lexington Books.

———. 2013. *Methods of Ethical Analysis: Between Theology, History and Literature*. Eugene: Wipf & Stock.

———. 2019. *Ethics and Society in Nigeria: Identity, History, Political Theory*. Rochester: University of Rochester Press.

PART I

Family and Community (Eros as in Belonging, Togetherness)

CHAPTER 2

Ethics of Family, Community and Childrearing

Victor Ojakorotu and Nelson Goldpin Obah-Akpowoghaha

INTRODUCTION

In the African traditional setting, parenting or childrearing is perceived to take different patterns, which is able to build the child to be a responsible person. Though there are various parenting styles, there are ways in which the African parent brings up a child in order for the child to imbibe the cultural values of the land and also be a responsible adult. Some of these forms of parenting are through storytelling (folk tales), the extended family, traditional rites and the mother's care, attention and love. One may ask: are these cultural practices still in vogue or have been impaired and distorted by external forces? (Amos 2013: 6; Ganga and Chinyoka 2017: 38).

Available literature and academic discourse on ethics and childrearing in Africa have stressed certain ancient practices in the continent of Africa undermining the impact of colonial system, Western and European modernisation in recent time (Caldwell and Caldwell 1987; Goody 1982; Lloyd and Blanc 1996 cited in Madhavan and Gross 2013). Africa as continent is endowed with valuable norms, cultures and values that serve as finest mechanism for community, childrearing and a body of ethics. But these qualities were massively eroded during slavery and colonial systems that seem barbaric to colonial masters. Colonial masters introduced Christianity, certain strange cultures and belief in Africa, and these have occupied the centre stage of childrearing and ethics of family in the continent. This has been properly captured by work of Patricia Mawusi Amos (2013), who revealed that "Research shows that majority of books concerning infancy are from the western world (Tomlinson & Swartz, 2003 cited in Amos 2015). In view of that African cultural values as far as

V. Ojakorotu (✉) • N. G. Obah-Akpowoghaha
North-West University, Potchefstroom, South Africa

© The Author(s) 2020
N. Wariboko, T. Falola (eds.), *The Palgrave Handbook of African Social Ethics*, https://doi.org/10.1007/978-3-030-36490-8_2

parenting is concerned are being forgotten and the western practice is rather adopted" (Amos 2013: 65).

The erosion of African values vis-à-vis ethics of family and childrearing have been intensified by the doctrine of globalisation centre on imperialism. Globalisation and imperialism have to do with integrating nations and individuals into global cultures and values with the purpose of capturing, subjecting other cultures and values in the international system. This has been evident in the area of language, eating habit, ceremonies, marriage, salutation, manner of greetings, worshipping and so on. In order to be a part and parcel of modernisation and benefit from the residues of globalisation, most African countries have aligned with Western, European and other cultures. This and among others have affected numerous families and communities in the continent of Africa in relation to childrearing. In line with this thought, Ganga and Chinyoka (2017: 38) argued that before the introduction of Western and European system of education in Africa, there existed traditional ways of child-rearing patterns. "Clear-cut roles, obligations, rights, expectations and sanctions were prescribed" (Durojaiye 1996 in Mwamwenda 2010 cited in Ganga and Chinyoka 2017: 38). With the advent of formal education and the influence of different cultures, the traditional parent-child relationships and child-rearing practices have been altered. Few traditional African communities still retain certain aspects of the rearing patterns intact, but many have been diluted by the Western culture (Ganga and Chinyoka 2017: 38).

Modern African child has been reared based on Christian, Islamic doctrines and foreign technologies. For those within Christian faith revolved around the lifestyle of Christians in Western and European societies, and while those within Islamic faith pattern their life style along Islamic nations.

The argument in this piece is that there is no absolute ethics and values in contemporary African states in childrearing. Existing families and communities in Africa, particularly the family of the rich or elites, absorbed what is at play in advanced countries, and which form the pattern of childrearing in communities and families in Africa. "Evidence from some African countries shows that there are no clear-cut child-rearing patterns but rather a combination of both African and Western styles"(Siyakwazi and Siyakwazi 2014 cited in Ganga and Chinyoka 2017: 38). The act of greetings or salutations, singing, marriage, building confidence in a child, eating and dressing, these and among others have been modified in the continent of Africa. In some African communities and families, there is absolute doctrine of assimilation of foreign norms and values. Most average African families hired the services of nannies, house help and other alien childrearing values in bringing up their children. In this case, the house help (caregiver) bath the child, feed and mode the child based on what is in vague on social media. Gay, lesbian practices and sex education have been accepted in some families in Africa, and parents have considered it as a duty to inform their children what it means. Sex education whatever the forms and pattern is a taboo in African families before colonialism and likewise a child who cannot greet and speak in her mother's tongue. Consequently, the twenty-first-century African communities and families are facing series of challenges in relation to childrearing due to an increase in knowledge from the advanced countries made available through science. The goal of childrearing entails nurturing, indoctrinating and socialising the child based on the ancestral traditions and values in that community, but most communities in Africa seem to be losing what constitute the norms and values of childrearing. It is on this note this chapter points out the challenges in childrearing in Africa and provide a way forward in reviving the handed-down childrearing norms and values in communities in Africa.

However, the arrangement of this chapter builds on the discussion of items such as ethics and the child, family and the community, the attachment theory, brief overview of African culture and practices of childrearing, science and information and communications technology (ICT), and we draw the conclusion. The methodological approach is premised on content analysis, arising from secondary sources of data collection.

Conceptual Review

Ethics and the Child

The philosophy of ethics vis-à-vis the child is anchored on caregivers to honour the cultural values, perspectives, beliefs of the immediate community and points the child to the beauty of life. The United Nations (UN) through her agencies, United Nations International Children's Emergency Fund (UNICEF) and in collaboration with World Health Organization (WHO) roll out plan to Care for Child Development (CCD) towards parenting practices and the good behaviour demonstrated in the course of the process. Some of its ideas on the rights of the child are premised on the child's desires and the parents should strive to fulfil it; in other words, the child's rights are more paramount over the parents, and this seems absurd in most African communities. African families are intertwined, child and the parents are shared same bold; and the notion of given a child separate identity on the grounds of specialised code of conduct in bringing up the child seems problematic.

Studies have identified that the general idea of UNICEF is to develop the innate ability of the child and create an atmosphere of holistic development in order to be a better person free from the gene of domestic violence characteristics. The population of study of the CCD is at the poor communities and low-middle-income level whose ethics of fairness and justice is inadequate to give the best to the child. A study by Jolly (2007) revealed that more than 200 million children under the age of five years in the aforementioned societies are not fulfilling their potential due to nutritional deficiencies, spread of uncontrollable diseases, environmental toxin and so on. The study placed emphasis on addressing biological and psychological risks of the child as a process of giving the best to the child. Again, on a similar note, Nutrit (2017) argued that placing more emphasis on the child over the parents in caregiving can cause ethical concerns in most communities and families.

Most of these new ideas about caregivers are Western and European inventions that are suitable in those societies and vividly made explicit by US research institutions and other English-speaking countries (Henrich et al. 2010). Although the works of Keller and Kartner (2013) recommended universal standards that recognised communities' values and norms, the point of implementations has generated behavioural academic discourse towards the parameters of children and parenting on its adoption.

Another study conducted in Senegal-based non-governmental organisation (NGO) Tostan by Weber, Fernald and Diop (2017) identified that most of the CCD interventions in the country rarely give adequate attention to people due to the Western patterns of lifestyle and practices, premised on one-on-one practices and playing mood using a discourse which is at variance to the Senegalese caregiver system of parents and child relationship. A critical knowledge of CCD ideas exposed the families belonging to low-income communities into a stigmatised situation and making them second-class citizens in their own communities upon these Western styles of caregivers.

Family and the Community

Family values provide cultural template for the child's development and life decisions, especially career, mode of operations, selections and reactions to the world. Introvert or extrovert parents genetically and socially affect the actions and inaction of the child. The essence of the activities of UNICEF in CCD is to make the child see beyond his/her family's incubations and environment. The family teaches the child the culture, norms and traditions of his/her nation; studies have identified that the intervention programmes of UNICEF to Care for the Child and Development (CCD) in low-income societies have created an ethical challenge, whereby the child experienced total assimilation of the Western and European cultures besides his/her family values and tradition. An investigation performed by Jolly (2007) on the Senegalese serves as a reference point. In most African communities, in addition to regional language or mother tongue, the child speaks fluently other languages such as English, French, and Portuguese. Similarly the mode of dressing and eating has been codified and re-socialised in line with Western and European norms and cultures, and these have elicited unanswered ethical questions about the suitability of UNICEF interventions to Car for the Child and Development (CCD) (Gilda et al. n.d.). Arising from this pitfall, the United Nations through UNICEF has expended her programmes in the developing countries that make provisions for involving communities' leaders and chiefs towards recognising the child's trait, culture and norms. Also the National Association for the Education of Young Children (NAEYC) (2011), in its Code of Ethical Conduct, Statement of Commitment and embraced by the Association for Childhood Education International and Southern Early Childhood Association utilised by the National Association for Family Child Care put up certain principles in position of the child, families and community towards given the best in the development of the child. On the child's ethical responsibilities, it says that:

> Childhood is a unique and valuable stage in the human life cycle. Our paramount responsibility is to provide care and education in settings that are safe, healthy, nurturing, and responsive for each child. We are committed to supporting children's development and learning; respecting individual differences; and helping children learn to live, play, and work cooperatively. We are also committed to promoting children's self-awareness, competence, self-worth, resiliency, and physical well-being. (NAEYC 2011)

The above assertion on the place of the child in caregiving can be associated with the initial setbacks accompanying the CCD initiatives in low-income societies that are predominantly living in Africa. These families and communities seem to be stigmatised being regarded as poor and tied to out-dated beliefs and lifestyle (Gilda et al. n.d.). In view of this, NAEYC (2011) has re-echoed and advocated strongly with respect to ethical responsibility towards families that:

> Families are of primary importance in children's development. Because the family and the early childhood practitioner have a common interest in the child's well-being, we acknowledge a primary responsibility to bring about communication, cooperation, and collaboration between the home and early childhood program in ways that enhance the child's development.

Corroborating the above observations, NAEYC has added that the immediate community is sacrosanct to the early childhood programmes, which are enshrined with the family and other institutions that show care to the development of the child. It further stated that their duties to the immediate community are anchored on the provisions of an enduring programme that catered for the numerous demands of nuclear families, in cooperation with designated institutions and specialised bodies that look after the needs and well-being of the child and the community as a whole (NAEYC 2011). The body reiterated that:

> As individuals, we acknowledge our responsibility to provide the best possible programs of care and education for children and to conduct ourselves with honesty and integrity. Because of our specialized expertise in early childhood development and education and because the larger society shares responsibility for the welfare and protection of young children, we acknowledge a collective obligation to advocate for the best interests of children within early childhood programs and in the larger community and to serve as a voice for young children everywhere. (NAEYC 2011)

The above declaration revealed some thoughts in parental literature, which have stood the test of time. The methods of creating emotional and psychological bonds between the child and the caregivers (mother) help in building the child's confidence, stability, refinement, and so on into his/her adulthood. In other words, there are scholarly works that have revealed unique ways of building a bond between the caregiver and child towards securing good environment for communication (Vivian and Danya 2006). This helps in the growth and proper development of the child that are seen as nonverbal devices, which include actions such as facial expression and eye contact demonstration.

This involves warm smiles which influences the entire day of the child leading to good sleep. Second is feeding; here, the caregiver has to observe the child and deduce when the child is hungry and also identify the best ways of the feeding process: holding the child close while breastfeeding gives emotional and psychological attachment; the caregiver has to introduce a memorable process so that the child will be zealous to feed and feel secure with the caregiver. Likewise, the bottle-feeding process should also go through the same mechanism with the breastfeeding whereby holding the child is an important device of ensuring emotional peace and secure mood of the child. Third, gentle handling entails avoiding harsh handling of the child, and if the child is very young in his/her age, a support in the head shows love, care, secure mood and the child feels safe in the hands of that particular caregiver. Fourth, rhythmic movement—it entails swinging, gentle jiggling (not shaking), dancing with the caregiver and rocking, leading to happy health of the child. Fifth, a soft soothing voice implies singing or talking to the child. The child enjoys the whole process; it serves as a source of building a distinctive language and skills, and the sound of the caregiver's voice activates his/her secure attachment mechanism. These observations have been found in Bowlby's attachment theory of the child and parental development. The work of John Bowlby on the child's development has attracted global attention and which has been introduced by health workers and other scientists towards making the child a better person in any community around the world.

Attachment Theory

The term attachment was coined by a paediatrician William Sears in one of his publications in 1993 where he identified certain variables such as preparing for pregnancy, birth and parenthood; feeding with love and respect; responding and reacting with sensitivity; nurturing devices; ensuring safety in bed rest and in environmental and psychological aspects; providing reliable and loving caring process; engaging in event rewarding discipline process; and ensuring balance in personal and the family life as a whole. In bringing up a child to his or her best form requires emotional and physical tie or bond formed with the child's primary caregiver—normally the parents—but it may be the nanny (house help). This has been observed as biological instinct to always be close to the caregiver for the sake of normal growth and development within the context of safety. However, the works of John Bowlby (1969) and Mary Ainsworth are notable and instructive, which tend to establish three attachment variables such as secure, resistant and disorganised. It has been argued that babies who experience secure attachment enjoy caregiver's company, thereby cry less, are happier, look healthier and cooperate more. Ainsworth et al. (1978) revealed that caregivers who are securely attached to the child tend to be highly sensitive and responsive to the child's desires. She added that when the caregivers serve as an embodiment of security and safety to the child, the atmosphere tends to be beautiful to the child, who readily explores and fearlessly launches into various units in societies. Literature has indicated that if this bond is not secure between the child and the caregiver(s), the mother who usually serves as the caregiver will experience psychological trauma and depression, that is, inadequate parenting skills can result in future dilemma for the child (Vivian and Danya 2006).

Argument on What Attachment Theories Constitute

Scientists first discovered cases of disordered attachment during the 1930s and 1940s when these groups of scholars identified the strange consequences of raising children in certain units. Scientists like Kleinina and John Bowlby who were psychiatrist and psychoanalyst, respectively, started to see from the perspective of the adverse influence on development of few maternal help and sought information on acute distress of children below the age of five years who are separated from their primary caregiver. He further observed that a close mother-infant relationship was essential for socio-emotional adjustment, which is strategically important for the mental development of a child that entails warmness, intimacy and continuous relationship with the mother leading both to maximum satisfaction (Bowlby 1953).

Recent developmental studies have come up with different kinds of challenges to attachment-based theories of child development, as the occurrence of longitudinal findings reveals the need to see the consistency and validity of attachment-based theory, Sroufe, Egeland, and colleagues' (Roisman et al. 2002), sequence to a chart of high-risk and lack of caregivers to children to adolescent, reveals considerable inconsistencies between expectations based on primary child's evaluation of attachment and adolescent appearances. Their discoveries provide information that attachment is feasibly present over some time, experiments, attachment evident or its representations are prone to hard and confuse life styles which weak in predictive power towards futuristic space of a child that needs care (Weinfield et al. 2000).

Sroufe et al. (1999) have advanced that the problem of applying attachment theory to forecasts: Initial encounter is not a function of later pathology in a rectilinear way; however, it contains an important process, which is complex, systemic, and transactional nature of development. And they further added that the involvement of roles like selection, engagement and interpretation of succeeding knowledge and applying natural things as an aid for advancement. More so, in difficult cases where the child is apprehensive from the beginning of attachment, this doesn't represent a primary infect of psychopathology but is an initiator of conduits probabilistically associated with later pathology.

Other findings reveal no precise evidence of a point that cut across psychological problems in older adopted children and insecure attachment relationships in a child. Singer et al. (1985) established a comparable value of attachment between biological and non-biological (adoptive and non-adoptive parents). They discovered that for average middle-class parents, absence of early contact with a non-biological child does not forecast anxious adoptive mother to child attachment. The investigations further revealed that higher amounts of psychological and learning problems among non-biological adopted child(ren) cannot be identified to insecure attachment styles between adoptive parents and children in infancy.

Another study by Juffer and Rosenboom (1997) unveiled that less than 80% of the adopted infants were securely attached to their caregivers regardless of the history of whether caregivers have given birth or not. These revelations suggest that the adoption experience itself, and all that the pre- and post-adoptive experiences may mean for the child and caregiver, is not a predictor of negative parent-child relationships, outside of other factors such as early expressive or bodily deprivation.

A Brief Overview of the African Culture and Childrearing Before Western and European Incursion

The way of life of group of persons of a particular ancestral lineage has been described as culture. In African states, after the advent of colonial system, numerous cultures strived to live together as a nation state, which has distorted some cultural values, especially those tribes of minority in terms of population. This has resulted owing to the need for national integration and nation-building whose aim is to collapse ethnic nationalities and royalties in support of a national identity (Obah-Akpowoghaha 2018). But generally, there are certain basics in African cultures that are dominant and connect Africans together (O'Neil [2006 cited in Amos 2013]). Children are meant to respect and greet elders at all times; virginity is a pride and must be preserved by the girl child with support from the community, which includes external family; and so on. Consequently, the African continent is rich and endowed with beautiful cultures and traditions that have been systematically put down from one generation to the other. This process takes the form of folk tales, storytelling, symbols, signs and other creations. A folk tale in African traditional system is an effective means of inculcating the virtues in children (Gyekye 1996 cited in Amos 2013). "It is obvious from the explanations given and their examples that these folktales carry with it values and morals which are being handed from one generation to the other. It teaches good morals which helps in parenting the child so (s)he will learn to be a responsible adult" (Amos 2013: 71).

However, the act of childrearing in Africa from infancy to adolescent or adulthood (i.e. marriageable age) is an interesting process characterised with the display of cultural heritage and enormous support from the man's nuclear and extended families, and likewise the woman. "Childrearing is a process by which parents transmit, and the child acquires, prior existing competence required by the culture to assume valued future tasks in the society" (Ogbu 1981 cited in Okafor 2003: 6). When a child is born into a family, he/she receives support and care from both families, and even in communities (Okafor 2003). Varieties of celebrations define the process and beautiful gifts of all sort, food items, clothes and other items that are given to the baby, and as the child grows up, the mother breastfeeds the child over a year. It is a belief that this act of nurturing makes the child morally healthy and strongly bonded with the immediate mother. The mother is not left alone in this care and love; the grandmothers, especially from the women's side, come around and stay in the house for some months to assist and nurture the child. For example, in West African countries, particularly in Nigeria, the child is seen as a very precious gift from God that reveals connections between ancestors of the past and mysteries of life that lies ahead. "The birth of a child is highly celebrated with flavour in all Nigerian cultures, and children are held in high esteem" (Okafor 2003: 6).

When the child is eight years old, most cultures circumcise the child. In some cultures the circumcision of the girl child is done when she reaches puberty and starts experiencing menstrual cycle. During this period, the mother will inform the father and the elders in the community, leading to ritual of some days and celebration whereby she will be taught what constitutes womanhood and the opposite sex. After strict observation of the rituals that involve bathing her in the river or stream and confirming her virginity before the elders, she is open for any man to come for her in marriage according to the cultural rules and regulations (Amos 2013).

The African child from the period of infancy to the adolescent age is trained by the relatives. The act of childrearing is not predominantly the work of the immediate parents, and this virtue is embedded in African cultures (Adinlofu 2009 cited in Amos 2013). This is evident when a child loses his or her parents as a result of natural disaster or epidemic. There are holistic care and love that strengthen the morale and vision of the child in achieving his or her dream in life. Outside the incident of death of child's parents, it is the cultural duty of the extended family to show love and care. The male child is trained in the act of war, bravery, governance, respect for women, and language power, and in some cultures, the priest or deity is also involved in the act of childrearing. The priest gives certain instructions to the parents, especially when there is prophecy concerning the child. In Africa, the male child attracts much interest and attention because of his utility in area of defence and protection of the community, as ambassador and decision-maker, custodian of traditions and heir to any family.

Special attention and training always characterised the upbringing of the male child in African communities due to the aforementioned variables. The act of childrearing also entails storytelling, folk tales, demonstration of cultural symbols, signs and revealing secrets of ancient warriors. Corroborating the analyses above, the research conducted by Okafor (2003) in Eastern part of Nigeria revealed certain acts of childrearing such as good or proper feeding connotes affection and love; mothers do not praise their children in public; facial expressions; control practices embodied scolding and calling of names in anger; spanking; and caning. It is believed that spanking affirmed the direction of the child in achieving his or her goals in life. Generally, the child is taught to be obedient, respectful and honour elders and the culture of the land. The act of childrearing in some cultures in the Eastern part of Nigeria is the duty of the extended clan, and not for the biological parents (Okafor 2003).

However, Okafor equally added that due to modernisation and the clash of civilisation, which has polluted African societies, much has been lost and the "parenting style of new African immigrants may create family tension and conflict in a Western society where group parenting is not practiced, and where children are raised to be assertive and independent, and where caning and spanking might be defined as child abuse" (Okafor 2003: 4). This has been put differently in the work of Amos (2013: 74), who lamented that "the extended family is tearing apart especially in our bigger, busy cities. Nuclear families should make it a point to visit their hometowns and patch up with their extended families. Parents should frequently introduce their children to their extended families on both sides" (Amos 2013: 74). By implication, he further stressed that "presently, teenage pregnancy is on the increase. Young girls do not regard their cultural values as far as virginity and marriage is concerned. Young couples give birth before they think about marriage" (Amos 2013: 75).

In another dimension that has broken the bond between mother and the child has to do with the duration of the time the mother spent with the child, especially during breastfeeding in contemporary African societies. For the work of Amos (2013) revealed that:

> During infancy, the child is breastfed for a longer time as compared to this modern time. This, it is believed, develop a bond between the baby and the mother. As the child grows, he/she sees the virtues being exhibited by the mother and all of these enhance good parenting. Presently mothers are not often seen in the house as they used to be. It must be emphasized that the involvement of more mothers in the modern labour force, deprives the children as well as the whole family of the daily love and care so necessary for proper child rearing and development. (Amos 2013: 73)

What is predominant in relation to foreign cultures that has affected the African child is the issue of the place of the child in contemporary African societies. The child is used as a domestic tool to provide income for poor families through hawking and begging in the streets, which dominated most African cities. This has been corroborated by the work of Okafor (2003), "that little children hawk and sell goods along the street.... in most urban areas of Nigeria, ...buying and selling in rural Nigeria takes place only in the market places and street selling is not practiced." Consequently, children in rural Nigeria do not hawk goods like their urban counterparts (Okafor 2003: 14).

Science, ICT and the Act of Caregiver

Information and Communications Technology as by-product of science has codified human society into a small unit. The use of social media, such as the Facebook, WhatsApp, Internets, Instagram and others, have served as a source of information to communities, families and global institutions. Science has positively impacted the development of Western cultures and societal development. Evidently, in 2004, the Ministry of Education in New Zealand embraced a projection prepared by Rachel Bolstad on the role and potential of ICT in early childhood education, a review of New Zealand and International Literature, which seeks to educate the early childhood programmes in the educational system of the country. The study identified areas such as teaching and learning, professional development, teacher education, sector capability, infrastructure and information management communication, all these were done towards early childhood settings and why ICT matters (Bolstad 2004).

In the study, Rachel Bolstad described ICT as anything that makes human beings to acquire information, disseminate it and impact on natural and other resources through the help of electronics or digital device. And added that in the course of early childhood caregiver process, ICT entails computer hardware and software, digital cameras and CCTV, telecommunication devices, Internet, programmable robotic items and so on (Bolstad 2004).

An important revelation about Rachel Bolstad project was premised on the encouragement of ICT as a strategic tool for caregivers in building the child's knowledge. She stressed that for early child development and growth, caregivers (teachers, parents and other practitioners) should deploy ICT tools towards enriching the child physically and mentally in line with primary objectives of *Te Whāriki* practices.

In another study conducted in South Africa, Uganda and Senegal on ICTs and the child's education, an extensive project that was put in place by World Bank carried out by David Souter, Lishan Adam, Neil Butcher, Claire Sibthorpe and Tusu Tusubira (www.eTransformAfrica.org) identified most African countries' weak policies towards ICT usage that have negatively affected the development and growth of children. The study also revealed the inadequacy of Africans in applying ICTs due to over-blurred budget and lack of commitment, which has affected homes, families and communities towards having access to ICTs and its training. It recommended among others that ICTs can serve as a hub for African integration, especially economies and improvement on issues that affect the environment.

In a review by World Health Organization on the importance of caregiver-child interactions for the survival and healthy development of young children showed that the caregiver and child failed to engage due to some factors. Poor nutrition, environmental hazards, violence prevention and so on are issues identified as part of the challenges of caregiver towards the child development in developing countries. It has been recorded that close to 11 Million children died before clocking their fourth or fifth birthday in the past year. It also revealed that about 40% of children in low-income societies die within the period of 5–13 days, although millions of children survived but experienced lessened lives and incapacitated to develop their full potential. Deficiency in food intake and general malnutrition limit the child chance to explore the world during tough period of learning and practice in basic social skill and intellectual. It further stressed that caregiver or communities find it difficult to prevent the worst effects of certain illnesses towards the child's growth and mental development (World Health Organization 2004).

Conversely, a study by Amos (2013) points out how the role of media has led to the neglect of some rich African culture. That the African child is exposed to foreign values and primarily engaged with exercising and demonstrating its essence at the expense of the African culture. He succinctly stated that:

> The media has taken precedence in our families that children no longer listen to folk stories anymore; they are rather with the television, internet, foreign books and computers. These modernization gadgets have limited information with regards to African cultural values and proper traditional parenting which can easily be assessed by all. In view of that a lot of young people have lost touch of the rich cultural values we have as Africans. A lot of young people presently no longer give a helping hand to the adult and do not offer their seat to the elderly whether in public or private. (Amos 2013: 74)

Extrapolating from the assertion given by Amos on the utility of the media or ICT, it reveals the wrong application and lack of parental responsibility on African children towards affirming African traditions and values on the African child. This has been ascribed to modern family setting and the nature of white-collar jobs that deny parents in giving proper attention to their immediate family. Like most banking work in Africa whereby the woman wakes up by 5 a.m. and must be at the workplace by 7:30 a.m., officially 8 a.m. She comes home by 7 p.m. or 8 p.m., and this depends on the volume of transactions on that day, while the father by African culture is little far from the children when it comes to domestic duties in areas of cooking, bathing the child, taking the child to bed, washing clothes and so on. Although modernisation has led some men to adjust and help the wife in this regard, it is rare in most homes in African societies where the father cooks, bathes and takes the child to bed in the absence of the wife every day.

Concluding Remarks

From this study, the concept of childrearing has been described as early childhood education, caregiver and so on. The family that constitutes the father and the mother has been seen as the primary caregivers who bring up the child based on certain values and rights known as ethics. This chapter has also revealed that the phrase Ethics of Family, Community and Childrearing have been dominated by Western and European thoughts whose ideas and ideals have been duplicated into developing countries, which is at variance from them especially the African continent. These thoughts of the developed societies have seen African societies as poor—plagued with diseases and ecological problems. Evidently, the Care for Child Development put in place by UNICEF and other initiatives from UN serve as a reference point. The pattern of dressing, speaking, languages, feeding and eating, and how the child should be handled and so on reflect the culture and ethics of the Western and European people.

These, among others, have made the implementations of these thoughts cumbersome; unanswered ethical questions arising from the extinction of ethical values of the African people built on communal living and not individualism. Although these programmes, to a certain extent, assisted in the area of poverty, technical aid and teaching methods, feeding the child and providing for the immediate caregivers, the attachment theory that was advocated and made known by John Bowlby has a remarkable influence on caregivers, family, communities and nations in giving the best to the child towards his/her growth and development, mental and physical well-being in the advanced countries. Another invention in early childhood education is the efficient use of ICTs, but studies have identified that most developing countries still lagged behind in launching this system into the world of science. ICT has been seen as a huge source for caregivers in childrearing and community development.

Conclusively, the declaration of UN through her numerous agencies, and other NGOs towards the development of the child, family and community, should undergo a critical survey in ensuring a balance within communities that need help, care and holistic development of the child. The African families and communities' patterns of caregiving should be incorporated in order to make the caregivers, practitioners and others excited. And these, among others, will produce fruitful results, reduce the place of stigmatisation and evolve the culture of the local people.

Bibliography

Ainsworth, M.D.S., M.C. Blehar, E. Waters, and S. Wall. 1978. *Patterns of Attachment: A Psychological Study of the Strange Situation*. Hillsdale, NJ: Erlbaum.

Amos, P.M. 2013. Parenting and Culture – Evidence from Some African Communities. www.intechopen.com. Accessed 10 June 2019.

Bolstad, R. 2004. *The Role and Potential of ICT in Early Childhood Education: A Review of New Zealand and International Literature*. Thorndon: New Zealand Council For Educational Research.

Bowlby, J. 1953. *Child Care and the Growth of Love*. London: Penguin.

———. 1969. *Attachment and Loss (Vol. 1). Attachment*. New York: Basic Books.

Ganga, E., and K. Chinyoka. 2017. An Analysis of How Contemporary African Child-Rearing Practices Affect a Child's Self-Concept and Learning. *Case Studies Journal* 6 (3): 38–47.

Gilda, M., Q. Naomi, C. Nandita, V. Marga, R. Mariano, K. Heidi, M. Marjorie, G. Alma, S. Gabriel, and T. Akira. (n.d.). Ethical Challenges of Parenting Interventions in Low to Middle-income Countries. Department of Applied Developmental and Educational Psychology, Boston College.

Henrich, J., S.J. Heine, and A. Norenzayan. 2010. The Weirdest People in the World? *Behavioral and Brain Sciences* 33: 61–83. https://doi.org/10.1017/S0140525X0999152X.

Jolly, R. 2007. Early Childhood Development: The Global Challenge. *The Lancet* 369: 8–9. https://doi.org/10.1016/S0140-6736(07)60007-5.

Juffer, F., and L.G. Rosenboom. 1997. Infant–Mother Attachment of Internationally Adopted Children in the Netherlands. *International Journal of Behavioral Development* 20: 93–107.

Keller, H., and J. Kärtner. 2013. The Cultural Solution of Universal Developmental Tasks. In *Advances in Culture and Psychology*, ed. M.J. Gelfand, C. Chiu, and Y. Hong, vol. 3, 63–116. Oxford: Oxford University Press.

Madhavan, S., and M. Gross. 2013. Kin in Daily Routines: Time Use and Childrearing in Rural South Africa. *Journal of Comparative Family Studies* 44 (2): 175–191.

National Association for the Education of Young Children (NAEYC). 2011. Code of Ethical Conduct and Statement of Commitment. Accessed and Retrieved 17 Feb 2019. https://www.naeyc.org.

Nurit, G. 2017. Ethical Issues in Health Promotion and Communication Interventions. *Oxford Research Encyclopedia of Communication*. Retrieved from https://oxfordindex.oup.com/oi/viewindexcard.

Obah-Akpowoghaha, G.N. 2018. Party Politics and the Challenge of National Integration in Nigeria's Fourth Republic. Unpublished PhD Dissertation in Department of Political Science, Faculty of Social Sciences, Obafemi Awolowo University, Ile-ife, Osun State.

Okafor, C.B. 2003. Child Rearing Practices in Eastern Nigeria: Implications for Social Work in the United States, *International Journal of Global Health* 2 (2). http://scholarworks.uni.edu/ijgh/vol2/iss2/2. Accessed 10 June 2019.

Roisman, G.I., E. Padron, L.A. Sroufe, and B. Egeland. 2002. Earned-Secure Attachment Status in Retrospect and Prospect. *Child Development* 73: 1204–1219.

Singer, L.M., D.M. Brodzinsky, D. Ramsay, M. Steir, and E. Waters. 1985. Mother-Infant Attachment in Adoptive Families. *Child Development* 56: 1543–1551.

Souter, David, Lishan Adam, Neil Butcher, Claire Sibthorpe, and Tusu Tusubira. ICT for Education in Africa. http://siteresources.worldbank.org/. Accessed 21 Feb 2019.

Sroufe, L.A., E.A. Carlson, A.K. Levy, and B. Egeland. 1999. Implications of Attachment Theory for Developmental Psychopathology. *Development and Psychopathology* 11: 1–13.

Vivian, P., and G. Danya. 2006. *Understanding Attachment and Attachment Disorder: Theory, Evidence and Practice*. London/Philadelphia: Jessica Kingsley Publisher.

Weber, A., A. Fernald, and Y. Diop. 2017. When Cultural Norms Discourage Talking to Babies: Effectiveness of a Parenting Program in Rural Senegal. *Child Development* 88: 1513–1526.

Weinfield, N.S., L.A. Stroufe, and B. Egeland. 2000. Attachment from Infancy to Early Adulthood in a High-Risk Sample: Continuity, Discontinuity, and Their Correlates. *Child Development* 71: 695–702.

WHO/UNICEF. 2013. Building Global Capacity for the Implementation of the WHO/UNICEF Intervention Care for Child Development. Retrieved from https://www.unicef.org/earlychildhood/files/CCD_workshop_June_24-29_2013_Final_Report_2.pdf

World Health Organization. 2004. The Importance of Caregiver-Child Interactions for the Survival and Healthy Development of Young Children. Department of Child and Adolescent Health and Development. https://www.who.int/maternal_child_adolescent/documents/924159134X/en/. Accessed 14 Feb 2019.

CHAPTER 3

Power Dynamics in Nuclear and Extended Families: A Feminist Foucauldian Analysis

Olayinka Oyeleye

Introduction

Debates within the social sciences and humanities on the concept of family and on family definitions have shifted considerably. It has moved beyond the norms of the binary mode of the nuclear and extended families as basis for adopting structural definitions which lay emphasis on persons that make up a family to functional definitions of the performative roles of each member as well as roles that the family as a collective engage in.

As a significant social object, the family is constructed through discourse. Discourse in this sense is a small but essential aspect of Michel Foucault's oeuvre. Discourses are beyond ways of producing thoughts and meaning. They are ways through which knowledges are constituted, alongside social practices, forms of subjectivity and the relations of power, which exist between such knowledges and the relations between them. In Kristine Baber's view, "it refers to interrelated systems of statements, terms, categories, and beliefs that reflect and reinforce existing social arrangements so that they come to be seen as normal and natural."[1] These beliefs, statements, terms and so on not only reflect and reinforce existing social arrangements but in becoming the norm also become conceptual and social constructs, which ultimately becomes the reality and worldview which then find expression and transmission through language.

The idea of family as discourse then "draws attention to the importance of language and meaning in understanding family lives."[2] Theoretically, creating 'family' and fluid family identities draw its implication from the emphasis on language and meanings, which derive from the postmodern constructionist approach. The postmodern view on language and meaning holds essentially

O. Oyeleye (✉)
Department of Philosophy, University of Ibadan, Ibadan, Nigeria

© The Author(s) 2020
N. Wariboko, T. Falola (eds.), *The Palgrave Handbook of African Social Ethics*, https://doi.org/10.1007/978-3-030-36490-8_3

that language is semantically self-contained; hence, the meaning of a word is not fixed in the world. "Meanings are a function of other meanings—which themselves are functions of other meanings, and so on."[3] As such, concepts like power, gender, family and so on do not have fixed meanings; they are neither objective nor universal. This view also grounds the constructionist idea of Gubrium and Holstein that "family is constantly under construction, obtaining its defining characteristics somewhere, somehow, in real time and place and through interpretive practice."[4]

Considered as a paradigm shift[5] from the traditional conceptions of family, which clings to the monolithic notion of family, the social constructionist view challenges canonical ways by which family has been conceptualized by querying the idea of family as a fixed social unit without much respect for race, culture, religion and even sexual orientation. Gubrium and Holstein raise some of the important questions among others that are germane to this chapter, which the social constructionist view of the family also asks—how is family defined? How is it experienced or perceived? Are our experiences or perceptions of family the same? How did we come about the singular or monolithic notion of the family? Who/What defines the essence and organization of domestic life? We ponder, indeed, on how correct the ideology of family which places the (white) heterosexual couple who are parents to children as the nucleus of the society? What nomenclature do we ascribe to homosexual couples who chose to be parents? What about the extended family? How has the focus on the nuclear family devalued the extended family? Are there Nuclear families in Africa? If there are, how were they conceived and how are they perceived? What about issues of gender? How is power exercised within nuclear and extended families, especially with attention to gender issues? These are questions of pertinence to the thesis of this chapter.

This chapter is organized into three sections. The first two sections excavate and discuss historical and ongoing sociological and anthropological ideas on the distinctions between the nuclear and extended families. The third section draws a dialogue between Michel Foucault and Amy Allen in a philosophical analysis of power, power relations and its dynamics within the family. It concludes that power, gender and family remain under construction.

The Western Nuclear Family and the Critique of Its Monolithic Notion

The social constructs of masculinity and femininity have been considered a fundamental aspect of the social organization of biological sex.[6] These constructs especially germinate and flourish within the context of the family organized around a breadwinner male husband and homemaker female wife. This monolithic model, based on family as a structural functional unit, with legal, procreative, socialization, sexual, residential, economic and emotional dimensions, is defined by Eichler as "a model according to which high interaction in one dimension of familial interaction is assumed to coincide with or result in high interaction in all other dimensions."[7] Eichler further posits that as far as the economic dimension of the monolithic model is concerned, one adult, usually the husband-father, is totally responsible for the economic support of all family members,[8] while the socialization dimension although concerned with the parental roles and responsibilities lays more emphasis on the mother's responsibility in the socialization of the children. Consequently, the monolithic model has been criticized by feminists as describing a type of idealized family that excludes and stigmatizes large segments of the population.[9] The monolithic notion has thus been described as a "male-dominated, Western, white, middle-class, heterosexual norm."[10]

This traditional view of the Western family some authors have opined originated and expanded "out of an unfortunate marriage between patriarchy and the industrial capitalist system."[11] Janssens further contends that there have recently been even more complex accounts of how the concept of the male breadwinner originated and broadened, with a wide range of factors identified as pertinent to the dispute. Some of these factors for Janssens include employers' strategies, seemingly gender-neutral labor market factors and processes of capital accumulation, concepts of masculinity and the complicated interactions between family strategies and the labor market or, indeed, the role of institutional structures of power.[12] These complexities have not only broadened the scope of the debate but also left it in a somewhat disenfranchised and confused state.

Elaborating further on the Western origin of the monolithic family, Trask noted also that much of what is believed to be suitable roles for men and women traces back to the industrialization epoch. Trask summarizes the argument thus:

> the movement toward industrialization was accompanied by a growing distinction between paid and unpaid work, a distinction that became increasingly associated with men's (paid) work and women's (unpaid) work. As Western societies moved ... towards a strong industrial base, the very nature of work changed ..., industrialization moved work out of the home. As the need for factory labor grew, men's work became more valuable and led to a societal discourse around naturalized roles for men and women.[13]

Proponents of essentialism ensured that emphasis on biological differences between males and females continued to dominate the discourse. Attributes of fecundity and procreation became the essence of females much so that, "women's biological ability to bear children increasingly became consistently equated with an equivalent ability to rear children."[14] So, while they (women) bore and reared children, it was the duty of the men to ensure that the household management in terms of finances be taken care of.

This progressively led to women being pushed into the private sphere, while men maintained the affairs of the public sphere of work and political matters whose end was to produce financial rewards. This followed from the belief that men had the strength and agility to work and survive the unpleasantly rough and severe factory conditions, which women were more than likely too weak to do. So, while men were recognized for their productivity, women were noted for reproductivity. Men's productive labor became paid labor and was ultimately placed above the reproductive unpaid labor of the women in the private domestic sphere. This led not only to an inequality between the sexes and in the home but, ultimately, to the subordination of women. The ideology about gender roles as well as the division of labor in the domestic arena continues to prevail in most cultures of the world.

Organizing the Domestic Sphere: How Gender Roles Were Formed and Maintained

The dichotomy between the public and private spheres following the earlier analysis prompts us to consider how these roles became somewhat institutionalized. Could these roles have existed in prehistoric societies? How did we come to accept the norm(s), which gendered these spaces male and female? Or as Gubrium and Holstein[15] put it, Who or what defines the essence and organization of domestic life? What abstract or physical entity determines the distinctive nature of familial roles? Let us premise our answer on the traditional definition of 'family.'

Traditionally, a family is defined as consisting of a child or children alongside the parents; thus, the parent-child relationship is fundamental to the family as a unit, which thrives upon procreation. We can argue then that much as the child requires the parent(s) to thrive, the preservation of the lineage is dependent upon the couple having child/ren. Thus, the nucleus of the family group can be said to be the child/ren to the extent that family life is organized not just around the heterosexual couple, but the couple organize life within the family around the child/ren. Following from the nature-nurture causation of sex differences debates, intrinsic to the feminine nature is said to be the maternal instinct of nurture, caregiving and protection of the child/ren,[16] a biological essence which Darwinian evolutionary scientists and functionalist theorists have used to carve out women's familial roles.

Talbot Parsons and Robert Bales, among other functionalist theorists, advanced an explanation of how family gender roles may have been formed and maintained in the course of biosocial evolution, suggesting that men took the more instrumental roles and women the expressive roles. In their opinion:

> the fundamental explanation of the allocation of the roles between the biological sexes lies in the fact that the bearing and early nursing of children establish a strong presumptive primacy of the relation of mother to the small child and this in turn establishes a presumption that the man, who is exempted from these biological functions, should specialize in the alternative instrumental direction.[17]

This alternative instrumental role, Parsons and Bales opined, simply puts the man in the position of the leader and breadwinner. Sociobiologists have argued in a similar vein that all human traits and behavioral tendencies are genetically determined. Thus, masculine traits such as dominance, agility, physical strength and aggression and feminine traits such as protection of infants, caregiving, passivity and nurturance are seen to be determined by one's genes. Now, since nurturing and caregiving were presumed to be feminine traits, it was naturally assumed to be feminine duty, and so evolutionary psychology as an offshoot of sociobiology suggests that in prehistoric societies, while the women attended to these expressive duties, the males were left with the duty of providing for the family.[18] Evolutionary psychologists argue then that "contemporary gender roles have evolved from early human history, when males provided food, through group hunting activities, and protected pregnant and lactating women (and their children) who were immobilized by their bodily conditions."[19]

A critical shortcoming of this approach as noted by Shehan and Kaestle is that we might never undoubtedly know how the domestic sphere was organized or what gender roles were like in prehistoric societies. Evidences, leading to the summation of the "man-the-hunter" theory by anthropologists and archeologists who looked into these prehistoric societies some decades ago, have been faulted. Feminist anthropologists and archeologists have particularly argued using their own reconstructions of early human history that women in these societies were not just sitting by the sidelines but shared center stage with the men.

Challenging the androcentric view, which placed women at the periphery while concentrating on the activities of men the hunters, Frances Dahlberg's innovative edited collection with its counter theme "*Woman the Gatherer*" became a response to this male-centered view and a reaction to Lee and Devore's Man the Hunter symposium. Dahlberg's edited collection is an attempt to balance this sexist view by providing theoretical arguments on the female role of gatherer which required as much intelligence as hunting. She argues that roles were not particularly fixed or rigid and as such women hunted and men were likewise caregivers. She argues also that contrary to the assumption by many anthropologists that "the sharing complex must include the division of labor by sex…[rather,] a strong sharing ethics enjoins each individual to share."[20] She suggests that even child care was shared duty.[21] Sharing in these societies, she concludes, could be "achieved without arbitrary work assignments by sex or reliance on marriage to assure both sexes necessary goods and services. Sharing need not require a sexual division of labor."[22]

Attempting then to answer the question who or what defines the essence of domestic organization, one significant fact stares us in the face, and it is the association of woman's body with the biological function of bearing and rearing children. This belief that the differences between men and women, especially when it comes to discussing family-related matters, is connected to the logic of biology, appears to be the dynamic at play in determining the place and hierarchy of woman, not just within the small household unit, but in the world at large. Also, attributing gender roles to biological essentialism was not in the real sense a general notion but the view of a few white elite male. Feminists are then saddled with the responsibility of challenging the norms that these male biases have created across different spheres and disciplines, thereby producing new knowledges. Nevertheless, one cannot but wonder how the view of a minority made history over the rest of humanity.

Heterosexuals Without Children, Homosexuals with Children: What Really Is Family?

Structural functionalism to an extent succeeded in positing the (white) heterosexual nuclear family with the father as breadwinner and decision-maker/head and the mother as housekeeper and carer/heart as the nucleus of the society.[23] Consequently, the nuclear family became a universal construct, albeit a false one. "Ignoring the economic circumstances and social discrimination that produced distinctive family patterns, [structural functionalists] confused difference with disorganization…even though race and class differences were at the very foundation of family experience."[24]

Arguing from the standpoint of difference, feminist family studies theorists have queried the ideology of family that places the (white) heterosexual couple who are parents to children as the nucleus of the society. Theorists working within the purview of lesbian, gay, bisexual, transgender and queer (LGBTQ+) have also queried heterosexuality as the paramount element of family organization. Since functionalism supports the status quo as justification for the smooth functioning of the society, it queries then the abilities of lesbian mothers and gay fathers as effective parents, even when they were parents prior to 'coming out.' Now, if the maternal instinct of nurture and caregiving, which had hitherto been attributed to females, is truly an inherent quality of women, why exempt lesbian mothers? Why assume "that lesbians are less maternal than heterosexual women"?[25]

It appears then, as Allen and Demo suggest, "that sexist and heterosexist assumptions continue to underlie most of the research on families by focusing analysis on heterosexual partnerships and parenthood,"[26] to the extent that heterosexuals without biological children of their own are considered fit and normal to adopt children over homosexual parents who are biological parents but now have to fight for custody of their children simply because they are of a different sexual orientation. Indeed, many prospective parents with the ability to offer children in need of adoption the stability of a permanent home have been refused as candidates because they indicated they were gay or lesbian.[27] They were refused not because they could not be good parents, but mainly on the grounds of their sexual orientation. Thus, reflecting the "belief that 'gayness' and family are mutually exclusive concepts.... Lesbians and gay men are thought of as individuals, but not as family members."[28]

Rethinking parenting or parenthood becomes significant at this point. What it takes to be a parent is beyond who one chooses to share one's intimacy with or how one chooses to be intimate. It should ideally be beyond what has been assumed as inherent qualities associated with males and females. Qualities presumed to be feminine like nurturing and caregiving can be found in males, while females can likewise be strong, aggressive and dominating. To complicate it further, one can be either female or male and inherently possess these qualities. Such persons so endowed, might be able to singly parent a child. Concepts such as motherhood and fatherhood should not only be critiqued and rethought but also ditched for parenting or parenthood within the field of family studies.

The Extended African Family

The a priori assumption of Westerners that any family unit larger than their conception of family, as consisting of father, mother and children living in a household, must necessarily be reduced or simplified to it or to something smaller, is perhaps the most probable reason why anthropologists are preoccupied with nucleation so much so that recognizing that there are other family forms asides their supposed nuclear family still necessitates that within family units termed as extended, a nucleus must yet be situated within its structure. As Niara Surdakasa notes, the procreative unit in all societies is normally a male and a female and that this procreative unit, alongside its offspring, is worthy of study or analysis. "It does not follow, however, that this unit should be conceptualized as the building block for families in every society where it is found. Labelling the father-mother-child unit as the 'nuclear family' does not make it invariably so."[29]

The extended family as a polarized concept to the nuclear family is often erroneously conceived as an expansion or extension of the nuclear family to include a considerable circle of relatives within the clan. The assumed nuclear family from which the extended family stems from in traditional African societies are more than likely polygamous rather than the monogamy that exists in the West. This assumed nucleus in itself stands at variance with the Western nuclear family since its more popular version would consist of the husband, wives and children and in other cases a polyandry. Summing up this polygamous unit as the nucleus of the extended family appears to be a far cry from the day-to-day conception of the Western nuclear family, which will consist of one husband, one wife and their children.

It becomes apparent then that Africans conceive of family totally different from the West. Adebola Bolajoko Dasylva discusses the family as "a social unit of parents, their children and extended family members."[30] Although Dasylva goes on to include the nuclear and extended family as if they are two separate entities living together under one roof, s/he does not explain in detail how the wives (who are allotted their own rooms) together with the husband and their children can make up a nuclear family. However, Dasylva points out clearly an important fact: "There is no distinction among the children of different wives; they all live together."[31] Similarly, Nelson Mandela in his book, *Long Walk to Freedom*, observed that his mother presided over three huts which were always filled with babies and children of his relations. Also that, "In African culture, the sons and daughters of one's aunts and uncles are considered brothers and sisters, not cousins." Thus giving a good degree of support to the fact raised by Dasylva that no distinction is made among children of the other wives and even cousins and nephews or nieces as long as they live together, they are all children of one compound, which the Yorùbás commonly refer to as *omo ilé*. This grounds Sudarkasa's generalization of indigenous Africa following P.A. Tetteh's observation concerning Ghana: "…when the word 'family' is used, it does not usually refer to the nuclear or elementary family based on the husband-wife relationship but to the extended family based on descent."[32] The extended family based on descent here appears to bear resemblance to a kinship system called the lineage. The lineage and the extended family are often confused kinship categories. Understanding their differences will further illuminate the structure and organization of the traditional African family.

Fundamental to understanding African kinship then entails an understanding of three important elements, which Sudarkasa states as; (1) the composition of the lineage and the extended family; (2) the differences between these two kin groupings and their relationship to one another; and (3) the relationship of the lineage and the extended family to the typical African residential grouping known as the *compound*.[33] Sudarkasa's work is quite significant because it not only places the extended family in another perspective to the norm, it also helps us better understand the structure of the family in Africa.

The lineage as Sudarkasa suggests is a kin group in which the members, both living and deceased, are related to each other through a common ancestor traced through a line of descent, which can be matrilineal or patrilineal but not through both. Through marriage ties, particularly where exogamous rules exist, members of different lineages come together into an *extended* family. Whereas marriage might be seen as starting a family in the West, for Africans, it was seen as joining an existing family. Upon marriage, depending if it's a matrilineal or patrilineal society, only one of the spouses changed residence. In patrilineal societies, because descent is traced through the male line, it is the wife that joins the husband's family who live together in a single compound, which the Yorùbás call *agbo-ilé*. This enables her children become part of the *omo-ilé*, that is, children whose descent can be traced through the (husband's) lineage. Thus, the in-coming wife from another lineage extends her own family by joining the husband's family, which would ordinarily be comprised of male resident members of the lineage, their wives (from other lineages), their children and yet-to-be married daughters (since upon marriage, they would have to move out of their compound into another family, which then becomes extended).

Summarily, African lineages are traced through a patrilineal or matrilineal line of descent and remain a part of the lineage as ancestors upon death, while a family extends through marriage. Marrying into a family makes one part of the existing family but not necessarily a part of the lineage. Children born into the family belong both to the family and the lineage. It is safe to infer thus that being a part of a lineage is more honorable than being a part of the family. This is largely because the extended family is built around the living adult members of the consanguineal relatives who are theirselves the core of the extended family.

The most apparent difference as Surdakasa notes is that, while lineages are based solely on descent, the extended family is a product of both descent and marriage. The blood/consanguineal members who are themselves the core of the family marry (in) their spouses and extend the family; this way the core members trace their descent through one line, which becomes their lineage, while the extended family traces relation or filiation rather than descent per se through both parents. Another difference worth noting is that members of a particular lineage are separate and distinct, they do not overlap. Members of the extended family through different marital affiliations end up with a cluster of relatives from other members of their lineage. Lastly, while lineages are conceptualized as "existing in perpetuity, involving the living and the dead, ... [E]xtended families are essentially constellations of living relatives."[34]

The relationship of the lineage to the extended family can be easily inferred from the preceding discussion as a connection that originates essentially through a 'blood line' and one that is created 'by law.' The continuity of the lineage is dependent upon its organization and how it contracts with other lineages to form its extension. The extended family then is based on marriage, for without marriage(s), the lineage would cease to exist. The traditional African family which has come to be known as the extended family consists primarily of the lineage by blood and its external connection through marriage.

Understanding the African Traditional Family: Consanguineal, Conjugal or Both?

The traditional familial arrangement found in most African societies is extended only to the extent that it serves the primary function of continuing and expanding a line of descent through marriage. This type of family structure is organized quite differently from the Western nuclear family and functions differently too. Although the concept of the extended family according to Aldous (1962), developed from studies of African peoples, the sense in which the concept is used does not adequately define what in the ideal sense ought to have been described as an African traditional family.

The traditional African family which has come to be known as the extended family consists of both the lineage (by blood) and its external connection through marriage (by law). The invention of the concept 'extended family' likewise its polar concept 'nuclear family' is often credited to G.P. Murdock. In his 1949 book, *The Social Structure*, Murdock had approached the study of family and kinship using a cross-cultural survey of 250 human societies, which he saw as representing all regions of the world as well as all levels of civilization. However, in a bid to "confirm his hypothesis concerning the universality of the nuclear family and its centrality in all other types of family groupings, Murdock imposed upon the empirical reality of the extended family an analytical paradigm which emphasized the primacy of the nuclear family."[35] Let us consider quickly Murdock's definition of the polygamous and extended families as composite families.

> The polygamous family, it will be recalled, consists of several nuclear families linked through a common spouse. The extended family includes two or more nuclear families united by consanguineal kinship bonds such as those between parent and child or between two siblings.[36]

Rather than viewing the family holistically, Murdock for some reason directed his gaze to what appears to be the parts, and these parts he saw as individual nuclear families with a spouse in common. These 'several nuclear families' from the Yorùbá African perspective isn't a 'family' as Murdock suggests, it is simply 'a unit' within a family and cannot be described as a nuclear family in the sense in which Murdock uses it. Recall that children within the traditional African family belong to the lineage and no distinctions made among them even when they are cousins, nephews or nieces, so also distinctions are not made among the units, although there might be distinctions among the wives since they are members of the family by law and not blood, but not among the blood members of the family. Murdock's model as Surdakasa suggests "does not fit the reality of African extended families."[37]

Understanding how easy it is for Western anthropologists/sociologists to make the ontological error or category mistake of assigning to African family systems qualities that can only belong to their own society, Ralph Linton in his 1936 book, *The Study of Man,* warned that:

> It is hard for Europeans to realize the sharp distinction which exists in many social systems between the reproductive unit composed of mates and their offspring and the authentic, institutional family. It happens that in our own society these two units coincide much more closely than in most. As a result, European students have shown strong tendency to assume that any grouping composed of father, mother and children must constitute the social equivalent of the family among ourselves.[38]

Linton proceeds to draw a distinction between the conjugal family and the consanguineal family as the necessary nucleus of any society. The West, it appears, "has stressed the conjugal relationship as the foundation of its functional family unit to such a degree that [they] tend to think of marriage and the family as inseparably linked, but many other societies draw a clear distinction between the two."[39] So, for Linton, societies can either be organized upon a conjugal basis, which would then consist of a nucleus of spouses and their offspring with a fringe of relatives surrounding them, or they can be organized on the consanguine basis which would in turn consist of a nucleus of blood relatives with a fringe of spouses surrounding them. Linton maintains that:

> [U]nder the first system it is the fringe of relatives which interlock and connect family to family. Under the second it is the marriages which, by their interlocking, link family to family. Under the first system the blood relatives of the spouses are of only incidental importance to the functioning of the family unit. Under the second, the spouses are of only incidental importance.[40]

The second categorization applies more to the African context, especially the sub-Saharan Yorùbá people than the first. Marriages are the means by which the families extend the link through which lineages become connected to other lineages; the consanguineal family thus form the nucleus of the family, while the spouses are only incidental. Much as Linton's work appears to give us a better understanding of how families are and can be formed and occurs earlier than Murdock's, Murdock's work and terminologies which center around presumed essential primary structural features of the family, however, seemed to have found a stronger foothold than Linton's. It appears, unfortunately, as Sudarkasa notes, "that Murdock's preoccupation with the nuclear family led him to misrepresent the structural characteristics he encountered"[41] within the African traditional families he studied. This primarily has led to a misrepresentation of the structure of the African traditional family, and, consequently, the African traditional family has not only been undermined and Western categories superimposed on it, it has also been devalued and its Western counterpart, the nuclear family, embraced and primacy attached to it.[42]

Organizing the Domestic Sphere: (Gender Roles) in African Traditional Families with Focus on the Yoruba

The African traditional family beyond being a social category is an organized unit designed to be pragmatic. In other words, beyond being structurally significant, the traditional African family is highly functional. Its purpose extends beyond its biological functions of procreation and the lineage continuity, to activities which can be legal, economic, social and educative. As Aldous observed, the traditional African "family substituted for a nonexistent government"[43] largely because it is in itself an arm of the government albeit at the local/traditional level. Taking into account the *Sociology of the Yoruba*, Fadipe describes the compound where it co-extends with extended family as the smallest political unit. The head of the family known as *baálé*, is duty bound to preserve peace and order, and to maintain discipline in his compound. He settles disputes and is recognized as " the chief law-giver and magistrate of the compound."[44] Similarly, Aldous cites Horace Miner's observation of the Songhoi people of ancient Mali that, "the extended family fulfilled a legal function meting out punishment or deciding upon reparations when a kinsman had engaged in robbery or murder or had himself been murdered."[45]

An apparent and noteworthy aspect of the economic organization of traditional African family[46] is its specialization by compounds.[47] While farming remains the dominant occupation and the main source of subsistence in household economy, compounds yet have a specialized occupation which are predominantly gendered. So, while the males follow a particular trade, the females and even wives who through marriage joined the family, irrespective of their specialization from their own lineage, adopt the craft of the lineage they have married into. Invariably, there is a continuity of the lineage's skill, which oftentimes reflect in the names given to the compound or to the individual members of the family. While the men tend to follow specialized industries like blacksmithing, hunting, cloth weaving and drumming, women are often seen in occupations such as pottery, mat weaving, food preservation, processing and cooking. While we may conclude that occupations in the Yoruba economic space are gendered, modernity has, however, allowed for fluidity in this regard such that industries that were once stereotypically male, like cloth weaving and drumming, now have females working them and most female-dominated occupation now have males flourishing in them. It is also important to note that the breadwinner concept was not essentially characteristic of the traditional African family because each person literally grew their own food. African women, and more precisely Yorùbá women, were saddled with the dual responsibility of breadwinner and nurturer.

The social and educative functions of the traditional African family—with focus on the Yoruba—are somewhat integrated. Being more communalistic as opposed to the individualism obtainable in the West, the average Yoruba, as Fadipe notes, maintains intimate contact with a much larger circle of blood and affinal relatives, as well as neighbors and friends. These various relationships are strengthened by communal living and in turn promote a 'we feeling' and communal good because it brings together families and, indeed, communities. The various relationships often gather to celebrate together and to mourn together, they also gather to help and support one another, thereby building a network of alliance built upon cooperation.[48]

The principal location for the socialization and informal education of the members of the family, particularly children, is the home. A large part of this early training is seen as the direct responsibility, first, of the mother, and then the other members of the immediate family.[49] The full training of the child, Fadipe posits, is a cooperative effort. According to him:

"The education of the young Yoruba in the codes of manners, convention, customs, morals, superstitions, and laws of his society is therefore achieved through various members of his family and household, …his kindred and his neighbourhood."[50] This is to say that it involves not just the members of the compound but the entire community.

This socialization and educative process starts through play. Children gather together to play and listen to stories after the day's work is done. Dasylva observes that the moonlight story sessions constitute one of the important ways by which "children experience cultural emersion and internalization of norms, acceptable ethics, and moral values through different lessons from folktales, myths, legends and proverbs, etc., usually narrated by an elder in Yoruba indigenous society."[51] Proverbs indeed are intended to serve as a beacon to guide members of the community into absorbing good morals, which ultimately lead to one becoming an *omolúàbí*.[52]

Dasylva further adumbrates the gendered division in this socialization and educative process by maintaining that; "… boys are placed outside of the family under the tutelage of a master; they listen to myths, proverbs, and jokes to sharpen their intelligence. The girls learn much from their mothers at home to increase their expertise in domestic chores before and after marriage."[53] By implication then, the education of boys tend to take them away from the domestic sphere of the home into the public sphere, which becomes their space, while girls are reserved for the domestic sphere.

Furthering the discourse on the socialization and education of children, Elizabeth Annan-Yao in *Gender, Economies and Entitlements in Africa* argues that: "[A]s the main educators of children of both sexes in the traditional African families, women socialise boys and girls to accept conditions of exploitation of females by males through the values they transmit."[54] This puts considerable amount of power into the hands of the women who, as John Stuart Mills puts it, are the educators of the character of children. It is adequate to suggest then that except the consciousness of the women who are the educators of these future generations is heightened, such that they realize that they have the *power to* question the norms which they grew up with—that, that which appears perfectly normal to them is a form of unequal gender socialization—to paraphrase Annan-Yao, then boys will continue to grow up feeling superior, while girls might continue to accept the inferior position in society. Annan-Yao concludes that girls consequently "accept the dominating role attributed to men (and boys) by society, become submissive to men and aim to fulfill social roles as wives and mothers, sometimes at incredibly rather early ages. Their education is therefore centered on their social and biological reproductive roles."[55]

Conclusion: Power Dynamics in (Western) Nuclear Families and (African) Extended Families

Power, as an abstract idea or as a general notion, has been intrinsically considered a highly contested concept, which has been of importance—as a perennial problem—to quite a lot of social scientists, historians and philosophers. It has generated a lot of scholarly debates to the end that Steven Lukes opined that discourses on power "inevitably involve endless disputes about their proper uses on the part of their users."[56] Michel Foucault, agreeing somewhat with Lukes although he argues in a different context, posits that, "the word power is apt to lead to a number of misunderstandings... with respect to its nature, its form, and its unity."[57] Lukes further maintains that power "is exercised within structurally determined limits,"[58] while Foucault holds that "power is not an institution, and not a structure; neither is it a certain strength we are endowed with; it is the name that one attributes to a complex strategical situation in a particular society."[59]

The conceptions of power are numerous and can be quite conflicting. Attempting to define power then will belabor the task of this chapter, and as Peter Morris[60] rightly suggests, greater clarity is not necessarily produced by arriving at the definition of a term. Our aim then is to focus rather on the applicability of the concept, power. We will for the purpose of a feminist analysis on power dynamics within nuclear and extended families limit ourselves to some aspects of Foucault's discourse on power—his conception of the omnipresence of power, resistance and power, familial power as sovereign and how networks of power constitute individuals—alongside Amy Allens's *Rethinking Power* as a critical prism through which we view power relations and dynamics within families.

Foucault discusses a conception of power in *The History of Sexuality*, indicative of a radical departure from our preconceived ideas. He discusses power not as collective institutions which we are subject to comply with or as forceful domination or as something which compels us to bow to a federation or authority. Much as we ordinarily would conceive such forms of power, they are for Foucault, "the terminal forms power takes."[61] The terminal forms power takes appear to mean one of two things, either they are a means to an end which makes these institutions and so on an outlet for power which Foucault claims is everywhere, invariably meaning that the institutions are the means and power the end, or it could on the other hand mean the institutions and so on are the end and power, the means on which they run. Either or both ways, Foucault asserts that:

> Power is everywhere; not because it embraces everything, but because it comes from everywhere. And "Power," insofar as it is permanent, repetitious, inert, and self-reproducing, is simply the over-all effect that emerges from all these mobilities, the concatenation that rests on each of them and seeks in turn to arrest their movement.[62]

The import of Foucault's analysis on this work is that while we might be tempted to view power from the top-down, that is, from the patriarch or breadwinner perspective in our discussion on families, Foucault hints that we consider power as coming from everywhere but not necessarily from top to bottom because for him, "[P]ower comes from below; that is, there is no binary and all-encompassing opposition between rulers and ruled at the root of power relations,...."[63]

For Foucault then, power is not centralized and does not come from centralized sources. Power should be thought of outside the restrictions of law or the state. It is also in Gardner's analysis of Foucault, "not something one individual 'has' over another; rather, it is a set of material discursive practices that construct individuals."[64]

Foucault further states that, "[W]here there is power, there is resistance"[65]; this resistance, he claims, is never positioned outside in relation to power, the existence of which depends on resistance from many yet varying points. These points of resistance "play the role of adversary, target, support, or handle in power relations."[66] Resistances, Foucault maintains "are possible, necessary, improbable; others [that] are spontaneous, savage, solitary, concerted, rampant, or violent; still others [that] are quick to compromise, interested, or *sacrificial*; by definition, they can only exist in the strategic field of power relations...."⁶⁷ Resistance then can be surmised as the antithetical position to power. Much as Foucault devoted quite a lot of attention to his analysis of power, the notion of resistance received little attention. We, however, find Foucault's notion of resistance, especially as the 'odd term,' the irreducible opposite to power very intriguing, particularly, how feminists have viewed resistance as a form of power in itself.

Foucault gives us another perspective on power, totally different from what we have been hinting at, in one of his lectures included in *Psychiatric Power*. He talks about disciplinary and sovereign power in relation to the family maintaining that the family is a sovereign institution. Foucault opines that "the family is a sort of cell within which the power exercised is not, as one usually says, disciplinary, but rather of the same type as the power of sovereignty."⁶⁸ Foucault, here, appears to contradict himself, having earlier argued that power ought to be theorized outside the restrictions of the state and laws or as sovereign, in the instance of the family, however, he states that rather than consider the family as disciplinary, we should see it as sovereign. He rhetorically asks the question, "What do we see in the family if not a function of maximum individualization on the side of the person who exercises power, that is to say, on the father's side?"⁶⁹

The power Foucault suggests here that the father exercises is not disciplinary power as he makes clear when he affirmatively states that, "I would put the functioning and microphysics of the family completely on the side of the power of sovereignty, and not at all on that of disciplinary power."⁷⁰ Although he refers in this instance explicitly to the family, following through his argument on the same page, it can be easily surmised that he thought of familial power here as paternal and patriarchal which invariably as sovereign power dominates and subjugates. If as earlier intimated, power is everywhere and exists from bottom to top, then there ought to be maternal power and a certain kind of power that children and others in the family depending perhaps on the role they play wield too. If also, power generates a form of resistance and paternal power dominates, what then does maternal caregiving power do?

Amy Allen in *Rethinking Power* argues that since gender is the primary field through which power is articulated, a feminist critique of gender should necessitate a feminist critique of power. Allen argues that "feminists have traditionally talked about power in one of two ways: either by focusing on the ways in which men have *power over* women – that is, on power understood as domination-or by concentrating on the *power that women have to* act-that is, on power understood as empowerment."⁷¹ She refers to power as domination as 'power over' and power as empowerment as 'power to.' Allen adds a third dimension which she calls 'power with.' We will keep our arguments however within the limits of power over and power to. Allen theorizes "the power that women retain in spite of masculine domination... with a more specific type of empowerment; namely, resistance."⁷² Resistance then, taking the form of empowerment, stands in opposition, as an antithesis, to male domination. She details further that, "whereas the feminist interest in empowerment arises out of the need to theorize the power that women have regardless of the power that men have over us, the interest in resistance emerges from the need to understand the power that women exercise as a response to male domination."[73]

Conceiving power thus as domination with its odd term or resistance being empowerment, Allen fuses for us the two conflicting conceptions of power which we have mined from the works of the early and later Foucault. So, while power is omnipresent, and can reside in the paternal patriarch as sovereign subjugating power—power over women as wives—and since Foucault posits that power must necessarily yield resistance, we find then in women a resistance to sovereign dominating power both as *power over* and *power to*. Much as Allen notes that these two conceptions of power are not all embracing of current feminist perspectives on the matter, it is however in the sphere of these two conceptions of power that we will base our analysis of power dynamics within the family.

The domination-theoretical view as *power over*, according to Allen, defines itself as opposing a conventional view of gender, where it is assumed that natural/innate differences between men and women are accountable for the domination of women by men. "In this understanding, differences between men and women are not in themselves problematic. Instead, what is problematic are the costs and benefits unjustly attached to those differences."[74] The unjust costs and benefits attached to difference continue in itself to be a form of power relation not just between men and women but between races—the dominating and the dominated—as well. To echo Allen, in the thoughts of MacKinnon: "difference is the velvet glove on the iron fist of domination. The problem is not that differences are not valued; the problem is that they are defined by power."[75] Domination theorists thrive, however, on their belief that resistance on the part of women to male domination is possible. "Indeed, if they did not believe that women had such a capacity, their discussion of male domination would have no point. Precisely the point is to get women angry enough about their situation to go out and start resisting."[76] One of such resistances has its theoretical foothold in the resource theory.

The resource theory moves the argument of power as dominance beyond the nature-nurture debate into the social and economic resource that each partner brings into the marriage. This view is suggested to have emanated from the field research conducted by Robert Blood and Donald Wolfe in *Husbands and Wives: The Dynamics of Married Living (1960)*. "The resource theory postulates that the balance of conjugal power is determined by the accumulation of many impacts stemming from a variety of resources."[77] Resources are generally believed to be financial, educational and occupational in nature. Robert Dahl however argues that there are no generally accepted ways of classifying resources[78]; this then makes the list of resources inexhaustible. For Katz and Peres, sexual adequacy is a necessary resource to make the list complete. The resource theory in its simplest form can be equated to the adage, 'the piper dictates the tune.' The kind of resistance that this has necessitated suggests that, if women across all societies had as much access to educational, financial and occupational resources as men, then a different dynamic would emerge. This implies then that one of the ways to reduce male dominance would be to open up women's access beyond the private sphere where they have been long confined. Nevertheless, within the private sphere, women have been able to demonstrate how powerful they can be.

An important observation Allen raises about the domination-theoretical view is that if men are powerful and women powerless, then an adequate conceptualization of women's resistance to oppression would have been denied. "Once power is defined as something that men have and women do not, instances in which women assert their own power over and against forces of domination will be invisible to the domination-theoretical apparatus."[79] African feminists often cite the all-female military regiment of Dahomey kingdom and the riots of the Aba women among others as instances where women have asserted their power over forces of domination. Other battles are fought and won within what one might call the "private space within the private sphere." Within this space, a lot of women without the occupational, educational and economic resource to be seen as dominant and powerful, wield power equal to a sovereign. In the corners of their bedrooms, they dominate rulers. Sex, beyond being a resource, becomes a weapon that is capable of turning around the table of power in the *other room*.[80] The other room and the household at large can be a space where feminine power is deployed. For women who understand negotiation, who know when, where and how to detonate patriarchal land mines and how to negotiate with or negotiate around patriarchy in different contexts,[81] power is everywhere, from the bottom to the top.

While the earlier discussion illustrates an instance of a woman's subtle assertion of dominance, it also intertwines with the empowerment-resistance argument. Allen contends that empowerment-resistance theorists ground capacities intrinsic to the feminine, such as the maternal instinct of caregiving, nurturing and protection of children, as feminine power. In the same vein, it is possible to argue that the power of the 'other room,' for women who know how to exercise it, is also feminine power as it is intrinsic to woman. If, according to Pateman,[82] the contract that founds patriarchal society is both social and sexual and this social-sexual contract establishes a series of social relations which gives men the power to dominate individual women, creating what Pateman calls the "law of male sex-right," and men exercise this right by sexually subjugating women, then women who know how and when to negotiate such dominance ought as well to exercise the power of 'the other room,' as a form of resistance and as domination too. For in love as in war, all is fair.

While empowerment theorists, in Allen's analysis, acknowledge the fact that men have power over women in patriarchal societies, they are however inclined to focus on power of a different sort, which is "women's power to transform themselves, others, and the world."[83] This transformative power, empowerment theorists believe, emerges from maternal and caregiving qualities intrinsic to women, and that this perspective "can provide the basis for a new way to think about power."[84] Maternal power or the power of mothers is seen by theorists of this view as transformative as opposed to dominating or controlling. A major criticism of this position is that not all women are mothers. Also, maternal power over children can be controlling and dominating; therefore, 'power to' and 'power over' are actually different sides of the same coin. Allen states it succinctly that: "Women's use of power is not necessarily benevolent; we are not unable or unwilling to use our power to hurt others simply because we are women; many women have access to power over other women by virtue of their race, class, and/or sexual orientation."[85] The traditional African extended family where seniority is one of the organizing principles gives us a good ground to discuss women's access to power over other women.

Seniority as an organizing principle among the Yorùbá people is held in high esteem and is applicable in all walks of life. The custom as Fadipe notes "cuts through distinctions of wealth, of rank, and of sex."[86] As earlier noted in our analysis of the traditional African family, family ties are extended through marriage. Among the Yorùbá, the in-coming wife is seen as birthed into the family at her point of entry by marriage. This then implies that all the living members of the family at her point of entry are seen as senior to her even if the in-coming wife was chronologically older.[87] Oftentimes, the power dynamics at play in such Yoruba familial settings is one of dominance, women's *power over* other women. Seniority here becomes the ideology masking other forms of power relations in which familial abuse is couched.[88]

Power relations within the family and, indeed, any social organization or institution can be both complex and dynamic. Complex because power is a relational tool and is dependent on other power forms. Dynamic because, as a relational tool, it is characterized by a highly developed ability to change. Power in itself is a fluid concept, flowing easily, everywhere. Power as domination, empowerment, resistance, coalition, as benevolent or malevolent, still has its defining characteristics in controlling or influencing others. Since power controls or influences, it entails then a dyadic master subject relationship and this relationship is apt to change without the conscious awareness of its principal actors. *Power over* and *power to* are just notional and idealistic perspectives of the problematic. Who dominates who is a matter of many complexities that we might never adequately conceptualize or even understand.

Notes

1. Baber, K.M. 2009. 'Postmodern Feminist perspectives and Families.' In *Handbook of Feminist Family Studies*. Eds. S.A Lloyd, A.L Few & K.R Allen. Los Angeles & London: Sage Publications. 58.
2. McCarthy, J.R & Edwards, R. 2011. *Key Concepts in Family Studies*. Los Angeles & London: Sage Publications. 58.
3. Duignan, B. 'Postmodernism.' Encyclopedia Britannica.
4. Gubrium, J. & Holstein, J. 1999. What is Family? Further Thoughts on a Social Constructionist Approach. *Marriage and Family Review*. Vol. 28. No. 3/4. The Haworth Press, Inc. 4.

5. See Allen, K.R. & Demo, D.H. 1995. The Families of Lesbian and Gay Men: A New Frontier in Family Research. *Journal of Marriage and the Family.* Vol. 57 No.1. Published by: National Council on Family Relations.
6. Bielby, D.D. 2006. Gender and Family Relations. *Handbook of the Sociology of Gender.* Ed. J.F Chafetz. New York: Springer. 393.
7. Eichler, M. 1981. The Inadequacy of the Monolithic Model of the Family. *The Canadian Journal of Sociology / Cahiers canadiens de sociologie.* Vol. 6, No. 3. Published by: Canadian Journal of Sociology. 371.
8. Ibid.: 377.
9. See Tyyskä, V. 2007. Sociology and the Monolithic Model of the Family. *Immigrant Families in Contemporary Society.* Eds. J. E Lansford, K. Deater-Deckard & M.H Bornstein. New York & London: The Guildford Press. 2007.
10. Ibid.: 83.
11. Janssens, A. 1997. The Rise and Decline of the Male Breadwinner Family? An Overview of the Debate. *International Review of Social History Supplement 5.* Ed. A. Janssens. Vol. 42. Cambridge: Cambridge University Press. 2.
12. Ibid.: 3.
13. Trask, B.S. 2010. *Globalization and Families: Accelerated Systemic Social Change.* New York & London: Springer. 49.
14. Ibid.
15. See Gubrium and Holstein (1999).
16. I paraphrase here McCarthy and Edwards (2011)
17. Parsons, T & Bales, R. 1955. *Family, Socialization and Interaction Process.* Illinois: The Free Press, Glencoe. 23.
18. In the idea of Shehan, C & Kaestle, C. 2009. 'Gendered Bodies in Family Studies: A Feminist Examination of Constructionist and Biosocial Perspectives on Families.' In *Handbook of Feminist Family Studies.* Eds. S.A Lloyd, A.L Few & K.R Allen. Los Angeles & London: Sage Publications.
19. Ibid.: 86.
20. Dahlberg, F. 1981. *Woman the Gatherer.* New Haven & London: Yale University Press. 10, 11.
21. Ibid.: 9.
22. Ibid.: 12.
23. To paraphrase Zinn, M.B. 2000. "Feminism and Family Studies for a New Century." *The Annals of the American Academy of Political and Social Science.* Vol. 571.
24. Ibid.: 44.
25. Patterson, C.J. 1997. "What research SHOWS: About Gay and Lesbian Parents and Their Children." *Family Advocate.* Vol. 20, No. 1. Published by: American Bar Association. 27.
26. Allen, K.R. & Demo, D.H. 1995. The Families of Lesbian and Gay Men: A New Frontier in Family Research. *Journal of Marriage and the Family.* Vol. 57 No.1. Published by: National Council on Family Relations. 112.
27. See Gibson (1999), as well as Patterson (1997).
28. Lesbian, gay, bisexual, transgender and queer (LGBTQ+) rights have significantly progressed over time in the West. Prior to June 2015, when the Supreme Court struck down all bans on same-sex marriages in the United States, partners in same-sex marriages could only adopt the biological children of the other

partner; in some cases, the couple could only adopt a child that is of the same sex, while some were not allowed at all.
29. Sudarkasa, N. 1980. African and Afro-American Family Structure: A Comparison. *The Black Scholar.* Vol. 11, No. 8, Black Anthropology. Published by: Taylor & Francis, Ltd. 44.
30. Dasylva, A.B. 2017. Family, Indigenous Education System, and Discipline. In *Culture and Customs of the Yorùbá.* Eds. T. Falola & A. Akinyemi. Austin, Texas: Pan African University Press. 709.
31. Ibid.
32. Tetteh, cited in Surdakasa (1980) *op.cit.* 47.
33. Ibid.: 38.
34. Ibid.: 41.
35. Ibid.: 46.
36. Murdock, G.P. 1949. *The Social Structure.* New York: The Macmillan Company, London: Collier-Macmillan Ltd. 23.
37. Surdakasa (1980). *Op.cit.* 46.
38. Linton, R. 1936. *The Study of Man: An Introduction.* New York: Appleton-Century-Crofts. 153.
39. Ibid.: 159.
40. Ibid.
41. Surdakasa (1980). *Op.cit.* 46.
42. As a result of modernization through which developments like industrialization and urbanization have occurred, the traditional African family forms and traditional African settlements have been and are still experiencing steady alteration.
43. Aldous, J. 1962. Urbanization, the Extended Family, and Kinship Ties in West Africa. *Social Forces,* Vol. 41, No. 1. Published by: Oxford University Press. 10.
44. Fadipe, N.A. 2012 (3rd Reprint). *The Sociology of the Yoruba.* Ibadan: Ibadan University Press. 106.
45. Miner, 1953 cited in Aldous (1962) *op.cit.* 8.
46. This work adopts the African traditional family as a more suitable concept to the extended family. Also, we refer explicitly about the Yoruba people here.
47. In the idea of Fadipe (2012). *Op.cit.*
48. See Joan Aldous's analysis in for other forms of socialization through support systems and how these familial support systems substituted for the nonexistent public welfare program.
49. Fadipe (2012) mentions this too.
50. Fadipe (2012). *Op.cit.* 311.
51. Dasylva, A.B. 2017. Family, Indigenous Education System, and Discipline. In *Culture and Customs of the Yorùbá.* Eds. T. Falola & A. Akinyemi. Austin, Texas: Pan African University Press. 710.
52. The *Omolúàbí* is a concept among the Yoruba, which describes an individual who is seen as responsible in character, deeds, dressing and appearance and language use.
53. Ibid.
54. Annan-Yao, E. 2004. Analysis of Gender Relations in the Family, Formal Education and Health in *Gender, Economies and Entitlements in Africa.* Dakar: CODESRIA. 2.
55. Ibid.

56. Lukes, S. 1977. *Essays in Social Theory*. London & Basingstoke: Macmillan Press Ltd. 4.
57. Foucault, M. 1978. *The History of Sexuality*. Trl. By Robert Hurley. New York: Pantheon Books. 92.
58. Lukes, S. (1977). *Op.cit.* 7.
59. Foucault, M. (1978). *Op.cit.* 93.
60. See Morriss, P. 2002. *Power: A Philosophical Analysis*. 2nd Edition. Manchester & New York: Manchester University Press.
61. Foucault, M. 1978. *The ... Sexuality*. *Op.cit.* 92.
62. Ibid.: 93.
63. Ibid.: 94.
64. Gardner, C.V. 2006. *Historical Dictionary of Feminist Philosophy*. Maryland, Toronto & Oxford: The Scarecrow Press, Inc. 94.
65. Foucault, M. 1978. *The ... Sexuality*. *Op.cit.* 95.
66. Ibid.
67. Ibid.: 96. Emphasis added.
68. Foucault, M. 2006. *Psychiatric Power: Lectures at the College de France 1973–1974*. Trl by G. Burchell. Basingstoke & New York: Palgrave Macmillan. 79.
69. Ibid.: 80.
70. Ibid.
71. Allen, A. 1998. Rethinking Power. *Hypatia*. Vol. 13, No. 1. Published by Wiley on behalf of Hypatia, Inc. 22. Emphasis added.
72. Ibid.: 32.
73. Ibid.
74. Ibid.: 22–23.
75. MacKinnon, 1989 cited in Allen, Ibid.: 23.
76. Ibid.: 25.
77. Katz, R & Peres, Y. 1985. Is Resource Theory Equally Applicable to Wives and Husbands? *Journal of Comparative Family Studies*. Vol. 16, No. 1. Published by: University of Toronto Press. 5.
78. See Robert Dahl's analysis on *Power*. Online source https://www.encyclopedia.com/science-and-technology/physics/physics/power
79. Allen, A. 1998. Rethinking Power. *Op.cit.* 25.
80. In 2016, standing next to Chancellor Angela Merkel, one of the most influential women in the world, Nigerian President Muhammed Buhari made a controversial statement that generated a lot of conversation on social media and the academe, leading to what Nigerians refer to as the 'power of the other room.' The president in response to his wife's criticism of his government had said: "I don't know which party my wife belongs to, but she belongs to my kitchen and my living room and the other room".
81. I use here the thoughts of Nnaemeka albeit in a different context. For details, see Nnaemeka, O. 2004. Nego-Feminism: Theorizing, Practicing, and Pruning Africa's Way. *Signs* Development Cultures: New Environments, New Realities, New Strategies. Eds. F. Lionnet, O. Nnaemeka, S. H. Perry, C. Schenck. Vol. 29, No. 2. Published by: The University of Chicago Press. 378.
82. Pateman, 1988, cited in Allen (1998).
83. Allen, A. 1998. Rethinking Power. *Op.cit.* 26.
84. Ibid.
85. Ibid.: 31.

86. Fadipe, N.A. 2012 (3rd Reprint). *The Sociology of the Yoruba*. Ibadan: Ibadan University Press. 129.
87. For detailed analysis, see Johnson, S. 2009. *History of the Yorubas: From the Earliest Times to the Beginning of the British Protectorate*. Lagos: CSS Bookshops. pp. 146. Also, Oyewumi, O. 1997. *The Invention of Woman: Making an African Sense of Western Gender Discourses*. London: University of Minnesota Press. pp. 46.
88. Bakare-Yusuf, B. 2004. "Yoruba's Don't Do Gender": A Critical review of Oyeronke Oyewumi's The Invention of Women: Making an African Sense of Western Gender Discourses. *African Gender Scholarship: Concepts, Methodologies and Paradigms*. Dakar: CODESRIA.

BIBLIOGRAPHY

Aldous, J. 1962. Urbanization, the Extended Family, and Kinship Ties in West Africa. *Social Forces* 41 (1): 6–12. Oxford University Press.

Allen, A. 1998. Rethinking Power. *Hypatia* 13 (1): 21–40. Wiley on behalf of Hypatia, Inc.

Allen, K.R., and D.H. Demo. 1995. The Families of Lesbian and Gay Men: A New Frontier in Family Research. *Journal of Marriage and the Family* 57 (1): 111–127. National Council on Family Relations.

Annan-Yao, E. 2004. Analysis of Gender Relations in the Family, Formal Education and Health. In *Gender, Economies and Entitlements in Africa*. Dakar: CODESRIA.

Baber, K.M. 2009. Postmodern Feminist Perspectives and Families. In *Handbook of Feminist Family Studies*, ed. S.A. Lloyd, A.L. Few, and K.R. Allen. Los Angeles/London: Sage Publications.

Bakare-Yusuf, B. 2004. "Yoruba's Don't Do Gender": A Critical Review of Oyeronke Oyewumi's The Invention of Women: Making an African Sense of Western Gender Discourses. In *African Gender Scholarship: Concepts, Methodologies and Paradigms*, ed. S. Arnfrede et al. Dakar: CODESRIA.

Bielby, D.D. 2006. Gender and Family Relations. In *Handbook of the Sociology of Gender*, ed. J.F. Chafetz. New York: Springer.

Dahl, R. Power. Online Source https://www.encyclopedia.com/science-and-technology/physics/physics/power

Dahlberg, F. 1981. *Woman the Gatherer*. New Haven/London: Yale University Press.

Dasylva, A.B. 2017. Family, Indigenous Education System, and Discipline. In *Culture and Customs of the Yorùbá*, ed. T. Falola and A. Akinyemi. Austin: Pan African University Press.

Duignan, B. Postmodernism. Encyclopedia Britannica.

Eichler, M. 1981. The Inadequacy of the Monolithic Model of the Family. *The Canadian Journal of Sociology/Cahiers canadiens de sociologie* 6 (3): 367–388. Canadian Journal of Sociology.

Fadipe, N.A. 2012 (3rd Reprint). *The Sociology of the Yoruba*. Ibadan: Ibadan University Press.

Foucault, M. 1978. *The History of Sexuality*. Trans. Robert Hurley. New York: Pantheon Books.

———. 2006. *Psychiatric Power: Lectures at the College de France 1973–1974*. Trans. G. Burchell. Basingstoke/New York: Palgrave Macmillan.

Gardner, C.V. 2006. *Historical Dictionary of Feminist Philosophy*. Maryland/Toronto/Oxford: The Scarecrow Press, Inc..

Gibson, J.G. 1999. Lesbian and Gay Prospective Adoptive Parents: The Legal Battle. *Human Rights* 26 (2): 7–11. American Bar Association.

Gubrium, J., and J. Holstein. 1999. What Is Family? Further Thoughts on a Social Constructionist Approach. *Marriage & Family Review* 28 (3/4): 3–20. The Haworth Press, Inc.

Janssens, A. 1997. The Rise and Decline of the Male Breadwinner Family? An Overview of the Debate. In *International Review of Social History Supplement 5*, ed. A. Janssens, vol. 42. Cambridge: Cambridge University Press.

Katz, R., and Y. Peres. 1985. Is Resource Theory Equally Applicable to Wives and Husbands ? *Journal of Comparative Family Studies* 16 (1): 1–10. University of Toronto Press.

Linton, R. 1936. *The Study of Man: An Introduction*. New York: Appleton-Century-Crofts.

Lukes, S. 1977. *Essays in Social Theory*. London/Basingstoke: Macmillan Press Ltd..

Mandela, N. 1994. *Long Walk to Freedom*. New York: Little Brown & Co..

McCarthy, J.R., and R. Edwards. 2011. *Key Concepts in Family Studies*. Los Angeles/London: Sage Publications.

Morriss, P. 2002. *Power: A Philosophical Analysis*. 2nd ed. Manchester/New York: Manchester University Press.

Murdock, G.P. 1949. *The Social Structure*. New York/London: The Macmillan Company/Collier-Macmillan Ltd.

Nnaemeka, O. 2004. Nego-Feminism: Theorizing, Practicing, and Pruning Africa's Way. In *Signs Development Cultures: New Environments, New Realities, New Strategies*, ed. F. Lionnet, O. Nnaemeka, S. H. Perry, C. Schenck, Vol. 29(2). Chicago The University of Chicago Press.

Parsons, T., and R. Bales. 1955. *Family, Socialization and Interaction Process*. Illinois: The Free Press, Glencoe.

Patterson, C.J. 1997. What Research Shows: About Gay and Lesbian Parents and Their Children. *Family Advocate* 20 (1): 27–28. American Bar Association.

Shehan, C., and C. Kaestle. 2009. Gendered Bodies in Family Studies: A Feminist Examination of Constructionist and Biosocial Perspectives on Families. In *Handbook of Feminist Family Studies*, ed. S.A. Lloyd, A.L. Few, and K.R. Allen. Los Angeles/London: Sage Publications.

Sudarkasa, N. 1980. African and Afro-American Family Structure: A Comparison. *The Black Scholar* 11 (8): 37–60. Black Anthropology. Taylor & Francis, Ltd.

Trask, B.S. 2010. *Globalization and Families: Accelerated Systemic Social Change*. New York/London: Springer.

Tyyskä, V. 2007. Sociology and the Monolithic Model of the Family. In *Immigrant Families in Contemporary Society*, ed. J.E. Lansford, K. Deater-Deckard, and M.H. Bornstein. New York/London: The Guildford Press.

Zinn, M.B. 2000. Feminism and Family Studies for a New Century. *The Annals of the American Academy of Political and Social Science*. 571: 42–56.

CHAPTER 4

Abuses of Children (Labor and Witchcraft Accusations)

Samson O. Ijaola

Common to both child labor and witchcraft accusations are abuses and in extreme cases violence, which are inimical to child's behavioral, cognitive, cultural, emotional, psychological, physical, social and spiritual developments. Inarguably, the preponderance of child labor and witchcraft accusations in Africa have been linked by scholars and several non-state actors to poor social and economic development facing the continent. Unemployment, low per capita income, poverty and other cultural practices are therefore the stimuli for both child labor and witchcraft accusations. The spiritual worldview of Africans, which entrench fears and suspicions of clandestine mystical activities that could harm their well-being, is also associated to witchcraft.

The ethical concerns, ranging from the increasing rate of street children and out-of-school children, leading to distorted socialization and propensity to and incidence of criminality among children and to the consequential effects on the current and future cultural development and socioeconomic growth of African society consequent upon child labor and witchcraft accusations, require critical thinking. This chapter notes that the prevalence of child abuse in the form of labor and witchcraft accusations in the black sub-Saharan Africa are alarming and portends a dangerous future for the continent.

Both child labor and child witchcraft accusations are robbing Africa of the prosperity of her posterity in children. The increasing number of violence against children, child abandonment, homelessness and other pathetic conditions faced by children, consequent upon these cultural practices, questions the role of the

---

S. O. Ijaola (✉)
Department of Philosophy and Religious Studies, Samuel Adegboyega University, Ogwa, Nigeria

state in making and implementing ethical sound policies that would protect African children from violence. It is however pitiable that African states, such as Zimbabwe and others in Southern Africa, afford legal backing to witchcraft accusations through witch doctors, who not only hunt innocent children but ensure jungle justice or prescribe treatment as the case may be.[1] Modern Africa appears trapped in lack of lucid understanding of her traditions on the conception of child and childhood.

It is also disheartening that despite the global concerns and investment through financial aids toward child right and development, Africa scores very low in programs, which aims at eradicating child labor and other cultural practices that promote abuses of children. Noting the important role that childhood plays in the trajectory of human development especially, in the formation of perception about and attitudes to the society, the need to ethically examine both factors aiding the spread of child labor and witchcraft accusations with the aim to reverse their effects cannot be over-emphasized. It is against this background that this chapter employs critical approach to discuss the concept of child and childhood, and examine child labor and witchcraft accusations in Africa within the global context.

Conceptual Discourse on Child and Childhood

The subject "child" has generated various viewpoints from disparate cultures, and it has elicited responses from various scholars. It appears that the term is not simply a biological category of a person within a particular age bracket and dependent on adults, especially, parents. Moreover, most scholars of child and childhood agree that these two concepts fall within the same social experience, but they are diverse from one nation and continent to the other. Hence, they cannot be discussed independently.[2] The idea of a conventional definition of child therefore becomes subjective in the light of various socio-cultural contexts and their worldviews. Little wonder, despite various cultural efforts and scholarly attempts to enhance the quality and understanding of childhood over centuries, there is no common front on the conception of childhood as a social practice today.[3] This chapter therefore adopts the International Labour Organization (ILO) convention to categorize children as human persons, either boys or girls under the age of 18.[4]

Social constructionists further note that the various stages and interactions within human traditions, society and technological advancement are responsible for different perspectives on the notion of child or childhood.[5] It is interesting that sociologists also do not have a synoptic approach to the study of children as they vary in their concentrations. While the emphasis on the child as social agent and participant in the epistemic formation through everyday phenomenon is the interest of scholars in "Sociology of Children," the diverse dialogs on children and childhood are the main focus of the "Deconstructive Sociology of Childhood."[6] In the same vein, there is "Structural Sociology of

Childhood," which is concerned with the major trajectories such as urbanization, scholarization and generation.[7] Rachita Bisht, quoting Mayall, suggests social generation is the best approach to the study of the child in relation to the society.[8]

To clearly answer the question—who is a child?—requires therefore the appreciation of social constructions of the various generations of a given society. Little wonder, African scholars, such as Boakye-Boaten, Amasa Ndofirepi and Almon Shumba in their works, reject both the biological, natural and universal classifications denoting who a child is. Their perspectives largely concur with the sociological inclination of child and childhood as historical, cultural and social variables. This is because it is inescapable to misconstrue these ideas if universalized.[9] Hence, they averred that cultural milieu provides the best appreciation of who a child is.[10]

The African socio-cultural context for child and childhood discourse can be classified into both the precolonial and postcolonial era. Going by the social generation approach, it is important to know the trajectory of the social construction of child and childhood in Africa. In their search to clearly depict an African child, both Ndofirepi and Shumba assert that "children and the notion of 'child' have been regarded in very different ways in different historical epochs, in different cultures and in different social groups."[11] Defining an African child merely from the modern view is cursory without noting the various epochal categorizations and their intersections. For Ndofirepi and Shumba, "a 'child' in Africa will be compartmentalised into the traditional person who is little affected by modernisation, the transitional person often living in, and shuttling between traditional African and western cultures, while the modern individual is one who participates fully in the activities of the contemporary, industrial or post-industrial world."[12] This classification follows the structural sociology of childhood, taking cognizance of not merely the social generation, but the traditional and modern nature of the society, as affected by other factors such as education, advancement in technology and politics. Inarguably, politics and in recent times globalization play important roles in the socio-cultural constructions of child and childhood. Boakye-Boaten opines that "Childhood in contemporary times has become a contentious concept, because of the political claims of culture and the notion of identity." Most importantly, the debate on children has intensified, as a result of the increasing rate of globalization, and the changing roles of children within the socio-cultural and political construct of modern societies. Modern global trends have affected many indigenous societies, transforming tremendously "the social structure and institutions of these societies."[13] Thus, Africa could not have maintained undisrupted conception of child and childhood, as a result of changes it experiences through colonization and, in the recent times, globalization. Further, the notion of child and childhood can be overtly or surreptitiously subjected to changes and redefinitions, consequent upon external interferences within the society.[14] Since pre-colonial Africa was utterly interrupted by colonial, Christian and Islam ideologies, the effects of such external intrusions into their socio-cultural order and the political philosophy definitely disrupt their traditional notion of child and child hood.

That the concepts of child and childhood exist before the colonization of African nations do not necessarily suggest that all of Africa possess a common notion of child. However, there are important common features that dominate their general outlook on the notion of child.[15] The traditional African societies' educational curricular for children contains their customs, values and cosmologies within their living environment. Tales and myths provide the channels of learning morals and etiquettes of the family and society by children. The interconnectedness of the cultural, spiritual, social, physical and political are established and passed on to the children through participation in certain religious activities. Children are also taught by examples the virtues of love, kindness, prudence, respect and obedience to elders and parents as encoded in religious doctrines and taboos.[16] "Characterised by a communalistic philosophy, traditional African communities place the child in close contact with a larger group, socialise the young into the group, and the group in turn has the responsibility towards the child."[17] "The child responds by offering a duty towards not only the immediate family members but also the larger community. Thus a reciprocal relationship prevails."[18] This is in exchange for "sharing resources, burden, and social responsibility, mutual aid, caring for others, interdependence, solidarity, reciprocal obligation, social harmony and mutual trust."[19]

CHILD LABOR

Engaging children in economic activities in Africa has come under global scrutiny. This is not unconnected to both the prevalence and the negative impacts labor has on the holistic development of children. It is inarguable that the future of a nation lies on the kind of upbringing given to its children population. The fact that a large population of African children are being exploitatively engaged in lieu of adults in strenuous labor and, as a result, being exposed to violence in the workplace, within and beyond their home countries, do not only defy International Labour Organization (ILO) standard,[20] but it raises some ethical questions about such a practice in contemporary Africa. Noting that the effects of child labor is not merely on the child, parents and the immediate family, but it also resonates to the community, nation, continent and the global community, which justifies the global concerns on child labor. This section of the chapter therefore examines child labor from the African root and locates it in the global ethical concerns on child labor:

> ILO defines child laborers as (1) children between 5-11 years of age who are economically active; (2) children between 12-14 years of age who work in an economic activity for 14 or more hours per week, and (3) children between 12-17 years of age engaged in hazardous work. The definition of child labor used by the ILO is derived from two conventions, Convention 138 on the Minimum Age for

Admission to Employment and Work, which sets the minimum working age at 15 years (14 years for some developing countries), and Convention 182 on the Worst Forms of Child Labor, which focuses on the worst forms of child labor.[21]

It important to note that the basic assumptions of ILO regarding this definition are the fact of economic exploitation and distraction from schooling. The definition does not negate the participation of children in domestic chores since they are neither economically exploitative nor distracting children from schools. Child labor, therefore, is primarily a response to economic challenges such as poverty and other needs for the survival of the family. While there are circumstances such as orphanhood, domestic violence, separation of parents and others, the major factors are related to economic problems affecting individual families.

Africa in the modern context tops the regional incidence of child labor in the world with 19.6% of the total 152 million children followed by Asia: 7.4%, Americas: 5.3%, Europe and Central Asia: 4.1% and Arab States: 2.9%.[22] Child labor is connected to poor economic growth and development, which is apparent in Africa. The child labor incidence appears to correspond directly with the regional incidence of poverty. Of the 728.4 million people in the world living below US$1.9 (abject poverty line), 413.25 million are in the sub-Saharan Africa, 25.90 million in Latin America and Caribbean, 18.64 million in the Middle East and North Africa, 7.32 million in other high-income countries and a negligible number in the South Asia.[23] It is therefore apparent that child labor is strongly connected to poverty in Africa. It is also arguable that the prevalence of poverty in sub-Saharan Africa is the causative factor of child labor.

The trajectory of child labor in Africa can be traced to but not necessarily rooted in the pre-colonial agrarian economy and other cultural economic practices. Interestingly, in this postmodern era, most nations' economy in Africa yet depends on agriculture as the main provider of jobs. Thus, agriculture as a means to earn a living in Africa appears as a culprit in the prevalence of child labor, noting its recent estimate of 59% of 98 million of children engaged in labor worldwide.[24] Child labor, defined as "work for which the child is too young–i.e., work done below the required minimum age"[25] can be applied to pre-colonial Africa. Nevertheless, there is need for a critical examination and application of what exactly constitutes child labor, considering the generational gap between the precolonial and postcolonial Africa, given the role of formal education, advance technology and modern economy.

The pre-colonial African society places good value on children. Having children among Africans is more or else a necessity. The reason that the inability of a couple to have a child becomes a problem attracting multifaceted approaches. In fact, both spiritual and traditional helps are often explored by couples having challenges with infertility. In some cases, help is sought from extended families. At such patronage of different faiths in search of cure, all in the attempt to have a child becomes orthodox. As children grow into adults, it is anticipated, in most cases, that they function as image makers of their families, provide for parents and sustain the family lineage. Against this background, children are expected to be given the best upbringing, but this can suffer some limitations due to a number of factors such as death of both or either of the parents, sickness and poverty.

Exploitative child labor is contradistinctive to values that Africans place on children and their upbringing. Whereas child labor existed before transatlantic slave trade in the pre-colonial Africa, such form of labor in most societies were neither aimed nor designed to be detrimental to the child development. Scholars have argued that the child labor in the pre-colonial Africa, where farmwork and other domestic shores were regarded as the process of educating the child.[26] Such works were not with the intention of exploiting the child. On the contrary, they were practical and vocational trainings designed along the theoretical modes of inculcating values, morals, customs and traditions in their traditional education curricula cannot be analyzed within the modern context of child labor.

The traditional African children just like American and European children worked in farms and at home over a long history prior to 1950s.[27] Child labor in the predominantly agrarian pre-colonial Africa, as in other continents before the 1950s, was therefore perceived as a means to introduce to the children and the children to a culture of responsibility.[28] The kind of works allotted to children during their training was also dependent on their age and strength. In this way, child engagement in farmwork or domestic chores, without exploiting them and exposing to danger but for the purpose of acquiring vocational and life skills are best classified as child work. Endlyne Anugwon observes the need to categorize child work and child labor as disparate concepts in order to put the latter in the right perspective and context.[29] He considers child work as neutral and good, but child labor as bad for the children.[30] The emphasis on the difference is to avoid such misapplication of either of the two concepts, especially, in African homes where children help out their parents with domestic chores.

Domestic chores could be regarded as child labor when it becomes abusive and lends to endangering the child physically, mentally, socially and spiritually. There are instances of domestic child labor in the precolonial Africa,[31] as occurrence of pawning children as bonded labor emerged in the pre-nineteenth century.[32] Recent findings show that there are some cultural practices that support child labor in contemporary Africa. For instance, the "money wife" (child marriage in exchange for money and food). While it is difficult to determine the prevalence of some of these cultural practices, the communal philosophy, strongly enshrined in pre-colonial Africa, would suggest a conclusion that they were mild. "The issue of sexual abuse of child domestic workers has received some attention recently, it remains an under-explored subject because of its sensitivity, and because of moral discourses and stigma surrounding girls' sexuality and sexual abuse, including while working on household chores."[33]

Both in the precolonial and postcolonial Africa, "child labour is largely driven by vulnerabilities caused by poverty and deprivation."[34] Poverty is, no doubt, endemic in the modern Sub-Saharan Africa. World Bank report on poverty, as of 2018, shows that abject poverty is increasing and not decreasing in the sub-Saharan Africa as of November, 2018.[35] Progress to eliminate child labor is therefore closely linked to reducing these vulnerabilities, mitigating economic shocks and providing families with social protection and an adequate level of regular income.[36]

According to Article 32 (1) of the Convention on Child Right, "a child must to be protected from economic exploitation and from performing any work that is likely to be hazardous or interfere with the child's education, or that is likely to harm the child's health or, physical, mental, spiritual, moral or social development." Other international instruments, especially the *Convention concerning the Prohibition and Immediate Action for the Elimination of the Worst Forms of Child Labour (Entry into force: 19 Nov 2000)* further recognizes a child's right to be protected from the "worst forms of child labour," such as conscription into armed conflict, narcotic trafficking and sexual abuse.

Child labor can be located in the present global understanding of slavery, and this takes so many forms. "This 'new slavery'… is quite different from the 'old slavery associated with the transatlantic slave trade." Bales and Robbins argued for the need to redefine the concept of "slavery," in order to detach it from other similar human rights misuses, and to inform better legislation on it, having observed the increasing confusion of the term in the modern society. Having critically explored the "the development of slavery definitions in international agreement from 1815 to the present," their aim is to propose a "more dynamic and universal definition of contemporary slavery from theoretical models and substantive examples" "as a state marked by the loss of free will where a person is forced through violence or the threat of violence to give up the ability to sell freely his or her own labor power." The three key dimensions in this definition of slavery are (1) "control by another person," (2) "the appropriation of labor power," and (3) "the use or threat of violence."

Forced labor such as debt bondage or peonage or pawning was a common cultural practice in the pre-colonial Africa. Oluyemisi Bamgbose categorized child labor to include agriculture labor, domestic labor and pawning or bonded labor known as *iwofa* among the Yoruba people.[37] Slaves and pawns represented the only regular sourced commercial labor outside the family in the pre-colonial days.[38] Pawning is generally described as a form of payment of interest rate on loan through a voluntary offer of labor, while the debtor is raising the principal to pay off the loan. There are various kind of peonage, depending on the arrangement of the lender and the debtor. But unlike a slave, a pawn is a free born, meant to provide labor services for a particular and agreed duration. Toyin Falola noted that the iwofa system as of the mid-nineteenth has been developed to ensure respect of contractual agreements.[39] But this was later abused as the wealthy sought stricter means of collecting the principal from defaulting debtors.[40] At the same time, they sought to enjoy a longer period of peonage for the various domestic and commercial services they received.[41] In the same vein, some bad debtors either became a permanent pawn or abandoned their children or relatives to be used as pawns to the creditor.[42] Where these pawns are mainly children, they became so vulnerable and exposed to abuse and violence. Whereas peonage had its advantages in its earlier structure in African communities, when it served as means of raising capital, acquiring assets, with affordable services to debtor, providing security for children during slave trade and as a scheme that helped the poor to train the young people in vocational skills with "free meals and accommodation."

Peonage does not confer ownership of a peon on the creditor like in the case of a slave. The peon is a free born with rights to own properties. Nevertheless, the abuses of peonage, which promoted the vulnerability of the peons, attracted the condemnation of both the European missionaries and the colonial government, which attributed the system to slavery.[43] While peonage was eradicated in the mid-1920s, some form of child labor survives till date.

The age-old tradition or practice of "money woman" or "money wife" among the Becheve tribe in Obaniluku Local Government of Cross River State, Nigeria, allows girls to be sold out at any time, before or after their birth and without their consent or personal benefits, to either clear debts or provide money and foodstuffs for immediate family or relations.[44] In most cases, girls are sold as low as US$6 and as high as US$60 with or without goat and foodstuffs, depending on the power negotiation and buyer's ability. Money wife is considered dead to her family as she can never be reabsorbed for whatever reason by them nor can separate herself from the buyer's family even after his death.[45] These money wives are often denied education and any form skills acquisition besides farming and domestic work.[46]

From the above discussion, it is apparent that the cultural factors responsible for the practice of child labor in the pre-colonial Africa is connected to economy. While the causes of economic challenges in each of the homes and societies in traditional Africa might not be known, the reality is that it translates into such child labor. In the same vein, the modern Africa experience of child labor is basically an economic induced practice. The rate of poverty in African countries is inarguably a major factor in the spread of child labor. It is suffice to say therefore that economic challenges are a major theme in the trajectory of child labor from the pre-colonial to the contemporary Africa.

CHILD WITCHCRAFT ACCUSATION

The phenomenon of child witchcraft accusation can be located in the bigger context of witchcraft accusation and discourses on witchcraft-related violence, gender and witchcraft, and structural justice. Witchcraft accusation is not peculiar to children. In fact, women appear to have experienced witchcraft accusation more than their male counterparts. This is because in the gender consideration of witchcraft accusations, patriarchalism has been considered as one of the contributing factors.[47] In the same vein, the power struggle in the household, which is often in favor of the man, has been identified as one of the possible causes of witchcraft accusations. This section of the chapter therefore seeks to examine some of the contributing factors of witchcraft accusations and how it has been managed by the state, considering the ethical questions the phenomenon raises.

WITCHCRAFT AND WITCHCRAFT ACCUSATION

Witchcraft accusation is not peculiar to Africa as it appears to cut across all over European and Asian continents in centuries past. The increasing incidence and the dynamics of witchcraft accusations in the modern Africa raise some major concerns, especially for scholars and social observers. Nevertheless, the experiences of child witchcraft accusations, in particular, have also attracted the reactions and engagements of several intergovernmental organizations such as United Nations International Children Emergency Fund (UNICEF) and several non-government organizations that are seeking to put an end to the treatment of or punishment meted out to accused child witches or, preferably, victims of child witchcraft accusations. These efforts are yet to have far-reaching effects due to reasons, including and chiefly, the cultural belief in and perceptions of witchcraft in most African societies. The growing modern consciousness, urbanization, education and government policies (in some African countries against ill-treatment and jungle justice) of the accused witches notwithstanding, the practice of stigmatization, maiming and family rejection of accused and killing of accused child witches are unabated.

Witchcraft is synonymous with dark magic—the practice of evil through some mystical skills. So, witches in most African societies are feared and hated because of the belief that they possess innate or acquired a kind of cosmic power—to manipulate, harm and kill people within and outside their families. Witches, in most cases, are regarded as the enemies of good, causes of bad luck for families and relatives, human eaters and blood suckers through mystical means. It is a common knowledge among Africans that while the operations of witches are within a spiritual space, the negative effects are cosmically experienced by their targets or victims. According to André Mary, a witch is described as "that disconcerting character, who operates more or less undercover, and who employs occult knowledge and controls certain objects and magic techniques…"[48] Also in most African societies, the fear and hate for witches are real and being expressed on a daily basis, in different societies. It is important, therefore, to critically examine the reality of witchcraft in order to justify its capacity to bring about a connection to evils as claimed within African societies.

If witchcraft is evil, questions which require our ethical considerations include: shouldn't it be the responsibility of the state to criminalize, punish and possibly stop or at least discourage it? In the same vein, shouldn't the severity of penalty for witchcraft, where and if criminalized by state, be subject to factors such as the age of the criminal or the gravity of the crime by law in order to avoid jungle justice? Answering these question is very instructive in order to address more fundamental ones—"what happens though after a witch is hunted and killed?"[49] What happens if an accused witch is "proved" innocent?[50] Nevertheless, the question about the truism of witchcraft is a long-term debate in various societies including Africa.

Anthropologists, sociologists and philosophers have lent their voices to the topical debate. Testimonies about witchcraft accusation seem universal. From the old to new Europe, the Americas, Asia and Africa, these testimonies strengthen the cultural beliefs in witchcraft. Partners of Law in Development (PLD) quoting Briggs note that witch hunting, which is related to witchcraft accusation, was at its peak in the seventeenth century all over Europe.[51] There were substantial proofs of witch accusation and witch hunting in British Isles, Estonia, France, Germany, Hungary, the Mediterranean, Netherlands, Russia, Switzerland and Portugal.[52] "Historians in the West delved deeper into the massive witch hunts that took place in the early modern period in Europe and colonial America, leading to the murder and trial of anything between 40,000 to nine million people."[53] The victims as well as the accusation varies from one place to the other. While females were dominant victims in a country, males were popular sufferers in the other.[54]

Early anthropological works reveal that in traditional Africa, witchcraft is part of the recognized social organization.[55] However, witchcraft in Africa since the nineteenth century has been discussed within the context of globalization—capitalism, modernity and state politics by both African and Western scholars.[56] Not surprisingly, Blair Rutherford describes witchcraft, particularly in Africa, as "a set of shifting and versatile practices and idioms deployed within local communities in response to wider social forces of state domination, capitalist commoditization and modernity itself."[57] Despite the thinking in some quarters that witchcraft and witchcraft accusations would fade away with time, it has survived, by transforming itself and changing modes of its presentation.[58] The notion of "witchcraft" is so flexible and elastic that it is able to integrate into all areas of life, including the most "modern."[59]

As a strong cultural belief, it is difficult to neglect several stories, instances of accusations and testimonies of witches and their victims. Thus, to vilify it as mere myths or folktales or as merely "invented traditions"[60] or as "reinvented traditions"[61] as Hobsbawm quoted in Aleksandra Cimpric will neither justify intellectual curiosity about its existential realties nor dismiss the cultural world views. Witchcraft accusations remain a major concern, for which several human rights groups and intergovernmental organizations are seeking state interventions. Witchcraft in the contemporary times has continued to generate heated debate and even aired in the news and social media. Its fame and presence have grown wider beyond its notion in traditional Africa. Witchcraft is present in churches, schools, hospitals and sometimes even in the courthouse.[62] It appears not difficult to believe therefore that "it is omnipresent in the daily lives of many African populations."[63]

A number of findings from both historians and social anthropologists have shown that witchcraft accusation can be motivated by a number of social and economic factors. The advancement of capitalist economy, for instance, was responsible for the economic challenges faced by people in the transition from premodern to modern.[64] PLD, quoting Foster, observes that:

> The existing social relations of pre modern Europe demanded charity and financial and other help from neighbours and familial members towards economically vulnerable people. However, within a new economic framework (the onset of capitalism) and increasing hardship, people found it difficult to practice this and refused pleas for aid, but not without guilt. Ensuing illness, death or misfortune was blamed on spells or witchcraft by those who had been refused aid. Witch hunts were also triggered by epidemics (the phrase 'cholera witches' refers to the 19th century association of witchcraft with the cholera epidemic), abnormal weather, crop destruction, children dying, a drought ('inexplicable' things) and anything worthy of attracting envy.[65]

Witchcraft accusation therefore is not unconnected with the complex relationship among economic, political and social factors.[66] This further extends to the child witchcraft accusation and the attendant violence against children in the urban area. The growing economic challenges such as economic recession, the associated low per capita income for employees, loss of job and unemployment cause frictions at different strata of social relationships in various families, neighborhoods and the society. Cimpric observes that the several military coups and counter coups and military incursions as well as political instability resulting in the loss of life have resulted into rising numbers of orphans and street urchins who are often accused as witches in some African societies.

The declaration of holy war by most Pentecostal, Charismatic, Zionists and spiritual churches has also continued to promote witchcraft accusations. "Their pastor-prophets fight against witchcraft in the name of God, identifying witches through visions and dreams, and then offering treatment – divine healing and exorcism – to the supposed witches. This 'spiritual' work, often of a violent nature, reinforces beliefs in witchcraft and increases accusations."[67] It is apparent that the witchcraft accusation has become a business line as "the more God's servants fight against witchcraft, the more they get involved in treating witches, and at the end of the day, the more they extend the resources of witchcraft"[68] "as well as their own income."[69] Ervin Van Dan Meer further corroborates the fact that both "traditional cultural beliefs and contemporary Pentecostal evangelical influences in Nigerian religious movies are important contributing factors" to witchcraft accusations. He alluded to Stepping Stones Nigeria documentary titled "Saving Africa's Witch Children" in 2008, which focused on child witchcraft beliefs and accusations made by Charismatic and Pentecostal pastors and prophets in Akwa Ibom state in Nigeria.[70] One of his findings in a research he conducted using purposive sampling and in-depth unstructured interview is that Nigerian films on witchcraft, viewed in a number of unauthorized cinema in Southern Malawi, contribute significantly to the southern Malawians' accusation of witches especially children.

Furzee kashyap and Jyoti Prasad Saikia in their own research findings also observe that "conspiracy holds a big stance in this whole discussion of witch hunt practices all over the globe."[71] Their position they found agreeable with Jim Harris work, "Witchcraft, Envy, Development, and Christian Mission in Africa" in 2012, which clearly marks the aspect of envy, jealousy in the cases of witch hunting. The point is that apart from the cultural beliefs in envy has its roles in witchcraft accusation. There are various instances of people.[72]

The actions and inactions of the State in terms of legislations, provision of medical facilities and education have been observed to have flamed violence against children through witchcraft accusations. While some African states in Southern Africa and others including Gambia have one time or the other criminalized witchcraft, some others appear to be neutral or tacit about it. Legislation on witchcraft in most cases complicate witchcraft accusation. For instance, in Zimbabwe, the various laws to suppress witchcraft are both controversial and judicially ineffective to define a witch.[73] In most cases where the State is tacit, the cultural view often prevails to determine the treatment of accused witches. Nevertheless, the economic and social importance of witchcraft accusation such as poverty, forced migration, internal displacement of people, increasing rate of street and out-of-school children and growing crime rate should be the basis for government policy.

African states are not unpopular regarding poor governance and bad leadership. In most African nations, lack of quality medical facilities, services and personnel have further strengthened the belief in witchcraft and promote witchcraft accusation. Death resulting from various sicknesses, and poor yield from farming, are not unknowingly linked to witchcraft instead of climate change, industrial pollution and urbanization. It is therefore not out of common sense to perceive state inaction on witchcraft accusations as a kind of distraction from government ineptness in handling the challenges of the state.

> Any response to accusations of witchcraft against children should strengthen national child protection systems that prevent and respond to abuse, exploitation and violence, including improving service provision, legal frameworks and access to justice. Moreover, programming and advocacy interventions should promote social change by raising awareness among families and community leaders, mobilizing and working with legal professionals and regulating churches and traditional healers.[74]

WITCHCRAFT ACCUSATION AND CHILDREN

The frequency of incidence of children being accused of witchcraft in the world and several parts of Africa, in particular, require ethical reaction from various stake holders. Elderly people, particularly female, used to be the victim of witchcraft accusation. Nowadays, the incidence of children accused of witchcraft is worrisome.[75] It is common that spiritual insecurity provides the premise for the frequent accusations that is "created notably through spreading the idea of ever-present danger, closely linked with that of witchcraft as the source of all evil."[76]

Save the Children and Human Rights Watch in 2006 had reported on the abandonment of children, resulting from witchcraft accusations the Democratic Republic of the Congo.[77] There were similar reports from Angola and other African countries and extended to African immigrants in England.[78] This has been identified as the primary cause of youths' homelessness in Congo and in Kinshasa, exorcism of children is a large part of the reported "cases of abuse in home and church."[79]

According to Cimpric, executions of accused witches is now alarming.[80] Gerrie ter Haar, an anthropologist who has collected proofs of killing of accused witches in "Botswana, Cameroon, Ghana, Namibia, Nigeria and the United Republic of Tanzania," and other writers have raised concerns on upsurge of violence trailing such accusations.[81] Again Cimpric, quoting Niehaus, and Ter Haar, states that "in Limpopo Province in South Africa, according to unofficial estimates, 389 people were allegedly killed between 1985 and 1995 and between 1996 and 2001 more than 600 people were killed by lynching in the same province, thousands of elderly people, especially women, have been accused of witchcraft and then beaten and/or killed in Tanzania."[82]

While Erwin Van Der Meer mentioned similar feature of children vulnerable to witchcraft accusation, Cimpric further categorizes them from his extensive anthropological findings into three. They include:

1. Fatherless or motherless children and those with physical disadvantages, especially with features such as distended belly, unusual eye colors and macrocephaly. Children with epilepsy and infectious coughs and those with developmental or genetic disorder with either communication or intellectual delays. In addition, children who are specially talented and those with bad manners.
2. Children through preterm birth in areas around the Bay of Benin and those with unusual birth presentation during delivery. Twins are also regarded to be in this second category.
3. Albinos, who are regarded to possess mystical power in certain parts of their bodies.[83]

Based on common knowledge, these categories may bring about suspicion and make children of these various physical features and delivery conditions susceptible to witchcraft accusation. It is important that with the advancement in medical science in modern Africa, such physical features and conditions are merely biological. They actually have no link with witchcraft. The scapegoat theory has been found useful in analyzing most cases of child witchcraft accusations.[84] The need to punish one or more offenders in some communities has led to witchcraft accusation. In most cases, children, women, strangers and the poor become the prey for power-driven males or wealthy class in the same society.

Conclusion

The point of convergence for both child labor and witchcraft accusation is violence against children. Any form of exposure of children to violence is ethically wrong because the effects of such exposure cannot be determined. Whereas some violence may not lead to physical harm for the child, their psychological impact cannot be easily measured. Since children learn from the goings-on in their environment, exposing them to violence may lead them into the path of violence in the near future. The rising trend of terrorism and other forms of insurrections all around the world are indicative of the need to prevent violence against children.

Eradicating child labor and witchcraft accusations in order to afford the children conducive cultural, economic, physical, political, social and spiritual environment for holistic development should become a priority of African states. Whereas intergovernmental organizations and nongovernmental organizations (NGOs) must not relent in raising the awareness on child labor and witchcraft accusations, the state must work toward making and implementing effective policies to stop them. More importantly, the African states need to rise up to tackle several economic challenges confronting them in order to create room for wealth creation and social welfare for the needy in their societies. Doing so would deal a final blow to resurgence of cultural practices that lack proper ethical bearing.

Notes

1. Juliet C. Sigauke, "Witchcraft and the Law in Southern Africa and the Greco-Roman World" (Online) https://www.academia.edu/17537760/witchcraft_and_the_law_in_southern_africa_and_the_greco-roman_world, accessed 2 June 2019.
2. Amasa Philip Ndofirepi and Almon Shumba, "Conceptions of "Child" among Traditional Africans: A Philosophical Purview," J Hum Ecol, 45, 3 (2014): 233.
3. Agya Boakye-Boaten, "Changes in the concept of Childhood: Implications on Children in Ghana," Uluslararası Sosyal Araştırmalar Dergisi The Journal of International Social Research, 3 no. 10 (Winter 2010): 105.
4. United Nations International Children Emergency Fund (UNICEF), Child Labour and UNICEF in Action: Children at the Centre. New York, UNICEF. 2014.
5. Rachita Bisht, "Who is A Child?: The Adults' Perspective within Adult-Child Relationship in India," Interpersona 2, 2 (2008): 152.
6. Bisht, Rachita "Who is A Child?: The Adults' Perspective within Adult-Child Relationship in India," 152–3.
7. Bisht, 153. Structural sociology of childhood analyses major movements and connections from bigger scope of the Societal structures (urbanization, scholarization and generation) to the child's holistic development as social being. of children's everyday lives. is a sociological theory based on places the society before individual.
8. Ibid., 153.

9. Ndofirepi and Shumba, 233.
10. Ndofirepi and Shumba, 233.
11. Ibid., 233.
12. Ibid.
13. Boakye-Boaten, "Changes in the concept of Childhood: Implications on Children in Ghana," 104–105.
14. Ibid.
15. Ndofirepi and Shumba.
16. P.C. Onwauchi, "African Peoples and Western education," The Journal of Negro Education, 41 no. 3 (1972): 242
17. Ndofirepi and Shumba, 235.
18. Ibid., 235.
19. O.A. Oyeshile, The individual community relationship as an issue in social and political philosophy, In O. Olusegun (Ed.): *Core Issues in African Philosophy.* Ibadan: Hope Publications, (2006): 104.
20. International Labour Office (ILO), *Global Estimates of Child Labour: Results and Trends, 2012–2016,* Geneva, ILO, 2014.
21. Peter Moyi, Child labor and school attendance in Kenya, Educational Research and Reviews Vol. 6, 1, (Online) http://www.academicjournals.org/ERR ISSN 1990–3839 ©2011 Academic Journal, 2011, p. 27.
22. ILO, *Global Estimates of Child Labour: Results and Trends, 2012–2016,* 33.
23. World Bank, Poverty Overview-World Bank (Online) https://www.worldbank.org/topic/poverty/overview/world/bank.html, accessed 31 May 2019.
24. ILO, *Global Estimates of Child Labour: Results and Trends, 2012–2016,* 11.
25. Ibid., 11.
26. Loretta Bass, *Child Labour in Sub-Saharan Africa*, Colorado, Lynne Rienner Publishers, 2004.
27. Bass Loretta, Child Labour in Sub-Saharan Africa.
28. Beverly Grier, "Child Labor in Colonial Africa," In Hugh D. Hindman, Ed., The World of Child Labor: An Historical and Regional Survey, New York, M.E. Sharpe, 2009.
29. Edlyne e. Anugwon, "Child Labour in the Context of Globalization in Africa," The African Anthropologist, vol. 4, No. 2, 2003, 108.
30. Edlyne E. Anugwon, "Child Labour in the Context of Globalization in Africa.
31. Falola, Toyin: The Political Economy of A Pre-Colonial African State: Ibadan, 1830–1900, Ife, University of Ife, Press, 1984.
32. Oluyemisi Bamgbose, "Labor: Child" In Toyin Falola and Akintunde Akinyemi (Ed) *Encyclopedia of Yoruba*, Indiana, Indiana University Press, 2016.
33. United Nations International Children's Emergency Fund (UNICEF), *Child Labour and UNICEF in Action: Children at the Centre,* New York: UNICEF, 2014, p. 9
34. UNICEF, *Child Labour and UNICEF in Action: Children at the Centre.*
35. Nirav Patel, Figure of the Week: Understanding Poverty in Africa, The Brookings Institution, Online, https://www.google.com.ng/amp/s/www.brokings.edu.blog/africa-in-focus/2018/11/21/figure-of-the-week-understanding-poverty-in-africa/amp, 2019, p. 14.
36. UNICEF, *Child Labour and UNICEF in Action: Children at the Centre,* p. 9.
37. Bamgbose, Encyclopedia.
38. Hamzat, Yoruba Customs.

39. Falola, The Political economy.
40. Ibid.
41. Ibid.
42. Abiodun, Encyclopedia of Yoruba p. 265.
43. Abiodun, 265.
44. Imani Odey and Ronke Sanya, Obanliku: Where Girls Are 'Forced' Into Marriage For Food, Money. Channels TV Programmes, Nigeria: Channels Incorporated Limited, 2018.
45. Odey and Sanya.
46. Ibid.
47. Aleksandra Cimpric, Children Accused of Witchcraft: Anthropological Study of Contemporary Practices in Africa. UNICEF WCARO, Dakar, 2013, 23.
48. André Mary, Sorcellerie bocaine, sorcellerie africaine: le social, le symbolique et l' imaginarie, Cahiers du LASA, Laboratoire de Sociologie Anthrpologique de l'Université de Caean, 7, 1987, 126.
49. Partners for Law in Development (PLD), *Piecing Together Perspectives on Witch Hunting: A Review of Literature*. New Delhi, Partners for Law in Development, 2013.
50. Partners for Law in Development, *Piecing Together Perspectives on Witch Hunting: A Review of Literature*, 83.
51. Ibid., 24.
52. Ibid., 24.
53. Ibid., 24.
54. Ibid., 26.
55. Blair Rutherford, "To find an African witch: anthropology, modernity and witch-finding in North West Zimbabwe." Critique of Anthropology, 1999, 1: 97.
56. Rutherford, "To find an African witch: anthropology, modernity and witch-finding in North West Zimbabwe," 97.
57. Ibid., 91.
58. Cimpric, Aleksandra Children Accused of Witchcraft: Anthropological Study of Contemporary Practices in Africa. 1
59. Cimpric, 1.
60. Ibid., 1.
61. Ibid., 1.
62. Ibid., 6.
63. Ibid., 6.
64. PLD.
65. Ibid., 16.
66. Cimpric, 1.
67. Cimpric, 3.
68. J. Tonda, *La guérison divine en Afrique central*, Congo, Gabon, Paris Karthala, 2002.
69. Cimpric, 3.
70. Erwin Van Der Meer, "Child Witchcraft Accusations in Southern Malawi," The Australasian Review of African Studies, 34, 1, 2013, 129.
71. Furzee kashyap and Jyoti Prasad Saikia, "Witch Hunting Practices: Culture, Superstition and Injustice Surrounding the Bodos of Kokrajhar District of Assam," International Journal of English Language, Literature in Humanities,5, 7, 2017, 378.

72. Furzee kashyap and Jyoti Prasad Saikia, "Witch Hunting Practices: Culture, Superstition and Injustice Surrounding The Bodos of Kokrajhar District of Assam," 378.
73. Juliet C. Sigauke, "Witchcraft and the Law in Southern Africa and the Greco-Roman World" (Online).
74. Cimpric, 3.
75. Cimpric, 2.
76. Cimpric, 2.
77. Van Der Meer, "Child Witchcraft Accusations in Southern Malawi."
78. Cimpric, 12.
79. Juliet C. Sigauke, "Witchcraft and the Law in Southern Africa and the Greco-Roman World."
80. Ibid., 13.
81. Ibid., 13.
82. Ibid., 13.
83. Cimpric, 2.
84. PDL.

Bibliography

Anugwon, Edlyne E. 2003. Child Labour in the Context of Globalization in Africa. *The African Anthropologist* 4: 2.

Bamgbose, Oluyemis. 2016. Labor: Child. In *Encyclopedia of Yoruba*, ed. Toyin Falola and Akintunde Akinyemi. Indiana: Indiana University Press.

Bass, Loretta. 2004. *Child Labour in Sub-Saharan Africa*. Colorado: Lynne Rienner Publishers.

Bisht, Rachita. 2008. Who Is a Child?: The Adults' Perspective within Adult-Child Relationship in India. *Interpersona* 2 (2): 151–172.

Boakye-Boaten, Agya. 2010. Changes in the Concept of Childhood: Implications on Children in Ghana. *Uluslararası Sosyal Araştırmalar Dergisi The Journal of International Social Research* 3 (10 Winter): 104–115.

Falola, Toyin. 1984. *The Political Economy of a Pre-Colonial African State: Ibadan, 1830–1900*. Ife: University of Ife Press.

Grier, Beverly. 2009. Child Labor in Colonial Africa. In *The World of Child Labor: A Historical and Regional Survey*, ed. Hugh D. Hindman. New York: M.E. Sharpe.

International Labour Office (ILO). 2014. *Global Estimates of Child Labour: Results and Trends, 2012–2016*. Geneva: ILO.

Kashyap, Furzee, and Jyoti Prasad Saikia. 2017. Witch Hunting Practices: Culture, Superstition and Injustice Surrounding the Bodos of Kokrajhar District of Assam. *International Journal of English Language, Literature in Humanities* 5 (7): 89–109.

Moyi, Pater. 2011. Child Labor and School Attendance in Kenya. *Educational Research and Reviews* 6 (1), (Online) http://www.academicjournals.org/ERR. ISSN 1990-3839 ©2011 Academic Journal.

Ndofirepi, Amasa Philip, and Almon Shumba. 2014. Conceptions of "Child" Among Traditional Africans: A Philosophical Purview. *Journal of Human Ecology* 45 (3): 233–246.

Odey, Imani, and Ronke Sanya. 2018. *Obanliku: Where Girls Are 'Forced' into Marriage for Food, Money*, Channels TV Programmes. Lagos: Channels Incorporated Limited.

Onwauchi, P.C. 1972. African Peoples and Western Education. *The Journal of Negro Education* 41 (3): 241–247.

Oyeshile, O.A. 2006. The Individual Community Relationship as an Issue in Social and Political Philosophy. In *Core Issues in African Philosophy*, ed. O. Olusegun. Ibadan: Hope Publications.

Partners for Law in Development (PLD). 2013. *Piecing Together Perspectives on Witch Hunting: A Review of Literature*. New Delhi: Partners for Law in Development.

Patel, Nirav. 2019. *Figure of the Week: Understanding Poverty in Africa*, 14. The Brookings Institution, (Online) https://www.google.com.ng/amp/s/www.brokings.edu.blog/africa-in-focus/2018/11/21/figure-of-the-week-understanding-poverty-in-africa/amp. Accessed 2 June 2019.

Rutherford, Blair. 1999. To Find an African Witch: Anthropology, Modernity and Witch-Finding in North West Zimbabwe. *Critique of Anthropology* 19 (1): 373–379.

Sigauke, Juliet C. Witchcraft and the Law in Southern Africa and the Greco-Roman World, (Online) https://www.academia.edu/17537760/witchcraft_and_the_law_in_southern_africa_and_the_greco-roman_world. Accessed 2 June 2019.

Tonda, J. 2002. *La guérison divine en Afrique central (Congo, Gabon)*. Paris: Karthala.

United Nations International Children's Emergency Fund (UNICEF). 2014. *Child Labour and UNICEF in Action: Children at the Centre*. New York: UNICEF.

Van Dar Meer, Erwin. 2013. Child Witchcraft Accusations in Southern Malawi. *The Australasian Review of African Studies* 34 (1): 129–144.

World Bank. Poverty Overview-World Bank, (Online) https://www.worldbank.org/topic/poverty/overview/world/bank.html. Accessed 31 May 2019

CHAPTER 5

Praying for Husbands! Single Women Negotiating Faith and Patriarchy in Contemporary Kenya

Damaris Parsitau

Based on ethnographic data gathered in the last ten years, this chapter examines how single women negotiate between faith and patriarchy in contemporary Kenya. In particular, I focus on selected Christian churches' responses to single women: responses which are broadly conceptualized to include a wide array of spiritual tools and resources ranging from 'praying for husbands' to real tangible and practical interventions such as provision of welfare to helping single women navigate relational spaces. Furthermore, I seek to understand not just how these churches and single women, respectively, construct and negotiate Christian singlehood in an increasingly contested religious space but also how such women make sense of their singlehood as they navigate their intimate lives in the face of tremendous challenges posed by a complexity of factors including rapid social transformations and social and religious stigma in a society that frowns upon them.

INTRODUCTION: EMERGING TRENDS IN FAMILY RELATIONS IN KENYA

In the recent past, Kenya has experienced an explosion of singlehood among women between the ages of 25–49 years, an explosion that is increasingly becoming a defining feature of gender and family relations in the country. A recent sociological study for example suggests that Kenya has one of the highest number of single mothers in Africa where six out of every ten Kenyan

D. Parsitau (✉)
Egerton University, Nakuru, Kenya

women are likely to be single by the time they are 45 years old.[1] This makes Kenya one of the countries with the highest number of single mothers in Africa. This research also found that Kenyan women have a 59.5 per cent chance of being single by the age of 45 either through premarital birth or through dissolution of marriage. Similarly, nearly 45 per cent of all children in Kenya do not live with both biological parents. At the same time, three in ten Kenyan girls become pregnant before the age of 18,[2] an indication that about 30 per cent of women in Kenya are giving birth before they are married. Similarly, Kenya also has roughly equal proportions of women becoming single mothers before marriage as those who become single mothers after marriage primarily from divorce or separation. This emerging trend has had significant impact on Kenyan family and gender relations even as researchers sound the alarm of an astounding trend that also shows that a significant number of women are increasingly drawn into single motherhood as more men abandon their traditional roles as providers for their families.[3]

Although this and other sociological research (Kahindi 2018; Meda 2013; Muriithi 2013; Kariuki 2016) offer scientific evidence on this emerging trend, it only confirms a shift that has become more and more visible in recent times. Yet, this changing face of the Kenyan family patterns and gender roles is a result of complex and multidimensional factors that are changing how Kenyan women are navigating family life and relational spaces. As a result, there are increasingly high numbers of female-headed households that also increase their vulnerability as well as those of their children. The most affected are women in their late 20s who are increasingly being abandoned by vanishing and fading spouses and are forced to raise children single-handedly after their male partners refuse to assume responsibilities for the children.

As in many parts of the world, and in the recent past, Kenya has undergone some major social transformations as a result of the changes in the wider sociocultural-economic systems (Beier et al. 2010; OECD 2009; Meda 2013). According to Meda (2013: 282), for example, 'urban Kenyan families are in transition from traditional structures that tended to favour large families living together to modern trends towards smaller nuclear families units'. Traditionally, she argues, 'marriage and family life in Africa is held in high esteem. Marriage is considered the basic social unit of society and was relatively stable with a wide network of relatives to support including in the rearing of children.' Children were regarded extremely important and seen as the responsibility of everyone. The main aim of marriage was procreation which also ensured family lineage and enlarged kinship ties. Men and women were socialized to aspire to marry and bring forth children who will perpetuate kinship and social ties. Marriage was then universal and was sustained through the widespread institution of polygyny. In these arrangements, young widows and widowers were encouraged to remarry and reproduce children to carry the family name and lineage.

Family life in Africa was therefore considered a social thing rather than a private arrangement. Even though marriage is a union of two individuals, this did not confine the couple to a world of their own (Meda 2013: 283). Instead, it was a web of social, kinship, communal and family relations that bound them together and relatively insulated the wife, husband and children from pressure and other issues such as conflict and marital stress. In this case, society reinforced the idea that marriage was a strong bond between families and communities. Any marital conflicts arising in the nuclear family were resolved by the larger extended family (Meda 2013).

However as the family structure is changing in many parts of the African continent, these social ties are increasingly becoming fluid and rare. Previous powerful agents of socialization which were associated with strong social and family ties are increasingly giving place to other agents of socialization like churches, institutions of learning, the media, peer pressure groups and more recently social media.

An array of factors including irresponsible fathers, peer pressure, rural-urban migration and the struggles to cope with modernization are blamed for the trend that has had significant impact on the Kenyan family life. Kenya has experienced increased urbanization and modernization since its independence in 1963. Rapid urbanization has had significant impact on family and social ties. According to Meda (2013: 287), 'it transforms societal organizations, the role of the family, demographic structures, the nature of work and the way we choose to live and with whom'. Furthermore, she argues that 'the evolution to an urban society goes frequently hand in hand with a decline in the status of the family and with the proliferation of non-traditional family forms and new types of households'. Consequently, this trend reflects diverse choices of living arrangements whether by blood or marriage.

In the past few decades now, Kenya has witnessed an explosion in the types of family formations and a sharp increase in the diversity of household and family types, including single-parent household types and many other types of family arrangements that are increasingly becoming visible in the Kenyan social scene. Female singlehood in Africa, Kenya in particular, is not a homogeneous group. Instead, it represents a diverse group ranging from age to experience and the cause of singlehood.[4] Women become single mothers because of divorce, separation, unplanned pregnancies, poverty, death of spouse, lack of marriageable partners and rape, among many other factors. Besides single mothers, there are many different types of single women in contemporary Kenya: namely widows, divorced/separated, never- married women, teenage mothers and of course the single-by-choice type of women that are becoming increasingly popular with young urban middle-class women. In such societies, the major cause of singlehood, particularly single motherhood, was the death of one of the spouses. Others include labour migrations, personal decisions and free choice, unequal gender relation and gender-based violence. Widowhood rendered many women single mothers and the head of their households, putting many of them in vulnerable situations. Divorce was another cause of singlehood, although it was rare in traditional societies. The 'mistress phenomenon' is also becoming quite common with men, especially the wealthy ones having several mistresses in different cities and towns. Though this phenomenon is socially frowned upon, it is becoming increasingly normalized to an extent that many married women subconsciously live with the possibility that their husbands have not one but probably several mistresses with children sired by their husbands.

But of all the categories of single women in Kenya mentioned above, the new single-by- choice type of women who are also known as 'spouse-free parents' is least accepted. A significant number of highly educated, financially stable and urban women are increasingly making personal choices to become solo parents. Such women may conceive on purpose but choose to raise the child alone. While these types of women do not want the baggage of a lived-in spouse, many believe that the men they have dated and sired children with bring no value to their lives or that of their children. This group is increasingly frowned upon as feminists who have taken free choice a little too far. They are also the targets of public ridicule, slander, attitudes and discrimination. Children of single mothers irrespective of the circumstances of their singlehood are often taunted by peers and frowned upon and objectified by society, even in schools and neighbourhoods.

This trend is also attributed to rapid social changes taking place in contemporary Kenya. The trend is further attributed to increasing female access to education and employment, urbanization, decreased polygyny, feminism and women empowerment, alcohol and substance abuse, violence and masculinities as well as other modern trends (Ntoimo and Abanihe 2013). This has ensured that the new face of the Kenyan family is female-headed. In traditional societies in Africa, marriage and family life were held in high esteem. Women were also socialized and brought up to aspire to get married and raise a family. In fact traditional societies taught that marriage was the ideal that every girl and woman aspired. That has changed now and current trends have raised concerns from academics, researchers, policymakers and other stakeholders such as religious organizations. The steady increase of the trend has been seen as a departure from the norm where a traditional family consisted of a husband, wife/wives and children.

Despite this, the Kenyan society has reluctantly accepted single motherhood as an inevitable outcome of the rapid social changes taking place in contemporary Kenya. Nevertheless, the majority of single mothers in Kenya never planned to raise their children single-handed. A few years back, the main cause of single parenthood in Kenya used to be parental death due to disease, war, accidents or just natural death. Recently, emerging factors appear to have shifted and we are now witnessing a proliferation of single mothers due to divorce, separation, abandonment, fading spouses as well as absentee fathers leaving many women in Kenya single. Unplanned pregnancies, intended pregnancies and adoption by those who are unmarried and without partners are also emerging trends. But younger educated women who are also financially stable are opting to have children without the baggage of men whose only role is that of a sperm donor. This could be a paid donor or an agreement between friends.

This emerging and astounding trend shows that a significant number of women are increasingly drawn into single motherhood as more men abandon their traditional roles as providers for their children. Yet, this trend is not unique to Kenya as it has been observed in other African countries such as Nigeria and Ghana (Ntoimo and Abanihe 2013).

Despite this emerging trend, singlehood broadly conceptualized and beyond a certain age is still frowned upon by the Kenyan society, including religious organizations. With the exception of widows, all the other categories of single women are pitied, judged, blamed for their status, slandered, objectified and treated with suspicions by society including men, married women and religious organizations such as Christian churches. Often, the blame is based on assumed personal character defect that makes these women unmarriageable. Consequently, many are called 'homewreckers', 'husband snatchers', 'baby mamas', 'slay queens' and other unflattering titles.

In social as well as church spaces, single women are often associated with infidelity, instability, premarital sex that resulted in a pregnancy and prostitution, among many others. The attitudes, labels and stereotypes about female singlehood are not only cruel but also thwart genuine efforts and do not allow for pragmatic engagements in a bid to understand this trend. Men are not objectified and society appears accepting of male infidelity but totally unaccepting of women's infidelity.

Remaining unmarried beyond a certain age is therefore frowned upon by the society because it is seen as negating the cultural and traditional norms of femininity. To many people, this is a social evil that should not be encouraged. As such, single women are stigmatized, scandalized and seen as women without morals and character. Often they are told to go get married first if they have any contribution to make in society. In marriage, unequal gender relations still persist between husbands and wives. Gender socialization prepares women to become wives and mothers first before anything else.

Yet, empirical studies suggest a cocktail of complex causal factors for this development including demographic, economic and personal factors. More importantly, it is the role of patriarchy, masculinities and current social changes taking place in the Kenyan society. Surprisingly and despite this growing phenomenon, it remains not just relatively under-researched but also that societal attitudes towards female singlehood continue to perpetuate stigma and discrimination against single women even where the causal factors of this situation are beyond their personal character and choices. But first let me situate this within the patriarchal systems and changing gender norms in contemporary Kenya.

Theorizing Patriarchy: An Overview of Patriarchy and Gender Relations in Kenya

Kenya is a heavily patriarchal country with persistent beliefs that perpetuate unequal treatment of women and girls (Parsitau and Van Klinken 2018; Parsitau 2012). Studies in sexuality, gender relations and family life in Kenya show that perceptions of sexuality, gender relations and ideas about marriage are similar across ethnic groups and are premised on patriarchal ideologies which privilege men over women, encouraging their socialization into forms of masculinities that are domineering and sometimes violent (Parsitau and Van Klinken 2018; Meda 2013).

There is also a general preference for male children over daughters who are less likely than females to experience rejection, prejudice, discrimination and abandonment (Parsitau 2017). Women are also often restricted in how they express their sexuality outside of and within marriage. Unlike single men, single women who are often seen or perceived as promiscuous are not only shunned by men but also unlikely to get married. Sexual infidelity by married women is considered unacceptable, even taboo. Such behaviour attracts violence, wife-beating, ostracism and many other severe punishments. Married men are free to engage in extra-marital affairs and can have as many partners as they wish. In many Kenyan communities, this is encouraged as appropriate masculine behaviour.

Besides, and in many Kenyan communities, men are still presumably considered as 'head' of families and households and the main decision-makers despite the fact that women contribute immensely to the family not just financially but also in terms of housework and childrearing. However, women often seem to play far bigger roles than men do as household heads. Yet, even where men and women work and bring home the same income, men still hold control of many household decisions. Domestic labour is the preserve of women and is neither appreciated nor enumerated.

Owing to the heavy patriarchal stronghold of the Kenyan society, women are expected to get married and remain married for the rest of their lives. The dissolution of marriage in many Kenyan communities is often blamed on the woman who did not 'persevere enough', 'pray enough' and 'work hard enough' to keep her family together. This places a heavy emotional and psychological burden on women who carry incredible responsibilities for their families. At the same time, women derive their status from their roles as wives and mothers. Inheritance rights are also tied to marriage and male children especially (Meda 2013). While the dominant form of marriage in Kenya is a monogamous one, polygyny is still popular. Mistresses are also becoming quite common with most men having as many mistresses as they can afford.

There is also a new emerging trend variously referred to as the 'sponsor culture' or the 'slay queen' phenomenon. This is an arrangement where attractive young women enter into intimate sexual affairs with wealthy older men in exchange for financial benefits.[5] This transactional sex culture has become pervasive in the Kenyan society. More and more young women, mainly campus students, are sexually engaged with old but wealthy and powerful men popularly known as 'sponsors' to fund a lifestyle worth posting on social media. The word 'sponsor' is the term used by millennials to describe their benefactors who are also variously called 'blessers' or 'sugar daddies'.[6] This has become an accepted practice, even a glamorous lifestyle choice, and it keeps evolving. The slay queen phenomenon has become the norm especially with campus girls. Older and wealthier women are also increasingly dating younger men in exchange for opulence in modern Kenya today.

Such encounters, driven by complex socio-economic factors, illustrate the emergence of an equally complex phenomenon: 'the exchange of youth, beauty and sex for financial gains'. While poverty might be the biggest driving factor in such relationships, they are also influenced by social media and the socialite phenomenon first popularized by US celebrity Kim Kardashian of *Keeping up with the Kardashians* reality series, but later and locally by Kenya's most prominent socialites Vera Sidika and Huddah Monroe.[7] Kenya's emerging socialite culture is also greatly influenced by Kenya's TV show *Nairobi Diaries* that tracks a group of young urban women living a lifestyle characterized by sex, glamour and opulence as its currency. This TV series is heavily influenced by the *Keeping up with the Kardashians* TV series. But it is also influenced by social media, particularly Instagram. Yet this is not only a Kenyan phenomenon as it has been observed in Nigeria and South Africa.[8]

At the same time, many Kenyan women experience diverse forms of violence and abuse in marriage and other intimate relationships. Despite significant progress for Kenyan women towards equal rights, widespread violence against women and girls continues to define the everyday lives of these vulnerable constituencies. Violence against Women and Girls (VAWG) in Kenya has in fact become a defining feature of life for so many women and girls with devastating consequences for many. In 2017–2018, an unprecedentedly high number of women and girls in Kenya died in the hands of intimate partners/spouses and family members that the *Daily Nation*, Kenya's leading newspaper, published in its headlines pictures of scores of young 'women butchered so young!'[9] This shocking headlines was a response to the murder of a number of young women and girls between ages 19 and 28 years, mainly university students, allegedly, brutally murdered by their spouses or intimate partners in less than one year. Statistics on violence against women and girls in Kenya (VAWG) are alarming as the *Daily Nation* pointed out. Yet, there was nothing new about these alarming deaths.

The Kenya Demographic and Health Survey (KDHS 2014) for example showed that 44 per cent of women in Kenya reported that they had experienced physical violence by men known to them since they turned 15. Similarly, and according to data from the Kenya Police, there were 2774 homicides in 2017 alone, which was a slight increase from previous years. The worst affected were women aged between 44–49 years.[10]

The rate of violence towards married women or those cohabiting with their partners in this report was 47 per cent, meaning that nearly half of married or cohabiting women have suffered both physical and sexual violence from their partners. The number of single women who experienced physical abuse was significantly lower at 31 per cent. According to this report, 'men are often the perpetrators of violence against women'. The report further states that even among married women, the most commonly reported perpetrators of physical violence are current husbands or partners at 57 per cent followed by former husbands or partners at 24 per cent.

There is a sort of normalization of violence in which violence against women is socially acceptable. Yet, violence against women is not only prevalent in homes and families but is rampant in institutions of learning, in public spaces including public transport space as well as religious spaces. In churches, women face sexual violence as well as emotional violence such as rejection of single women, sexual abuse by some clergy as well as violence accruing from certain theologies of churches.[11] In particular, theologies of deliverance and exorcism, sexual purity and women's bodies remain sources of violence for many women. Church spaces are no longer a safe space for women (Parsitau and Van Klinken 2018; Wane et al. 2018). Single women face huge stigma and stereotypes in Christian churches than they would in communities in which they live in.

In the next section I examine not just the response of Christian churches to the explosion of single women but also how women are navigating Christian singlehood and motherhood in a society that frowns on unmarried mothers. Through an examination of selected church sermons and interventionist programmes, I attempt to understand not just how these churches respond to these developments but also how they construct Christian singlehood as well as how they help single mothers to navigate their singleness and motherhood in rapidly changing social, religious and cultural environments. Here, I seek to bring in the voices of single Christian women not just as they navigate their singlehood but also how they contest space, agency, patriarchy, voice and faith. Furthermore I explore how marginalized women find meaning and acceptance in religious organizations and how these organizations help them reconstruct their lives in the face of tremendous urban challenges.

In the next section, I examine the role and response of selected Christian churches to women singlehood in a largely Christian nation. In particular, I focus on interventions including 'praying for husbands' and 'delivering the spirit of singlehood' and real tangible interventions such as helping single women navigate Christian singlehood through the provision of practical skills and tools to navigate relational spaces. Others include welfare for single women to stringent control of women's personal liberties and sexual lives to spiritual and economic empowerment through the building of women's capacities to do business and become leaders both in the private and public spheres. Yet, Christian churches' response to the explosion of female singlehood is also not that radically different from that of the wider society.

Preaching a Heterosexual Gospel? Masculine Christianity, Patriarchy and Single Women in Contemporary Kenya!

Christian churches such as Protestant, Catholic, Pentecostal and other traditions are spaces that not only idolize traditional marriage and family life, but they also preach a heterosexual gospel. The idea of a heterosexual gospel tends to put more emphasis on monogamous marriage as the goal of every Christian person. These churches uphold that God instituted marriage for the welfare and happiness of humankind. Pentecostal churches for example believe that marriage was instituted and commissioned by God in the biblical Garden of Eden as a permanent institution that forms the core of human existence and progress. According to this position, 'marriage was designed to meet critical human needs such as companionship, procreation, mutual love between a husband and wife, encouragement, practical help and sexual satisfaction' (Muriithi 2013). While Catholics adopt a similar position, singlehood is however acceptable for those divinely ordained including priests and nuns who take vows of celibacy and chastity.

Christian churches believe that marriage, strictly understood in its monogamous and heterosexual sense to be between one man and woman, is the ideal. Marriage also serves as a demonstration of Christ's relationship to his church. Although traditional family patterns have changed in recent time, including new forms of emerging patterns such as single-headed (mainly female-headed) as well as non-heterosexual relationships such as same-sex families, the position of Christian churches with respect to family still remains the same.

Pentecostal churches for example idealize marriage as the ideal state in a way that excludes single women who are often made to feel incomplete in spaces that are exclusively designed for the married. Pentecostal clergy for example also like to publish and widely circulate images of immaculate clergy with their wives in a manner that depict them as deeply in love, romantic, happy, blessed and the envy of many. Some like Bishops Allan and Kathy Kiuna of the Jubilee Christian Centre (JCC), nicknamed the 'power couple', project an image of a couple that is deeply in love with each other as their images lovingly and romantically staring at each other in a lusty manner are circulated on social and traditional media.[12] They also image themselves as the nation's 'marriage counsellors' who are sought after for marital advice by television and radio stations (Parsitau 2019). Many other leading Kenyan televangelists, famous and non-famous alike, often project images of couples deeply in love with each other, happily married, romantic, successful and God-loving. This is all a performance especially in Pentecostal churches as well as for televangelists where image is everything.

Through a series of interviews with this author, Reverend Linda Ochola-Adolwa, an ordained priest of the Anglican Church and a highly influential woman in the Kenyan social and religious scene, shares her thoughts on single women and how the church fails them. In a long interview, based on her own personal experiences both as a married woman and as an influential clergy member with massive following, she had this to say when I asked her how Christian churches respond to women singlehood: 'marriage is idealised by Christian churches in a way that excludes single people'. Speaking to this author during an interview, Reverend Ochola gave her personal observations about the state of marriage in a largely Christian country:

> As a woman pastor, my personal feelings are that Christian churches idealized marriage. The bulk of the messages preached in Christian churches idealized marriage as an institution commissioned by God. The bulk of messages coming from the pulpit are designed to make one dissatisfied with ones' single status. Marriage is privileged over singlehood in a way to suggest that singlehood is undesirable. The message it seems to me is saying to single women that singlehood is undesirable. The image it seems to me is saying to single women that singlehood does not adequately reflect the image of God. It is as if single women are made to feel dissatisfied in their realities. This is why women will do everything in their power to get out of their present realities. Sermons preached are meant and designed to make women aspire for marriage.[13]

When I asked her why marriage is framed as the ideal, Rev. Ochola explained:

> In the Kenyan society, marriage confers status, credibility, worth, value and respect to women. While I am not a feminist, (I am a happy married wife and mother), I believe that a woman's worth and value should not be linked to her marital status. As far as I am concerned Jesus conferred value and worth on women regardless of their marital status. Clergy should affirm the humanity of women. That they have value and dignity irrespective of their marital status. Marriage doesn't give women value! God gives them value. Clergy should preach about singlehood as a complete state of life. Churches do not affirm single women as complete human beings made in the image of God. Few have also created programmes that help women move forward towards a more complete, ideal happy state of life. It is as if singlehood distorts the image of God in such women, many of whom decide to remain unchurched because churches are exclusive space for the married.[14]

Rev. Ochola believes that while clergy and churches idealize marriage in their pulpits, the reality is however different:

> As a clergy who served for many years at Mavuno Church including undertaking marital counselling, I can confirm that: Marriage is overemphasize. I know many Christian homes that are less than ideal. In the same way I know many Christian single women who are thriving and raising wonderful and successful families just like married couples would. I also know many Christian homes that are devoid of love. I also know many Christian homes that are devoid of love.

In further illustrating her perspectives, Rev. Ochola further observed:

> I got married at the age of thirty-three and I had already suffered huge pressure from family, friends and society to get married because I was getting too old.

There was also a general feeling that as a single person, I was not as responsible as those who were married. But even then and as a young woman, I felt marriage was highly valued by the church in a way that made single people feels that they are left out. Also, as a young woman growing up in a Christian family, I observed my Parents relationship. I had the ability to keep distance and observe and critic the status of their marriage and it was less than ideal. So from early on I developed alternative perspectives about marriage. I realised that it is not the ideal that Christian churches project. In fact the Bible itself offers an alternative perspective on marriage that is often not heard enough. 1Corinthians 7:28 clearly states that those who marry will face many troubles in this life, and I want to spare you this!

Besides, Rev. Ochola explains that most of the sermons preached then and now in Christian churches were always about the power of 'a prayerful wife', 'the power of a prayerful mother', or 'how to become a prayerful wife', 'unlocking the power to get married' or 'making marriage work'.

In my many years of researching Kenyan Pentecostalism, I do not ever recall coming across sermons about justice for women, or the woman that God loves. Yet, and according to Rev. Ochola, there is a broad spectrum of women in the Bible that Jesus loved and affirmed. In a reflective mood, Rev. Ochola posed:

> How come as pastors we don't interrogate what is unjust, or the violence, infidelity, rejection, marital strife, and neglect that is apparent in many Christian homes? Why are churches not preaching messages of acceptance? Sermons that are inclusive of all the body of Christ including single women?

Rev. Ochola also believes that there are just so many biblical resources that outline godly principles that are available for Christians to access. There are also many women in the Bible that Jesus Christ affirmed and loved and Christians can use these as models for a theology that ministers to single women in our churches. Examples include Mary Magdalene, Martha and Mary, his own mother, among many others. Rev. Ochola believes that Christians need to re-evaluate their own lives before they objectify single women.

Based on my personal observations as a researcher of Kenyan Christianity, I can argue that there was a serious disconnect between what was preached by the churches and the real situation. Yet a casual glance at the sermons preached in many pulpits suggests that there are very few programmes and plans to cater for the needs of single women.

Instead church spaces are full of stigma and stereotypes about single women who are often ridiculed, objectified and treated with suspicion by men and married women who view them as husband snatchers and homewreckers. At the same time, I have witnessed violence and emotional and spiritual abuse in church spaces, especially those that practice deliverance and exorcism.[15] A case in point is the Neno Evangelism Ministry where its head and founder Apostle James Maina Ng'ang'a often slaps out demons of sex and marital challenges in women even as he objectifies women followers. In several disturbing videos that went viral, Apostle Ng'ang'a dares a woman follower to fight him, brushing over her breasts and telling her there is nothing she can do to him. In this violent well-choreographed video, Ng'ang'a slaps the woman several times, while pinning her to the floor ostensibly, to exorcise demons that, invariably, have been sent to kill him. The woman finally calms down, gets up and rumbles in mumbo jumbo about her demon-possessed life. The video attracted mass outrage, where the public questioned Ng'ang'a's sanity (Parsitau 2019).

The response of various Christian churches to the phenomenon of female singlehood remains ambiguous with few churches responding in different ways. The church congregations mostly composed of the conventional two-parent family view single women negatively. Similarly, church programmes are designed to meet the needs of the conventional two-parent Christian family. A quick scan of the kind of programmes designed and offered by many churches shows that there are no specific programmes designed for single women. The programmes I came across during field research show programmes for children, youth, men and women fellowships and couples without any specific ones targeting single parents. Single females often experience stigma in social and religious settings and circles.

According to Rev. Ochola, churches need to be safe spaces for all including single women. Churches should also be intentional in offering opportunities for community and discipleship for all of their members irrespective of their marital status. Rev. Ochola further argues that God's plan for the world was not to make single people married but to bring reconciliation, love and community to all. Churches must be intentional in making sure singles feel welcomed and included in all their activities. In the next section, we examine the response of selected churches to the phenomenon of single women in Kenya.

Selected Christian Churches' Response to Single Women in Kenya

Christian churches' response to the phenomenon of female singlehood has been ambivalent and characterized by silence, denial, stigma, reluctant acceptance and in many cases subtle to outright condemnation. Below, I examine the varied responses of Christian churches to this relatively new phenomenon and argue that churches' response to singlehood has been ambivalent. Some engage in praying for husbands while others attempt to provide spiritual resources to single women.

Praying for Husbands: Pastor Chris Ojigbani of Singles and Married Ministries International

Nigerian-based Pastor Chris Ojigbani, the President and founder of Singles and Married Ministries International,[16] has twice (2010 and 2016) held 'prayers for husbands' rallies in Nairobi, Kenya.[17] According to biographical data on his ministry's website, Pastor Chris is described as a 'seasoned counsellor and an international speaker' who was commissioned by God to hold seminars in various parts of the world to help women in particular find husbands and the married to stay happy. His ministry's vision is to 'remove the devices that cause delays in marriage and empower singles to marry according to biographical date on his ministry's website'. In this ministry, it is further suggested that the 'singles marry easily and the married enjoy their marriages'.[18] It is also alleged that attendees of his seminars 'learn the right knowledge about marriage and achieve their goals easily'.

His programme 'Single and Married' is aired on various television channels across the globe. He is also an author of various books such as *I Want to Marry You*, *Activating the Grace of Marriage*, *Secrets of Blissful Marriage* and *Access Relationships Secrets 101* which has several series that are also sold on Amazon. The book *Relationship Secrets 322*[19] for example is said to 'reveal one of the most concealed secrets and is a powerful solution to the marital problems in the world'.[20]

When Pastor Chris Ojigbani, who has been variously dubbed the 'Apostle of marriage' or the 'marriage doctor', first came to Kenya in 2010, and returned in 2016, on both occasions hundreds of single women and a few men flocked to the Kenyatta International Convention Centre (KICC) in Nairobi (Kenya's premium conference facility) in search for 'prayers for husbands'. Pastor Chris Ojigbani whose sole mission is 'empowering singles to marry and making marriages work' has packaged himself as a sort of marriage doctor, the only one with hidden 'secrets', 'knowledge' and 'prayers' to help single women find husbands and the married to enjoy their marriages. In an interview with a Kenyan journalist in 2016, Pastor Chris diagnosed:

> Single women don't need to wait on God to give them the right man at their convenience. What women need are the right teachings not miracles. Whenever I hold seminars, people easily marry, mainly because they learn the right doctrines that help them. These teachings are also important in fostering happy marriages. In my seminars, prayers are not the main focus even though we pray. Our emphasis is on the special knowledge which comes through teachings about secrets to getting a husband and making marriages work.[21]

When Pastor Chris first came to Kenya in September 2010, during a much-publicized event that attracted hundreds of single women, the event was packaged as one that would help thousands of single women find husbands instantly. His pre-arrival adverts read like the usual Pentecostal crusades with promises of instant miracles including instant husbands. Pastor Chris was also imaged as the dispenser of wisdom, knowledge and tips to help single women attract husbands. Testimonies of women, once hopeless and single are now happily married thanks to the powerful prayers by the Apostle of marriage, were published and widely circulated in Kenya's media. The emphasis was that his teachings and prayers have the power to unlock husbands instantly.

During participant observations by this author, a largely women audience was witnessed with a few men from all social, economic and educational backgrounds flock to this much-publicized meeting for prayers for husbands. These women looked urban, fashionable, accomplished, educated and smart, who I thought were capable of making right and informed decisions about their future spouses. Yet, according to Grace Nduku[22] who attended both the 2010 and 2016 meetings, 'the pastor was full of advice and wisdom and good tips' that would help many of us find elusive husbands. The few men I interviewed intimated that they attended the meetings to gain knowledge and wisdom as they plan on getting married in the near future and needed help on how to navigate relational spaces. Nevertheless, the focus on 'single women' who are imaged as desperate, lacking agency, lonely and helpless people who need help from the 'dispenser of tips and wisdom' to instantly find a husband baffled many Kenyans. Many asked questions as to why otherwise educated and financially stable women need tips and prayers to find husbands. Others wondered if there were no other resources available to these women from the thousands of Christian churches in Kenya to help them find husbands that it took a Nigerian Apostle of marriage to come pray for them. Why do women and men easily fall for prayers for miracles from charlatans of the Christian industry who are out to make money by cashing in on the desperation of vulnerable women desperate to find love and marriage?

The answers to many of these questions can only be understood within the larger crisis of singlehood that Kenyan women are grappling with as well as the premium placed on marriage in African societies. Marriage confers status and security on women, without which many have been socialized to believe that they are not complete human beings unless they are married. The social and religious stigma also puts significant pressure on many women to marry so that they gain respect and acceptance from their families and society. But it is also a pointer to the failure of other institutions to focus on the crisis facing women in contemporary times.

Yet, 'praying for husband' as well as every other thing appears to be a typical Pentecostal Christian response to issues in the public and private spheres including singlehood. This is not just unique to Kenya but is a phenomenon observable in Africa and its diaspora (Adogame 2008; Gifford 2009). Take for example the case of the Redeemed Christian Church of God (RCCG), a popular Pentecostal church in Kenya led and founded by Rev. Pastor Arthur Kitonga. Every last Sunday of the month, the Redeemed Christian Church of God holds prayer vigils for single women. The aim of the prayers vigils is to pray for single women to find husbands.

Rev. Linda Ochola finds this line of thinking problematic because it perpetuates the idea that as long as a woman is single, she is not complete. This line of thought does not affirm singlehood as a complete state of life, she argues. Instead single women are made to feel incomplete because of their marital status. A more complete state of life for single women in many Christian churches is marriage. She explains that because few Christian churches neither affirm women singlehood nor their humanity, many single women will do all they can to get married to gain both recognition and respect. Christian charlatans take advantage of this desperation to make money out of vulnerable women. This is important to point out given that Pastor Chris Ojigbani charged very expensively to pray for women to get husbands.

REVEREND LUCY NATASHA OF PROPHETIC LATTER GLORY MINISTRIES

Rev. Lucy Natasha, the founder and overseer of the Prophetic Latter Glory Ministries International, is a single woman who images herself as a prophetess, a much sought-after conference speaker, a miracle worker and a proponent of the 'gospel of prosperity'. She also calls herself 'an oracle of God' and 'a vessel' used by God to preach to the nations of the world.[23] Her ministry is said to be an interdenominational outreach ministry that holds frequent conferences, revival meetings and seminars. Her meetings are often held in flashy hotels and other rented spaces since she does not have a church per se. Rev. Natasha often uploads glamorous photographs of her affluent life including cars, houses and security aides on social media.[24] She is also one of the richest and most flashy female ministers in Kenya even though the source of her wealth is not clear, given that she does not have any known registered church.

Her unique, expensive, fashionable and extravagant life has attracted significant controversies, with people questioning her relationship with politicians whom it is claimed she offers 'spiritual service'. Rev. Natasha is young, flashy, urban, single and searching for a husband. Raised by a single mother and the firstborn in a family of three, Natasha is said to hold a diploma in public relations as well as theology although I could not find evidence of this in my research.

She is also the author of many books, but her favourite one is titled *Before You Say I Do*, which prepares couples who want to get married with tips to navigate marriage spaces. In the book, she covers an array of issues such as the 'type of men to run away from', the 'type of woman to marry' and many other such tips. Although she is single and considers herself a kind of an expert in relationship matters, Rev. Natasha is still 'praying for a husband' to settle down with and start a family. And she believes God gives the right partner. In a television interview, she avers that:

> I would like to marry a man after God's own heart. A man who will be my best friend and is also sincere.[25]

Despite of her single status, Natasha is not shy to dispense tips on the traits both women and men should look for in a prospective spouse. Natasha appeals to younger flashy unmarried women. Yet, single women like Lucy Natasha who claim to perform miracles, signs and wonders see no paradox in their own inability to pray for their own husband. Her tips about marriage also continue to perpetuate the thinking that women are only complete when they are married, which is problematic in many ways as we discussed above.

Between Agency and Vulnerability: Single Women Navigating Christian Singlehood in the Ministry of Repentance and Holiness (MRH)

The Ministry of Repentance and Holiness founded by 'self-proclaimed' and controversial Prophet David Edward Owuor is very popular with womenfolk who find his message of repentance, holiness and moral probity attractive. Yet, this controversial church is good to women, most of all single women: widows, divorcees, single unmarried mothers and others. In fact, women occupy a visible public role in this ministry. Many are ordained bishops, pastors, deacons, heads of altars and disciples/apostles and evangelists. Currently, the ministry has already appointed 12 women bishops serving as heads of regions such as counties and districts.[26] Some counties are huge both geographically and in terms of the districts as well as large concentrations of altars. There are perhaps thousands of female pastors who lead and head hundreds of altars (as churches are referred to in this movement) dotting much of the country, be it in rural or urban centres. Women are also empowered to become spiritual leaders who adjudicate cases of conflict between members in various altars. Women also sing in altars and lead worship services and crusades, as well as provide ushering services and translate sermons into Swahili for the prophet who preaches in English during large repentance and holiness crusades and rallies.

One such woman clergy member Bishop Gladys is among the 12 women bishops heading expansive counties. Gladys is currently commanding an entire county which is made up of 5 districts and 80 altars. Bishop Gladys, who also doubles up as a businesswoman and an interior designer, described to me her responsibilities as a bishop. These include overseeing and providing leadership to over 300 pastors serving under her and coordinating the activities of all the altars under her care (Parsitau 2019; Deacon, and Parsitau 2017).

Other such roles and activities performed by Bishop Gladys and other deacons serving as heads of counties include weekly preaching, discipleship and mentorship to the youth, providing leadership, counselling to couples and those planning to get married, officiating weddings and funerals, presiding over the Lord's table or the Holy Communion as well as presiding over activities and programmes for widows, orphans and the vulnerable. Asked why the Ministry of Repentance and Holiness is popular with women, Bishop Gladys had this to say:

> The reason women love this ministry is because it embraces and accepts women irrespective of their present circumstances. Women therefore feel loved, accepted and not judged. The church also takes care of windows and orphans and the vulnerable.[27]

Bishop Gladys further explained that the church services always have two offering baskets, one for widows, orphans and the vulnerable and the other for paying utility bills for the staff working in the Altars. Every once a month she explained that they have contributions for the widows and vulnerable women's basket. After the collection, all the monies are banked and the altars apportion the money to those very needy women who need to pay school fees for their children, pay hospital bills and buy food and other supplies. This action and undertaking makes the ministry very popular with women because it takes care of their welfare. At the same time, the fact that this ministry does not judge single women, that is, divorcees, never married but with children, widows and other such categories and in a society that frowns upon single women, makes this ministry attractive to women. Women are accepted and embraced just the way they are. The fact that the church does not discriminate against single women remains interesting because women's bodies and sexualities in this church are extremely controlled with sermons about the ungodly images of their bodies or women's bodies as locales for sex and sin (Parsitau and Van Klinken 2018; Parsitau 2016, 2019). At the same time, the disbursement of welfare services is pegged on women remaining single and sexually pure. All single women, except younger never-married ones, are not allowed to marry. Young widows are forbidden from having intimate relationships with men and they are policed by neighbours and other church members. Should they be seen with a man, the church welfare services are terminated. The reason for this is that sex is considered sinful and polluting of the body of Christ (Parsitau 2019).

Rev. Linda Ochola-Adolwa: Helping Christians Navigate Relationship Spaces

Rev. Linda Ochola-Adolwa is a very influential personality in evangelical circles and a popular woman of faith to her followers. Rev. Ochola thinks that Christian churches in Kenya are family- and marriage-centric spaces that exclude single women. Her teachings and sermons at the Nairobi Chapel drew huge crowds and became popular among her followers because of programmes that sought to 'turn ordinary people into fearless influencers of society'. Rev. Linda, as she is popularly referred to by members of her former church, is a passionate minister who has been engaged in the ministry for a long time. She has a mission to bring about social impact through well-researched and inclusive sermons. For example, in a series of sermons dubbed 'Survivor, Love Edition',[28] Rev. Linda seeks to equip her members with spiritual tools and resources to help them navigate complex relationship spaces.

In this series of sermons, Rev. Linda delves into the complexities of intimate and personal relationships and endeavours to help women navigate this complex space. In one of her sermons which is also uploaded on YouTube, Rev. Linda delves into this terrain by asking her audience questions:

> OMG: who can I talk to? Who do I talk to? All around us, marriages are breaking, people are having sexual struggles! We know children or loved ones who are making wrong decisions. Relationships are complex, people are hurting and wounded by broken relationships. It is a chaotic space out there. Do you feel like you are in

a relationship wilderness? Are you looking for love? Are you stuck in a bad or dead relationship? Is your marriage going nowhere? Welcome to Survivor love editions series. Sit and listen to me as I help you navigate relationship spaces in a complex world.

In these series of sermons, Pastor Linda provides her church followers and viewers with spiritual resources to help them navigate relationships. In one sermon, she poses;

where do good men meet good women? What do you say to them when you meet them? How does a woman know that you are interested in her? What non-verbal cues are you communicating? How do you gain emotional intelligence to understand body language? Women are socialized to wait for men to make the first move but men are scared of rejection. How do you navigate this? Through reading of scriptures, Pastor Linda takes her audience through many of these tensions and how to build confidence to navigate this.[29]

Speaking of the platforms she created at Mavuno Church, Rev. Linda spoke in detail about her Survivor Love Edition series in which she sought to use the pulpit to empower men and women, in particular, and the youth to reclaim power and knowledge to navigate relationship spaces. In these series of sermons, she taught young men and women about dating, unpacking messages such as wives' submission to husbands, asking younger girls to date with their heads and not hearts (make wise decisions about who you marry) and rethinking about commitment before signing the marriage certificates. In one sermon, she urged young women especially not to suspend their thinking when dating but instead to ask hard questions and observe due diligence. Do not give away so much ground but instead negotiate space, power and voice with your partner, she said in one of the Love Series.

Theorizing Singlehood, Patriarchy and Masculine Christianity in Contemporary Kenya

Except for a handful of female-led and female-founded ministries and churches, Pentecostal churches are female spaces mostly led by men (Parsitau 2012). Many Pentecostal churches are also spaces that idolize marriage and family. Such spaces can be exclusive of single women who are often viewed with suspicion and imaged as 'wicked women' out to tempt Christian men and break their families. In many cases, such women are compared to Jezebel in the Bible, a treacherous and wicked woman who used her beauty and sexuality to get what she wanted. Many Pentecostal churches have couples' days, marriage retreats and date nights that totally disregard single women in the churches. Single women are often referred to as 'wicked women' and homewreckers, who pray for pastors' wives to die so they can marry the pastor.[30]

This can be isolating and stigmatizing for many women who feel rejected by their pastors and spiritual communities. For these reasons, some women have left such churches to find their own space where they try to create safe spaces for single women to have fellowship and community. Examples include Jesus Is Alive Ministries (JIAM), Faith Evangelistic Ministries (FEM), Single Ladies Interdenominational Ministries (SLIM), Prophetic Latter Glory Ministry International and many others. Others have created spaces for women to find fellowship and community but are bound by oppressive teachings and practices that require them to remain holy and unmarried if they have to access church welfare services as we have seen in the Ministry of Repentance. According to Rev. Nancy Gitau,[31] a widow and a young mother of five when her husband died early and left her with five children, single women are ostracized by Christian churches and these fuels their desperation to find husbands. Yet, according to Nancy Gitau, God's plan was not to make single people married. Scores of single women I interviewed shared with me their frustrations of being single Christian women.

Lydia Wanjiku[32] shared with me her frustrations with her local church where married women did not want to associate with her: 'You know, they despise me and are suspicious of me because they think I will steal their husbands. What they don't know is that

> I am also married to Jesus! God is my father and the father of my children God is also my husband and unlike earthly husband, he does not leave or abandon you like earthly husbands do. Also they do not know that the Holy Spirit is my companion. When I go to bed, I pray and tell Jesus to come And lie down with me. And he protects me from all evil. Bless the name of the Lord.'[33]

In my conversations with single women, I got a glimpse of how they make sense of their singlehood using biblical images of God, Jesus Christ and the Holy Spirit as their company. Many also strive to find biblical female heroines such as Ruth, Mary, Mary Magdalene and many others in which they can draw inspiration from (Griffiths 1997). Rev. Ochola Linda agrees that such powerful biblical tools can be important resources to help single women not just make sense of singlehood but also to navigate that space even in the face of rejection and exclusion from their church.

Conclusion

In this chapter, I have demonstrated using ethnographic data and sociological research how single women in Kenya are negotiating between faith and patriarchy in Christian churches in contemporary Kenya. Through examples of the varied ways in which different Christian churches are responding to the explosion of female singlehood, I show how prayers appear to be the most common response to a phenomenon that requires real tangible interventions including policy and laws to protect vulnerable women and children. It is also clear that single women in Kenya face myriads of challenges ranging from social, economic, emotional to social rejection and identity issues. Yet, stigma and rejection from their families, society and churches not only isolate them but also make them feel incomplete without husbands.

NOTES

1. https://mobile.nation.co.ke/lifestyle/family/3116132-1958704-format-xhtml-hd39ygz/index.html
2. Kenya has some of the highest numbers of teen mothers in Africa. Parsitau, D.S. (2018), 'How Teenage Pregnancy Is Keeping Girls out of School in Kenya and Why We Should Care', Kajiado County News.
3. https://mobile.nation.co.ke/lifestyle/family/3116132-1958704-format-xhtml-hd39ygz/index.html
4. In this chapter, I use the term single women to refer to a wide and diverse group of women that are unmarried either by default or by design.
5. http://oyungapala.com/slay-queens-socialites-and-sponsors-sexual-violence-in-kenyan-society/
6. https://www.bbc.co.uk/news/resources/idt-sh/sex_and_the_sugar_daddy
7. https://www.theelephant.info/features/2018/11/01/slay-queens-socialites-and-sponsors-the-normalisation-of-transactional-sex-and-sexual-violence-in-kenyan-society/
8. https://www.bbc.co.uk/news/resources/idt-sh/sex_and_the_sugar_daddy
9. https://www.nation.co.ke/news/Victims-yet-to-find-justice/1056-4782762-3a1iofz/index.html
10. Ibid.
11. https://www.the-star.co.ke/news/2019-08-30-prophet-owuors-bishop-in-sex-scandal/ https://www.bbc.com/pidgin/tori-47141008
12. https://www.standardmedia.co.ke/article/2000028915/we-live-and-work-together-in-love
13. Interview with Reverend Linda Ochola-Adolwa, Tuesday 10, 2019 in Nairobi.
14. Interview with Pastor Linda.
15. https://www.theelephant.info/features/2019/09/12/for-the-love-of-money-kenyas-false-prophets-and-their-wicked-and-bizarre-deeds/
16. http://www.singlesandmarried.org/
17. https://www.standardmedia.co.ke/article/2000043413/why-women-flocked-to-hear-the-marriage-pastor
18. http://www.singlesandmarried.org/about/
19. https://www.amazon.com/Relationship-Secrets-Pastor-Chris-Ojigbani/dp/1609574206
20. https://www.standardmedia.co.ke/article/2000043413/why-women-flocked-to-hear-the-marriage-pastor
21. https://www.standardmedia.co.ke/article/2000043413/why-women-flocked-to-hear-the-marriage-pastor
22. Not her real name.
23. https://www.youtube.com/watch?v=IlDlkkVGK0E
24. https://www.facebook.com/Revlucynatasha/
25. https://www.youtube.com/watch?v=IlDlkkVGK0E
26. According to Bishop Gladys, Overseer of Nakuru County, during a series of interviews held between June and September 2016 in Nakuru town.
27. Personal interviews with Bishop Gladys in 2016 in Nakuru.
28. https://mavuno.wordpress.com/tag/pastor-linda-ochola-adolwa/
29. Interview with Pastor Linda Ochola Adolwa.

30. I heard a pastor preach about this sermon in Deliverance church in the early 1990s. The wife of the presiding bishop of the church was battling cancer and eventually died. During this time filled with anxiety and sadness for the family and the church, which also had a significant number of single women, a pastor preached a sermon and prayed for the healing of the bishop's wife. He then suggested that some single women were silently praying that the wife of the bishop dies so one of them can get married to the bishop.
31. Rev. Nancy Gitau is an ordained minister who runs a small ministry for widowed women in Nakuru town.
32. Not her real name.
33. Interview with Lydia Wanjiku (not her real name) in Nakuru town 20 September 2019.

Bibliography

A Baseline Survey on Gender Based Violence in Kenya, 2010, National Commission on Gender and Development Report, Nairobi.

Adogame, A.O. 2008. I Am Married to Jesus! The Feminization of the New African Diasporic Religiosity. *Archives de Sciences and Social des Religions* 143: 129–148. https://www.research.ed.ac.uk/portal/files/12331979/ADMOGAME_afeosemime_I_am_married_to_Jesus_The_feminization_of_new_African_diasporic_religiosity.pdf

African Union. 2003. *Protocol to the African Charter on Human and Peoples Rights on the Rights of Women in Africa*. Maputo: African Union.

Beier, L., et al. 2010. *Family Structures and Family Forms: An Overview of Major Trends and Development*. http://www.familyplatforms.eu

Constitution of Kenya. Revised 2010. *National Council for Law Reporting*. Nairobi: Government of Kenya.

Gifford, P. 2009. *Christianity, Politics and Public Life in Kenya*. London: Hurst. 193.

Gregory, D., and D.S. Parsitau. 2017. Empowered to Submit: Pentecostal Women in Nairobi Navigation Culture. *Journal of Religion and Society* 19. The Kripke Center, Creighton University. http://wwwhdl.handle.net/10504/109164

Griffith, Marie. 1997. *God's Daughters: Evangelical Women and the Power of Submission*. Los Angeles: University of California Press.

Jewkes, R. 2002. Intimate Partner Violence; Causes and Prevention. Available at www.thelancet.com/journals/lancet/article/PIISQ40673602083575/. Accessed Oct 2016.

Kahindi, L.W. 2018. Christian Response to the Phenomenon of Single Parenthood in Kenya. Unpublished Ph.D, Thesis.

Kariuki, W.P. 2016. In Search of a Sense of Identity: Coping with Single Parenthood in Kenya. *Early Child Development and Care* 50: 25–30. https://profiles.uonbi.ac.ke/wanjirukariuki/publications/search-sense-identity-coping-single-parenthood-kenya

Kenya Demographic and Health Survey 2008–2009, Kenya Bureau of Statistics.

Kenya Demographic and Health Survey 2014, Kenya National Bureau of Statistics, December 2015.

Kenya National Bureau of Statistics (KNBS) and ICF Macro. 2010. *Kenya Demographic and Health Survey (KDHS) 2008–09*. Calverton: KNBS and ICF Macro.

Kenya Times, Newspaper. 2005, April 28. Castrate Rapists Say Kenyan MPS. Nairobi: Kenya Times Office.

Meda, S.G. 2013. Single Mothers of Nairobi: Rural-Urban Migration and the Transformation of Gender Roles and Family Relations. Urban People, Lide Mesta 15, 2013.

Muriithi, E.N. 2013. Pastoral Marital Programmes Used among Members of the Redeemed Gospel Church in Embu. MA Thesis, Kenyatta University.

Ntoimo, F.C., and Abanihe. 2013. Patriarchy and Singlehood among Women in Lagos, Nigeria. *Journal of Family Issues* 35 (14): 1–33.

OECD. 2009. *Family Data*. http://www.oecd.org/social/family/database.htm

Parsitau, D.S. 2012. Agents of Gendered Change: NGOs and Pentecostal Movements as Agents of Social Transformation in Urban Kenya. In *The Pentecostal Ethic and the Spirit of Development: Churches, NGO and Social Change in Neo-Liberal Africa*, ed. D. Freeman, 203–220. Palgrave Macmillan. http:/www.palgrave.com

———. 2014. Embodying Holiness: Gender, Sex, Bodies and Patriarchal Imaginaries in a Neo-Pentecostal Church in Kenya. In *Body Talk and Cultural Identity in the African World*, ed. Augustine Agwuele. Equinox Publishers, Texas State University. ISBN-13-9781782791851. www.equinoxpub.com

———. 2016. Prophets, Power, Authority and the Kenyan State: Prophet Owuor of the National Repentance and Holiness and Ministry, in Coertzen, P et al (2016) *Religious Freedom and Religious Pluralism in Africa: Prospects and limitations*, African Consortium for Law and Religion Studies (ACLARS) Sun MeDIA, Stellenbosch University, South Africa. www.afriacnsunmedia.co.za

———. 2017. *Engaging the Custodians of Tradition and Culture: Leveraging the Role Multiple Actors in Maasai Girls' Education, Global Scholars Policy Brief.* Washington, DC: Center for Universal Education (CUE), Brookings Institutions. https://www.brookings.edu/research/engaging-the-custodians-of-tradition-and-culture-leveraging-the-role-of-multiple-actors-in-maasai-girls-education/

———. 2019. Women without Limits and Limited Women: Pentecostal Women Navigating between Empowerment and Disempowerment, in the *E-Journal for the Study of African Religions and its Diaspora*, Vol 5. (1) 2019; http://www-a-asr.org/journal/

Parsitau, D.S., and N.J. Mwaura. 2010a. "Gospel without Borders": Gender Dynamics of Transnational Religious Movements in Kenya and the Kenyan Diaspora, with Mwaura, P.N. In *Religions Crossing Boundaries: Transnational Religious Dynamics in Africa and the New African* Diaspora, ed. Afe Adogame and Jim Spickard, 185–210. Leiden: Koninklijke Brill NV.

Parsitau, D.S., and P.N. Mwaura. 2010b. Perceptions of Women's Health and Rights in Christian New Religious Movements in Kenya. In *African Traditions in the Study of Religion in Africa: Emerging Trends in Indigenous Spirituality and the Interface with Other World*, ed. A. Adogame, 175–186. Farnham: Ashgate Publishers.

Parsitau, D.S., and Van Klinken. 2018. Pentecostal Intimacies! Women and Intimate Citizenship in the Ministry of Repentance and Holiness in Kenya. In *Christianity, Sexuality and Citizenship in Africa*, ed. Adriaan Van Klinken. Abingdon: Routledge/Taylor and Francis. https://www.routledge.com/Christianity-Sexuality-and-Citizenship-in-Africa/Klinken-Obadare/p/book/9780367141523.

Republic of Kenya. 2001. *The Children's Act, 2001, CAP 286 Laws of Kenya*. Nairobi: Government Printer.
———. 2006. *The Sexual Offences Act, 2006*. Nairobi: Government Printers.
Violence Against Women and Girls in Kenya: The Roles of Religion and Response of Faith Actors. WFDD 2017 Policy Brief No 21. August 2016.
Wane, N.N., et al. 2018. Dangerous Spaces: Kenya's Public Universities as Locus for Sexual and Gender Based Violence: A Case Study of Egerton University, Njoro Campus. Canadian Women Studies(CWS) Journal Issues. *Sexual and Gender Violence in Education: Transnational and Global Perspectives* 32 (1, 2): 21–28.

CHAPTER 6

The Meaning of Human Person in the African Context

David Nderitu

Introduction

Reflection about who a human person is has been and still continues to be central in discourses since time immemorial. Anthropocentric school of thought has controversially strived to show that all reality is about discovery, fulfilment and actualization of the human person. Its position is that a human being is the centre of reality. This is construed to mean that all other aspects of reality are meant to serve, explain or fulfil the human person; everything else is meant to serve the human course. The main controversy here is that anthropocentricism is a display of human egoistic stance, which has more often than not led to undermining of the rest of the reality by humankind.

Notwithstanding the above perception, and perhaps as a remedy to unwarranted dominance of the human beings over the rest of reality and the resultant undoing towards other beings and even against themselves over time, it is worth discussing more about who a human person is. As soon as the mind starts to think about this being then does it discover that it stares at a complex phenomenon. A human person has proven to be an enigma. According to Kahiga and Eberl (2013) ultimately who a person is, is beyond our ability to characterize definitively as the being of a person possesses some 'infinite' character which is beyond our scope.

Despite a significant success in revealing who a human person is across civilizations, the mystery of this being remains. This is because of the dynamic nature of the human person and the unique contextual situations surrounding the diversity of human existence. Since it is not possible to discover completely who or what a human person is, what is left for us is to understand a human

D. Nderitu (✉)
Egerton University, Nakuru, Kenya

person according to particular dispositions in different contexts. This chapter interrogates the meaning of a human person in the African context. This is compared to the Western world view of personhood because of the contrasting perspectives.

Who Is a Human Person?

This is a fundamentally difficult question. A fair answer to this question really lies within the understanding of a human being from specific cultures and civilizations. Various cultures have different understanding of a human person. But even within these cultures, a human being is portrayed as a diverse and complex phenomenon. John Locke (1632–1704) a modern-period British philosopher observed that a person is "a complex of ideas or as a band of perceptions".

Formal and scholarly attempts to understand a human person have been made in terms of the sociological, scientific, religious and psychological nature of human beings. Since the classical Greek period, thinkers and scholars have attempted to define who a person is. Aristotle (384–322 BCE), for example, perceived a human person as a rational animal. Boethius (480–524), a medieval Philosopher, attempted to offer a certain definition of a human person as an individual substance of rational nature. Another medieval thinker Thomas Aquinas (1225–1274) preferred to follow this understanding because he adopted it and also went beyond it by acknowledging the importance of the physical body, thus bringing the understanding that a human being is "an individual entity composed of a rational soul informing a material body" (Eberl 2006).

The above definitions of a human person have something in common—they all tend to perceive a human person as an 'individual' rational entity. This is so much a reflection of the Western world view. The Western perception of a human person is often associated with the philosophy of a modern French philosopher, Rene Descartes (1596–1650). The Cartesian philosophy of "cogito ergo sum", or I doubt/think therefore I am, is often interpreted to imply that a human person 'is' as far as he/she is able to think as an 'individual' being. This is the hallmark of the entire Western world view of individualism. It is this world view that is contrasted with the African world view of a person, which I now embark on discussing in the next section.

Anthropocentric Foundation in Perceiving a Person in Africa

The African perception of a person is established on the underlying African ontology of nature explained by Tempels (1959) and Mbiti (1969), which depicts human beings to be at the centre of the universe. The African ontology of nature is described as a hierarchy showing the relationship between the higher beings including God, divinities and spirits and the lower beings to humankind in the hierarchy including animated non-human beings and inanimate beings. The human beings sit at the centre of this sequence and therefore they are seen as the focus of the whole cosmic reality. In summary, the ontology is guided by five elements:

(i) God
(ii) Spirits
(iii) Human beings
(iv) Non-human beings (animated things)
(v) Inanimate things

Running across this hierarchy is a *vital force*, which links the various beings (Mbiti 1969; Tempels 1959). Apart from God and divinities, among other creatures within the hierarchy, only human beings bear the knowledge about this relationship, and they also have special ability to tap and control the vital force for the betterment of reality or at its detriment. Witches and sorcerers are believed to cause evil-like sickness by reducing the vital force, while the medicine men and diviners restore the vital force where there is deficiency (Mbiti 1969).

This is construed to mean that it is the human beings who consciously control the rest of lower reality in the hierarchy. It also means that the entire reality exists and has meaning in as far as it has bearing and relationship to the human existential reality. Every phenomenon serves this course. Human beings therefore become the focal point of every aspect of reality in Africa. In essence, the African foundational conception of reality is anthropocentric.

THE AFRICAN COMMUNITARIAN PERSON

Generally, there is emphasis of the fact that African traditional world view is largely communitarian; even the identity of a person is found within the community. The African communitarian culture has best been expressed by Mbiti who summarized it with this statement: "I am because we are, and since we are therefore I am" (Mbiti 1969). According to him, every aspect of life in Africa is guided by this philosophy. An individual cannot exist without the others. Therefore, there is no individual person but the community; there is no 'I' but 'we'. This is contrasted with the individualistic Western world view mentioned earlier; the Cartesian *cogito ergo sum* is in fact a contrast of the Mbitian, "I am because we are and since we are therefore I am".

This blatant 'communalism' versus 'individualism' dichotomization of world views and the resultant association of these philosophies with African and the Western culture, respectively, is contestable. It may not be in black and white that every aspect of African life is communalistic since there are instances where individual choices and decisions would be more valuable than community ones. In the same breath, there are evident cases where communitarianism would be inevitable in Western cultures.

Furthermore, though traditionally it is evident that most of the African cultures have been based on the communitarian foundation but in the current situation characterized by globalization and dynamism of the African culture, things may have changed. Particularly in the case of the African urban communities which are so much exposed to and fancy the Western lifestyle, most of the people are growing to be more individualistic. Nevertheless, fundamentally, the African culture is still by and large based on communitarian foundations than the Western culture.

The communitarian culture in Africa therefore influences the perception of a person to be viewed within the community; a human person finds meaning within the community. While the meaning, fulfilment and dignity of a person in the Western world view is founded on the basis of the ability of that person to demonstrate rationality and claim individual rights, in Africa, this is different. The African person finds identity meaning and dignity only in the community. Traditionally, African people are known to live and share resources together. There is still evidence of very strong community ties among Africans even in the midst of modernization and globalization.

Even for African people who are deemed to have embraced modernization and globalization in critical moments in life, they still exhibit the traditional communitarian mentality. During important events in life like birth, initiation and even during crises like sickness and death, Africans still gather to celebrate and agonize or mourn together. In an interview for a research, a principal investigator from North America, in a collaborative health research, shared her experience with this kind of a situation. This is what she said concerning her experience with the Kenyan research team: *I don't always understand some cultural contexts; there some cultural issues like someone's mother dies and the entire staff wants to go to the funeral and they take a day or two off work. In North American I can tell you that would never happen; But here it's normal, it is expected, it is part of how people support each other, and it is very much part of social fabric.*[1]

The above situation demonstrates that Africans are still communalistic, and they continue to maintain that kind of culture to date. It is in this kind of realities that a person is defined and fulfilled compared to what would be the case with the Western culture. Therefore, in Africa, personhood is conceptualized within the context of the community.

One growing area where the conflict between the African communalistic world view and the Western individualistic world view is clear is in the conceptualization of informed consent in health research. The ethical guidelines for health research require that each research should have mechanisms of seeking individual informed consent form each research participant. Chattopadhyay and De Vries (2008) have given the specific case of the 'Universal Declaration on Bioethics and Human Rights' promulgated by United Nations Educational, Scientific and Cultural Organization (UNESCO) where one aspect of it directs that: "The interests and welfare of the individual should have priority over the sole interest of science or society" (UNESCO 2005).

This directive has proven difficult to apply during research in most of the contexts in Africa because it often requires individual persons to give consent as autonomous entities when they are accustomed to seeking opinion from the wider community. In Africa, an individual is not entirely autonomous because a person finds meaning and accomplishment through the community. Therefore, in the African context, it becomes 'non-sensical' to require an individual to be self-determinant by insisting on individual informed consent.

According to Chattopadhyay and De Vries (2008), this is the case because the ethical principles referred to in bioethics and research ethics are predominantly founded upon Western philosophy. These ideas are replete with Socrates, Plato, Aristotle, Augustine, Aquinas, Kant, Locke, Mills, Bentham, Heidegger, Levinas, Sartre and Foucault. They have succeeded in solidifying bioethics into ideals that are rooted in the Western world view. Unfortunately, this world view cannot be applied in all setups, and this has proven to be the case in an attempt to apply some bioethics concepts in Africa. In order to ensure that research policies and practice address the contextual issues in Africa, there are growing concerns to align them with the African world views and in this case the communalistic mindset. One way of doing this is through growing suggestion of having provision for 'group' or 'community' consent in the research guidelines for contexts where the individual informed consent is not valued.

What Is the Extent of the African Communalism?

Inasmuch as African mentality is largely perceived to be communitarian, the community aspect of the African mentality only extends to some limited boundaries. When we say 'I am because we are', the 'we' in this context refers only to the immediate family members, extended family members, the clan and the tribal community. More often than not, members of one community view people from other communities as outsiders, aliens and, to some extent, enemies. In that sense, they are less human persons compared to the people from one's own community.

In the African cultures, the name given for a human being (person) is always in reference to 'one of us' tribe, race, clan or family. The one that is not 'one of us' is referred to as 'enemy', 'thing' devoid of the 'word' or 'cultural identity or spirit' (Kiruki 2012). Therefore, there is a specific perception of the person in this context. Those who belong to the same ethnic community regard each other as human persons, while those of the outside communities are given an inferior place as far as being human is concerned.

Thus, the 'other' is regarded not as a subject (person), but as an object in the diminutive sense (Kiruki 2012). In this regard, a human person is not any other being belonging to the *Homo sapiens* species as is scientifically and universally thought but a member of a one's own ethnic community. Others are just beings with lesser status to human persons. This vindicates the fact that it would be a serious offense to kill a person from one's own community because one would have killed a kinsman. In such a case, the murderer would have demoted himself to a lower level of non-human person. There would be a very heavy punishment that would follow such an act. For example, among the Agikuyu community of Central Kenya, when a person was killed by a member of the community, the standard fine was 100 goats and sheep (Leakey 1977).

Sometimes, the fine was stricter as one would be ex-communicated from the rest of the human persons since he was no longer one of them. He was expected to go out there and live with other beings who are lesser human in outside communities. Alternatively, the murderer would be killed since he/she would have declared himself less human by killing a person from his/her ethnic community. In order to appease the human spirit that was once in the killed murderer, a white sheep or any other animal would be slaughtered.

A person who killed human beings from a different ethnic community, especially during raids, cattle rustling, or intercommunity fights, was regarded a hero and was accorded high status in community like being the head of his peer group or being given the most beautiful lady for marriage. This shows that the members of other communities were disregarded as persons.

In fact, most African communities have some derogatory names for people belonging to other communities, while they give positive names to people from their own communities. According to Kiruki (2012), among the Agikuyu, the name of a person is 'Mundu', the 'other' who is not a 'Mugikuyu' is diminutively referred to as 'Nyamu'-'animal'; hence, the phrase, 'Nyamu cia Ruguru', literally the 'animals of the West'. Among the Pokot from the Northern-Rift Valley Province in Kenya, a person is called 'Chito', (or 'pojon' meaning the one who belongs). The 'other' is called 'Punyon', which literally means 'an enemy'. The Turkana who neighbour the Pokot refer to fellow Turkana as 'itiokang' meaning 'mother' or 'ikaatong' meaning 'brother' or 'sister', which are soothing names. They refer to other people as 'ng'imoe', which means an 'enemy' or 'alien'.[2] This is the trend with most of the communities in Africa.

This kind of branding of people from other communities with derogatory names depicting lesser humans is the one that justifies some social evils in most African communities like ethnic conflict and civil strife, which lead to murder of people. In Rwanda the inter-ethnic war between the Hutus and Tutsis in 1994 was premised by one group referring to the other as 'cockroaches' destined to be crushed (Kiruki 2012), a mentality that contributed to the genocide. This is the same case with many African contexts where such war has been experienced.

The Pokot and the Turkana in Kenya have been in constant conflict as neighbours. Since the Pokot regard each other as 'chito' or 'pojon' (our own), while the others are taken as 'Punyon' (enemy), it means that killing a 'punyon' is not a serious offence because the 'punyon' does not bear the essence of a human person. Likewise, the Turkana regard others as 'ng'imoe' (enemies/aliens) and therefore they would find it easy to kill them and hence the exacerbation of ethnic fights among these two neighbours upon slight incitement and provocation. The demeaning of people from other communities is even more pronounced among these pastoralists because they accord high dignity to cattle more than people from the other ethnic community. Thus, they are ready to kill a person from a different community in order to raid cattle. They would also find it normal to kill a person who has been found raiding cattle.

Among the Agikuyu, the 'mundu' (fellow Kikuyu) carries with it the meaning of a real human person, while the 'nyamu' (animal) refer to beings with lower status like animals. In fact, the Agikuyu refer to the non-Kikuyu as 'nduriri', which refers to outsiders or 'those other beings' or people of other nations (ruguru). This would be the story in other parts of Africa where we often experience inter-ethnic conflicts. People regard the others as enemies, and since "it was permissible to kill an enemy" (Wandibba 2012), then people kill each other indiscriminately. This is the basic reason that explains the persistence of fights and killings among most neighbouring communities in Africa.

Changing the Perception of the Human Person

A number of suggestions have been put forward particularly in addressing inter-ethnic animosity and conflict in Africa caused by the way communalism is to be perceived. The general predication of communalism as the dominant African world view is an optimistic start. But when the communalism turns out to be a limited concept, extending only to one's ethnic community, then it throws some pessimism, particularly because it is the platform on which hatred for other human beings is advanced. The mindset that is committed to show the difference and divide human beings will succeed in doing that to a gullible mind until one is left alone since people are not identical and therefore looking for complete similarity is impossible. These are mental deceptions that make humans take themselves as superior beings to others.

The human mind is in a cave of personal deception like the cave that Plato talked about. At that point, the mind relies on *doxa* or opinion as the source of truth and reality about a human person. This is opposed to the state of *episteme* or knowledge, which brings forth the true status of affairs. At the opinion level, the human mind is stuck with the images, while at the *episteme* level the human mind is concerned with the originals or archetypes. Kirui (2017) has used Plato's illustration of *the Allegory of the Cave* not only in demonstrating how people take others as inferior, while terming themselves as superior human persons, but also in suggesting how Plato's ideas could be used to educate people on the importance of getting out of the cave particularly regarding negative ethnicity in Kenya.

Borrowing a leaf from Kirui (2017), we can interpret more the adoption of the allegory in addressing the concept of a person in Africa. The human mind is enslaved in superiority complex just like the people in the cave. Because they have been enslaved for long, they think that this state of mind is the real one. The Agikuyu in Kenya think that being a Kikuyu is absolute. The same applies to the Pokot who think that if you are not a Pokot, you are an enemy. It is the same illusion that leads one community to refer to the other as 'cockroach' as was with the case in Rwanda before the genocide. This is a form of enslavement of the mind in the cocoon of illusions about community entitlement at the expense of other communities. This mentality reveals how imprisoned the human minds are in the bondage of their own perceptions.

These opinions that people in various cultures bear, which prevent them from savouring the truth of reality, are also comparable to the idols that Francis Bacon talked about. They are the idols of the mind, which refer to the prejudices that can conceal truth (Marias 1967). Particularly the 'idol of the cave' represents the kind of prejudice that most human beings have regarding people from other communities. The idol of the cave just like the Platonic cave, is a kind of a situation that each community finds itself in, especially based on traditional myths and understanding of one's community versus the other. They are the tendencies and predispositions that lead people to mistaken perceptions about others.

Perhaps the human mind could be liberated from this kind of disposition. In the allegory of the cave, there is strife to make the mind of the prisoners trapped in the cave ascend from illusion to pure reality outside the cave (Kahiga 2004). Of course, this is a difficult process since it involves a painful movement from darkness to light. The movement from ignorance to knowledge has never been all time easy. Even in Plato's explanation, one would find resistance were he to make an attempt to bring the prisoners who are in the cave to the light. They are simply not willing to abandon their current state of slavery of mind. Most of the people have a conviction that their understanding of human persons as those belonging to their own communities is right. They are adamant to change this perception and any understanding that is contrary to this is bound to be met with firm resistance. However, this liberation of the mind from the fetters of tradition and narrow mindedness (Kahiga 2004) is the only way out in changing the perception of the human person.

Plato suggested education as the way to overcome the illusory understanding about reality. This could be effective in this case too. Plato's roadmap to this liberation envisioned a life curriculum where the young people in the society would be gradually directed to embrace a new perception about reality that bears eternal and absolute truths, leaving behind the shadows of world error, falsehood, prejudice and blindness (Kahiga 2004). This can be done to our minds, which are prejudiced against other people who do not belong to our heritage whom we perceive as less human. African traditional education system can be given a new curriculum that puts true values to the mind of the people to make them appreciate others as fellow human beings who share the same essence, rights and dignity.

We have to appreciate the fact that human beings are essentially the same even though we look different. The difference that we have is only accidental. But again, we can never be identical. The whole concept of identity has always elicited debate. There is identity where a thing is in harmony with itself or with those of its like. But no two or more things may exist with similarities in terms of both form and content; hence, no two or more things may be identical in this sense (Ochieng'-Odhiambo 1997). In other words, no two or more things can be absolutely identical. Once we understand this fact, then we should be able to appreciate the differences that we have among ourselves.

But we have common properties some of which share is in our essence as human beings, in that we have some harmony as human persons. Our essential identity as human beings could be differentiated with other creatures like animals of the same species. But we also share some identity with animals, and this is the genetical identity. Therefore, humans and monkeys are genetically identical because they both belong to the animal genus, whereas a Kikuyu and a Kalenjin, a Pokot and a Turkana, a Hutu and Tutsi have a specific identity, in that they all belong to the human species.

The latter fact is the emphasis that should be stressed on the human minds so that they have a clear understanding of who a human person is. The perception reigning in the minds of many Africans is that the human person is limited to the ethnic group. But going with the categorization of the human beings as belonging to the same species, then the reigning perception should be expanded in the minds of people who still refer to other people as less humans. Such a move would go a long way in ensuring that people respect each other, hold high the dignity of other people and embrace the rest of humanity as belonging to the same heritage. This will leave people with second thoughts whenever they want to propagate atrocities against their fellow human persons like the case of ethnic cleansing that continues to be experienced in Africa.

Conclusion

A human person is a complex being, and there have been various attempts to understand who a 'person' is. The African world view of associating the conceptualization of a person with a being in the community is plausible. This is a value that the Western culture of individualism misses. But the extension of the communal conceptualization is limited to the narrow ethnic boundaries, and this contributes to the disregard of the others as real human persons. This, in turn, influences animosity and conflict between people from different ethnic communities, which has been the greatest failure in Africa.

This mentality can be liberated through proper education as Plato suggested. If such a development was to be pursued, then the perception of a person would change, and people would not consider themselves different and superior to others. Africa has a ready platform in its foundational communalistic mindset, which can be developed and expanded beyond the perception of a person beyond the ethnic boundaries. This will reduce ethnic conflicts in many parts of Africa.

Notes

1. Interview with a respondent from University of Toronto, Canada for a PhD thesis by David Nderitu (author) titled: 'An analysis of Aristotelian analogy of friendship among unequal parties: the case of IU-Kenya Partnership' on 16 March 2017.
2. Interview with an opinion shaper from the Turkana community on 23 May 2012 in Naivasha Sub-County, Kenya.

Bibliography

Chattopadhyay, S., and R. De Vries. 2008. Bioethics Concerns Are Global, Bioethics Is Western. *Eubios Journal of Asian and International Bioethics* 18 (4): 106–109.
Eberl, Jason T. 2006. *Thomistic Principles and Bioethics*. Oxon: Routledge Annals of Bioethics, Routledge.
Kahiga, Joseph K. 2004. *Introduction to Critical Thinking*. Eldoret: Zapf Chancery.
Kahiga, Joseph K., and Jason T. Eberl. 2013. Personhood: African and Western Threads of Thought. In *Contemporary Issues in Philosophy, Religion and Theology*, ed. Joseph K. Kahiga and M.N. Wanyama. Eldoret: Utafiti Foundation.
Kirui, I.K. 2017. *Ethnicity in Kenya*. Eldoret: Utafiti Foundation.
Kiruki, Joseph K. 2012. Making a Difference to Patients: Perspectives of Health Care Ethics. *Current Research Journal of Social Sciences* 4 (2): 93–98.
Leakey, L.S.B. 1977. *The Southern Kikuyu Before 1903*, 111. London: Academic Press.
Marias, Julian. 1967. *History of Philosophy*. New York: Dover Publications.
Mbiti, J. 1969. *African Religions and Philosophy*. Nairobi: East African Educational Publishers.
Ochieng'-Odhiambo, F. 1997. *African Philosophy: An Introduction*. Nairobi: Consolata Institute of Philosophy Press.
Tempels, P. 1959. *Bantu Philosophy*. Paris: Presence Africaine.
UNESCO. 2005. *Universal Declaration on Bioethics and Human Rights*. Paris: United Nations Educational, Scientific and Cultural Organization.
Wandibba, Simiyu. *Kenyan Cultures and Our Values*. Wajibu: A Journal of Social and Religious Concern. Retrieved on April 24, 2012., from africa.peacelink.org/Wajibu/articles/art_4484.html

CHAPTER 7

Personhood in Africa

George Kotei Neequaye

INTRODUCTION

Léopold Sedar Senghor, the famous African philosopher, poet and statesman, and former President of Senegal, used the word *communalism*[1] to distinguish African communal living from the socialism and communism of the West. Senghor expounds that by communalism, he means, "a community-based society, communal not collectivist. We are concerned here not with a mere collection of individuals, but with people conspiring together, *con-spiring* in the basic Latin sense (literally "breathing together"), united among themselves even to the very centre of their being."[2] Communalism, as Augustine Shutte defines it, refers to a group of people who depend on each other for their survival; any selfish attitude by one of them is seen as a threat to the very survival of the community. Harmony and interdependence are at the centre of African life. This harmony is also extended to the gods and ancestors, who are the custodians of the people and the continued existence of the community. A community, for the African, involves the people, the gods, the ancestors and even the unborn. Within the African context, what has been described as tradition is the cultural history of the community. It is the values and tenets which the ancestors have tested and practised and believed to be useful for the common good of the community. Such traditions and cultures are open-ended, meaning that they are dynamic. No tradition or culture remains static, except, of course, those values that are the very foundation of the community. In general, each person is expected to play within the rules outlined by the community. A person is regarded as recalcitrant if he/she fails to obey the rules and regulations of the community. A person who remains a trouble-causer within the community and fails to adhere to the standards of the community is usually ostracized

G. K. Neequaye (✉)
Trinity Theological Seminary, Legon, Ghana

from the community. Within this context, therefore, personhood is never defined in isolation; it is defined in relationships and that is what this chapter sets out to do. It concludes that even though this togetherness still pertains in certain cultures in Africa, care must be taken not to exchange the individualism of the West with communalism as practice in Africa.

In this chapter, we elaborate personhood in Africa in the context of African communalism. How is personhood defined in the Western world? Who is a person in African communalism? How is personhood defined within the African community? Should we talk about African personhood or African personhoods? As an introduction, we try to explore the last question above on whether or not we could talk about African personhood or African Personhoods. We, then, go on in the next sections to discuss personhood in communalism, personal identity in the African context and whether or not personhood, as practised within communalism, disenfranchises the person of his/her rights, obligations and responsibilities. The contribution this chapter makes to the academia are twofold: first, it provides a much-detailed discussion on personhood among the Ga people of Ghana in a way that has not been done before. Second, this chapter provides a unique dialogue among various African communities on personhood in Africa that gives the reader a bird's-eye view of the meaning of personhood in Africa.

In an attempt to write on personhood in Africa, the methodological problem confronted with is the concept of African personhood. The question is, can we talk about one African personhood or should we talk about African personhoods? When commenting about whether or not African Traditional Religion has to be in the singular or plural, John Vernon Taylor,[3] has this to say,

> But is it possible to speak of African Religion as if it were one and the same throughout the continent south of the Sahara? Certainly, there is not one homogeneous system of belief throughout Africa. One tribe gives prominence to an element which is only vaguely conceived in another. Nevertheless, anyone who has read a number of ethnological works dealing with different parts of Africa must be struck not only by the remarkable number of features that are common but by the emergence of a basic world-view which fundamentally is everywhere the same.[4]

It is generally believed that African tradition is culture specific and heterogeneous. Taylor was right to indicate that even though African culture is diverse, there are belief systems that cut across the continent. When culture is used as a resource, we can talk about one African culture from which we draw, for instance, moral resources for a particular project on the African people. Neville Richardson distinguishes two approaches to the study of African ethics, which is appropriate to this discussion: one in which a factual study of the moral situation of Africa is done that involves an almost impossible task as one has to do "massive research on phenomena in African society deemed to be indicators of the moral state of that continent, or at least of certain parts of Africa."[5] The second approach is to do a study of African morality, looking at a specific area within the African continent. Kwame Gyekye made a cogent argument on the second point by emphasizing that one does not have to speak about the whole of African philosophy before it could be called African. He stressed that "for me a philosophical doctrine does not have to be shared by all Africans for it to be African; it need only be the product of the rational, reflective exertions of an African thinker, aimed at giving analytical attention or response to basic conceptual issues in African cultural experience."[6] Even though Gyekye is right on this point, to avoid arguments, we might as well give specific headings to our African philosophies in order to prevent overgeneralization. For instance, when one knows that the research he/she is about to do covers a particular region in Africa, like East Africa or West Africa or Francophone Africa, and so on, that region must be identified in the title of the work. But even then, when one titles a work as West Africa or East Africa or North Africa, they are still discussions about Africa and intrinsically African. So, using the title *Personhood in Africa* with a focus on certain parts of Africa still stands. We, therefore, intend to dwell on Richardson's second approach in this research. "Personhood in Africa," therefore, stands as the heading of this chapter since this chapter deals with certain cultures within Africa. That means, we do not make the almost impossible task of discussing personhood in all African cultures, but to draw from certain cultures within Africa to make a point on personhood as understood by those cultures.

NATURE AND CONSTITUTION OF PERSONHOOD

The Nature of Personhood

Personhood refers to the recognition of a person within a given community. Personhood is never achieved in an island; it always has to be achieved, in general terms, in the "I-Thou" relationship. In most of the Western world, the "I" is emphasized, especially in the context of humanism and existentialism, but the "I" cannot be defined as a person unless it is connected to a family and in relationships. "No one is an island," the adage goes. That is not to say that the person is not a human being before his/her being declared a member of a particular community. Personhood is used in the sense of one's attachment to a community or to a relationship. Within Western culture, one's personhood is defined within the context of the "I-Thou" relationship. "I-Thou" refers to a person-to-person relationship, person-to-family relationship and person-to-community/society relationship. That is why every family in the West in most cases have a common surname. However, within the context of communalism in Africa, personhood is achieved by the "I-Thou-Other" relationship. "I-Thou-Other" refers to the person-to-person, person-to-nature gods, person-ancestors and person-God relationships. On no count is the social, metaphysical and normative relationship excluded in the definition of personhood in Africa. It is, therefore, not surprising to refer to African culture as "incurably religious." Personhood in Africa is tied to the family, the community and the spiritual world. It is a relationship that is defined within the context of the past, present and future. The past has to do with the relationship between the living and the ancestor and the perpetuity of the traditions of the fathers. The present has to do with the relationship among the living, and that of the living with the nature gods; and the future has to do with the relationship with the unborn and everything that is done in the present to preserve the future existence of the community. As Polycarp Ikuenobe,[7] aptly emphasized,

> If we properly understand this idea of transcendence, then we can appreciate how a moral person and the African community are harmoniously connected by an enduring spirit and moral traditions to their ancestors, forefathers, and posterity. Hence, the communal 'we' is not limited to the immediate here and now, nor is it simply a temporary group or an aggregation of people that happen to exist and live in a particular historical time frame. Rather, the community is an enduring 'fused' group that is connected to a past historical time and the future; it transcends time.[8]

There is nothing like superstition in the African community; everything is interpreted within the context of the 'I-Thou-Other' relationship. The more one obeys the normative, social as well as the metaphysical rules of the community, one's personhood is applauded. Once a person lives contrary to the wishes of the community, one is regarded as a bad person. Thus, personhood, whether in African or in the West, is defined in relationships. The "Other," representing God, is, however, not so much emphasized in Western cultures. Ikuenobe was apt in this discussion when he stated that "instead of defining the individual self in terms of Descartes' 'thinking I' (cogito) and using it as the basis for individual identity, we find in the African culture, and affirmation of the existing community ('we are') as a basis for defining the identity of the existent and thinking self ('I am')."[9]

Most Africans, without doubt, believe that the Supreme Being created human beings.[10] Africans are, however, not in agreement on the means of creation. These divisions could be found in their myths. While some believe that humans were created, others believe that humanity was brought out of a hole, a vessel, a leg or a knee.[11] The majority, however, believe that the African was fashioned with a clay.[12] Africans are also in agreement that a person is made up of male and female.

Consequently, there are names allotted to men and women, and in most cases, no female is given a male name, nor is a male given a female name. All indigenous African names are very clear about female names and male names. Most often, the African child is born into an already existing structure of names or into a formula of names. For some, the day on which one is born determines the name one will have. For instance, among the Akan of Ghana, when a child is born on a Saturday,[13] he will be named Kwame if he is a male, and Ama if she is a female. For instance, among the Ga people, the first male or female takes the name of their grandfather or grandmother. The second male or female takes the name of their grandaunts and granduncles and so on. My first son's name is Niikoi, which is the name of the first boy born in my father's line. My second boy's name is Amon, which is my father's name, the second in line, and so on. In other words, the Ga parents name their children after their fathers, mothers, uncles and aunts. These names are acquired from the father's extended family and not from the mother's extended family. Conversely, in situations when the father of the child is not known, the child is named by the mother's family. In that case, the maternal grandfather of the child names the child.

Composition of a Person

Regarding the constitution of a person among the Akan, Wiredu avers that three elements constitute a person. One vital element, which he calls the *life principle*, comes from God, the creator. And it is this *life principle* which points to the fact that all human beings are from the same source and, therefore, are one universal family. "Literally: all human beings are the children of God; none is the child of the earth," he stresses.[14] Comparing the *life principle* of Wiredu to the *vital force* of Tempels, one notices that whereas the *life principle* of the Akan refers to the *principle of life* or *the source of life from the Supreme Being for all persons on earth*, the *vital force* of Tempels is limited only to Africans, in particular, the Bantu people. On the other hand, life, for both Tempels and Wiredu, cannot be conceived without the *vital force* or the *life force*.

On the subject of linking the source of ontology in the African context to a common ultimate universal being, Nimi Wariboko, cautioned this way:

> This ontology manages to avoid two extremes. On one hand, the wisdom of the continent opposes a simple sort of metaphysical ontology which reduces all conceptions of personhood to changeless common substance. On the other hand, it avoids a radical kind of relational ontology which takes the human to be totally relationally constituted or socially constructed.[15]

I have discussed the second part of this caution in another section below. I have a problem with the first caution, which restricts people from pointing to an ultimate metaphysical ontology as the source of all being. This is because the African concept of God is utilitarian; almost all Africans take their source from an ultimate being. That is why God is termed *the Supreme Being* in African Traditional Religion, and Africans have peculiar names for this *Supreme Being* which are normally not given to ordinary beings. John Mbiti is right to emphasize that "Over the whole of Africa, creation is the most widely acknowledged work of God,"[16] and Wariboko also confirms that "Kalabari men and women will easily agree with their ancient Greek counterparts that there is a common substance to humanity in the sense that creator-God (*Ogina, Tamuno* or *Temeoru*) created (*temem*) humans out of a substance.[17] *The Supreme Being* is the creator and source of all *beings*. When discussing personhood among the

Kalabari in Niger Delta, Nigeria, Wariboko was on point when he argues that Robin Horton missed the point when he criticizes Victor Turner's affirmation that "*Kavula* (God) is the Ndembu's attempt 'to represent pure-act-of being, the primal entity that underlies and supports all things in man's world'."[18] This is much like Aristotle's concept of the Uncaused Cause, and yet the idea of *Kavula* differs from Aristotle's conception by emphasizing that *Kavula* is not an inanimate entity but a primal living being who is the source and sustainer of all beings in this world. Wariboko goes on to uphold this all-important epistemology of Africans when he surmises that "What Horton fails to understand is that *Kavula* as a pure being has acquired particularities of its various manifestations and yet has not denied its content as the 'ground of all things and the transcender of all things.'"[19] Wiredu is, therefore, not acknowledging the extreme when he intimated that the *life principle* of the Akan is the source of all being on earth. For the Akan, any person on earth is a person who shares in the same substance with other being, whether the person is an Akan or a stranger. That is why the African is taught from infancy to treat the stranger with care.

The other two elements that make up the person, according to Wiredu, are the *blood principle* and the *charisma principle*, which are from the mother and the father, respectively. The *blood principle* constitutes the person's body, and the *charisma principle* constitutes the person's personality.[20] And this biological input of the mother and the father grounds the person in a particular clan within the community and, therefore, establishes his/her identity.[21] The *blood principle* and the *charisma principle* secure the mother-child bond and the father-child bond relationship, respectively.

Writing about the Asante, who also comes from the Akan tribe, Busia avers that the person is made up of *mogya, the blood of the mother*, and *ntro, the spirit of the father*.[22] Busia also affirmed that the child gains his/her citizenship of the Akan tribe through the *mogya* of the mother. In his own words, he surmises that "The mother-child bond therefore confers the rights and obligations of citizenship. It also determines a man's status and his title to office or property, since succession and inheritance are transmitted in the matrilineal line."[23] Nevertheless, when the person commits an offence, it is the father who is held responsible for the action of the person and not anyone from his/her mother's side.[24] Thus, like Wiredu, he also affirms the matrilineal nature of the Akan culture. In addition to the *ntro*, a male also receives from his father a *sunsum, spirit* and a *kra, soul*.[25] The *sunsum* from the father gives the child his/her distinctive character, thus, representing the person's ego and personality, while the *kra*, which comes from God, represents the person's *life force* and identifies him/her with God. After the death of the person, the *kra*, which never dies, returns to the Supreme Being.[26] What Busia failed to indicate at this point, which Wiredu did, was that the *kra* proceeds to be an ancestor after death.[27] That means that the *kra or life force* of Busia is the same entity as the *life principle* of Wiredu, and the *sunsum* of Busia represents the *charisma principle* of Wiredu and means the same thing—the person's character and personality. It is imperative to note that Wiredu elsewhere also refers to the *okra* of the Akan, which is the same as the Asante's *kra*.[28] According to Busia, during intercourse, the man gives his *sunsum* to the child at conception, and the Supreme Being gives the child his/her *kra*.[29] It is believed that the person's *sunsum* perishes with him at death. When a witch attacks a person spiritually, it is the *sunsum* that is attacked. When a person dreams, it is again the *sunsum* that functions in the dream.[30] It is pertinent to add here that the function given to the *heart* of a person in Alexis Kegame's *shadow concept* of the Bantu people is similar to the meanings allotted to the *vital principle* of the *sunsum* of the Akan. That is because Kegame's *shadow concept* particularizes the person's *heart* with intelligence, character and immortality. According to him, intelligence refers to the reasoning faculty of the person and forms the subset of the functions of the *heart*. In its function, the *heart* combines all the internal activities of the person and constitutes the personality of the person, thus, differentiating one person from the other.[31] In the *shadow concept*, therefore, the *heart* represents the *vital force* and constitutes *the very nature* of the Bantu ontology.[32]

The *life principle* or the *vital force* can also refer to the *teme* of the Kalabari as described by Wariboko. According to Wariboko,

> The unreal, the illusive shadow of one's true substance, the *teme* (spirit, shadow, image, to fashion) could refer to nonbeing. *Teme* also means to create—apparently creating what does not exist, bringing into existence … And since everything real in Kalabari (from trees and animals to humans) has a spirit (*teme*) it means that in every form of existence, being- ness is mingled with nonbeing.[33]

Like the *life principle* or the *vital force*, *teme*, as a nonbeing spiritual force, participates in and energizes all things—whether animals or nature or humans or the nature gods and ancestors; they are all held together and function by the power and spirit of *teme* in Kalabari society. In particular, *teme* is that which strengthens and rejuvenates being and gives being his/her active relational qualities. Wariboko communicated it more clearly in the following: "Being is also often explained in discourse as an ontological principle, the spirit that adhere in all things, animate or inanimate that enables them in self-determination, self-affirmation or existence."[34] *Teme* is the spiritual force in being that enables being to function as a creative and empirical being, yet, paradoxically, it is an *ontological principle* that precedes nonbeing. Teme-órú, the Supreme Being, also shares in the spiritual force of *teme* with His creatures. For the Kalabari, work takes place in three forms: *communality, participation* and *possibilities,* and all three are held together and function in relationships through the power of *teme*. *Teme* enables the spirit of *amatemeso*-centric love, which is the mutual cooperation and relationships resulting in community development (amatemeso); it enables the ontological divine creativity of the community, which opens more room for participation in divine creativity in the work of the community, but the work of *teme* is not limited only to the Kalabari community, but to the whole earth community. In other words, even though *teme* is restricted to the Kalabari community, it also stretches its wings to cover activities of the cosmos, not excluding the sustenance of nature and the care of the unborn.[35]

In much the same way, the *vital force* or the *life principle* of Wiredu also describes the meaning and function of *ubuntu* as it relates to the value of sharing in the relational qualities of being. In his article, *The ethics of Ubuntu*, Mogobe Ramose explains the inner meaning of *Ubuntu*. According to him, "*ubuntu* evokes the idea of *be-ing* in general."[36] For him, "to be is to be in a condition of *–ness*." Like Heraclitus, he emphasizes that everything, including human nature, is in the state of flux, towards whole-*ness*. He further notes that this is in line with the philosophic view that *motion is the principle of be-ing*. This means that the moral nature of human beings, and for that matter Africans, is dynamic in nature. Applied to morality and to what he states as *ubu-untu*, it means that humanity is supposed to daily grow into perfection, much like the ontological *being* described by Wariboko: "The Kalabari person is believed to be continually growing toward an ideal so as to fully actualize their potentialities, to become all that they can be, to become the perfect, complete person (*krakra tombo*)."[37] Ramose explains that *ubu-*, which is the prefix of *-ntu*, stands for the unfolding nature of *be-ing* in general, and *–ntu*, which is the essence of *be-ing*, is the source from which *ubu-* evolves. According to him, *ubu-*, the prefix, is ontological in nature, and *–ntu*, the stem, is epistemological in character. But he goes on to stress that they form an indivisible whole, the two coming together to give the true picture of *Ubuntu*. This means that it is the function of the *–ntu* to feed the *–ubu*, the being, with knowledge. And within *Ubuntu* it is a special kind of knowledge—a daily growth towards perfecting, sharing and caring in *being*. This resonates with Augustine Shutte's[38] observation: "Our deepest moral obligation is to become more fully human. And this means entering more and more deeply into community with others. So, although the goal is personal fulfilment, selfishness is excluded."[39]

Ramose further notes that *Ubuntu* is "linked epistemologically to *umuntu*," *umuntu* representing "the be-ing which renders the coincidence between ontology and epistemology meaningful."[40] *Umuntu* "is an activity rather than an act," he clarifies. "Through the faculty of consciousness or self-awareness, *umuntu* releases the speech of being and, pursues its rationality by means of dialogue of be-ing with being."[41] This means that in the act of *Ubuntu*, a person experiences his/her true nature, but ironically, that true nature is a *be-ing* that is in flux towards perfection, the enabler is *umuntu*. This means that *umuntu*, like the Holy Spirit in Christian theology, is acting as the "one" who enables *being* to practise *Ubuntu*. It is that which moves *being* into action to attain the *summum bonum* of *Ubuntu*. "Whatever is perceived as a whole is always a whole-ness in the sense that it ex-ists and per-sists towards that which it is yet to be,"[42] Ramose explains. He indicates that *umuntu* is an ongoing process which is unstoppable until motion itself stops. This means that Africans, and for that matter humanity, are continually growing in compassion, fellow-feeling, sharing and caring, to mention a few. This resonates with the Christian assertion that the more believers pray, read God's Word and eschew sin, the more they grow into perfection (cf. Mat. 5: 43). The "one" that enables the continued growth of compassion, fellow-feeling, sharing and caring in being is *umuntu*. So, the ultimate essence of *ubu-ntu* is *umuntu* rendering *ubu-ntu* active. It means that at the heart of every human be-ing is the activity of the *umuntu*, making it possible for every individual to show *Ubuntu* towards each other. Humanity is, therefore, intrinsically a *responsive being,* an *inter-relational being*. It is in this sense that when one's actions are inimical to society that he/she is regarded as non-human in the African community. The foregoing implies that *Ubuntu* ethics of responsibility is a process whereby humans, and for that matter Africans, have the responsibility to daily practise caring, sharing, selflessness, compassion and forgiveness as they try to live their day-to-day lives.[43]

On the Yoruba front, according to Segun Gbadegesin, *eniyan, a person*, was put together under the collaboration of *Olodumare*, the Supreme Being and *Orisa-inla*, the arch-divinity.[44] Gbadegesin further records that *eniyan* is made up of three other parts: *opolo, emi* and *ara. Opolo* stands for the human brain and is, therefore, the source of reasoning. For example, when the Yoruba says someone has no *opolo*, it means the person's *opolo* is not functioning correctly. Someone with an incomplete *opolo* is a developmentally disabled person, and someone who lacks simple reasoning is referred to as *alaelopolo*.[45] The direct Yoruba translation for the Ga *jwenmo* is *ronu*; they both refer to thought or the thinking faculty of the person.[46] *Ara* in Yoruba refers to the *body* of the person. *Emi* is part of the divine *breath* that was put into *ara* to give it life.[47] Emi is, therefore, the *life force* of *ara*. It is only when *emi* is given that the body begins to breathe. *Emi* is, therefore, spiritual. The source and function of *emi* is the same as the *kla* and the *okra* of the Ga and Akan, respectively. But whereas *kla* and *okra* are referred to as the soul, *emi* is not. When *emi, kla* and *okra* are withdrawn from the human body, death ensues.

It is imperative to note here that the Kalabari people also have a tripartite system of personhood: *Teme*, (shadow or spirit or image), *oju* (body) and *dumo-digi* or *bala* (soul). *Bala* is also the life-giving cord of the person, the foundation of consciousness and emotion, including psychic behaviour.[48] *Oju* is the material part of the person. *Teme* and the *bala* are in *oju* and keeps the *oju* alive. Once they leave the body, the death of the body results. *Teme* and *bala* live on even after the body is dead. As discussed above, *teme* is the spirit, the immaterial part of the body that enables the person to be in communal relationship. The person is a person because it is a relational being, and relationships cannot take place without *teme*, the *life principle* of the person. Like the Holy Spirit in Christianity, *teme* is the enabler as well as the helper in relationships. Mutual relationships occur, therefore, in the spirit of *teme*. Because *teme* is a spiritual entity, it can be at two places at the same time. It cannot be seen by ordinary persons, but spiritualists can see and communicate with them in the spirit. According to Wariboko, in Kalabari worldview, "Priests and mediums who have undergone the training of 'clearing the eyes and ears' can see and communicate with spirits."[49] The body, on the other hand, cannot be at two places at the same time. It is confined to space and time.

Margaret Field rightly affirmed that, among the Ga, a person is made up of three entities: *gbɔmɔtso*, *kla* and *susuma*,[50] a biological as well as a spiritual entity.[51] *Gbɔmɔtso* generally means body. Etymologically, *gbɔmɔtso is made up of gbɔmɔ*, meaning *person*, and *tso*, meaning *tree* or *wood*. Thus, *gbɔmɔtso* literally means *a person's tree*. As in *ara*, *gbɔmɔtso* also has normative aspect to some of its constituent parts. For instance, for the Ga people, *tswi*, the heart, which is *okan* in Yoruba, are all the seat of character, thought and emotions.[52] When the Ga say, *Otswi mli tseee*, it means your heart is not clean. In other words, you have a bad moral. *Otswi wa*, means one whose heart is hard, and it is therefore very difficult to deal with or very stubborn or someone who stands his/her grounds no matter what. *Gbɔmɔtso* and *ara*[53] both have other parts that support the functioning of the person. For example, among the Ga, *jwenmɔ*, the brain, which is the same as *opolo* in Yoruba, are all believed to be the source of thought and reasoning.[54] When the Ga wants to say someone is ethically unsound, they say, *gbɔmɔ gbonyo*. *Gbɔmɔ* means person, and *gbonyo* means a dead person. *Gbɔmɔ gbonyo*, therefore, literally means someone who is dead. Thus, a person who has no feelings towards others is referred to as a dead person.

Etymologically, *susuma* of the *Ga* is made up of *susu*, which means *to think, to analyse or to expatiate*[55] and *ma* means *to build*. *Susuma*, therefore, means *to build thought* or *to analyse things*. However, *susuma* uses *jwenmɔ* (the mind) to think and to do the analysis. *Susuma* in Ga also refers to *spirit*, and therefore, it is a spiritual entity. *Susuma* is, thus, the person's centre of thought and spirituality. It is also part of the functions of the *susuma* to logically differentiate between good and evil. Since *susuma* is known to have originated directly from *Ataa Naa Nyɔŋmɔ*, the Supreme Being, it is, therefore, the seat of our conscience. Field is, therefore, right to refer to the *susuma* as the centre of the person's wisdom and personality.[56] Consequently, the person has to tap wisdom from his/her *susuma*.[57] Failure to do so results in bad behaviour or wrong choices. I disagree with Field when she notes that, "Also the *susuma* 'knows more than the man himself knows' and 'is wiser than the man himself'."[58] That is because it is logically inconceivable for what constitutes a person to be wiser than the person himself/herself as if it is an entity of its own. If the *susuma* is the personality and the source of wisdom for the person, it merely corresponds to who the person is; it functions as the conscience of the person and not as *a wiser entity* dwelling inside a person.

Given this meaning, the ethical character of the Ga is believed to have been given by *Ataa-Naa Nyɔŋmɔ* (*Father-Mother God*).[59] Even though a lot of the moral laws are made by human beings to enable the community's existence, it is also believed that God gives humanity their moral instincts before they come into the world. *Susuma*, therefore, is the seat of morality.

The *kla*, which is *the soul* of the person, is the seat of the person's character. The *kla* is thus normative and determines the nature and state of the person's behaviour. For example, when one does something wrong, and he/she is being insulted, it is said, *Okla hie flɛflɛ*. *Flɛ* in Ga means literally *to burst continually*, as when, for instance, the flicking sound that sometimes comes out of burning charcoal or when a windscreen breaks into pieces. The double *flɛ*, is an emphasis which means *something that is bursting or flicking beyond control*. Dakubu translates *flɛ* as "to gambol, as to skip or jump about in a playful manner." He also translates it as "a rowdy person, or to retort disrespectfully, or one who answers back."[60] *Flɛflɛ*, therefore, refers to something that has lost its sanity. Thus, *Okla hie flɛflɛ* is an insult, which means *one's soul is a fool*, since it is exhibiting a bad character, or a soul that has lost self-control. Arries-Tagoe translates *flɛflɛ* as *frivolous*.[61] The Ga also believes that the *kla* and *susuma* can acquire a quasi-physical body in dreams and go out of the person in a mission.[62] When the *susuma* leaves the body in dreams, the *kla* has to stay to keep the body alive, and vis versa. If, on the other hand, both the *kla* and the *susuma* leave the body, the body loses its breath and therefore dies. The *kla* and *susuma*, thus, keep the body alive.[63] The *kla* and *susuma* are spiritual. The source of the *kla* and the *susuma* of both male and female makes sense when one considers the fact that the Ga regards the Supreme Being a mother as well as a father. In other words, the female originates from the motherhood of the Supreme Being, and the male originates from the fatherhood of the Supreme Being.[64] It is hardly conceived that way in other cultures.

The *kla* is believed to carry *gbeshi*, which is one's destiny. It is known as *nkrabea* in Akan and *ori* in Yoruba. However, in Yoruba, *ori* is also regarded as the carrier of the person's divinity and the holder of the key to one's success or failure. Hence, it is the centre of one's personality.[65] One either has a bad or a good *gbeshi*. *Gbeshi* is differentiated from a normal way of life. It is a behaviour that one is not able to control, nor is one held responsible. The same explanation of destiny given by Fortes about the Tallensi of northern Ghana applies: "There is no implication of his having to repair a conscious failure which he might have been able to avoid originally. He does not consider himself, nor is he considered to be, guilty through sins of commission or omission. Indeed, he is not even exclusively and solely responsible."[66] When a person is judged to be consistently unscrupulous, or always unlucky or goes through a tough time, or behaves in a queer way,[67] one says *mone gbeshi nyiɛ esɛɛ*, meaning, this person's *destiny* is following him/her. Field dwelt on the saying that "this person's destiny is following him/her" to conclude that *gbeshi* is external to the person and literally follows the person.[68] She also indicated the same thing in the following words, "The *gbeshi* is nevertheless personified, though it is something external to its owner and is not a part of his own make-up like the *kla* and *susuma*."[69] However, like many others, the phrase *gbeshi nyiɛ esɛɛ* is used metaphorically in the same way as saying, "bad luck is following a person." So, it was erroneous for Field to conclude that *gbeshi* is external to the person. *Gbeshi* is part of the personality of the person and therefore is associated with the *kra* of a person. It is internally placed like the *kla* and the *susuma*. A typical example of someone with a bad *gbeshi* is kleptomania. A mentally challenged or insane person is also not morally held responsible for his/her actions, as pertains elsewhere in the world. The difference with a mentally challenged person is that he/she usually is not born mentally challenged; one becomes mentally challenged at one point in the person's life. When one has a lousy destiny, he/she is regarded in the community as someone who needs spiritual help. Such a person will be sent to a traditional priest for treatment.

Since the Akan practise matrilineal inheritance, *the blood principle* identifies one with the family of the woman, and *the charisma principle* identifies one with the man's family. On the contrary, among the Ga people, the tribe this researcher hails from, patrilinear inheritance is practised among the clans. Because the Ga operate a patrilineal system, there is no emphasis on any *blood or charisma principle*; the paternal grandfather of the child names him/her. Subsequently, the child is identified with both families right from the eighth day when he/she is named at the *kpojiemɔ*, the Outdooring Ceremony for babies, but, in particular, he/she is identified with the father's clan and given a name from the father's family.

The child is still recognized as belonging to the mother's extended family too and calls the mother's brothers and sisters, uncles and aunts in the same way that he/she recognizes the father's brothers and sisters as uncles and aunts. When a child is born, it is after the naming ceremony that the clan accepts the child as a member of the clan. Before the initiation rite, the child is regarded as a stranger who has been sent from a Sky Family.[70] The child has to go through seven days of spiritual trials, each with its own danger. And it is after the child survives the seven dangers that he/she is qualified to be initiated and accepted as a person who has come to stay among them.[71] No wonder then that when a baby is being initiated into the Ga family, he/she is raised up and shown to *tsotsoobi, the morning star.*[72] During the naming initiation rite of the baby on the eighth day, which is performed at dawn—about four o'clock—when *the morning star* could be seen, he/she is raised up three times to *tsotsoobi* to thank the Sky Family and ultimately the Supreme Being for the gift of the child.[73] Once a person is initiated into the African family or the clan or the community, the work of introducing him/her with the normative rules and rites of the society begins. The initiation of the baby into personhood does not end there, and it continues throughout the person's life in his/her initiation into adulthood, then 'elderhood' and, finally, 'ancestorhood.'[74] On the other hand, if a child dies before the naming ceremony on the eighth day, the child is not counted as belonging to any family. He/she came as a stranger and has gone back as a stranger. The name that was supposed to be given to that child will be given to the next child that is born. The child that died before the eighth day is, therefore, wiped out from existence; it is as if the child was never born.[75] The personal identity of the person, therefore, begins with the initiation into the clan.[76] That does not mean that the person is not a human being right from the day he was born. He/she is regarded as a human being sent from the Sky Family, but at the same time, a stranger waiting to be incorporated into the family and the clan through the initiation. Writing about the Tallensi of northern Ghana, Meyer Fortes also avers that destiny is either good or bad. It is part of a person's personhood, and that one chooses his/her destiny in his/her prenatal state in heaven before birth.[77] That means that, among the Tallensi, a person's destiny or fate is already fixed before one enters into the world.[78] Destiny, however, could be reversed by performing prescribed rituals. Fortes again was on point when he reported that "Given these ideas, it is consistent that Tallensi defines the ritual of ridding a patient of a bad Predestiny as a ritual of 'sweeping way,' divesting the patient of his or her lot and casting it out to make way for its reversal."[79]

Self-Identity

The preceding on African communalism means that the responsibility of a person is tied to his/her relationship with and for the community. As Ikuenobe puts it, "A person is described in terms of his community, his responsibility, and social status in the community."[80] Therefore, the self-identity of the person is derived from his/her obedience and connectedness to the community. What is ethically right or good is not, like the Western practice, tied to what the individual thinks or decides, it is intrinsically tied to the acceptable norms of the community. "There is no other self to be true to, except the communal self. The community, its continuing harmony and well-being, are the measures of what is good," Richardson reiterates. Whatever the individual does is aimed at contributing to the holistic nature and survival of the community. In the words of Ambrose Moyo, "There is no identity outside community."[81] The individual's identity is, therefore, defined by his positive involvement in the community. Richardson aptly observes that "The notion of the sovereign will of the individual is obviously very far removed from the view that one's very identity is known and expressed through one's belonging in the community."[82] According to Munyaka and Motlhabi, "Only through the co-operation, influence and contribution of others, can one understand and bring to fulfillment one's own personality. One is able to discover a sense of self-identity only in reference to the community in which one lives."[83] The identity of the person in communalism is, therefore, grounded in the person's relationship with other members of the community and with the *Other* (i.e., the gods and the ancestors, and ultimately to the Supreme Being).

Among the Ga, and ultimately among Africans, what you do and acquire in work further gives you an identity and status within the community. When a person is described as *anihaolo* (a laziness person) among the Ga, it refers to someone who will not work or who does not help himself/herself or one who does not contribute to the welfare of the community. *Anihaolo* is a disgrace not only to his/her family, but to the community at large. It means that the family or the community has failed in her duty to train one to contribute positively to the welfare of the community. Wariboko stated it more succinctly this way, "Of course, the name or identity is always embedded in some community reference framework but is nonetheless one's name, and one has to guard it as to guard the bigger name of the family or *house*."[84] Failure to guard the good name results in the Ga community designating such a person as *moni he bɛ sɛnamo*, meaning an unprofitable person or a useless person. Among the Ga, no man will give the hand of his daughter to be married to such a person. In fact, *anihaolɔ* cannot even have money to pay for the bride price to enter into marriage. On the other hand, when one is described as *mɔni tsuo nii waa* (the one who works hard), whether you become rich or not, it gives you a status as a hard worker and a morally good person in the community. Everyone is proud of you in the community and most men will like to give their daughters to such people in marriage. Acquisition of property through work and using it to support members of the community changes one's status in the community. In fact, among the Ga, work is not only about labour, it is also defined in the context of the help you give to others. As Wariboko clearly stated, "Work is not just the exercise of energy or production of products. It is essentially a stream of products, events and psychological states that are unified by legacy of work as a whole realm of human creativity. A person's value figures in the creation and sustenance of this legacy."[85] One's attitude towards work, therefore, either attracts praise or attracts shame to the one and to the one's family. When the Ga say someone is *pɛsɛ-kumenya*, it means he/she is a selfish person.[86] That person is ethically unsound because he/she has failed to grasp the concept of giving and sharing in the community. Justice is denied in such a situation. This means that the status of a person changes based on whether a person works hard or not. The concept of work, therefore, participates in a person's identity and forever defines the character of the person.

Among the Ga, the more money and property you have, the more you are expected to help the less privileged in the community. This depicts what is described as *fellow-feeling*[87] in the concept of African communality: those who are well-to-do are expected to help those who are in need. This has been described as the extended family system among Africans. In fact, this practice of helping those in need may be one of the reasons why most Africans are not rich. No matter how small the resources of an African is, he/she is expected to help the less privileged in the extended family system. The Ga sees it as support for one another, and it is done without complaining because one grows up seeing everyone supporting one another. This support system is a way of making sure that no one starves to death in the community. In fact, solidarity is one of the cardinal principles of African communality. As Shutte ably puts it, "The extended family is probably the most common, and also the most fundamental expression of the African idea of community … The importance of this idea for ethics is that the family is something that is valued for its own sake."[88] This means that in the concept of *fellow-feeling*, the well-being of a member of the extended family system is linked to the well-being of another member of the extended family community. We can, therefore, state the concept of *fellow-feeling* along the lines of the one John Mbiti gave in the following way: *Because you are well, I am well; because you are satisfied, I am satisfied; and because you are clothed, I am clothed.*[89] So within the African communality, " 'Family first' and 'charity begins at home' are recurrent maxims of African moral thinking, where, at a fundamental level, the agent's own, existing communal relationships are given precedence over others."[90] This means that your identity in the community is also defined by working hard to make sure that you also contribute to the welfare of the community. Failure to do so defines you as morally unsound and a failure within the community. Wariboko is on point here too: "Grounding an ethics of work in self-identity is a necessary foundation and point of departure for relating the particular to the universal,"[91] where the particular refers to the individual and the universal refers to the community. Moral identity is therefore directly related to the work you expend to the community. Good legacy within the society is, therefore, acquired through participation in the work of the community.

This emphasis on the interpersonal relationship with the *Other* harmonizes with the views of Martin Buber, Emil Brunner and Amitai Etzioni's on the foundational significance of the "I-Thou" relationship in the formation of a person's identity. According to Buber, a person's identity is expressed in his "I-It" and "I-Thou" utterances. His/her identity comes from the "I," the self, being address by the "Thou." Drawing from this idea of Buber, Brunner concludes that the fundamental being and responsibility of a person is found in the "Thou" calling him/her and communicating Himself to him/her.[92] This *I-Thou* relationship or the relationship with the *Other* is key for the identity of the individual within African communalism. Others like Bradley, however, argue that if the Latin word for "person," *persona*, means an actor's mask or a person in a play, then the identity of a person should be pinned to his role in society. So, for instance, when you say, "I am a father," it shows one of your roles in the society, and that should identify your personhood. That means the identity of a person could be derived from his/her "duties, virtues, and values that role entails."[93] Appended to this meaning is a "representative action." That means that a person comprises a self through dialogical relationships and representative actions. One is identified through one's answering others and acting for others.

However, more importantly, the self-image of the person is identified with his/her responsibility towards the community; the more his actions benefit the continued peaceful existence of the community, the more he/she has identified positively with the community and, consequently, his self-identity. The person whose actions are inimical to the cohesiveness of the community is likely to be banished from the community. Again, Wiredu aptly puts it this way, "Habitual absences or malingering or half-hearted participation marked an individual down as a useless person (*onipa hunu*) or, by an easily deduced Akan equation, a non-person (*onye onipa*)."[94] That is also true of Yoruba concept of a person. Segun aptly avers that to be regarded as *eniyan*, a person, one must lead "a life of selfless devotion and sacrifice to the communal welfare. Here selfishness and individualism are abhorred and expected to be superseded by a developed sense of community."[95]

Individual Responsibility as Personhood

Does the above description of the community within the African set-up mean that there is no individual responsibility? Does it mean that the community has absorbed the rights, initiatives and accountability of the individual, and that the individual only depends on the community for survival? Does it also mean that the individual has no opinion at all in the community? That is not the case at all. Even though the welfare of every African community is paramount, the individual is also held responsible for his/her actions. For instance, among the Ga people in Accra, there is an adage which says, "anuuu tsofa ahaa helatsɛ," which literally means "one does not drink medicine for a sick person." An Akan adage also says, "The lizard does not eat pepper for the frog to sweat."[96] The two proverbs mean that even though each member of the community is expected to work towards the welfare of the community, one is also held responsible for his or her actions. A Bantu proverb, noted by Didier Kaphagawani also emphasizes the individuality of the African in communalism: "What your neighbour has experienced is gone, tomorrow it will be your turn."[97] Any individual whose action disturbs the peace or destabilizes the harmony of the community will be held responsible for his/her actions. According to Gyekye, "The achievements, success, and well-being of the group depend on the exercise by its individual members of their unique talents and qualities. And these talents and qualities are assets of the community as a whole."[98] That means that whereas the individual needs the community to be successful, the community also depends on the talents of the individual for its continued existence. For instance, in Chinua Achebe's classic book titled *Things fall apart*, a particular song was sung for Akafo because he won a crucial wrestling match for a particular community. The song goes like this:

> Who will wrestle for our village?
> Akafo will wrestle for our village,
> Has he thrown a hundred men?
> He has thrown four hundred men.
> Has he thrown a hundred Cats?
> He has thrown four hundred Cats
> Then send him word to fight for us.[99]

The song above indicates that a warrior is expected to use his/her talents for the well-being and continued existence of the community. John Mbiti puts it succinctly this way, "Whatever happens to the individual happens to the whole group, and whatever happens to the group happens to the individual."[100] Furthermore, Kwasi Wiredu emphasizes the individual nature of responsibility within the African community. According to him, within the Akan context— and this may apply to all Africans—each person is held responsible for his/her actions. He cites a famous proverb among the Akans, which says that "it is because God dislikes injustice that he gave everyone their own name (thereby forestalling any misattribution of responsibility)."[101] More importantly, he also adds that corporate punishment by the gods of the society may also occur as a result of the irresponsibility of an individual. Often the wrong action of an individual has an immediate impact on his/her immediate family. For instance, a proverb in Burundi goes this way: "If one member of the family has eaten dog-meat, all the members of the clan are disgraced."[102] That is why each family has a direct responsibility to teach the moral tenets of the society to their children right from the onset to be responsible to the needs of the community. That means that the responsibility of the individual and the community, it seems to us, is reciprocal—one gains from the community as one gives to the community. Wiredu succinctly puts it this way:

> Along with this clear sense of individual responsibility went an equally strong sense of the social reverberations of an individual's conduct. The primary responsibility for an action, positive or negative, rests with the doer, but a non-trivial secondary responsibility extends to the individual's family and, in some cases, to the environing community.[103]

Like Mbiti, Peter Sarpong emphasizes personal and corporate responsibilities in Akan community. Among other things, he observes that in the Akan community, the things that are inimical to the continued existence of the community are catalogued under taboos.[104] Failure to observe taboos is not so much an offence against another person, but against the gods (*abosom*), the ancestors (*nsamanfoo*) or the Supreme Being (*Nyame*), which warrants corporate punishment, resulting in calamity or illness against the whole community. In order for the community to avoid this, each member of the community acts as a watchdog against flouting the taboos.[105] Fortes was right to show that there are two aspects of personhood—the objective part and the subjective part. The community builds up the objective personhood, which is then internalized. The subjective person so formed then uses his/her acquired talents to support the continued existence of the community that formed him/her. That means that the objective lessons from the community are directly proportional to the contributions that the person so formed could give back to the community.[106] As Presbey puts it, "Recognition of a person comes at different levels, both when one achieves the benchmarks of success (as outlined by the society in a conformist sense), and for some, when they excel in an individualistic way, for example, as heroes or healers, in what Honneth describes as the transition from 'person; to 'whole person'."[107] The more he/she learns from the community, the more he/she is likely to give back to the community. G. H. Mead puts it more clearly this way: "the 'I' of introspection is the self which enters into social relations with other selves."[108] Let me put it this way: the objective "I" receives from the community so that the subjective "I" could give back what it has gained to the community.

Furthermore, even though personhood in Africa is determined in relationships in a community, the community cannot also exist and be called a community without persons. Persons first come together to form a community before the community begins to nurture and form the person. Wariboko is apt here when he surmises that "At the level (intersection) of individual and commonality of dimensions, the focus is not to subsume the being or the individual particularity into that of the community or suprapersonal being like God, but enabling the particular person to be him or herself and contribute his or her best to the community well-being."[109] The individual capabilities of a person in a relationship is very active; it remains alive if the relationship with the community can flourish. The individual gains his/her personality in relations to the community, and at the same time, the community gains its continuity from peaceful relationships. The talents of the individual are, therefore, paramount if the community will continue to flourish and exist. The community and the individual are not centrifugally related; they are mutually inclusive. Wariboko is apt here:

> Relationship is not a gift of social life; it is the very giver of social life ... A person's being could be more complete, more perfect in its kind by giving and receiving inputs, qualities, and characteristics from the communal milieu. The paramount moral goal of the person is to contribute his or her best to the well-being of the community and the community's aim is to let him or her be all that he or she can be, develop all his or her capabilities so that his or her personhood is not diminished or threatened, but enhanced.[110]

Wariboko got it right about the African communality when he stated the following from Robert Neville: "As Neville has shown, to deny individuality or individual pursuit of values that relate to identity is ultimately to deny community, the set of conditional features of individuality."[111] The conditional features of a person are what you acquire or give to the community in your interaction with the community. The essential features are what defines one's being. The conditional and the essential features form the determinate person in the community.

The foregoing proves that the identity of the individual is directly proportional to his/her interaction with the community in much the same way as the collective existence of individuals constitute a community. It is, therefore, erroneous to affirm that in an African community, the individual has no say. The individual is, therefore, not passive in the African collective pool. Extreme individualism, like in the West, is, however, not a feature of an African community.

Personhood and Death

As Fortes rightly put it, "full personhood is only finally validated by proper death and qualification for ancestorhood."[112] Personhood is consummated in the qualification to the ancestral world. Not everyone who dies within the African community enters into the ancestral world. At the time of death, the individual must have fulfilled certain conditions that make it possible for him/

her to enter into the ancestral world. Before one is able to enter into the ancestral world, the basic conditions are that he/she must be an adult, must have attained old age and he/she must also have children. The person is also responsible for his/her moral life, as one must have lived an exemplary life if one is to enter the ancestral world.[113] He/she must also die a "natural" death. One cannot enter into the ancestral world if one dies through accident or suicide, or through an unclean disease, such as lunacy, dropsy, leprosy or epilepsy, and when a woman dies at childbirth.[114] It is believed that if someone fails to attain any of the above conditions and dies, he/she will be reborn into the world to relive his/her life. It is also believed that some ancestors are also reborn into the world to finish something they started but which they could not complete.[115] According to Sarpong, "those who cannot get entry into Asamando, the ancestral world, roam about as ghosts frightening people until they are born again to relive their lives."[116] That is the point where, like Hinduism, reincarnation comes into play within the African community. It is, therefore, the responsibility of the individual to live in such a way that he/she enters into the ancestral world. But suffice it to note that because the ancestor is consulted almost daily by the community, the relationship he/she shares with the community continues to define his/her personality.[117]

Conclusion

From the foregoing, there is no doubt that harmony and interdependence are at the centre of African life. This harmony is also extended to the gods and ancestors, who are the custodians of the people and the continued existence of the community. A community, for the African, involves the people, the gods, the ancestors, the unborn and nature. Within the African context, what has been described as tradition is the cultural history of the community. It is the values and tenets which the ancestors have tested and practised and believed to be useful for the common good of the community. Such traditions and cultures are open-ended—meaning that they are dynamic. In general, each person is expected to play within the rules outlined by the community. A person is regarded as improperly trained and therefore ethically unsound if he/she fails to obey the rules and regulations of the community. A person who remains a trouble-causer within the community and fails to adhere to the standards of the community is usually ostracized from the community. Within this context, therefore, personhood is never defined in isolation; it is defined in relationships and that is what this chapter sets out to do. But even though the African community faces the onslaught of individualism through globalization, care must be taken by all Africans to uphold this sense of togetherness, for in unity lies strength. A single broom will find it almost impossible to sweep the African compound; the compound is cleaned property when several brooms are tied together to sweep the compound.

NOTES

1. This word comes from a socialist tradition and was originally used in Paris as a political term in 1871 to describe a revolutionary political theory and practice.
2. L. S. Senghor 1963, Negritude and African socialism, in *African Affairs*, 2nd ed., (K. Kirkwood, 1963), 16.
3. He was an English theologian, a missionary to Uganda, Secretary General of Church Missionary Society and Bishop of Winchester from 1974 to 1984.
4. John V. Taylor. *The Primal Religion: Christian Presence amidst African Religion* (London: SCM, 2001), 9–10.
5. Neville Richardson. Ethics in an African Context, in *Questions about life and morality: Christian ethics in South African today*. Edited by L. Kretzschmar & L. Hulley (Pretoria: J. L. Van Schaik Publishers, 1998), 37.
6. Kwame Gyekye. *An Essay on African philosophical thought. The Akan conceptual scheme* (New York, Cambridge University Press, 1987), x–xi. See also Kwame Gyekye. 1996. *African cultural values: An introduction* (Accra, Ghana: Sankofa Publishing Company, 1996), 55–56.
7. A Nigerian philosopher at the Department of Philosophy, Kent State University, Ohio, U.S.A.
8. Polycarp Ikuenobe. *Philosophical Perspectives on Communalism and Morality in African Traditions* (Oxford: Lexington Books, 2006), 64–65.
9. Polycarp Ikuenobe. *Philosophical Perspectives*, 55.
10. John Mbiti. *African religions and philosophy*, 2nd ed. (Oxford: Heinemann, 1999), 91.
11. John Mbiti. *African religions*, 91–2.
12. John Mbiti. *African religions*, 91.
13. Wednesday, which mythologically is the birthday of spider, is called *Wukuda* (in Fante) and *Wukuada* (in Twi). According to Philip F. W. Bartle (in Forty Days: The Akan Calendar, *Africa: Journal of the International African Institute*, Vol. 48, No. 1 (1978), pp. 81–82), the Akan Calendar dwells on a 40-day period, known in the Akan language as Adaduanan (ada means day, and aduanan means 40). The calendar has a 42-day system, with the 43rd day being the same as the first day. The adaduanan calendar cycle may have started with a six-day weekly system, which has currently been superimposed with a seven-day system, influenced by traders from the savannah region of Ghana. The seven-day period starts on a Monday.
14. Kwasi Wiredu. The moral foundations of an African culture, in Coetzee, P H & Roux, A P (eds.) 2002. *Philosophy from Africa: A text with readings*, 2nd ed., (Oxford: Oxford University Press, 2002), 287–296. Wiredu 2002: 289, 313. See also K. A Busia. The Asante of the Gold Coast, in Daryll Forde (ed.). *African. Worlds: Studies in the Cosmological ideas and social values of African peoples* (London: Oxford University Press, 1968), 200. The same point is made by Segun Gbedegesin about the Yoruba culture: Segun Gbadegesin. *Eniyan: The Yoruba conception of a person*, in P. H. Coetzee and A. P. J. Roux (eds.), The African Philosophy Reader.(London: Routledge, 2003), 178.
15. Nimi Wariboko. *The Depth and Destiny of Work: An African Theological Interpretation* (New Jersey: African World Press, Inc., 2008), 96.

16. John Mbiti. *African religions and philosophy*, 2nd ed. (Oxford: Heinemann. 1999), 39.
17. Nimi Wariboko. The Depth and Destiny of Work, 104.
18. Nimi Wariboko. The Depth and Destiny of Work, 103.
19. Nimi Wariboko. *The Depth and Destiny of Work*, 103.
20. Kwasi Wiredu. *The Moral foundations*, 289.
21. Kwasi Wiredu. African Philosophical Tradition: A Case Study of the Akan, in *African Philosophy: A Classical Approach*. Edited by Parker English and Kibujjo M. Kalumba (New Jersey: Plentice Hall, Inc., 1996), 108.
22. K. A Busia. *The Asante*, 196.
23. K. A. Busia, *The Asante*, 196.
24. K. A. Busia, *The Asante*, 199.
25. K. A. Busia, *The Asante*, 197.
26. K. A. Busia, *The Asante*, 200.
27. Kwasi Wiredu. *African Philosophical Tradition*, 108.
28. Kwasi Wiredu. *African Philosophical Tradition*, 108.
29. K. A. Busia, *The Asante*, 197.
30. Kwasi Wiredu. *African Philosophical Tradition*, 109.
31. Alexis Kegame. The Problem of 'Man' in Bantu Philosophy, *Journal of African Religion and Philosophy*, 1: 35–36.
32. Placide Tempels. Bantu Philosophy (Paris: Presence Africaine, 1959), 51.
33. Nimi Wariboko. The Depth and Destiny of Work, 98.
34. Nimi Wariboko. The Depth and Destiny of Work, 98.
35. Nimi Wariboko. The Depth and Destiny of Work, 227–228.
36. Ramose, B. R. The ethics of ubuntu, in Coetzee, P H & Roux, A P (eds.) 2002. *Philosophy from Africa: A text with readings*, 2nd ed. (Oxford: Oxford University Press, 2002), 324.
37. Nimi Wariboko. The Depth and Destiny of Work, 70–71.
38. According to Metz and Gaie, Shutte is 'one of the first professional philosophers to seriously engage with Ubunto/Botho (2010: 275). I noted this here because it is of historical importance.
39. Munyaka, M., & M. Motlhabi. Ubuntu and its socio-moral significance, in *African ethics: An anthology of comparative and applied ethics*. Munyaradzi F. Murove, 63–84 (Scottsville: University of Kwazulu-Natal Press, 2009), 65.
40. Ramose, B R. The ethics of ubuntu, 325.
41. Ramose, B R. The ethics of ubuntu, 324–325.
42. Ramose, B R. The ethics of ubuntu, 324. See Prozesky, M. H. Cinderella, Survivor and Saviour: African ethics and the quest for a global ethic, in *African ethics: An anthology of comparative and applied ethics*. Edited by M. F. Murove (KwaZulu-Natal: University of KwaZulu-Natal Press, 2009), 306.
43. For an elaborate discussion on the concept of *Ubuntu*, see George K. Neequaye. *Towards an African Christian Ethics for the Technological Age: William Schweiker's Christian Ethics of Responsibility in Dialogue with African Ethics*: https://repository.up.ac.za/handle/2263/1770/discover
44. Segun Gbadegesin. *Eniyan*, 178.
45. Segun Gbadegesin. *Eniyan*, 176, 178.
46. Segun Gbadegesin. *Eniyan*, 177.

47. This is the same as the *kla* and the *okra* of the Ga and Akan people, respectively, only that is not referred to as the soul. When it is withdrawn by Olodumare, death ensues.
48. Nimi Wariboko. The Depth and Destiny of Work, 113.
49. Nimi Wariboko. African World View and the Structure and Strategy of Traditional Business Enterprise: The Case of Kalabari of Southern Nigeria. *Nordic Journal of African Studies*, 8(2), 18–50 (1999), 29.
50. M. J. Field. Religion and Medicine of the Ga People (London: Oxford University Press, 1937), 92.
51. My literature search shows that this is the first time a work on personhood is being done among the Ga people. Most of the work in this section are my own research on the subject. I hope that this section on personhood among the Ga people will generate a lot of discussions by Ga scholars on the subject.
52. Segun Gbadegesin. *Eniyan*, 177.
53. Segun Gbadegesin. *Eniyan*, 175.
54. Segun Gbadegesin. *Eniyan*, 176.
55. A. A. Arries-Tagoe. *The Ga-English Bilingual Dictionary* (Accra: Harvest Home Vision, 2016), 141.
56. M. J. Field. Religion and Medicine, 92.
57. M. J. Field. Religion and Medicine, 92.
58. M. J. Field. Religion and Medicine, 92.
59. E. A. Ammah. *Kings, Priests, and Kinsmen: Essays on Ga Culture and Society*. Edited by Marion Kilson (Accra: Sub-Saharan Publishers, 2016), 264.
60. M. E. Kropp Dakubu (ed.). *Ga-English Dictionary with English-Ga index*. Revised Edition revised and expanded (Accra: Language Center, University of Ghana, 2009), 69.
61. A. A. Arries-Tagoe, *The Ga-English Bilingual Dictionary*, 35.
62. M. J. Field. Religion and Medicine, 92.
63. M. J. Field. Religion and Medicine, 92.
64. A full discussion on the Supreme Being is being dealt with by this author in another article.
65. Segun Gbadegesin. *Eniyan*, 181, 182.
66. Meyer Fortes. *Religion, morality and the person: Essays on Tallensi religion*. Edited with an introduction by Jack Goody (London: Cambridge University Press, 1987), 155. See also Margaret Field, *Social Organisation*, 95.
67. M. E. Kropp Dakubu, *Ga-English Dictionary*, 77.
68. M. J. Field. Religion and Medicine, 94.
69. M. J. Field. Religion and Medicine, 94.
70. M. J. Field. Religion and Medicine, 97.
71. M. J. Field. Religion and Medicine, 171.
72. Tsotsoobi refers to Venus, the second planet from the sun in the solar system. According to the New Oxford American Dictionary, it is "the brightest celestial object after the sun and moon and frequently appearing in the twilight sky as the evening or morning star. In Greek mythology, Venus represents the goddess of love. This Ga tradition and its link with Greek mythology has to be investigated to see how they are linked. See M. E. Kropp Dakubu, *Ga-English Dictionary*, 214 for the translation of *tsotsoobi* into English.
73. A. A. Amartey. *Omanye Aba* (1990), 32.
74. Cf. Polycarp Ikuenobe. *Philosophical Perspectives*, 57.

75. Prince T. Squire. Ke Ene Ale Ga: Kusum Ke ŋaaŋ Saji (Translated as *Use this to know Ga Culture and Wisdom Matters*), Van Roberts Series, Volume 2. Publishers unknown. ISBN: 978-9988-1-2267-6.
76. I am currently doing a full research and analysis of the Ga *Kpojiemo*, which will be published in the very near future.
77. Meyer Fortes. *Religion, morality and the person*, 149.
78. That raises the question of individual responsibility. At what point can such a person be held responsible for his/her actions?
79. Meyer Fortes. *Religion, morality and the person*, 149.
80. Polycarp Ikuenobe. Philosophical Perspectives, 52.
81. A. Moyo. Material things in African society: Implications for African ethics, in Mugambi, J N K and Nasimiyu-Wasike, A (eds.). *Moral and ethical issues in African Christianity* (Nairobi: Initiatives Publishers, 1992), 52; cf. Kretzschmar & Hulley. *Questions about life and morality*, 43; Munyaka & Motlhabi, *African Philosophy: A Classical Approach*, 69. See also Shutte 2009: 90–92).
82. Neville Richardson, *Ethics in an African context*, 43; cf. Senghor, Negritude, 93–94, in Coetzee and Roux 2002: 298).
83. Munyaka & Motlhabi. *African Philosophy*, 70.
84. Nimi Wariboko. The Depth and Destiny of Work, 183.
85. Nimi Wariboko. *The Depth and Destiny of Work*, 184.
86. M. E. Kropp Dakubu, *Ga-English Dictionary*, 176.
87. It means caring for one another.
88. Metz, T & Gaie J B R. The African ethic of ubuntu/botho: Implications for research on morality, *Journal of Moral Education* 39 (3), (2010), 276, 284.
89. The concept of *fellow-feeling* fits very well into Matthew 25: 31–46 where Jesus told those on His right hand that so far as they did good to other people, they have done it to Him.
90. Metz, T & Gaie J B R. The African ethic of ubuntu/botho, 276.
91. Nimi Wariboko. *The Depth and Destiny of Work*, 184.
92. E. Brunner. *Truth as encounter* (Philadelphia: The Westminster Press, 1964), 19.
93. William Schweiker. Responsibility, 62.
94. Kwasi Wiredu. *African Philosophical Tradition*, 292. Cf. Gyekye's explanation of *onye nipa* in the book under consideration. His assertion that personhood can only be partly conferred by the community is implied since other things like the biological inheritance discussed above also play a role in personhood. See pp. 303, 306.
95. Segun Gbadegesin. *Eniyan*, 191.
96. Kwasi Wiredu. *African Philosophical Tradition*, 49.
97. Didier Njirayamanda Kaphagawani. African Conceptions of a Person: A Critical Survey, in *A companion to African Philosophy*, edited by Kwasi Wiredu (Oxford: Blackwell Publishing Ltd., 2006), 338.
98. *African cultural values: An introduction* (Accra, Ghana: Sankofa Publishing Company, 1996), 49–50.
99. Chinua Achebe, C. 1994. *Things fall apart* (New York: Anchor Books, 1994), 36.
100. John Mbiti. *African religions and philosophy*, 106.
101. Kwasi Wiredu. *African Philosophical Tradition*, 289.
102. Benezet Bujo. *Foundations of an African Ethic: Beyond the universal claims of Western morality* (Kenya: Paulines Publications Africa, 2001), 115.

103. Kwasi Wiredu. *African Philosophical Tradition*, 289.
104. Peter Sarpong. Aspects of Akan ethics, *The Ghana Bulletin of Theology* 4 (3), 41.
105. Peter Sarpong, Aspects of Akan ethics, 4 (3), 41.
106. Meyer Fortes. *Religion, morality and the person*, 251.
107. Gail M. Presbey. Maasai Concepts of Personhood: The Roles of Recognition, Community, and Individuality, International *Studies in Philosophy* 34, 2 (2002), 257.
108. G. H. Mead. *Mind, Self and Society* (Chicago: Chicago University Press, 1934). Taken from Meyer Fortes. *Religion, morality and the person*, 250.
109. Nimi Wariboko. *The Depth and Destiny of Work*, 108.
110. Nimi Wariboko. The Depth and Destiny of Work, 109, 111.
111. Nimi Wariboko. The Depth and Destiny of Work, 181.
112. Meyer Fortes. *Religion, morality and the person*, 259.
113. Kwasi Wiredu. *African Philosophical Tradition*, 162.
114. Peter Sarpong. *Aspects of Akan ethics*, 98.
115. John Mbiti. *African religions and philosophy.* 160; see also Peter Sarpong, Aspects of Akan ethics, 4 (3), 99.
116. Peter Sarpong, Aspects of Akan ethics, 4 (3), 99.
117. Benezet Bujo, Foundations of an African ethic, 122.

Bibliography

Achebe, C. 1994. *Things Fall Apart*. New York: Anchor Books.
Amartey, A.A. 1990. *Omanye Aba*.
Ammah, E.A. 2016. *Kings, Priests, and Kinsmen: Essays on Ga Culture and Society*, ed. Marion Kilson. Accra: Sub-Saharan Publishers.
Brunner, E. 1964. *Truth as Encounter*. Philadelphia: The Westminster Press.
Bujo, B. 2001. *Foundations of an African Ethic: Beyond the Universal Claims of Western Morality*. Nairobi City: Paulines Publications Africa.
Coetzee, P.H., and A.P. Roux, eds. 2002. *Philosophy from Africa: A Text with Readings*. 2nd ed, 287–296. Oxford: Oxford University Press.
Dakubu, M.E.K., ed. 2009. *Ga-English Dictionary with English-Ga index*. Revised and Expanded Edition. Accra: Language Center, University of Ghana.
Field, M.J. 1937. *Religion and Medicine of the Ga People*. London: Oxford University Press.
Forde, D., ed. 1968. *African Worlds: Studies in the Cosmological Ideas and Social Values of African Peoples*. London: Oxford University Press.
Fortes, M. 1987. *Religion, Morality and the Person: Essays on Tallensi Religion*. Edited with an Introduction Jack Goody. London: Cambridge University Press.
Gbadegesin, S. 2003. Eniyan: The Yoruba Conception of a Person. In *The African Philosophy Reader*, ed. P.H. Coetzee and A.P.J. Roux. London: Routledge.
Gyekye, K. 1987. *An Essay on African Philosophical Thought. The Akan Conceptual Scheme*. New York: Cambridge University Press.
———. 1996. *African Cultural Values: An Introduction*. Accra: Sankofa Publishing Company.
Ikuenobe, P. 2006. *Philosophical Perspectives on Communalism and Morality in African Traditions*. Oxford: Lexington Books.

Kegame, A. 1989. The Problem of 'Man' in Bantu Philosophy. *Journal of African Religion and Philosophy* 1: 35–36.

Kretzschmar, L., and L. Hulley, eds. 1998. *Questions about Life and Morality: Christian Ethics in South African Today*. Pretoria: J. L. Van Schaik Publishers.

Mbiti, J. 1999. *African Religions and Philosophy*. 2nd ed. Oxford: Heinemann.

Mead, G.H. 1934. *Mind, Self and Society*. Chicago: Chicago University Press.

Mugambi, J.N.K., and A. Nasimiyu-Wasike, eds. 1992. *Moral and Ethical Issues in African Christianity*. Nairobi: Initiatives Publishers.

Murove, M.F. 2009. *African Ethics: An Anthology of Comparative and Applied Ethics*. Scottsville: University of Kwazulu-Natal Press.

Neequaye, G.K. 2014. *Towards an African Christian Ethics for the Technological Age: William Schweiker's Christian Ethics of Responsibility in Dialogue with African Ethics*. https://repository.up.ac.za/handle/2263/1770/discover

Presbey, G.M. 2002. Maasai Concepts of Personhood: The Roles of Recognition, Community, and Individuality. *International Studies in Philosophy* 34 (2): 57–82.

Prozesky, M., and H. Cinderella. 2009. Survivor and Saviour: African Ethics and the Quest for a Global Ethic. In *African Ethics: An Anthology of Comparative and Applied Ethics*, ed. M.F. Murove. KwaZulu-Natal: University of KwaZulu-Natal Press.

Ramose, B.R. 2002. The Ethics of Ubuntu. In *Philosophy from Africa: A Text with Readings*, ed. P.H. Coetzee and A.P. Roux, 2nd ed. Oxford: Oxford University Press.

Sarpong, P. 1972. Aspects of Akan Ethics. *The Ghana Bulletin of Theology* 4 (3): 40–54.

Senghor, L.S. 1963. Negritude and African Socialism. In *African Affairs*, ed. K. Kirkwood, 2nd ed. London: Oxford University Press.

Taylor, J.V. 2001. *The Primal Religion: Christian Presence Amidst African Religion*. London: SCM.

Tempels, P. 1959. *Bantu Philosophy*. Paris: Presence Africaine.

Wariboko, N. 1999. African World View and the Structure and Strategy of Traditional Business Enterprise: The Case of Kalabari of Southern Nigeria. *Nordic Journal of African Studies* 8 (2): 18–50.

———. 2008. *The Depth and Destiny of Work: An African Theological Interpretation*. Trenton: African World Press, Inc.

Wiredu, K. 1996. African Philosophical Tradition: A Case Study of the Akan. In *African Philosophy: A Classical Approach*, ed. Parker English and Kibujjo M. Kalumba. Upper Saddle River: Plentice Hall, Inc.

———. 2006. *A Companion to African Philosophy*. Oxford: Blackwell Publishing Ltd.

CHAPTER 8

African Communal Ethics

Polycarp Ikuenobe

INTRODUCTION

It is commonly accepted that African cultural traditions are communalistic, especially their ethical systems. It is debatable what communalism in African traditions involves, and its ethical implications for individual rights, autonomy, dignity, choices, and way of life. This chapter examines the idea of communalism in African traditions and how it is exemplified in various ethical norms, values, and ways of life. It discusses how communal ethical norms inform African moral conceptions of personhood, environmental ethics, individual rights, and obligations, and their ontological and religious foundations.

A reference to African communal ethics does not suggest that Africa is monolithic in its values and beliefs. Such reference indicates some common dominant ideas among African traditions, in terms of how they are similar as opposed to how they are different. This commonplace generalizing use-sense of 'African' applies to 'Western' thought, and the comparison between 'African' and 'Western' thoughts.

COMMUNALISM AND COMMUNAL ETHICS

'Communitarianism' is used commonly in place of 'communalism' to describe African traditions. In Wiredu's view, a distinction could be made.[1] 'Communitarianism' in philosophical literature has social-political connotations involving how a state is organized to engender a sense of common belonging and collective obligations to the state as the locus of the monopoly of force, and the prioritization of collective interests over individual rights.

P. Ikuenobe (✉)
Kent State University, Kent, OH, USA

The concept of 'communalism' in African traditions has a broader connotation: it is rooted in the traditions of a group of people with common kinship, aspirations, values, and beliefs, living together proximately, sharing, and organizing aspects of their lives cooperatively in a community. 'Communalism' connotes a sense of *commune* of people sharing social, political, moral, epistemological, spiritual, and metaphysical relationships and *communion*, which are manifested in beliefs, attitudes, values, and ways of living.

Menkiti's distinction between *constituted* and *collectivist* communities can illuminate the idea of *communalism*.[2] A *constituted* community is an association of individuals who choose voluntarily to be part of the community. A *collectivist* community (in his words, "collectivities in the truest sense"[3]), which captures the notion of communalism, is a complex organic set of individuals, relationships, values, cultural traditions, institutions, interests, and obligations that transcend individuals or their simple aggregation. This indicates an epistemic element (methodological holism) of communalism, in terms of how to explain and understand the relation between community and persons, and how individuals acquire and justify beliefs and values.

Communal ethics involves principles and norms of conduct that regulate behaviors, relationships, and institutions to achieve harmonious communal living. In Thaddeus Metz's view, the ethical features that define the communal relations between community and persons, and among individuals, can be couched in terms of 'love' and 'friendliness.'[4] These features involve relationships, sharing ways of life with others, feeling integrated, caring for one another's quality of life, achieving the good of all, being committed to the good of others, and being concerned for others' welfare. The central idea of African communal ethics is cryptically captured by John Mbiti's aphorism: "I am because we are, and since we are, therefore I am."[5] The idea of 'we' as a basis for 'I' involves the communal basis for ethical norms and individual ethical reasoning and actions.

One way to understand this communal ethical outlook is to contrast it with the individualistic ethical outlook dominant in Western ethical theories. In contrasting African communalistic and Western individualistic bases for ethical perspectives and personhood, Menkiti says:

> [W]hereas most Western views of man abstract this or that feature of the lone individual and then proceed to make it the defining or essential characteristic which entities aspiring to the description 'man' must have, the African view of man denies that persons can be defined by focusing on this or that physical or psychological characteristic of the lone individual. Rather, man is defined by reference to the environing community.[6]

Menkiti's reference to one's environing community indicates *substantive social-moral views of* personhood, autonomy, and rights that consider the lived world and context of a person's ethical relations with others in a community. This idea is opposed to the Western *abstract metaphysical view* that removes the individual, his or her autonomy, or rights from a communal context.

The ethical idea of communalism has linguistic references and equivalences in many African languages. This communal idea, that *a person is a person through other persons*, is *Ubuntu* in Bantu languages. In Shona language in Zimbabwe, it is *Unhu*, and it is *Botho* in the Tswana language of Botswana. It is captured in Kiswahili by the concept of *Harambee*, which means 'everyone pulling together,' but the idea is exemplified in many cultures of Eastern Africa. This ethical idea is implicated in Julius Nyerere's (1968) idea of *Ujamaa*.[7] He sought to extend the traditional African communal values of extended family relationships of caring, mutual support, and cooperation to the wider society as a principle of governance.

Nyerere used the idea of *Ujamaa* to capture African traditional communal values of welfare, responsibility, and harmonious living. He articulates this value as follows: "In traditional African society we were individuals within a community. We took care of the community, and the community took care of us. ... Nobody starved, either of food or of human dignity, because he lacked personal wealth; he could depend on the wealth possessed by the community of which he was a member."[8] Everyone with the requisite capacity has the responsibility to contribute to the communal welfare in order to ensure that everyone is taken care of. Such communal contributions provide the material conditions of a good, value-driven, and harmonious context for individuals' well-being.

African communal ethics finds expression in egalitarian spirit, which involves the fair and equal production and distribution of goods, responsibilities, and burdens.[9] According to Nyerere (1968), "the organization of traditional African society—its distribution of the wealth it produced—was such that there was hardly any room for parasitism."[10] This engenders harmonious living and relationships, love, friendship, solidarity, mutuality, and caring for the well-being of all. According to Dismas Masolo the ethical principle of communalism involves "living a life of mutual concern for the welfare of others, such as in a cooperative creation and distribution of wealth. ... Feeling integrated with as well as willing to integrate others into a web of relations free of friction and conflict."[11] Communal ethics emphasizes individuals' responsibility, promoting, and contributing to, the welfare of everyone in the community, on which one's own well-being depends. The proper performance of such responsibilities defines, socially and morally, one's personhood, character, and well-being.

African communal ethics of responsibility is bound by considerations of human concern, caring, and welfare. As Gyekye indicates, "concern for human welfare constitutes the hub of the Akan axiological wheel."[12] This value of human welfare allows the community to be organized such that the choices that are beneficial to the individual are reciprocally beneficial to the community and vice versa. The community and the conditions or goods it provides promote self-respect, solidarity, social-psychological support, health, security, caring, food, shelter, love, friendship, mutuality, and meaningful decision-making regarding one's good. Without a community, relationships with other people, and the material conditions they provide, one cannot realize one's choice of a good life, and have or experience a meaningful sense of dignity, self-worth, or well-being. This idea is expressed in ethical principles that emphasize communal mutual dependence, relationships, solidarity, and caring.

Criticisms of Communal Ethics

In this communal view, individuals have responsibilities to themselves, others, and communal relationships because such responsibilities are simply the proper things to do. According to Segun Gbadegesin, "Every member is expected to consider him/herself an integral part of the whole and to play an appropriate role towards achieving the good of all."[13] Critics, such as Gyekye and Matolino, consider a responsibility view of African communal ethics as radical or extreme. It is understood as overemphasizing obligations to others and the community over individual rights, autonomy, and dignity. They argue that its overemphasis on communal responsibility, interests, and obligation to others and communal harmony is inconsistent with the acknowledgment and preservation of individual rights.[14] The prioritization of responsibility to, and interests of, the community diminishes individual interests and rights.

Critics argue that it is in virtue of an individual's innate natural rights, but not responsibilities, that one has moral dignity; such rights are not dependent on the community. Thus, Gyekye has argued for a moderate view of communalism that seeks to balance the interests of the community with the rights, freedom, and autonomy of individuals.[15] However, there is a debate regarding whether a plausible distinction can be made between moderate and radical forms of communalism or its ethical principles, whether the views that are considered radical are truly radical, and whether Gyekye's view is truly moderate.[16] Ikuenobe has argued that the responsibility interpretation of African communal ethics as radical is mistaken.[17] He argues that the interests of, and obligation to, the community are not necessarily in conflict with individual freedom, autonomy, and rights. Rather, when they are properly construed, the interests of the community or relevant obligations and individual rights or freedoms are coextensive and mutually supportive. Rights have relevance and meaning only in the context of social arrangements, material conditions, and individuals' ability to meet and exercise their different duties, which contribute to the health, well-being, peace, and harmony of the community.

Obligation, Rights, Dignity, and Personhood

The commonplace political and moral notion of 'obligation' or 'duty' is that it derives from rights that others have intrinsically. Rights give rise correlatively to obligations in terms of what we owe others, such that without a right, no obligation exists. However, there are two approaches to the issue of human rights: (1) natural rights approach, and (2) social justice approach. African communal ethics adopts a social justice approach, which relies on the idea that 'duty' viewed as the *jural correlative* of 'rights' depends on the community. Rights and duties are two sides of the same coin. Right claims (as entitlements) exist in a social-communal context. The norms of a community impose obligations on others to respect individuals' rights. This involves the ability and willingness of the community to use its social-moral rules and norms to protect rights and to demand relevant duties by others.

Although African communal ethics is, primarily, duty-based, it recognizes rights as socially recognized entitlements that are parasitic on communal duties and harmonious social arrangements. Masolo's idea of African communalism involves a community that morally calls on everyone to honor mutual and reciprocal responsibilities toward others.[18] Communal ethics prescribes the moral relationship of embeddedness in a community that involves reciprocity and mutuality of 'give and take.' Reciprocity involves the *jural correlative* relationship between 'duty' and 'rights,' where 'take' involves 'rights' regarding what people can 'claim,' are 'entitled to,' or 'are owed.' However, 'give' involves (non-supererogatory) 'duty,' 'payments,' and 'contributions' based on what are owed to people, which the community uses its social-moral norms and laws to protect. When you have the two (reciprocal) sides of a coin, 'rights' ('take') and 'duties' ('give'), the issue or debate usually is, which perspective gets a priority?

Critics who consider the duty perspective of African communal ethics as radical adopt the dominant Western individualistic view, which takes the perspective of prioritizing 'rights,' whereas African communal ethics takes the perspective of 'duties.' The obligations of reciprocity, solidarity, mutuality, and caring, which are essential to communal ethical principles of harmonious living and relationships, do not necessarily imply a corresponding right that individuals have intrinsically. Communal ethics insists that obligations and respect by others do not derive necessarily from individuals' natural inalienable rights or dignity. Having a right is not the only basis for having obligations to, or respecting, others. There are other prudential, utilitarian, and pragmatic bases for moral and social obligations and communal well-being. The mutual dependence between personhood (rights, identity, or dignity) and community implies that "an individual is obligated to contribute to the community not because it is expected of him or her, but because it [the community] is him or her."[19] Because one's social-moral personhood derives from the community, one has a responsibility to contribute to the community.

One's obligation to be a communal person depends on one's capacity for such obligation: 'ought' implies 'can' principle. One cannot have obligations that one is incapable of meeting. While those who lack such abilities, such as children, those with mental or physical disability, and senile elders do not have such obligations, those with the requisite abilities owe obligations to these groups of people. Communal well-being, caring, and harmony are exemplified by how a community treats its people, especially children, people with disability, the elderly, and the sick. Anyone who shirks his or her responsibility to such people diminishes his or her personhood or dignity; he or she cannot fully realize his or her own dignity or experience well-being or freedom in the community. Communal ethical obligations indicate that it is a violation of human dignity to enslave people because such acts fail to meet one's responsibility to provide the conditions for people to use their capacity for their well-being, harmonious relationships, realizing moral personhood, and experiencing dignity.

Metz articulates African communal ethical principle of *Ubuntu* as follows: "An action is right just insofar as it promotes shared identity among people grounded on good-will; an act is wrong to the extent that it fail to do so and tends to encourage the opposite of division and ill-will."[20] This principle involves, on the part of those *who are capable* or *have the capacity* to *use it actively*, the obligation to develop the relevant attitude, in order to *act* in ways that promote harmonious communal relationships, mutuality, solidarity, caring, human welfare, and good living. This principle, which indicates a responsibility ethics, requires people to actively cultivate and perform communal obligations that promote human dignity.[21] However, the features of dignity that Metz articulates as a basis for the communal ethics of *Ubuntu* assume or imply a right-based or deontological ethical perspective.[22] His articulation of African communal ethics of *Ubuntu* emphasizes the centrality of dignity in African conceptions of personhood, communal ethics, and harmonious relationships.[23]

It appears that Metz's deontological ethical view of *Ubuntu* is inconsistent with his articulation and defense of the African communal ethics of *Ubuntu* as the grounding for human dignity as the absolute, inalienable, intrinsic worth of the human capacities for communal love and friendship. The ethical principle of *Ubuntu* gives priority to responsibility toward others and the community, but it also seeks the goal or utility of promoting communal interests or well-being, on which individual interests and well-being depend. Thus, it is unclear how Metz's view of the absolute, intrinsic worth, and inherent nature of dignity, which involves a right-based (deontological) ethics, can be grounded in the communal teleological ethics of *Ubuntu*, which seeks to promote utility in terms of the communal goals and interests of mutual caring, friendship, solidarity, and harmonious living.

It is more reasonable to construe African communal ethics as consequentialist, in terms of acting to promote the goals of harmonious relationship, solidarity, well-being, and also, as deontological, in that it involves goodwill and responsibilities. Communal ethical principles are a hybrid of moral teleology (the moral view that an action is good if it maximizes human interests, utility, and harmony or balance in the community or reality) and moral deontology (the moral view that an action is good if it involves duty, or affirms intrinsic moral worth). William Frankena has called this hybrid ethics "mixed-deontology."[24] It has the advantage of avoiding the pitfalls of each of deontology and consequentialism, but combines the values of both. This hybrid view of communal ethics provides a reasonable basis for African conceptions of dignity, rights, freedom, autonomy, and the priority of responsibilities.

A plausible African communal ethical idea of human dignity is broader than Metz's idea of merely having the capacity for communal love and friendship. In addition to 'having the relevant capacities,' dignity involves *how properly one uses* one's capacity practically to enhance and promote communal love, caring, friendship, solidarity, and harmonious living. In this view, one's inherent capacities do not have an intrinsic, absolute, or inalienable moral worth that is separate from how these capacities are used in the context of communal well-being and harmonious relationships. Human capacities are instrumental goods; they are a means for good life, choices, and actions that manifest respect for self and others, mutuality, and harmonious communal living and relationships. They are to be used productively and positively as members of a community that make one's own good life and choices possible.

The community is essential for dignity and rights because it provides laws, structures, material conditions, and the moral, psychological, and social support and guidance for how properly people use their inherent capacity to live a good life. Communal harmonious living depends on how well people use their capacities to create and sustain the proper conditions for their capacity, dignity, and rights. As Menkiti argues,

> the transgression of accepted moral rules gives rise not just to a feeling of guilt but to a feeling of shame—the point being that once morality is conceived as a fundamental part of what it means to be a person [of dignity] then an agent is bound to feel himself incomplete in violating its rule, thus provoking in himself the feeling properly describable as shame, with its usual intimation of deformity and unwholeness.[25]

Social-moral personhood depends on how well one uses one's capacities and communal norms to contribute to such conditions. Individual capacities, rights, dignity, and autonomy are not inherently valuable or inalienable; otherwise, there would be no argument for enforcing rules, which limit one's dignity and rights.

The idea of having and using properly one's capacity for communal living indicates the African idea of 'moral personhood', which involves someone who is capable of feeling guilt or shame for transgressing communal norms, being accountable, and accepting punishment as atonement for transgressions. According to Gessler Nkondo, *Ubuntu,* viewed as a communal practical ethical principle for organizing life, involves a "commitment to the good of the community in which their identities were formed, and a need to experience their lives as bound up in that of their community."[26] If one chooses to act in uncaring ways that manifest wanton disregard for one's own life, well-being, lives of others, and harmonious living by committing violent, life-threatening crimes, then the responsibility of others and the community to respect that person's dignity or rights is diminished.

As such, the dignity and rights of a dangerous violent criminal are not inherently valuable; we should not respect absolutely his or her dignity, rights, freedom, and autonomy by allowing him or her to continue his or her criminal behavior to the detriment of the dignity, freedom, and rights of others and the community. African communal ethics indicates that *dignity, rights, autonomy,* and *freedom* and their correlative *respect and protection* are not unconditional or absolute. Their respect or protection is a matter of degree and conditional on proper use. A community must evaluate and determine the degree of respect or protection one earns and deserves, and the extent of responsibility that people have toward an individual, which is conditional on the quality of one's moral behavior and virtuous character.

The conditional and gradational conceptions of *moral dignity, rights,* and *freedom* in the framework of communal ethics, and their *respect by others and protection by the community,* which are based on one's responsibilities to self and others, are predicated on the responsibility to promote harmonious relationships and well-being within a community. This implies that a community, under certain conditions, may do things to diminish, *to some degree or extent,* elements of a person's capacity or rights to free choice and action. Although the community might justifiably imprison and violate the dignity, freedom, or rights of a dangerous criminal, the gradational and conditional views indicate that the community must exercise some degree of caring and respect for him, his well-being, and dignity, by not torturing or allowing him to suffer needless excruciating pain, dehumanization, or humiliation.

Similarly, a community may (albeit, humanely or respectfully) put a dangerous mentally ill person in a straitjacket, or force a dangerous drug addict and mentally ill person into treatment. These measures may violate their dignity, freedom, or rights, *to some degree,* by limiting the scope of their rights and capacity for actions and choices, but they are consistent with communal respect and protection for dignity, rights, and harmonious living. In some situations, harmonious communal living is *morally and logically prior* to the dignity, rights, or autonomy of, or the respect or protection for, someone who does not use his capacity properly. The community should respect, to some degree, one's dignity or autonomy to make *some* choices; such respect is not absolute. Some limits are necessary for communal well-being or harmony, which provides the material context, goods, and conditions for individual moral dignity.

The communal ethical ideas of morally circumscribing one's dignity, rights, or freedom when one misuses one's capacity, and respecting one's dignity, rights, or capacities when one uses them properly, are supported by the idea of holding *capable people* accountable for their actions. If one feels a diminished sense of dignity and self-respect, in terms of lack of autonomy, loss of physical or mental capacities, and self-control, based on factors beyond one's control, such as illness or natural mishap, then one still deserves a high degree or duty of respect by others and protection by the community. The idea of respecting unconditionally those who are *not capable* of acting to earn respect is supported by the moral principle of 'ought implies can,' which indicates that you cannot hold people responsible for what is impossible for them. For those who are able to use such capacity freely, there is an added element of accountability, which is that respect or protection depends on meeting one's responsibility to use one's capacity to promote loving and caring communal living.

ONTOLOGICAL, COSMOLOGICAL, AND RELIGIOUS FOUNDATIONS

African communal ethical norms regarding how one ought to act in the context of a community are founded on conceptions of reality, the cosmos, nature, and the relationships among various entities in a harmonious and ordered reality. Reality's natural order consists of humans (community), physical objects, spirits, ancestors, deities, gods, and God. A transgression of the natural order that is reflected in communal norms creates disharmony. According to Senghor (1995), "If the moral law of the African has remained unknown for so long, it is because it derives, naturally, from his conception of the world."[27] Such conception indicates that reality is a harmonious interconnected unity of things. A community, social institutions, relations, people's actions, ways of life, values, and their beliefs reflect the efforts to exist in harmony with nature and the supernatural.

Reality is a holistic composite of mutually reinforcing life forces involving human communities, ancestral spirits, deities, stones, mountains, rivers, plants, and animals. In the view of Placide Tempels, "It is because all being is force and exists only in that it is force, that the category 'force' includes of necessity all 'beings': God, men living and departed, animals, plants, mineral."[28] Vital forces differ in their essences; we have divine, celestial or terrestrial, human, communal, animal, vegetal, and material or mineral forces. The community is not reducible simply to the constituent individuals, institutions, norms, relationships, and all the elements that make it up, because it is not the simple addition of all these elements.[29] The idea of community has transcendental metaphysical and social ontological features and forces: moral norms, values, and relationships that unite people and mold individuals' character, conception of good, choices, and actions. Reality is a communion among supernatural (God, gods, spirits, ancestors), natural, social, and human energy and forces aiming at harmonious relations.[30]

In the African view of reality, the *natural* and *supernatural* are coextensive; they are interrelated and one is an extension of the other as a community of entities that exist in harmony. This idea is captured by Innocent Onyewuenyi's description that reality involves dynamic life forces: "The concept of force or dynamism cancels out the idea of separate beings or substances which exist side by side independent of one another."[31] Thus, there is no gap between natural human features and supernatural features in the harmonious composite of things in reality. As Menkiti states, "of course, there is procreation, old age, death, and entry into the community of departed ancestral spirits—a community viewed as continuous with the community of living men and women, and with which it is conceived as being in constant interaction."[32] Human relationships with supernatural entities, that is, God, gods, spirits, and ancestors, are manifested in reality and experienced in natural events. Living humans have communion with the spirits of ancestors and the gods by pouring libations and making sacrificial offering. These activities are aimed at achieving and maintaining harmony in reality.

In analyzing African worldviews, Mbiti indicates, "to understand their religions we must penetrate that ontology."[33] In articulating the connection between ontology and religions, he argues: God is the originator and sustainer of humans. Humans are at the center of this ontology, and animals, plants, and other natural phenomena and objects constitute the environment in which humans live. The environment provides the means for human existence and survival, and humans have mystical relationships with the environment, God, and supernatural entities.[34] The African view of ontology is implicated in cosmological and religious views of the sacred, divine, the origin of things, and how they are organized in the universe. According Leopold Senghor, "the whole of the universe appears as an infinitely small, and at the same time an infinitely large, network of life forces which emanate from God and end in God, who is the source of life. It is He who vitalizes and devitalizes all other beings, all the other life forces."[35]

In this harmonious order in reality, God is the source and origin of life in living creatures, gods, deities, and spiritual entities. As such, "there is no such thing as dead matter: every being, everything—be it only a grain of sand—radiates a life force, a sort of wave-particle; and sages, priests, kings, doctors, and artists all use it to help bring the universe to its fulfillment."[36] African views of ontology and cosmology reflect a naturalistic pantheism: everything is holistically natural and God is in everything and the source of everything, which are in order and harmony. This involves the belief in God's omnipresence, although God's presence is stronger in some place than others.[37] Although God's presence is transcendent, it is immanent in nature, and He is all-good. Because of the omnipresence of God, most traditional Africans consider nature as sacred and divine, it is in harmony with humans, and it has inherent moral worth, which derives from its role in cosmic and ontological order and its moral and religious primacy.

The qualities and attributes of God are potentially manifest in humans and communities, hence morally, humans attempt to actualize such potential in all their actions and communal obligation to emulate God and manifest reverence for Him.[38] Given the pantheistic view of nature, moral obligation or respect for nature, others, and the community is moral obligation or respect for the gods, spirits, ancestors, and God. Most moral and religious practices seek to maintain harmony that exists in and among nature, reality, and community. It is not in our interest to offend the gods, spirits, and ancestors or incur their anger by mistreating others and nature. In many traditional religious practices, people consider objects as things in which gods, deities, spirits, and ancestors are made manifest. People see mountains, trees, rivers, and some animals as embodiment of deities or spirits, and as such, they are divine, sacred, and are accorded reverence and moral respect. Natural objects have religious and spiritual significance and they are designated as religious shrines in which the divine or sacred is manifested.

According to Mbiti, natural objects are deemed sacred because "people hold that the spirits dwell in the woods, bush, forest, rivers, mountains, or just around the villages."[39] Religious beliefs are manifested in ethical norms, attitudes, actions, and religious rites. Religious rites are performed to appease spirits, deities, gods, and God with prayers, offerings, and sacrifices in places designated as religious shrines. Some shrines are the bases of trees, mountains, and banks of rivers, which are adorned with gifts and offerings of natural objects. Sometimes, sacred animals are sacrificed and offered to gods, deities, and ancestors, which are embodied in natural objects and shrines. Such appeasement and reverence are ways in which humans are in communion and fellowship with the spiritual world, the sacred, and the divine. These acts, which are partly religious and moral, contribute to the harmony in nature, community, and peoples' lives. This view is reflected in the belief and practice of totemism, where different families, clans, or villages respect different animals, plants, or natural objects as totems or sacred objects in which ancestral spirits reside.

Many traditional Africans believe that a spiritual connection exists between people and animal totems, which engender the attitudes, norms, and acts of moral respect. According to Burnett and wa Kang'ethe (1994), for the Bantu, animal totems, "was not killed except in self-defense, and it was never eaten. Kindness toward the totem was expected, and in turn, it was expected that the totem might assist in times of need or desperation."[40] People need totems, deities, gods, ancestors, and spirits as intercessors and intermediaries in the spiritual realm to communicate directly with God because people cannot do this directly with Him. In most activities and ceremonies, people invoke the spirits by offering prayers and sacrifices to convey people's prayers and requests to God. According to Mbiti, "it is held that God specifically created the spirits to act as intermediaries between Him and men."[41] It is believed that God works with the gods, deities, ancestors, and other spiritual entities to cause and bring about harmony in nature and the community.

These spiritual or religious elements have misled some to argue that African communal ethics cannot be characterized strictly as 'ethics' involving universal moral principles that are rationally justifiable. They misunderstand African moral principles, values, and their ultimate justifications as necessarily tied to supernatural phenomena such as gods, spirits, deities, and ancestors. In their misunderstanding, they argue that because moral principles and values are tied to supernatural entities and the dogmatic belief in them, they are accepted dogmatically without question or rational justification. This view comes from lack of proper understanding of the African view of ontology—in terms of the harmonious connections among humans, community, nature, and supernatural entities—and how this view of ontology provides the rational teleological and deontological foundations and justifications for the normative prescriptions of principles and human actions within African communal ethics.

Cosmological Foundation and Environmental Ethics

According to African views of ontology and cosmology, human actions and natural events are explained by reference to harmony or disharmony in the order of nature. People believe that things happen to people and in the community because of disharmony in nature that is caused by people's bad actions. For instance, human ill health or natural disaster could be caused by the frailty of human nature or disharmony in the micro-sense of our natural body or disharmony in the macro-sense of our communal body or our interactions with all other aspects of or among entities in nature. These forms of disharmony or ill health can be rectified or cured with natural ingredients such as herbs, or by the spell of supernatural powers, which can also be altered or restored using supernatural powers. Based on this mode of explanation, communal ethics prescribes proper moral actions regarding how individuals ought to treat their own bodies and how they should act in a community and interact with other people and entities in nature.

A moral prescription for one to act in order to maintain harmony in one's own body (between body and mind/spirit) could also lead to harmony with the human community and nature, and harmony in reality. This moral view is consistent with the African practice of sorcery or divination which involves efforts by people with supernatural powers to decipher the order of nature, whether there is disharmony, which is the source of problems, and what humans should do to bring about harmony. As Vernon Dixon indicates, the aim of Africans and their actions

> is to maintain balance and harmony among the various aspects of the universe. Disequilibrium may result in trouble such as human illness, drought, or social disruption. ... According to this orientation, magic, voodoo, and mysticism are not efforts to overcome a separation of man and nature, but rather the use of forces in nature to restore a more harmonious relationship between man and the universe.[42]

Diviners and sorcerers are able to acquire knowledge of, and communicate with, the spiritual world in order to prescribe the proper moral attitudes, actions, and norms.

In this view of ontology and cosmology, there is no dichotomy between the natural and supernatural as *objective reality* (object) and a human *subjective view or perspective* (subject). The lack of ontological separation between 'object' and 'subject' has epistemological implications for how humans know and justify communal ethical norms as the basis for their actions. Reality involves and depends on human subjects and human conceptions, understanding, knowledge, and interpretations of it. Communal ethical norms regarding how humans ought to act and interact with each other and with reality depend on their knowledge and understanding of reality and others as a unity in harmony with relevant value. The African communal view indicates that the phenomenal world is not independent of, or external to, the self; rather, it is affected by one's interpretations, understanding, and interactions with it.

Reality is what humans know it to be, based on what is experienced by humans' robust moral, spiritual, and physical interactions with it. Thus, reality is not external to humans or its conceptions formed by the mind. In this epistemological view, objects do not exist unknown by a human subject. The implication for communal ethics is that what is known about reality determines how people act morally and interact with reality, and vice versa. This involves the moral and epistemological blurring of 'object' and 'subject,' the 'observed' and 'observer.' There is no 'unexperienced reality' and there is no reality if it is not experienced in some form. This African communal ethical and epistemological view is, fundamentally, *experientialist*, because people acquire moral values and knowledge in a community from their robust communion with reality. Moral understanding involves the phenomenological embeddedness of the subject (observer) in the object (observed).

The idea of an objective reality that exists independent of its 'being known' by anyone does not make sense and has no practical and ethical significance in terms of how people act. The practical significance and human interaction with reality is underscored by human's sensitivity to external reality. As Senghor (1995) indicates: "The African is, of course, sensitive to the external world, to the material aspect of being and things. ... he is sensitive to the tangible qualities of things—shape, color, smell, weight, etc."[43] A subject who is a human person that lives in and is shaped by the community is not passive toward an objectively unknown reality. A person (as a subject) is an active aspect of reality who understands, experiences, and knows reality by interacting with it and shaping it morally as a member of a community.

African ontology and communal ethics are implicated in environmental ethics, where the environment is seen as a part of the broader human community that includes nature and reality. Communal ethics indicates that individual responsibilities to nature, others, and human community could be based on pragmatic, utilitarian, or prudential grounds. One's obligation to others, community, or the environment is an obligation to oneself, in that the well-being of others, community, and the environment provides the material goods and conditions for one's well-being. Failure to meet one's obligations to the environment, others, and nature that provide material conditions for humans would engender social or moral condemnation; this attenuates moral personhood and dignity, and respect by others. The moral attitudes or obligations toward nature or the environment as a part of the holistic unity of reality are illustrated in the thought system of the Oromo people.

According to Workineh Kelbessa's (2006) account, "the Oromo protect their environment for utilitarian reasons. They think that the value of the environment lies in human use. Trees are a source of capital, investment and insurance against hard times. Trees ... provide the supply of timber, wood and food. Peasant farmers and pastoralists are conscious that, when their environment deteriorates, their life and future generations of humans will be harmed."[44] In addition to this utilitarian moral attitude, African communal ethics also exemplifies a deontological moral attitude or obligation. According to Kelbessa, "For them [Oromo people], land is not only a resource for humans' utilitarian ends, but also it has its own inherent value given to it by *Waaqa* (God)."[45] Many traditional African worldviews do not see the earth or natural entities *only* as commodities or tools that people can use and dispose of at will as they wish. Kelbessa (2006) accounts for the deontological moral view among the Oromo people in the idea of *Saffuu*, which reflects the idea or obligation of justice.

This idea of *Saffuu*, which regulates human interactions with other animals, reflects a deep respect for and an effort to maintain a balanced existence with other natural things. According to him, "The Oromo do not simply consider justice, integrity and respect as human virtues applicable to human beings but they extend them to nonhuman species and mother Earth."[46] From a deontological point of view, African communal ethics considers nature or environment, humans, and harmonious communal relationships as part of the holistic community as ends in themselves which should be respected for its own sake. From a teleological point of view, nature is given due respect by Africans because it is in the interests of humans because of the utility to be derived it. This moral attitude involves considerations of the bad consequences of not having such obligations and an appreciation of the good consequences of such obligations.

Thus, it is in our interest to use natural resources to our benefit and to maintain a balance and harmony in nature because what affects nature affects us as part of the cosmic whole. Maintaining balance and harmony in reality and a healthy environment make the world a good and hospitable place to live; it helps our well-being both physically and spiritually. One's ability for reverence for nature and the efforts to maintain harmony, which make one a moral person, are also what morally distinguish humans from other living creatures: animals and plants. The African views of reality, human community, and religion indicate normative prescriptions regarding how humans should act toward or interact with each other, and how to act toward and interact with other entities, including gods, deities, ancestors, nature, and the environment.

Conclusion

We have obligations to the community and nature (water, air, trees, and the environment), not because they have dignity or rights, but because we must depend on them as the material conditions for our well-being, rights, freedom, or dignity in a community. Because God is the guardian and source of everything in nature, reverence for God means that people cannot destroy nature or interact with others simply to satisfy their needs and interests. This moral attitude calls for a sense of justice, duty, as well as enhancing utility, human and communal interests, well-being, and harmony in reality. The responsibility to maintain the harmonious relationship among humans and between humans and other things in nature arises from the hybrid communal ethical perspective of both deontology and utility.

NOTES

1. Wiredu (2008: 333).
2. Menkiti (1984: 179–180).
3. Ibid., 180.
4. Metz (2007: 369–387).
5. Mbiti (1989: 141).
6. Menkiti, 171.
7. Nyerere (1968: 165–166).
8. Ibid., 165–166.
9. Onwuanibe (1984: 187).
10. Nyerere, *Ujaama*, 163.
11. Masolo (2010: 240).
12. Gyekye (1997: 143).
13. Gbadegesin (1991: 65).
14. Gyekye (1997), Matolino (2011: 163–184).
15. Ibid., 81–88.
16. Matolino (2009: 160–170), Famakinwa (2010a: 65–77, 2010b: 152–166).
17. Ikuenobe (2006).
18. Masolo (2010: 231).
19. Verhoef and Michel (1997: 395).
20. Metz (2007: 338).
21. Metz (2012: 26–27).
22. Ibid., 20–21.
23. Metz (2007: 369–387, 2012: 19–37).
24. Frankena (1963: 35).
25. Menkiti (1984: 176).
26. Nkondo (2007: 91).
27. Senghor (1995: 49).
28. Tempels (1995: 67).
29. Menkiti (1984: 179).
30. Burnett and WA Kang'ethe (1994: 149).
31. Onyewuenyi (1995: 424).
32. Menkiti (1984: 174).
33. Mbiti (1989: 15).
34. Ibid., 16.
35. Senghor (1995: 49).
36. Ibid., 49.
37. Burnett and WA Kang'ethe (1994: 150).
38. Mbiti (1989: 29–37), Idowu (1973: 140–161).
39. Mbiti (1989: 74).
40. Burnett and WA Kang'ethe (1994: 156).
41. Mbiti (1989: 70).
42. Dixon (1976: 62–3).
43. Senghor (1995: 48).
44. Kelbessa (2006: 21).
45. Ibid., 22.
46. Ibid., 24.

Bibliography

Burnett, G.W., and Kamuyu WA Kang'ethe. 1994. Wilderness and the Bantu Mind. *Environmental Ethics* 16 (2): 145–160.
Dixon, Vernon. 1976. World Views and Research Methodology. In *African Philosophy: Assumptions and Paradigms for Research on Black Persons*, ed. Lewis M. King, Vernon J. Dixon, and Wade W. Nobles. Los Angeles: Fanon Center Publication, Charles R. Drew Postgraduate Medical School.
Famakinwa, J.O. 2010a. How Moderate Is Kwame Gyekye's Moderate Communitarianism? *Thought and Practice: A Journal of the Philosophical Association of Kenya* 2 (1): 65–77.
———. 2010b. The Moderate Communitarian Individual and the Primacy of Duties. *Theoria* 76 (2): 152–166.
Frankena, William. 1963. *Ethics*. Englewood Cliffs: Prentice Hall.
Gbadegesin, Segun. 1991. *African Philosophy*. New York: Peter Lang.
Gyekye, Kwame. 1997. *Tradition and Modernity: Philosophical Reflections on the African Experience*. New York: Oxford University Press.
Idowu, Bolaji. 1973. *African Traditional Religion*. New York: Orbis Books.
Ikuenobe, Polycarp. 2006. *Philosophical Perspectives on Communalism and Morality in African Traditions*. Lanham: Lexington Books.
Kelbessa, Workineh. 2006. The Rehabilitation of Indigenous Environmental Ethics in Africa. *Diogenes* 207: 17–34.
Masolo, Dismas. 2010. *Self and Community in a Changing World*. Indianapolis: Indiana University Press.
Matolino, Bernard. 2009. Radicals Versus Moderates: A Critique of Gyekye's Moderate Communitarianism. *South African Journal of Philosophy* 28 (2): 160–170.
———. 2011. Exorcising the Communitarian Ghost: D. A. Masolo's Contribution. *Quest: An African Journal of Philosophy* 25 (1–2): 163–184.
Mbiti, John. 1989. *African Religions and Philosophy*. Oxford: Heinemann.
Menkiti, Ifeanyi. 1984. Person and Community in African Traditional Thought. In *African Philosophy: An Introduction*, ed. Richard A. Wright. New York: University Press of America.
Metz, Thaddeus. 2007. Ubuntu as a Moral Theory: A Reply to Four Critics. *South African Journal of Philosophy* 26 (4): 369–387.
———. 2012. African Conception of Human Dignity: Vitality and Community as the Ground of Human Rights. *Human Rights Review* 13 (1): 19–37.
Nkondo, Gessler. 2007. Ubuntu as a Public Policy in South Africa: A Conceptual Framework. *International Journal of African Renaissance Studies* 2 (1): 88–100.
Nyerere, Julius. 1968. Ujaama—The Basis of African Socialism. In *Freedom and Unity*. New York: Oxford University Press.
Onwuanibe, Innocent. 1984. The Human Person and Immortality in IBO Metaphysics. In *African Philosophy: An Introduction*, ed. Richard A. Wright. New York: University Press of America.
Onyewuenyi, Innocent C. 1995. Traditional African Aesthetics: A Philosophical Perspective. In *African Philosophy: Selected Readings*, ed. Albert Mosley. Englewood Cliffs: Prentice Hall.
Senghor, Leopold Sedar. 1995. Negritude: A Humanism of the Twentieth Century. In *I Am Because We Are Readings in Black Philosophy*, ed. Fred Lee Hord and Jonathan Scott Lee. Amherst: University of Massachusetts Press.

Tempels, Placid. 1995. Bantu Philosophy. In *African Philosophy: Selected Readings*, ed. Albert Mosley. Englewood Cliffs: Prentice Hall.

Verhoef, Heidi, and Clausin Michel. 1997. Studying Morality Within the African Context: A Model of Moral Analysis and Construction. *A Journal of Moral Education* 26 (4): 389–407.

Wiredu, Kwasi. 2008. Social Philosophy in Postcolonial Africa: Some Preliminaries Concerning Communalism and Communitarianism. *South African Journal of Philosophy* 27 (4): 332–339.

CHAPTER 9

Between Community and My Mother: A Theory of Agonistic Communitarianism

Nimi Wariboko

INTRODUCTION

As I contemplated the subject of this chapter, I knew that I was going to say something that might annoy many specialists in African social ethics. I want to begin this chapter with a provocative statement; to some it may, indeed, be deemed shocking. Now wait for it: it is time to stop this bromide about all-authentic African social ethic being about communitarianism. Those who advocate this ethic define it as an ethic that accents the community as the ultimate concern, pronounce it as the criterion of truth, laud it as the source of value, and hold that its structures constitute the meaningful order for individual lives in it, secure the integrity of interpersonal interactions, and provide the foundation for communion. With this definition they deny that individualism ever had a place in precolonial Africa and as such they insist that any scholarship today about social ethics in contemporary Africa must have as its point of departure and destiny communitarianism for it to be considered authentically, indigenously African. But I strongly disagree with this view. There are individualistic, competitive aspects of African moral philosophy, both in the past and in the present, and many of the scholars who write on the subject have conveniently ignored this fact.

African social ethic is (was) not purely and thoroughly communitarian. There were societies in precolonial times which had spheres that were competitive and individualistic; at least they were branches that were grafted in among the root and trunk of the communitarian tree.[1] Yes, there were societies where individualism and communitarianism coexisted and the competitive spirit was regarded as valuable. For instance, the Kalabari-Ijo of the Niger Delta in

N. Wariboko (✉)
Boston University, Boston, MA, USA

© The Author(s) 2020
N. Wariboko, T. Falola (eds.), *The Palgrave Handbook of African Social Ethics*, https://doi.org/10.1007/978-3-030-36490-8_9

Nigeria was one of such communities. As far back as the 1960s Anthropologist Robin Horton had pointed this out in his scholarship. The precolonial Kalabari society was very competitive and fluid. Horton has this to say in comparing Kalabari culture with that of the Tallensi of Ghana: "Kalabari society, whether in its village or in its city-state variant, encourages aggressive individualism and personal achievement. If the emphasis in Taleland is on 'fitting in,' in Kalabari it is on 'getting up.'"[2]

Contrary to what some scholars are telling us, Africa was not an uncontaminated haven of communitarianism. Indeed, as Peter Ekeh has taught us, in many parts of Africa the state and society drifted apart, starting in the era of slave trade, which only intensified in the colonial period, and was exacerbated by post-independence politics. The forces of the state, which have refused to recognize his/her worth or citizenship, have steadily attacked the individual. As some precolonial African states engaged in the slave trade, they became hostile to their citizens and did not recognize the worth of the individual, and their politics was driven by the calculus of profit and power. The terms of exchange between the individual and the society or state in these states were not always on communitarian terms.[3] Some scholars miss this insight because they are diverted by the "shining object" of communitarianism at one level of sociality to the neglect of other levels. In the precolonial and colonial periods, the moral focus of individuals was on the *primordial public* such as kin and ethnic groups and at this site communalism prevailed. This is well and good until you realize that the so-called triumph of communalism at the lower levels may well be the fallouts of citizens' alienation from their states. Thus, the very triumph of communitarianism that some scholars celebrate at the local (village or ethnic) level may well be an indication of the failure or decay of "pure" communitarianism at higher reaches of social totalities. This much is implicit in Ekeh's seminal essays.

The problem that confronts scholars who emphasize communitarianism to the exclusion of other forms of social ethic in Africa is fourfold. First, implicit in this emphasis is the notion of "I am because we are" that they have stretched to the point of distortion. At the extreme uses of this notion of intersubjective formation of humanity, individuals in traditional African communities are not considered as having value or worth in and of themselves. Individuals are made by the community, belong to the community, and have value because they are embraced by the community. While this writer does not deny that a human being becomes a person only in a community of other human beings, he refuses to accept that individualism necessarily thwarts the process of human personhood. For instance, in precolonial Kalabari society individualism occurred as individual fulfillment in the context of community, as an expression of the substance of justice and actualization of human potentiality in ways consistent with human dignity and with the unity of community members. The individualism in this context is not the *expressive individualism* wherein the needs of the self trump those of the community. What I have in mind is what I will call *covenantal individualism* wherein the needs of the communal relationship and social justice take priority over the needs of the individual without necessarily stifling individual creativity and actualization of potentiality. The take-home point here is that communitarianism in Kalabari did not operate in the exclusion of (every sort of) individualism.

Second, too often scholars of African communitarianism ignore the historical records and refuse to acknowledge the coexistence of competitive individualism and communitarianism, especially in some communities that were engaged in long-distance trade. These kinds of communities recognized the uniqueness and difference of each individual and the value of his/her individual self-interest or good within the ethos of communitarianism. The Kalabari was one of such groups.

Third, the advocates of African communitarianism have mistaken the notion of individualism as operated in African societies like the Kalabari with the narcissistic individualism at work in contemporary Western society. In Kalabari, individualism was the play of dialogical subjective autonomies where each player agrees to rationally and consistently will that which coheres with the common good (broadly defined) of the community.[4] Individualism was the means or freedom by which Kalabari citizens were allowed to invent, discover, deliberate, and seek to attain their various goods within the nontotalitarian meaning-making framework of their community.[5] This form of individualism (always embedded in social practices that are largely defined by shared norms and sense of mutual belonging) was a good internal to the values of Kalabari and was grounded in the individuals' striving to be good human beings, virtuous agents, and persons in a right relationship with others.

Finally, scholars talk about communitarianism as if the spirit of capitalism and other ethos of modernity have not penetrated contemporary Africa. I understand the need and emotion behind the intense or exclusive focus on communitarianism, but it does not warrant playing fast and loose with historical records or the contemporary situation in the continent. The ethic of communitarianism is not the melanin gene of African social ethics; it is not the only source of everything distinct about African social values, it is not the unchanging, eternal pigmentation of the color of African ethics.

I Love My Mama

Do not get me wrong. I know that a lot of Africans harbor communitarian values. I do too. But if you asked me to choose between my mother and my community, I will choose my mother. There are many Africans who believe in their communities or in communitarianism, but like Albert Camus they will defend their mothers before they defend justice or community.

You may doubt that there were such Africans in the precolonial times or before the encounter of many traditional African societies with capitalism. Your doubt does not diminish the gap or hole in our understanding of the ethic of communitarianism in precolonial Africa. At what point in the evolution of the moral fabric of precolonial Africa did genuine commitment to communitarianism give way to private life, to pursuit of private interests, or to degradation of communitarianism? Or are you ready to argue that at the height of your preferred exemplary society of African communitarianism there was no personal or private life? Are you saying that precolonial Africa had no private, personal, individual life? Was every person one with the community? Indeed, if you said yes, then it means you are implying that there were no persons, only community. I wish you good luck with such a philosophical stance.

Such a strict view of communitarianism amounts to smuggling of Kantianism into precolonial African social ethic. It was Kant who in the name of the categorical imperative ruled out of ethics any emotion, personal sympathy, and personal feeling. He regarded any move away from the universal imperative of duty as pathological inclination. He would regard the choice of my mother over justice as a pathological inclination that interferes with reason as the supreme foundation of morality.

Was there an African community in which the warmhearted feeling for a mother was regarded as an obstacle to some universal moral law? It is only in the academy that I find an interpretation of communitarianism as a kind of Kantian universal moral law and the pursuit of private interest automatically interpreted as an obstacle to the realization of the moral ideas of communitarianism. It is high time we stopped this line of moral reasoning. Most of us who study African social ethics fall into this Kantian dream because we have not paid sufficient attention to the reality of the tension between particularity and universality (communitarianism) in African societies.

How many of us who champion communitarianism to the exclusion of other forms of ethic in Africa can say that there was (is) no unconditional call of the particular face as Emmanuel Levinas argues? Precolonial Africa is not the graveyard for the "sovereignty" of particularity. By African communitarianism, do we mean that Africans killed all selfish interests in the pursuit of ideals or the paramount goals of their community? If this is not what you mean, then how have you addressed the inevitable tension between defending community and defending mother? How did Africans negotiate the tension either when the two imperatives (mother and community) coincide or when they diverge?

The thorny issue that I see in African social ethics is that often well-meaning scholars prematurely dissolve the tension between particular interests and the communitarian call for group flourishing or universal justice in the community. Communitarian ethicists need to educate us on how Africans on a continuous basis resolve the tension between the particular and the universal, private, and public. Social ethics everywhere harbor a tension between the particular and the communitarian (or universal). The nonsense is to believe that Africans as moral animals are somewhat different. The Africans that I know are like other human beings that are daily dealing with tensions of the universal and the claims of their mothers or other loved ones.

My protest against the current overemphasis on communitarianism in the study of African social ethics is that its proponents have, ultimately and a priori, dissolved the tension by elevating the universal (communal) above the particular. Of course, I am also aware that to prioritize the particular is to also prematurely settle the tension. Africans, especially today, are caught in the gap between the particular and the universal, individualism (individuality) and communitarianism. So every form of social ethics that wants to be faithful to the everyday moral behavior of Africans must acknowledge the inevitable tension between particularity and universality in their moral fabric. The unconditional call to responsibility to the singular/beloved must be balanced against the valorization of community's call for its paramount goal.

As a son to my 87-year-old mother, I feel myself placed under infinite responsibility for her. When I was a helpless baby, she had the same infinite responsibility toward me. To say all this is not to argue that my mother and I were autonomous moral subjects that rationally entered into a mutually beneficial contract. Given her maternal instincts and the ethos of her Kalabari community, she loved me as a baby without concerning herself with profits from the mother-child relationship. She loved me without concerns that I would love her. Today, I care for her, without equivocation, not with a sense of an abstract universal duty I must perform, not because communitarianism runs in my blood, but because of my "pathological inclinations." More importantly, neither my mother nor I considered the movement toward the other as self-negation or self-inflation. We do not feel that heeding to the unconditional call of the other person in the relationship amounts to negating ourselves. We do not feel that either of us is going beyond what is human to extend ourselves to the other. And we are not practically committing ourselves to love everyone in our community equally.

Did the particular loving focus of my mother on me as a baby cut her off from the communitarian stream of compassion in her community? The particular focus of my mother on me, her inability to equally love all children in her community at the same time, was never a form of turning away from communitarianism. Within her limited abilities and well-grounded understanding of the ethos of her community, she worked for and hoped that every child would have a loving home so he or she could grow up to actualize his or her potentialities and be a blessing to the community. Thus, my mother's love for me was ultimately not at the expense of other children in her community.

In this way of understanding communitarianism neither my mother nor myself was commended to take a degree of responsibility that only God or the gods could bear. One hubris of the proponents of free-ranging communitarianism in Africa is that they portray Africans as capable of loving as God or capable of realizing the ideals of communion as God. The proponents' notion of communitarianism has no a priori limits and in its light Africans are mistaken as divine beings. The kind of responsibility, commitment, and communion demanded by the communitarian ethic amount to denying the humanity of Africans as it calls upon them to be God-like.

Without intending to do so, communitarian ethic almost sounds as death of God theology. The ethic of communitarianism as it is often propagated is unequivocally inclined toward divine responsibility. Never mind that in it there is a lot of focus on gods and deities. Human beings, that is Africans, are perfect gods who are perfectly committed to the ideals of communion, who are in some sort of perichoretic relationship with their neighbors. This does not make sense. Communitarian ethic must not burden finite, contingent Africans, past or present, with the divine task of infinite and absolute responsibility of building and sustaining perfect interpersonal or community-wide relationalities.

From Communitarianism to Agonistic Communitarianism

It does not also make sense to present (traditional) Africans as incapable of ignoring the common interest for their own interests or welfare. The assumption of the advocates of African communitarianism is that the traditional African is consistently selfless. Traditional Africans, adherents of African traditional religion (ATR), like Christians are not "always" able to be selfless, to consider the community and its welfare before their own. Such advocates of African communitarianism are as wrong as the Christian ethicists who hold that the arc of the ethos of Christianity inviolably bends toward communitarianism. Reinhold Niebuhr argues against ethicists who advocate ideas similar to African communitarianism in Christianity with these words:

> The ... error consists in defining a Christian in terms which assume that consistent selflessness is possible. No Christian, even the most perfect, is able "always" to consider the common interest before his own. At least he is not able to do it without looking at the common interest with eyes colored by his own ambitions. If complete selflessness were a simple possibility, political justice could be quickly transmuted into perfect love; and all the frictions, tensions, partial cooperations, and overt and covert conflicts could be eliminated. If complete selflessness without an admixture of egoism were possible, many now irrelevant sermons and church resolutions would become relevant. Unfortunately there is no such possibility for individual men; and perfect disinterestedness for groups and nations is even more impossible.[6]

The key question before us is this: Is self-interest absent from communitarianism (in its past or present form), or is self-interest antithetical to the welfare of community? What is the community? Is it my compound, village, town, ethnic group, or nation? If my town is confronted by another town and I support mine, are we (I and my town members) not guilty of collective self-interest? Is it too difficult to imagine that the values and norms that I was raised with as a Kalabari person, that habituated me into the community's moral life and taught me to prefer my town (Abonnema, *Nyemoni*) to other towns can also prepare me—at least—to prefer my family to my town? In choosing my family (typically an extended one) over my town, am I not subjecting myself to common interest? What is the common interest?[7] Is what is common telos to my family members not common interest? To answer the key question at the beginning of this paragraph, I would say that communitarianism does not dismiss self-interest, but must necessarily entertain it even as it resists it, that is resisting its illegitimate expressions.[8] Communitarianism does not consider it illegitimate when I execute what I owe to my town, family, or town.

I will illustrate this point with a Kalabari proverb that is often mistaken as advocating absolute communitarianism or teaching that community unarguably surpasses the individual: *Ama bebe buru ngeribo buru pakiri*, meaning "only the community tantamount a whole yam, the individual is always but a piece of it," "the whole community constitute the full yam and the individual is half yam." There is something philosophically intriguing about this proverb in terms of the argumentative thrust of this chapter. There are five ways to interpret the proverb with the central item of yam in mind. First, it suggests that there are two yams. For if the town owns a full or whole yam, the piece that individual is said to possess must have come from another yam. It brings up the idea that the confrontation is between a full yam and a piece from another yam, suggesting that whole (collective interest) is likely to overcome the part. Nonetheless, we do not see here the non-existence of self-interest in the Kalabari version of communitarianism, but an indication of an agonistic struggle between two types of interest.

Second, whether the individual has a piece of the yam that the town claims to own or hers is a piece from a different yam, she nonetheless has a piece of yam. She is allowed her part, and, if you like, her self-interest, and she is given a space to make her decision whether to participate with the whole or to die in one corner with her piece of yam as her banner of resistance.

Third, while the proverb makes a subtle allusion to individuality or respect for self-interest, the whole framing of its logic suggests that the parts that individuals possess might (can) not add up to a whole yam when even they are added together. Note that the town is always credited with a whole, fulsome yam and individuals only hold parts of a yam. There is the logic of zerosumness and non-zerosumness embedded in the proverb. Individualism without a bend toward cooperation leads to zerosumness, but when individuals act in concert and cooperate to achieve a common purpose they create the benefits of non-zerosumness. The yam that is owned by the town (the signifier of cooperation) always works as a whole that is increasing because of the logic on non-zerosumness. The pieces of yam owned by individuals would not add up to a whole, not to talk of a whole that is always increasing because the pieces themselves lack the feature of non-zerosumness. The point to note here is that communitarianism, at least in the Kalabari version, does not deny self-interest, but acknowledges it even as it points it to the benefit of cooperativeness, inclusion, and non-zerosumness.[9] The idea of communitarianism embedded in this proverb, as I am interpreting it, points to the relentless search for non-zerosumness in relations, the benefits of interdependence, internal coordination, and cooperation. Communitarianism (cooperative intimacy) is an inherent process or ethos of not leaving anything or any person outside the benefits of its relationality. Such an ethos, no doubt, accents increasing communality and upbuilding of communal structures, but it does deny self-interest or competitive intimacy.[10]

This last point brings us to the final interpretation of the Kalabari proverb. The communal yam in question is divisible: individuals are said to own pieces of it. Given the logic of the third interpretation, the community may not have begun with two yams as the first interpretation makes us believe. From the outset it might be one yam, and when the dissenting individual takes her share of the whole, the incomplete yam that is left for the community grows back into a whole yam, and even a bigger one; the incomplete yam remakes itself because of synthesis and cooperativeness of non-zerosumness. (This should not be construed to mean that individualism which in the Kalabari context is competitive intimacy does not or cannot create non-zerosumness in all circumstances.)

There is another interpretation of the proverb that occurs to the mind when its rumination is not directed by the central item of yam, but the idea of organizing principle of interests in the community. *Ama bebe buru ngeribo buru pakiri* suggests to me that the love for one's community or the community's paramount goal is the *ultimate concern* that unconditionally orders, prearranges, and preapproves all other concerns and loyalties; and all other such loves, goals, and loyalties are partial, fragmentary, and incomplete. On a second thought, the interpretation of the proverb in terms of ultimate concern does not require us to move away from the central idea of yam. Yam may be interpreted as a metaphor for ultimate concern. *Buru* can also be translated as food or sustenance in general. In this sense, the proverb alludes to the paramount goal of the community as always the indivisible, comprehensive moral vision of the community, and personal goals are always partial and incomplete. The interpretations suggest that the proverb is not about the denial of self-interest, but a call for its right, proper ordering.

In the light of the preceding fivefold interpretation, the key difference between communitarianism and individualism is not the absence of self-interest, but how self-interest is coordinated to create the kind of communal structures and communality that each ethological system prefers. So it is an overreach on the part of some supporters of communitarianism to pick a quarrel with me because I prefer my mother to the community. Once again if you asked me to choose between my mother and my community, I will choose my mother. My decision is not a turning away from communitarianism, and my Kalabari people never burden me with the divine task of absolute responsibility toward upbuilding communal structures or community-wide relationalities.

My endeavor here to point out the overreach of communitarian ethic should not be counted as a failure on my part to recognize that traditional African social ethic calls upon an individual to consider his or her call to responsibility as extending beyond his or her immediate family context. I am only arguing that without the proper delimitation of the kind of absolute responsibility to the community demanded by distorted communitarianism, communitarian ethics is strictly impossible. The kernel of my critique is to point us to an approach to African social ethics that accents the simultaneous necessity of the spheres of the universal (community) and the particular, the community and my mother. My mother in loving her child, the person whose face she saw, also paid attention to those who were not in a face-to-face relationship with her: acknowledged her primordial ethical obligation to them as members of her community. Love and justice (social justice), love for her own child and love for other children, and justice for her son and justice for her community are compatible in this conception of the African communal ethic. This interplay or "mutual" recognition of love and social justice points us to the deeper play between community and individual in the traditional African social ethics. Communitarianism in Africa is an interplay of self-becoming and community's telos or common social goals. It is not a strict opposition between collective obligation and free individual actions, not a war between the self and the social. My mother's "free" personal action, her love for her son, was located in a process of structuration. None of her behavior was totally or inviolably personal or individualistic; yet nothing was permanently an outcome of a *given* collective structure, or fixed beyond her interactions with others, or outside the daily grind of interactions between persons.

On a different note—perhaps at a less concrete philosophical level—communitarians loathe individualism because they think that in the divide or tension between justice (*meritism*) and mercy (charity) individualism is on the side of the former. They reason that when it comes to helping the needy or poor individualism insists on giving people only what they deserve and often the poor or those who need help are deemed undeserving. But they will argue that communitarianism is always on the side of mercy, that the poor should get undeserved gifts from other members of their communities. As I shall demonstrate later, the contextual individualism in precolonial Kalabari society required the unity of justice and mercy. Kalabari individualism requires or habituates the well-off to make sacrifices that reconcile justice with mercy, as per the notion of *Perebo-kalakeibari*, "let the well-endowed give me a little of his resources, wealth."[11] Kalabari individualism works with a moral spirit which the communal ethos supplies and even strengthens. The bread of individualism was leavened by the eros toward the community's constitutive goods.[12] Yet the community and the individual were not one; they were in constitutive relationships.

Neither individualism nor communitarianism was allowed to run "amok" in Kalabari society. Communitarianism had its place in the precolonial competitive Kalabari society that accents individualism because of its trading culture and the *canoe house system* of wealth accumulation.[13] In the colonial and postcolonial eras of the society's engagement with more robust capitalism and West-induced individualism, communitarianism still has its place. The Kalabari notion of individualism starts with the definition or an understanding of the paramount goal, telos of the community, the moral law members of the community have given themselves. Only after the citizens have arrived at this understanding that defines or elucidates their obligations, rights, and freedom that they work out the practices (or conceptions) of individualism that are compatible with it (telos). The self in this individualistic view is not abstracted from communal identities and inheritances and not cut off from the stories of the community that claim it, and the self is deemed deformed if cut off from the narrative that gives it quest for life coherence or moral particularity.[14] Individualism was a continuous process of individual self-realization and movement toward increasing, uniting relationality. The separation that arose in each individual dynamic actualization was overcome or limited by its realization within the whole society and by virtue of mutual participation in each other's lives.[15]

Let me illustrate this combined working of individualism and communitarianism with the original name of the Kalabari people. The name is *Perebo-kalakeibari*, meaning, "let the well-endowed, the wealthy share his or her rewards, gifts, winnings, or resources with me," "let him or her give me a little of his or her." As we can discern, the key idea in this name does not accent communitarianism as total disregard for individualism. It actually lauds the coexistence of both individualism and communitarianism. The ethos or principle of *Perebo-kalakeibari* encourages those who are talented or gifted to develop their skills and get rewarded with the understanding that their endowments, rewards, or winnings will be shared with the community, to give a little part of their rewards or winnings to improve the situation of other members of the community. This expectation or obligation of generosity does not mean that in the traditional Kalabari society an individual's assets, endowments, or rewards belong to the whole community as common assets.

In the light of my foregoing interpretation of the original name of the Kalabari people, we may interpret Kalabari "communitarianism" as individualism with a powerful vision of equality. It is individualism that improves the lot of the community or the least fortunate members in it. It is not a communitarianism of leveling equality that stifles the kind of individualism (competitive intimacy) that ultimately helps the least advantaged.

Perebo-kalakeibari and *Ama bebe buru ngeribo buru pakiri* are two words/sentences important to the argument I am making in this chapter. When the two sentences or a sentence and a proverb face each other, and when they flow into one another, we get the philosophy of *agonistic communitarianism*. In Kalabari the strong hand of communitarianism culturally formed a contextual variant of individualism: communitarianism birthing and defending individualism, you might say. Agonistic communitarianism is an attitude and a position that speaks to the intense and relentless struggle of individualism with the weight of communitarianism on one hand and the struggle of communitarianism against the fires of individualism that want to melt and erode the established structures of the community on the other. Agonistic communitarianism is the artful irruption into communitarianism of individualism. It is a term of ethics, signifying not the ethos of transcending (idealistic) communion, but the practices of transimmanent egalitarianism under the weight of competitive entrepreneurism and creative destruction engendered by centuries of long-distance trade, investment risk-taking, and struggles for political power.[16]

Agonistic communitarian (a combination of sense of self-interest and norm-grounded conception of the common good) as worked out or evolved in precolonial Kalabari was structured around what the culture considered as the three integral parts of the whole human person (*tombo*) and their ethical orientations. These are body (*oju*), heart (*biogbo*), and spirit, soul (*teme*). The soul is oriented toward righteousness, morality, and justice. The heart, the seat of desire, yearns for fellowship, togetherness (*gboloma*), and connection with others. When the heart is bad it turns away from this desire or yearning. The body is the fount of deeds, material gains, the ego-self striving for its success, the realization of its destiny. Communitarianism in the Kalabari context engendered or brewed a combination of the impulse of innovative deeds of the body, the energy of connectivity, others-centeredness of the heart, and the power of shared common values and sense of mutual belonging that the soul embodies. In the competitive world of long-distance trade that the Kalabari inhabited in the precolonial time and in much of the colonial period, these triune roots of the agonistic communitarianism conduced to quest for economic, entrepreneurial accomplishments, the upbuilding of communal structures and welfare, and the moral formation, virtuous habits of the individuals.

This Kalabari world of artful mix of cooperation and conflict (that is, competition) reminds us of the central dynamic of Akan communal relations that Kwame Gyekye illustrates with the art motif of the two-headed crocodile with one stomach. He argues that in Akan social thought communality and individuality coexist.[17] As he puts it:

> The symbol of the crossed crocodiles with two heads and a common stomach has great significance for Akan social thought. While it suggests the rational underpinnings of the concept of communalism, it does not do so to the detriment of individuality. The concept of communalism, as it is understood in Akan thought, therefore does not overlook individual rights, interests, desires, and responsibilities, nor does it imply the absorption of the individual will into the "communal will," or seek to eliminate individual responsibility and accountability. Akan social thought attempts to establish a delicate balance between concepts of communality and individuality. … Akan social philosophy tries to steer clear of the Scylla of exaggerated individualism and the Charybdis of exaggerated communalism (= communism). It seeks to avoid the excesses of the two exaggerated systems, while allowing for a meaningful, albeit uneasy, interaction between the individual and the society. (pp. 160–161, 162)

In all these, communitarianism gives cover, aid, and comfort to individualism to flourish even as it holds up a two-way mirror to individualism to show it the paucity of its own social imaginary or logic of zerosumness. Everyday practical men and women who are not slaves to some defunct intellectual influence see through the same mirror that individualism is not limping after communitarianism. It is illuminating or gaslighting communitarianism by displaying its future or manipulating its fragility. The time for pure communitarianism in Africa—if there was ever such a period—was, perhaps, in the pre-twentieth-century era. It is far too late now. Our individualism-inflected culture, agonistic communitarianism, "not only exists, it thrives. The question is whether it thrives as a virus or as a bountiful harvest of possibilities."[18]

AGONY AND ANTAGONISM OF DIVIDED CONSCIOUSNESS

With the foregoing arguments I hope I have succeeded in convincing my brothers and sisters who champion unbridled communitarianism as the true ethical foundation of Africans that scholars like me who disagree with them deserve to be heard, if not embraced for our "un-African" stance. Let me say that I am afraid that communitarian ethicists may still demand for my raw hide to be flayed in the hot tropical African sun. I am not sure if I have persuaded them to wake up from their dogmatic slumber. But I can still count on their love. The true ethical step for them under the canopy of communitarian ethic is to throw away my "stupid talk" and embrace me as a brother. By embracing me, have they not suspended the ethos of communitarian universality? That is, have they not chosen against their communal ideals under the hammer of my particularity? Have they not chosen to honor my face as the singular other? In so choosing, have they not acknowledged that there are Africans like me who accent particularity under certain circumstances and we need to be protected? Compelled to choose between communitarianism and particularity, between justice and love, and between their all-embracing position and me, have they not chosen me, affirmed my right to exist, and my right to go contrary to their communal ideals? Have they not demonstrated some equivocation? Do they think their African ancestors did not show similar equivocation? What kind of equivocation was this? This was an equivocation between universality and particularity that did not give way to the ultimate prioritizing of the private sphere or individualism. Nonetheless, there was particularism or individualism. This is the slight adjustment of thought I am pleading for in this chapter.

We must not view African social ethics as monolithic. We should endeavor to capture the tensions in African stories and not try to smoothen its edges for the touristic and voyeuristic academic audience. Africa is not a single narrative we can package and market to conference attendees in Western cities who are usually impatient with the complex and multilayered reality of Africans. Africa is rich with multiple experimentations of social existence and organization. Africa is not a simple place and its ethics is not simplistically one-sided.

I am not simple either. I harbor tensions within me as I try to find the proper balance between the "community" and the "individual" in my scholarship and in my personal orientation to life such that the community is granted its right authority in all my endeavors. Many Africans today are stirred and wracked by layers of double consciousness: (a) mother as the matrix of individual inclinations warring against community as the ammunition against such inclinations, which I have described in the preceding paragraphs, and (b) one of crucial impacts of colonialism and Christianity on African personhood is a twoness; there is a received (precolonial) *being-with* and a modernist

(European-capitalist) consciousness: "two unreconciled strivings; two warring ideals in one dark body, whose dogged strength alone keeps it from being torn asunder."[19] The dialectic of African personhood oscillates between subjectivity fashioned by an African sense of communion and individualistic orientation, being African yet feeling Western, and yearning for native Africanness but grasping for alien European cosmopolitanism. Africans labor under the weight of a crisis of personhood, self-identity, and a split self that is precipitated by Christianity, colonialism, and Westernization/globalization.[20]

The cumulative effect of the weight of racism, domination, and the oppression Africans suffered under colonialism and the various attempts by the colonial state and colonial Christian missions to transform African personhood to fit the Western-styled autonomous, self-focused individual have weakened the bond between individuals and their societies. In the 1970s Ekeh wrote an insightful essay on the existence of two publics: communal (primordial) and civic. In his thinking the communal or ethnic public is considered moral and beloved. The other is amoral, hostile, and largely hated. In the primordial one, because it recognizes the worth of his personhood and citizenship, the individual feels a sense of citizenship and membership in the community. The individual is morally linked to the society and she sees her duties as moral obligations to benefit and sustain a community of which she is a member. On the other hand, the civic public, primarily imposed by colonialism and its apparatus of coercion, which refused to recognize the worth or citizenship of the individual, has no moral link with the individual. The individual steadily being attacked by the colonial and postcolonial state is alienated from the state and her attention is focused more on the primordial public, such as kin and ethnic groups, which are independent of the state. Unlike the attitude of cooperation in the primordial realm, the attitude toward the civic realm is purely materialistic and exploitative, and the individual experiences no moral urge to give back to the civic realm in return for its benefits. In fact, the individual is obliged to draw resources from the civic public for the benefit of the primordial community.[21]

For those Africans today who are more comfortable, for whatever reason, with the individualistic rather than the communal ethos of life, there is also a struggle within themselves not to slide into what I have elsewhere called the *lotus-self*.[22] This is the vexing disposition of Africa's political leaders and elites "enjoying" themselves amid the physical and metaphorical filth and decadence of African communities. Like the lotus flower, leaders and elites now strive, luxuriate, and "flourish" amid dirt, decay, and death. There is a frightening *withdrawal of self* from the public space and public concerns, which is marked, defined, and even energized by a "banality of evil." There is a certain thoughtlessness about committing evil, ubiquity of evil that is now the quiddity of living, and senselessness of it all that is destructive of social existence, thwarting life itself. It is important to realize that this withdrawal of the self from the public is not of the case that the self has absolutely no relation to the public, specifically the state and its treasures. On the contrary, what is excluded in the lotus-self maintains itself in relation to state resources in the form of stealing state resources. The lotus-self is a kind of exclusion that is inclusive. The lotus-self in withdrawing from the public takes the state resources outside of public control and rule. The lotus flower (the lotus-self) does not subtract itself from its environment (state), rather, the environment, suspending its rule of touching everything in it (the state ruling over all citizens equally), gives rise to the withdrawal (don't-touch-me stance) and keeping itself in relation to the flower (self), first constitutes itself as a withdrawal (the state abdicating its reach). This is the nature of the paradoxical zone of indistinction between the lotus-self of deadly politicians and the privatized postcolonial state, which "maintains itself in its own privation," to govern in no longer governing.[23] The withdrawal of the lotus-self is thus not the withdrawal of political leaders from the chaos of primitive accumulation that precedes rational, market-based accumulation, but rather the condition that results from the suspension of rationality and the center in which the state finds its raison d'etre, the coming to light of a "free and juridically empty space" unbounded by law that haunts the colonial-postcolonial state and functions as if it considers the state already dissolved.[24] This is at once anarchy of self-interest and banality of evil as the center of the political scene of twenty-first-century Africa. This is a grave moral problem. It is no longer the mere case of a decision-maker split between mother and community, but the shaking of the moral foundations of African communities.

Conclusion

The function of moral philosophy in a situation like this is that of analyzing the import of communitarianism, individualism, or agonistic communitarianism for liberation and human flourishing of Africans. All three are in play in contemporary African societies and it does no one any substantial good to insist that the authentic African social ethic is communitarianism.

My efforts to set the debate between these three forms in terms of mother versus community underline my understanding that as an ethicist I am called to make a tragic choice between them. It is tragic in the sense that I am called to choose between three good options and by opting for one I have turned away from the singular goods of the others. I am losing something. But in choosing agonistic communitarianism I am trying to minimize the "loss." I take as the core of African communitarianism others-centeredness, the summon to make what is outside the self, the care for others rather than the self, as the ultimate appeal of the human person. Agonistic communitarianism carries forward this summon, this worthy ideal as *mattered* by twenty-first-century sensibility and individual creativity, as *enfleshed* by individual agency. Agonistic communitarianism, as I am using the term here, is individualism (not selfishness) that is framed within communitarianism that undergirds and propels it. Individualism (an inadequate word chosen for a lack of a better term) in the flashlight of agonistic communitarianism is not set as an opposite or rejection of communitarianism. It is an exfoliation of the abiding care and concern for individuality in African communitarianism, the individual-in-communion given an ample space to better actualize his or her potentiality for the flourishing of the self and what transcends it. Individualism here is covenantal individualism rather than expressive individualism. Individualism here is only a capstone of the community's relationships and not their keystone: it is not what forms and disciplines the societal relationships but what is fixed on top of them as symbol of unemasculated individual creativity.

Thus, the real task for social ethicists who aspire to bring African communal ethics to face the challenges of the twenty-first-century's socioeconomic development and civilizational shifts is to figure out how to create sturdy social structures, institutions, and policies that will not only promote fellowship but also entrepreneurial innovativeness and self-transcending individualism—in other words, promote agonistic communitarianism.

NOTES

1. As this chapter was about to go to press I came across the work of Moses E. Ochonu where he basically agrees with the position I have taken in this chapter. He argues that too much epistemic visibility has been given to the "incorrect notion of precolonial Africa as a site of subsistent communalism, an undifferentiated societal continuum supposedly unspoiled by the twin capitalist evils of the profit motive and private wealth accumulation. … Evidence … indicates that a communitarian ethos underpinned and mediated the entrepreneurial pursuits of precolonial Africans. … Even the most communally organized precolonial societies and economies had enterprising members who improved their lives through entrepreneurial initiatives, indicating that neither communalism not subsistence, two hyperbolized and overgeneralized features of precolonial Africa, was incompatible with private property or the pursuit of individual wealth for self-improvement." See Moses E. Ochonu, "Introduction: Toward African Entrepreneurship and Business History" in Moses E. Ochonu (ed.) *Entrepreneurship in Africa: A History Approach* (Bloomington, IN: Indiana University Press, 2018), pp. 1–27; quotation from p. 16.
2. Robin Horton, "Social Psychologies: African and Western" in M. Fortes and Robin Horton (eds.), *Oedipus and Job in West African Religion* (Cambridge: Cambridge University Press, 1983), 54, pp. 41–82.
3. Peter Ekeh, "The Public Realm and Public Finance in Africa" in Ulf Himmelstrand, Kabiru Kinyanjui, and Edward Mburugu (eds.), *African Perspectives On Development* (London: James Currey Ltd., 1994), pp. 234–248; Peter Ekeh, "Social Anthropology and the Two Contrasting Uses of Tribalism in Africa," *Comparative Studies in Society and History* 32.4 (1990), pp. 660–700; Peter Ekeh, "Colonialism and the Two Publics in Africa: A Theoretical Statement," *Comparative Studies in Society and History* 17.1 (1975), pp. 91–112.
4. This definition was inspired by Michael Onyebuchi Eze, "What is African Communitarianism? Against Consensus as a regulative ideal," *South African Journal of Philosophy*, Vol. 27, no. 4 (July 2008): 386–399.
5. Marc Stier, "Reconciling Liberalism and Communitarianism." A paper presented at the Annual Meeting of the American Political Science Association, Marriot Waldman Park, August 31–September 3, 2000, p. 12 [1–24]. Note that

my notion of agonistic communitarianism is quite different from his. Stier's notion is based on the usefulness of conflicts between different conceptions of goods and schemes of virtues between liberalism and communitarianism that lead to refinements of viewpoints. Mine, as I will later demonstrate, is about the existence of the ethos of individualism within the framework of communitarianism in Kalabari ethical consciousness.

6. Reinhold Niebuhr, *Love and Justice* (quoted in 259 of Forell and Childs, *Christian Social Teachings*, second edition).
7. Niebuhr, *Love and Justice* (quoted in 259 of Forell and Childs).
8. Niebuhr, *Love and Justice* (quoted in 259 of Forell and Childs).
9. Robert Wright, *Nonzero: The Logic of Human Destiny* (New York: Vintage Books, 2001).
10. The terms of cooperative intimacy and competitive intimacy came from my Gambian friend, Mariama Khan. I have deployed them here in ways that are somewhat different from her usage.
11. This is the original name of the Kalabari people.
12. J. Budziszewki, *The Revenge of Conscience: Politics and the Fall of Man* (Dallas, TX: Spence Publishing Company, 1999), 121–124. This paragraph was inspired by these pages.
13. See Nimi Wariboko, *The Mind of African Strategists: A Study of Kalabari Management Practice* (Madison, NJ: Fairleigh Dickenson University Press, 1997).
14. Michael J. Sandel, *Justice: What's the right thing to do?* (New York: Farrar, Straus and Giroux, 2009) gave me the language to express my ideas here.
15. Paul Tillich, *Theology of Peace*, edited by Ronald Stone (Louisville: Westminster John Knox Press, 1990), 94; I have borrowed language from this book to articulate my understanding of individualism in precolonial Kalabari.
16. Advocates of African communitarianism have the dream of transcendence. This is the dream of transcendence of acting and thinking from non-individual location, of an individual engagement with fellow community members without the original sin of self-interest, self-preference, and partiality that communitarians hold fast or tot up.
17. Kwame Gyekye, *An Essay on African Philosophical Thought: The Akan Conceptual Scheme* (Cambridge: Cambridge University Press, 1987), 145–146, 158–61.
18. Toni Morrison, *The Source of Self-Regard: Selected Essays, Speeches, and Meditations* (New York: Alfred A. Knopf, 2019), 335. I have implanted her words from a different context to make my point here.
19. W. E. B. Du Bois, *The Souls of Black Folks* (New York: Penguin, 1989), 5.
20. See Nimi Wariboko, "Colonialism, Christianity, and Personhood" in Charles Ambler, William A. Worger, and Nwando Achebe (eds.), *Blackwell Companion to African History* (Hoboken, NJ: John Wiley and Sons, 2019): 59–76.
21. Ekeh, "Social Anthropology and the Two Contrasting Uses" and "Colonialism and the Two Publics."
22. Nimi Wariboko, *Ethics and Society in Nigeria: Identity, History, Political Theory* (Rochester: University of Rochester Press, 2019): pp. 19–34.
23. Giorgio Agamben, *Homo Sacer: Sovereign Power and Bare Life*, trans. Daniel Heller-Roazen (Stanford: University of Stanford Press, 1998), 28.
24. Carl Schmitt, *The Nomos of the Earth in International Law of the Jus Publicum Europaeum* (New York: Telos Press, 2003), 95.

Bibliography

Agamben, Giorgio. 1998. *Homo Sacer: Sovereign Power and Bare Life*. Trans. Daniel Heller-Roazen. Stanford: University of Stanford Press.

Budziszewski, J. 1999. *The Revenge of Conscience: Politics and the Fall of Man*. Dallas: Spence Publishing Company.

Du Bois, W.E.B. 1989. *The Souls of Black Folk*. New York: Penguin.

Ekeh, Peter. 1975. Colonialism and the Two Publics in Africa: A Theoretical Statement. *Comparative Studies in Society and History* 17 (1): 91–112.

———. 1990. Social Anthropology and the Two Contrasting Uses of Tribalism in Africa. *Comparative Studies in Society and History* 32 (4): 660–700.

———. 1994. The Public Realm and Public Finance in Africa. In *African Perspectives On Development*, ed. Ulf Himmelstrand, Kabiru Kinyanjui, and Edward Mburugu, 234–248. London: James Currey Ltd.

Eze, Michael Onyebuchi. 2008. What Is African Communitarianism? Against Consensus as a Regulative Ideal. *South African Journal of Philosophy* 27 (4): 386–399.

Gyekye, Kwame. 1987. *An Essay on African Philosophical Thought: The Akan Conceptual Scheme*. Cambridge: Cambridge University Press.

Horton, Robin. 1983. Social Psychologies: African and Western. In *Oedipus and Job in West Africa*, ed. M. Fortes and Robin Horton, 41–82. Cambridge: Cambridge University Press.

Morrison, Toni. 2019. *The Source of Self-Regard: Selected Essays, Speeches, and Meditations*. New York: Alfred A. Knopf.

Niebuhr, Reinhold. *Love and Justice* (Quoted in 259 of Forell and Childs, *Christian Social Teachings*, Second Edition).

Ochonu, Moses E. 2018. Introduction: Toward African Entrepreneurship and Business History. In *Entrepreneurship in Africa: A History Approach*, ed. Moses E. Ochonu, 1–27. Bloomington: Indiana University Press.

Sandel, Michael J. 2009. *Justice: What Is the Right Thing to Do?* New York: Farrar, Straus and Giroux.

Schmitt, Carl. 2003. *The Nomos of the Earth in International Law of the Jus Publicum Europaeum*. New York: Telos Press.

Stier, Marc. 2000. Reconciling Liberalism and Communitarianism. A Paper Presented at the Annual Meeting of the American Political Science Association, Marriot Waldman Park, August 31–September 3.

Tillich, Paul. 1990. *Theology of Peace*, ed. Ronald Stone. Louisville: Westminster John Knox Press.

Wariboko, Nimi. 1997. *The Mind of African Strategist: A Study of Kalabari Management Practice*. Madison: Fairleigh Dickenson University Press.

———. 2019a. Colonialism, Christianity, and Personhood. In *Blackwell Companion to African History*, ed. Charles Ambler, William A. Worger, and Nwando Achebe. Hoboken: John Wiley and Sons.

———. 2019b. *Ethics and Society in Nigeria: Identity, History, and Political Theory*. Rochester: University of Rochester Press.

Wright, Robert. 2001. *Nonzero: The Logic of Human Destiny*. New York: Vintage Books.

PART II

Polity (Violence, Power, Figures)

CHAPTER 10

Pluralism and African Conflict: Towards a Yoruba Theory of African Political Ethics of Neighbourliness

Olufemi Ronald Badru

Introduction and Problem Statement

One of the issues of much concern in the postcolonial African state is the problem of pluralism, exemplified by the common anti-neighbourliness of conflictual interaction between the self (contextually plurally conceived) and the other (contextually plurally conceived), a phenomenon that is contrary to the idea of monistic pluralism (*MP*) in Africa. At both intra-state and inter-state citizenship levels of human relations in Africa, conflictual interaction is easily seen among Africans that are territorially contiguous in terms of various instances of morally irrational interethnic violence and religious intolerance/violence. Some of the practical examples of conflictual interaction between the self and the other on the continent are the Somali Civil War (2009–present), the Rwandan genocide against the Tutsi by the Hutus (1994), the Sierra Leone Civil War (1991–2002), the Eritrean-Ethiopian War (1998–2000), the Nigerian Civil War (1967–1970), the Burundian genocides (against the Hutus by the Tutsi in 1972, and against the Tutsi by the Hutus in 1993), the unjustifiably rampant killings of other African citizens/nationals in South Africa and so on. Given that some of the noted instances of the conflictual interaction are still continual, and that rationality readily informs us that there is nothing in the present African experience, which may preclude a future recurrence of the past instances of conflictual interaction, and, perhaps, in other African states,

O. R. Badru (✉)
Lead City University, Ibadan, Nigeria

© The Author(s) 2020
N. Wariboko, T. Falola (eds.), *The Palgrave Handbook of African Social Ethics*, https://doi.org/10.1007/978-3-030-36490-8_10

especially in the presence of thick ethnic and religious pluralism in Africa, then every effort to confront the anti-neighbourliness is worthwhile.

Given the above, the work advances and defends the thesis that pluralism in Africa, which is usually deployed by some internal and external forces to promote the anti-neighbourliness of conflictual interaction, at the micro level of intra-state citizenship relations, and at the macro level of inter-state citizenship relations, could actually be positively managed through a Yoruba theory of African political ethics of neighbourliness (*APEN*), drawing on the idea of monistic pluralism (itself derived from African metaphysics). Thus, this chapter garners some relevant moral virtues and values from this idea, as instantiated in the Yoruba culture of South West Nigeria, to first theorize on the *APEN* framework, and later coherently develop some concrete ways of socio-politically operationalizing the framework at the micro and the macro levels of human relations in Africa. It must be preliminarily noted that the three basic factors that inform and motivate the present attempt are (i) peace-related scholarship in Africa largely domiciles in social sciences, and social sciences in Africa are methodologically Western-inclined; (ii) African peace scholars, who are mainly social scientific in orientation, are generally averse to philosophically normative peace-related research, especially from the angle of African philosophy; and (iii) many philosophically normative African scholars rarely research, in any significant sense, in the area of peace thinking and practice. Given this background, the present chapter includes a two-sided objective of showing that African philosophy is also capable of advancing a coherent normative framework for the conduct of peace thinking and practice in Africa (internalist objective), and that it could also autochthonously contribute to the global pool of knowledge in the area of philosophy of peace and non-violence (externalist objective).

This chapter is divided into eight sections. Section "Introduction and Problem Statement" is the introductory aspect; section "The Conceptual Framework" focuses on some basic conceptual explications; section "Africa and the Problem of Conflict as Anti-Neighbourliness" makes a survey of the anti-neighbourliness of conflictual interaction in Africa; section "The Problem of Conflictual Interaction in Africa: Towards a Yoruba Theory of African Political Ethics of Neighbourliness" develops a Yoruba theory of African political ethics of neighbourliness (*APEN*), underpinned by the idea of monistic pluralism (*MP*), to address the conflictual interaction in Africa; section "Likely Objections and Responses" examines and responds to some likely objections to the theoretical framework; section "Operationalizing a Yoruba Theory of Political Ethics of Neighbourliness for Peaceful Conduct in the Self-Other Interaction in Africa" discusses a methodology of sociopolitical realization of the political ethics of neighbourliness in Africa; section "Socio-Political Environment for the Development of *APEN* for Peaceful Conduct in the Self-Other Interaction in Africa" examines the public goods, so to say, that should background the *APEN* framework; and section "Summary and Conclusion" summarizes and concludes the discussion.

The Conceptual Framework

Before engaging in the main discussion, it is important to be preliminarily clear about the basic concepts involved in the discussion, which are African cosmology and ontology, African conflict, African political ethics of neighbourliness, and monistic pluralism.

African Conflict: Contextually, this refers to any extended, largely violent, antagonistic interaction between the self and the other, on the African continent, such as interethnic violence, inter-religious violence, civil wars, or inter-state violent clashes.

African Cosmology and African Ontology: African cosmology (AC) and African ontology (AO) are the two subsets of African metaphysics. It seems to be a consensus among many African philosophers and related others that AC is committed to the idea of duality of being: that the physical and the spiritual worlds exist and actively interact, while AO is committed to personhood as self-other relationality.[1] If AC and AO are harmonized, then we have two conclusions: (i) that the theoretical template of being-duality of AC grounds the superstructure of self-other account of personhood by AO, and (ii) that the idea of monistic pluralism, which emphasizes that the diverse entities in nature are ultimately united (the ontological relationality of all entities in Africa), aptly captures the essentials of both AC and AO.

Ethics: According to Coady and Corry, ethics is the study of right action and virtuous living.[2] Also, according to Boston et al., ethics is about what we ought to do or ought not to do … it is concerned with what is good and bad, right and wrong, just and unjust, or noble and ignoble, and how we can tell the difference.[3] For Wasudha Bhatt, the field of ethics, also called moral philosophy, involves systematizing, defending, and recommending concepts of right and wrong behaviour.[4] Ethics could also be defined as a critical and systematic exercise in philosophy, which involves examining and interrogating human conduct, with a view towards rationally making a valuation of right or wrong, on the conduct so concerned.

From the conceptions of ethics given, certain features are basic. First, ethics could be a formal course of study, and it could as well be a system of foundational virtues, values, and norms, prescribing the right conduct as distinguished from the wrong conduct. In the latter sense, ethics is both normative and prescriptive; it always attempts to rationally generate and prescribe norms of proper conduct to the human person, be it individually or institutionally understood, in society. Second, ethics is contextually a critical exercise: (i) the foundational virtues, values, and norms are usually epiphenomena of deep reflections, and (ii) the foundational virtues, values, and norms are always subject to continual constructive analysis and interrogation, which might sometimes lead to some fresh reconstruction and, perhaps, reconstruction of them. It is the latter, especially, that distinguishes philosophical ethics from descriptive/sociological ethics, which basically refers to traditions or customs of a people that are not usually subject to constant critical analysis and interrogation, by those that subscribe to them.

Neighbourliness: This may be understood as a positive sense of community between the self (in the singular or plural sense) and the other (in the singular or plural sense), who share non-extensive or extensive proximity[5]; it is a cultivated sense of togetherness between the self and the other. Thus seen, neighbourliness is a virtue and a value. It is a virtue, given that it is a kind of excellence of conduct that ought to be consciously (knowingly) and conscientiously (unreservedly) nurtured by a rational agent, who seeks to live happily with the other, within a shared political collectivity. It is a value in both instrumental and intrinsic senses. Instrumentally, the telos of neighbourliness is some extended/future good (however this is defined), from the other, to whom the self has presentatively shown some good. Intrinsically, being neighbourly is being morally attentive to the principle of beneficence, even if there would be no reciprocal good from the focused other.

Drawing on the philosophical understandings of ethics and neighbourliness, therefore, African political ethics of neighbourliness (*APEN*) refers to a theoretical framework, composed of some moral virtues and values, drawn from the idea of monistic pluralism (*MP*), meant to prescribe what the right account of personhood morally entails in Africa, either at the intra-state citizenship level or at the inter-state citizenship level. The contextual essence of *APEN* is that, though we are ethnically and religiously plural (and thus divided) in Africa, we are still ontologically relational, and that virtues and values from this ontological relationality ought to define and characterize both intra-state and inter-state citizenship interactions in Africa. And, given that the framework ought to further suppress the cleavage of pluralism in the sociopolitical relations among the people within a political collectivity, in the first instance, and also across the boundaries of political collectivities in Africa, then it is reasonable to take the framework as political, apart from being ethical.

Critically examined, one could see that if the self and the other in interaction in Africa are committed to this framework, then there is a strong likelihood of the development and promotion of sustainable peaceful relations between them. If we agree to this latter claim, then it logically follows that the proposed *APEN* is consistent with an attempt to evolve an African ethical theory of peace thinking and practice. It is this sense of *APEN* that is adopted in this work.

Monistic Pluralism: The concept of monistic pluralism (MP), as coined by the present author in a recent work, captures the basics of the metaphysics of being in Africa; MP emphasizes two claims: (i) that there are different existential forces, human and non-human (plural aspect), and (ii) that the different existential forces are necessarily connected, being forces-in-interaction or forces-in-relation, forming a coherent whole (monistic aspect).[6] There are some virtues (understanding 'virtue' as 'excellence of conduct') and values (understanding 'value' as 'that which is desirable') of neighbourly interaction that are derivable from MP; these would be discussed within the APEN framework, after the next section.

AFRICA AND THE PROBLEM OF CONFLICT AS ANTI-NEIGHBOURLINESS

The high incidence of the phenomenon of conflict (usually ethnically and religiously motivated) between the self and the other in Africa, especially at the intra-state level, is absolutely undeniable. Really, the facts about the phenomenon are alarmingly disturbing in many plural African states.

According to Venkatasawmy, 'More than half of all African countries have experienced at least a year of armed conflict during the past three decades'.[7] In fact, in the estimation of Picciotto, conflict-related casualties in Africa exceed those of all other regions put together. Moreover, the contention goes further that about one-fifth of the African population lives in areas severely disrupted by conflict. Really, sub-Saharan Africa alone has an unenviable record, where almost half of all developing countries affected by conflict are located: it has 32 (out of 47) countries affected by 126 wars since 1980.[8] Analytically, the conflictual interaction in Africa between the self and the other could be: (i) at the micro level of intra-state citizenship relations or (ii) at the macro level of inter-state citizenship relations.

Micro Level of Intra-State Citizenship Relations At this level, there are many examples of conflictual relations in Africa to draw on, and some notable ones are: the Somali Civil War (2009–present); the Rwandan genocide against the Tutsi by the Hutus (1994); the Sierra Leone Civil War (1991–2002); the Eritrean-Ethiopian War (1998–2000); the Nigerian Civil War (1967–1970); and the Burundian genocides (against the Hutus by the Tutsi in 1972, and against the Tutsi by the Hutus in 1993).[9] Presently, Nigeria is internally battling with the Boko Haram terrorism, which has decimated thousands of lives, destroyed millions of worth of items of property, and negated economic progress in North East Nigeria.[10]

Macro Level of Inter-State Citizenship Relations At this level, there are also many examples of conflictual relations in Africa to point out. According to Aremu, some notable ones are:

1. Nigeria-Cameroon dispute over the Bakassi peninsula since the 1970s;
2. Algeria-Morocco conflict over the Atlas Mountains area in October 1963;
3. Eritrea-Ethiopian crisis between 1962 and 1979;
4. Somalia-Ethiopia' dispute of 1964–1978 over the Ugandan desert region;
5. Chad-Libya crisis of 1980–1982;
6. Kenya-Somalia border war of 1963–1967 in which Somalia aimed at recovering its lost territories including the Northern Frontier District of Kenya; and
7. Tanzania-Uganda crisis in 1978–1979.[11]

There are many factors responsible for the conflictual interaction in Africa. According to Aremu, some of them are arbitrary borders created by the colonial powers, the heterogeneous ethnic composition of African states, inept political leadership, corruption, the negative effect of external debt burden, and poverty.[12] It is noteworthy that many of the causes are directly connected to the subject of pluralism in one way or another. And, those that are not so connected are connected to the causes directly connected to pluralism. The point is revealing enough. If the self could be the only existential entity, then the subject of pluralism would not arise. However, since the other would always also be an existential entity, then the subject of pluralism could never be wished away. The problem of corruption for instance is moral diminution, resulting in the manipulation of common resources for singular ends, by either the self or the other. Similarly, poverty may result from the irresponsibility and unresponsiveness of the privileged one, extending no good to the needy other, or the manipulation of common resources for personal ends, paying no attention to the needs of the other. Similarly, the problem of arbitrary colonial boundary delimitation in Africa is ultimately about who is to exclusively possess what space, as constituted by the boundaries in contention, between the self and the other.

The problem of inept political leadership in Africa also falls within the present fold of the pluralism subject. As Aremu rightly notes, one fundamental problem of political leadership in Africa is the inability to internally forge, through ethnically/religiously blind domestic policies and actions, a cohesive people (obviously between the self and the other) out of the diversity within the society.[13] As experience has amply shown in Africa, the problem of corruption mentioned earlier is also causally related to the problem of inept political leadership in Africa; a corrupt political leader could hardly be functionally effective. Even the problem of burden of external debt is also somewhat connected to the problem of inept political leadership, given that political leadership in Africa is generally known to be usually bereft of necessary economic epistemology to sustainably engage in domestic policies that: (i) diversify the economy as much as feasible, (ii) patronize more of domestic goods than foreign ones, and (iii) develop and encourage domestic industrialists to produce competitive goods that could earn more foreign exchange.

As might be expected, the conflictual interaction in Africa has impacted negatively on the continent. Some of the negative results are: loss of thousands of lives, massive destruction of infrastructural facilities, economic backwardness, massive displacement of people, and so on. All these, inferentially, alienate the self from the other. To morally confront both the causes (at least, most of them) and the negative consequences of the conflictual interaction in Africa, an attempt would be made in the next section to theorize on an African political ethics of neighbourliness, which contextually could also be regarded as an African ethical theory of peace-building in a conflictual environment.

The Problem of Conflictual Interaction in Africa: Towards a Yoruba Theory of African Political Ethics of Neighbourliness

Having examined some facts about the conflictual interaction between the self and the other in Africa, an attempt would now be made to theorize on the *APEN* framework, which draws on some specific moral virtues and values derived from *MP*. It must be reiterated that, in line with the motivating basic factors given earlier, the framework is a systematic attempt to develop and advance an autochthonous solution to an autochthonous problem in Africa.

But, what relevant moral virtues and values make up the *APEN* framework, which is derived from *MP*? To address the question, the discussion would proceed in four interrelated ways; the first is to focus on a given cultural context in Africa, where the moral virtues and values are to be drawn[14]; the second is to identify and discuss the relevant moral virtues and values; the third is to connect the identified moral virtues and values with *MP*; and the fourth is to give some rational background for the practical flourishing of the *APEN* framework in the modern African state.

Contextually, the African culture of focus is that of the Yoruba. Resident mainly in South West Nigeria, West Africa, the Yoruba people are one of the multi-ethnic groups in Nigeria. Philosophically, the culture of the Yoruba could be trifurcated into: Yoruba metaphysics, Yoruba epistemology, and Yoruba ethics. Each would be briefly examined.

Yoruba metaphysics is divisible into *Yoruba cosmology* and *Yoruba ontology*. In *Yoruba cosmology*, there is generally a strong belief in the worldview that reality is neither wholly physical nor wholly spiritual. Rather, the belief is that it is a composite of the physical and the spiritual: the former is the realm of the sensible and the latter is the realm of the non-sensible, the spiritual. For the Yoruba, the spiritual segment of reality is hierarchically arranged, with *Olodumare* occupying the topmost rung of the ladder, followed by lesser spirits (divinities) that are also hierarchically arranged in relation to one another, according to their respective attributes and powers.[15] An important feature of the physical and the non-physical aspects of reality in *Yoruba cosmology* is a strong belief in their relatedness (interaction), hence the contextual semantic propriety of 'duality of reality'.

In *Yoruba ontology*, the centrality of the relationality of personhood is always emphasized, given that every existential being is taken to be relational with another. While examining a similar relationality-related word, which is *ubuntu*, used by the Zulu people of South Africa, Metz roughly translates it as 'a person is a person through other persons'.[16] Moreover, according to Masaka and Chemhuru, the Shona people of Zimbabwe hold that the individual within the Shona society, just as in other African societies, is not a moral island. Rather, a human being can only be fully comprehended as an inseparable part of the whole.[17] Similarly, Nimi Wariboko also notes that, in the case of the Kalabari, relationship and fellowship constitute the identity of the self.[18] As could be readily seen, the conclusion in *Yoruba ontology* aligns with the emphasis on relatedness in *Yoruba cosmology* and is consistent with similar positions among some other African ethnic groups. Significantly, both reflect the plural and the monistic aspects of the essence of *MP*, as examined earlier.

There are various ways of approaching the discourse of Yoruba epistemology. It could be examined thematically by critically looking at some basic epistemic terms, such as *Otito* (truth), *Igbagbo* (belief), *Eri* (evidence), *Imo* (knowledge), *Ooye* (understanding), *Ogbon* (wisdom), and so on; systemically, such as philosophically interrogating the epistemic status of the *Ifa* system of divination, for example; and methodologically, such as philosophically interrogating the methods of knowledge impartation within the Yoruba world, such as the epistemic significance of *Iriri Aye Agba* (experientialism, relative to the elderly), as a source of epistemic guidance for the inexperienced young ones, and so on. Presently, we shall understand Yoruba epistemology as a branch of Yoruba philosophy that deeply reflects on the systems of knowledge, specific methods of knowing, fundamental epistemic concepts, ideas, or notions, and so on within the context of the Yoruba world.

Yoruba ethics, in the general sense, is character-apt. This, invariably, makes it a virtue ethics. According to Kwame Gyekye, the notion of character is generally central to African ethics. Specifically, Gyekye confirms that the word *iwa* means both character and morality ... in Yoruba language and thought[19]; thus, Yoruba ethics places much premium on the *iwa* (character) of a person in the moral valuation of the person. Given this, in Yoruba ethics, a morally good person is adjudged as *eniyan to ni iwa ni*. Sometimes, the word *eniyan* (human person) may also be used to express the same thing as *eniyan to ni iwa ni*. In this case, the normative dimension of the word, which means 'a morally good person', is intended, rather than a descriptive dimension of the word 'a human being'.[20] Critically dissecting the Yoruba ethics as character ethics, there are significant virtues and values, which could be signally relevant to the proposed *APEN* framework, and these virtues and values are conceptually correlative in that excellence of conduct ought to be desirable to a morally good person. Specifically, the relevant virtues and values come in three stages: the first stage of virtues and values is for pre-conflictual peace conduct; the second stage of virtues and values is for peace intervention during a conflictual situation; and the third stage of values and virtues is for post-conflictual peace conduct.

Stage I: APEN and Pre-conflictual Peace Conduct Since crisis cannot but sometimes ensure in the world of the human person, the central focus of APEN at this stage is to stall any brewing crisis from developing fully into a conflictual situation in Africa, alienating the self from the other and inverting the relationality between them. The relevant virtues and values at this stage are the following:

Émi Suru: Lexically, émi suru refers to 'spirit of patience'. In Yoruba ethics, a moral agent that possesses émi suru or iwa suru is one who usually finds a way of controlling his/her anger. S/he always approaches issues, no matter how volatile, with caution and calmness of mind. Thus, such a personality in Yoruba ethics is morally commendable: émi suru is a virtue, given that its cultivation is an excellence of conduct; similarly, it is a value because it is desirable; a morally good person, at least, would always strive to cultivate it. In the present context, if the self and the other in interaction in Africa conscientiously cultivate the virtue/value of émi suru, any brewing crisis between them might be easily and amicably resolved, rather than it transforming into a full-blown conflict that might weaken the string of relationality between them.

<u>Iwa-irele</u>: *In simple English, iwa-irele means 'humility of conduct' and the opposite is iwa-igberega, which means conduct of pride. In Yoruba ethics that is character-apt, iwa-irele is one of the virtues of Omoluabi, an ideal moral agent. Thus, it is encouraged that it ought to be morally inculcated in children, being part of moral education in Yorubaland, so that the children might not become haughty people that easily treat others with disdain in adulthood. Thus, implicitly, an important moral component of iwa-irele in Yoruba ethics is respect, which is also a virtue. This is a rational conclusion, given that a proud person feels reluctant to respect the moral agency of the other. If this is accepted, then it follows that both the self and the other ought to treat one another with respect, if they are to be taken as committed to iwa-irele. Since respect is given much premium among the Yoruba, a person that lacks iwa-irele is strongly morally reprehended in Yorubaland. It is noteworthy that the virtue/value of iwa-irele may also be epistemic, apart from being moral. It becomes epistemic when the self or the other with iwa-irele is committed to the belief that neither of them is a fount of knowledge, that either of the moral agents has something of epistemic value to reciprocally impart. Contextually, if the self and the other in Africa reciprocally learn to develop and sustain iwa-irele in their interaction, then they would not reciprocally treat (each) one (other) another with disdain, which might be a step towards the use of toxic communication (hate speech), essentially denigrating the self or the other, alienating them from (each) one (other) another, and eventually leading into a conflictual interaction. And, experience has amply shown that one of the causative factors of most forms of conflictual interaction (from electoral campaigns of political parties to interethnic/inter-religious relations) in Africa is toxic communication (hate speech) from the self to the other, or from the other to the self.[21] This invariably takes us to another related virtue (and value) of pre-conflictual peace conduct, which is Oro-rere.*

<u>Oro-rere</u>: *Roughly translated into English, oro-rere means 'good word', generally in communication. It could also be taken as oro-tutu, which means 'mild words'. In Yoruba ethics, oro-rere or oro-tutu is a linguistic virtue as well as a value. It is a virtue to the extent that parents in traditional Yoruba communities always tried to teach and inculcate in their children and wards oro-rere or oro-tutu so that they would not grow up to talk indecently to/about others. It is also a value because a person that wishes to be regarded as an Omoluabi in the Yoruba world ought to embrace it in his/her communication with others. The inverse of oro-rere*

is oro-buruku (bad words). It is because of the negativity of oro-buruku that makes it a moral vice in Yoruba ethics. To show the moral-social significance of oro-rere, the Yoruba usually state that: Oro-rere n' yo obi l'apo, oro-buruku n' yo ida l'ako (good words bring about exchange of gifts/establish friendly relations, while bad words bring about fight). Contextually, if the self and the other in interaction in Africa develop and nurture the virtue of oro-rere, on the one hand, and take it as a value that ought to define their communication mode with each (one) other (another), then on the other hand, they would rarely come into any conflict.

Stage II: APEN and Peace Intervention During a Conflictual Situation It must be noted that there might still be some level of conflict, negating neighbourliness between the self and the other, despite adherence to the foregoing prescriptions. When this occurs, there should be a transition from the first stage of the APEN framework to the second stage. At this second stage, the main objective of APEN is to ensure that the conflictual interaction between the self and the other is morally mitigated as much as possible so that either the self or the other does not overdo things, taking steps that might make it difficult to heal the ruptured relationality between the self and the other in the post-conflict period. The following prescriptions are relevant presently:

<u>Iwa-pele</u>: In English translation, iwa-pele simply means gentleness/moderation in conduct: a person that is disposed to gentleness will invariably try to do things in moderation. In Yoruba ethics, a person with iwa-pele does not always rush into decision-making and act unthinkingly; rather, s/he always thinks deeply about the likely consequences of his/her intended conduct. Thus, one could rightly state that a person with iwa-pele is, invariably, a person with emi-arojinle (commitment to the virtue of deep thinking), an epistemic virtue in Yoruba epistemology.

Relevantly here, a person that has the moral virtue of *iwa-pele* is also always moved to take all excesses (such as rushing into decision-making) in human conduct as moral vices. In the present context, if the self and the other in conflict in Africa, whose link of relationality is hereby temporarily weakened, take *iwa-pele* to be an essential moral value, then they would not employ the conflictual interaction as an opportunity to act in morally wrong ways (such as ethnic cleansing, during an interethnic conflict in Africa) that would totally damage the link of relationality between them.

<u>Emi-arojinle</u>: Explained more fully than done above, in English translation, emi-arojinle refers to the spirit of deep thinking, or the virtue of criticality in thought. Apart from contributing to the depth of knowledge imparted in Yoruba epistemology, making it an epistemic virtue, emi-arojinle is also a logic virtue, given that a person aspiring to be a good thinker ought to embrace it as a value. In (traditional) Yoruba epistemology, people that could think deeply to address knotty (especially, familial) issues were well respected, being called agba ologbon (wise elders). Emi-arojinle is also a moral-epistemic value in the Yoruba world; a person that

wishes to be a good moral agent in the Yoruba world must be able to always distinguish between 'what is good' and 'what is bad', in the first instance, and this invariably may involve emi-arojinle as to 'what is good' and 'what is bad' in order to properly distinguish between them.

Contextually, if the self and the other in conflict in Africa take *emi-arojinle* as a highly relevant value that ought to be embraced for a progressive and developmental self-other interaction, then they ought to always think deeply on how to humanely and humanly conduct the extant conflict between them so that their link of rationality, though presently weakened by the conflict, is not totally damaged and thus irreparable in their post-conflict interaction.

Stage III: APEN and Post-Conflict Peace Conduct At this stage, the essence of APEN is to foreground a just, reconciliatory, and cohesive self-other interaction in the post-conflictual environment. This is a stage at which the metaphysics of relationality is fully restored between the self and the other.

<u>Emi-atunse</u>: *In English translation, 'to tunse' means 'to rectify' or 'to correct'. Thus, atunse means 'rectification' or 'correction', perhaps, of a mistake or an error earlier committed. In Yoruba ethics, emi-atunse is a moral duty that is expected, wherever applicable, of an offending party to an offended party in their shared post-conflict world. In this context, emi-atunse graphically shows that: (i) the offending party is truly sincere in saying that s/he wrongly acted in offending or injuring the other party in the past, (ii) s/he is now willing to rectify or correct the wrong conduct in the present, and (iii) the mistake of offending or injuring the other party might not recur in future. Thus, one could aver that emi-atunse as a moral good is both backward-looking, as in the case of (i) as well as forward-looking, as in the case of (iii). Given the foregoing, emi-atunse is a moral good that ought to be taken as an important post-conflict value in Africa, by the offending party.*

<u>Emi-idariji</u>: *If the offending party takes emi-atunse as a significant post-conflict value in the shared post-conflict world with the offended party, then the offended party also ought to take emi-idariji as an important value in the shared post-conflict world with the offending party. In English translation, emi-idariji (or emi-iforiji) refers to a spirit of forgiveness. Emi-idariji (or emi-iforiji) is one of the virtues normally predicated of Omoluabi, a paradigmatic moral agent in Yoruba ethics. Thus, a person that wills to become an Omoluabi, in relation to an offending other, ought to develop and nurture the virtue. Teleologically, it is also a value in that it is a good step towards repairing the damaged link of relationality between the self and the other that had previously been in conflict in Africa. In the absence of emi-idariji (or emi-iforiji) by the offended party to the offending party in Africa, in their shared post-conflict world, the damaged link of relationality between them may not be successfully repaired.*

Emi-irepo: If the self and the other, who had previously been in conflict in Africa, committedly embrace both emi-atunse and emi-idariji, then emi-irepo would normally develop between them in their shared post-conflict world. Translated into English, emi-irepo is a relationship-bonding spirit, given that 'to repo' means 'to cement together or bond'. In Yoruba ethics, emi-irepo is an important virtue expected to be developed and nurtured by a moral agent, who subscribes to the metaphysics of MP, the defining philosophy of the communal life in Africa. However, it is a moral vice in Yoruba ethics if a person inverts the value of emi-irepo, given that this invariably separates him/her from the other. In the context of a shared post-conflict world in Africa, the self and the other, who had previously been in conflict, are praised if they morally subscribe to emi-irepo, and there are, at least, two reasons for that. First, it shows that the previously ruptured link of relationality between them has been repaired. Second, it practically actualizes the defining philosophy of MP in the communal life in Africa.

Likely Objections and Responses

There are some objections that could possibly be raised against the *APEN* framework. These would be critically examined next.

The Question of Continental Plausibility: This argument is simple enough. The point is that the APEN framework is too culturally restrictive, drawing solely on the ethics in the Yoruba culture, which may or may not, from the perspective of this critique, appeal to other ethnocultural groups in Nigeria, not to say outside of Nigeria. This argument, doubtless, makes a fine point in that the framework actually draws solely on the ethical system of the Yoruba, a given cultural milieu. But, the point of the counterargument, doubting the continental plausibility of the framework on the basis of its source, is suspect. The counter to the counterargument, or a counter-negation to it, is that the source of the framework has little, if at all, to do with its continental applicability. Liberal democracy has its roots in the Western culture, but it is now gaining almost universal applicability. Perhaps, what matters most for the proposed framework is whether or not it is disposed towards achieving a moral good for the African continent. Given that the framework is teleologically disposed towards the building of a sustainable peace between the self and the other in Africa, which is a moral good, then it ought to be morally acceptable to all in Africa.

The Question of Inter-State Feasibility: The argument here is that, even if we grant that the framework is feasible at the level of intra-state citizenship relations, given that the citizens, on the one hand, and the non-citizen Africans (/non-Africans), on the other hand, at this level share more or less a territorially close social environment, it may not be feasible in the context of inter-state citizenship relations, given that citizens of African states at this level are largely territorially disparate from one another. The point of disparate territoriality in the counterargument is obviously non-contestable. But, the factuality of disparate territoriality *does not, and cannot, render inconsequential the idea of ontological relationality, represented in the metaphysics of MP, shared by territorially disparate Africans. Given that the framework evolves from the basis of this ontological relationality, in the final analysis, then it could still pass the test of inter-state feasibility in Africa.*

Operationalizing a Yoruba Theory of Political Ethics of Neighbourliness for Peaceful Conduct in the Self-Other Interaction in Africa

Having attempted to discuss a Yoruba theory of *APEN*, the next thing is to examine how the theoretical framework could be operationalized within the context of modern African society. The present task is to be approached from the micro level of intra-state citizenship relations and at the macro level of inter-state citizenship relations and inter-state relations.

The Micro Level of Intra-State Citizenship Relations At this level, the following constitutes the moral duties of all the relevant citizens within the modern African state in the practical realization the APEN framework. The duties are divided into three broad categories: (i) familial moral duties, (ii) social moral duties, and (iii) moral duties at the state level.

<u>Familial Moral Duties</u>: *At the family level, parents are morally obligated to inculcate in their children and wards the APEN virtues, such as emi suru, iwa-irele, oro-rere, iwa-pele, emi-arojinle, emi-atunse, emi-idariji, emi-irepo, and the like, so that all these moral virtues will later become moral values of proper social conduct to them in their self-other interaction in adulthood. Moreover, the parents also have a moral duty to try, as much as humanly possible, to act out all the moral virtues they teach to their children and wards. As one could see, this kind of upbringing has a strong promise of turning the children and wards into neighbourly adults later in life.*

<u>Social Moral Duties</u>: *At the social level of interaction in the modern African state, the citizenry are morally obligated to take the virtues, such as emi suru, iwa-irele, oro-rere, iwa-pele, emi-arojinle, emi-atunse, emi-idariji, emi-irepo, and the like, as foremost social values of interaction: the values that ought to define and characterize their ethnic, religious, and political relations in their shared society. These virtues and values, as noted at the family level, also have a strong probability of making good neighbours out of those that subscribe to them at the social level of interaction.*

<u>Moral Duties at the State Level</u>: *At the state level of interaction between the leadership and the followership, it is morally obligatory for the relevant followership to appoint/elect leaders on the basis of strict commitment, in one way or another, to both the adumbrated familial moral duties and social moral duties. This may be a relevant part of the moral and political legitimacy test for the leaders; it is a sort of pre-leadership moral and political legitimacy. Analogously, it is also morally*

obligatory for the leadership to operate within the same moral framework of duties in their interaction with the people, after they have been appointed/elected. Non-operation within the framework of moral duties, after they have been appointed/elected, inverts their pre-leadership moral and political legitimacy and, in the same token, in part delegitimizes their future prospects as appointed/elected leaders. Thus, strict operation within the framework of moral duties, after they have been appointed/elected, constitutes a significant part of their future leadership moral and political legitimacy.

The Macro Level of Inter-State Citizenship Relations and Inter-State Relations At this level, the following constitutes the moral duties of all Africans in the practical realization of the *APEN* framework.

Social-Level Moral Duties
It is morally obligatory for the citizens and non-citizens of the modern African state to always perceive and treat one another as moral agents, who are all bound by ontological relationality, but not as fellow citizens and non-fellow citizens. As one could rationally deduce, the former form of human perception and treatment is more in tune with the neighbourly virtues and values given earlier, than the latter form of human perception and treatment.

State-Level Moral Duties
It is morally obligatory for all African leaders to perceive and treat all non-citizen African people that are resident within their individual states as moral agents that are all ontologically relational to their national citizens, rather than perceiving and treating them merely as aliens/foreigners that are just resident in their individual states. This also significantly contributes to the promotion of the neighbourly virtues and values given earlier, in the interaction among the fellow national citizens and non-citizen African people that are resident in their states.

Similarly, it is also morally obligatory for all Africans to perceive and deal with other Africans, outside their territorial boundaries, as equal moral agents that are ontologically relational to them, all things considered. But, what constitutes the necessary background for the flourishing of the *APEN* framework in the modern African state? This is addressed next.

SOCIOPOLITICAL ENVIRONMENT FOR THE DEVELOPMENT OF *APEN* FOR PEACEFUL CONDUCT IN THE SELF-OTHER INTERACTION IN AFRICA

In order to properly, socially develop the virtues and values that constitute the *APEN* framework in the modern African state, there are some public goods (defined as those essentials in the open sphere of any human society, as distinguished from the private sphere of same, which conduce to the collective flourishing of the humanity of the people therein), so to say, that should be the background.

The Good of Third Culture The modern African state should try as much as possible to consciously develop and sustain a sort of third culture, a culture of positive integration of the essentials of the self culture (SC) and the other culture (OC). This could be promoted through an open-minded, critically constructive, and systematic studying and learning of the cultural values of the other by the self, or the self by the other.[22] This exercise helps to nurture a multiculturally functional individual, and build a socially cohesive relationship.[23] It substantially provides the background to socially integrate the self and the other in Africa. It is a move that is especially imperative towards transcending the cleavage of pluralism (ethnic and religious), which has become one of the defining features of the state in Africa. This good, undoubtedly, supports the development of the constitutive virtues and values of the APEN framework.

The Good of 'Public Responsibility to Human Flourishing' This is a very important public good, given that the good could yield other public goods that may, ultimately, be human-integrative. Moreover, the good is both vertical and horizontal in nature. But, what kind of good is 'public responsibility to human flourishing', to start with? In the present context, the term refers to the functional devotion of governance to the service of the people, being both the means and the ends of administrative legitimacy, and the commitment of the people to the sustenance of such governance. This public good becomes vertical when the administrative leadership fulfils the governance aspect of the good, and it becomes horizontal when the people conscientiously work together to promote the existential continuity of the governance. But, how does this public good connect to the evolution of the APEN framework in practice? The explanation is simple. Commitment to the good of 'public responsibility to human flourishing' could motivate the administrative leadership in the modern African state to be more positively disposed to the smooth operation of the rule of the law (among others), leading to the promotion and protection of the social, political, economic, and cultural rights of the people in the state, on the one hand. On the other hand, the people feel motivated and encouraged, on the basis of the former, to conscientiously work together to support such administrative leadership. Inferentially, when the people become so inclined in their interaction with one another, the spirit of relationality, defining their personhood in Africa, is embraced, and when the spirit of relationality is so embraced, then the virtues and values that constitute the APEN framework become easy of development. The people know fully well that the virtues and values would help them strengthen the spirit of relationality so embraced futuristically.

Summary and Conclusion

This chapter makes an attempt to advance a Yoruba theory of political ethics of neighbourliness, to morally address the problem of conflictual interaction between the self and the other, in Africa. To go about the task, we first discussed the conceptual framework of the study, before examining the anti-neighbourliness of conflictual interaction in Africa. Thereafter, we attempted to develop a Yoruba theory of African political ethics of neighbourliness, which, as argued in the work, is underpinned by the idea of monistic pluralism, to address the anti-neighbourliness of conflictual interaction in Africa. Later on, we examined and responded to some likely objections to the theoretical framework and discussed a methodology of sociopolitical operationalization of the theoretical framework, in Africa, before foregrounding the public goods that could aid the development of the framework. In conclusion, it is reiterated that Africans are morally obligated to make every effort to ensure that the incessant problem of conflictual interaction in Africa is frontally addressed so that the self and the other could enjoy a sustainable peace on the continent. The *telos* of the present chapter is in line with this moral duty.

Notes

1. These conclusions are drawn from the works of many authorities on African metaphysics. See, for example, Teffo, Lebisa J. and Roux, and Abraham B.J., 'Metaphysical thinking in Africa', *The African Philosophy Reader*, P.H. Coetzee and A.P.J. Roux, eds., Cape Town: Oxford University Press, 2002, p. 196; however, this position, as related to African political philosophy of eco-democracy, is captured in Badru (2018) above, and in Badru forthcoming (*Ethical Perspectives*), as related to an African theory of just war.
2. David Coady and Richard Corry, *The Climate Change Debate: An Epistemic and Ethical Enquiry*, ed. Jonathan Boston, Andrew Bradstock, and David Eng (Palgrave Macmillan, Basingstoke, UK, 2013), p. 2.
3. Jonathan Boston, Andrew Bradstock, and David Eng, 'Ethics and Public Policy', *Public Policy: Why Ethics Matters* (ANU E Press: Canberra, 2010), p. 1.
4. Wasudha Bhatt, 'WHAT IS DEVELOPMENT ETHICS?: A theoretical inquiry into the philosophical traditions', *The Indian Journal of Political Science*, Vol. 70, No. 2 (APRIL–JUNE, 2009), 317–343 (at p. 317), citing G.E. Moore, *Principia Ethica* (Cambridge University Press, London, 1962), 1–2.
5. Contextually, non-extensive proximity between the self and the other occurs when both legally share a given territorial space (as Nigeria by various Nigerians); thus, neither of them deserves to have more of the space than the other, except on some strong legal (or moral) grounds. In short, the shared space is their point of proximity. Extensive proximity between the self and the other occurs when both share some identical cosmological or ontological link; though, they may or may not legally share the same territorial space (as Africans, who are of different African states). In brief, the identical cosmological and ontological link shared forms their point of proximity.
6. R.O. Badru, 'Environmental Deficit and Contemporary Nigeria: Evolving an African Political Philosophy for a Sustainable Eco-Democracy', *Environmental Philosophy: The Journal of the International Association for Environmental Philosophy*, vol. 15, Issue 2, Fall, 2018, 195–211, at p. 203.
7. Rama Venkatasawmy, 'Ethnic Conflict in Africa: A Short Critical Discussion', *Transcience* 6, 2 (2015), pp. 26–37, at p. 26.
8. See R. Picciotto, 'Conflict Prevention and Development Co-Operation in Africa: an Introduction', in *Conflict, Security and Development*, vol. 10, no. 1. (2010), pp. 1–25, at p. 2.
9. Facts about all these are online.

10. For a critical review of the Boko Haram phenomenon, see, for example, Chidiebere C. Ogbonna, 'The Inordinate Activities of Boko Haram: A Critical Review of Facts and Challenges', *RIPS*, vol. 16, núm. 2 (2017), pp. 9–24.
11. Johnson Olaosebikan Aremu, 'Conflicts in Africa: Meaning, Causes, Impact and Solution', *African Research Review: An International Multi-Disciplinary Journal*, Ethiopia, vol. 4 (4), Serial No. 17, October 2010, pp. 549–560, at p. 550.
12. See Aremu…, pp. 551–554.
13. See Aremu…, pp. 552–553.
14. The basic reason for this is that it is impossible, given the limitation of space for the present work, to philosophically examine all the different cultural groups in Africa. However, there might be some objections, arising from focusing on a given African culture; these would be addressed later in the work.
15. See Bolaji Idowu, *Olodumare: God in Yoruba Belief* (revised and enlarged edition). Ikeja: Longman, 1996. For a philosophical examination of some issues involved in interpreting 'God' as 'Olodumare', see Benson O. Igboin, 'Is Olodumare, God in Yoruba Belief, God?' *Kanz Philosophia*, vol. 4, no. 2, 2014, pp. 189–208.
16. T. Metz, 'Towards an African Moral Theory', *The Journal of Political Philosophy*, 15/3, 2007, pp. 321–341, at p. 323.
17. See Dennis Masaka and Munamato Chemhuru, 'Moral Dimensions of Some Shona Taboos (Zviera)', *Journal of Sustainable Development in Africa*, vol. 13, no. 3, 2011, pp. 132–148, at p. 134; I.A. Menkiti, 'On the Normative Conception of a Person', in K. Wiredu (Ed.), *A Companion to African Philosophy*, Oxford: Blackwell Publishing, 2006, pp. 324–331.
18. See Nimi Wariboko, *The Depth and Destiny of Work: An African Theological Interpretation*, Trenton, NJ: Africa World Press, Inc., 2008, pp. 105–106.
19. Kwame Gyekye, 'African Ethics', *Stanford Encyclopedia of Philosophy* (2010), accessed on 17 June 2013 from 2013 http://plato.stanford.edu/entries/african-ethics/
20. See Segun Gbadegesin, *African Philosophy: Traditional Yoruba Philosophy and Contemporary African Realities*, New York: Peter Lang, 1991, p. 27.
21. In the rundown to the 2015 general elections in Nigeria, politicians, especially those from leading political parties at that time, People's Democratic Party (PDP) and All Progressives Congress (APC), were freely using toxic communication against one another in both print and electronic media. Moreover, one of the issues that really heated up the polity among the different ethnonational groups in Nigeria was the so-called Kaduna Declaration on 6 June 2017 by some group of youths in the North, calling on all the Igbo to leave the Northern region by 1 October 2017. For more details on this, see: *THE KADUNA DECLARATION—Full Text of Northern Youth Declaration Asking Igbos To Leave Northern Nigeria*. Retrieved on 24 Feb 2019 from https://www.tekedia.com/the-kaduna-declaration-full-text-of-northern-youth-declaration-asking-igbos-to-leave-northern-nigeria/
22. See R.O. Badru, 'Nigeria and the Deficit of National Cohesion: Exploring the Political Philosophy of a Third Culture in the Post-Centennial Era', *Culture and Dialogue* 6 (2018) 151–173.
23. Badru…, p. 169.

CHAPTER 11

Religion and Politics in Africa: An Assessment of Kwame Nkrumah's Legacy for Ghana

Ebenezer Obiri Addo

This chapter seeks to locate the role of religion in traditional and contemporary African politics. Using Ghana as a context, it raises and struggles with certain key questions such as: How was religion conceived and applied in traditional sub-Saharan Africa? How was it conceived, shaped, and applied by Kwame Nkrumah, Ghana's first post-independence leader? How has Nkrumah's approach to religion been utilized and/or contested in post-Nkrumah Ghana? What is the future on Nkrumah's legacy?

I contend that political leadership in traditional (indigenous) politics was tinged with sacredness. Contemporary Ghanaian politics emerged with the nationalism of Kwame Nkrumah, who creatively used religion as an element to weave a tapestry of political culture as a "traditionalist-nationalist."[1] He was overthrown and succeeded by military and civilian leaders. Since then other leaders have followed their own choreography of the religion-politics nexus. However, Nkrumah's blueprint remains the canon of the role of religion in Ghanaian politics. This blueprint is his enduring legacy. But since every generation tends to face old questions in new ways, Ghana's current political leadership which has roots in the anti-Nkrumah camp is attempting to contest this legacy.

Through empirical research, archival documents, and newspaper reports, I argue that (a) the Ghanaian is incredibly religious as evidenced in language, symbols, and behavior; and (b) religion is a key variable that has fueled both traditional and contemporary politics, guided its direction, and generated its successes and/or failures. Successive leaders have therefore sought to demonstrate the religious-political dynamic, sometimes in amusing, even nonsensical, ways. I conclude that Ghana has been spared the interreligious conflicts such as

E. O. Addo (✉)
Seton Hall University, South Orange, NJ, USA

© The Author(s) 2020
N. Wariboko, T. Falola (eds.), *The Palgrave Handbook of African Social Ethics*, https://doi.org/10.1007/978-3-030-36490-8_11

we have in Nigeria because of the foundation established by Kwame Nkrumah. However, I also caution against what Lamin Sanneh has described as "Christian triumphalism" in which Ghanaian Christians essentially demonize indigenous religions as well as Islam. This attitude could potentially axe the relative peace which contemporary Ghana has enjoyed. In my discussion, I dwell at length on Nkrumah's use of the religious dynamic in his political leadership. I call it "cultural engineering," following Ali Mazrui's use of the term.[2]

I am using the concept of religion as pertaining to "models of social and individual behavior that helps believers to organize their everyday lives."[3] It relates to supernatural realities, and the "ultimate conditions of existence."[4] In short it is a human quest for meaning. Politics, from my perspective, is the art of the management of power. In a culture in which people are primarily "transreligious," that is, the ability to hold different religious traditions simultaneously without feeling any contradictions, it is normal to combine the potencies in all these religions to maximize one's power. Conflict therefore arises when a political leader seems to vouch for only one religious brand and, for example, refuses to have a libation poured at a national event, or not visit a mosque on a significant Islamic festival. All these have been part of the political life in post-Nkrumah Ghana. One can trace specific moments in national life to identify the historical dynamics of the interrelationship of politics, political leaders, and religious institutions. I believe this may offer a wise counsel for national leaders, for Akan elders have cautioned that *Dua a Ananse adi awu no, Ntikuma nkotena ase nto nko*; "Ntikuma (Ananse's son) should by all means avoid sitting under the very tree of which fruit his father ate and died."

KWAME NKRUMAH

The first group of post-independence African leaders was confronted with several issues of nation-building. Formal colonization of the continent followed closely after the "scramble" and "partition" of the continent by the major European powers with the tacit support of the United States.[5] Nationalist leaders were therefore confronted with the task of making sense out of the arbitrarily drawn colonial administrative units, as well as ethnic fragmentation left by the departing powers.

Nation-building, in this connection, was the attempt to build nation-states out of ethnic conglomerates with very tenuous cultural bonds.[6] The new leaders had to deliberately and self-consciously cultivate new sets of symbols, identities, and values to unite disparate ethnic groups whose primary allegiances were based on primordial sentiments. Also, and even more importantly, they were expected to validate the ostensible gains of independence through ideological innovation, for these new nations had no pre-given identities as "nations."

Kwame Nkrumah was one of those nationalists who inherited a "nation" based on competing interests and sometimes without a unifying center. How did he perceive his task as a nation-builder and national developer, who would lead the new nation-state toward economic modernization? What methods and goals would enable him to legitimize his leadership and influence the direction of national politics? Realizing how institutional or organized religion could generally compete with secular authority for supreme power in the political process, how did he pursue his political agenda in light of existing institutions, particularly traditional and religious ones?

I contend that Kwame Nkrumah believed that a modern, African nation such as Ghana must be a secular state. However, this state should be effectively built on an ideology that took all existing religio-cultural influences as ready-made material to lay the foundation of the new nation. The concept of ideology, as used in this context, means a road map for political action.

For Nkrumah, the key strands in the ideological tapestry for the new nation of Ghana were: (a) the African segment, which comprised the traditional way of life; (b) the Islamic segment which dated back to the eighth century; and (c) the Euro-Christian segment which came primarily through European imperialism and colonization of the nineteenth century. All these competing segments had religious strands. However, while using these different religious ideas and cultures, the new nation would avoid the institutionalization of any particular religion. Nkrumah's perception of the place of religion in a modern state was one which was "not based on any revealed religion or metaphysical rationalism evident in Christianity and Islam."[7] He sought to encourage a pluralistic and comprehensive African worldview that could provide meaning for people's lives. *Consciencism: Philosophy and Ideology for De-Colonization*[8] was Nkrumah's testament on secular modernization. Modernization in this context meant the new demands, particularly economic and social, which necessitated changes in structures of authority. It included economic modernization that required a realignment and redesigning of social and cultural aspects of national life. This process, therefore, goes hand in hand with political modernization. In advocating a secular state, Nkrumah was also aware that Ghanaians have cultivated religious reverence for their institutions as well as their political leadership. He realized this, and used religious ritual, symbols, and myths to bridge the gulf between himself and his followers. In examining *Consciencism*, I therefore discuss his personal as well as his followers' application of religion. I point out that this leader-follower dynamic became a bone of contention between Nkrumah and the institutional, missionary church. It accused him of building a personality cult.

Consciencism

It is generally believed that Nkrumah's ideological thought evolved over time. Political observers, including David Apter, believed that it was a direct result of the earlier version of Nkrumah's socialist philosophy called "Nkrumaism." His lieutenant, Kofi Baako, described it as "applied religion." Baako explained "Nkrumaism" as a

> non-atheistic socialist philosophy, which seeks to apply the current social, economic, and political ideas to the solution of our problems, be they domestic or international by adapting these ideals to the realities of everyday life .... As a philosophy it has no boundaries and allows a flexibility of application anywhere in the world where similar conditions exist. I refer to conditions such as domination by colonial powers, exploitation of the natural resources by foreigners against the will of the people, discrimination of any kind .... Nkrumaism Is not a Religion and has not come to replace any Religion, but it preaches and seeks to implement all that true Religion teaches. I can safely therefore describe Nkrumaism as applied Religion.[9]

Apter sees the ideological phase of Nkrumah's political career as specifically emerging when his charisma (in the Weberian sense) was waning.[10] John Kraus offers a general insight to sort out the maze about emergence of ideology. Ideology, he notes, "invariably develops during periods of social or political change and tension, when existing beliefs no longer seem as capable of comprehending new behavior or social needs."[11] Commenting on developing political systems in new states, Clifford Geertz saw ideology as arising against the "background of a chronic effort to correct socio-psychological disequilibrium."[12]

While all these observations help us to appreciate the background to Nkrumah's development of his philosophy of "Consciencism," I perceive it as a fulfillment of his long search for a definitive ideological statement that would clarify his understanding of African emancipation. Emancipation and decolonization of the African continent were his lifelong ambitions. He had stated in his first major work, *Towards Colonial Freedom*, drafted in 1945:

> Thus, the goal of the national liberation movement is the realization of complete and unconditional independence, and that the building of a society of peoples in which the free development of each is the condition of the free development of all. People of the colonies, Unite: The Working Men of all Countries are Behind You.[13]

For Nkrumah, emancipation would be meaningless unless Africa solved its "crisis of conscience" that had caused a sense of "malignant schizophrenia" in African life and thought.[14] For him, Africa at its independence had no identity. Competing ideologies had raptured its original self. Islam and Euro-Christian cultures competed with traditional African religions and culture for the soul of the continent.

Traditional Africa, he argued, was egalitarian, a communal society in which land as well as the means of production were communally owned. He recalled the socialist tendencies in traditional Africa and blamed the processes of colonization that virtually destroyed the communal ethos of traditional Africa:

> Revolution is thus an indispensable avenue to socialism, where the antecedent social-political structure is animated by principles which are a negation of those

of socialism, as in capitalist structure .... But from ancestral line of communalism, the passage to socialism lies in reform, because the underlying principles are the same .... Because of the continuity of communalism with socialism, in communalistic societies, socialism is not a revolutionary creed, but a restatement in contemporary idiom of the principles underlying communalism.[15]

Hountondji has also described Consciencism as an "ideology of continuity," that is:

> Continuity between "traditional" African culture and present and future African culture, continuity between the communal organization of the pre-colonial economy and the socialist organization of the new African economy envisaged by African revolutionaries. In fact, according to the logic of Consciencism, these revolutionaries are the truest traditionalists.[16]

However, religion played such a crucial role in traditional African societies, to the extent that we now have a cliché attributed to John Mbiti that "the African is incredulously religious," and that "African people do not know how to exist without religion."[17] For this reason in *Consciencism*, Nkrumah does not wholly embrace the Marxian understanding of religion as the "opium of the masses;" he rather promotes a new secularism suitable to the new Africa. This secularism does not totally negate religion. However, it accounts for its reality as a social fact. First, he reechoes Marx and Lenin by saying,

> Fear created the gods, fear preserves them: fear in bygone ages of wars, pestilences, earthquakes and nature gone berserk, fear of "acts of God," fear today of capital-blind because its action cannot be foreseen by the masses.[18]

He then goes on to paraphrase Marx and at the same time points out the "historical condition of Africa," and the need to "contain" the three religious strands:

> Religion is an instrument of bourgeois social reaction. But its social use is not always confined to colonialists and imperialists. Its success in their hands can exercise a certain fascination on the minds Africans who begin by being revolutionary, but are bewitched by any passing opportunist chance to use religion to make political gains ... For certain, it will check the advancing social consciousness of the people ... It is essential to emphasize in the historical condition of Africa that the state must be secular.[19]

In order not to be misunderstood as advocating anti-religious sentiments, Nkrumah explained further that religious pluralism should be the basic foundation of the new state. His political philosophy was therefore his desire for a synthesis of all three religious traditions. He therefore tried to clarify his position on his "philosophical consciencism" as follows:

> With independence ... a new harmony needs to be forged, a harmony that will allow the combined presence of traditional Africa, so that this presence is in tune with the original humanist principles underlying African society ... Such a philosophical statement I propose to name philosophical consciencism, for it will give the theoretical basis for an ideology whose aim shall be to contain the African experience of Islamic and Euro-Christian presence as well as the experiences of the traditional African society, and, by gestation, employ them for the harmonious growth and development of that society ... Consciencism is the map in the intellectual terms of the disposition of forces which will enable African society to digest the Western and the Islamic and the Euro-Christian elements of Africa, and develop them in such a way that they fit into the African personality.[20]

It would seem that Nkrumah's position on state-religion relationship was akin to Weber's classic typology of caesaropapist, in which secular power dominates religion itself.[21]

How, then, did organized, institutional religion, particularly the Christian Church—Western missionary churches—react to Nkrumah's ideas in *Consciencism*?

It is safe to limit the politics of religion to tensions between Nkrumah and the established churches because even though Islam was a major religious institution, the Convention People's Party (CPP) had managed to split the Gold Coast Muslim Association (GCMA) into two rival factions. A pro-CPP faction—the Gold Coast Muslim Council—had been formed. It became a more powerful and vocal ally of the ruling party, thus rendering the GCMA impotent as a political force. It had eventually become the Muslim Association Party in 1954, but was localized primarily in Kumasi, the Ashanti capital.[22]

The relationship between Nkrumah and the mission churches had never been cordial. He had moved to wrestle control of "mission schools" to the government, and had ordered the churches to open branches of the CPP in each community's church building. The churches had been concerned with Nkrumah's "communist" agenda, and the enactment of the Preventive Detention Act in 1958[23] had created further tensions. The publication of *Consciencism* was therefore a continuation of the crisis in church-state relations.

One specific, open confrontation in the ongoing tensions which is often cited occurred over his deportation of the then Anglican Bishop of Accra, Reginald Richard Rosevere. The bishop, who was also chairperson of the Christian Council of Ghana, had criticized Nkrumah over his formation of a national youth movement, the Ghana Young Pioneers (GYP). Statements such as "Nkrumah Never Dies" and "Nkrumah Is Our Messiah" were central in the slogans of the GYP. In his Synod Charge at the 1962 Annual Conference of the Anglican Church, the bishop stated:

> It is a truism to say that the future will be in the hands of the boys and girls of today .... There are, I regret to say, certain aspects of the Ghana Young Pioneers Movement which are the cause of sorrow and fear to very many thoughtful people, Christian and non-Christian alike .... It seems that the movement confuses

the work and example of a great man with divine acts, which are unique in history …. The incipient atheism is quite foreign to the traditional concepts of the African Personality.[24]

This added further tension to the ongoing debate over *Consciencism*. Nkrumah was quick to redeem his position on a "secular state":

> Insistence on the secular nature of the state is not to be interpreted as a political declaration of war on religion, for religion is also a social fact, and must be understood before it can be tackled. To declare a political war on religion is to treat it as an ideal phenomenon, to suppose that it might be wished away, or at worst scared out of existence. The indispensable starting point is to appreciate the sociological association between the religious belief and practice on the one hand, and poverty on the other.[25]

Elsewhere, Nkrumah had argued that in the new African society, there was the need for, in his view,

> An ideology which, genuinely catering for the needs of all, will take the place of the competing ideologies and so reflect the dynamic unity of society, and be the guide to society's continual progress.[26]

However, it was obvious that the church was, in his estimation, one of the identifiable instruments of the colonial administration, which had to reshape itself for the new society to emerge. This is how he described the church's association with colonial power:

> Because of these instruments, the colonial administrations were seen by all to be closely associated with the new sources of power, they acquired a certain prestige and rank to which they were entitled by the demands of the harmonious development of their own society[27]

Arguably, if Nkrumah favored one of the three religious tapestries and used it as a legitimizing force, it was traditional religion. It was the dynamic people readily recognized. Yet we may also add that Nkrumah was adroit at playing the politics of religion through cultural engineering. He used traditional Ghanaian religion and spirituality to connect with his followers.

> The traditional face of Africa includes an attitude towards man, which can only be described, in its social manifestation, as being socialist. This arises from the fact that man is regarded in Africa as primarily a spiritual being, a being endowed originally with certain inward dignity, integrity, and value. It stands opposed to the Christian idea of the original sin and degradation of man.[28]

The politics of religion, then, was the political tug-of-war between Nkrumah and the missionary churches, for he saw the church as an ideological block that had to yield to his new ideology:

> While societies with different social systems can co-exist, their ideologies cannot. There is such a thing as peaceful co-existence between states with different social systems; but as long oppressive classes exist, there can be no such thing as peaceful co-existence between opposing ideologies.[29]

The Christian Council of Ghana and the National Catholic Secretariat did not react to the publication of *Consciencism* per se. However, the document offered ammunition for the churches to accuse Nkrumah of being anti-Christian. It is arguable, though, that the ideological phase of Nkrumah's career was also a time for his creation of a kind of "political religion"; *Consciencism* became the sacred text of this religion. My use of the term "political religion" follows David Apter who argues that in new states, the governments "are weakly legitimized." Therefore,

> an ideological position is put forward by government that identifies the individual with the state. Modern political leaders come to recognize quickly, however, that no ordinary ideology can prevail for long in the face of obvious discrepancies between theory and practice. A more powerful symbolic force less rational, although it may include rational ends, seems necessary for them. This force is what shall be called political religion.[30]

Political religion may also be understood in light of Bellah's use of the term "civil religion," a set of beliefs and practices designed to inspire and sustain the nation-state.[31] Before this ideological phase, the politics of religion had created enormous tensions and alienations in the new nation. He had come to power with a complex attitude toward religion. However, his understanding of it as a powerful social force was undeniable.

By his own admission in his *Autobiography*,[32] Nkrumah was a person who feared three things in life: money, women, and organized and obligatory religion, because of his "dread of being trapped." He was afraid of having his "freedom taken away or being in some way overpowered." Pressed to declare his denominational affiliation, he would only say he was a "non-denominational Christian and a Marxist socialist."[33]

The use of religious metaphors, idioms, and parodies colored the speeches and writings of both Nkrumah and his followers. During the heat of the nationalist agitation, Nkrumah was imprisoned for declaring "Positive Action," which was his version of political nonviolence in the tradition of Mahatma Gandhi. *The Accra Evening News* which was the official mouthpiece of his party, Convention People's Party (CPP), published its own, parodied version the Beatitudes[34]:

> Blessed are they who are imprisoned for self-government's sake, for theirs is the freedom of the land. Blessed are ye, when men shall vilify and persecute you, and say all kinds of evil against you, for Convention People's Party sake. Blessed are they who hunger and thirst because of self-governing, for they shall be satisfied. Blessed are they who reject the Coussey Report, for they shall know freedom. Blessed are the parents whose children are political leaders, for they shall be thanked. Blessed are they who took part in Positive Action, for they shall have better rewards, Blessed are they who love C.P.P., for they shall be leaders in the years to come. Blessed are they who cry for self-government, for their voice shall be heard.[35]

Furthermore, the "Apostle's Creed" became "A Verandah Boy's Creed":

> I believe in the Convention People's Party, the opportune savior of Ghana. And in Kwame Nkrumah its founder and leader, Who is endowed with the Ghana spirit, Born a true Ghanaian for Ghana, Suffering under victimization; Was vilified, threatened with deportation, He disentangled from the clutches of the U.G.C.C. and the same day he rose victorious with the "verandah boys". Ascended the political Heights; And sitteth at the supreme head of the C.P.P. From whence he shall demand full self-government for Ghana. I believe in freedom for all peoples, Especially the new Ghana; The Abolition of Slavery; The Liquidation of Imperialism; The victorious ends of our struggle, its glory and its pride, and the flourish of Ghana, for ever and ever.[36]

On the eve of the 1951 general elections, *The Accra Evening News* carried the headline "Chameleon Organizations Shall Pass Away, But the Political Holy Ghost, the C.P.P. Shall Stay Forevermore." This was a reference to Mathew 24:35. Then again, the term "Messiah," given to Nkrumah as one of his ascriptive titles, was another key issue in this politics of religion. *The Accra Evening News* of March 29 and April 29, 1960, carried the headline "This is our Messiah-Kwame Nkrumah, in the Hour of Transfiguration." A March 7, 1960, issue went further:

> Some people call him the second Christ, coming just at the time when children in the womb all over the globe are suffering from the atom bomb's strontium 90, as foretold in the Bible. Others call him Son of God, the Messiah, the Organizer, the Redeemer of Men, the Positive Actionist ... yet Kwame Nkrumah puts it to every follower: "I am one of you; I belong to you and Africa. I am flesh of your flesh, son of an ordinary woman and a goldsmith of the village of Nkroful."

The divinization of Nkrumah went as far as making his mother, Nyaniba, a comparable figure with Mary, the mother of Jesus. On September 30, 1963, *The Accra Evening News* stated, "A year before the S. S. Bakana grounded in heavy gale, the blessed womb of Nyaniba gave birth to a son. And his name was KWAME NKRUMAH." One of Nkrumah's closest associates was his private secretary, Erica Powell. She did not lose sight of this divinization of the *Osagyefo*, and offered this apologetic statement in her memoir:

Kwame Nkrumah did more in ten years ... to give a true interpretation of Christ's teaching than the hard-working and dedicated missionaries were able to achieve in a century or more .... Dr. Nkrumah never set himself up to be a god or a saint in the eyes of his people. It was the black people, not only of Ghana, but throughout Africa and the world, who raised him on a pedestal and looked to him as their savior.[37]

Another issue in the politics of religion was Nkrumah's elevation of Ghanaian traditional religiosity to a new level of respectability. At all state functions prayers were offered as follows: (a) the sounding of "talking drums," with appellations from the "State Linguist" B. S. Akuffo as follows: "Osagyefo (Savior), you have cunningly managed to push aside the big, red flag of the British, in order to establish the flag of Ghana in its rightful place ... Kwame, you are wonderful. Kwame, a whole army will see you and scatter. Kwame, speak! Speak! Speak once and for all! Speak righteously. Speak, for we are listening. Speak! Speak! Speak!" (b) Libation was poured by a traditional priest, then (c) a Christian and/or Muslim prayers were said.

Additionally, Nkrumah popularized the wearing of traditional dress, particularly the *Kente* (Akan or Ewe ones) and the *Batakari* (from the Northern Region). The singing of appellations to the *Osagyefo* (Messiah) completed what the church perceived as the "Divinization of Nkrumah."

After Nkrumah's overthrow, there were attempts by Dr. Kofi Abrefa Busia, the leader of the opposition who later became the Prime Minister, to present himself as a "Westerner." Even though his own academic research and teaching at Oxford had indicated the "trans-religious" tendencies Nkrumah identified and applied, he seemed to have distanced himself from Nkrumah's approach. In an interview with Jean Lacouture regarding the different approaches between Nkrumah's CPP and the United Gold Coast Convention (UGCC) nationalist movement, Busia stated, "Oath-taking? libation-pouring? The purpose of all that is to bind the masses to the CPP. Tribal life is religious through and through ...These practices ... insure, with rough authority, that the masses follow and accept the leadership. The leaders of the CPP use tribal methods to enforce their ends." Lacouture then asked Busia, "I take it that you wouldn't use such methods?" To which Busia replied, "I? I'm a Westerner."[38]

Conclusion

I have argued that national integration was the key task that Nkrumah and other African leaders of the first decade of independence faced. This was a necessary first step toward modernization and development. The integration needed some available raw material: first for political legitimacy, and second, to act like glue to weld ethnically diverse groups with primordial attachment together. For Nkrumah, religion—its symbols, language, metaphors, and other cultural underpinnings—became the raw material. As a realist, however, he critiqued and formulated his understanding of Ghanaian history in the form of an ideology. I contend that this ideology he termed as "consciencism" gave a great value to the ensuing social milieu.[39] This intentionally integrative and inclusive ideology competed with the ideas of the Christian Church, which claimed to offer normative standards for political and social action. Thus, competition between religious pluralism and monism formed the arena for religious politics in Nkrumah's Ghana. It was the first religious conflict in postcolonial Ghana, yet it eventually served as the model of religious pluralism for later Ghanaian leaders. Former President J. J. Rawlings on his part raised Islamic holidays to the level of national holidays. This to a large extent furthered Nkrumah's vision.

During the debate on *Consciencism*, Nkrumah's Minister of Education Dowouna-Hammond told the annual conference of the Methodist Church in an address on August 6, 1965 that, "True Religion is Never Neutral." He challenged the churches to adopt a "nationalist" attitude rather than maintain their "colonial mentality." He stated that the church had a responsibility in the era of "Consciencism." He stated:

> Your paramount role is to help in the dissemination of the ethical concepts and values on which our national ideology is based ... the church and state are one indivisible instrument, each playing an integrated part constructively not only not only in the service of all our peoples but also for their over-all and total welfare.[40]

Challenging the church to promote the ideology of Consciencism, the minister referred to the perception about the historical role of the church as an ally in the colonial process.

> Missionaries of the colonial era, being loyal to the Queens and Kings of England and heads of their respective states, used the pulpit to disseminate such ideology to the people in order to enhance the exploitation of our country. The schools mostly mission, served their purposes by means of textbooks, recitation, and songs in the spreading of capitalist ideology. True religion, and the church which is an instrument of religion, can never remain neutral in the struggle for the emancipation of man. The justification of religion lies in its reinforcement of man's effort to achieve material and moral upliftment in society.[41]

Nkrumah was overthrown in a military coup on February 24, 1966. His detractors singled out *Consciencism* as a book he never wrote by himself because of its sophistication. Peter Omari claimed that Nkrumah wrote to please his ego.

For example, Habib Niang, his advisor on French West African affairs, insisted on a book to outclass Senghor's political philosophy: *Consciencism* was the result.[42]

Another ardent critic, David Rooney, suggested,

> Nkrumah's drive towards a scientific socialist solution to all his problems included the publication of *Consciencism*. It is believed that this book, purporting to provide the philosophy of the African revolution and full of abstruse philosophical

concepts, was substantially the work of Professor Willi Abraham, the first African Fellow of All Souls College, Oxford, and of some Marxist scholars who had recently arrived in Accra. Its publication illustrates another aspect of Nkrumah's problem—that his Marxist colleagues allowed him to hear only sycophantic adulation. After the publication a delegation of market women came to congratulate him on the best book he had ever written. There was not a literate woman among them.[43]

Akan elders have said that no matter how much you detest the *Okwaduo* (a swift-running animal of the antelope family), you may have to acknowledge its speed. Nkrumah's political philosophy was systemized in *Consciencism*. It was an affirmation and yet critique of religion as a whole, and Euro-Western Christianity in particular. His goal was national integration, which, it seems to me, no other Ghanaian since Nkrumah has been able to match. He laid enough solid foundation for Ghana's integration based on religious ideas, which has enabled the nation to prevent the ethnic conflicts in many parts of sub-Saharan Africa. His understanding of religion as a social force led him to lay a foundation for what Ali Mazrui calls "the ecumenical state," whereby a government is not religiously monopolistic; rather it upholds and trusts religious pluralism.[44] David Apter's observation about Nkrumah's integrative effort is another way to acknowledge the speed of Okwaduo:

> The nation replaces the ethnic community. The presidential monarch replaced the chief. The authority of charisma ritualized into the special role of warrior-priest. Ideology became a political religion increasingly intolerant of all other religions, monopolistic, expressed through the militant elect of the party. The writings and speeches of Nkrumah took on the quality of sacred texts to be interpreted in slogans and revolutionary symbols and to be taught to the women and children. Around Nkrumah were socialist militants, both the moderate and Puritants.[45]

This, I believe, is one of the best ways to understand what Nkrumah not only stood for; it would also help us to appreciate how he perceived the task of building a modern state which had just emerged out of centuries of domination, and the role of religion—its experiences and practices in the postcolonial state. His legacy should be kept in focus in order to preserve his dream of One Ghana, One People, otherwise the dream will become a nightmare.

I contend that this "dream-to-nightmare" scenario is at play in Ghana today. In March 2018, Ghana's current President Nana Addo Dankwa Akufo-Addo unveiled the design of a planned National Cathedral. At a fundraising dinner to support this project, he revealed to the nation that it was in fulfillment of a pledge he made to God ahead of the 2016 elections: "The building of the national cathedral in the capital city is to serve as a gesture of thanksgiving to God for His blessings, favor, grace and mercies on our nation and to give me an opportunity to redeem a pledge I made to Him before I became president."[46] He donated US$100 toward the project, adding, "As I launch this fundraising campaign for the national cathedral project, I am confident that, like the statement of the prophet Nehemiah in the rebuilding of the walls of Jerusalem, it is Almighty God who will prosper us and make us succeed in this endeavor."[47] The reactions of the Muslim community and other non-Christian groups have sparked a fierce debate about the role of organized religion in Ghanaian politics. Speaking at the International Luncheon of the National Prayer Breakfast in Washington, D. C. on February 11, 2018, President Akufo-Addo reiterated that, "I was born into a family of deep Presbyterian convictions." He explained that he comes from a line of paternal and maternal ancestors whose "ministries remain enduring legacies and inspirations for succeeding generation of priests. I was baptized a Presbyterian, and became an Anglican, much to the vehement protests of my parents ... Religious activities during my four-year stat at Lancing, England, helped build up my faith in God, and reinforced my belief in his word that 'without me you can do nothing.'" He argued that 71% of the Ghanaian population is Christian,[48] who continue to enjoy God's "blessings in that God has blessed our nation by sparing us the horrors of civil wars that have afflicted virtually all our neighbors." He then restated his promise and pledge before the 2016 election, adding, "I have decided to build an interdenominational National Cathedral of Ghana to His glory and honor. It will serve as a fulcrum for propagating the Christian faith in unifying the country."

It is important to note that the current government is a historical successor to the opposition government to Kwame Nkrumah, the United Party. Its members were predominantly drawn from the United Gold Coast Convention (UGCC) that invited Nkrumah to join them in 1947. He broke away to form his Convention People's Party (CPP) in 1949. When he was overthrown in 1966, his party was virtually banned and has never been able to regroup. It seems that everything he stood for is now being contested, including "Republic Day" and "Founder's Day." The government argues that Nkrumah was not the "founder" of modern Ghana; rather there were "founders."

The first sign of monist, exclusivist, and religious triumphalism that Nkrumah identified and therefore advocated a secular state has occurred. A story in the January 7, 2019 edition of the *Daily Graphic* was about the rejection of a US$25 million donation from "a gay community in Ghana, through its United Kingdom (UK) counterparts." The National Cathedral Secretariat, through its Executive Director, Dr. Paul Opoku-Mensah, explained that "the secretariat did not have room for interest groups and individuals, whose motivation to donate towards the construction of the cathedral would draw attention to themselves and their issues."[49]

Akan ancestors have said, "Every bird flies with its own wings." They have also cautioned that, "Borrowed water does not quench thirst." It was the visionary desire of Nkrumah to weave a nation out of the many through its own historical resources. He identified the new nation's religious heritage—indigenous, Islam, and Euro-Western Christianity—and refused to promote none of them over the others. Virtually all the so-called horrors and wars

President Akufo-Addo refers to have religious and ethnic roots. Ghana has been spared not for being Christian, but rather because of its founder's vision.

The President ended his remark with a quotation from US President Lincoln, which sounded very triumphantly Christian: "In the words of the 16th President of the United States, Abraham Lincoln ... I quote, 'My concern is not whether God is on our side; my greatest concern is to be on God's side. I want Ghana to be on God's side, and we will be an example to the black peoples of the world.'" In contesting the legacy of Nkrumah's integrative vision, Akan ancestors would remind us: "You don't develop a hunch-back the very day you throw a stone over the Volta River." In other words, time is long.

Notes

1. This is a term I have used in place of "neo-traditionalism," which seems a bit too trite. Thandika Mkandawire has argued that "African nationalism always contained some notion of cultural reaffirmation and race-liberation ... there can be no doubt thats leaders such as Kwame Nkrumah, Leopold Senghor and Cheikh Anta Diop did try in their own way" (See "African Intellectuals and Nationalism" in *African Intellectuals: Rethinking Politics, Language, Gender and Development*, Dakar: Codesria Books in Association with Zed Books, London, 2005: 18).
2. Ali A. Mazrui, *Cultural Engineering and Nation-Building in East Africa* (Evanston, Ill.: Northeastern University Press, 1972).
3. Jeff Haynes, *Religion and Politics in Africa* (London: Zed Books, 1996: 1).
4. Haynes, Ibid, 2.
5. See Adekeye Adebajo, *The Curse of Berlin: Africa After the Cold War* (Scottsville, South Africa: University of KwaZulu-Natal Press, 2010: xi).
6. Deutsch and Foltz (1963); Kautsky (1963); Emerson (1960); Spiro (1962); Jackson and Rosberg (1982); and Geertz (1963). Almond and Powell argue that nation building "emphasizes the cultural aspects of political development. It refers to the process whereby people transfer their commitment and loyalty from smaller tribes, villages, or petty principalities to the larger central political system." See Almond and Powell, *Comparative Politics: A Developmental Approach* (Boston: Little, Brown & Co., 1966) 36.
7. Ebenezer Addo, *Kwame Nkrumah: A Case Study of Religion and Politics* (1997: 68).
8. Kwame Nkrumah, *Consciencism: Philosophy and Ideology for Decolonization*, Monthly Review Press, 1964.
9. "Address to Conference of Ghana Envoys," Vol. I, #II (Accra: Ministry of Foreign Affairs, 1962: 120).
10. David Apter, *Ghana in Transition* (1972) 303–305; *The Politics of Modernization* (1965).
11. John Kraus, "Socialism in Ghana," in *Socialism in the Third World*, Helen Desfosses and Jacques Levesque, Eds., (New York, Praeger, 1975) 183.
12. Geertz, *The Interpretation of Cultures* (New York: Basic Books) 201.
13. Nkrumah, *Towards Colonial Freedom* (Accra: Ministry of Information, 1957: 32–33).
14. *Consciencism*, 59.

15. *Consciencism*, 74.
16. Houtondji, *African Philosophy: Myth and Reality* (Bloomington: Indiana Univ. Press, 136).
17. John Mbiti, *African Religions and Philosophy* (London: Heinemann 1969: 2).
18. *Consciencism*, 14.
19. *Consciencism*, 14.
20. *Consciencism*, 70, 79.
21. Weber's three typologies included *hiercratic*, in which secular power, though dominant, is cloaked in a religious legitimacy, and *theocratic*, whereby ecclesiastical authority is preeminent over secular power (See *Economy and Society*, Berkeley: University of California Press, 1978) 1159–1160.
22. See John S. Pobee, *Religion and Politics in Ghana* (Accra, Asempa Publishers, 1992) 107.
23. This law allowed the government to jail political opponents without trial. Arguably, Nkrumah suffered more political violence than any postcolonial leader. Yet it is noteworthy that there was never an application of the capital punishment under his rule. I can only cite his experience of executions during his political imprisonment in Jamestown prison. "I believe that its a relic of barbarism and savagery and that it is inconsistent with decent morals and the teaching of Christian ethics. The aim of punishment should be that of understanding and correction" (*Autobiography*: 132).
24. See John S. Pobee, *Kwame Nkrumah and the Church In Ghana: 1949–1966* (Accra: Asempa Publishers, 1988) 131.
25. *Consciencism*, 79.
26. See his *Handbook of Revolutionary Warfare*, 68.
27. *Consciencism*, 69.
28. *Consciencism*, 68.
29. *Consciencism*, 57.
30. *Ghana in Transition*, 61.
31. Bellah in Richy and Jones, eds., *American Civil Religion*, 1974.
32. *Ghana: The Autobiography of Kwame Nkrumah*, 1957: 12.
33. *Kwame Nkrumah*, 12.
34. See Maathew 5: 1–12.
35. *The Accra Evening News*, Accra, January 17, 1950.
36. See J. S. Pobee, *Kwame Nkrumah and the Church in Ghana: 1949–1966* (Accra: Asempa Publisher) 104–110. Also see his "Bible and Human Transformation" in *Mission Studies*, 1–2 (1984). Prof. Pobee also cites these parodies as evidence of the impact of Christianity on Ghana, which made Biblical language to be used to inculcate nationalism. It stands to reason, then, that Nkrumah wanted to reorder the new nation's political culture by taking history seriously.
37. Erica Powell, *Private Secretary* (New York: St. Martin's Press, 1984) 163–164.
38. Jean Lacoture, *The Demigods: Charismatic Leadership in the Third World* (New York: Alfred A. Knopf) 260.
39. *Handbook*, 56.
40. *The Spark*, (Friday, August 13, 1965) 4–8.
41. *The Spark*, 5.
42. Peter Omari, *Kwame Nkrumah: Anatomy of an African Dictatorship* (New York: Africana Publishing, 1970) 142.

43. David Rooney, *Kwame Nkrumah: The Political Kingdom in the Third World* (London: F. B. Tarius and Co., 1988) 221.
44. See Mazrui, "Piety and Puritanism Under a Military Theocracy: Uganda Soldiers as Apostolic Successors," in C. Kelleher, (ed.), *Political Military Systems* (Berkeley: University of California Press, 1974) 35–70.
45. Apter, *Ghana in Transition* (1972) 358–359.
46. See *Daily Guide*, Accra: Western Publications Limited, Thursday, January 3, 2019.
47. Ibid.
48. The late William Lavundi once opined that "there are three kinds of lies: a big lie, a small lie, and statistics." One can cite figures to make any point, but does that really tell the whole story? For the Ghanaian religious experience and religious practice are not either-or propositions. Rather it is "and-but-also," which makes the Ghanaian, like most West Africans, "trans-religious," the ability to belong to disparate religious traditions without feeling any contradictions.
49. *Daily Graphic* (Accra, Ghana, January 7, 2019: 14).

Bibliography

Addo, Ebenezer Obiri. 1997. *Kwame Nkrumah: A Case Study of Religion and Politics in Ghana*. Lanham: Roman and Littlefield.

Adebajo, Adekeye. 2010. *The Curse of Berlin: Africa After the Cold War*. Scottsville: University of KwaZulu-Natal Press.

Apter, David. 1972. *Ghana in Transition*. Princeton: Princeton University Press.

Bella, Robert Bellah. 1974. Civil Religion in America. In *American Civil Religion*, ed. Donald G. Jones and Russel E. Richey. New York: Harper and Row.

Blay, Benibengor J. 1973. *The Legend of Kwame Nkrumah*. Accra: Abico, Ltd.

Cordersria Books, Dadar, *in assciton with* Zed Books (London, 2005).

Daily Graphic. 2019. Accra: Graphic Publications, January 9.

Daily Guide. 2019. Accra: Western Publications Limited, January 3.

Desfosses, H., and J. Levesque. 1975. *Socialism in the Third World*. New York: Praeger.

Deutsch, Karl, and William J. Foltz, eds. 1963. *Nation-building*. New York: Atherton Press.

Dzirasa, Stephen. n.d. *The Political Thought of Dr Kwame Nkrumah*. Accra: Guinea Press.

Emerson, Rupert. 1960. *From Empire to Nation: The Rise of Self – Assertion of Asia and African Peoples*. Cambridge: Harvard University Press.

Geertz, Clifford. 1943. *The Interpretation of Cultures*. New York: Basic Books.

———, ed. 1963. *Old Societues and New States*. New York: Free press.

Haynes, Jeff. 1996. *Religion and Politics in Africa*. London: Zed Books.

Huntington, Samuel P. 1968. *Political Order in Changing Societies*. New Haven: Yale University Press.

Jackson, R., and C. Roseberg. 1982. *Personal Rule in Black Africa: Prince, Autocrat, Prophet Tyrant*. Berkeley: University of California Press.

Kautsky, John H. 1963. An Essay in the Politics of Development. In *Political Change in Underdeveloped Countries*. New York: Wiley.

Lacoture, Jean. 1970. *The Demigods: Charismatic Leadership in the Third World*. New York: Alfred A. Knope.

Liebenov, Gus J. 1986. *African Politics: Crises and Challenges*. Bloomington: Indiana University Press.

Marable, Manning. 1987. *African and Caribbean Politics: From Kwame Nkrumah to Maurice Bishop*. London: Verso.

Mkandawire, Thandika, ed. 2005. *African Intellectuals: Rethinking Politics, Language, Gender and Development*. Darkar: Codesria Books.

Nkrumah, Kwame. 1957. *Ghana: The Autobiography of Kwame Nkrumah*. New York: International Publishers.

———. 1964/1974. *Consciencism: Philosophy and Ideology for Decolonization*. New York/London: Monthly Press/Panaf.

———. 1979. *Towards Colonial Freedom*. London: Panaf.

Omari, Peter T. 1970. *Kwame Nkrumah: The Anatomy of an African Dictatorship*. New York: African Publishers.

Pobee, John S. 1988. *Kwame Nkrumah and the Church in Ghana: 1949–1966*. Accra: Asempa Publishers.

———. 1992. *Religion and Politics in Ghana*. Accra: Asempa Publishers.

Rooney, David. 1988. *Kwame Nkrumah; The Political Kingdom in the Third World*. London: F. B. Tarius and Co.

Sigmund, Paul E.T. 1963. *The Ideologies of the Developing Nations*. New York: Praeger.

Spiro, Herbert J. 1962. *Politics in Africa: Prospects South of the Sahara*. Englewood Cliffs: Prentice Hall.

———. 1967. *Patterns of African Development: Five Comparisons*. Englewood Cliffs: Prentice Hall.

CHAPTER 12

Ethics of Superpowers and Civil Wars in Africa

Comfort Olajumoke (Jumoke) Verissimo

INTRODUCTION

The Africa we know is primarily a design of influential and powerful countries. This is the result of the long years of colonial rule the continent suffered until the 1950s, when a wave of freedom fighters began agitating for independence from the colonial masters. The consequence of this agitation was a spate of independent nations who also bore the cross of navigating political and social relationships that had created fault lines in the system. These fault lines are the result of the forceful union of dissimilar ethnic, racial and social groups into one country for the convenience of colonial administration. This factor is considered as a foundation of many of the civil wars that has happened on the continent.[1] The first of these civil wars began in Sudan in 1956 and was followed by the war in the Democratic Republic of Congo (former Zaire) in 1960. Then the Nigerian-Biafran War broke out in 1967,[2] with more recent ones like the South-Sudan and Libya Civil War.[3] Some of these civil wars can be traced to issues of land/resources, discords sown during the struggle for independence, allegations of marginalization and revolts against despots instituted by foreign support, among several others. For example, the Angolan Civil War (1975–1994) heightened following the rivalry of two political groups that were formed during the struggle for independence against the Portuguese, and it extended after the country's independence in 1975.[4] In another dimension, the civil wars which happened in Uganda between 1966 and 1990 were a consequence of four different political phases: the first one was the destruction of the powers of the king by Milton Obote, Uganda's political leader who was prime minister and twice president of the country; the second phase was the atrocities of mass killings and massacres carried out by Idi Amin who tried to

C. O. (Jumoke). Verissimo (✉)
University of Alberta, Edmonton, AB, Canada

© The Author(s) 2020
N. Wariboko, T. Falola (eds.), *The Palgrave Handbook of African Social Ethics*, https://doi.org/10.1007/978-3-030-36490-8_12

remain in power; and the third phase was the attempt to overthrow him which resulted in a civil war, while the fourth phase was as a result of the takeover from Obote, who returned to rule after Amin, leading to the assumption of power by Yoweri Museveni.[5] While the contexts of the civil wars differ, superpowers have influenced and played a considerable dimension in the way these wars evolve. Influence from superpowers come in diverse ways, either in the form of military assistance which fuels and sustains the conflict or as an instrument for political recognition in the strife for global hegemony. As Arnold noted, "few African countries have developed any important arms industries of their own—the exceptions being Egypt and South Africa—and in consequence, they are all dependent upon imports to meet their military requirements." With the instability that has followed colonialism on the continent, the military has played a center stage in Africa's politics. Hence, when civil wars occur, participants "have been largely dependent either upon importing arms from their traditional suppliers or seeking alternatives." Most times, these alternatives are sought by the relationship formed with more influential nations. These relationships are built on the notion of a shared benefit or common purpose, with a recognition that both parties—superpowers and the warring state—are allies fighting for the same cause. The idea here is that, the support from an influential nation presents leverage over the other participants. The result of the relationship between superpowers and African states strongly impacts how the notion of justice and morality is defined in civil wars in Africa. What is just, what is honest and what is moral in a war where external intervention is offered by a superior power? What really do foreign powers stand to gain, and why would any nation get involved in another country's war?

The aim of many superpower or regional interventions in African wars is to give humanitarian aids or military backing. These supports do not always quell these wars. In some cases, it heightens it. Therefore, the interventions of external forces complicate civil wars in Africa. An illustration is how the Cold War between superpowers became an inducement for conflicting African states to negotiate alternative sources of arms supply, from the rival, the US, and its allies, the Union of Soviet Socialist Republics (USSR) and China.[6] This raises the question of morality behind the "support" that is given to African participants during civil wars, especially when we consider the dynamics of power at play and how it conditions response to conflicts. In addition, another point of consideration is the lopsided economic benefits and political status that come with intervening in Africa's civil wars. Hence, what are these interventions in the wars for, justice or order? What should be considered wrong, what is right and what is honest when these wars are fought?

To explore these questions and focus on the ethical influence and dynamics of superpowers and civil wars in Africa, we begin by exploring how the term "superpower" came about. According to Joseph S. Nye, the word was first used toward the end of the Second World War when it became apparent that two countries—the US and the USSR—would emerge with a much greater capacity to shape the postwar world than any of the other great powers.[7] It is however important to state that this chapter would broaden the term "superpowers" outside its historical usage of global powers that emerged from the Cold War (1947–1991), the US and the USSR. These two countries have positioned and projected their influence on the global stage and seek to extend their hegemonic status on Africa, like a trophy. The reason for broadening the term superpower is more of a need to accommodate the historicity of the external influence of powerful nations in Africa, rather than a disruption of the central idea of how the world evolved. Hence, we categorize Africa's colonial masters in the context of the superpowers being examined in this chapter, because they have continued to extend their influence in shaping the social and political fate of the continent. Hence, we begin our exposition by tracing the concept of superpowers in Africa to three major sources: colonialism, struggle for independence and the post-independence power struggle. These three sources are recognizable effects on how external power dynamics have shaped Africa as it is known today. However, as we cannot examine all the civil wars that have happened in Africa in detail in this chapter, we evaluate how the sources mentioned above act as key factors in the ethical relations of superpowers in civil wars in Africa, with a focused attention on the Nigerian Civil War (1967–1970).

The first source of external power force in Africa, colonialism, broadens our concept of superpower on the continent. We move with the claim that colonialism laid the foundation for the many civil wars that happened in Africa. In fact, the disruption of the lives of Africans is traceable to colonialism's 75 years of military and economic dominance across the continent, except for Liberia and Ethiopia,[8] which escaped the scrabble on the continent which led to colonialism.

Colonialism is one of the factors that set a foundation for the perpetual conflict that has ravaged the continent for economic prospects, evolving from small trading posts across the coasts from the slave trade, to becoming the basis for Europe's colonialists to gain the desire to "liberate" Africans from Arab slave trade—an attempt to right a wrong—which led to 200 years of the Atlantic slave trade, and eventually, the colonial scramble for Africa. In all, this idea to "free" Africans is a ploy on assumptions of how the idea of what is right or wrong and honest was designed in, and for, Africa. There were many tools to achieve this conception of morality in Africa, one of such was religion. Religion was a major influence in instituting the idea of Europe as the "savior." This way, Europeans slowly eroded the ethical values that existed in Africa, by its separation of Africans from their religion, and in effect, what constituted their traditional ethics. Benson O. Igboin makes this argument in his article "Colonialism and African Cultural Values." He argues that colonial rulers promoted their economic and religious values to enable "economic exploitation and socio-religious vitrification" which was needed to achieve their economic and political objectives for success. Igboin, quoting Irvin Markovitz, writes that colonialism is "one expression of an ever more encompassing capitalism" which not only allowed colonialists to carry out their economic exploitative agenda, but it also enforced "the ethnocentric belief that the morals and values of the colonizer were superior to those of the colonized."[9] Perhaps, what we can derive from this argument is the idea that the colonialist's morals and values positioned it as the harbinger of freedom, even when there were obvious cases of exploitation. Considering the ideological and economic policies that determine some of the terms of relations that have happened with African states and influential powers, there is a continuation of these courses of actions that perpetuate the narrative of offering "true freedom" to African states in a civil war, either through military assistance or humanitarian aids. This colonial template seems to be the terms of relations between superpowers and many African states. Citing the case of a former colonial power in Africa as an example: the Angolan Civil War lasted for 27 years and saw a considerable influence of foreign intervention from different countries like, the US, the USSR and their allies. A significant reference point in the war is, however, the struggle of the country's freedom fighter with their colonial power, Portugal. The significance of this war, which we seek to point out here, is that Portugal's role in the war was of self-preservation, based on an understanding of its position as one of the two poorest non-communist states in Europe. The country "saw its African colonies, and most notably Angola, as essential to its economic well-being and so determined to hold unto them at all costs. It was a member of the North Atlantic Treaty Organization (NATO) but in fact, with the connivance of the United States and Britain in particular, used armaments that were designated for NATO purposes only to fight its African wars."[10]

In another vein, the creation of many countries in Africa was for the purpose of colonial administration: to govern the partitioned lands which were shared following the scramble for Africa,[11] this brought together entities without commonalities to exist forcefully. In the case of Nigeria, the Southern Protectorate, which shares different "land tenure systems, local government administration, educational systems, and judicial systems," was forcefully joined with the Northern Protectorate in 1914.[12] With the creation of what is best described as contrived borders came the propensity for power struggle on the national stage between ethnic groups who observed that the colonial master supported a specific group and designated them to rule. The idea of justice and equity became a matter of conflict resolution, and the idea of peace was built around favorable relationships with the colonial master.

The second historical phenomenon that can help us understand the ethical dimensions of civil wars in Africa is the struggle for independence which came after colonialism. The struggle for independence among African nations also came with the knowledge that there were other influential powers outside the colonial masters. This struggle for national independence not only gave meaning to the context of power struggle among the people, but also perpetuated an awareness of freedom of association. Hence, when the Cold War broke out following the end of the Second World War, many African countries, as a way to push their own regional agenda, considered the capability of their inherent powers, based on partnerships with a global superpower. Hence, the Cold War transformed the idea of power in Africa, dispersing the supremacy that was accorded solely to colonial masters like Britain, France, to countries like the USSR and the US.[13] Significantly, the insidious power tussle that followed in Africa was as Gavin Raymond describes, not a result of "colonial ambitions in Africa," rather it was of "Africa as a proxy battlefield that they could not afford to directly wage war in." This led "both sides "to rapidly militarized regimes that were chosen for expediency rather than legitimacy, and whose internal rule was not held to account." In fact, an encyclical letter issued by Pope John Paul II in 1988 criticized the rivalry between the superpowers, the East and the West, and looked at the ethical significance on third world countries. He expressed that the nations that "need effective and impartial aid from all the richer and more developed countries find themselves involved in, sometimes overwhelmed by, ideological conflicts, which inevitably create internal divisions, to the extent in some cases of provoking full civil war."[14] For the countries in Africa, the hostilities that accompanied the Cold War proved functional in the growing contentions among ethnic groups and regions that desired sovereign power on the national stage. Warring factions could now play around lobbying for support, counting on the political significance of superpowers that showed interest in their country's geography, economic relevance and social stature. The consequence of these associations of convenience, borne as diplomacy, can be found in countries like Somalia, Ethiopia and Democratic Republic of Congo (former Zaire) depending on Cold War aid while intensifying the power struggle that eventually blew out of proportion.[15] In the context of two long-lasting conflicts—Angola and Ethiopia—the US and the USSR provided one or the other support, and this was "a constant and sometimes decisive factor in the fortunes of the combatants."[16]

In the context of the phenomenon discussed earlier, and narrowed further down to the Nigerian-Biafran War context, we again reiterate the questions we raised in an earlier paragraph; on what basis is the "good" intention of superpowers formed? What is honest, what is right and what is wrong with the involvement of superpowers in the civil wars in Africa. And lastly, how have the motivations of superpower rights and wrongs influenced what has become of Africa today?

ETHICS, SUPERPOWER AND POWER SHOWMANSHIP?

According to John Deigh's definition, ethics "is the philosophical study of morality." Deigh, knowing how ambiguous the concept of "morality" can be, clarifies his definition by explaining that there are "two distinct notions of morality." One is of an existing institution of a society, the conventional morality, and the other is that of morality as a universal ideal established in reason. The first, he explains, covers phenomena studied in anthropology and sociology. The second defines the subject of ethics.[17] Since our focus is on ethics, the second notion is of more interest to us.

As in our earlier claim, colonial relations and, subsequently, superpower actions in civil wars in Africa are directed by the rationale that they have the power and influence to do good. This "good" on a broader level is also based on the assumption that it is in the best interest of not just Africa but the world at large. It is also seen as being in the "best interest" of all, which implies that it has been ubiquitously accepted by "reasonable countries"—which would be countries that share their ideology or political ideals. Ideology in this case does not involve the ancient traditional values of Africa, but the newly imagined world which it wants to make African states a part of. But first, who determines and conceives the idea of "good intentions," and are the mediations of bodies like the Geneva and Hague Conventions effective in limiting the effects of armed conflict? As it is, there is already a power dynamic that exists between superpowers and third world countries, where most of the warring African countries fall into. This raises questions of whether superpowers can ever be made accountable for their actions, and how can their actions be judged if they decide what is wrong, right or honest. How do their actions benefit the African states they involve themselves in? Do their honest or right decisions, despite the influence or dominant positions of their political system, enable development and an improvement of the political welfare and structure of African states? For example, morality in warfare in many pre-colonial Nigerian societies required that warring parties see themselves as brothers, as most wars were fought with neighboring clans. Hence, there was a declaration of war, as well as definite place and time for the warfare. The ethics of war in pre-colonial Nigeria also ensured that at the end of the war, emissaries from both parties meet and discuss lasting peace in the community, compensations are decided and war prisoners are released. "In general, it may be said that limited wars, preceded by ample warning and conducted with due observance of protocol, were waged between tribes and communities which considered themselves related. Guerilla wars and all-out wars were reserved for stranger clans, with whom in any case there could be no easy communication because of language barriers."[18] Hence, the idea of the war in pre-colonial Nigeria was not to destroy or overcome factors that determined the power and strength of a nation, rather it was characterized by a desire for industry and social relevance.

Writing on the context of ethical tradition in the Western tradition, Joseph Nye explains that there is no traditional Western system with which to measure "superpower ethics." Nye explains:

> Within the Western ethical tradition, there is attention to motivation, means, and consequences. The consequentialist tradition—which includes but is broader than utilitarianism—places emphasis on outcomes. The deontological, or Kantian, tradition stresses following rules and having the right motives as sufficient for judging the morality of actions. The aretaic, or Aristotelian, tradition stresses an ethics of virtue rather than an ethics of consequences. It can be described as the difference between an emphasis on the integrity of "who I am" as against an emphasis on the consequence of my choices—an ethics of being versus an ethics of doing.[19]

As the aphorism goes, the road to hell is paved with good intentions. Nye further explains that the motives of the two superpowers, in this case the US and the USSR, are "stripped of ideological camouflage" and have the same objective, which is to "preserve or expand spheres of power and influence." Hence, the idea of an intention—whether purported as good by the two superpowers—is not a question of the consequences of their actions on African states, but how they can become more powerful—it is a showmanship of "who I am."

Examining superpower ethics in the context of the third world, Mazuri explains that political liberation, economic redistribution, military security and violence are factors that unify third world countries and superpowers. With a focus on the two global superpowers, the US and the USSR, Mazuri highlights how they support each other through their policies and ideologies. He argues that the political liberalism of the US was like the Soviet Union that promoted economic redistribution. His explanation is that the ethical code of the two countries was contradictory to their international policies, and rather than being dualistic in their approach, he argues that, the ethics of violence of the superpower was action that ensured international policies that did not cater for third world countries, even though it propagated different ideologies.[20] Hence, though the "United States is a liberal polity domestically, but at the global level does American policy pursue the redistribution of political power in favor of marginalized nations? The Soviet Union is a socialist system, but at the global level does Soviet policy work for the redistribution of economic power in favor of the dispossessed nations?"[21] Mazuri also explains that "Both superpowers regard Third World states as fair markets for the sale of conventional armaments, subject to wider political allegiances."[22] In the conclusion of his essay, he writes that "The two ethical worlds can have no human meaning unless they jointly agree on one thing—that the survival of the human species is a precondition for both liberty and economic justice." The central idea of these arguments is that there is no point propagating a better form of life for people when the idea behind the "good" is to emphasize a larger conflict. What really is the essence of discouraging violence only to initiate even more by arms sales, which destroy the lives of those who are trying to make meaning of their existence?

In the case of the Nigerian-Biafran War, it was a result of successive, unresolved internal conflicts between the eastern region and the northern region of Nigeria. It eventually culminated into a war between the federal government of Nigeria and the eastern region, resulting in the death of about two million deaths. This war saw Britain, the country's colonial power, and the two global superpowers at the time—the US and the USSR—though reluctantly at first, throwing their weight around to enjoy some significance. In his narration, on how the war started, John de St. Jorre explained that the Nigerian-Biafran war officially became imminent following a meeting convened by the leader of the secessionist group, Emeka Ojukwu, the Eastern Consultative Assembly (which comprised of chiefs, elders and representatives of Eastern Nigeria), "unanimously passed a resolution mandating Ojukwu to declare the sovereign

Republic of Biafra"[23] While this did not immediately initiate the secession, it is believed that the response of Nigeria's head-of-state, General Yakubu Gowon, with a state of emergency and a division of the country into 12 states to disperse the concentration of power in the major ethnic groups, aggravated the issue. It resulted in the eastern region of Nigeria declaring their independence as the Republic of Biafra on May 30, 1967. Nigeria responded with a military campaign to reverse the secession, which resulted in long months of conflict that would come to an end on January 15, 1970.[24] The influence of colonialism in this war can be traced to the 1914 amalgamation by the British, which was more of a broker of convenience for the colonialists, than the foundation of solid nationhood. With the British giving more power to northern Nigeria elites due to its large population and support from the British, it was only a matter of time before the subject of marginalization and subjugation ripped the country apart. According to Robert Benjamin Shepard: "At the root of the antagonisms between the regions lay the fact that Nigeria was a completely artificial state created by Britain from three distinct and wholly unconnected colonies, each dominated by different and unrelated people." There was also difference in the natural resources in the different regions, as well as the cultural and social structures.[25] Even after independence, Britain maintained strong economic and political ties with Nigeria and played a significant role during the civil war by taking the side of the Nigerian federal government, with the claim that it wanted to ensure the unity of the country. However, there are claims that the main reasons for the war were largely because of oil; Chibuike Uche argues that the interest of the British government in the war was for the protection of its investments of Shell-BP in Nigerian oil and not its highly propagated fight to keep Nigeria remain one.[26] It is also important to mention that at the time of the war, the US and the USSR had become recognized world powers, and it needed to remain an influential country in Nigeria's politics.

The Nigerian Civil War, which is regarded as the first televised war in Africa, also points to the part superpowers played in "designing" the war to suit their purpose. While this is not in any way the focus of this chapter, it raises questions on how the images of starving children and women across the globe became a ticket for contesting power in this widely "advertised," African war. In the section "Biafra's Darkest Hour," in *The Nigerian Civil War*, De Jorre narrated the reluctance of superpowers to become fully involved in the conflict. For France, one of Africa's former colonial power, the declaration of support for the secessionist state, Biafra, came on July 31, 1968, through its French information minister. This was followed up with weaponry routed through Abidjan and Libreville. Nevertheless, the French's support was a cautious relationship that never materialized into anything tangible afterward. It, however, motivated the Biafrans to continue to fight. In the case of France, Christopher Griffin's analyzes that France's motivation for the support of the Biafran side was based on the notion that it will become the greatest ally of the secessionist state if it won the war. And in the case where Nigeria won, it would retrace its step and mend its relations with the Nigerian government.[27] The US was facing the Vietnam War when the Nigerian Civil War broke out. The US treaded with caution, as its own "benefit" was not as clearly laid out as that of France either to the Biafran side or the Nigerian government. According to Shepard, for over one and half year war, Johnson, the president of the US at the time, tried to distance himself from the war. Shepard writes that, "Johnson always took the steps he believed would most distance the United States from the conflict. He refused to sell arms to either side. He refused to recognize Biafra and jeopardize America's long-term relationship with Nigeria." It was not until the starvation photos circulated globally and received wide attention that prompted Johnson to begin a relief program in the country.[28] It is also important to note that at this time, America's major concern was not about the question of what could be done in terms of an intervention that protects human life, but what needs to happen for the relationship with Nigeria to be sustained. This relationship was its non-communist stance, and its support of some of America's policies in Africa, leading it to be an ally. In addition, America also saw Nigeria as a country with a bright future, and it made efforts to expand its trade and investment in the country. Hence, when the civil war broke out, the US chose the policy of "minimalization."[29]

On the other hand, with the end of the war, Nigeria praised the Soviet Union for its support, an irony, considering the resistance of previous Nigerian government before the civil war to accept the socialist orientation that was peddled among the new states following independence. Despite the USSR's reflection on the plight of the Igbos, it "seemed to believe (or at least intimated so in their official pronouncements) that their safety could be guaranteed under the unitary arrangement. And as usual, the ultimate rationalization came from the standard appeals to (imagined) class solidarity."[30] The Nigerian government took advantage of the friendly disposition of the Soviet Union, when it met a brick wall requesting military support from the US and the UK. However, before the civil war, the interest of the global superpowers—the USSR and the US—were to attain ideological victory. While the USSR was interested in building a socialist society, the US wanted Nigeria to build a Western-styled democracy.[31] Hence, previous Nigerian government openly declared its rejection of socialist ideals. It was therefore no surprise that the USSR initially treated its relationship with the Nigerian federal government with caution, as it was not willing to jeopardize the friendliness with which it was now being treated. Ironically, before its eventually friendly ties with the Nigerian state were created, Moscow had shown sympathy to the Biafran cause; however, this changed. The result was Biafran shifted to the USSR's long-term adversary, Israel, and subsequently, it would also explore the Cold War as an avenue to sustain itself. It further employed the conflict between the People's Republic of China and Russia to seek the support of China—with Ojuwku pointing out that the support was China's way of standing against the hegemony of Russia and the US. The support by the different superpowers and influential countries, though constructed around ideological belief, appeared to have a motivation to enhance their hegemonic positioning on the world's stage, as against the genuine preservation of lives in the warring groups.

Also interrogating the ethical flaws of superpowers from the tension that comes from their interactions and "differing" policy stance in his article "The Rules of the Game," Stanley Hoffman advocates for superpower rules that are effective and ethical.[32] This idea of what is ethical in the context of Africa's political climate, where there is a history of subjugation, is indeed difficult to navigate. Warfare in today's world, and the question of ethics, can be complex. However, in Africa's case, the complexity is not just in the process or the scale of modern warfare but the foundational narrative of "doing Africa good." It is this challenge that Joseph Nye argues for in his "Superpower Ethics: An Introduction," where he explains that there is no traditional Western system that meets the challenge of establishing an ethics for the US and the Soviet Union. He made this observation with reference to Aristotle's "virtue," Kant's "good intent" as well as the consequentialist's "good result" was deficient in establishing the moral codes of superpowers. What then can be done?

At this point, we turn to practical advocacies like that of Nimi Wariboko, whose "principle of excellence" proffers a framework for social ethics. In his book, Wariboko offers an insight on what could be useful in designing a workable framework for superpowers with his concept of excellence. Before going further with Wariboko's concept, we may posit that the idea of the ethical would also imply justice, and this is a respect for human lives and a desire for excellence, which we can argue is being sort in the war. The idea to do good, to be just and honest is a concern for the preservation of human lives. In his explanation of the concept of excellence, in the chapter "Excellence and Economic Development," Wariboko states that expansion and enhancement of human life has always been a part of human history. Quoting Amartya Sen's argument, Wariboko elaborates that a major part of this development "has been the overcoming of problems, the removal of 'unfreedoms' that thwart human flourishing." For this reason, as Wariboko explains, "the degree of excellence is the degree to which somebody is striving for and able to affirm increasing levels of human flourishing. Excellence in this light is the ontological foundation of human flourishing and virtue altogether. Excellence is a virtue; the highest and more prior virtue, is living, acting, and doing according to one's true nature."[33] Hence, the idea of an excellent ethical practice would imply one that concerns itself with creating a place for African countries to thrive, as against an ethical practice which is largely focused on the aggrandizement of the superpowers.

Conclusion

The existence of ethics in warfare is universal. However, the question is: does the idea of this universality capture the needs of civil wars in Africa? What are these needs—or is it just the singular need to exist? We are at a time when we need to revisit the implication of external interventions from superpowers and how the interplay of the power dynamics interferes with the applications of ethics in Africa. What is right? What is moral? What is honest?—when it concerns Africa. These questions are important because, Africa needs to move beyond the narrative of her as an invention of the West, based on the history of the scramble for its land by colonial powers, which have now become former empires with a desire to amplify their presence on the global stage.

The scramble and tussle for Africa is ongoing, and countries like China are slowly instituting their relevance on the continent. Perhaps a future research and examination could look at the growing relevance of China on the continent as a superpower and its prospect in Africa. The question would then be, whether Africa would ever have sincere allies that would deal with it on its own terms—a true and right term—based on benefit that does not promote the superpowers but can help Africa flourish as a continent.

Lastly, the reality today is that Africa is in a vulnerable position and still needs the help of superpowers, as "war of all kinds attract intervention, and this may come in many guises. Apart from military assistance to one or the other side, or efforts at peacekeeping, a war situation attracts offers of aid—for humanitarian purposes, to enable an interested outside power to maintain a footing in the country, or to assist in the subsequent rebuilding and rehabilitation of a war-ravaged territory."[34] In essence, Africa's inability to support itself at this time requires that external interventions are revisited and conceived as a conviction to ensure the existence of the African states in a war, and not the amplification of economic benefits, and hegemonic expansion of superpowers—for really, what is the idea of being a superpower when the only value of its "super" lacks excellence and is nothing but a superlative loss of human existence?

Notes

1. This is a central argument in Mamdani's book: Mahmood Mamdani, *Citizen and Subject: Contemporary Africa and the Legacy of Late Colonialism*. (Princeton, NJ: Princeton University Press, 1996).
2. Mohamed Ahmed Ali Taisier and Robert O Matthews. *Civil Wars in Africa: Roots and Resolution*. (Montreal [Que.]: McGill-Queen's University Press, 1999): 3–4.
3. "South Sudan Country Profile." BBC News. Accessed September 21, 2018. https://www.bbc.com/news/world-africa-14069082
4. Guy Arnold. *Historical Dictionary of Civil Wars in Africa*. (Lanham, MD: Scarecrow Press, 1999): 36–48.
5. Guy. *Historical Dictionary of Civil Wars in Africa*. 279–280.
6. Ibid. 168–169.
7. Joseph S. Nye. "Superpower Ethics: An Introduction". *Ethics & International Affairs* Volume 1, Issue 1: (March 1987): 1–7. doi:https://doi.org/10.1111/j.1747-7093.1987.tb00510.x
8. Liberia and Ethiopia also suffered the fate of civil war though they were not colonized by other countries. They, however, suffered the effect of typical issues

which led to an outbreak of war and resulted in the influences of foreign powers in their affairs.
9. Benson. O. Igboin. "Colonialism and African Cultural Values" African Journal of History and Culture, Vol. 3(6), 2011: 121.
10. Guy. *Historical Dictionary of Civil Wars in Africa*. 83.
11. For more on the "Scramble for Africa" read Barbara Harlow, and Mia Carter. *The Scramble for Africa*. (Durham, N.C.: Duke University Press 2003).
12. Paul Eric, "The Amalgamation of Nigeria: Revisiting 1914 and the Centenary Celebrations" *Canadian Social Science* Vol. 12, No. 12, 2016, pp. 66–68, DOI:https://doi.org/10.3968/9079
13. Fred Marte. *Political Cycles in International Relations: The Cold War and Africa, 1945–1990*. (Amsterdam, Netherlands: VU University Press, 1994).
14. Roberto Suro. "Papal Encyclical Says Superpowers Hurt Third World" https://www.nytimes.com/1988/02/20/world/papal-encyclical-says-superpowers-hurt-third-world.html
15. Gavin Raymond. "Causes of Civil War in Africa." Academia.edu – Share Research. Accessed October 22, 2018. https://www.academia.edu/3372289/Causes_of_Civil_War_in_Africa
16. Guy. *Historical Dictionary of Civil Wars in Africa*. 82.
17. John Deigh. "What is Ethics" *An Introduction to Ethics*. (Cambridge: Cambridge University Press) 7 https://www-cambridge-org.login.ezproxy.library.ualberta.ca/core/books/an-introduction-to-ethics/BF9730043EBE96B6C9DE420748C9A990. Print 2010, Online Publication, June 2012.
18. Elechi Amadi, *Ethics in Nigerian Culture*. (Ibadan: Heinemann Educational 1982): 30–41.
19. Nye, "Superpower Ethics: An Introduction", 2.
20. Mazuri, Ali, "Superpower Ethics: A Third World Perspective" *Ethics and International Affairs, vol. 1, 1987, pp. 9–21*.
21. Ibid. p. 11.
22. Ibid. p. *17*.
23. De St. Jorre, John, *The Nigerian Civil War*. (London: Hodder and Stoughton, 1972). 121.
24. De St. Jorre, *The Nigerian Civil War*.
25. Robert Benjamin Shepard, "Superpower and Regional Power: The United States and Nigeria, 1960–1979." (PhD diss., John Hopkins University. 1984) 35. University Microfilms International, Ann Arbor, Michigan, USA.
26. Chibuike Uche. "Oil, British Interests and The Nigerian Civil War." *The Journal of African History* 49, no. 1 (2008): 111–35. doi:https://doi.org/10.1017/S0021853708003393
27. Griffin Christopher, "France and the Nigerian Civil War" in *Postcolonial Conflict and the Question of Genocide: The Nigeria-Biafra War, 1967–1970*, ed. Moses, A. Dirk, and Lasse Heerten. (New York: Routledge, 2018), 156–177.
28. Shepard, "Superpower and Regional Power: The United States and Nigeria, 1960–1979." 51–52.
29. Shepard, "Superpower and Regional Power: The United States and Nigeria, 1960–1979." 22, 24.

30. Matusevich Maxim, "Strange Bedfellows: An Unlikely Alliance Between the Soviet Union and Nigeria During the Biafra War", *Postcolonial Conflict and the Question of Genocide: The Nigeria-Biafra War, 1967–1970*. 156–177.
31. Olajide Aluko. "Nigeria and the Superpowers." Millennium 5, no. 2 (September 1976): 128. doi:https://doi.org/10.1177/03058298760050020401
32. Stanley Hoffmann. "The Rules of the Game." *Ethics & International Affairs* 1 (1987): 37–51. doi:https://doi.org/10.1111/j.1747-7093.1987.tb00513.x
33. Nimi Wariboko. *The Principle of Excellence: A Framework for Social Ethics.* Lanham, Md.: Lexington Books, 2009., 182.
34. Arnold, Guy. *Historical Dictionary of Civil Wars in Africa.* Lanham, MD: Scarecrow Press, 1999.

Bibliography

Achebe, Chinua. 1994. *Things Fall Apart.* New York: First Anchor Books Edition.
Aluko, Olajide. 1976. Nigeria and the Superpowers. *Millennium* 5 (2): 128. https://doi.org/10.1177/03058298760050020401.
Amadi, Elechi. 1982. *Ethics in Nigerian Culture.* Ibadan: Heinemann Educational.
BBC News. South Sudan Country Profile. https://www.bbc.com/news/world-africa-14069082. Accessed 21 Sept 2018.
De St. Jorre, John. 1972. *The Nigerian Civil War.* London: Hodder and Stoughton.
Eric, Paul. 2016. The Amalgamation of Nigeria: Revisiting 1914 and the Centenary Celebrations. *Canadian Social Science* 12 (12): 66–68. https://doi.org/10.3968/9079.
Griffin, Christopher. 2018. France and the Nigerian Civil War. In *Postcolonial Conflict and the Question of Genocide: The Nigeria-Biafra War, 1967–1970*, ed. A. Dirk Moses and Lasse Heerten, 156–177. New York: Routledge.
Guy, Arnold. 1999. *Historical Dictionary of Civil Wars in Africa.* Lanham: Scarecrow Press.
Harlow, Barbara, and Mia Carter. 2003. *The Scramble for Africa.* Durham: Duke University Press.
Hoffmann, Stanley. 1987. The Rules of the Game. *Ethics & International Affairs* 1: 37–51. https://doi.org/10.1111/j.1747-7093.1987.tb00513.x.
Igboin, O. Benson. 2011. Colonialism and African Cultural Values. *African Journal of History and Culture* 3 (6): 93–103. http://www.academicjournals.org/app/webroot/article/article1381858600_Igboin.pdf
John, Deigh. 2010. What is Ethics. In *An Introduction to Ethics.* Cambridge: Cambridge University Press, Print 2010, Online Publication, June 2012. https://www-cambridge-org.login.ezproxy.library.ualberta.ca/core/books/an-introduction-to-ethics/BF9730043EBE96B6C9DE420748C9A990
Mamdani, Mahmood. 1996. *Citizen and Subject: Contemporary Africa and the Legacy of Late Colonialism.* Princeton: Princeton University Press.
Marte, Fred. 1994. *Political Cycles in International Relations: The Cold War and Africa, 1945–1990.* Amsterdam: VU University Press.
Matusevich, Maxim. 2018. Strange Bedfellows: An Unlikely Alliance Between the Soviet Union and Nigeria During the Biafra War. In *Postcolonial Conflict and the Question of Genocide: The Nigeria-Biafra War, 1967–1970*, ed. A. Dirk Moses and Lasse Heerten. New York: Routledge. e-book.

Mazuri, Ali. 1987. Superpower Ethics: A Third World Perspective. *Ethics and International Affairs* 1 (1): 10–21.
Nye, Joseph S. 1987. Superpower Ethics: An Introduction. *Ethics & International Affairs* 1 (1): 1–7. https://doi.org/10.1111/j.1747-7093.1987.tb00510.x.
Raymond, Gavin. Causes of Civil War in Africa. Academia.edu – Share Research. https://www.academia.edu/3372289/Causes_of_Civil_War_in_Africa. Accessed 22 Oct 2018.
Rowlandson, Mary. 2016. The Narrative of My Captivity. In *The Making of the American Essay*, ed. John D'Agata, 19–56. Minneapolis: Graywolf Press.
Shepard, Robert Benjamin. 1984. Superpower and Regional Power: The United States and Nigeria 1960–1979. PhD Dissertation, John Hopkins University, Baltimore. University Microfilms International, Ann Arbor, Michigan, USA.
Suro, Roberto. Papal Encyclical Says Superpowers Hurt Third World. https://www.nytimes.com/1988/02/20/world/papal-encyclical-says-superpowers-hurt-third-world.html
Taisier, Mohamed Ahmed Ali, and Robert O. Matthews. 1999. *Civil Wars in Africa: Roots and Resolution*. Montreal: McGill-Queen's University Press.
Uche, Chibuike. 2008. Oil, British Interests and the Nigerian Civil War. *The Journal of African History* 49 (1): 111–135. https://doi.org/10.1017/S0021853708003393.
Wariboko, Nimi. 2009. *The Principle of Excellence: A Framework for Social Ethics*. Lanham: Lexington Books.

CHAPTER 13

When the Ancestors Wage War: Mystical Movements and the Ethics of War and Warfare

Georgette Mulunda Ledgister

The meeting with the leaders of the eastern factions of the Mai-Mai was set to last for an hour. It was the eve of my 20th birthday, and I could not help but wonder whether or not I would live long enough to see the day—or any other day for that matter. Sensing my discomfort, Paul[1] turned to look me square in the face before exiting our taxi.

"Are you alright?"

I nodded.

"I need you to speak, and to tell me that you're alright."

Frustration at his line of questioning provided the emotional reprieve from sheer terror that I needed. I cleared my too-dry throat.

"Yes. I'm okay. I can do this."

By "this" I meant that I could regain and keep my wits about me long enough to interpret for Paul Mawere during our hour-long meeting with the leadership and political envoys of the Mai-Mai. It was only the second day of our six-day preelection assessment mission to the Democratic Republic of Congo (Congo henceforth)—a country reeling from an estimated 5.4 million deaths as a result of war, starvation, and disease. Our delegation of four had already met with leaders and representatives of each of the key players of the 1+4 transitional government—as the Congolese transitional government at that time was popularly called—and we were not yet halfway down our list of appointments.[2] Ironically, the Mai-Mai, arguably the deadliest faction of the war, was excluded from this power-sharing agreement, and its leaders were intent on making their discontent known.[3]

"All I have to do is interpret, right?"

G. M. Ledgister (✉)
Agnes Scott College, Atlanta, GA, USA

As Paul knitted his brows in concern, I realized how facile my question had been. Serving as an interpreter required translation of words and meaning but also interpretation of facts and accounts. We were meeting with groups that had very specific agendas that they wanted to sell to the international organization we represented. Interpretation was everything to the Mai-Mai.

Paul frowned.

"Yes. And—"

"I know, Paul." I sighed. "I know. I'm ready." I exited the taxi.

Paul was a father of three, and of Zimbabwean origin. He was a veteran of the Zimbabwean army, and had a surgically repaired left knee to show for it. However, he was renowned in international development and conflict resolution circles for his skill and capacity to befriend and negotiate with almost anyone he met—from warlords to headstrong soon-to-be-20-year-old interns. It was not lost on me that our chief of delegation had "assigned" the meeting with the Mai-Mai to me and Paul—two persons of African descent—Congolese and Zimbabwean, respectively. They—two White men—were meeting with majority party leaders at the same time.

Our shoes crunched on the gravel walkway that led to the entrance of what looked like a large, vacant warehouse, in a quiet quarter of the Gombe business district of Kinshasa, the capital of Congo. We were greeted at the entrance of the building by two armed guards in khaki fatigues. My eyes darted to the AK-47s they carried, when I remembered Paul's coaching not to stare at weapons or at faces. Paul introduced us, and we were escorted inside the warehouse as soon as I finished interpreting his introduction.

The warehouse appeared to be a single room with bare concrete floors, concrete walls that were painted a creamy white, and boasted small rectangular windows cut more than three-quarters of the way up the four walls. There were no panes or frames in the windows—just rough-hewn rectangular openings that allowed some light to filter into the otherwise unlit room. My eyes went from scanning the windows—perhaps searching for an escape—to examining the seating arrangements. Our hosts had arranged two rows of ten chairs facing one another across a distance that could have been 10 or 15 feet. Four Mai-Mai leaders dressed in *abacosts*—short-sleeved khaki suits that required neither suit nor tie, and were the fashion of choice of many Congolese politicians at the time—were seated in the center of their row, with three vacant chairs at each end.[4] Behind them stood two more armed guards, sporting weapons and facial expressions that suggested they would not hesitate to use those weapons when necessary. Our hosts gestured for us towards the seats across from them, and the conversation began.

Not surprisingly, the Mai-Mai leaders began by expressing displeasure at having received only half of our delegation—notably the nonwhite half of the delegation. As I interpreted their remarks to Paul, and in turn conveyed Paul's responses, I stole glances at each of the men seated in front of us, and noticed—with a visible start—that the man seated directly across from me (who appeared to be their chief spokesperson) had not closed the zipper of his pants. Paul felt my movement to his left, but did not skip a beat in the conversation. He waited for his turn to speak, and in the same breath that he asked the Mai-Mai—in English—what their vision for a stable Congo was, he added a few short words for me.

"I see it too. Don't react." I resumed my task of interpretation, feeling the terror that had threatened to incapacitate me disappear with every passing moment that this fearsome man's zipper remained agape. At that moment, I began to question the mental image of the Mai-Mai that I had created from the editorials, news reports, and aid agency reports that filled international outlets. The men seated in front of me were far shorter, and far more ordinary-looking than the towering, ruthless cannibals I had imagined. Furthermore, one of them had committed the most human of all errors—he had neglected to pull up the zipper of his pants!

Twelve years later, following eight months of ethnographic research in Congo with Chatty, a Mai-Mai warlord in the southeastern province of Upper Katanga, I reflected on the absurdity of the "zipper moment." While countless eyewitness testimonies of atrocities committed by Mai-Mai groups existed—testimonies that included fantastical tales of Mai-Mai mystical powers—fewer accounts spoke of the morality or, at a more fundamental level, the humanity of these indigenous warriors. Yet on March 11, 2006, I met with people—fearsome, mystically powerful, and infamous *people*. The dissonance that remained with me from my initial meeting with the Mai-Mai was not caused by my inability to justify the atrocities that millions of Congolese and international news outlets attributed to the Mai-Mai. I was troubled by my willingness to accept dehumanizing accounts of the Mai-Mai—who were only one group among many others that committed acts of violence during the Congolese Five-Year War of 1997–2002, to legitimate the creation of a political system that would empower some, and politically and socioeconomically disenfranchise others.

My deep hanging out with Chatty—to use Clifford Geertz's term—prompted me to interrogate my theoretical assumptions of the Mai-Mai and other indigenous combatant movements in Africa—theoretical assumptions that were not only informed by media representations of African warfare as nothing short of grotesquerie but were bolstered by the relative dearth of scholarship on the ethics of war in African conflicts.[5] What made the acts of violence committed by the Mai-Mai any more abhorrent than the rapes, killings, and lootings perpetrated by soldiers of the Forces Armées de la République Démocratique du Congo (FARDC), or worse yet, those acts committed by invading Rwandan and Ugandan forces and peacekeepers of the United Nations Organization Stabilization Mission in Congo (MONUC, later renamed MONUSCO)? Why did scholarship on the ethics of war fail to substantively engage the contemporary African context? Given the numerous armed conflicts on the African continent since the independence movements of the late nineteenth and twentieth centuries—conflicts funded by Western governments and business interests—how does one justify the epistemological silence of Western ethicists, and ethicists trained in the West, pertaining to Africa in scholarly discourse on wartime ethics?

This chapter engages the aforementioned questions by locating the moral source of a Mai-Mai, and more broadly speaking, an African ethic of war in the spiritual lifeworld that encompasses the African world-sense, and analyzing the imbrications between the material and immaterial in African warfare.[6] I contend that the epistemological silence on African wartime ethics is neither due to the absence of African moral agents in combat nor the lack of African moral sources that govern human conduct in times of war and peace. Rather, Western scholarship on the subject has sublimated African voices because Western scholarship retains a myopic and panoptic view of the African person and her morality. The accounts of Mai-Mai warriors like Chatty Masangu wa Nkulu, daughter and second-in-command of the forces of the infamous Wilson Vwende wa Mutompa Kalunga, leader of the Mai-Mai in the Upper Katanga Province of Congo, invite one to inhabit the interstices of several intersecting worlds: war and peace, life and death, and person and community.

By focusing on the spiritual lifeworld—the social imaginary which Catholic moral theologian Laurenti Magesa (1997) and practical theologian Fulgence Nyengele (2014) argue frames much of African lived experience—I turn to African spirituality and its accompanying ontology to anchor the humanity and morality of combatants during war. Contra normative studies on the ethics of war, which focus primarily on large-scale, organized violence between institutions that legitimately possess a monopoly on violence, or are vying for such a monopoly—studies which begin with *jus ad bellum* justifications for war—this chapter begins and remains firmly grounded in conceptions of personhood and the formation of the African moral self.

Beyond *Jus Ad Bellum*: The Roots of an African Ethic of War

While considerations of what qualifies a war as just, namely legitimate authority, just cause, proportionality, last resort, the conduct of war, noncombatant immunity, and considerations for peacemaking, are indeed important, numerous scholars have already written richly, thoughtfully, and critically about just war theory. Most recently, A.J. Coates's (2016) volume *The Ethics of War*, William Shaw's (2016) *Utilitarianism and the Ethics of War*, and Pamela Creed's (2013) *Ethics, Norms and the Narratives of War: Creating and Encountering the Enemy Other* not only focus on conflicts that carry direct foreign and domestic policy implications for Western nations, they study the possibilities and limitations of just war principles, given Western scholarship's preoccupation with the changing landscape of war and its accompanying technologies.

Since the United Nations Charter of 1945 that created the United Nations and delineated reasonable conditions under which states could justify engaging in a war or using armed violence—collectively referred to as *jus ad bellum*, or the right to war, ethical analyses of war have focused on institutional or meta causes of war, sublimating the persons that actually engage in the act of killing on behalf of their country. Not to be confused with *jus in bello*, a set of guidelines that regulate moral conduct during war, paying particular attention to issues of collateral damage and treatment of combatants, *jus ad bellum* sets the ground rules for war for all member nations of the United Nations, before such a war should even be declared. However, given the plurality of sociopolitical factors and complex historical contexts in which most wars are fought, making clear determinations of what constitutes a just or ethical war is a problematic task at best. As history has shown, not only does the victor of a war claim the right to shape history, but the victor also single-handedly inhabits the moral high ground. Universal guidelines for war have done little more than empower the authors of such guidelines. However, scholarship on war and ethics has begun to take a turn away from the universal, toward the particular—albeit a slow turn.

Although she focuses specifically on the Iraq War of 2003–2011, Pamela Creed (2013) analyzes wartime myths and the role of public memory in the creation of narratives that justify war—which in the case of American post-9/11 rhetoric was the dismantling of networks of terror and the defense of democracy. Her text returns narrative—personal and public—to the core of ethical inquiry on war, emphasizing that the discourses that people create about themselves, and the corresponding dehumanizing discourse they weave around the enemy other, comprise a moral backdrop that demands and even obligates a moral agent to resort to war, well before *jus ad bellum* comes into play. According to Creed, "Myth, public memory and militarism begin with language and are grounded in perceived categories of reality that constitute belief systems."[7] Quoting President Bush's infamous reference to the romanticism of American soldiers fighting for "a young democracy" and his envy of their role in "making history" in Iraq, Creed makes a compelling argument for analyzing the belief systems that inform the particular, private motivations and dispositions toward war, before making a turn toward the public and institutional actions that make war a reality.[8]

Similarly, Séverine Autesserre's (2010) research on the local causes and sources of conflict, particularly in Congo, focuses on the micro concerns of communities that engage in armed conflict, and the danger that such communities pose to national peace and reconstruction when their demands are not deemed urgent enough in the face of national and international concerns. Both Creed and Autesserre make a similar epistemological move in their scholarship—moving from the global to the local, and from the universal to the particular—expanding the study of wartime ethics in revelatory ways. However, even Creed and Autesserre's analyses are invariably influenced by *jus ad bellum* preoccupations. Their scholarship belies a Western prioritization of the state and its actors as the primary agents in war, and the elevation of reason as a source for moral formation and conduct, in service to an idealized polis created and sustained primarily by a select few.

Models of communal life—particularly public life—that do not conform to the idealized polis are eschewed in a normative approach to wartime ethics, precluding engagement with forms of warfare—mystical warfare—that are gaining momentum and heightening the precarity of daily life for many Africans on the continent. To quote historian Torkel Brekke, one of the few Western scholars whose research focuses on comparative wartime ethics in Western and non-Western contexts, "the academic study of the ethics of war often takes the European just war tradition as its point of departure."[9] Manuel Barcia, also a historian, responds to the epistemological asymmetry of Western scholarship on the ethics of war, by researching the ethics intrinsic to the resistance warfare conducted by enslaved West Africans in the Americas and the Caribbean in the nineteenth century. Decrying the Western theoretical assumption that African modes of knowing, and more specifically African modes of being, must be "backward" given the state of African economies when compared to their Western counterparts, Barcia writes:

> Such a biased understanding of warfare has frequently led authors to offer hypothetical lose-lose situations as examples in which their protagonists—which are almost always white western observers, facing non-white, non-western actors—are presented with moral dilemmas for which there are no viable ways out. Certainly[,] none through which they can redeem their western humanity and superior moral standing. Confronted with the brutality and ethical dubiousness of non-white, non-western antagonists, these white western protagonists are often forced to commit a minor atrocity, in the hope of a avoiding a major one perpetrated by those putting them [on] the spot.[10]

Barcia argues, and I agree, that academic discourse on the ethics of war must include an African ethic of war—an ethical framework that attends to the spiritual lifeworld in which African combatants experience daily life, and subsequently informs and determines what qualifies as moral action during war. In search of an African ethic of war, the discipline must not only embrace and deepen its commitment to shifting from the universal to the particular, and from the public to the private. More importantly, I contend that such an epistemological shift, particularly in African contexts, must be accompanied by a methodological shift from the etic toward the emic.

THE LAW OF THE MAI-MAI: AN ETHNOGRAPHIC ACCOUNT OF A MAI-MAI ETHIC OF WAR

In my research on agency, gender, and war, I had the privilege of living with Chatty, a former warlord of the Mai-Mai movement—a diffuse self-defense movement that spanned the four eastern-most provinces of Congo, and incidentally, the most mineral-rich regions of the country (*mai* is Swahili or Lingala for water). Mai-Mai groups were convened around local leaders and their beliefs were grounded in the reverence of the land of their ancestors. Subsequently, Mai-Mai groups in neighboring provinces, and even in neighboring districts within the same provinces, had little to no contact with other Mai-Mai, or were at times at odds with satellite groups, fighting to protect their own villages and constituencies. Mai-Mai recruits were largely poor civilians in remote parts of the country, like my informant Chatty, who had no military training, and were too far outside of the military, political, and economic purview of the Congolese government, which struggled to administer a country that could encompass all of Western Europe within its borders. Rather than succumbing to the destruction, pillaging, looting, and rape of their communities—hallmarks of their material and physical conditions as vulnerable citizens of a distant government—the women, men, and youth in villages like Kabumbulu, Chatty's home village in the district of Malemba-Nkulu in mineral-rich southeastern Congo, elected to join the Mai-Mai to access mystical ancestral power that would enable them to defend their villages from invading Rwandan and Ugandan forces during the Congolese Five-Year War.

The choice to join an armed movement and to fight in a war points to the moral agency of Chatty and others like her who link their well-being to the flourishing of their community and to that of their land. In my interviews with Chatty, she named protection of the land and defense of her people as the primary objectives of the Mai-Mai: "Becoming a Mai-Mai is a sacrifice. You *choose* to suffer. *Leza*[11] gives you the power to endure suffering because you choose to fight to defend your country and your people," she recounted during one of our interviews (Ledgister 2018). Sacrifice and choice were recurrent themes in Chatty's narrative, in part describing the harsh realities of a war that took its toll on already poor and vulnerable communities that fought to protect themselves, and also disabusing me of any Western propensity to romanticize warfare, and least of all, mystical warfare. In an excerpt of an interview I conducted with Chatty about the Law of the Mai-Mai, she shared the following about the moral code that simultaneously informed the Mai-Mai's impetus for using ancestral power to engage in armed conflict (*jus ad bellum*) and regulated conduct during war (*jus in bello*):

"What is the Law of the Mai-Mai?"

"You can't touch someone who is not Mai-Mai. You can't even touch their food, their money, or anything. The only thing we can take is weapons. At [the village of] Kachumbuyu Longo-Longo where they [the…Mai-Mai] had surrounded the rebels, they found bags of American dollars, food, and many other things. They could not touch any of it. If they were hungry or thirsty, they had to eat on the other side of the river. They burned everything they saw—even the money."

"Why? Wouldn't that money have helped the [local] Mai-Mai?" She was emphatic in her response.

"No! You don't become a Mai-Mai to enrich yourself."[12]

The sole benefit that becoming a Mai-Mai afforded anyone who joined the movement was protection during combat. Chatty explained that the power of the Mai-Mai resided in the ritual water or *mai* with which each warrior was doused prior to combat. The ritualized water served as bullet protection for all who underwent the ritual, preventing bullets from piercing one's skin. The *mai* ritual, and other rituals that Mai-Mai fighters underwent, permitted them to straddle the material world as the embodied living and the immaterial world of the disembodied living—the world of the ancestors. Unsanctioned contact with the material world could jeopardize the delicate balance that enabled the Mai-Mai to access mystical power, hence the prohibition against touching the uninitiated, or attempting to enrich oneself with the spoils of war. Violation of the Law of the Mai-Mai could mean life or death for fighters who depended solely on mystical power as their military strategy, to overcome their lack of training and resources.

Whereas the embodied living were constrained by the laws of physics and their socioeconomic conditions, the world of the ancestors transcended the limitations of the material world. The mystical rituals that the Mai-Mai underwent allowed them access to a power that enabled them to overcome the restrictions of embodied existence, and made them redoubtable foes during combat. Chatty recalled an instance during the war when her village was attacked by armed soldiers of the Congolese military, sent to subdue her father's forces and to compel them to pledge allegiance to a government that had heretofore neglected the existence of her people. She was surrounded by a platoon of soldiers pointing weapons at her, and she reported freezing these soldiers in place using only a handful of soil and an invocation to the ancestors. I could not verify the veracity of Chatty's accounts, nor did I attempt to so. The instance that she recounted was only one of several supernatural acts that her positionality as a mystical warrior afforded her. Furthermore, Chatty was far from being the only Mai-Mai who purportedly performed supernatural feats in combat during the Congolese Five-Year War.

In her article "'Is it Witchcraft? Is it Satan? It is a Miracle.' Mai Mai Soldiers and Christian Concepts of Evil in North-East Congo," Emma Wild (1998) analyzes accounts of Mai-Mai mystical power in the liberation of the northeastern Congolese provinces from Rwandan invasion, and specifically Christian responses to this power. Unable to explain or rationalize what force could permit a group of untrained civilians to defeat a well-armed military invasion, Wild's Christian informants struggle to reconcile Mai-Mai mystical combat with their spiritual grammar that does not offer them the means to conceptualize human action from beyond the grave. Wild's informants find a tenable middle ground between their Christian ideology and their need for Mai-Mai protection by grudgingly embracing the "evil" power of the Mai-Mai, and framing this power as a miracle permitted by their Judeo-Christian God (and performed through Mai-Mai action). Yet, Congolese Christians' oversimplification or misconceptions of Mai-Mai notwithstanding, the fact remained that the Mai-Mai wielded a supernatural capacity that enabled them to survive a war that they should have lost. In many instances, as Wild's informants and Chatty note, ancestral and mystical power enabled the Mai-Mai to rebuff the attacks of invading military forces, driving out trained and well-resourced armies, where the Congolese military itself had failed. To analyze the source of Mai-Mai power, and the agency at work in ordinary civilians' decision to turn toward local non-Western spiritualities and sources of knowledge during war, I turn to the work of catholic moral theologians, Laurenti Magesa (1997) and Bénézet Bujo (2001).

From Reason to Relationality: The Shift from Ideology to Ontology in an African Ethic of War

Mai-Mai warfare, and African mystical warfare in general, finds its origins in the spiritual practices and belief systems that encompass much of the African lifeworld. Constructing an African ethic of war necessitates engagement with the values and virtues of indigenous belief systems that regulate life in times of peace and in times of war. The stories of ancestral intervention in combat through the actions of warriors like Chatty point to the communotheistic nature of African spirituality, to use Dianne M. Stewart's (2005) term. Stewart introduces communotheism as a concept that captures the centrality of communal life in the African quotidian, not just in the material world but in the construction of African spirituality, which encompasses communities of the invisible interacting with communities of the visible.[13] By resisting the structuralist tendency to number the deities in the African lifeworld, a numbering that justifies the monotheistic-polytheistic binary that informs the thinking of many Congolese Christians, Stewart argues that the immaterial and material worlds function in a symbiotic relationship that serves as a model for daily life. Laurenti Magesa (1997) and Bénézet Bujo (1992, 2001) similarly name the interrelatedness of the African lifeworld not only as a value in African moral philosophy but as the source of the supernatural essence that fuels mystical warfare.

Using Christian theological framings, Magesa defines vital force, the building block of life and the essence that unifies all creation—embodied and disembodied living alike—as a spark of the Divine in creation.[14] Bujo advances Magesa's thesis of vital force by using the concept of the *imago Dei* to develop an African Christian theology that not only claims that human beings are created in the likeness and image of the Divine, but that human beings and all of creation contain the likeness of the Divine. As a result, all interactions within creation are necessarily interactions with divinity. This theological understanding of vital force has sociological and philosophical implications, placing ontology as the foundational concern in African moral philosophy—a concern that constitutes justification for moral action in times of peace and in times of war.

By understanding the African world-sense as ontological or oriented toward the nature of being, the rules of engagement that ensure the flourishing—namely the increase of the vital force—of persons and of the communities in which persons live become paramount. Vital force consequently functions not just as an ordering principle, life-giving energy, and a spark of the Divine within creation, but it also functions as a connecting and moralizing principle. In this sense, therefore, communities are understood to be made of persons, persons who understand that they exist within community, and are formed and supported in community, and that their flourishing is intricately tied to that of the community. With the promotion of community flourishing as the primary goal, communities develop mores and practices to that end. Moral education takes place within the community and with the participation of the entire community, which understands the education and moral formation of its members as a philosophical, spiritual, and cultural task. To be clear, war disrupts the conditions under which moral formation occurs in times of peace by placing pressure on existing social networks of care in communities like the village of Kabumbulu—Chatty's home—further compromising already socially and economically vulnerable communities. However, the moral commitment to preserve the flourishing and vital force of communities, despite the constraints of war, remains the same. Given that one's community is not limited to the embodied living, the recourse for communities like the village of Kabumbulu, which are under-resourced, powerless, and economically vulnerable, is to turn to the supernatural capabilities—and agency—available to them through the ancestors.

Ordinary persons, like Chatty, who chose to undergo the esoteric water ritual that transforms one from a civilian to a formidable fighter, equally chose to live in their present vulnerable circumstance, from and through the supernatural power and action of the ancestors. They purportedly performed feats such as using ordinary soil to immobilize their aggressors and to relieve them of their weapons, to conjuring hives of bees to tactically attack invading forces and fight alongside the Mai-Mai (Ledgister 2018). The ancestors—spirits of women and men who changed their address from the world of the living to the world of the disembodied living—transcended materiality and time, uniting the past with the present and future. As a Mai-Mai, Chatty could circumvent the limitations of the present by tapping into an atemporal power to take action in the present, thereby securing her future and that of her community. To become Mai-Mai was her ultimate expression of agency—a refusal to be a casualty of war, and a reclaiming of her moral duty to preserve her own vital force, and that of her community. To be a Mai-Mai was to be a moral agent, and vice versa.

Emerging Trends in Mystico-Political Warfare: Concluding Remarks

Unearthing an African ethic of war that fully embraces the African spiritualities in which such an ethic is embedded not only critically expands ethical discourse on the subject but offers a framework for understanding and engaging mystical warfare in the public sphere. On May 17, 2017, followers of Bundu dia Kongo (BDK)—a movement that MONUSCO has labeled a religious sect—staged the largest prison break in Congolese history, freeing thousands of inmates (some local sources say over 4000) from the Makala maximum-security prison in Kinshasa, the nation's capital.[15] According to news reports, an unknown number of BDK members, called "cultish rebel[s]" in *The New York Times*, stormed the gates of Makala prison, and reportedly stabbed and beheaded prison guards with the use of blunt sticks.[16] Eyewitnesses cited the BDK's intent to free their leader, Ne Muanda Nsemi, who was imprisoned at Makala as the motivation for the group's attack. Naming their mission as a missiological campaign to reverse the ills of colonization in Congo, and to restore the Kingdom of Kongo to its precolonial glory and preeminence on the continent, followers of BDK, mostly youth, have resorted to the use of mystical power to violently assert their political aims.[17] In October of that same year, Mai-Mai fighters stormed the local prison in Pweto, a town in Chatty's home province of Upper Katanga, also using seemingly harmless objects to harm and kill prison guards, freeing an indeterminate number of Mai-Mai who had been arrested at the prison, and capturing noninitiated prisoners. Only two people escaped the attack alive and evaded capture. My cousin's spouse was one of them. He escaped by tearing down the flimsy drywall and plywood of the provincial prison cell's ceiling, and concealing himself in the rafters until the attack ended (Ledgister 2018). Mystical warfare, or the use of supernatural capacities, is neither a new phenomenon on the continent nor is it a military strategy unique to Congo. Since the independence movements of the late nineteenth and early twentieth centuries in Africa, groups such as the Mau Mau of Kenya, and militias commanded by leaders like Joshua Milton Blahyi, a young priest of the Krahn people of Liberia who fought under the sobriquet of "General Butt-Naked" during the first Liberian civil war, the mystical and political have gone hand in hand in African conflicts. However, the use of deadly mystical power to stage large-scale violence in times of peace or stability is an emerging trend to which scholars and public officials alike must attend.

The diffuse nature of mystico-political movements, the esoteric nature of recruitment—given the spiritual dimensions of such movements—and the unclear political agendas of many mystico-political movements in the postcolonial period render groups such as the Mai-Mai a daunting and unpredictable player in the public sphere. However, as the recent prison breaks in Congo have shown, ignoring these groups—and the deadly agency of groups like the Mai-Mai who have the capacity to wield a seemingly unstoppable force—could spell disaster. Yet, as this chapter shows, by understanding vital force as the essence of mystical power in African warfare, by unearthing the community-oriented ethic that instantiates such a power, and by elevating the agency of ordinary persons who turn to indigenous sources as recourse during war, scholars of African social ethics and war have the potential of informing policy that can lead to peace and prevent war.

Notes

1. Names have been changed to maintain anonymity.
2. In a last-ditch effort to prevent a five-year conflict that international journalists were calling "the deadliest war since World War II," national and international mediators negotiated a peace agreement to end the Congolese Five-Year War in 2002 (Jeffrey Gettleman, "Africa's Worst War," *The New York Times* Sunday Review, December 12, 2012, https://www.nytimes.com/2012/12/16/sunday-review/congos-never-ending-war.html; Séverine Autesserre, *The Trouble with the Congo: Local Violence and the Failure of International Peacebuilding*, New York: Cambridge University Press, 2010).
3. The Congolese transition government of 2003–2006 was the first to have an executive branch comprising one president from the majority party, Joseph Kabila, and four vice presidents, each representing the largest rebel factions during the war. The brainchild of a compromise designed to end further war at all costs, the 1+4 government (as it was commonly called) consolidated all armed factions in the Congolese Five-Year War into one national army, and saw to the organization of the first set of elections in Congo since its independence in 1960 (United States Institute of Peace, "Truth Commission: Democratic Republic of Congo," 2003) (see Georges Nzongola-Ntalaja, *The Congo From Leopold to Kabila: A People's History* [Chicago: Zed Books, 2002]).
4. The *abacost* was a deeply political fashion statement of Congolese (then Zairean) men—political elite or otherwise—that had its genesis in the late 1970s and early 1980s. The shortened form of the French phrase *abats le costume* (literally, "down with the suit"), the *abacost* rejected the attire and conformity of colonial rule, and became one of the key symbols of the Zaireanization initiatives of the regime of Mobutu Sésé Séko (Eyamba G. Bokamba, "D.R. Congo: Language and 'Authentic Nationalism,'" in *Language and National Identity in Africa*, ed. Andrew Simpson (Oxford: Oxford University Press, 2008), 228.
5. Manuel Barcia's research on African warfare and the ethics of war in Africa remains one of the notable exceptions in the field of wartime ethics, in its analysis of West African warfare in the Americas in the nineteenth century. See Manuel Barcia, *West African Warfare in Bahia and Cuba: Soldier Slaves in the Atlantic World, 1807–1844*, Oxford and New York: Oxford University Press (2014).
6. In lieu of employing the term worldview to indicate Western conceptions of and apprehension of the world, I am using Oyèrónkẹ́ Oyěwùmí's concept of worldsense. She critiques the Western prioritization of sight as the primary sense operating in social interaction that creates a subject that gazes upon an object (Oyèrónkẹ́ Oyěwùmí, *The Invention of Women: Making an African Sense of Western Gender Discourses* [Minneapolis: University of Minnesota Press, 1997]), 3.
7. Pamela Creed, *Ethics, Norms and the Narratives of War: Creating and Encountering the Enemy Other* (London: Routledge, 2013), 2.
8. Creed, *Ethics, Norms and the Narratives of War*, 2.
9. Torkel Brekke, "The Ethics of War and the Concept of War in India and Europe," *Numen: International Review for the History of Religions*, 52, 1 (2005), 60.
10. Manuel Barcia, "'To Kill all Whites': The Ethics of African Warfare in Bahia and Cuba, 1807–1844," *The Journal of African Military History*, 1 (2017): 75.

11. The closest English translation of *Leza* from Chatty's native language of Kiluba is Deity or God. Chatty was careful to differentiate between *Leza*, the Luba Deity or God, and the ancestors. She defined the latter as the departed living (Chatty Masangu wa Nkulu, interview with author, Lubumbashi, Democratic Republic of Congo, September 29, 2017).
12. Chatty Masangu wa Nkulu, interview by author, Lubumbashi, Democratic Republic of Congo, September 29, 2017.
13. Dianne M. Stewart, *Three Eyes for the Journey: African Dimensions of the Jamaican Religious Experience* (New York: Oxford University Press, 2005), 24.
14. Laurenti Magesa, *African Religion: The Moral Traditions of Abundant Life* (Maryknoll, NY: Orbis Books, 1997), 25.
15. Steve Wembi and Kimiko de Freytas-Tamura, "An Unfortunate Record for Congo: Thousands Flee Cells in Biggest Jailbreak," *New York Times*, May 19, 2017, https://www.nytimes.com/2017/05/19/world/africa/congo-prison-break-kabila.html
16. Ibid.
17. Bundu dia Kongo, "About Us: What is Bundu dia Kongo?" Bundu dia Kongo, August 10, 2017, http://bundu-dia-kongo.org/about/index.html.

Bibliography

Amnesty International. 2003. *On the Precipice: The Deepening Human Rights and Humanitarian Crisis in Ituri*. New York: Amnesty International.

Autesserre, Severine. 2010. *The Trouble with the Congo: Local Violence and the Failure of International Peacebuilding*. New York: Cambridge University Press.

Barcia, Manuel. 2017. "To Kill All Whites": The Ethics of African Warfare in Bahia and Cuba, 1807–1844. *The Journal of African Military History* 1: 72–92.

Bockie, Simon. 1993. *Death and the Invisible Powers: The World of Kongo Belief*. Bloomington: Indiana University Press.

Bokamba, Eyamba G. 2008. D.R. Congo: Language and 'Authentic Nationalism', In *Language and National Identity in Africa*, ed. Andrew Simpson. Oxford: Oxford University Press.

Brekke, Torkel. 2005. The Ethics of War and the Concept of War in India and Europe. *Numen: International Review for the History of Religions* 52 (1): 59–86.

Bujo, Bénézet. 1992. *African Theology in Its Social Contexts*. Eugene: Wipf & Stock.

———. 2001. *Foundations of an African Ethic*. Nairobi: Pauline Publications Africa.

Bundu Dia Kongo. n.d. *Bundu Dia Kongo*. http://bundu-dia-kongo.org/about/index.html. Accessed 10 Aug 2017.

Coates, A.J. 2016. *The Ethics of War*. Manchester: Manchester University Press.

Creed, Pamela. 2013. *Ethics, Norms and the Narratives of War: Creating and Encountering the Enemy Other*. London: Routledge.

Guy, Kitwe Mulunda. 2014. Mai-Mai Militia and Sexual Violence in Democratic Republic of the Congo. *International Journal of Emergency Mental Health and Human Resilience* 16 (2): 137–142.

Gyeke, K. 1992. Person and Community in Akan Thought. In *Person and Community*. Ghana: CRVP Press.

Human Rights Watch. 2016. *World Report 2016*. New York City: Human Rights Watch. https://www.hrw.org/sites/default/files/world_report_download/wr2016_web.pdf.

———. 2018. *Democratic Republic of Congo: Country Summary.* Country Summary. Human Rights Watch. https://www.hrw.org/world-report/2018/country-chapters/democratic-republic-congo#.
Ledgister, Georgette Ilunga-Nkulu Mulunda. 2018. Warriors of the Water: A Luba Mai-Mai Story of Agency, Personhood and Ancestral Power. PhD diss., Emory University.
Magesa, Laurenti. 1997. *African Religion: The Moral Traditions of Abundant Life.* Maryknoll: Orbis Books.
Mawere, Munyaradzi. 2011. *African Belief and Knowledge Systems: A Critical Perspective.* Mankon: Langaa Research & Publishing CIG.
Mbiti, J.S. 1990. *African Religions and Philosophy.* Oxford: Heinemann.
Menkiti, I. 1984. Person and Community in African Tradition Thought. In *African Philosophy.* London: Rowan and Littlefield.
Murove, Munyaradzi Felix. 2009. *African Ethics: An Anthology of Comparative Ethics.* Scottsville: University of KwaZulu-Natal Press.
———. 2016. *African Moral Consciousness: An Inquiry Into the Evolution of Perspectives and Prospects.* London: Austin Macauley Publishers.
Nyengele, Fulgence M. 2014. Cultivating Ubuntu: An African Postcolonial Pastoral Theological Engagement with Positive Psychology. *Journal of Pastoral Theology* 4: 1–35.
Nzongola-Ntalaja, Georges. 2002. *The Congo from Leopold to Kabila: A People's History.* Chicago: Zed Books.
Oyěwùmí, Oyèrónké. 1997. *The Invention of Women: Making an African Sense of Western Gender Discourses.* Minneapolis: University of Minnesota Press.
Perry, David L. 2016. *Partly Cloudy: Ethics in War, Espionage, Covert Action and Interrogation.* New York/London: Rowman & Littlefield.
Reynaert, Julie. 2010. *MONUC/MONUSCO and Civilian Protection in the Kivus,* Interns & Volunteers Series, 47. Antwerp, Belgium: IPIS.
Rohart, Frédéric. 2017. Heurts Sanglants à Kinshasa, en Pleine Instabilité Politique. *L'Écho,* August 8.
Shaw, William H. 2016. *Utilitarianism and the Ethics of War.* London: Routledge.
Stewart, Dianne M. 2005. *Three Eyes for the Journey: African Dimensions of the Jamaican Religious Experience.* New York: Oxford University Press.
Tull, Denis M. 2010. Troubled State-Building in the D R Congo: The Challenge from the Margins. *Journal of Modern African Studies* 48 (4): 643–661.
Wembi, Steve, and Kimiko de Freytas-Tamura. 2017. "An Unfortunate Record for Congo: Thousands Flee Cells in Biggest Jailbreak." *New York Times,* May 19.
Wild, Emma. 1998. 'Is it Witchcraft? Is it Satan? It Is a Miracle.' Mai-Mai Soldiers and Christian Concepts of Evil in North-East Congo. *Journal of Religion in Africa (Brill)* 28 (4): 450–467.
Wiredu, Kwasi. 1980. *Philosophy and an African Culture.* Cambridge: Cambridge University Press.
Yager, Thomas R. 2016. *2013 Minerals Yearbook: Congo (Kinshasa) [Advance Release].* U.S. Geological Survey, U.S. Department of the Interior, U.S. Geological Survey Minerals Yearbook.

CHAPTER 14

State and Society in Africa: A Comparative Perspective

Olufemi Vaughan

This chapter analyzes the interactions between the agencies of the modern nation-state and structures of society in Africa from the period of decolonization in the 1950s to the crisis precipitated by neo-liberal economic reforms at the end of the twentieth century. Analyzed in the context of local, national, and global forces that shaped the material conditions of local people, the chapter underscores the implications of the political calculations and decisions of the custodians of state power for governance and development in African states after the attainment of independence in the 1960s. Specifically, the chapter contends that challenges and potential for governance and development in African countries are intricately connected to the contradictions between the post-colonial African state and Africa's dynamic societies. This phenomenon is sustained by statism, neo-patrimonialism, and the neo-liberal economic programs imposed by Bretton Woods agencies in the 1990s. Despite the deepening crisis of the state, local communities in African countries have been resourceful in their quest for development and good governance. This chapter is consequently a critical analysis of the role of the political class of African states and the collective action of local communities in the development and governance of African states since the decolonization process after the Second World War.

The chapter analyzes three interrelated objectives. First, to provide the appropriate historical context on which we articulate the challenges and potential for development and governance in African states, I shall discuss the structural and moral foundation on which Africa's post-colonial states are constructed. This section underscores a critical point that is often glossed-over by scholars of African political studies, namely the historicity of African states and societies,

O. Vaughan (✉)
Amherst College, Amherst, MA, USA

emphasizing complicated social spaces derived from the imposition of amoral colonial system since the turn of the twentieth century. The incorporation of this historical analysis of modern African states in the dynamic processes of development and governance in a rapidly shifting post-colonial context is critical because it reveals a deeper engagement with the political and social contexts (and consequently the structural imbalance between state and society) in which state policies are formulated and implemented. Second, drawing from case studies from Africa's most populous and heterogeneous country, Nigeria, and Botswana, a small and relatively homogeneous African state, the chapter analyzes the challenges and opportunities for development and governance in two very different post-colonial African states. These two African states are chosen to provide a comparative perspective that challenges the over-generalization of African conditions that has become an essential feature of Africanist scholarship and pedagogy. Finally, focusing on a critical assessment of community development programs in these two African countries, the chapter sheds light on the evolving culture of politics and governance in African states. Given the complex interactions between the holders of state power and local communities, this chapter draws on a distinctive interdisciplinary social science perspective that engages intersecting social, political, and economic spaces in which African state-society relations are constructed. This study therefore endeavors to integrate relevant social science scholarship to local discourses on development and governance in Nigeria and Botswana. The historical trajectories and divergent social and political experiences of these two countries will illuminate contextual and conceptual issues in the development and governance of African states.

While Nigeria is the most populous, diverse, and complex state in Africa, with a history of authoritarian military regimes and complicated liberal democratic governments, Botswana on the other hand, is one of the least populous, stable, and culturally cohesive African countries with sustained experience in constitutional democratic governments since it attained independence from Britain in 1966. Despite their divergent political, social, and historical experiences, the chapter contends that these two countries provide good comparative perspective to explore the complexities of governance, politics, and development in post-colonial African countries.

STRUCTURAL COMPLEXITIES OF THE AFRICAN NATION-STATE

Premised on a liberal idea of citizenship, the modern nation-state is widely regarded as the sovereign political entity where the moral authority of national government is articulated in an emergent modern world. Articulated in the political, constitutional, and economic modernization of the West, especially since the turn of the nineteenth century, its foundational framework is based on a formidable state system that derives its moral authority from a robust civil society. Constructed on the idea of rights and obligations of national citizenship, this evolving democratic system of governance is sanctioned as legitimate when the privileged sectors of society are mobilized for national, political, and economic development. In many Western societies, this hegemonic nation-state project that arose out of this historical experience was nurtured by the unifying values and interest of a dominant national political, economic, and bureaucratic elite (Hoarre and Smith 1971).

Conversely, given a history of domination and exploitation since the early seventeenth century, expressed through Atlantic slavery and colonialism, African regions were the antithesis of this phenomenon in the age of imperialism. Peter Ekeh's seminal article "Colonialism and the Two Public in Africa: A Theoretical Statement" provides a groundbreaking theoretical perspective to interrogate the processes of state-society formation in colonial and post-colonial Africa. In it, Ekeh argues that colonialism precipitates the emergence of two peculiar public realms in Africa, the civic and the primordial. Published in 1975, only a decade after the wave of independence of African states, Ekeh contends that the unfolding political crisis in Africa's newly independent states can be traced to the contradictory relationship between these two publics. To effectively articulate Ekeh's central argument, it is essential to fully grasp what he meant by these two publics. In the case of the civic public, Ekeh contends that this realm constitutes the formal institutions of political and administrative authority that were imposed by an arbitrary colonial state at the turn of the twentieth century on African societies before decolonization only five decades later. These include formal state institutions such as the military, police, civil service, and so on. Given its superficial and arbitrary qualities, this realm is fundamentally weak and largely disconnected from the vibrant structures of society in African states. In this context, Ekeh asserts that this realm is largely amoral in local communities. Conversely, Ekeh contends that in a desire to respond to the exigencies of modern governance and politics following the challenges of decolonization in the 1950s, African political leaders and their communities devised an instrumentalist second public realm, the primordial public. Intelligible and commonsensical, this public realm emerged from the familiar structures and practices of old Africa. To establish essential linkages between the new rulers of African states and local communities, the primordial public draws its moral authority from age-old structures of society, largely predicated on ethnic, hometown, and kinship loyalties and ties. Despite the tendency to generate centrifugal pressures that precipitate political instability and neo-patrimonialism within the context of Africa's emergent and rapidly changing states, the primordial public is perceived to be moral among local people. The implication of Ekeh's theorizing for the legitimacy of the post-colonial state in African countries is apparent. With the agencies of the state devoid of moral authority, Ekeh concludes: "The primordial public in Africa may indeed be fruitfully seen of the elements of citizenship. The individual sees his duties as moral obligations to benefit and sustain a patrimonial public of which he is a member ... For the civic public, meanwhile, duties... are de-emphasized while rights are squeezed out of the civic public with the amorality of an artful dodger" (Ekeh 1975, 107).

Concomitantly, in post-colonial Africa, a major limitation of the political elite lies in their inability to sustain their hegemony over the instrumentalities of the state and the moral order of society. With the post-colonial state system unable to construct the social, political, and economic precondition that can sustain the engines of the developmental state, the custodians of the states in many African countries have failed to build viable national institutions, doctrines, and practices capable of reconciling contending interests of fragmented society (Kothari 1974). In many post-colonial African states, this phenomenon is apparent in the incongruity between the holders of state power and the structures of society (Hayden and Williams 1994). The crisis of the state in many African states in the decades following the attainment of independence is thus intimately connected to the ambiguous nature of the public sphere and the weakness of unifying national institutions and ideologies. Political, social, and economic development initiatives in African countries reflected narrow elite interest sustained by post-colonial state institutions. In this context, the preoccupation of the political class is to advance their material interest at the expense of local communities. Modern state agencies have hardly been used as institutions of governance and development. Rather, they have functioned primarily as a means for allocating patronage to the clients of the political class and as instruments of political domination in local communities. In the early years after independence, African power brokers expropriated national resources to advance narrow class interest. In the divided societies of many African states, rapacious regimes rationalized communal alliances based on age-old mythologies and local histories. The resultant centrifugal forces have undermined the viability of these post-colonial African states. Conscious of the inability of the state to provide sustenance and security, many local communities sought refuge in kinship structures, communal identity, and local patronage networks. This political system, premised on rent-seeking strategies, has undermined local entrepreneurial initiatives, entrenched structural poverty, intensified communal conflicts, and promoted the dependence of many African states on advanced industrial countries (Mbaku 1999). Despite this trend, there are some exceptional African cases where nationalist elites have managed to reconcile their governance agendas with local aspirations. In these cases, the structural balance between the objectives of nationalist modernizers and local communities has sustained a viable developmental state.

This is the prevailing context in which many African state-society relations, alongside their development and governance systems, were structured since the decolonization process of the 1950s. In this evolving state-society framework, local political and social actors, notably peasants, urban workers, elders, chiefs, women traders, and so on, have struggled to define their interest outside the confines of the state. While this state-society framework is pervasive in post-colonial Africa, their significance varies among African states—as will be evident in our Nigerian and Botswana case studies. I now turn to a discussion of the role of the holders of state power and local communities in Nigerian governance and development after the formulation of a comprehensive decolonization policy by the British colonial authorities in 1947.

From Decolonization to Independence in Nigeria

After the Second World War, British colonial authorities were compelled by African nationalists to institute political reforms that ultimately led to independence in many of their African colonies. These nationalist agitations brought the indirect rule system of local administration that was imposed by British colonial authorities on their African colonial territories in the early twentieth century to an abrupt end by the early 1960s. In many African colonies, this new perspective led to a shift in administrative priorities from old guard, chiefs as the custodians of the "natives" authority system on which indirect rule was based, to Western-oriented African nationalists who insisted on independence for African colonies. This new thinking was articulated in Prime Minister Clement Attlee's Labour Government colonial reforms in British West Africa. Reluctant to accede to the agitations of radical nationalists for independence, Attlee's government imposed policies that responded to the pressure for reforms, while safeguarding British imperial interest. Consequently, Britain abandoned the previous colonial policy of benign neglect in favor of a more progressive local administrative policy in its African colonies. This reform policy was defined in the historic 1947 Local Government Dispatch from the Secretary of State for the Colonies, Arthur Creech Jones (Creech Jones 1947). Ostensibly, the document revealed a general disenchantment by the British authorities with the indirect rule system and the chieftaincy structures on which it had been based. In short, by emphasizing the importance of a more responsive local administrative system, British policy marginalized traditional title-holders and embraced Western-educated elites as leaders of a reformed local government administrative system.

In major regions of Nigeria, during the decolonization process, this reform policy was essentially an alliance between the emergent Western-educated elite and traditional rulers. These emergent nationalist elites drawing their authority from a new ethno-regional structure had to contend with traditional rulers because of the latter's strong connections of indigenous social and political structures in local communities. However, such strong connections of local people to traditional rulers soon exposed the growing fragmentation of Nigerian society. This framework on which the decolonization process was rationalized in the 1950s when nationalist parties were formed reveal the arbitrary construct on which the Nigerian nation-state was ultimately established when the country gained independence in 1960. Since decolonization embraced a constitutional democratic system that shifted power to emerging ethno-regional political classes (drawing on intelligible hometown, ethno-linguistic, and ethno-religious loyalties), the attention of the new holders of state power moved away from local communities where grassroots struggles over official policies were expressed during the earlier decades of colonial rule. By the time Nigeria obtained independence in 1960, these political developments had deepened the contradictions among various constituencies, especially rural peasants, urban workers, communal groups, local chiefs, and regional political leaders. Consequently, by the fall of Nigeria's first liberal democratic system in 1966, the ensuing statist strategies of economic planning had entrenched a corrupt neo-patrimonial political arrangement. In turn, this trend undercut the aspirations of local people for development and governance (Mackintosh 1962).

State-Society Relations: Governance and Development in Nigeria

A major feature of post-colonial Nigerian politics was expressed in the persistence of authoritarian tendencies by dominant regional political parties utilizing extra-electoral methods to stifle opposition and consolidate control over local communities under their administrative jurisdiction (Post and Vickers 1974). For example, during Nigeria's first attempt at constitutional democracy (The First Republic), the dominant party in the Northern Region, the Northern People's Congress, utilized local government institutions under its control to intimidate political opponents and dominate local communities. Following the coup of January 1966 and subsequent imposition of military rule from 1966 to 1979, various military regimes marginalized local communities in state affairs, undercutting local initiatives in entrepreneurship and community development (see Gboyega 1975; Fadahunsi 1977). Indeed, the return to a civil-democratic government from 1979 to 1983 revealed a partner similar to the First Republic in which power was concentrated in the lands of the dominant national and regional political parties. Consequently, despite constitutional provisions to prevent abuse of power, the state governments that were elected to power in October 1979 were no less relentless in their attempt to dominate local politics. This trend was exacerbated by the confrontation between the National Party of Nigeria (a national party with firm base in the Muslim North) and other regional-based political parties, especially the Unity Party of Nigeria (A party largely based in the Southwest, Yoruba region). During this period, dominant political parties dissolved duly elected local authorities and replaced them with management committees. Since these committees were staffed with party supporters, they reflected the narrow political agendas of national and regional politicians rather than the aspirations of local people. In addition, politicians that controlled the state governments created new local authority jurisdictions at will. This domination of local government institutions by leaders of the major parties was thus "a means not only of distributing patronage, but was also an exercise in gerrymandering" (Bach 1989, 228–229). As Jane Guyer notes, local authority delimitation became "a logical party political or federal constitutional issue and not a means of linking the corporate structures of government with local forms of governance" (Guyer 1990). These political trends consolidated the interest of the dominant regional political classes and undermined the community development programs imposed by successive military and civilian governments.

The interaction between a fragile state system and structures of society further reveals how local forces confront and accommodate state policies in the context of conflicting communal and class interests. To illustrate this trend, I provide analyses of two landmark national development policies, namely the 1976 Local Government Guidelines and the 1978 Land Use Decree imposed by the military regimes of Generals Murtala Mohammed and Olusegun Obasanjo.

With the enduring problems of local government administration, especially after the Nigeria-Biafra War, the federal military government imposed guidelines for state military governments to guide the implementation of a responsible local government system prior to creating new institutions to usher in a civil-democratic system in 1979 (Guidelines for Local Government Reform 1976). Although this national local government policy extolled the virtue of local autonomy, several years after its implementation around the country, local authorities were still firmly under the control of the state governments. With a military style of governance that promoted a centralized authoritarian federal structure, the 1976 Local Government Guidelines did not devolve control of local government administration to grassroots communities. As discussed earlier, the trend during Nigeria's second democratic government (1979–1983) was for the state governments to dominate local communities by dissolving duly elected local authorities and replacing them with partisan management committees (Olurode 1989). The contradiction between state and society also featured prominently in Nigeria's historic national land tenure policy promulgated by the Obasanjo military government in 1978.

Premised on sustaining national development initiative that will alleviate poverty in local communities, the 1978 Land Use Degree (later Land Use Act) vested all communal land in the state governments. The major assumption of this national policy was based on the notion that state government officials would provide the initiative necessary for economic transformation in their respective states. The reform erroneously assume that the political class would judiciously act as custodians of communal land under their authority. Indeed, in the early decades after the promulgation of the decree, local people had little faith in this national land policy. "Landowner," tenants, and peasants, especially in rural communities continue to observe customary systems of land tenure. Paul Francis concludes that the persistence of the pre-existing land tenure system "is not due to irrational inertia but rather to perceived mutual advantage, the need for security, and a rational assessment of long term interest" (Francis 1984, 23).

Despite these implications of enduring challenges of state-society relations for local governance and development, Nigeria's local entrepreneurs and grassroots organizations continue to demonstrate ingenuity in a rapidly changing society (Hopkins 1988, 10–12). In the 1980s and 1990s, despite the negative consequences of neo-liberal economic reforms, local enterprise demonstrated significant resourcefulness by reconciling indigenous networks to modern economic conditions (Forrest 1994). These strategies were expressed in how local entrepreneurs responded to major state policies and the shifts in Nigerian industry and commerce. In this environment of economic uncertainty, some local enterprises responded to the pressing economic conditions across the country. Notable examples of this spirit of indigenous entrepreneurship were evident in the haulage and motor spare parts industry in the Igbo towns of Nnewi, Onitsha, and Aba. The surge in these industries occurred at a period when import restrictions from foreign exchange crisis had followed the decline in oil revenue in the 1980s. Although largely a rural community at the time, Nnewi emerged as a leading center in the production and trade in motor spare parts. Throughout this period, Nnewi experienced rapid industrialization with approximately twenty medium to large-scale industries established, and native entrepreneurs controlling about ninety percent of the Nigerian motor spare parts trade. Tom Forrest identifies three major characteristics of this "silent industry" in Nigeria: (a) apprenticeship in the industry was generally drawn from people with limited formal education who maintain strong ties to their hometowns; (b) basic infrastructure such as equipment, tarred roads, land, water boreholes, transformers, and generators were acquired through mutually benefiting networks based on community values; and (c) local technical resources shifted away from Britain and Europe to the Far East (especially Taiwan) where these materials were more affordable (Forrest 1994).

Onitsha and Aba were also critical to Nigeria's haulage and passenger transportation network during this period of severe economic downturn. Initially major trading towns in motor spare parts, these Igbo towns emerged as nerve centers of a lucrative but unstable transportation industry. Like Nnewi, the success of these enterprises can be attributed to perseverance, industry, and strong kinship ties in local communities. Thus, unlike earlier national industrial planning schemes, especially during the oil boom years from 1973 to 1977, these grassroots enterprises succeeded because local customary practices were adapted to the changing economic conditions specific to the time. However, the moral basis of these local industrial enterprises was soon stymied by the amoral actions taken by powerful national and international political and economic actors. These Igbo entrepreneurial innovations were soon undermined by the policies of successive military regimes, mounting national debt burden, and growing marginalization of Nigeria in the global economy.

While lacking the strong enterprise culture of these local Igbo industrial initiatives, social welfare organizations also emerged as important centers of community development in the 1980s and 1990s (For insightful works see Thomas 1987; Berry 1985). Similar to the hometown and ethnic-based progressive associations of the transformative years of decolonization in the 1940s and 1950s, a new generation of social welfare organizations that came under the nomenclature of non-governmental organizations in the 1980s and 1990s emerged to fill the growing social space vacated by state agencies because of the neo-liberal economic reforms imposed on Nigeria by Bretton Woods agencies. With civic commitment, these organizations harnessed scarce resources through local, regional, and global networks as the economic crisis deepened in the country. But despite their success as providers of basic social programs, these organizations exhibited limitations in key areas of local community development, notably agricultural schemes, community-based industrial initiatives, employment of local work force, and the provision of educational and public health services (Enemuo and Oyediran 1990). Finally, the long-term performance of these non-governmental organizations was hampered by their dependence on global and national neo-liberal economic networks. These alliances reflect a patronage system of economic rewards that serve narrow interest of influential personalities and cliques at the expense of local communities. With a comparative perspective in mind, I now turn to a discussion of a second case study, Botswana. Like the initial discussion on Nigeria, I proceed with the historical context from which I explore the nexus of state-society relations in Botswana's governance and development.

From Decolonization to Independence in Botswana

Michael Crowder, Jack Parson, and Neil Parsons provide an important conceptual perspective through which I historicize the evolution of the modern Botswana state and society, emphasizing their critical role in the country's governance and community development initiatives. Framed in the context of evolving mechanism of governance, they contend that modern Tswana community harbors a political culture based on well-established traditional system of male primogeniture. These scholars argue that the resilience of this prevailing pre-colonial social and political system serves as foundation for the culture of politics in contemporary Botswana state-society relations (Crowder et al. 1990). During colonial rule, Tswana politics followed a strict traditional system in which royal and chiefly potentates succeeded to their office through well-established claims to traditional positions of authority and power. Despite colonial modifications, they contend strong adherence to established rules determined the daily affairs of the state under the direction of British colonial administrators. With the primacy of primogeniture in succession to traditional rulership, Tswana chieftaincy structure did not only determine the pace of colonial rule from 1885 when Britain imposed its rule on Botswana to 1966 when the country gained independence but also shaped the evolution of state and society in the critical decades after independence. Consequently, during the colonial period, British authorities conceded significant political autonomy to Tswana chiefs by effectively incorporating them into important administrative functions of the colonial state. Indeed, during the first decade of Botswana's incorporation as a British protectorate, colonial administrators performed minimal role in local administration. The dominant position on which this pre-colonial arrangement was grafted not only had important implications for the persistence of chieftaincy structures in the post-colonial era but also shaped the direction of governance and development policies, once an emergent nationalist elite assumed power under the leadership of Seretse Khama, the charismatic traditional potentate and visionary modernist who laid the foundation of the post-colonial Botswana state and society (Crowder et al. 1990, 10).

With this historical experience consolidating the political leadership of a dominant Tswana nationalist elite, an emergent nationalist party, the Botswana Democratic Party (BDP) appropriated this prevailing culture of politics as a framework for governance in the decades immediately after colonial rule. Additionally, since a modern construct of Tswana identity had been consolidated by the end of the colonial period, competing ethnic fissures were largely insignificant in post-colonial Botswana. Thus, the centrifugal forces that were unleashed in many sub-Saharan African states were a minor issue in post-colonial Botswana. These developments were further reinforced by Botswana's vibrant economy immediately after independence. Indeed, the booming diamond and cattle industries, coupled with a steady flow of economic aid, meant that resources were readily available to advance the objectives of the Botswana developmental state. This strong economy sustained a "paternalistic developmental" system that consolidated the power of the BDP while advancing development agendas in local communities, especially in urban areas (Carlton 1991, 277). However, these prevailing historical forces soon encouraged the emergence of two distinct social domains, the rural sector, where chiefs retained considerable influence, and the urban sector, where modern government institutions and state development projects were relatively well developed. We now turn our attention to a discussion of the political system that set the stage for the tension between politicians and traditional chiefs in Botswana.

During decolonization, what became Botswana's post-colonial constitution was a partnership between British administrators in Whitehall and a small group of Western-educated elites who dominated Botswana's two major nationalist parties, the Botswana Democratic Party (BDP) and the Botswana National Front (BNF). Based on a parliamentary system, political authority was derived from a popularly elected National Assembly drawn from single member districts of roughly equal populations. In addition, the Independence Constitution also created a House of Chiefs, where senior chiefs or Kgosi deliberated over legislations enacted by the National Assembly and policies formulated by the central government. Although the House of Chiefs had no power to block National Assembly legislations, it emerged as an important forum where chiefs discussed state policies. The president, the highest state office holder, was elected by members of the National Assembly. In turn, the president was empowered to appoint a vice-president from the National Assembly, who acted in his absence and assumed the presidency upon his resignation or death. Along with the National Assembly's legislative authority, the president had extensive statutory control over local authorities and chieftaincy institutions. The Independence Constitution also established a single-tier city council structure, four town councils, and nine district councils, varying in population and resources. Although constituted by statute of parliament, district councils were under the jurisdiction of the central government's ministry of local government. Dominated by elected councilors, and consisting of chiefs as ex-officio members, district councils were expected to function as agencies of democratic decentralization, charged with the responsibility of administering community development projects, primary education services, construction and maintenance of rural roads, and provision of water supply.

Conversely, though chiefs retained control over customary courts and kgotla meetings (a regular public forum where adult men, under the leadership of chiefs and headmen, deliberate over important issues in community affairs), the Independence Constitution effectively eroded chiefly power in state affairs by subordinating chiefs to the central government and local authorities (Sharma 1997). However, despite their marginalization, chiefs as custodians of cherished local traditions and customs remain influential as mobilizers of public opinion in their local communities. More importantly, the resilience of chieftaincy lies in the incorporation of the traditional kgotla system to modern governance and their important role in community development efforts in rural community where formal state institutions are particularly weak (Molutsi and Holm 1990). This trend in governance was most profoundly expressed in the tension that ensued between chiefs and modern state officials over local government administration, rural development, and land reform policies.

State and Society: Politicians and Chiefs in Botswana

Reflecting lingering tensions between state and society, debates over governance and development strategies and outcomes by the modern political elite who control state agencies and chiefs as self-appointed voice of local communities—especially rural communities—dominated state affairs in the decades immediately after Botswana's independence. The proceedings of the House of Chiefs in the 1970s and the 1980s will illustrate the tension between the kgosis, the senior chiefs, who dominated the House of Chiefs, and BDP state officials on the crucial issues of local government reforms. In House of Chiefs deliberations, chiefs incessantly complained that the tribal administration structures, which represented chiefs in local administration were poorly funded, that salaries of chiefs were low, and chiefs and headmen were unable to perform their functions efficiently because of inadequate resources. BDP state officials, conversely, responded that given their workload (in comparison to other local agencies) tribal administrations were adequately compensated for the work they perform in local communities.

Chiefly opposition to government policies was, however, not limited to their eroding status in local and national politics. In July 1991, following a controversial policy by the central government to implement a separate development program for the outcast Basarwa community (the so-called Bushmen of the Kalahari Desert), Tswana chiefs mounted a vocal opposition against the BDP government. Complicated by two decades of feuding with the central government over local government and land reform, the chiefs in deliberations in the House of Chiefs, local authorities, and kgotlas meetings, gave considerable attention on the plight of Botswana's most vulnerable minority group. The chiefs thus appropriated the Basarwa controversy throughout the 1990s to enhance their status as the voice of a dispossessed and marginalized rural minority. Intense debates over rural electrification also generated much disagreement between chiefs and the BDP central government during this period. In short, these issues—Bararwa controversy and rural electrification—reveal a common thread in the tension between chiefs and the BDP government: the persistent attempt of the chiefs to underscore their relevance as the legitimate voice of Botswana's marginalized rural communities (House of Chiefs Report, 2 July 1991a).

STATE AND SOCIETY: LAND REFORM IN BOTSWANA

As in most African states, immediately after independence, land reform, like local government reform, was the centerpiece of the struggle for grassroots development and governance in Botswana. With the recurring crises over land rights since independence, the BDP central government, following several failed land reform policies, established a high-powered presidential commission to investigate land issues and make recommendations to the central government. The recommendations, which became the blueprint for the government's land tenure policy, provide critical insight into the complex problem of land tenure, governance, and community development in Botswana. Before we analyze the reform, it is necessary to examine the pre-existing arrangement of land tenure in Botswana since decolonization.

Prior to the promulgation of Botswana's first major tenure policy, the Tribal Land Act of 1968, administrative control over land was vested in chiefs as communal land trustees in local communities. As communal land trustees, chiefs did not only have authority over residential, arable, and grazing land, but they also had power to allocate and repossess land. The extensive constitutional powers of chiefs over communal land came to an end when the central government passed the Tribal Land Act of 1968, which transferred the authority over communal land from the chiefs to government constituted land boards. With the passing of the new land law, tensions over the administration of communal land would dominate the relationship between the chiefs and the land boards. In kgotla meetings, district council meetings, and in the House of Chiefs, the kgosis consistently registered their disapproval to BDP land policies from the 1970s to the 1990s, emphasizing the ignorance of members of the land boards on local land matters. Thus, the chiefs called on the BDP central government to integrate them into the government land tenure policy. However, when the Presidential Commission submitted its report, it essentially upheld the 1968 land law, though it entertained a limited role for chiefs in the administration of land, especially in rural communities (Land Problems in Mogoditshane and Other Per-Urban Villages).

In summation, a critical assessment of the dynamics of state-society relations in Botswana reveals considerable gains in the consolidation of constitutional democratic system of government. Despite the disaffection of chiefs, Botswana, because of a relatively good balance between the structures of society and the agencies of the modern state, has sustained a steady process of governance and development. Yet despite these accomplishments, a careful reading of the struggles between chiefs, who claim to be the moral voice of local communities, and BDP politicians, who control the agencies of the post-colonial state, reveals significant discontent among chiefs because of their marginalization from formal institutions of state power and claims of growing rural alienation.

Conclusion

This chapter explores the legitimacy and moral authority on which African states are structured since the process of decolonization after the Second World War. By analyzing the interactions between state and society in two distinctive African countries, Nigeria and Botswana, the chapter underscores the dialectical tensions between state agencies and structures of societies in the context of governance and development. The Nigerian case study discussed here shows how structures of society paradoxically express constructive social and economic activities on the one hand while imbricated in the processes of fractionalization that is endemic in Nigerian politics and society. The chapter contends that this contradictory outcome in post-colonial governance and development has deep roots in the structural imbalance between the agencies of the post-colonial state and structures of Nigeria's deeply divided society. Consequently, while the holders of state power have entrenched a neo-patrimonial political system structured on ethno-regional alliances, local people drawing from age-old structures and practices have devised creative strategies of sustenance in a rapidly shifting political, economic, and social environment. In this context, local people in grassroots communities have consistently drawn on their economic and social resourcefulness in a post-colonial state system structured on uncertainty and insecurity. Conversely, with a smooth transition from the colonial to the post-colonial era and relatively fluid connections between agencies of the modern state and structures of society, Botswana's post-colonial state-society dynamics has exhibited relatively higher level of moral authority when compared to most African states. Despite tensions between chiefs and the nationalist political elite, Botswana continues to be one of Africa's most viable developmental states. Premised on a methodological approach that privileges the historicity of African states in colonial and post-colonial contexts, these two case studies underscore the structural basis on which African states and societies are articulated in this rapidly shifting post-colonial world. Despite the consequences of this structural incongruity between state and society, local communities in many African countries have consistently exhibited considerable ingenuity in local governance and development.

Bibliography

Bach, Daniel. 1989. Managing a Plural Society: The Boomerang Effect of Nigerian Federation. *Journal of Comparative and Commonwealth Politics* 27 (2): 218–245.
Berry, Sara. 1985. *Fathers Work for Their Sons: Accumulation, Mobility and Class Formation in an Extended Yoruba Community*. Berkeley: University of California Press.

Bratton, Michael. 1989. Beyond the State: Civil Society and Associational Life in Africa. *World Politics* 41: 407–430.

Carlton, Roger. 1991. Bureaucrats and Politicians in Botswana's Policy-Making Process: A Re-Interpretation. *Journal of Commonwealth and Comparative Politics* 29: 265–282.

Creech Jones, Arthur. 1947. The Place of African Local Administration in Colonial Policy. *Journal of African Administration* 1: 3.

Crowder, Michael, Jack Parson, and Neil Parsons. 1990. Legitimacy and Faction: Tswana Constitutionalism and Political Change. In *Succession to High Office in Botswana: Three Cases*, Ohio University Center for International Studies Monograph Series, ed. Jack Parson. Athens: Ohio University Center for International Studies.

Ekeh, Peter. 1975. Colonialism and the Two Public's in Africa. *Comparative Studies in Society and History* 17: 91–112.

Enemuo, F.C., and O. Oyediran. 1990. Community Development Association as Agents of Rural Transformation: A Case Study of Town Unions in Anambra State. Paper Presented at the National Seminar on Integrated Rural Development Policy in Nigeria, Abuja.

Fadahunsi, Olu. 1977. The Politics of Local Government Administration in Western Nigeria, 1958–1968. *Quarterly Journal of Administration* 2: 61.

Forrest, Tom. 1989. The Advance of African Capital: The Growth of Nigerian Private Enterprise. Paper Presented at the Workshop on Alternative Development Strategies in Africa, Queen Elizabeth House, University of Oxford.

———. 1994. *The Advance of African Capital: The Growth of Nigerian Private Enterprise*. Charlottesville: University Press of Virginia.

Francis, Paul. 1984. For the Use and Common Benefit of All Nigerians: Consequences of the 1978 Land Nationalization. *Africa* 54: 5–28.

Gboyega, Alex. 1975. Local Government and Political Integration in Western Nigeria. PhD. Thesis, University of Ibadan.

Guidelines for Local Government Reform. Lagos: Federal Government Printer, 1976.

Guyer, Jane. 1990. Representation Without Taxation: An Essay on Democracy in Rural Nigeria, 1952–1990. Boston University, African Studies Center Working Papers.

Hayden, Goran, and Donald Williams. 1994. A Community Model of African Politics: Illustration from Nigeria and Tanzania. *Comparative Studies in Society and History* 36: 68–96.

Hoarre, Q., and G.N. Smith, eds. 1971. *Selection from the Prison Notebooks of Antonio Gramsci*. New York: International Publishers.

Hopkins, A.G. 1988. African Entrepreneurship: The Relevance of History to Development Economics. *Geneve Afrique*: 26, 7.

House of Chiefs Report, 2 July, 1991a.

———, 5 July, 1991b.

Kothari, Rajni. 1974. *Footsteps into the Future: Diagnosis of the Present World and a Design of an Alternative*. New York: Free Press.

Land Problems in Mogoditshane and Other Per-Urban Villages, Government Paper, No 1, March 1992.

Mackintosh, John P. 1962. Electoral Trends and the Tendency to a One Party System in Nigeria. *Journal of Commonwealth Political Studies* 1 (3): 194–210.

Mbaku, John Mukum. 1999. *Preparing Africa for the Twentieth First Century: Strategies for Peaceful Coexistence and Sustainable Development*. Aldershot: Ashgate.

Molutsi, Patrick, and J.D. Holm. 1990. Developing Democracy When Civil Society Is Weak: The Case of Botswana. *African Affairs* 89: 323–340.

Olurode, Olayiwola. 1989. Grassroots Politics, Political Factions, and Conflict in Nigeria. *Rural Africana* 25–26: 113–124.

Post, Kenneth, and Michael Vickers. 1974. *Crisis and Conflict in Nigeria*. London: Heineman.

Sharma, Keshar. 1997. Mechanisms for Involvement of Traditional Leaders in the Promotion of Good Governance. Symposium on Traditional Leadership and Local Government, Gaborone, Botswana.

Thomas, Barbara P. 1987. Development Through Harambee: Who Wins and Who Loses? Rural Self-Help Projects in Kenya. *World Development* 15: 463–481.

CHAPTER 15

Political Ethics of Kwame Nkrumah

Ebenezer Obiri Addo

"Seek ye first the political kingdom and all other things shall be added unto thee."[1] This often-quoted biblical passage that says "But strive first for the kingdom of God and his righteousness, and all these things will be given to you as well" was parodied by Kwame Nkrumah to define his political philosophy. This was inscribed on his statue in front of the parliament building during his term in office.[2] The statement became a bone of contention between Nkrumah and the Ghanaian Christian community throughout his leadership. It gave his detractors another weapon in their perceived "divinization" of his personality.[3]

I argue, however, that this parody rather defined Kwame Nkrumah's perspective on political ethics: the primacy of power. The Akan paradigm of societal power relations is premised on the proverb, *Se woton tumi a, ton wo maame koto; se wonya tumi a, wobetumi agye wo maame*, "If power is being sold, sell your mother to buy it; once you attain power you can use it to retrieve her."

The attainment of political power as a nationalist was an all-consuming energy for Nkrumah. How, then, do we unpack his understanding and application of power in historical perspective? What were some of the influences on his life, particularly during his twelve-year sojourn overseas? Are there some convergences of and developments in his political thought that help us to reassess his career? I define political ethics as the human struggle with the problem of morality in relation to issues of statecraft. These dynamics include the uses and abuses of power in terms of justice and injustice in a given society. Political ethics is therefore not divorced from a particular political history and sociocultural structure/environment. One can therefore understand Nkrumah's position on political ethics by examining his struggle to "birth" a new nation which he saw as his "autobiography".[4] How did he perceive Ghana's historical and political developments? In his single-minded devotion to his goal of "Serve Government

E. O. Addo (✉)
Seton Hall University, South Orange, NJ, USA

Now," how did he deal with his political opponents, and how did this political climate define his understanding of the political game? What was his relationship with the Ghanaian Christian community, and how did his perspective on religion and politics dictate the relationship?

I contend that if there is one source of tradition in political thought that defined Nkrumah's ethics in politics, it would be "Machiavellianism." Niccolo Machiavelli is credited with shaping political thought vis-à-vis the rise of the nation-state, and how leaders could attain and hold power.[5] For Machiavelli, moral imperatives are embedded in the collective historical wisdom of a people. As Akan ancestors have said, *Obi nkogye obi se nkonwenwene*, "One does not borrow someone else's teeth to smile." Historical legacy, for him was premised on the imitation of a people's historical heroes:

> Let no one marvel if in speaking of new dominions both as to prince and state, I bring forward very exalted instances, for men walk almost always in the paths trodden by others, proceeding in their actions by imitation. Not being able to follow others exactly, nor attain to the excellence of those he imitates, a prudent man should always follow in the path trodden by great men and imitate those who are most excellent, so that if he does not attain to their greatness, at any rate he will get some tinge of it.[6]

Furthermore, he opined that in the modern state, politics becomes primary while moral considerations take a backstage in political leadership. Essential to this position was the prohibition of the church from interfering in the functions of the state. In this quest to disengage civil government from the constraints of the Christian church, Machiavelli did not repudiate religion per se from politics. Religion was most helpful when it could serve as a cohesive force in society, as glue that binds. He thus becomes an original advocate of civil religion.

The historical, cultural and political contexts of Kwame Nkrumah's leadership should not be divorced from his political ethics. He was among the first group of postcolonial African leaders who were primarily tasked with nation-building. They were to construct "nations" out of ethnic "states," arbitrarily drawn by departing European colonial powers.[7] Almond and Powell also argue that nation-building "emphasizes the cultural aspects of political development. It refers to the process whereby people transfer their commitment and loyalty from smaller tribes, villages, or petty principalities to larger central political systems."[8]

Carl Friedrich has argued that while nations of Europe were "formed", postcolonial African nations had to be "built":

> ...Western nations were not built, but grew...Even the modern nation-state, the political order of such a nation, was not deliberately built, but rather came into being as expansionist rulers sought to strengthen their government. [They were] ultimately dependent upon an inclusive religious community, which was Christian, and an exclusive secular community, which was nation. The growth of Western nations was undoubtedly facilitated by the prevalence of one unifying religions, even if it was split into various denominations.[9]

NKRUMAH AND THE LEADERSHIP CHALLENGE

When Nkrumah joined the political struggle in 1947 after a twelve-year sojourn in the United States and Britain, immediate "self-government" for his people was his primary goal. But who were the people, and what was the historical context? The Gold Coast, as it was then called, was an amalgamation of ethnicities based on "primordial attachments." Clifford Geertz defines primordial attachments as ones that

> stem from the "givens"—or more precisely, as culture is inevitably involved in such matters, the assumed "givens"—of social existence: immediate contiguity and kin connection mainly. But beyond them the givens that stem from being born into a particular religious community...and following particular practices.[10]

Competing loyalties arising from these attachments will eventually be exploited by his opponents to undermine his efforts for national integration. It also provoked the first opposition to Nkrumah. One way to assess his understanding of power is to highlight his relationship with the "opposition" throughout his leadership.

The United Gold Coast Convention (UGCC) was the main political organization that had invited Nkrumah to become its national secretary. The campaign slogan of the UGCC was "Self-Government Within the Shortest Possible Time." Nkrumah broke away to form his own party, The Convention People's Party (CPP), with the slogan "Self-Government Now!". The new party would also not be exclusively for chiefs and the intelligentsia; it would be an all-inclusive one that embraced all ethnicities and classes.[11] The split between the UGCC and Nkrumah's CPP was to deepen the political divisions in the emerging "nation". Following World War II and the rise of nationalist agitations, political affiliations in the Gold Coast included the following: Gold Coast Ex-Servicemen's Union (1946), led by B. E. A. Tamakloe; the United Gold Coast Convention, led by Joseph Boakye Danquah (1947); and The Convention People's Party (1949), led by Kwame Nkrumah. These were the main political grouping that contested the 1951 elections. The second major elections that occurred in 1954 saw more political groupings: Ghana Congress Party (GCP), 1952, led by Kofi Abrefa Busia and the National Liberation Movement (NLM) led by Bafour Osei Akoto. Other smaller parties emerged as well: Togoland Congress, The Muslim Association Party and the Northern People's Party.

In this hotly contested climate leading up to independence, the stage was set for either a federal system—advocated by the Busia-Danquah faction—or Kwame Nkrumah's CPP. John Gunther a political analyst observed in 1955 that

> The Gold Coast revolution had three aspects—youth against age, the people against the chiefs, the nationalists against the British. It is Nkrumah's greatest source of power that he combines in himself leadership in all these spheres.[12]

In the ensuing struggle, Nkrumah and his CPP won the elections to lead the country to independence. But the victory rather intensified the tensions between primordial loyalties and civil sentiments. This resulted in a challenge to Nkrumah's quest for an integrated, unitary Ghana. One group that became part of the political conflict was the Joint Provincial Council of Chiefs, a government advisory body. Nkrumah perceived this group as closely aligned with the opposition. This was the context of is classic statement:

> It was here that I said in a speech at the Arena that if the chiefs would not cooperate with the people in their struggle for freedom, then a day might come when they 'will run away and leave their sandals behind'.[13]

We can thus see how Nkrumah perceived power in terms of who was for or against him. When the motion for independence was introduced in 1957, the opposition boycotted the debates. The motion was therefore supported solely by CPP votes. The National Liberation Movement (NLM) and Northern People's Party (NPP) threatened to secede. There was so much tension in the country that Bankole Timothy's advice to the two opponents, Busia and Nkrumah, is noteworthy:

> It is give and take which makes the world go round. Give in then and strike a compromise. Will you do that? If you do then yours is a stable and United State of Ghana with everything in it and, more than this, posterity will honor and bless you for it…. Kwame and Kofi, the choice before you now is this—olive or sword.[14]

I contend that this concept of "olive or sword" is metaphoric in Ghana's political history; it also explains the ethical dilemma of Nkrumah's leadership. In the Akan language, "enemy" and "opponent" are used interchangeably. It is therefore difficult to draw a distinction when it comes to political debate. To a large extent, Nkrumah's desire to integrate the country heightened antagonisms which have continued even today. But Nkrumah's political opponents conceded that he meant well for Ghana, even in his desire for absolute power and control. William Ofori Atta (Paa Willie), a member of the UGCC and later Nkrumah's opponent said this when I interviewed him on January 27, 1988:

> Nkrumah was a great nationalist, always striving for leadership in life to liberate Ghanaians from what he called imperialism…. The advantage of Nkrumah over all of us in the UGCC was that the British authorities feared him more than all others…. The masses rallied behind him because they saw him as more devoted than the rest of us whom he described as stooges.[15]

He contended that power was everything for Nkrumah, and his understanding of power made him "terrorize chiefs initially, for he knew the power and symbol of the chief. Nkrumah was against all powers likely to compete with him; the church was one".¹⁶ Indeed, Akan ancestors' adage comes to mind here, *Se wotan okwaduo a woyi ne mrika*, "No matter how much you detest the Okwaduo, you have to acknowledge its speed."

The conflict between Nkrumah and the Christian church highlights another aspect of his approach to power politics. In his attempt to resymbolize politics in the new nation, he maintained that politics must be secular. He argued in his *Consciencism: Philosophy and Ideology for Decolonization* that the ideological tapestry of the new nation of Ghana was made up of (a) the African segment, which comprised the traditional way of life; (b) the Islamic segment, which dated back to the eighth century; and (c) the Euro-Christian segment, which came primarily through European imperialism and colonization of the nineteenth century. These were competing religious strands as well. The new nation would avoid the institutionalization of any particular religion:

> Our society is not the old society, but a new society enlarged by Islamic and European Christian influences. A new emergent ideology is therefore required, an ideology which can solidify in a philosophical statement, but at the same time an ideology which will not abandon the original humanist principles of Africa. Such a philosophical statement will be born out of the crisis of the African conscience confronted with the three strands of present African society.¹⁷

His goal was what I term as secular modernization. Thus, religion in the modern state will not be based on any revealed religion or metaphysical rationalism evident in Christianity and Islam. Rather, he sought to encourage a pluralistic and comprehensive African worldview.¹⁸ In fact, he described his religious development and position in this way:

> In those days I took my religion seriously and was very often to be found serving at Mass. As I grew older, however, the strict discipline of Roman Catholicism stifled me. It was not that I became less religious but rather that I sought freedom in the worship of and communion with my God, for my God is a very personal God and can only be reached direct. I do not find the need of, in fact I resent the intervention of a third party in such a personal matter. To-day I am a non-denominational Christian and a Marxist socialist and I have not found any contradiction between the two.¹⁹

The conflict with the Christian Council of Ghana was further complicated by his cultivation of the youth wing of the CPP called "The Ghana Young Pioneers". Statements such as "Nkrumah Never Dies" and "Nkrumah Is Our Messiah" proved too much for the church. The direct response came from the Anglican Bishop of Accra, Reginald Richard Rosevere. In his Synod Charge at the 1962 Conference of the Anglican Church, he stated that:

> It is a truism to say that the future will be in the hands of the boys and girls of today… There are, I regret to say, certain aspects of the Young Pioneers Movement which are the cause of sorrow and fear to very many thoughtful people, Christian

and non-Christian alike... It seems that the movement confuses the work and example of a great man with divine acts, which are unique in history.... The incipient atheism is quite foreign to the traditional concepts of the African personality.[20]

The Bishop was deported by Nkrumah on August 13, 1962. The deportation order stated that his "presence in Ghana was not conducive to the public good" (Pobee 1988: 131). On appeal, he was permitted to return on October 13, 1962. But the Christian Council's letter of gratitude to Nkrumah summarized the power dynamic in Nkrumah's Ghana:

> On behalf of the Ghana Christian Council we request you kindly to convey to Osagyefo the President warmest gratitude for granting the Council's humble petition and permitting Bishop Rosevere's return. This most generous gesture will rejoice the hearts of multitudes of Christians throughout Ghana and many lands... We pray Almighty God's continued guidance, support and blessing for Osagyefo.[21]

The Moslem community had also been cowed into submission with the deportation of two leading members in Kumasi, Alhaji Amadu Baba and Alhaji Othman Larden Laramie. In his staunch opposition to Nkrumah and his CPP, Laramie was reported to have said that "True Moslems can never be friends with the C. P. P. The Moslem Association is prepared to hold the devil by the throat until everybody is free in this country".[22]

One major act which cemented Nkrumah's power and also defined his perception of "opposition" was the passing of the Preventive Detention Act (PDA) in 1958. This Act empowered the government to arrest and detain any enemy of the state or any person who was a threat to state security, for up to five years. It stipulated that, "no arrest or detention made under this bill was actionable in any court of Law."[23] The bill was promulgated in July 1958. By November, thirty-eight members of the opposition United Party including J. B. Danquah had been detained. Later, his Attorney General Geoffrey Bing reflected:

> Preventive detention, which when established was only to be used in an emergency, now began more and more, to be regarded as the sheet-anchor of stability.[24]

By 1960, the parliamentary opposition had become a mere shadow and negligible force. Dr. K. A. Busia, leader of the opposition, had left the country in July to avoid detention. S. D. Dombo replaced him. Nkrumah went ahead to declare Ghana as a republic. In a referendum in January 1964, Ghana became a one-party state under Nkrumah's CPP:

> ...there shall be one national party which shall be the vanguard of the People in their struggle to build a socialist society and which shall be the leading core of all organizations of the people.[25]

Conclusion

After the downfall of Nkrumah in February 1966, David Apter revised his previous work, *The Gold Coast in Transition* to *Ghana in Transition*,[26] and concluded that Nkrumah's leadership will remain a subject for reinterpretation and analysis. It would seem that his political ethics is one of the under-researched areas. This chapter attempts to do that.

Akan ancestors have cautioned that, *Tumi te se kosua; woso mu dennen a, ebo; woanso me yie nso a efi wo nsa*, "Power must be handled in the manner of holding an egg; if you hold it too firmly it breaks, it you hold loosely it falls." They have also warned that, *dua koro gye mframa a ebu*, "If a tree gathers all the wind it easily falls." I believe Nkrumah's attitude to power as well as the religious dynamic was Machiavellian. He made no commitment to any particular religion and insisted on a secular state, but he employed religion mainly as a political tool. By his own admission, Nkrumah feared three things in life equally: women, money and obligatory religion, because of his "dread of being trapped."

> I have never outgrown that feeling towards women. It is not fear to-day, but something deeper. Perhaps it is a dread of being trapped, of having my freedom taken away or being in some way overpowered. And I have the same feeling about money and obligatory religion. All three of them represent to my mind something that should play a very minor part in a man's life, for once one of them gets the upper hand, man becomes a slave and his personality is crushed.[27]

While we cannot divorce Nkrumah from the historical context of his leadership, we can also argue that his own inborn tendency to control his own destiny offers an angle to understand his political ethics. Col. A. A. Afrifa, one of the architects of the coup that toppled Nkrumah, described him in his post-coup radio interview as "ruthless," "dishonest," "a kind of Joshua and Father Divine and Cassius Clay rolled into one"[28] One can dismiss Afrifa's comment in terms of the Akan proverb that, *Obi mpe w'asem a, osua w'asaw a okyeakyea n'eto*, "Your enemy imitates your dance for you to appear bad." Also, Akan elders would say that, *Se akoko nim asa se den koraa a, ennye akroma fe da*, "No matter how beautiful the chicken dances, it would never please the hawk." But, among the influences that shaped Nkrumah's life during his sojourn in America was Father Divine. His relationship with the Father Divine movement reveals the mind of a person who sought to maintain his security and interests at all costs. The movement was a popular Black organization that gained ascendency during the Depression and thrived up to the period after World War II. Sarah Harris, who has documented the movement, describes Father Divine as "the black Messiah who, like Marcus Garvey before him, was a utopian seeker of magnificent proportion".[29] It would rather seem that Nkrumah followed an ethic of expediency, and this character trait was evident in his political career. Nkrumah wrote in his *Ghana* that:

Poverty and need drive one to surprising ends. For want of something better to do and because it provided me with an evening's free entertainment, I used to go round quite a lot to various Negro religious gatherings and revivalist meetings. The only one that I gave much attention to was a movement headed by Father Divine, and then only because of the privileges attached to membership. By being a follower of Father Divine I discovered that it was possible to obtain a good chicken meal for half a dollar, instead of the usual two or three dollars charged at other restaurants, and also a hair-cut at a certain barber's shop for only ten cents instead of a dollar. To an impoverished student this was quite enough to attract him to any sort of movement and as long as I could be fed and shorn at cut prices by merely raising my arm above my head and whispering 'Peace'. I fear I did not concern myself with the motives of Father Divine's group.[30]

Kwame Nkrumah was also a Garyeyite, an advocate of Black pride. In fact, one of his first acts as Ghana's political leader was to name the new country's national shipping line "The Black Star Line" in memory of Garvey's attempt to create Black nationhood. He wrote:

It was unfortunate that I was never able to meet Garvey as he had been deported from the country before I arrived, in connection with some kind of alleged fraud that he had got involved in.[31]

Kwame Nkrumah was as complex as his career. An assessment of his political ethics should be understood in terms of his personal development including the influences that shaped his political evolution. The sociocultural and political context should also play a role in our understanding. Many years after his life and work, Ali A. Mazrui offered his own perspective on Nkrumah which seems to encapsulate the complexity of the man. He wrote, inter alia:

What went wrong in Ghana after independence? How did this hero of African independence and African unity become the villain of the one-party state and preventive detention?...[Nkrumah] was a great African but not a great Ghanaian.. he succumbed to two contradictory tendencies within Ghana at the time—the monarchical tendency, which increasingly turned him into a royal figure, on one hand, and the Leninist tendency towards the vanguard party and the single-party state, on the other. When the monarchical and the Leninist tendencies are fused, they basically produced "a Leninist Czar"....[32]

In this image, we perceive a man as complex as his political ethic, informed by Machiavelli, Father Divine, Marcus Garvey and the Ghanaian political landscape. The complexity makes sense of an Akan ancestral wisdom: *Osekan-tia biako nngua esono nngua ekoo, nngua odenkyem-mirempon, na wasan agua onnaka na wasan atwa wo wura nsa na wonhon wo ade mu ana?* "You cannot use one little knife to skin an elephant, a buffalo, a big-throated crocodile, and yet go out of your way to skin a python, and also cut your master's hand, and expect the knife to remain in its handle without being cast out of the way?" A complex man evoked a complex ethics: that was Kwame Nkrumah.

Notes

1. *Holy Bible: New Revised Standard Version* (Nashville, TN: Thomas Nelson Publishers, 1989).
2. Ebenezer Obiri Addo, *Kwame Nkrumah: A Case Study of Religion and Politics in Ghana* (Lanham: University of America Press, 1997) 58.
3. T. Peter Omari, *Kwame Nkrumah: The Anatomy of an African Dictatorship* (New York: Africana Publishing Corporation, 1970); David Rooney, *Kwame Nkrumah: The Political Kingdom in the Third World* (London: I. B. Tauris & Colta, 1988).
4. See his *Ghana: The Autobiography of Kwame Nkrumah* (New York: International Publisher, 1957).
5. Niccolo Machiavelli, *The Prince and the Discourses* (New York: The Modern Library, 1940).
6. *The Prince*, 19–20.
7. Deutsch and Foltz 1963; Kautsky 1963; Emerson 1960; Spiro 1966; Jackson and Rosberg 1982; Geertz 1963.
8. See Gabrield A. Almond and Bingham G. Powell, *Comparative Politics: A Developmental Approach* (Boston: Little, Brown & Co., 1966) 36.
9. See "Some Reflections on Constitutionalism for Emergent Political Orders" in *Patterns of Development*, Herbert Spiro, Ed., (Prentice Hall, 1967) 14.
10. Clifford Geertz, *Interpretation of Cultures* (New York: Basic Books, 1973) 255 ff.
11. Kwame Nkrumah, *Ghana: The Autobiography of Kwame Nkrumah* (New York: International Publishers, 1957) 102–122.
12. John Gunther, *Inside Africa* (London: Hamish Hamilton, 1955) 782.
13. Kwame Nkrumah, *Ghana*, 120.
14. See his *Kwame Nkrumah: His Rise to Power* (London: George Allen and Unvin Ltd., 1955) 161.
15. See Ebenezer Addo, *Kwame Nkrumah*, 200.
16. Addo, Op. Cit. 200.
17. Kwame Nkrumah, *Consciencism: Philosophy and Ideology for Decolonization* (New York: Monthly Press, 1964) 59.
18. Ebenezer Addo, Op. Cit. 68.
19. Kwame Nkrumah, *Ghana*, 12.
20. John S. Pobee, *Kwame Nkrumah and the Church in Ghana* (Accra: Asempa Publishers, 1988) 131.
21. James Aquandah, *40 Years: Ghana Christian Council Anniversary Handbook* (Accra: Asempa Publishers, 1971) 23.
22. *Ashanti Pioneer* (Kumasi, January 9, 1954).
23. *Cabinet Minutes*, May 27, 1958.
24. Geoffrey Bing, *Reap the Whirlwind* (London: MacGibbon & Kee Ltd., 1960) 267–268.
25. Jon Woronoff, *West African Wager: Houphouet Versus Nkrumah* (Metuchen, NJ: Scarecrow Press, 1972) 67.
26. David Apter, *The Gold Coast in Transition* (Princeton: Princeton University Press, 1955/63/77).
27. Kwame Nkrumah, *Ghana*, 1957, 12.

28. A. A. Afrifa, *The Ghana Coup: 24th February, 1966* (London: Frank Cass & Co., 1966).
29. Sarah Harris, *Father Divine* (New York: Collier Books, 1971) xvii.
30. Kwame Nkrumah, *Ghana*, 40.
31. Kwame Nkrumah, Op. Cit., 45.
32. Ali A. Mazrui, *Nkrumah's Legacy and Africa's Triple Heritage Between Globalization and Counter Terrorism* (Accra: Ghana Universities Press, 2004) 4.

Bibliography

Addo, Ebenezer Obiri. 1997. *Kwame Nkrumah: A Case Study of Religion and Politics in Ghana*. Lanham: University Press of America.
Afrifa, A.A. 1966. *The Ghana Coup: 24th February, 1966*. London: Frank Cass.
Almond, Gabriel A., and Bingham G. Powell Jr. 1966. *Comparative Politics: A Developmental Approach*. Boston: Little, Brown.
Apter, David. 1955/63/77. *The Gold Coast in Transition*. Princeton: Princeton University Press.
Aquandah, James. 1971. *40 Years: Ghana Christian Council Anniversary Handbook*. Accra: Asempa Publishers.
Bing, Geoffrey. 1960. *Read the Whirlwind*. London: MacGibbon & Kee.
Emerson, Rupert. 1960. *From Empire to Nation: The Rise of Self-Assertion of Asian and African Peoples*. Cambridge: Harvard University Press.
Geertz, Clifford, ed. 1963. *Old Societies and New States*. New York: Free Press.
———. 1973. *Interpretation of Cultures*. New York: Basic Books.
Gunther, John. 1955. *Inside Africa*. London: Hamish Hamilton.
Harris, Sarah. 1971. *Father Divine*. New York: Collier Books.
Jackson, R., and C. Rosberg. 1982. *Personal Rule in Black Africa: Prince, Autocrat, Prophet, Tyrant*. Berkeley: University of California Press.
Machiavelli, Niccolo. 1940. *The Prince and the Discourses*. New York: The Modern Library.
Mazrui, Ali A. 2004. *Nkrumah's Legacy and Africa's Triple Heritage Between Globalization and Counter Terrorism*. Accra: Ghana Universities Press.
Nkrumah, Kwame. 1957. *Ghana: The Autobiography of Kwame Nkrumah*. New York: International Publishers.
———. 1964. *Consciencism: Philosophy and Ideology for Decolonization*. New York: Monthly Press.
Omari, Peter. 1970. *Kwame Nkrumah: The Anatomy of an African Dictatorship*. New York: Atlanta Press.
Pobee, J.S. 1988. *Kwame Nkrumah and the Church in Ghana: 1949–1966*. Accra: Asempa Publisher.
Rooney, David. 1988. *Kwame Nkrumah: The Political Kingdom in the Third World*. London: I. B. Tauris.
Timothy, Bankole. 1955. *Kwame Nkrumah: His Rise to Power*. London: George Allen & Unwin.
Woronoff, Jon. 1972. *West African Wager: Houphouet Versus Nkrumah*. Metuchen: Scarecrow Press.

CHAPTER 16

Political Ethics of Léopold Sédar Senghor

Aliou Cissé Niang

Biographies, poems, and other literary genres written by many intellectuals, and specially in this case first African heads of states such as Léopold Sédar Senghor, Kwame Nkrumah, and Julius Kambarage Nyerere,[1] I read over the years embed much of their lived experiences shaped by cultural encounters—African and imperial Europe. Much of their moral vision and quest for a way beyond colonization was shaped by their lived experiences.[2] In other words, their thoughts, messages, and leadership style bespeak of a resilient attempt to create alternative communities to the ones empires constructed for them.[3] These first African leaders negotiated the independence of their respective countries from colonists reluctant to relinquish power and incapable of seeing how their imposition of European cultural values on Africans that justified economic exploitation is morally unacceptable. Senghor woke up to this reality once concealed by the French geopolitical discourse that legitimized colonization and lampooned African cultures as devoid of any valuable contributions to world civilization.

I have yet to read a systematic political ethics of Senghor from his proponents or opponents. As I was writing this chapter, I decided to ask one of the experts on Senghorian Negritude, Souleymane Bachir Diagne, whether he knew of any work on Senghorian political ethics to date. A Senghorian political ethic has yet to be written, I learned from Diagne,[4] and therefore the only actionable venue is to excavate and construct it from his prolific writings and those of his commentators. In the process, I realized that one major hurdle that stifles any retrieval and construction of Senghor's political ethics is the daunting task of repositioning his work from dismissive criticisms that plagued the

A. C. Niang (✉)
Union Theological Seminary, New York, NY, USA

most instructive aspects of his thought. Senghor was as determined as his closest companions from West Indies, Léon-Gontran Damas and Aimé Césaire in particular, to free and rehabilitate the image of Africans from European colonial objectifications. A venture into a Senghorian political ethics is a momentous task for at least two main reasons. First, *Orphée Noir*[5] written by Jean Paul Sartre to preface Senghor's *Anthologie de la nouvelle poèsie nègre et malgache de langue Française* turned out to be a piece penned for a European audience, as Polybius did in writing a Roman history for Greek readers. It began with a persuasive rationale for emergent African voices out of French colonial alienation but then escalated into a demotion of Negritude, painting it as nothing less than a fad—*un racisme antiraciste* "a racism anti-racism" headed to its annihilation.[6] It is not surprising to hear similar criticisms from some African authors from mostly British colonies such as Ezekiel Mphahleles[7] and Wole Soyinka,[8] and Americans such as Reiland Rabaka[9]—just to name a few.

Sartrian interpretation on Negritude, I argue, did much to influence how Negritude should be read by both Africans and Westerners alike. Second, such a conditioned reading resulted in too much focus on two oft-quoted lines yanked out of their respective genres and contexts to serve as the basis for poignant criticism against Senghorian formulation of Negritude with the first being, *l'émotion est nègre, comme la raison hellène*[10] "emotion is negro as reason is Greek" (appeared in a speech); and second, *Car j'ai une grande faibless pour la France*[11] "For I have a great weakness for France" (a line from one of the poems that embed his theological ethics). To some, to Soyinka in particular, Senghor appeared to have caved-in to the French claim for epistemological superiority and the inferiority of black people—a complex that drove him to embrace French culture and language.[12]

In this chapter, I am modestly constructing a primer or more accurately a sketch of Senghorian political ethic, and as I noted earlier, I have yet to read a systematic one but that does not mean attempts have not been made in this regard beyond my knowledge. That being said, I provide a concise statement on the birth and life of Negritude, then move to African Socialism/communalism that underpinned Senghor's political ethic expressed as an African-Serer Christian humanism and *civilization of the universal* and then close with some remarks.

Senghorian Political Ethic in the Making[13]

Admittedly, my response to the criticisms leveled against Senghorian Negritude in no way ignores their necessity. Criticism against his positive take on French culture and language are not that nuanced. They overlook his stern rejection of colonial abuse evinced in many of his writings and poems, in particular, his poem entitled, Prière de Paix "Prayer for Peace." Many studies published on his works and persona tend to ignore key dimensions of his life and thought—contexts and conditions that gave rise to the Negritude movement, its impetus, and the religions that shaped Senghor's faith and moral vision. It is conceivable to argue that much of the moral vision and praxis of a person of faith is somewhat a function of their vocation under the aegis of the deity they revere and serve. What then are the contexts of the conditions that gave rise to Negritude? One must start with the Senegalese colonial context and condition fictionally captured by Cheikh Hamidou Kane's *Ambiguous Adventure*.

At the heart of Kane's novel are the depths of the African struggle with transferred European cultural values that elicited various responses from Senegalese people. His thought-provoking account provides actionable insights into the multifaceted struggle many colonized people faced from their African contexts to Metropolitan France.[14] In a nail-biting Diallobé deliberation, the main fictional character, Samba Diallo, the symbol of *Diallobé* people, colonized Senegalese, and Negro people sent to France. Faced with an overwhelming task of negotiating life under the French Empire, the Diallobé decided to place the future of their people and country in the hands of Samba Diallo. In the heights of this deliberation, Kane invites his readers to his fictionalized autobiography, in the voice of la Grande Royal "The most Royal Lady." The imaged scenery captures how his Diallobé community members gathered to deliberate on ways to survive French colonization that threatened their culture and faith. La Grande Royal proposed that her cousin Samba Diallo "*must go to learn from them the art of conquering without being in the right* ... joining 'wood to wood'."[15] He must enter the "new school," namely the French colonial school—the most effective French weapon for transferring French culture to Senegalese people. To know this art might lead to freedom, identity, and cultural reclamation. As the story enfolds, it became increasingly clear that La Grande Royal was a radical visionary prophet:

> The School in which I would place our children will kill in them what today we love and rightly conserve with care. Perhaps the very memory of us will die in them. When they return from the school, there may be those who will not recognize us. What I am proposing is that we should agree to die in our children's hearts and that the foreigners who have defeated us should fill the place, wholly, which we shall have left free ... remember our fields when the rainy season is approaching. We love our fields very much, but what do we do then? We plough them up and burn them: we kill them. In the same way, recall this: what do we do with our reserves of seed when the rain has fallen? We would like to eat them but, we bury them in the earth. Folk of the Diallobé, with the arrival of the foreigners has come the tornado which announces the great hibernation of our people. My opinion—I, The Most Royal Lady—is that our best seeds and our dearest fields—those are our children. Does anyone wish to speak?[16]

Samba Diallo ended up being murdered by the fool at the end of the novel—a death that echoed much of Okonkwo's in *Things Fall Apart* but was not in vain.[17] His death has soteriological and eschatological implications for colonized people not just the Diallobé—a world beyond colonization as The Most Royal Lady saw it. The Chief of the Diallobé also echoed her vision admitting that sending their children to learn the art is fraught with dangers. Once in

France, and as the children "learn all the ways of joining wood to wood ... they would also forget. What they forget is themselves, their bodies, and the futile dream which hardens with age and stifles the spirit. So what they learn is worth infinitely more than what they forget."[18] The Chief personified Western education as a powerfully seductive weapon that numbs and corrupts and colonizes the mind to embrace imperial ontology and epistemology as normative. In this *imaginaire*, forgetting one's cultural and spiritual roots does not necessarily preclude or inhibit relearning those very suppressed values.[19] Kane's fictional autobiography mirrors the life and thought of Senghor and many African leaders. Senghor's thought grew over time—from using the language of founders of the Harlem Renaissance, such as the "new Negro," to his own reformulation of Negritude.

Negritude was coined by Césaire but proto-Negritude was the work of Senghor, Césaire, and Damas ("The Three Musketeers", as Senghor called them in a eulogy to Damas[20]) in response to the French colonial geopolitical discourse of objectification of African people and their culture. It was not just a response or protest, as some authors maintain, but the beginning of an introspective and repositioning journey from the oppression or *chosification*, "thingification" in the words of Césaire,[21] of colonized Africans and people of African descent to their liberation and rehumanization. After embracing Negritude and anticipating a pushback or trivialization of its genuine cause, Senghor ensured their would-be critics would have an initial understanding of Negritude's raison d' être. He writes:

> In what circumstances did Aimé Césaire and I launch the word negritude in the years 1933–35? Together with a few other black students, we were at the time panic-stricken. The horizon was blocked. No reform in sight and the colonizers were legitimizing our political and economic dependence by the theory of *tabula rasa*. They deemed we had invented nothing, created nothing, written, sculpted, painted and sung nothing ... To establish an effective revolution, *our* revolution, we first had to get rid of our borrowed attire—that of assimilation-and assert our being, namely our negritude. Nevertheless, negritude, even when defined as "the total of black Africa's cultural values" could only offer us the beginning of a solution to our problem and not the solution itself. We could not go back to our former condition, to a negritude of the sources ... To be really ourselves, we had to embody Negro African culture in twentieth-century realities. To enable our negritude to be, instead of a museum piece, the efficient instrument of liberation, it was necessary to cleanse it of its dross and include it in the united movement of the contemporary world.[22]

Clearly, the founders conceived of Negritude as a repositioning process, a conscientization process to liberate and rehabilitate Africans in Africa and the diaspora. Senghor and Césaire will each formulate a Negritude, consonant with their respective lived experiences—either embracing "the fact of being black ... destiny... black history ... culture... and history"[23] or ways of "self-expression of the black character," "world," and "civilization."[24] Differences between these definitions are somewhat negligible, given the fact that both Césaire and Senghor were taken up with the same effects of colonial alienation.[25] From his home in the Senegalese protectorate to metropolitan France, Senghor learned "the art of conquering without being in the right" and saw its dehumanizing capacity and shrewd attempts to permanentize colonization.

Questioning the relevance of Negritude then and especially now (in our neocolonial and globalized world), as many have done, is the right course of action. Any concept, movement, or method should not be exempt from scrutiny, and to dismiss Negritude on the basis of Senghorian words lifted out context, as far as I am concerned, misses the point. Any criticisms based on yanked out lines, such as the ones I noted earlier, would risk misconstruing what Senghor was trying to communicate from the early 1930s up to his retirement from public service. The years leading up to and during the aftermath of the independence of many African countries was a delicate period. African leaders must get it right as they work assiduously to minimize potential failures in order to set their respective countries on the right path to political and economic independence. This required a daunting gradual and delicate task of dismantling Western hegemonic historiography and its epistemological claim to superiority over non-Western cultures it deemed uncivilized.[26]

SENGHORIAN POLITICAL ETHIC AS AFRICAN COMMUNALISM

As I noted earlier, much of Senghorian political ethics may be constructed from his narratives, poems, and speeches—*On African Socialism*, "Negritude: A Humanism of the Twentieth Century," *Liberté 1-5*, *Ce Que Je crois*, "Ce que l'homme noir apporte," "allocution de Monsieur Léopold Sédar Senghor," *La condition Humaine*,[27] and *Hosties Noirs* "Black Wafers."[28] To return to my earlier point, one of the two lines that engendered much criticism is *l'émotion est nègre, comme la raison hellène* "emotion is negro as reason is Greek."[29] If I am not mistaken, these words occur in most criticism leveled against Senghor, in spite of his tireless clarifications. I recall a conversation I had with a taxi driver in Manhattan, a native of République de Guinée "Republic of Guinea", West Africa, on the role Senghor and Sékou Touré played in the years leading up to the independence of most African countries. He did not hesitate emphasizing his disappointment with Senghor for painting Africans as emotional people devoid of reason. It was a sober realization that all my taxi driver knows about Senghor was that Senghor believed "emotion is negro as reason is Greek" and nothing more. I was not that surprised. I had, and still have, many conversations with thinkers that often gravitate around that oft-quoted sentence. The phrase attracted and still does much rejection of Senghorian Negritude. Senghor's "emotion is negro as reason is Greek" is a line stated in a much broader and complex argument contrasting Western and African ontology and epistemology. He was responding to Western colonial geopolitical discourse essentializing French culture and demoting the Africans in the same way Europeans did.

Senghor's lived experiences and education in both Africa and Europe shaped his framing of negritude, and the speech he delivered at the First International Congress of Negro Writers and Artists in 1956 laid down key elements of his political ethic further developed systematically in his *On African Socialism*. The speech itself is nothing short of a manifesto of African communalism, cultural values, and artistic contributions, all couched in the spirit of deconstructing and emphatically rejecting the theory of *tabula rasa*.[30] During the same conference, his closest colleague Césaire bluntly protested, "We refuse to yield to the temptation of the *tabula rasa*. I refuse to believe that the future of African culture can totally and brutally reject the former African culture."[31] Both were taking on an important colonial dimension many Africans tend to shrug off today as passé and therefore irrelevant to the current state of affairs in post-independent Africa, namely imposition of European culture on Africans, economic exploitation, and domination. The transfer of European cultural values was the root cause of African identity and cultural crisis, and both Senghor and Césaire found it expedient to reject the imposition of French culture on African culture as a moral problem. Senghorian political ethic anchors his philosophy shaped by what he conceived to have been a moral violation of human dignity. Negro ontology and epistemology—Negro humanism—predated the slave trade and colonialism. What is Negro ontology and epistemology of which Senghor persistently spoke?

African ontology and epistemology are at the center of Senghor's deconstructive and constructive project. If "emotion is negro as reason is Greek," was his attempt to tackle the root of French moral conundrum (an epistemology that helped legitimize colonization), Senghor begins with what he conceived to be African Negro ontology as *mother* of African epistemology. The African Negro, Senghor avers, "does not realize that he thinks; he feels that he feels, he feels his existence, he feels himself."[32] This is hardly a reduction of African Negro epistemology to pure emotion without rational capacity. Senghor's point, however, is that European reasoning is analytical, namely discursive by utilization, while African Negro "reasoning is intuitive by participation."[33] Intuitive reason is by no means superficial but transcends "appearance to understand the totality of the real."[34] In this case, epistemology is a function of ontology. I know through what "I feel"—relating to the other through my touch—therefore I am. In other words, one knows an object or a person through intimate relationship mediated by touch. The African knows through feeling, touching, or dancing with the other, while the European isolates the object or person first in order to know and then relates as in Cartesian epistemology.[35] This distinction is a necessary step toward African liberation and rehabilitation. I now turn to Senghorian communalism that underpins his humanism and *civilization de l'universel*.

Communalism

If epistemology is a function of ontology, as Senghor consistently argued, then the distinction he made between African and European ontologies and epistemologies is central to his political ethic. Senghor and his partners found colonial geopolitics of the time marshaled to justify the erasure of African culture by imposing European culture through association (British) and assimilation (French) policies unethical. Senghor conceived of the African Negro as a person who relates intuitively to humans and the cosmos. The life force that rhythmically animates the cosmos simultaneously illuminates African Negro existence and knowledge and moves and guides their participatory agency—interrelationship. He writes:

> The vital force of the African Negro, that is, his surrender to the Other, is thus inspired by reason. But reason is not, in this case, the *visualizing* reason of the European White, but a kind of *embracing* reason which has more in common with *logos* than with *ratio*. For ratio is compass, T-square and sextant; it is measure and weight. *Logos* on the other hand was the living word before Aristotle forged it into a diamond. Being the most typical human expression of a neural and sensory impression, *logos* does not mold the object (without touching it) into rigid logical categories. The *word* of the African negro, which becomes flesh as we shall see presently when we come to language, restores objects to their primordial color, and brings out their true grain and veins, their names and odors. It perforates them with its luminous rays so as to make them again transparent, and penetrates their sur-reality, I mean, their *sub-reality* in its primeval *wetness*."[36]

To live this way is to practice "participation" or "communion"—a "life in the rhythm of the object" as well as humans.[37] African Negro ontology and epistemology is a bifocal lived experience that fully embodies the subject-object relationship. Echoes of biblical myths are clearly intimated here (Gen 1–2 and John 1:1–14). The White European, Senghor argues, keeps the object

> at a distance, immobilizes it outside time and in some sense outside space, fixes it and slays it. Armed with precision instruments, he dissects it mercilessly so as to arrive at a factual analysis. Learned, but moved by practical considerations European White uses the Other, after slaying it, for practical ends: He treats it as a *means*. And he *assimilates* it in a centripetal motion; destroys it by feeding on it.[38]

This was precisely the point Joseph de Maistre (1753–1821) made as he was critiquing the danger some of his compatriots posed to humanity and nature. As he saw it, placed above the various animals of the fauna is the human being, and I suspect he meant the White European,

> whose destructive hand spares nothing that lives; he kills to nourish himself, he kills to clothe himself, he kills to adorn himself, he kills to attack, he kills to defend himself, he kills to instruct himself, he kills to amuse himself, he kills for the sake of killing: superb and terrible king, he wants everything and nothing could resist him.[39]

The strong verbs describing human selfish actions are analogous to the colonial—the violence guised as civilization in reality proved to be nothing less than a domineering transfer of European cultural values, plunder, and ultimately murder of those who would dare to speak against or question empire. Denouncing imperial Rome's occupation of the British Isles, Tacitus offered these devastating critiques of empire saying, these deadlier

> Romans, whose arrogance you cannot escape by obedience and self-restraint. Robbers of the world, now that the earth fails their all-devastating hands ... alone of humanity they covet with the same passion want as much as wealth. To plunder, butcher, steal, these things they misname empire: they make a desolation and they call it peace. (Tacitus, *Agr.* 30.4–5 [trans. Peterson, LCL])[40]

Senghor never saw himself as a politician but rather as a priest and teacher. In spite of his being turned down to enter the priesthood, teaching and upholding ethical values central to the priestly vocation never departed from his heart. In the end, he not only became teacher, poet, and head of state, he was also the "priest *manqué*," "missed priest"[41] as Soyinka observed, and both dimensions shaped his political ethic. The Negro plight under colonial rule forced him into the political arena with a view to freeing and conscientizing Africans. He dreamed of seeing Africans take ownership of their affairs. Hammering out and clarifying aspects of his Negritude, Senghor learned from senior Senegalese politicians (Blaise Diagne and Lamine Guèye) but avoided their preferential treatment of the citizens of the colonial towns. In spite of the enormous length of time he spent in Metropolitan France, Senghor never forgot his rural roots. He identified with his rural more than urban compatriots and relentlessly fought for their freedom, education, and the improvement of their economic conditions.[42] In context, one can see clearly that seeming essentialist tendencies of which he had been accused from many fronts were actually his attempt to hammer out a way out of colonial dominance that many African leaders such as Nkrumah and Nyerere (just to name a few) also tried to achieve.

In his *African Indigenous Ethics*, Leonard Tumaini Chuwa provides helpful insights on Ujamaa, Ubuntu, and Senghorian socialism/communalism.[43] To me, the distinctions Chuwa made between the concepts are relevant but need not to be overemphasized since context determined the formulation of such ideas. The main point I take away from Chuwa's study is that these concepts share a key feature that transcends their respective contexts—that is, the individual's relationship to the community and vice versa.[44] How this relationship is explained and nuanced by Senghor, Nkrumah, and Nyerere is merely semantics. I am keenly aware of Serer and Diola self-understanding and communalism. The Diola or Serer never prioritizes the community over the individual. The individual's participatory agency in precolonial Diola or Serer communities is one in which both the community member's individuality and that of the community are intertwined. I am not idealizing or essentializing Africa and African communalism—a community ethos that encourages communal solidarity, administration of equity, and practical communion. Senghor envisioned "a *community* where each individual will identify himself with the collectivity and the collectivity will identify with all its members."[45] The contrast he draws between European and African Negro individuals in community evinces Senghor in no way strips African Negro community members of their individual rights, contributions, and needs. He writes:

> To return to the distinction between Negro-African and collectivist European society, I would say that the latter is an *assembly of individuals*. The collectivist society inevitably places the emphasis on the individual, on his original activity and his needs. In this respect, the debate between "to each according to his labor" and "to each according to his needs" is significant. Negro-African society puts more stress on the group than on the individual, more on *solidarity* than on the activity and needs of the individual, more on the *communion* of person than on their autonomy. Ours is a *community* society. This does not mean it ignores the individual, or that collectivist society ignores solidarity, but the latter bases this solidarity on the activities of individuals, whereas the community society bases it on the general activity of the group. Let us guard against believing that the community society ignores the *person* ... The individual is, in Europe, the man who distinguishes himself from others and claims his autonomy to affirm his himself in his basic originality. The member of the community society also claims his autonomy to affirm himself as a *being*. But he feels, he thinks that he can develop his potential, his originality, only in and by society, in union with all other men—indeed, with all other things in the universe: God, animal, tree, or pebble.[46]

Communion of persons or community society bespeaks of Senghorian socialism and spiritually informed humanism.

Humanism

Senghor uses strong verbs (*live, feel, reflect, know, e-move, sympathize*) and nouns (*embrace, contact, participation, communion*) to describe African Negro ontology and epistemology.[47] Ontology, in particular, grounds his ethics. He avers, African Negro ethics is

> on its ontology, and realizes itself in social action ... The *existence* of the Being is nothing but an integral part of the clan force, which in its turn must harmonize with the whole of the vital forces of the universe... Ethics, in Negro Africa, is *active wisdom*. It consists, for the living man, in recognizing the unity of the world and in working towards its ordering. His duty thus is to strengthen his own persona, life, certainly, but also to recognize *being* in other men. It is this which explains the place occupied in society by religion, which is truly the link between the Living and the Dead, and which through the latter, unites God with the grain of sand; which explains the organization of this same society in a network of vertical and horizontal communities; which explains the cultivation of certain virtues, such as labour, honour, filial piety, charity, hospitality.[48]

Senghor went on to describe honor as being "the intellectual expression of divine sentiment" that arises from the African Negro self-consciousness as free persons who reacted to preserve their human integrity. If honor is central to human integrity, then it is "consciousness," "vital act ... and act of life."[49] To exercise honor is to treat others as one would want to be treated—an echo of the Golden Rule—a fusion of his Serer and Christian moral vision.

> In everything do to others as you would have them do to you; for this is the law and the prophets. (Matt 7:12 cf. Luke 6:31)

The practice of honor should translate into living justly—a lifestyle that "establishes—or restores—peace, so dear to the heart of the African Negro, that balanced order which achieves the unity of the individual, the community and society. It is an act of justice to succor your neighbor, to give him nourishment and shelter and moral comfort."[50] Furthermore, Senghor avers:

> It is visible that Negro-African ethics is not the same as European morals. It is not a catechism which is recited; it is an ontology which is realized in and through society, and first and foremost, in and through oneself. Once again, in contradiction to the European world, the Negro-African world is one of *unity*.[51]

Seen this way, it is conceivable to argue that African Negro ethics is a salient aspect of the multivalency of Senghorian Negritude. Vaillant provides a gradual development of elements of Senghorian political ethic citing his *Condition Humaine*. One can detect hints of his subtle critique of French assimilation policy and its negative effects on African education and economic development. French colonial geopolitics shrewdly promoted the permanentization of French cultural values, while concealing cultural dominance and economic exploitation. Senghor was convinced that African autonomy can only be realized when Africans become producers and movers of their own destiny.[52] Senghor's preference for the word autonomy over freedom might have been a calculated choice, perhaps to avoid spooking or alerting French colonial intelligentsia of his realization that the freedom of Africa would require politics. Vaillant writes that Senghor

> never abandoned his conviction that the purpose of politics was to create a setting in which humans beings could develop their individual cultures, but his growing sophistication had led him to a conclusion that paralleled that of Kwame Nkrumah who had coined the memorable slogan "Seek ye first the political kingdom and all things will be added unto you." Senghor now realized that his vision of a free and self-directing African culture could not be realized without attention to political issues.[53]

Many Africans, including Senghor, contributed to the liberation of France from the Nazis, and it has become apparent to him that Africans were being denied any reward for having sacrificed their lives to free France from the

Germans. The indecisiveness of Charles de Gaulle after he delivered supporting words that would have paved the way for the autonomy of Africans at the conference of Brazzaville and atrocities such as the French massacre at Camp de Chiaroye "Camp of Chiaroye," forced Senghor to overcome his reluctance and enter politics. An adequate course of action for African autonomy, as Senghor conceived of it, would be for Africans to assimilate the best of French values, affirm precolonial cultural domestic art and politics, and maintain a relationship with France; and he was critiqued for this. The relationship with metropolitan France Senghor had in mind was a tactical move and means to help jump-start African educational and economic independence. Africans should use the French education curriculum and supplement it with ethnography and study of indigenous languages.[54]

France's reluctance to free her colonies proved problematic for Senghor, so he appealed to France's traditional "equality and fraternity" slogan in the hopes of exposing this ethical conundrum. Through such a relationship, the French should provide "concrete improvements in the overseas territories: more schools, more economic investments, and a more genuine voice for Africans in running their own affairs. Words without deeds were not enough."[55] Senghor has gradually come to the realization that African freedom, autonomy, and self-governance have a political dimension that must be taken seriously. African liberation, self-governance, French education implemented with the study of indigenous languages and histories, and participation in the *civilisation de l'universel* are entrenched in his political ethic.

Civilisation de l'universel *as Alternative Community*

Senghor's *Civilisation de l'universel* is an idea shaped by many factors—atrocities of the slave trade, colonization, World War II, and incipient Pan-Africanism. Senghor was born in 1906 in the protectorate instead of the colonial towns (Saint-Louis, Gorée, Dakar, and Rufisque) and was, as a result, a subject. He worked his way up—educated at home (taught by Catholic Priests of the Holy Ghost Fathers) and in Paris where he earned his aggregation in French Grammar, a degree equivalent to a Ph.D. He was later granted French citizenship, joined the French Army, fought alongside many African recruits from French colonies (derogatorily labeled "Tirailleurs"[56]) to free France from the Nazis during World War II, and was captured as prisoner of war (POW) by the Germans. These events significantly shaped his *Civilisation de l'universel* "civilization of the Universal"—a vision he discussed at great lengths in his *Liberté 3: Négritude et civilisation de l'universel*.

As a person who grew up rooted in his Serer culture, an African follower of Jesus, teacher, poet, and politician who became the first President of Senegal in 1960, and I would add, perhaps an honorary *priest-apostle-ambassador*,[57] Senghor developed an ethical moral vision to change a world torn by the slave trade, colonization, and war—life-negating events in human history based on greed, violence of words and armed wars, and genocides. These evil acts perpetrated against humanity inspired his hope and firm belief in an alternative world in which humanity will be guided by her practice of love and judged by her character to affirm and exercise her racial-ethnic and cultural mixture, the gift of dialog, and symbiotic cultural exchange.[58] Senghor's "civilization of the universal," an alternative world to the one imperial Europe created for most non-Europeans, imaged a different and new *diverse unity of cultures*. As we have seen, his vision for a new community is not just limited to words; he worked hard to persuade many of his contemporaries, critics and supporters alike, to join the cause.

When the Mali Federation failed to unite French West African countries, Senghor turned his attention to Senegal to serve as the basis for carrying out his vision for his new alternative world-community. One of Senghor's earlier moves toward the realization of his *Civilization de l'universel* was to match words with action. The failure of the Algerian conference led to his successful hosting of the *First World Festival of Negro Arts* on 01–24 April 1966 in Dakar, Senegal.[59] This event emphasized one of Senghor's central beliefs to debunk the theory of the *tabula rasa* that inspired Negritude but also charted the way for Africans to take their destiny on their own. Many dignitaries, mostly of Negro descent in continental African and the Diaspora (America and West Indies), participated in the festival.

Although my point is not to provide an in-depth look at the festival, it is important to emphasize its relevance to Senghor's overall project. Of the many aspects this First Festival symbolized, the most important were the liberation of Africans, the exhibition of their artistic productions, intellectual contributions to world civilization, and unity of the people of African descent.[60] It built on the central aim of Pan-Africanism,[61] and his new world was realized when he co-founded the Francophony institution on 20 March 1970 in Niamey, Niger.[62]

Francophony was a significant step toward his vision. The use of French as a working language, though problematic for most of his critics, should not be viewed as an end but a means to achieving freedom. As Papa Alioune Ndao maintains, a shared French language might be conceived of as yet another Senghorian calculated move to diffuse and circumvent French colonial angst and suspicion and facilitate networking and communication among African heads of states. His persistent call for rigorous education (that would gradually displace the need for "Assistants techniques," "Technical assistants"), economic improvement via salary increase for national functionaries and peasants, organizing the First Festival of Negro Artists, and the founding of the Francophony institute all represent aspects of his *Civilization de l'universel*. Senghor's critics mistook his embrace of French language as being too cozy of a relation with empire, failing to see it as a clever liberative move.

I started this chapter with a Senghorian epigraph that clearly highlights the interconnectedness of theory and praxis. Fusing Serer and Christian beliefs, Senghor deeply believed in the power of love to transform the kind of hate, violence, and greed unleashed on humanity, especially on people of African descent, into a world of genuine and yet delicate *Liberté, Égalité, Fraternité*[63]—a slogan France herself proclaimed but failed to deliver. Some critics thought Senghor's positive attitude toward colonial France manifested his thorough assimilation and love for the French language at the expense of his own culture. In reality, what the slave trade and colonization did to Africans cannot be wiped out at once. No nation is built overnight, and Senegal must gradually rise from the shambles of the slave trade and colonization. Senghor uses France to illustrate his point saying:

> A nation is not realized in a day; like fruit, it needs an inner ripening. The building of a state resembles that of a cathedral in the Middle Ages. It is a long-term enterprise, requiring centuries of effort and patience. It took France 2,000 years—up to Napoleon's time—to become a nation-state, and she was the first in Europe to do so. We were wise to begin at the beginning, with the foundation, with a federation of states, the Mali Federation. This did not suppress the federated republics; it simply coordinated their policies by transferring to the federal authorities only the general prerogatives, strictly defined and limited. We must await the adherence of the other states of the former French West Africa to see in what direction and how far we should go. We must also test the results of the first phase by experience. the fact remains that the Mali Federation is a state, with its own government, parliament, system of justice, and administrative services.[64]

Senghor has an aversion to the politics of isolation. He opted for *collaborative accommodation* to pave the way for his country to move from autonomy to independence. Since "tests of force are not the best solution," preparing for "independence through a period of autonomy and by negotiated agreements" is a healthy diplomatic approach.[65]

I argued earlier in this chapter that Senghorian political ethic is a function of his life and thought. In other words, his political ethics is autobiographical—precisely psychobiographical. Experiences of his Childhood Kingdom, missionary Christianity in Senegal and metropolitan French Christianity, the Nazis as prisoner of war, and his French education that allowed him to read classical and modern philosophers, ethnographers, and Africanists gave him a unique perspective on leadership and ethical vision. Marx, Senghor argued, built on Hegelian view of human *alienation* and Feurbach's *praxis* from which he developed "the particular theory of *value* and *capital*."[66] Labels such as nationalist, nativist, "a racism anti-racism", essentialist, or Europeanized black African are, to me, overblown characterizations of Senghorian persona. Context matters when it comes to the interpretation of any text or analysis of a person's life, thought, literary works, deeds, and words. For instance, in his praise of Senghor, Soyinka highlights his humility, respect, compassion, and capacity for conciliation, insisting that he was probably the only African Head of State who cared much to assist war-torn East Timorese people with an "office and funds in Dakar"[67]—a concrete demonstration of the moral vision of his *Africanité*. Elhadj Abdoul Hamidou Sall's homage to Nelson Mandela also emphasized Senghor's collaboration with Mandela in the struggle against Apartheid. Sall relates how Senghor, during Mandela's visit to Senegal in 1962, supported the

South African cause against the apartheid regime through diplomacy by providing an office in Dakar to jump-start, equip, and strengthen the diplomatic front to overthrow the Apartheid Regime.[68]

At home, other than some of his closest Senegalese friends and critics, most functionaries seemed to have had little grasp of what Senghor meant by African Socialism, thinking it was just a form of social justice and equitable land tenure.[69] Senghor's presidency was anything but perfect. The resilience of the Baobab Tree has been often used to metaphorically characterize his leadership, especially in difficult times and his ability to rebound from near-crushing situations[70] Senegal intermittently faced, especially in 1968, early 1970s, and 1980. Some of the problems he faced ranged from economic crises, natural phenomena (drought), and world market instabilities. Senghor appeared to have given up on his earlier commitments to fight for his compatriots as he seemed to teeter toward authoritarian tightfisted rule by quelling some riots and protests. Opinion is divided among observers. Some blamed his apparent detachment from the realities of his country to either his advanced age or events that impacted his leadership. Senghor's earlier position to ensure Africans take ownership of their own destiny has increasingly become a reality and spur for leaders to create organizations to promote economic and cultural exchange such as the Organization of African Unity (OUA). Senghor apparently learned from his limitations and mostly protesting young Senegalese technocrats, some of whom he appointed to his administration. In the end, he relinquished power to the younger generation.

As the context changes, humans often scramble to adapt in any way they can—a way of negotiating life that manifests the kind of hybridity Senghor often spoke of in terms of *métissage culturel* "cultural mixture" that his *Civilization de l'universel* called for or *métissage biologique* "biological mixture of his family." The former informs his argument for the latter. Colonial objectification, as Fanon reminds us, not only forces the colonized to question their identities but also develop various accommodative behaviors[71] and has the potential of metamorphosing a black person into someone with black skin with a white masquerade. Confronting colonization has a therapeutic dimension that is very much a function of repositioning. By repositioning, I mean the sort of conscientization that enables the colonized to debunk the colonial theory of *tabula rasa* and proudly reclaim some elements of their cultural heritage. To debunk an ideology presented as normative by colonists is a daunting task that requires, as Senghor gradually realized, a political answer—an answer he worked out through his formulation of African Negro ontology and epistemology.

As I noted earlier, to Senghor, African Negro epistemology is a function of African ontology. In other words, whereas the African knows if she/he/they cultivate a relationship with objects and persons first, the European isolates or distances her/him/themselves from objects and people in order to know them. The ethic of the African Negro on behalf of whom Senghor spoke rests on communalism. For each community member to participate in the common good of the entire community does not cancel out her/his/their individuality; rather, it actually affirms it. In this *imaginaire*, politics and ethics constitute two complementary sides each community member should uphold and practice. In precolonial Diola as well as Serer worlds, each community member, or even better, each ritually initiated generation[72] would have been socialized to practice communalism. Ancient cultures, according to many social scientists, were collectivist as opposed to modern and especially Western cultures that tend to be more individualistic.[73] Arguably, many African cultures such Diola and Serer have similar ways of making sense of and practicing interpersonal relations.

As a Serer Christian, Senghor's political ethic reflects much of his understanding of persons in community, which is foundational to his *African Socialism*, summed up as development as "integral humanism" with both economic and cultural dimensions.[74] This he believes would lead Senegalese people to economic freedom that serves as the basis for cultural and spiritual fulfillment. This socialism or precisely communalism should not be confused for capitalism and power-grabbing monopoly but "democratic socialism"[75]—a practical vehicle for "production and distribution" with deference to all community members instead of a handful of powerful elites as in capitalism. Senghorian socialism is the kind of "economic growth for development" that administers social justice, namely "the possibility offered to every citizen to fully benefit in the common good."[76] Each person would be awarded according to her/his/their own labor. Senghorian social justice, as Markovitz rightly understands it:

> requires intellectual and moral rigor, lucidity and courage, an objective analysis of the fact and austerity. This is what socialism is. Socialism is simply honesty. One cannot have the optimum development of the production of goods and the equitable division of these goods without an implacable battle against waste and embezzlement. There is "no major formula including socialism that can replace work and national unity," but the work will not be forthcoming and there will be no "unity of hearts and spirits in a renovated democracy" if corruption cannot be stopped. This is why socialism also requires and is a moral tension, a constant struggle for improvement. Rooted in human laws, amenable to human control, the process for development will be taken in hand by socialist masses to construct a new society.[77]

Senghor believed a moral society is one in which its members, from elites to peasants, participate in its political and economic development as we have already seen.

As I noted earlier, Senghorian socialism has strong African-Serer roots as he himself confirms in his Childhood Kingdom where he learned, under the tutelage of his dear uncle Toko Waly, and practices communalism with humans and nature. I would be remiss not to mention his Christian ethic and the explicit biblical ethical themes that permeate much of his work such as the communalism one reads of in many biblical passages.

> For as in one body we have many members, and not all the members have the same function,
> so we, who are many, are one body in Christ, and individually we are members one of another. (Rom 12:4–5)

The following lines from his often-cited Prayer for Peace bespeak of his capacity to forgive and reconcile:

> Lord, at the foot of this cross-and it is no longer You
> Tree of sorrow but, above the Old and New Worlds,
> Crucified Africa,
> And her right arm stretches over my land
> And her left side shades America…
> At the feet of my Africa, crucified for four hundred years
> And still breathing
> Let me recite to You, Lord, her prayer of peace and pardon ….[78]

Senghor's approach to leadership may be characterized as "tact and respect" as Vaillant has it.[79] The poetic lines proclaim the abolition of violence, hate, and all sorts of marginalization as well as peace, forgiveness, and reconciliation between colonist and colonized, oppressed and oppressor. He imaged a world in which people of African descent would work together with other people to reconcile with each other, nature, and God. The poem is subversive in its call for the abused to reconcile with the abuser and experience the healing power of forgiveness in a world prone to colonial violence. Colonial war of words and violence (Fanon and Amilcar Cabral)[80] leave no room for reconciliation and forgiveness but rather life destruction. The power of forgiveness and reconciliation is a denunciation of violence, oppression, and all sorts of exploitations as loudly attested by the cross of Jesus Christ (Luke 23:34).

Conclusion

In this chapter, I provided a modest primer of Senghorian political ethic. African Negro ontology, the anchor of Senghorian Negritude, embeds African Negro epistemology and ethics. From its inception, Negritude aimed at repositioning and rehabilitating the colonized so they can assert their "being"—reclaim their "black Africa's cultural values." Doing so, according to Senghor, would pave the way for Africans to actualize their liberation and "embody Negro African culture in twentieth-century realities." This daunting task rested on the practice of African socialism—an "integral humanism" informed by African religious and Christian humanistic traditions that call for the administration of social justice and equity.

In his eulogy to Senghor, Wole Soyinka, one of Senghor's most vocal critics, emphasized two areas I believe are embedded in the political ethic Senghor practiced. He writes:

I can think of two areas in which Senghor can be considered an exemplar, a medium, and mediator for the future of the continent. One is his philosophy of conciliation, which, considered profoundly, may be regarded as the precursor of South Africa's seemingly miraculous resolution of a potentially destructive conflict.

The second, worthy of consideration and emulation by African leaders is Senghor's

> lesson in power, one that brings with it the transcendence of the humanist over the trappings of office, a lesson that one wished so desperately that other African Heads of State would heed ... Senghor's relinquishing of power was not simply symbolic. After years of pomp and circumstance of power, he accepted and fully lived his transformation into a private citizen. As recent events in Zimbabwe have demonstrated, the sermon that Léopold Sédar Senghor, priest *manqué*, has preached with his life remains as urgent and pertinent as ever: there is life after power.[81]

I agree with Soyinka that Africans desperately need leaders to emulate the model Senghor offered not just to Africans but a world experiencing the resurgence of nationalism. Senghorian political ethics were inspired by a symbiosis of his African-Serer and Christian moral visions. To lead an ethnically and religiously mixed people to independence and govern them with somewhat clean hands, as Senghor did, required divinely inspired political ethics. It empowered him to defy greed, relinquish power, practice conciliation at home and beyond, and live modestly.

Notes

1. Janet G. Vaillant, *Black, French, and African: A Life of Leopold Sedar Senghor* (New Haven, CT: Harvard University Press, 1990); Kwame Nkrumah, *Ghana: The Autobiography of Kwame Nkrumah* (New York: International Publishers, 1957); Julius K. Nyerere, *Uhuru Na Ujamaa: Freedom and Socialism* (New York: Oxford University Press, 1968).
2. Stanley J. Grenz, *The Moral Quest: Foundations of Christian Ethics* (Downers Grove, IL: Intervarsity Press, 1997).
3. James Wm. McClendon, *Biography as Theology: How Life Stories Can Remake Today's Theology* (Philadelphia, PA: Trinity Press International, 1974); idem, *Ethics: Systematic Theology Volume 1* (Nashville, TN: Abingdon Press, 1986); idem, *Doctrine: Systematic Theology Volume II* (Nashville, TN: Abingdon Press, 1986); 1994; idem, *Witness: Systematic Theology Volume III* (Nashville, TN: Abingdon Press, 1986), shows how a person's theology and ethics are a function of their biography.
4. Souleymane Bachir Diagne, *African Art as Philosophy: Senghor, Bergson and the Idea of Negritude* (trans. Chike Jeffers; New York: Seagull Books, 2011); idem, "Negritude," *Stanford Encyclopedia of Philosophy;* http://plato.stanford.edularchives/spr2014/entries/negritude; idem, "In Praise of the Post-racial Negritude Beyond Negritude," *Third Text* 24/2(March 2010): 241–248.

5. Jean Paul Sartre, "Orphée noir," in *Anthologie de la nouvelle poèsie nègre et malgache de langue française* (Paris: Presses Universitaires Française, 1948), IX. See Léopold Sédar Senghor, *Anthologie de la nouvelle poèsie nègre et malgache de langue française* (Paris: Presses Universitaires Française, 1948).
6. Sartre, "Orphée noir," xl-xli, cf. xiv.
7. Ezekiel Mphahleles, *The African Image* (London: Faber and Faber Limited, 1962).
8. Wole Soyinka, *Burden of Memory, the Muse of Forgiveness* (New York: Oxford University Press, 1999).
9. Reiland Rabaka, *The Negritude Movement: W. E. B. Debois, Elon Damas, Aime Cesaire, Leopold Sedar Senghor, Frantz Fanon, and the Evolution of an Insurgent Idea* (New York: Lexington Book, 2015).
10. Léopold Sédar Senghor, *Liberte l: Négritude et Humanisme* (Paris: Éditions du Seuil, 1964), 24, originally entitled "Ce que l'homme noir apporte" and published in 1939.
11. Léopold Sédar Senghor, "Hosties Noirs," in *Œuvre Poétique* (Paris: Editions du Seuil, 1964, 1990), 99.
12. Soyinka, *Burden of Memory*, 93–144.
13. Léopold Sédar Senghor, "What is Negritude?" *Atlas* (1962): 54–55, offers a concise definition and detailed treatment of Negritude including five volumes entitled *Liberte 1*; *Liberte 2*; *Liberte 3*; *Liberte 4*; and *Liberte 5*.
14. Cheikh Hamidou Kane, *Ambiguous Adventure* (trans. Katherine Woods; Portsmouth, NH: Heinemann, 1962), 48.
15. Kane, *Ambiguous Adventure*, 38.
16. Kane, *Ambiguous Adventure*, 46–7.
17. Chinua Achebe, *Things Fall Apart* (New York: Anchor Books, 1959/1994).
18. Kane, *Ambiguous Adventure*, 34.
19. Cheikh Hamidou Kane, *Les Gardiens du Temple* (Côte d'Ivoire, Abidjan: Nouvelle Éditions Ivoiriennes, 1997), 48–9, 51–4. Compare with idem, *Ambiguous Adventure*, 34, 45–7.
20. Léopold Sédar Senghor, "La mort de Léon-Gontran Damas," in Hommage Posthume à Léon-Gontran Damas-1912–1978 (Paris: Présence Africaine, 1979), 11, "Des 'trois mousquetaires' que nous étions, Léon Damas, Aimé Césaire et moi-même, c'est Léon Damas qui, le premier, illustra la Négritude par un recueil de poèmes qui portait, significativement, le titre de *Pigments*. Car cette poèsie conservait toutes les qualités de l'œuvre nègre: images symboliques et rythmes faits de parallélismes asyndétiques, mais encore humour. Cet humour nègre, le point noir, car reaction et revanche du reel: la vie," ["Of the 'three musketeers' that we were, Léon Damas, Aimé Césaire and myself, it is Léon Damas who, first, illustrated Negritude by a collection of poems which bore, significantly, the title of Pigments. Because this poetry retained all the qualities of the Negro work: symbolic images and rhythms made of asymmetrical parallelisms, but still humor. This black humor, the black point, because reaction and revenge of reality: life"].
21. Aimé Césaire, *Discours sur le colonialisme suivi de Discours sur la Négritude* (Paris: Présence Africaine, 1955/2004), 23, means by this word colonization.
22. Senghor, "Rapport sur la doctrine," 14, cited by Lillian Kesteloot, *Black Writers in French: A Literary History of Negritude* (trans. Ellen Conroy Kennedy; Philadelphia, PA: Temple University Press, 1974), 102–103 also cited by Sylvia

W. Bâ, *The Concept of Negritude in the Poetry of Léopold Sédar Senghor* (Princeton, NJ: Princeton University Press, 1973), 12. Although the rise of Negritude is embedded in the lived experiences of Senghor, Césaire and Léon-Gontran Damas, their definitions of it differ as noted by Vaillant, *Black, French, and African*, 224. Whereas for Senghor, Negritude is "the manner of self-expression of the black character, the black world, the black civilization," to Césaire it is the "recognition of being black, and the acceptance of that fact, of our destiny of black, of our history and our culture."

23. Senghor, *Liberté 3: Négritude et civilisation de l'universel* (Paris: Éditions du Seuil, 1977), 269, 270. See Vaillant, *Black, French, and African*, 244.
24. Senghor, *"What is Negritude?"* See also Vaillant, *Black, French, and African*, 244.
25. Léopold Sédar Senghor, "La Négritude comme culture des peoples noirs, ne saurait être dépassée," in *Hommage à Léopold Sédar Senghor homme de culture* (Paris: Présence Africaine, 1976), 49–66, responding to Aimé Césaire, "Césaire reçoit Senghor," in *Hommage à Léopold Sédar Senghor homme de culture* (Paris: Présence Africaine, 1976), 41–47.
26. Edward Said, *Orientalism* (New York: Vintage Books, 1979), 7; 4–8; 330–331; idem, "Orientalism Reconsidered." *Race & Class: A Journal for Black and Third World Liberation* 27(1985): 1–15.
27. Extensively discussed in Vaillant, *Black, French, and African*, 224.
28. Léopold Sédar Senghor, *On African Socialism* (trans. Mercer Cook; New York: Frederick A. Praeger Publisher, 1964); idem, *Liberté 1: Negritude et Humanisme*; originally entitled "Ce que l'homme noir apporte" originally published in 1939; idem, "Allocution de Monsieur Léopold Sédar Senghor Président de la république du Sénégal," *Présence Africaine* 92/2(1974): 23–30; idem, "Negritude: A Humanism of the Twentieth Century," in *I am Because We Are: Readings in Black Philosophy* (Amherst, MA: University of Massachusetts Press, 1995). The latter is so important that it was reprinted in at least three different volumes: Fred Lee Hord (Mzee Lasana Okpara) and Jonathan Scott Lee, eds., *I am Because We are: Readings in Black Philosophy* (Elmhurst: University of Massachusetts Press, 1995); Wilfred Cartey and Martin Kilson., *The African Reader: Independent Africa* (New York: Random House, 1976); Roy Richard Grinker and Christopher B. Steiner, *Perspectives on Africa: A Reader in Culture, History, and Representation* (Malden, MA: Blackwell Publishers, 1997).
29. Léopold Sédar Senghor, *Liberte l: Negritude et Humanisme*, 24, originally entitled "Ce que l'homme noir apporte" and published in 1939.
30. Léopold Sédar Senghor, "The Spirit of Civilisation, or the Laws of African Negro Culture," *Presence Africaine: The First International Conference of Negro Writers and Artists* 19th–22nd (September 1956): 51–64.
31. Aimé Césaire, "Culture and Colonisation," *The First International Conference of Negro Writers and Artists* 19th–22nd (September 1956): 206.
32. Senghor, *On African Socialism*, 74.
33. Senghor, *Liberté 1*. 24, 246.
34. Senghor, *Liberté* 1.246.
35. Senghor, *On African Socialism*, 73, 93–94. His oft-quoted dictum, "I feel, I dance the Other; I am" is similar to John S. Mbiti's "I am, because we are; and since we are, therefore I am" published four years after Senghor's in his *African Religions and Philosophy* (2nd ed.; Oxford: Heinemann Educational Publishers,

1969), 106. Senghor and Mbiti agree that the African's self-understanding hinges on the corporate personality of the group—a counter Cartesian individualized epistemology.
36. Senghor, "On Negrohood: Psychology of the African Negro," *Diogenes* 10/37(1962): 7–8. Translated by H. Kaal. See the entire in-depth argument in pages 1–15. See Abiola Irele, "Negritude-Literature and Ideology," *The Journal of Modern African Studies* 3/4(1965): 499–526.
37. Nadine Dormoy Savage, "Entretien avec Léopold Sédar Senghor," *The French Review* 47/6(1974): 1070, 1065–1071.
38. Senghor, "On Negrohood," 2–3.
39. Joseph de Maistre, *Les Soirées de Saint-Pétersbourg ou Entretiens sur le Gouvernement Temporel de la Providence* (Tome II; Paris: J. B. Pélagaud, Imprimeur Librairie, 1854), 28–9. "main destructrice n'épargne rien de ce qui vit; il tue pour se nourrir, il tue pour se vêtir, il tue pour se parer, il tue pour attaquer, il tue pour se défendre, il tue pour s'instruire, il tue pour s'amuser, il tue pour tuer: roi superbe et terrible, il a besoin de tout, et rien ne lui résiste." [My translation].
40. I made a minor language sensitive adaptation from "mankind" to "humanity" in the translation.
41. Wole Soyinka, "Senghor: Lessons in Power," *Research in African Literatures* 33/4(2002): 2.
42. Vaillant, *Black, French, and African*.
43. Leonard Tumaini Chuwa, *African Indigenous Ethics in Global Bioethics: Interpreting Ubuntu* (New York: Springer, 2014), 40–42, 76, 149. See also Stanley Uche Anozie, "African Esotericism with a Concentration on the Igbos," in *Spiritual and Global Ethics* (ed. Mahmoud Masaeli; UK: Cambridge Scholars Publishing, 2017),163–180.
44. Chuwa, *African Indigenous Ethics*, 40–42, 76, 149.
45. Léopold Sédar Senghor, *Constituent Congress of the P.F.A. (The Party of African Federation)* (Paris: Présence Africaine, 1959), 35, 63–84; idem, *On African Socialism*, 92–94. See Chuwa, *African Indigenous Ethics*, 82–83.
46. Senghor, *On African Socialism*, 92–94.
47. Senghor, "On Negrohood," 2–3.
48. Léopold Sédar Senghor, "Constructive Elements of a Civilization of African Negro Inspiration," *Présence Africaine* 2(26 March–1 April 1959): 285–286.
49. Senghor, "Constructive elements," 286.
50. Senghor, "Constructive elements," 286–287.
51. Senghor, "Constructive elements," 287.
52. Vaillant, *Black, French, and African*, 214–242.
53. Vaillant, *Black, French, and African*, 241–242.
54. Vaillant, *Black, French, and African*, 191–203.
55. Vaillant, *Black, French, and African*, 206.
56. *Harraps' Shorter Dictionnaire Anglais-Francais/Francais-Anglais*, 757. *Tirailleur* means "sharpshooter" or "skirmisher." In colonial context it meant "native Algerian" or "Senegalese infantry." Lexically, the word is made up two terms *tire* "shoot" and "*ailleur*" elsewhere and conjures up the idea that Algerian or Senegalese infantry aimed away from their targets, namely the Nazis.
57. Senghor is either called "Apostle," "ambassador" or priest "*manqué*." To me he is a *priest-apostle-ambassador* inspired to transcend human proclivities, vicissi-

tudes, and ethnocentrism to propose a vision of a world consonant with the much propagandized and less lived French *Liberté, Égalité, Fraternité* slogan, especially when it comes to French views and treatment of humans in their colonies in Africa and West Indies.
58. Léopold Sédar Senghor, *The Foundations of "Africanité" or "Négritude" and "Arabité"* (Paris: Présence Africaine, 1971).
59. Senghor, *Liberté 3: Négritude et Civilization de l'universel*, 58–62; idem, "2nd Pré-Colloquium," 31–38.
60. David Murphy, ed., *The First World Festival of Negro Arts, Dakar 1966: Contexts and Legacies* (Liverpool: Liverpool University Press, 2016). Essayists in this volume provide some good but mixed views on the overall significance of the festival for the Africa and the diaspora. Murphy, in particular, notes the renewed interest in this epoch-making event and importance today.
61. Colin Legum, *Pan-Africanism A Short Political Guide* (rev. ed.; London: Pall Mall Press, 1962, 1965).
62. Senghor, *Liberté 3*, 62. For details on the making of Francophony, see Papa Alioune Ndao, *La francophonie des Pères fondateurs* (Paris: Éditions Karthala, 2008), who offers a good treatment of the collaboration that shaped this institution that has now outgrown its modest beginnings to include many nations around the world.
63. Since the French Revolution, established during the Third Republic, this slogan was finally written into the French Constitution in 1958.
64. Senghor, *On African Socialism*, 12–13.
65. Irving Leonard Markovitz, *Léopold Sédar Senghor and the Politics of Negritude* (New York: Atheneum, 1969), 109, 102–118, has a detailed discussion of Senghorian politics and his prudent thinking as he designed, so to speak, Senegal.
66. Senghor, *On African Socialism*, 27.
67. Soyinka, "Senghor: Lessons in Power," 1.
68. Elhadj Abdoul Hamidou Sall, "Mandela et le Senegal, Mon Hommage a Madiba" http://www.leral.net/Mandela-et-le-Senegal-Mon-Hommage-a-Madiba-Par-Hamidou-Sall_a100899.html
69. Vaillant, *Black, French, and African*, 325.
70. Janet G. Vaillant, "Homage to Léopold Sédar Senghor," *Research in African Literatures* 33/4(2002): 17.
71. Frantz Fanon, *Black Skin, White Masks* (trans. Charles Lam Markmann; New York: Grove Press, 1967).
72. By initiated generation, I am appealing to the rites of passage to adulthood in both Diola and Serer worlds. These initiation rites are central to individual and corporate construction of reality, self-understanding, and agency.
73. John J. Pilch and Bruce J. Malina, *Biblical Social Values and Their Meaning: A Handbook* (Peabody, MA: Hendrickson Publishers, 1993), 49–52.
74. Markovitz, *Léopold Sédar Senghor and his Politics of Negritude*, 155.
75. Markovitz, *Léopold Sédar Senghor and his Politics of Negritude*, 157. Pages 155–187 offer a detailed analysis of Senghorian political ethics drawn from his speech.
76. Markovitz, *Léopold Sédar Senghor and his Politics of Negritude*, 159.
77. Markovitz, *Léopold Sédar Senghor and his Politics of Negritude*, 159–160.

78. Léopold Sédar Senghor, "Prayer for Peace," in *Léopold Sédar Senghor Collected Poems* (trans. Melvin Dixon; Charlottesville, VA: University of Virginia Press, 1991), 69–72.
79. Vaillant, *Black, French, and African*, 217.
80. Fanon, Frantz. *fa.*, 35, 63. See Tsenay Serequeberhan, *The Hermeneutics of African Philosophy: Horizon and Discourse* (New York: Routledge, 1994), 79, 55–85.
81. Soyinka, "Senghor: Lessons in Power," 1–2.

Bibliography

Achebe, Chinua. 1959/1994. *Things Fall Apart*. New York: Anchor Books.
Anozie, Stanley Uche. 2017. African Esotericism with a Concentration on the Igbos. In *Spiritual and Global Ethics*, ed. Mahmoud Masaeli, 163–180. Newcastle upon Tyne: Cambridge Scholars Publishing.
Bâ, Sylvia W. 1973. *The Concept of Negritude in the Poetry of Léopold Sédar Senghor*. Princeton: Princeton University Press.
Cartey, Wilfred, and Martin Kilson. 1976. *The African Reader: Independent Africa*. New York: Random House.
Césaire, Aimé. 1955/2004. *Discours sur le colonialisme suivi de Discours sur la Négritude*. Paris: Présence Africaine.
———. 1956. Culture and Colonisation. In *The First International Conference of Negro Writers and Artists*, 19th–22nd (September 1956): 193–207.
———. 1976. Césaire reçoit Senghor. In *Hommage à Léopold Sédar Senghor homme de culture*, 41–47. Paris: Présence Africaine.
Chuwa, Leonard Tumaini. 2014. *African Indigenous Ethics in Global Bioethics: Interpreting Ubuntu*. New York: Springer.
de Maistre, Joseph. 1854. *Les Soirées de Saint-Pétersbourg ou Entretiens sur le Gouvernement Temporel de la Providence*. Vol. II. Paris: J. B. Pélagaud, Imprimeur Librairie.
Diagne, Souleymane Bachir. 2010. In Praise of the Post-Racial Negritude Beyond Negritude. *Third Text* 24 (2): 241–248.
———. 2011. *African Art as Philosophy: Senghor, Bergson and the Idea of Negritude*. Translated by Chike Jeffers. New York: Seagull Books.
———. Negritude. In *Stanford Encyclopedia of Philosophy*. http://plato.stanford.edu-larchives/spr2014/entries/negritude
Harraps' Shorter Dictionnaire Anglais-Francais/Francais-Anglais. Edinburgh: Harrap Books, 1993.
Fanon, Frantz. 1967. *Black Skin, White Masks*. Translated by Charles Lam Markmann. New York: Grove Press.
Grenz, Stanley J. 1997. *The Moral Quest: Foundations of Christian Ethics*. Downers Grove: InterVarsity Press.
Grinker, Roy Richard, and Christopher B. Steiner. 1997. *Perspectives on Africa: A Reader in Culture, History, and Representation*. Malden: Blackwell Publishers.
Hord (Mzee Lasana Okpara). 1995. In *I am Because We are: Readings in Black Philosophy*, ed. Fred Lee and Jonathan Scott Lee. Elmhurst: University of Massachusetts Press.

Irele, Abiola. 1965. Negritude-Literature and Ideology. *The Journal of Modern African Studies* 3 (4): 499–526.
Kane, Cheikh Hamidou. 1962. *Ambiguous Adventure*. Translated by Katherine Woods. Portsmouth: Heinemann.
———. 1997. *Les Gardiens du Temple. Côte d'Ivoire*. Abidjan: Nouvelle Éditions Ivoiriennes.
Kesteloot, Lilyan. 1974. *Black Writers in French: A Literary History of Negritude*. Translated by Ellen Conroy Kennedy. Philadelphia: Temple University Press.
———. L'après-guerre, l' anthropologie de Senghor et la Préface de Sartre. http://ethiopiques.refer.sn
Legum, Colin. 1962. *Pan-Africanism: A Short Political Guide*. Revised ed. London: Pall Mall Press.
Markovitz, Irving Leonard. 1969. *Léopold Sédar Senghor and the Politics of Negritude*. New York: Atheneum.
Mbiti, John S. 1969. *African Religions and Philosophy*. 2nd ed. Oxford: Heinemann Educational Publishers.
McClendon, James Wm. 1974. *Biography as Theology: How Life Stories Can Remake Today's Theology*. Philadelphia: Trinity Press International.
———. 1986a. *Ethics: Systematic Theology*. Vol. 1. Nashville: Abingdon Press.
———. 1986b. *Doctrine: Systematic Theology*. Vol. II. Nashville: Abingdon Press.
———. 1986c. *Witness: Systematic Theology*. Vol. III. Nashville: Abingdon Press.
Mphahleles, Ezekiel. 1962. *The African Image*. London: Faber and Faber Limited.
Mudimbe, Valentin Y. 1988. *The Invention of Africa, Gnosis, Philosophy and the Order of Knowledge*. Bloomington: Indiana University Press.
Murphy, David, ed. 2016. *The First World Festival of Negro Arts, Dakar 1966: Contexts and Legacies*. Liverpool: Liverpool Press.
Mveng, R.P. Engelbert. 1976. Léopold Sédar Senghor l'homme de la fraternité humaine, l'homme de la dignité des peoples noirs. In *Hommage à Léopold Sédar Senghor: homme de culture*, 231–237. Paris: Présence Africaine.
Ndao, Papa Alioune. 2008. *La francophonie des Pères fondateurs*. Paris: Éditions Karthala.
Nkrumah, Kwame. 1957. *Ghana: The Autobiography of Kwame Nkrumah*. New York: International Publishers.
Nyerere, Julius K. 1968. *Uhuru Na Ujamaa: Freedom and Socialism*. New York: Oxford University Press.
Palacios, Arnoldo. 1976. Monde et sang en fusion: Négritude et Latinité. In *Hommage à Léopold Sédar Senghor: homme de culture*, 350–354. Paris: Présence Africaine.
Patzia, Arthur G. 2001. *The Emergence of the Church: Context, Growth, Leadership and Worship*. Downers Grove: Intervarsity Press.
Pilch, John J., and Bruce J. Malina. 1993. *Biblical Social Values and Their Meaning: A Handbook*. Peabody: Hendrickson Publishers.
Rabaka, Reiland. 2015. *The Negritude Movement: W. E. B. Debois, Elon Damas, Aime Cesaire, Leopold Sedar Senghor, Frantz Fanon, and the Evolution of an Insurgent Idea*. New York: Lexington Book.
Said, Edward. 1979. *Orientalism*. New York: Vintage Books.
———. 1985. Orientalism Reconsidered. *Race & Class: A Journal for Black and Third World Liberation* 27: 1–15.
Sall, Elhadj Abdoul Hamidou. Mandela et le Senegal, Mon Hommage a Madiba. http://www.leral.net/Mandela-et-le-Senegal-Mon-Hommage-a-Madiba-Par-Hamidou-Sall_a100899.html

Sartre, Jean Paul. 1948. Orphée Noir. In *Anthologie de la nouvelle poèsie nègre et malgache de langue française*, iv–xliv. Paris: Presses Universitaires Française.
Savage, Nadine Dormoy. 1974. Entretien avec Léopold Sédar Senghor. *The French Review* 47: 1065–1071.
Senghor, Léopold Sédar. 1948. *Anthologie de la nouvelle poèsie nègre et malgache de langue française*. Paris: Presses Universitaires Française.
———. 1956. The Spirit of Civilisation, or the Laws of African Negro Culture. In *Presence Africaine: The First International Conference of Negro Writers and Artists*, 19th–22nd (September 1956): 51–64.
———. 1959. Constructive Elements of a Civilization of African Negro Inspiration. *Présence Africaine* 2 (26 March–1 April): 262–295.
———. 1962a. What Is Negritude? *Atlas*: 54–55.
———. 1962b. On Negrohood: Psychology of the African Negro. *Diogenes* 10 (37): 7–8.
———. 1964a. *On African Socialism*. Translated by Mercer Cook. New York: Frederick A. Praeger Publisher.
———. 1964b. *Liberté 1: Negritude et Humanisme*. Paris: Éditions du Seuil.
———. 1971a. *Liberté 2: Nation et Voie Africaine du Socialisme*. Paris: Éditions du Seuil.
———. 1971b. *The Foundations of "Africanité" or "Négritude" and "Arabité"*. Paris: Présence Africaine.
———. 1974a. 2nd Pré-Colloquium on 'Black Civilisation and Éducation'. *Présence Africaine*: 31–38.
———. 1974b. Allocution de Monsieur Léopold Sédar Senghor Président de la république du Sénégal. *Présence Africaine* 92 (2): 23–30.
———. 1976. La Négritude comme culture des peoples noirs, ne saurait être dépassée. In *Hommage à Léopold Sédar Senghor homme de culture*, 49–66. Paris: Présence Africaine.
———. 1977. *Liberté 3: Négritude et Civilisation de L'Universel*. Paris: Éditions du Seuil.
———. 1979. "La mort de Léon-Gontran Damas." In *Homage Posthume à Léon-Gontran Damas-1912–1978*, 10–11. Paris: Presence Africaine.
———. 1985. *Liberté 4: Socialisme et Planification*. Paris: Éditions du Seuil.
———. 1990a. Hosties Noirs. In *Œuvres poétiques. Poèsie*, 57–100. Paris: Les Editions du Seuil.
———. 1990b. Lettres à trois poètes de'hexagone. In *Œuvres poétiques*. Paris: Éditions du Seuil.
———. 1991. Prayer for Peace. 69–72 Léopold Sédar Senghor Collected Poems. Translated by Melvin Dixon. Charlottesville: University of Virginia Press.
———. 1993. *Liberté 5: Le Dialogue des Cultures*. Paris: Éditions du Seuil.
———. 1995. Negritude: A Humanism of the Twentieth Century. In *I am Because We Are: Readings in Black Philosophy*, 45–54. Amherst: University of Massachusetts Press.
Serequeberhan, Tsenay. 1994. *The Hermeneutics of African Philosophy: Horizon and Discourse*. New York: Routledge.
Soyinka, Wole. 1959. *Constituent Congress of the P.F.A. (The Party of African Federation)*. Paris: Présence Africaine.
———. 1999. *Burden of Memory, the Muse of Forgiveness*. New York: Oxford University Press.
———. 2002. Senghor: Lessons in Power. *Research in African Literatures* 33 (4): 1–2.
Thiam, Cheikh. 2014. *Return to the Kingdom of Childhood: Re-envisioning the Legacy and Philosophical Relevance of Negritude*. Columbus: The Ohio State University Press.

Thioune, Birahim. 2014. *Léopold Sédar Senghor: Un Combattant parmi les hommes, un poète devant Dieu*. Paris: L'Harmattan.
Vaillant, Janet G. 1990. *Black, French, and African: A Life of Leopold Sedar Senghor*. New Haven: Harvard University Press.

Homages Paid to Léopold Sédar Senghor

Hommage à Léopold Sédar Sénghor: homme de culture. Paris: Présence Africaine, 1976.
Présence Sénghor: 90 écrits en hommage aux 90 ans du poète-président. Paris: UNESCO, 1997.
Léopold Sédar Senghor: La pensée et l'action politique. Paris: Organisation Internationale de la Francophonie, 2006a.
Mémoire Sénghor 50 écrits en hommage aux100 ans du poète-président. Paris: UNESCO, 2006b.
Rencontre des traditions religieuses de l'Afrique avec le Christianisme, L'Islam et la laïcité à partir des écrits de Léopold Sédar Senghor. *La Voix de l'Afrique dans le dialogue interreligieux*. Paris: UNESCO, 2008.

CHAPTER 17

The Political Ethics of Frantz Fanon

Chika C. Mba

Introduction

Frantz Fanon's political ethics is not one of the themes usually paid much attention by scholars of his work, at least, not as the basis of a discourse that merits an independent treatment. Yet, understanding Fanon's political ethics, in spite of possible reservations in certain quarters about the legitimacy of the nomenclature of that discourse, is crucial to gaining a holistic understanding of his wide-ranging decolonial thought. For Fanon's political ethics is rooted in his decolonial ethics, which undeniably complements his decolonial thought. In Fanon's decolonial thought, Lewis Gordon writes, 'one finds the effort to decolonize not only knowledge and the organization of society, but also normative life.'[1] Notably, Fanon's decolonial ethics is a paradoxical conjuncture of an ethic of political violence and an ethic of what Christopher J. Lee calls *radical empathy*. This chapter critically explores how Fanon wields these seemingly non-overlapping normative frameworks in developing his powerful political ethics. Here, we begin with his ethics of violence.

Understanding Fanon's Ethics of Political Violence

Fanon's ethics of (political) violence—that is, his conception of why and how violence *ought* to be deployed in social politics—is a major plank of his decolonial moves and transformative political praxis, but it is also his most controversial and most discussed standpoint among his scholars. Thus, in order to understand Fanon's political ethics, we need, at first, to unpack his ethics of violence. Fanon's notion of political violence is often misunderstood and interpreted outside of the context of the shattering anti-colonial moment within which his

C. C. Mba (✉)
Institute of African Studies, University of Ghana, Legon, Ghana

© The Author(s) 2020
N. Wariboko, T. Falola (eds.), *The Palgrave Handbook of African Social Ethics*, https://doi.org/10.1007/978-3-030-36490-8_17

ideas erupted and were fermented, and further stretched beyond the scope of his phenomenological, empathetic cogitations on human dignity. For he held liberty and human dignity, including the dignity of the human *body*, to be of the highest value; in fact, 'Fanon couldn't separate the person from the corpse and the associated dignity violated by its evisceration.'[2] He abhorred the many instances of lurid violations of the human body, the body of people of colour especially, that oozed out of the settler-colonial moment in Algeria, and he sought to bring this situation to an end at all costs, even if it meant naturalising violence or creating a balance-of-terror situation, a desire borne out of the unavoidable decolonial realism that defines his politics.[3]

However, as Christopher J. Lee recognises, Fanon was able to look beyond the actual political events happening in Algeria to state his own political beliefs unapologetically—and that makes him a theorist of the ought, a philosopher.[4] In all events, some of the earliest interpretations of Fanon's views on violence paid only a perfunctory, if any, attention to Fanon's sophisticated and insightful treatment of the subject, and so they unsurprisingly took his views at face value, disconnecting his well-known advocacy of violence as a means of revolutionary struggle, as already noted, from the Manichean settler-colonial situation that birthed his response.[5] The import of Fanon's wider assessment of violence as a default *anti*-value in the context of the colonial situation often eluded these critics; they equally completely miss out on the mitigating/underlying value of radical empathy on Fanon's admittedly complicated notion of violence. And so, these critics, Lewis Gordon regrets, 'have seen his [Fanon's] work as a form of antiethics, advocacy of irrationalism, and the glorification of violence.'[6] Happily, though, this shoddy treatment of Fanon's ethics of political violence has waned considerably, at least among his committed scholars like Achille Mbembe, Lewis Gordon and Nigel Gibson.

Taking Fanon's ethics of violence seriously, we acknowledge that his original contribution on the significance of violence in politics is not to celebrate violence as an effective means of galvanising political action, per se, but to assert that when applied (as the last option) against the *violent oppressor*, violence simultaneously serves as a tool of rebirth and of the total fulfilment of humanity in the oppressed whose human dignity has before now been suspended.[7] Given the high status human dignity occupies in Fanon's ethics, his battles (in the Second World War and the Algerian War of Independence) and his defence of political *counter*-violence are informed by his untrammelled desire to defend and preserve human dignity, at all cost. Fanon deserves to be allowed to speak for himself here at some length:

> For a colonized people the most essential value, because the most concrete, is first and foremost the land: the land which will bring them bread and, *above all, dignity*. But this dignity has nothing to do with the dignity of the human individual: for that human individual has never heard tell of it. All that the native has seen in his country is that they can freely arrest him, beat him, starve him: and no professor of ethics, no priest has ever come to be beaten in his place, nor to share

their bread with him. As far as the native is concerned, morality is very concrete; it is to silence the settler's defiance, to break his flaunting violence—in a word, to put him out of the picture. The well-known principle that all men are equal will be illustrated in the colonies from the moment that the native claims that he is the equal of the settler. One step more, and he is ready to fight to be more than the settler. In fact, he has already decided to eject him and to take his place; as we see it, it is a whole material and moral universe which is breaking up.[8]

In fact, the revolution would be deemed successful, Fanon argues, and a true national consciousness emerge if only

> The masses ... [are] ... able to meet together, discuss, propose, and receive directions. The citizens ... [are] ... able to speak, to express themselves, and to put forward new ideas. The branch meeting and the committee meeting are liturgical acts. They are privileged occasions given to a human being to listen and to speak. At each meeting, the brain increases its means of participation and the eye discovers a landscape more and more in keeping with human dignity.[9]

Fanon defines human dignity broadly to include *enforced* equality, liberty and freedom from assault, freedom of speech and association, and, above all else, the right to a means of livelihood. And his argument is quite simple: any social and political situation that subverts human dignity is immoral, in fact antihuman, and deserves to be overthrown by any means possible, including violent confrontation, especially if that regime is itself violently oppressive.

The starting point, for Fanon, is where the Self is revealed and elevated, a positive image and reassertion of oneself in the face of rejection and misrecognition. But the rediscovery and restoration of the Self and its dignity must begin from a reflexive heteronomy to a radical rejection of all forms of oppression and cultural prejudices. To make things clearer, in *Black Skin, White Masks,* Fanon enunciates what Ziauddin Sardar calls 'a particular definition' of human dignity that flows from an assumption of human freedom.

> Dignity is not located in seeking equality with the white man and his civilization: it is not about assuming the attitudes of the master *who has allowed his slaves to eat at his table*. It is about being oneself with all the multiplicities, systems and contradictions of one's own ways of being, doing and knowing. It is about being true to one's Self.[10]

The point here is that human dignity could not hold much value in a world laden with the drivers of colonialism such as oppression, racism and cultural prejudice.[11] Yet human dignity or its restoration, equality and equity are vital to achieving Fanon's new *universal* humanity.[12] Fanon would not wait much longer before he finds an actional root to restoring dignity for the damned of the earth, those forced to occupy the zone of non-being by the violent oppressor.[13]

In due course, he outlines a form of political activism that is at odds with the political ethics of non-violence preferred by other iconic revolutionaries of the twentieth century like Mohandas Gandhi, Martin Luther King Jr. and Desmond Tutu. But, of course, as Lewis Gordon frequently explains, Fanon's considered opinion on violence has everything to do with the internal structures and modus operandi of colonialism in the different geographical spaces within which each revolutionary emerged and fought. The colonial situation Fanon found himself was one of pervasive violence, offering little or no hope of ever getting justice either via a recourse to the law or an appeal to the oppressor's conscience. In short, this is to say that like most people, the impetus for Fanon's work is in the context of his age, his struggles; his ideas are in certain respects moulded by metamorphosing and militating factors, even as he defines and transcends the specificities of that epoch.[14] To reiterate, Fanon dealt first-hand with settler-colonialism and the racism, oppression and inhumanity it created. He was up against an obdurate and suffocating system of things that, he could clearly see, only an authentic upheaval could shake up and transform, and he earnestly sought this inexorable transformative praxis. He thought that counter-violence provides the beginnings of that praxis.

But Fanon was acutely aware of the limits of violence, and in the last part of *The Wretched of the Earth*, he highlights *his* in-depth awareness of the psycho-pathology of violence as an ethic of political engagement. He demonstrates clearly, from his accounts of treating psychiatric victims of the Algerian War of Independence, the mutual debilitation of violence for both the oppressor and the oppressed. In other words, he understood the pan-damaging consequences of violence as a tool of politics. He then proceeded to try and make violence an undesirable approach to socio-political ordering, once he could show that the oppressor's monopoly of the use of violence is unsustainable and broken-backed. By encouraging the native to wield the weapon of warfare, Fanon aimed to stop the colonialist, the oppressor, in their tracks, forcing them to finally recognise the humanity of the oppressed, who truth be told, had not before now been regarded as human. For it is only by organising a fight back against the denigrators and violators of their humanity, that the colonised would prove that they are not game-animals after all, game-animals who could be attacked, killed or maimed almost without repercussions. The maxim implicit in the Golden Rule, which applies to *all* human beings, as Fanon notes in *Black Skin, White Masks*, stipulates that we do unto others what we wish for ourselves.[15] In committing continuing serial acts of violence against the native, the coloniser is without doubt inviting the native to fight back as any *human being* is expected to. Thus, without fighting back or putting up any kind of self-defence against a relentless attacker, the native would be casting doubts on their inherent, inviolate humanity; other than counter-violence, there is no other way to force the murderous colonial enemy to consider the colonised an equal, as fellow humans, worthy of reciprocal recognition and respect. As Lewis Gordon intones:

> The basic problem of nonviolent critique is this: to treat the prohibition on violence as deontological—that is, absolute—leads to a failure of addressing

situations in which violence is already the status quo. In such instances, what is called nonviolent intervention simply maintains—and, even worse, perpetuates—violence. Critics would object that the point is about committing violence at all, that agents of social change must be ethically better than those preserving injustice. Fanon's retort is that such arguments fail to address the core issue of violence in the first place: it is only recognized as such when it is unleashed against those whose humanity is already guaranteed.[16]

To refocus Fanon's ethics of violence, there is a sense in which we can speak of early and late Fanon, the former conciliatory while avoiding the cross of history in *Black Skin, White Masks*, the latter radically confrontational against colonialism and oppression in *The Wretched of the Earth*. The early, negritudist Fanon sought forgiveness for the coloniser on the side of the colonised. The oppressed who have suffered past injustices and oppression, Fanon preaches, should look beyond the resentment and dark memories of the past. Iris Marion Young articulates Fanon's recommendations here as follows:

> The purported revolutionary who anguishes over the vast crimes of the past will get bogged down in backward-looking resentment. ... Fanon recommends instead the existentialist stance of radical freedom and self-invention. ... Only a radical leap out of this pathological structure into a future where everyone is only human will disalienate the person of color. ... A project of producing guilt among us for the sins of former generations is not likely to succeed, and even if it did, what would be the point of allowing such a guilt to fester? Why not put this past behind us and *start over* on terms of equal humanity?[17]

Young disparages Fanon here for the latter's anodyne ahistoricity. But what Young seems to have missed, however, is that Fanon never really believed that starting over on terms of equal humanity would be that easy, without something else even more earth-shaking occurring. Because even at that early stage of his evolving political ethics, Fanon had a soft spot for negritude, a powerful ideological construct for reclaiming the African personality and the dignity of Black people that have before now been lost to the conjunctural afterlives of enslavement and colonialism.

Indeed, negritude forms a strong scaffold for Fanon's early political ethics. But Fanon saw that negritude seems to feed into the Manichean delirium of the colonial moment and obstructs the kind of radical mutation and political newness for which the decolonial intellectual yearns and must in the end account. On the one hand, negritude was a good thing, Fanon saw, because it would, among other positives, help Black people to guard against being ensnared by 'Western culture,' but, on the other hand, negritude was problematic in that its apostles ignored the urgent existential, social and economic challenges besetting Africa, while burrowing too deep into an almost non-existent romantic African past. In *Toward the African Revolution*, Fanon dismisses negritude as '"the great black mirage," arguing for a national, rather than a civilizational basis for cultural resistance and autonomy.'[18]

Conversely, the more experienced late Fanon does not assume that reciprocal recognition can be achieved by mere exhortations, partisan pacifism or legalism, but via a politics of the streets, 'the radical overthrowing of the system.'[19] In his conception of an inclusive revolutionary politics, Fanon argues that genuine change occurs through a politics of the streets driven by the masses, from below. For it is in politics from below that the true power of the people as thinking and acting critical mass is revealed, the fact that the people—the illiterate and the rural poor—are able to confront and channel their sociopolitical problems through a bond of solidarity solidified by the sweat and blood of the struggle for emancipation. Given some hope by this emancipatory solidarity Fanon would settle for nothing less than radical mutations on the part of the oppressor and the oppressed, the rise of a new humanity that must first transcend the conceits and deceits of European humanity via a dialectical progression. This process of arriving at a new species of human beings that recognise and dread the consequences of prejudice, injustice and exceptionalism must begin from the colonised people's conscious effort to fight (their) humanity back into existence. Fanon believes that only when the worth of human life is equalised in this way would decolonisation become truly therapeutic and the new humanity he envisages would emerge. For the 'most horrible crime' Europe has committed against humanity is 'in the heart of man, and consisted of the pathological tearing apart of his functions and the crumbling away of his unity.'[20]

As already hinted, 'Fanon believed in the possibility of a new form of human interaction, a new society that could be achieved only through a revolutionary dismantling of the colonial state, and ... [consequently] held out hope that Algerian Jews as well as Algerians of European descent would become part of the new Algerian nation.'[21] Citizenship or nationhood, not civilisation, should for Fanon, determine politics. For '[t]he nation is not only a precondition for culture, its ebullition, its perpetual renewal and maturation. It is a necessity.'[22] Fanon's idea is that culture should only serve as one more instrument for a people's struggle for freedom, but once victory is attained, a true politics of reciprocal recognition that requires inclusivity, transculturalism and respect for the dignity of all human beings must emerge. For Fanon, culture is supposed to serve the purpose of a compass for human solidarity at the stage of liminality or what Plato would call the state of aporia, during that moment of incomprehension when humanity is shut out, before freedom is regained, before the new humanity is birthed.[23]

Fanon saw clearly that morality or ethics in politics can only exist in the context where at least the humanity or the Otherness of everyone is, in the very least, recognised and effort put in place to always guarantee human dignity; otherwise, for him, even the most basic conversations about justice and human rights cannot logically and truly begin.[24] Political morality or human equality, for Fanon, makes sense only in the context where the oppressed can finally claim equality with the oppressor, the native with the settler, the Arab with the French, the African with the European and so on.[25] That is also why Fanon, like Sartre, thought it the height of public immorality or 'degradation' when people are silent about atrocious actions of their country's government or armed forces.[26]

RADICAL EMPATHY AND HUMAN DIGNITY[27]

Radical empathy is an integral part of Fanon's political ethics. But how can we reconcile radical empathy with his philosophy of violence? In his writings and actions, Fanon himself tries to balance the paradoxical relations that appear to exist between his ethics of violence and radical empathy. In both thought and action, Fanon sought new forms of connection and solidarity; his '... "only frontiers were the boundaries of freedom, justice and of dignity."'[28] Indeed, Fanon lived out a life of boundless, radical empathy; it is difficult to pin him down to a particular location—Martinique, France, Algeria or Tunisia—or even to the particular epoch he lived, precisely because of his commitment to cosmopolitanism. To be sure, radical empathy is not coterminous with cosmopolitanism, for the former is a political outcome of the latter, in short, 'a political ethic beyond the antiracial and anticolonial violence he famously promoted. ... It is a mechanism for the new humanism he aspired to at the end of *The Wretched of the Earth*.'[29] The recognition here is that 'Fanon's politics were not purely contrarian'; radical empathy is 'the precise opposite of those contrarian qualities often attributed to Fanon—namely, an unqualified support of violence and an entrenched Manichean world view that affirmed difference.'[30] And Fanon strongly holds that linkages and connections between contrasting or even oppositional subjectivities are not possible without radical empathy or love, for it is radical empathy that can subvert the politics of difference. For Fanon, in *Black Skin, White Masks*, 'true love, real love' is not being subject to others, *contra* Sartre; it is instead, 'wishing for others what one postulates for oneself.'[31] How about the toxic spaces created by feelings and assumptions of inferiority and superiority? 'Why not,' Fanon counsels, 'simply try to touch the other, feel the other?'[32] He makes this case because he is committed to 'alternative forms of identification and solidarity in order to transcend difference.'[33]

In the end, decoloniality, human dignity and radical empathy are the bedrocks of Fanon's political ethics. This is why, we must recognise, he sought 'to transcend the racial, political and intellectual ontologies imposed on him by colonialism,' in short, a politics of recognition and solidarity beyond one's familiar enclave.[34] Like Nelson Mandela, Fanon sought to expand distinctions rather than reinforce them, to promote a 'more inclusive humanism unburdened by preceding hierarchies of racial, cultural, economic and political discrimination.'[35] Fanon argues in this way with an eye to the universal, another important strand of his uniquely cosmopolitan ethics. According to Fanon's conception of the universal, it could neither be the product of a particular civilisation imposed on the rest of us nor be the hasty attraction to a particular culture or religion.[36] The universal is something that we choose to accept because it extends our freedoms and reinforces our dignity as human persons.

For 'every time a man has contributed to the victory of the dignity of the spirit, every time a man has said no to an attempt to subjugate his fellows, I have felt solidarity with his act.'[37] It is in this solidarity with all struggles for emancipation that universalism is achieved. Universalism becomes a fact whenever and if the dignity of all human beings is elevated, respected or restored. Thus, Fanon's new humanity does not consist in a competition of any kind—not even a positive competition, but a genuine desire, a human wish to '"want to walk always, night and day, in the company of man, of every man."'[38] In short, the utopian vanishing point, on the horizon of Fanon's decolonial ethics, is the ultimate revolutionary prize: human solidarity.

Fanon follows Marxian aesthetics to criticise contemporary capitalism and insists that every peasant *jacquery* (revolt) remains a constant reproach against capitalism and its values.[39] He warns those who currently benefit hugely from the lopsided gains of capitalism (i.e. the oppressors) to be wary of the oppressed and deprived because they are never really tamed, only waiting for the right time to fight for justice, for freedom and for their dignity.[40] Overall, for Fanon, what defines humanity is freedom for the human subject in the continual quest for an ethic of the good life, living in ambivalent attachment to our most cherished values. This Fanon's deep and intriguing understanding of humanity as freedom is strikingly similar to Jan Patočka's insistence that human beings be understood always as free beings 'living in problematicity' of truth beyond cultures.[41] Living in problematicity or always questioning our most cherished beliefs and values is, of course, in keeping with Fanon's innermost desire in the closing passage of *Black Skin, White Masks*.[42] Throughout his writings and speeches, he emphasised that human interest and human dignity trump all else in every of our consideration of how we ought to treat others, even as we constantly question the basis of our most cherished values. In short, Fanon installs empathy as the compass of political action, empathy as the bedrock of any political ethics.

In comparison, Emmanuel Levinas and Jacques Derrida introduce a subtle inversion of Fanon's approach to conceiving humanity, otherness and ethics that simultaneously transcends and complements Fanon's political ethics. Rather than conceive 'a free subject ... [as] the origin of responsibility, on a Levinasian/Derridian conception, responsibility is prior to and ground for freedom' exemplified in Fanon's and Patočka's lives and writings, as living in constant commitment to duty and responsibility to the Other, while interrogating the basis of all truth.[43] In an insightful reading of Levinas, Roger Burggraeve writes:

> Through interpreting human rights beginning from the Other, it becomes clear [to Levinas] how responsibility is also the core of charity: "Everything begins with the rights of the Other and with my infinite responsibility." To love my neighbor is to respond to his Face, to accept his ethical lordship over me and recognize that he has rights over me. A truly humane justice is thus possible on the basis of a "humanism of the Other" which stands in contrast with the classical

humanism of the ego. The humanism of the Other implies a dethroning and decentering of the ego: "There can be talk of culture only when one reaches the conviction that the center of my existence does not lie in myself." ... "The human par excellence—the source of humanity—is the Other" ... justice begins as "heteronomy" and "inequality." It begins not in my freedom but in the Other him or herself: it is "an-archic."[44]

The simple idea here is that for Levinas, my very existence, my humanity is not so much about my own value or my place in the world, but that my humanity is ethically grounded in my relationship, my responsibility to the Other. But who is the 'Other' here? The Other is my neighbour with whom I stand in proximity and by whom I find signification of my own existence. But this 'neighbour' is not my next-door neighbour, as such, but the whole of humanity. My proximity to this neighbour is not defined conventionally, logically, legally, geographically or biologically, it is defined morally and transcendentally via a preconditional non-indifference.[45] 'The face [of my neighbour] is a singular universal and in "the proximity of the other, all the others than the other obsess me."'[46] Justice is necessary, not to save me from the infinite responsibility to one other 'but for the sake of judging in the presence of the whole of humanity—in each face.'[47]

In a memorable passage, Levinas writes, 'The Other, revealing itself by its face, is the first intelligible, before cultures and their alluvions and allusions.'[48] For this reason, Kwame Anthony Appiah rightly doubts the imperative to respect cultures, as opposed to persons, and urges us to always consider persons as abstract rights-holders.[49] Appiah's assertion is to affirm the independence of ethics in relation to history. And for Levinas,'[s]howing that the first significance arises in morality, in the quasi-abstract epiphany of the face, which is stripped of every quality-absolute—absolving itself of cultures, means tracing a limit to the comprehension of the real by history and rediscovering Platonism.'[50] Thus, for Levinas as for Appiah and Fanon, and rightly so, the status of the heteronomous Other is 'absolute' in the strict sense, 'absolved from any relation to world, context, culture, homes, symbolic order, rituals, and from any order of reason. The subject is thus constituted in relation to a personal rather than a non-personal alterity such as a "culture" or a "world."'[51] And because the face (the Other) is independent of worlds, context and culture, because it comes from an 'elsewhere into which it already withdraws' even before it arrives, Levinas sees in it a guarantee that the Other is more than a 'cultural meaning' who approaches me from out of his cultural whole. Ethics, therefore, must precede culture: as face, the Other is an *abstract man*, in the sense of someone 'disengaged *from all culture*.'[52]

In disavowing Sartre's assertion that the individual is condemned to freedom, Levinas argues persuasively that freedom is an investiture conferred on her by the encounter, the entrance of the Other. It is indeed how I choose to use my freedom in relation to the Other that will either subvert or enhance my authentic freedom. 'The heteronomy of our response to the human other, or to God as the absolutely other, precedes the autonomy of our subjective freedom.'[53] But Sartre is not to be easily swept aside, for he could ask Levinas and, indeed, the question arises for the former, why would the, *initially*, metaphysically free human subject be unwilling to help their neighbour? Levinas' response would be to invoke Martin Heidegger and to transcend him. We do not always think of humanity in Heideggerian phraseology as *Dasein*, Levinas contends, that is, in terms of personhood and mortality, or contemplate the originary ethics of human values, high enough. But, then, as we saw, Levinas moves a powerful step further than Heidegger. For 'while what defines man's reality in *Being and Time* is his concern for his own death, for Levinas what constitutes man's very humanity is the concern for the death of the other.'[54] Thus, if we follow Levinas and late Fanon long enough, what we would have is a world in which everyone realises how important the other really is, over and above any purported attachment to a comprehensive doctrine,[55] in short, a world of *cultural humanism*,[56] always guided by radical empathy.

Conclusion

Fanon's political ethics deserves more attention than it has thus far been accorded, as it is primarily concerned with the kind of relationships that exist between actual human beings and human institutions, which is and should clearly be one of the most important issues in political theory. Fanon's work also raises a number of key unresolved questions about the kind of relationship that ought to exist between morality and politics in our world today. Scholars and activists ought to think more patiently and carefully about a world where alternative theoretical/ideological narratives and political action channels seem either passé or tilted dangerously towards extremism. In the context of Fanon's ethics of political violence, what are the bounds of moral conduct in our pursuit of political freedom? What are the real choices of political thought and actions open to the damned of the earth and the untouchables, in specific and wider contexts, in a world of rapidly alternating binarisms where might is often right? In an era blighted by forced migrations, statelessness and a global refugee crisis, where, exactly, should the politics of inclusion begin and end? What exactly should freedom and self-determination mean? In demanding for inclusion, even were recognition to be taken for granted, what kind of political actions are open to the freedom fighter, locally against oppressive regimes and internationally against an unjust world order?

Notes

1. Gordon, Lewis, 2015a, Fanon, Frantz, *The international encyclopedia of ethics*, H. LaFollette, Ed., John Wiley & Sons, Ltd. p. 1.
2. Gordon, Lewis, 2015a, Fanon, Frantz, p. 2.
3. Cf. Ciccariello-Maher, George, 2013, Decolonial realism: Ethics, politics and dialectics in Fanon and Dussel, *Contemporary Political Theory*, 13(1): p. 2–22;

also Tucker, Gerald E., 1978, Machiavelli and Fanon: ethics, violence and action, *The Journal of Modern African Studies*, p. 397–415.
4. Lee, Christopher J. 2015, *Frantz Fanon: toward a revolutionary humanism*, p. 19–34.
5. Cf. Fashina, Oladipo, 1989, Fanon and the ethical justification of anti-colonial violence, *Social Theory and Practice*, 15,2, p. 179.
6. Gordon, Lewis, 2015a, Fanon, Frantz, *The international encyclopedia of ethics*, p. 5.
7. Irele, Abiola, 2011, *The Negritude moment: explorations in Francophone African and Caribbean literature and thought*, p. 140.
8. Emphasis added, see Fanon, F. 1963 [1961], *The wretched of the earth*, Preface by Jean Paul Sartre. C. Farrington, p. 45–46.
9. Fanon, F. 1963 [1961], *The wretched of the earth*, p. 195.
10. Italics are quotations of Fanon and are Sardar's. See Sardar, Z. 2008, Foreword to the 2008 edition, *Black skin, white masks*, C. L. Markmann, Trans., p. vii.
11. Fanon lampoons the very notion of racial prejudice, arguing not just that it is absurd, but also that it has constituted a kind of ailment, a tarnishing accretion to the purported purity of European humanity. See Fanon, F. 2008, *Black skin*, p. 18–20.
12. Cf. Sardar, Z. 2008, Foreword to the 2008 edition, p. xvii.
13. Cf. Gordon L.R. (2015b) *What Fanon said: A philosophical introduction to his life and thought*, Johannesburg: Wits University Press, p. 19–46.
14. Lee, Christopher J. 2015, *Frantz Fanon: toward a revolutionary humanism*, passim.
15. Fanon, Frantz, 1952 [2008], *Black skin, white masks*, p. 28.
16. Gordon, Lewis, 2015a, Fanon, Frantz, p. 5.
17. Iris Marion Young's further critique of Fanon that follows her summation here is not entirely true, but I shall let it alone here for want of space. She argues that Fanon's 'compelling vision' is 'also ultimately flawed,' and that '[t]he existential humanism on which it is based is too radically individualist and dehistoricized.' For the verbatim citation in-text, see Young, I. M. 2011, *Responsibility for justice*, p. 171–72; and for the footnote quotation, see p. 171.
18. Lee, Christopher J. 2015, *Frantz Fanon: toward a revolutionary humanism*, p. 155.
19. Fanon, F. 1963 [1961], *The wretched of the earth*, Preface by Jean Paul Sartre. C. Farrington, Trans., p. 59.
20. Fanon, F. 1963 [1961], *The wretched of the earth*, p. 315.
21. Alice Cherki, cited in Lee, Christopher J. 2015, *Frantz Fanon: toward a revolutionary humanism*, p. 152.
22. Fanon is cited from The wretched of the earth in Lee, Christopher J. 2015, *Frantz Fanon: toward a revolutionary humanism*, p. 170.
23. Cf. Ndlovu-Gatsheni, S.J. 13/10 (2015), Decoloniality as the future of Africa, *History Compass*.
24. Cf. Gordon L.R. (2015) *What Fanon said*, p. 119.
25. Fanon, F. 1963 [1961], *The wretched of the earth*, p. 44.
26. Sartre J.P. 1963 [1961], Preface to Fanon, F. 1963 [1961], *The wretched of the earth*, p. 29–30.

27. Analysis in this section is indebted to Christopher Lee for introducing and elaborating on the term 'radical empathy.' See Lee, Christopher J. 2015, *Frantz Fanon: toward a revolutionary humanism*, passim.
28. We will have more to say about this. Lee cites Mohamed Bedjaoui approvingly here; See Lee, Christopher J. 2015, *Frantz Fanon: toward a revolutionary humanism*, p. 28–29.
29. Lee, Christopher J. 2015, *Frantz Fanon: toward a revolutionary humanism*, p. 29–33.
30. Lee, Christopher J. 2015, *Frantz Fanon: toward a revolutionary humanism*, p. 193.
31. Fanon, Frantz, 1952 [2008]. *Black skin, white masks*. C. L. Markmann, Trans. London: Pluto Press, p. 28.
32. Fanon, Frantz, 1952 [2008]. *Black skin, white masks*, p. 28 and passim.
33. Lee, Christopher J. 2015, *Frantz Fanon: toward a revolutionary humanism*, p. 192–193.
34. Lee, Christopher J. 2015, *Frantz Fanon: toward a revolutionary humanism*, p. 190–191.
35. Lee, Christopher J. 2015, *Frantz Fanon: toward a revolutionary humanism*, p. 196.
36. 'Burgers and coke are eaten and drunk throughout the world but one would hardly classify them as universally embraced, healthy and acceptable food: what the presence of burgers and coke in every city and town in the world demonstrate is not their universality but the power and dominance of the culture that produced them.' See Sardar, Z. 2008, Foreword to the 2008 edition, p. xvi; cf. Fanon, F. 1963 [1961], *The wretched of the earth*, p. 215.
37. Fanon, F. 2008, *Black skin*, p. 176.
38. Fanon is cited by Hountondji, but is reported here from Coetzee, P. H. 2003, Africa in the global context, *The African Philosophy reader: a text with readings*. 2nd Ed. P. H. Coetzee and A. P. J. Roux. Eds. London and New York: Routledge, p. 651.
39. Fanon, F. 1967 [1961], *The wretched of the earth*, p. 63.
40. Fanon, F. 1967 [1961], *The wretched of the earth*, p. 41 and 47.
41. See Patočka, J. 2007, *Living in problematicity*, E. Manton, Ed., Fanon, F. 1963 [1961], *The wretched of the earth* and Fanon, F. 2008, *Black skin, white masks*.
42. Fanon, F. 2008, *Black skin*, p. 181.
43. See Young, I. M. 2011, *Responsibility for justice*, p. 119; Patočka, J. 2007, *Living in problematicity*, passim.
44. Burggraeve R., 2002, *The wisdom of love in the service of love: Emmanuel Levinas on justice, peace, and human rights*, p. 105.
45. Cf. Hand, S. 2009. *Routledge critical thinkers: Emmanuel Levinas*, p. 54–55.
46. Thomas, E. L. 2004, *Emmanuel Levinas: ethics, justice and the human beyond being*, R. Bernasconi, Ed., p. 157.
47. Thomas, E. L. 2004, *Emmanuel Levinas*, p. 157.
48. Levinas, E. 1990, *Difficult freedom: essays on Judaism*, S. Hand, trans., p. 295.
49. Appiah, K. 2005, *The ethics of identity*, New Jersey: Princeton University Press, p. xv.
50. Levinas, E. 1990, *Difficult freedom*, p. 295.

51. See Newman, M. 2000, Sensibility, trauma, and the trace: Levinas from phenomenology to the immemorial, *The face of the Other and the trace of God: essays on the philosophy of Emmanuel Levinas*. J. Bloechl, Ed., p. 94–104.
52. Visker, R. 2005, Dis-possessed: how to remain silent 'after' Levinas, *Emmanuel Levinas: critical assessments of leading philosophers; Levinas, phenomenology and his critics*. C. Katz and L. Trout, Eds., Vol. 1, p. 379.
53. Levinas is paraphrased here by Paul Marcus in Marcus, P. 2008. *Being for the Other: Emmanuel Levinas, Ethical living and psychoanalysis*, p. 43.
54. Mosés, S. 2005, Emmanuel Levinas: ethics as primary meaning, G. Motzkin, Trans., *Emmanuel Levinas: critical assessments of leading philosophers; Levinas, phenomenology and his Critics*. C. Katz and L. Trout, Eds., Vol. 1, p. 327.
55. See Rawls, J. 1992, Justice as fairness: political not metaphysical, *Communitarianism and individualism*. S. Avineri and A. De-Shalit. Eds. New York: Oxford University Press, p. 186–204; Rawls, J., 1996 [1993], *Political liberalism: with a new introduction and the "Reply to Habermas."*
56. For more on this idea, see Mba, C., 2018, Conceiving global culture: Frantz Fanon and the politics of identity, *Acta Academica*, (50)1: 83–103.

Bibliography

Appiah, K. 2005. *The Ethics of Identity*. Princeton: Princeton University Press.
Burggraeve, R. 2002. *The Wisdom of Love in the Service of Love: Emmanuel Levinas on Justice, Peace, and Human Rights*. Milwaukee: Marquette University Press.
Ciccariello-Maher, G. 2013. Decolonial Realism: Ethics, Politics and Dialectics in Fanon and Dussel. *Contemporary Political Theory* 13 (1): 2–22.
Coetzee, P.H. 2003. Africa in the Global Context. In *The African Philosophy Reader: A Text with Readings*, ed. P.H. Coetzee and A.P.J. Roux, 2nd ed. London/New York: Routledge.
Fanon, F. 1963 [1961]. *The Wretched of the Earth*, Preface by Jean Paul Sartre. Trans. C. Farrington. New York: Grove Press (Présence Africaine).
———. 2008. Black Skin, White Masks. Trans. C. L. Markmann. London: Pluto Press.
Fashina, O. 1989. Fanon and the Ethical Justification of Anti-Colonial Violence. *Social Theory and Practice* 15: 179.
Gordon, L. 2015a. Fanon, Frantz, *The International Encyclopedia of Ethics*, ed. H. LaFollette. Wiley. https://doi.org/10.1002/9781405186414.wbiee812.
Gordon, L.R. 2015b. *What Fanon Said: A Philosophical Introduction to His Life and Thought*. Johannesburg: Wits University Press.
Hand, S. 2009. *Routledge Critical Thinkers: Emmanuel Levinas*. London/New York: Routledge; Taylor & Francis Group.
Irele, A. 2011. *The Negritude Moment: Explorations in Francophone African and Caribbean Literature and Thought*. Trenton: Africa World Press.
Lee, C.J. 2015. *Frantz Fanon: Toward a Revolutionary Humanism*. Athens: Ohio University Press.
Levinas, E. 1990. Difficult Freedom: Essays on Judaism. Trans. S. Hand. Baltimore: The Johns Hopkins University Press.
Marcus, P. 2008. *Being for the Other: Emmanuel Levinas, Ethical Living and Psychoanalysis*. Milwaukee: Marquette University Press.

Mba, C. 2018. Conceiving Global Culture: Frantz Fanon and the Politics of Identity. *Acta Academica* (50)1: 83–103. https://doi.org/10.18820/24150479/aa50i1.5.

Mosés, S. 2005. Emmanuel Levinas: Ethics as Primary Meaning. In *Emmanuel Levinas: Critical Assessments of Leading Philosophers; Levinas, Phenomenology and HIS CRITICS*, ed. C. Katz and L. Trout. Trans. G. Motzkin. London/New York: Routledge & Francis Group.

Ndlovu-Gatsheni, S.J. 2015. Decoloniality as the Future of Africa. *History Compass* 13: 485–496. https://doi.org/10.1111/hic3.12264.

Patočka, J. 2007. *Living in Problematicity*, ed. E. Manton. Prague: PRAHA.

Rawls, J. 1992. Justice as Fairness: Political Not Metaphysical. In *Communitarianism and Individualism*, ed. S. Avineri and A. De-Shalit. New York: Oxford University Press.

———. 1996[1993]. *Political Liberalism: With a New Introduction and the "Reply to Habermas"*. New York: Columbia University Press.

Sardar, Z. 2008. Foreword to the 2008 edition, *Black Skin, White Masks*. Trans. C. L. Markmann. London: Pluto Press.

Sartre J.P. 1963 [1961]. Preface to Fanon, F. *The Wretched of the Earth*. Trans. C. Farrington. New York: Grove Press (Présence Africaine).

See Newman, M. 2000. Sensibility, Trauma, and the Trace: Levinas from Phenomenology to the Immemorial. In *The Face of the Other and the Trace of God: Essays on the Philosophy of Emmanuel Levinas*, ed. J. Bloechl. New York: Fordham University Press.

Thomas, E.L. 2004. *Emmanuel Levinas: Ethics, Justice and the Human Beyond Being*, ed. R. Bernasconi. London and New York.

Tucker, G.E. 1978. Machiavelli and Fanon: Ethics, Violence and Action. *The Journal of Modern African Studies* 16: 397–415.

Visker, R. 2005. Dis-possessed: How to Remain Silent "After" Levinas. In *Emmanuel Levinas: Critical Assessments of Leading Philosophers; Levinas, Phenomenology and His Critics*, ed. C. Katz and L. Trout. London/New York: Routledge & Francis Group.

Young, I.M. 2011. *Responsibility for Justice*. Oxford/New York: Oxford University Press.

PART III

Economy (Energies of Exchange, Market)

CHAPTER 18

Spirit/Religion and Ethics in African Economies

J. Kwabena Asamoah-Gyadu

In this chapter, we interrogate the intersections between religion and economics in African traditions in both its primal/traditional and modern/contemporary forms. The entry first considers the relationship between African traditional religions (ATRs) and culture(s) on the one hand, and economics on the other, before applying the thoughts to how these have played out within contemporary society. The underlying thesis is against the backdrop of a worldview in which the world is filled with numberless spirits that influence life either for good or for ill; African peoples still maintain an understanding of things in which no human activity including their economic lives may be separated from their religious practices. The factors that have affected the economic landscape in Africa and that have changed its face and socio-economic orientation include colonization, the impact of religious missions and religious pluralism, the globalization of cultures, migration, technological change, and the media in all its forms.

In spite of the strength of these forces of change and transformation, certain traditional ways and worldviews, such as the belief in mystical causality, we have noted, have remained resilient in African life and thought. One would think, for example, that modernity and globalization would have led to the obfuscation of traditional forms of religion such as ancestral practices and allegiance to deities. Whereas in many urban spaces overt practices associated with these primal religions may have dwindled, their underlying worldviews have persisted. Thus, in contemporary Pentecostalism to take just one example, the faithful payments of tithes and offerings have a direct bearing on one's economic fortunes. If business fails, it probably means the entrepreneur has been "robbing God" in "tithes and offerings." The failures would then be explained not in terms of the workings of world economies and inflation, but to the

J. K. Asamoah-Gyadu (✉)
Trinity Theological Seminary, Legon, Ghana

activities' "spiritual locusts" that, in keeping with the hermeneutics of Malachi 3:8–11, eat up or frustrate one's commercial efforts and endeavors.

In other words, in the midst of globalization traditional religio-cultural and biblical ideas and practices have persisted. People continue to combine in their personal worlds, Christian, Islamic, traditional, and other religious beliefs with what they have learned from the past. In many cases, a complete break with the past has not happened with some African immigrants in Europe, for example, still explaining stagnations in their economic lives in terms of the activities of witches in their rural families back in their home countries. Thus, Christian prophets and neo-traditionalists like Kweku Bonsam of Ghana still travel many miles across the Atlantic to "minister" in particular to the health and economic needs of African immigrants abroad. There are fortunes to be made through ritualistic engagement with the spirit world of spirits, many believe.

The search for *sikaduro*, literally medicine money, through human sacrifices, and its more modern forms, *sakawa*, are all ways and means by which Africans sustain some sort of ritualistic relationship with the world of spirits for economic benefits. Not only do people need the spirit world to make money but also to protect what they have from envious competitors and relations who may seek to use the same transcendent means to bring them down and to shame. We live in a world in which traditional religio-cultural worldviews and modernity remain in a constant state of engagement. Thus, in spite of scientific advances in agriculture, for example, when crops refuse to grow as a result of lack of rainfall resulting from climatic changes, certain African societies could still explain it in terms of how they have reneged on ancestral responsibilities rather than see things in the light of those scientific reasons usually cited in the more developed economies.

African Cosmologies and Economic Worldviews

Traditionally, the inseparability between religion and life in African philosophical thought means it is virtually impossible to talk about morality/ethics on the one hand and African economic life on the other without reference to spirituality or lived faith.[1] Religion is pervasive in African ways of life, culture, and being. Religion brings together the asymmetrical worlds of the seen and unseen, visible and invisible, or physical and spiritual realms in relationships of constant and perpetual interaction. The abundance of rain, food, fish, and other resources for sustenance all depend on the sorts of relationships that the living have with the world of spirits. In traditional or what we are also referring to as primal economies, when the spirits are angry because they have been neglected by the living, what results is environmental and climatic chaos including striking with thunder, floods, and causing drought. The Christian equivalent of that is the economic stagnation that Pentecostal pastors teach that people suffer for the non-payment of tithes and offerings. In the African traditional context, it is to avoid these calamitous situations, we note presently, that traditional African societies still maintain cordial relationships with the supernatural worlds of spirits and ancestors. The major themes in a typical African cosmological order, then, would include beliefs in an enchanted universe, the sacrality of life, reverence for the natural environment stemming from its mystical nature, a sense of community that involves the living and the dead, solidarity and participation, an emphasis on fecundity, and hospitality.

In view of the ontological worldview, African traditional economies have always been foregrounded in the cosmological idea that we live in a "sacramental universe" in which the physical serves as a vehicle for the spiritual. In traditional thought of the Nuer of Sudan, for example, "spirits of the above" are usually associated with the sun, rain, lightening, thunder, and so on, while their "spirits of the below may be identified with rivers, streams, lakes, land, etc." The intersection of the activities of the spirits of the above and below on traditional economies lies in the fact that it is the sun and rain that make it possible for the land to retain its fertility and produce food for the sustenance of human beings and their communities. The sources of physical economic living are therefore governed by the relationship between human beings and the world of spirits. The breach of such simple traditional ethical codes as not fishing or farming on certain sacred days, it is believed, could affect the productivity of the land and rivers. In other words, famine and hunger could in African societies be seen as religious issues. In pre-missionary Mende Society in Sierra Leone, Kenneth Little reported, for example, that the making of rice farms offers an important illustration of their routine approach to the ancestors. The preparation of the land, the sowing of the rice, and its harvesting all involved extensive rituals that "suggest that the Mende believe that the ancestral spirits are in a position to help the living, even to intercede on their behalf" for economic wellbeing.[2]

In the African traditional context, the relationship between Spirit/religion on the one hand and ethics and economics on the other may therefore be best appreciated from the perspective of a key theme in African ontology. This relates to the sense of affinity that Africans possess with nature. Nature does not only owe its source to the Supreme Being, but it is also enchanted with divine presence and power. Thus, in the Mende worldview that relates to the cultivation of rice, Kenneth Little notes that the ceremonies do not suggest that ancestral spirits necessarily have power in their own right. Rather, the implication is that whatever influence the spirits possess and exercise on behalf of the people of the earth is due to *Ngewo*, the Supreme Being.[3] The natural sources of economic activity and of living and survival, like the land, forests, rivers, and even the sea, are all deified.

When certain rivers dry up, the traditional explanation would usually be that the spirit that inhabits that particular natural environment may have departed, in which case it would be up to those with the powers of divination to explain the reasons for the turn of events to the community and provide directions for religious rectification. These "natural resources," as we would like to refer to them within modern civilizations, are therefore supposed to be handled with the utmost reverence and care. Traditional economies have never been seen as separate from religious beliefs and faith. In *Theology in Africa*, Kwesi A. Dickson points out, the description of the gods of Africa as "nature gods" must be understood to mean that the various aspects of Nature are held to be the means whereby reality is experienced: the stone, the sea, the tree, and generally the various elements in the human environment are meaningful to the African because they point to something beyond themselves.[4] The human being and communities are in kinship with nature because humanity is sustained by nature's bounty.

Eking out a Living from Nature

In African philosophical thought, nature or the environment ought to be treated with ethical and moral respect because, first, it belongs to the now dead, but spiritually living cult of ancestors; second, the living are the custodians of it, holding it in trust for their living-dead ancestors; and third, human life, survival, and destiny depend on it. We eke out our living from the natural resources of Mother Earth. If the African perceptions of the universe consist of the interactions of various vital forces—physical and spiritual, seen and unseen, earthly and heavenly—then the African ethical consciousness cannot but be a religious one.[5] On account of the dynamic relationship between sacred and secular realities, Laurenti Magesa notes how the world becomes even more important in African ethical thought because it is recognized that human life depends directly upon its vital forces.[6]

Human beings, we have noted, eke out their living from natural resources that are owned by the Supreme Being and that are inhabited by the presence of deities and which the ancestors have bequeathed to the living. Until fairly recently when urbanization has thrown its peculiar commercial challenges at Africans, land was only leased for temporary use, not perpetually commercialized for individual economic profit. Traditional chiefs and elders constantly bemoan the fact that when things worked properly with due reverence for the ancestors, no human being touched a tree, rock, or the land, without first deferring to the controlling spiritual powers who, ultimately, are the custodians of the environment on which life depended.

Economically speaking, human flourishing in traditional thought was impossible to explain apart from our relationship to, and consequently a proper and reverential handling of, the earth and its fullness as belonging to the Supreme Being and the supernatural world in its various expressions, whether as deities, spirits, or ancestors. Quoting Magesa:

> In African ethical understanding, the earth is given to humanity as a gratuitous gift and all human beings possess an equal claim to it and the resources it offers. This is especially true of the essentials of life such as land, air, water, fire. ... These cannot be alienated from the clan and ethnic group. What this means is that and individual person can only hold land in trust for one's descendants on behalf of the clan or ethnic group. Water sources, mineral resources, forests ... are in

principle public property [communally owned] and have to be cared for and used as such. ... African morality does not and cannot sanction private ownership of land, and the natural resources under the ground.[7]

One way to appreciate the relationship between the resources of nature on which human life and wellbeing depends and the supernatural forces of beneficence is to look at the religious nature of the celebration of festivals. In most African cultures traditional or ancestral festivals are related to how people eke out their living, thus creating and sustaining a relationship between these ritual celebrations and economic life. Libation prayer is the way in which humans communicate with the world of spirits. The officiant at a typical libation prayer among the Akan peoples of Ghana, for instance, first invokes the forces of beneficence beginning with the Creator God followed by Mother Earth, the ancestors, and the pantheon of lesser deities in that order. What such libation prayer petitions the world of ancestors for include good health and agricultural abundance for feeding the living.

MOTHER EARTH

The Earth is gendered feminine among the Akan of Ghana and is the center of many a traditional celebration because she is the one who "mothers" the community by providing the means of economic sustenance. Among the Gikuyu of Kenya the earth is the "mother of the tribe"; it is the soil that feeds the child through its lifetime and so the earth is the most sacred thing above all that dwell in or on it.[8] In most communities, therefore, Mother Earth has sacred days on which no tilling is to be done on it. This is to avoid de-sacralization through overexploitation. It is also forbidden to de-sacralize the earth through the spilling of innocent human blood and engaging in sexual intercourse on the bare ground. There are trees in African forests that cannot be felled, even for economic reasons, without asking "permission" from the earth through prescribed rites of libation and rituals and sacrifices. The Earth has spiritual power, Kofi A. Busia argued, because it is her spirit that makes the plants grow; she has the power of fertility and offerings are made to her not only so that she could help crops grow but also so that farmers may be protected from misfortune.[9]

A typical libation prayer directed at the Earth by the Asante of the Gold Coast (Ghana) goes as follows:

> Earth, condolences; Earth condolences;
> Earth and dust; The Dependable One; I lean upon you.
> Earth, when I am about to die, I lean upon you.
> Earth, when I am alive, I depend upon you.

The invocation of the beneficent powers of Mother Earth during libation prayer is instructive because it emphasizes the point that the main source of human livelihood is sacred. This is done in recognition of the religious connection between the traditional economy and transcendent realities. After pointing the receptacle that holds the drink to the skies in acknowledgment of the Supreme Being, libation drink is then poured on to the Earth. The message segment of libation prayer that is directed at these transcendent powers is even more poignant in terms of its economic implications. A typical libation prayer among the Akan of Ghana requests from the supernatural realm of the Supreme Being, ancestors, and deities—seen as the sources of power, fruitfulness, and vitality—such things as make for a good life:

> God, the dependable, drinks
> *Asaase Yaa*, [Sacred Earth], drinks
> As you receive drinks,
> We seek life and prosperity.
> We seek long life ...
> Business prosperity, love within the lineage ...
> Drive the evil one far beyond
> To our health, those here assembled
> To the health of our gods and our souls![10]

All of life's forces in African traditions are intended to serve and enhance the life force of the human person and society.[11]

Spirits/Religion and Ethics

Laurenti Magesa writes that "African moral values and ethical behavior are therefore vitalistic, existential (dynamic), holistic, relational, anthropocentric and mystical."[12] Thus, instructively, the closing segment of traditional prayers of libation may be reserved for cursing evil—physical and spiritual sources that work against the wellbeing of the living—so that an auspicious environment may be created for human flourishing. In the relationship between spirit/religion and economies in the traditional context human behavior is important for its ontological consequences, which could be for good or for ill. In Chinua Achebe's classic novel *Things Fall Apart*, he weaves into the storyline the empathy that the ancestral culture of the Igbo reveals in the harmonious relationship that the humans were supposed to have with their environment. We encounter in Achebe's novel this inseparable relationship through a particular action of Okonkwo its main character:

> Okonkwo's prosperity was visible in his household. He had a large compound enclosed by a thick wall of red earth. ... At the opposite end of the compound was a shed for the goats, and each wife built a small attachment to her hut for the hens. Near the barn was a small house, the "medicine house" or shrine where Okonkwo kept the wooden symbols of his personal god and of his ancestral spirits. He worshipped them with sacrifices of kola nut, food and palm-wine, and offered prayers to them on behalf of himself, his three wives and eight children.[13]

The linkage of Okonkwo's economic prosperity with his religion in the text is evident. In several Ghanaian societies, Yam and Maize festivals are celebrated annually with religious rites and rituals meant to acknowledge and appreciate the gods and ancestors for harvests, feed them, and then petition for more abundance in ensuing years. As with the Jewish First Fruits that are meant to be presented to Yahweh in appreciation for deliverance and salvation, the first Yams that are harvested or fishes netted from rivers and lagoons may first be offered to the deities whose interest in the economic wellbeing of their communities made it possible for the lands and water bodies to yield food in the first place. In other words, the economic lives of traditional Africans are founded on the principle that the sources of economic living are controlled by the gods. Land is invested in the ancestors and one cannot work it or even dispose of it without some ritual of permission or amusement.

When Okonkwo in a fit of rage defied traditional ethics, religious, and social norms to physically assault his wife on a sacred day, the consequences of his action were interpreted in the light of its effects on the wider society. The woman had gone to plait her hair at a neighbor's home, as a result of which Okonkwo's evening meal was delayed. On return she received heavy beating from Okonkwo who in his anger had forgotten that this was the week of peace or sacred week. This is usually a period of silence imposed on traditional societies in which people ceased from working the land, fishing, or engaging in any economic activity. Achebe writes that it was unheard of for one to beat another during the sacred week. At dusk, Ezeani the priest of the earth goddess, Ani, called on Okonkwo in his *obi* or hut. Against the backdrop of customary courtesy toward visitors, Okonkwo had brought out kola nut and placed it before the priest in observance of the traditional mode of welcoming strangers. The rest of the story is best told in Achebe's own words:

> "Take away your kola nut. I shall not eat in the house of a man who has no respect for our gods and ancestors. ... Listen to me ... you are not a stranger in Umuofia. You know as well as I do that our forefathers ordained that before we plant any crops in the earth we should observe a week in which a man does not say a harsh word to his neighbor. We live in peace with our fellows to honor our great goddess of the earth without whose blessing our crops will not grow. ... The evil you have done can ruin the whole clan. The earth goddess whom you have insulted may refuse to give us her increase, and we shall all perish.[14]

The concluding words of the priest drew out the religious implications of the actions of Okonkwo. For, by breaking sacred taboo, the actions of a single individual had the potential to affect the economic fortunes of a whole community: "the earth goddess whom you have insulted may refuse to give us her increase, and we shall all perish."[15]

African Pneumatic Christianity and Economics

African innovations in Christianity that started at the beginning of the twentieth century with different sorts of prophetic movements have, above all else, privileged the pneumatic aspects of the faith. The ministries of these prophets, including William Wadé Harris of Liberia and William Sokari Braide of the Niger Delta, Ogbu Kalu notes, "illustrate the battle for sacred powers" that became important at the turn of the twentieth century. He observes how they removed "the strangeness of charismaticism by inserting into it the broad spectrum of African initiative."[16] And there were major ethical dimensions to these prophetic ministries as by turning to Christ, and away from traditional resources of supernatural succor, there also occurred drastic changes in the moral choices that people made in their personal lives. The reason for the emphasis on the work of the Spirit by the independent church movements that followed the work of the indigenous prophets is no different from the African worldview in which that which relates to power, wealth, health, and wellbeing, in short, material and spiritual prosperity are related to the human interaction with the supernatural realities of life. In that sense, African charismatic Christianity initiated a paradigmatic from a missionary theological viewpoint in which poverty and material lack became a mark of genuine spirituality with material wealth as an obstacle to the kingdom of God, especially in its eschatological sense. Indeed, in the intersection between spirituality and material wellbeing, we have an idea of what the African, when left to himself or herself, may consider important in religion. Religion is instrumental and serves as a survival strategy in the African imagination.

The principles set out in Max Weber's Protestant Ethic Thesis and its promotion of thrift and Christian capitalism had been very much a part of Western mission Christian spirituality that evangelized most of Africa from the early years of the nineteenth century in particular. Mission Christianity discouraged conspicuous consumption and materialism, but it did, at the same time, support the efforts of Christians to work toward earning decent income and investment. In spite of the promotion of hard work and industry, materialism, and mission Christianity preached, could be a great setback to Christian walk for after all, Jesus had preached that "a person's life did not consist in the abundance of his possessions" (Luke 12:15). The story of John Bunyan's *Pilgrim Progress*, which was translated into many African languages, was taught at Sunday School and Bible classes as supplementary material to biblical teachings on the dangers of wealth in general and money in particular. Western missionary Christian evangelization was founded on the provision of formal education and the provision of social intervention programs such as clean water and modern medicine. The result was that missionary work became the principal means of civilization. The relationship between religion generally and Christianity in particular and economics was therefore a very practical one. Being "evangelized" meant receiving formal education and the adoption of Western European ways of living that then saw traditional cultures steeped in religious beliefs as backward, devilish, and retrogressive.[17]

The educated African who had gone through the mission school system, to a large extent, abandoned some of the connections that the "uncivilized" traditionalists made between religion and economic wellbeing dismissing these as belonging to a past that had misunderstood how the God of the Christian evangel worked. In spite of these developments, religious change in twentieth-century Africa belonged to the autochthonous pneumatic churches founded by African charismatic prophets and leaders. The independent churches, as they were generally called, reinvented within Christian settings worldviews of mystical causality that were associated with the traditional culture. African independent church prophets specialized in praying rituals that sought to reverse economic and other misfortunes. There was much emphasis in their work on practical salvation, which meant they prayed for employment, childbirth, promotion, and success for their clients. They created the ritual contexts for those believing that their economic progress in life depended on dealing with the supernatural forces of retrogression in their lives, families, and workplaces to come for prayer and spiritual fortifications against the forces of evil generally and witchcraft in particular.

Preaching a Christology of power, African charismatic prophets specialized in invoking power in the name and blood of Jesus to deal with those malignant powers that hold back the economic fortunes of their clients. To that end, African prophets are known to be the producers, suppliers, or custodians of sacramental substances or religious tangibles, as I call them, that people planted on their farms, kept on their persons, or homes to prevent the activities of witches from affecting their labor or spiriting away their material resources.[18] Popular Islam in Africa spread by the same means as clerics supplied charms and amulets not just for personal protection against evil but most importantly to enhance people's economic fortunes in all sorts of ways.[19] That was the way in which witches were known to inflict the curse of poverty on people. Traditional and personal economies had everything to do with prayer and ritual. There are some who opted to go for protective or anti-witchcraft prophylactics from some of the popular medicine cults at the time, *Tigare*, *Aberewa*, and *Hwemeso*, as they have been labeled among the Akan of Ghana.[20]

In the Christian church, however, traditional medicine cults were demonized as belonging to the realm of the satanic and the independent churches provided their own array of sacramentals to make up for the need. It was common knowledge that the general practice was for people to opt for the religious resources that worked for them, whether Christian, Islamic, traditional, or even most commonly a combination of all three, for potency and quick action. People combined, in their personal religious worlds, spiritual resources that they believed would deliver economic and material successes. Those who worked in government service or even had private businesses relied on powerful prophets to protect their personal economic interests and help them to do well in their various careers. It is not uncommon to hear about ordinary market women relying on traditional priests, diviners, medicine shrines, or even indigenous Christian prophets for spiritual arsenal for economic ends. Those who seemed to prosper economically in the traditional African context could easily come under suspicion as relying on religious substances obtained from these sources to support their activities.

Prosperity Gospel and Economics

Africa has since the closing decades of the twentieth century witnessed the rise of a new breed of independent church movement and these are the contemporary pneumatic or Pentecostal/charismatic churches. In the new forms of pneumatic Christianity in Africa, the relationship between religion/spirit and economics has become even more pronounced with the gospel of prosperity. The popular descriptions of these churches as preaching a health-and-wealth gospel clearly sustain a new worldview of a relationship between divine action and economic wellbeing. The immediate results of the born-again message preached by these churches are not hard to find. Testimonies flowed on how people, as a result of giving their lives to Christ, had been able to rechannel their material resources into constructive purposes away from vain and canal living that affected social and family lives in negative ways. When people became ethically and morally responsible, following their experiences of regeneration, personal economies improved with consequences for wider society. Additionally, these are movements that actively deploy the biblical material to justify their direct use of Christianity for capitalist economic ends. There has been an extensive commodification of religion at the hands of the new Pentecostals. Their media setups are completely economic as books and sermons recorded on various portable media technological devices are circulated with great monetary returns among patrons. In other words, among the contemporary prosperity-preaching Pentecostals, there exists a whole range of sacramental substances that have great commercial value. It has been argued, and with veracity, that African Pentecostalism is "marketed and advertised" as an effective means of material success.

In other words, religion and, in this case, Pentecostalism has economic value. The route to Pentecostal prosperity is not monolithic or simply formulaic. Hard work, as in the Weberian example cited earlier, counts a lot in the new discourses on prosperity. Donald E. Miller and Tetsunao Yamamori have referred to these economically and developmentally minded contemporary Pentecostal movements as Progressive Pentecostals.[21] Progressive Pentecostals claim to be inspired by the Holy Spirit and the life of Jesus to pursue a holistic approach to spiritual, physical, and social development.[22] People are urged to work hard, pursue the Christian ethical principle of honesty, and expect God to bless their toil. Even within Progressive Pentecostalism, hard work alone may not be sufficient for prosperity. For hard work to yield the required dividends of blessing, it must be supported by faithful giving. This preaching is reciprocal as it also allows the churches to focus on giving by those economically blessed by God. Thus, the mandatory giving in tithes and offerings has been institutionalized through innovative fundraising methods often requiring specialists who employ different marketing strategies to impress upon people to give.

The ethical dimensions lie in being personally truthful, especially in the payment of tithes by big earners. This is a gospel in which personal and business prosperity is related directly to the levels at which people give of their earnings. The prosperity-preaching churches raise enormous resources through their fundraising activities that go to sponsor not only their imposing and competitive church infrastructures but also the various social developmental programs that some of them take on. The point to note is that Progressive Pentecostalism makes a direct connection between Holy Spirit or pneumatic Christianity and economics. Economic prosperity however does not just depend only on giving. There is a reason why contemporary Pentecostal pastors cast themselves as motivational preachers, for, they use the Bible to inspire their hearers to cultivate the spirit of investing in high-yielding financial instruments and explore and participate in new economic ventures.

The prosperity gospel is a major hallmark of contemporary Pentecostal preaching. Nimi Wariboko serves as well by identifying five basic theological paradigms that frame the discourses on Africa's economic development and its relationship to human flourishing on the continent. They are the covenant, spiritualist, leadership, nationalist, and developmental paradigms of prosperity.[23] It is not my intention to discuss the various prosperity paradigms in any detail here but simply to state that in deploying these paradigms so well classified by Wariboko in their hermeneutics, contemporary Pentecostals propose to help shape our individual and collective futures through life-affirming rather than poverty-bringing religious rituals that grasp the future through prayer, faith, and purposeful actions.[24] In the covenant paradigm, for example, poverty is problematized as a religious phenomenon that is caused by lack of faith in God's promises of prosperity.[25] The metaphor used in the covenant prosperity paradigm is the agricultural one of sowing and reaping. Patrons and clients are called upon to sow tithes and offerings into the church or even the personal ministry of a charismatic leader and expect to reap bumper harvests of wealth and prosperity.

In this sowing and reaping approach to prosperity, as Wariboko argues it, Christians are encouraged to be positive in their verbal declarations, fulfill their tithing obligations, and sow seeds of money and other gifts in the life and ministry of their anointed charismatic leaders and simply reap the results in material blessings.[26] The prosperity preachers in this covenant paradigm, Wariboko notes, do not merely address poverty and fuel greed. They produce desires and dreams and connect them to the transcendental God. Those who tithe faithfully do so within a Pentecostal covenant paradigm of prosperity in which giving becomes an obligation toward God and is supposed to generate requisite returns in blessings of wealth. Some have castigated this as a message that subdues the biblical emphasis on personal holiness and morality, but there is some positive element here in that the preachers motivate believers to become agents of their own personal economic improvement. The downside of it is that it takes a simplistic approach to development and leaves those who fulfill their covenant obligations and yet continue in poverty and suffering without adequate answers to the quagmires of life.[27] The emphasis on prosperity as covenant giving continues in prosperity preaching, but the message is in some cases a bit more nuanced than when these churches started preaching in the late 1970s.

There is a second model of prosperity that Wariboko terms the "excellence model," which is meant to deal with the fallout in the simplistic name-it-and-claim-it approach to wealth and wellbeing. This model, according to Wariboko, dwells on human capability development and Afrocentric sentiments. He explains how this model works in prosperity gospel hermeneutics within the context of contemporary Pentecostalism or charismatic Christianity in Nigeria, noting that, if Nigerians are sowing and reaping material blessings, they must do so, according to the proponents of this model, with the best machinery and organization. The excellence model of prosperity encourages taking advantage of and the use of technical and technological abilities within globalized economies. The operation of these technologies must be sustained and advanced by the ethos of professional excellence. This model says that Nigeria has failed in economic development because there are too few sane, resourceful, and patriotic managers who can bring together and develop the right talents to orchestrate development in the various spheres of the economy. The excellence model, Wariboko explains, is based on a triad of factors: nationalism (Afrocentric view), professionalism (human capacity building), and the prosperity gospel orientation to development.[28]

The simplistic positive confession and sowing-and-reading forms of prosperity have been balanced by other charismatic pastors with a more pragmatic approach in which the stress is on hard work, the constructive and wise use of gifts and talents, and the pursuit of relevant educational programs. Indeed, elsewhere, Nimi Wariboko presents prosperity-oriented Pentecostalism as "an art of disciplined subjectivity rather than as dogma or rhetoric of deception."[29] One way to appreciate the practicalities of this is to consider the new system of presenting the sermon through motivational speaking that is found in preachers like Bishop T. D. Jakes of the Potter's House in Texas, USA. We find an African example of motivational speaking in Pastor Mensa Otabil of Ghana. His approach to prosperity has been very well analyzed by Paul Gifford in his book *Ghana's New Christianity*. The importance of the spiritual for human development lies at the heart of the new hermeneutics we come across in the sort of contemporary Pentecostalism that Pastor Otabil represents. In *Nigerian Pentecostalism* Nimi Wariboko gives the following succinct summary of the sort of hermeneutics of development or empowerment that I speak of here:

> It is the belief in the power of Pentecostalism—the movement of the Holy Spirit and the power to initiate something new—to transform and elevate African society and the dignity of the black race. Within a certain segment of Nigerian

Pentecostalism, the only way of living acceptably to God was life not merely of holiness and personal salvation and wealth but by the fulfilment of an obligation to be God's battle-axe to uproot and destroy economic backwardness and the black race's indignity. This was their calling. They saw themselves as an instrument of the divine in the history of Africa.[30]

Following the assertions in this quotation, Wariboko then discusses how Pentecostals are "bearing the weight of blackness" by articulating ideas of Christian citizenship and the desire for the "greatness of the black race."[31]

One of the books written by Mensa Otabil, *Beyond the Rivers of Ethiopia*, deals precisely with this sort of hermeneutics of empowerment.[32] In this book, Otabil writes that the average black person has to contend with Western values and would be shaped by them. The suffusion of African societies with things Western is that blacks end up feeling inferior to the white race. Even Christian missionaries, he writes, assumed that everything African was evil and our indigenous names were demonized as satanic.[33] He then gives Africans a charge in relation to seizing the moment and taking our place in God's world: "We were not made in God's image to receive mercy drops! The times have changed, and God is calling on us to change our attitudes and expectations."[34] The reference to Ethiopia in the narrative is very instructive. That country became the symbol of black emancipation on account of the fact that it was the only African country that resisted colonial rule and domination. Besides Ethiopia appears in the biblical narrative as quickly stretching out her hands to God (Psalm 68:31) and also bring God an offering (Zephaniah 3:10).

These texts including the baptism of the Ethiopian eunuch by Philip in the *Acts of the Apostles* have inspired the thinking that Africa looms large in God's imagination and Westerners must not be allowed to hold him in their custody. These thoughts are also present in the writings of Matthew Ashimolowo of the Kingsway International Christian Center (KICC). In his book *What is Wrong with Being Black*, he writes as follows:

> It is my opinion that there is no culture that transcends any other culture or stand superior to other cultures. The Bible is raised as the standard here because it is in it that we find what I consider the key root to Black pathologies and the final solution that will cause Blacks to come into the fullness of who they will be. It is the Bible that will cause them to come to a place of the true identification of their gift in God, transformation and a manifestation of the gifts and abilities that have been deposited in them from time immemorial.[35]

The subtitle of Ashimolowo's book—*Celebrating our Heritage [and] Confronting our Challenges*—is very instructive. It follows the same thought as Pastor Otabil's writings regarding the sort of black empowerment hermeneutics that the new crop of motivational speakers is developing in Africa within the context of independent Pentecostalism. Their theses of black empowerment constitute a new form of popular African liberation theology that has had great success in its empowering effects on Africa's middle class.

CONCLUSION

According to Andrew F. Walls, Christianity in Africa has in some way inherited the old goals of traditional religion.[36] In this chapter, we have noted in particular that the association of traditional or primal religions with power, protection, and wealth lies undiminished in the independent Christian expressions of the faith. The effectiveness of the Christian faith or any particular manifestation of it, Walls notes, is accordingly open to the test of whether it gives access to power and prosperity to protection against natural or spiritual enemies (purposes to which much traditional practice was directed) and satisfactorily enforces familial and social duty.[37] Prosperity in the context of African Christianity, as I have argued, always has a strong existential and not just an eschatological dimension.

The African ontology is very much a religious one, as we have discussed, and its implications for the traditional economy are taken very seriously. One reason why the African might be more inclined toward the Old Testament, Kwesi A. Dickson argued, for example, is that in Africa as in ancient Israel, religion pervades life.[38] African Christians find in the Old Testament a kindred atmosphere because the latter contains bodies of rules and regulations which were meant to govern the ritual and moral lives of the ancient Israelites.[39] Many of these relate to how communities eke out a living from natural resources. Agricultural pursuits, Dickson noted, bring the African face to face not only with God who brings rain and sunshine but also with the Goddess of the earth.[40]

The resonances, between the traditional forms of faith and the pneumatic forms we have discussed as they relate to economic life, lie in the fact that in traditional belief systems salvation is about wholeness that embraces both spiritual and physical blessings. In Wariboko's view, the Pentecostal churches "may be tapping into the sources deep in the veins of traditional thought" but "struggling to conceptualize the imported meaning of salvation." He helps us to understand how, unlike say the historic mission denominations, African Pentecostal Christians reject the separation between the sacred and secular binary thinking preferring rather to see salvation not just in spiritual/eschatological but also in physical/existential terms. The material realm, the realm of the bread and butter, Wariboko notes, must be opened to the spiritual.[41] The implications for this unitary perception of the salvific order for ethics are not too hard to find. In the Christian message, change begins with accepting Christ as Lord and personal Savior. The Pentecostal emphasis on the born-again experience as fundamental to Christian living means that in reality, we cannot talk about prosperity without commitment to doing justice, loving kindness, and walking humbly with our God (Micah 6:8).

Notes

1. Laurenti Magesa, *African Religion: The Moral Traditions of Abundant Life* (Maryknoll, NY: Orbis Books, 1997), 3.
2. Kenneth Little, *The Mende in Sierra Leone*, in Daryll Forde ed., *African Worlds: Studies in the Cosmological Ideas and Social Values of African Peoples* (Oxford: Oxford University Press, 1954), 118–9.
3. Little, *Mende*, 119.
4. Kwesi A. Dickson, *Theology in Africa* (Maryknoll, NY: Orbis Books, 1984), 161.
5. Magesa, *African Religion*, 57.
6. Magesa, *African Religion*, 60.
7. Magesa, *African Religion*, 61.
8. Jomo Kenyatta, *Facing Mount Kenya* (London: Mercury Books, 1938), 21.
9. Kofi A. Busia, "The Ashanti," in Daryll Forde ed., *African Worlds: Studies in the Cosmological Ideas and Social Values of African Peoples* (Oxford: Oxford University Press, 1954), 195.
10. Kwesi Yankah, *Speaking for the Chief: Ókyeame and the Politics of Akan Royal Oratory* (Bloomington and Indianapolis: Indiana University Press, 1995), 176–177.
11. Magesa, *African Religion*, 51.
12. Magesa, *African Religion*, 51.
13. Chinua Achebe, *Things Fall Apart* (London: Heinemann, 1958), 10.
14. Achebe, *Things Fall Apart*, 30.
15. See J. Kwabena Asamoah-Gyadu, "The Evil You Have Done Can Ruin the Whole Clan: African Cosmology, Community, and Christianity in Achebe's Things Fall Apart," *Studies in World Christianity*, vol. 16, 1 (2010), 46–62.
16. Ogbu Kalu, *African Pentecostalism: An Introduction* (Oxford: Oxford University Press, 2008), 31.
17. Birgit Meyer, *Translating the Devil: Religion and Modernity Among the Ewe in Ghana* (Edinburgh: Edinburgh University Press, 1999).
18. J. Kwabena Asamoah-Gyadu, "Signs, Tokens and Points of Contact," *Studia Liturgica: An International Ecumenical Review for Liturgical Research and Renewal*, Volume 48, 1 & 2 (2018), 127–146.
19. Lamin Sanneh, *The Crown and the Turban: Muslims and West African Pluralism* (Boulder, Colorado: Westview, 1997).
20. Opoku Onyinah, *Pentecostal Exorcism: Witchcraft and Demonology in Ghana* (Dorset, UK: Deo Publishing, 2012), 69–75.
21. Donald E. Miller and Tetsunao Yamamori, *Global Pentecostalism: The New Face of Christian Social Engagement* (Berkeley: University of California Press, 2007).
22. Miller and Tetsunao, *Global Pentecostalism*, 2.
23. Nimi Wariboko, "Pentecostal Paradigms of National Economic Prosperity in Africa," in Katherine Attanasi and Amos Yong, ed. *Pentecostalism and Prosperity: The Socio-Economics of the Global Charismatic Movement* (NY: Palgrave Macmillan, 2012), 35–59.
24. Wariboko, "Pentecostal Paradigms," 35.
25. Wariboko, "Pentecostal Paradigms," 37.
26. Nimi Wariboko, *Nigerian Pentecostalism* (Rochester, NY: University of Rochester Press, 2014), 234.
27. Wariboko, *Nigerian Pentecostalism*, 236.

28. Wariboko, *Nigerian Pentecostalism*, 238.
29. Nimi Wariboko, *Economics in Spirit and in Truth: A Moral Philosophy of Finance* (NY: Palgrave Macmillan, 2014), 88.
30. Wariboko, *Nigerian Pentecostalism*, 230.
31. Wariboko, *Nigerian Pentecostalism*, 232.
32. Mensa Otabil, *Beyond the Rivers of Ethiopia: A Biblical Revelation on God's Purpose for the Black Race* (Accra: Altar International, 1992).
33. Otabil, *Rivers of Ethiopia*, 15
34. Otabil, *Rivers of Ethiopia*, 68.
35. Matthew Ashimolowo, *What's Wrong with Being Black: Celebrating Our Heritage; Confronting Our Challenges* (Shippensburg, PA: Destiny Image, 2007), 12.
36. Andrew F. Walls, *The Cross-Cultural Process in Christian History* (Maryknoll, NY: Orbis Books, 2002), 122.
37. Walls, *Cross-Cultural Process in Christian History*, 122.
38. Dickson, *Theology in Africa*, 154.
39. Dickson, *Theology in Africa*, 153.
40. Dickson, *Theology in Africa*, 156.
41. Wariboko, "Pentecostal Paradigms," 41.

Bibliography

Achebe, Chinua. 1958. *Things Fall Apart*. London: Heinemann.
Asamoah-Gyadu, Kwabena J. 2010. The Evil you Have Done Can Ruin the Whole Clan: African Cosmology, Community, and Christianity in Achebe's Things Fall Apart. *Studies in World Christianity* 16 (1): 46–62.
———. 2018. Signs, Tokens and Points of Contact. *Studia Liturgica: An International Ecumenical Review for Liturgical Research and Renewal* 48 (1 and 2): 127–146.
Ashimolowo, Matthew. 2007. *What's Wrong with Being Black: Celebrating Our Heritage; Confronting Our Challenges*. Shippensburg: Destiny Image.
Busia, Kofi A. 1954. The Ashanti. In *African Worlds: Studies in the Cosmological Ideas and Social Values of African Peoples*, ed. Daryll Forde, 190–209. Oxford: Oxford University Press.
Dickon, Kwesi A. 1984. *Theology in Africa*. Maryknoll: Orbis Books.
Kalu, Ogbu. 2008. *African Pentecostalism: An Introduction*. Oxford: Oxford University Press.
Kenyatta, Jomo. 1938. *Facing Mount Kenya*. London: Mercury Books.
Little, Kenneth. 1954. The Mende in Sierra Leone. In *African Worlds: Studies in the Cosmological Ideas and Social Values of African Peoples*, ed. Daryll Forde, 118–119. Oxford: Oxford University Press.
Magesa, Laurenti. 1997. *African Religion: The Moral Traditions of Abundant Life*. Maryknoll: Orbis Books.
Meyer, Birgit. 1999. *Translating the Devil: Religion and Modernity Among the Ewe in Ghana*. Edinburgh: Edinburgh University Press.
Miller, Donald E., and Tetsunao Yamamori. 2007. *Global Pentecostalism: The New Face of Christian Social Engagement*. Berkeley: University of California Press.
Onyinah, Opoku. 2012. *Pentecostal Exorcism: Witchcraft and Demonology in Ghana*. Dorset: Deo Publishing.

Otabil, Mensa. 1992. *Beyond the Rivers of Ethiopia: A Biblical Revelation on God's Purpose for the Black Race*. Accra: Altar International.

Sanneh, Lamin. 1997. *The Crown and the Turban: Muslims and West African Pluralism*. Boulder: Westview.

Walls, Andrew F. 2002. *The Cross-Cultural Process in Christian History*. Maryknoll: Orbis Books.

Wariboko, Nimi. 2012. Pentecostal Paradigms of National Economic Prosperity in Africa. In *Pentecostalism and Prosperity: The Socio-Economics of the Global Charismatic Movement*, ed. Katherine Attanasi and Amos Yong, 35–59. New York: Palgrave Macmillan.

———. 2014a. *Nigerian Pentecostalism*. Rochester: University of Rochester Press.

———. 2014b. *Economics in Spirit and in Truth: A Moral Philosophy of Finance*. New York: Palgrave Macmillan.

———. 2019. *Ethics and Society in Nigeria: Identity, History, Political Theory*. New York: Rochester Press.

Yankah, Kwesi. 1995. *Speaking for the Chief: Ókyeame and the Politics of Akan Royal Oratory*. Bloomington/Indianapolis: Indiana University Press.

CHAPTER 19

Corruption, Nepotism, and Anti-Bureaucratic Behaviors

Bola Dauda

INTRODUCTION

Bureaucracy pervades every aspect of a modern human's life, not only from cradle to the grave, but from before birth through to after death. In the guideline for contributors, the editors of this handbook have rightly identified "the five major spheres of life: family, polity, economy, creativity, and dominion (religion)." If social ethics simply means a set of human shared values of what is right or wrong, or what the editors have defined as "the spiritual and moral energies behind human flourishing and civilization," bureaucracy is the ubiquitous platform or the constituted institution for all forms of human interactions. For example, bureaucracy is involved in human life from the determination of the social status or rights of a child conceived within or out of a legal wedlock, and the mother's attendance at anti-natal health clinics through to the registration of death, and whether, or not, one died intestate, and what happens to one's legacy. What the editors have described as the "dynamic and open social reality" of African social ethics, in other words, as "lived, [or] as experienced historical-social existence" are often espoused as everyday post-traumas of slavery and trade in human beings otherwise euphemized as "slave trade," and as the living ruptures of racialized categorization of human beings, colonialism, imperialism, and the postcolonial inequities of satellite-metropolis international trade and global political-economic relations.

This chapter demonstrates that "if we want to focus on ethics as lived, as experienced historical-social existence" nothing "tells the story of African ethics as a dynamic and open social reality that bear the marks of changes, rup-

B. Dauda (✉)
Independent Scholar, London, UK

© The Author(s) 2020
N. Wariboko, T. Falola (eds.), *The Palgrave Handbook of African Social Ethics*, https://doi.org/10.1007/978-3-030-36490-8_19

tures, contradictions, and passages of time" more than the issues of corruption, nepotism, and anti-bureaucratic behaviors. Nothing tells the story of the deplorable and failing state of the African nations more than the incidence of systemic and institutionalized corruption, nepotism, and anti-bureaucratic behaviors.

The chapter is in seven parts: (1) understanding the universality of the primordial African social ethics; (2) the roots of corruption, nepotism, and anti-bureaucratic behaviors; (3) review of the interface of the African social ethics and the politics of the contemporary African nation-states; (4) paradox of the interface of the oral African governance institutions and the Weberian bureaucratic principles; (5) understanding the everyday lived political economic realities and the dilemmas of corruption, nepotism, and anti-bureaucratic behaviors; (6) interrogating African social ethics in today's global village and worldview of good governance; and (7) conclusion: Is decolonization, reorientation, privatization, and computerization the way forward?

This chapter does not dwell on specific "petty and grand" incidences and cases of corruption, nepotism, and anti-bureaucratic behaviors involving individuals and national public servants because there is a lot of information on such cases in the academic, social media, and public domains.[1] Also, there is no point in dwelling either on the effects of corruption or on the multifarious anti-corruption initiatives.[2] However, in an outlook for African social ethics for sustainable nation-building and for an enduring socio-economic development and a cohesive political transformation, the chapter concludes with proposed bureaucratic institutional precepts and practices to avert corruption and nepotism.[3] These institutional precepts and practices are archetypes of what the editors of this handbook have encapsulated as "spiritual and moral energies to guide the African human drive toward transcendence and the future."[4]

Understanding the Universality of the Primordial African Social Ethics

With 54 nation-states and over 500 ethnic nationalities, caution must be exercised in the use of an umbrella field of study as *African social ethics*. African ethnic nationalities are not monocultural but have diverse cultures with differing multifarious values and beliefs that shape the rubrics of the social norms and regulations of their everyday lives and behaviors. However, anthropological studies of the social ethics of African ethnic nationalities such as the Yoruba in south west Nigeria, the Akan in Ghana, and the Bantu in South Africa have reports of the communal, judicial, spiritual, socio-economic, and political commonalities and sometimes the universalities of the primordial African social ethics as a body of norms, mores, and rules for the control and management of the everyday human relations and interactions.[5] For example, Ubuntu represents the Bantu ontology of humanness and the essence of African humanity, while Omoluwabi presents the Yoruba versions of the African traditional moral codes. They (Ubuntu and Omoluwabi precepts) remain evident in the everyday lives of the postcolonial Bantu and Yoruba communities. As archetypes of other African ethnic nationalities, they constitute a corpus of unwritten constitutionally enduring indigenous systems of African social ethics for governance which are not only aberrant to corruption and nepotism but are somehow *democratic, equitable, and morally responsive and self-regulating.*

Ifeanyi Menkiti renders this point very clearly:

[t]he various societies found in traditional Africa routinely accept this fact that personhood is the sort of thing which has to be attained and is attained in direct proportion as one participates in communal life through the discharge of the various obligations defined by one's stations. It is the carrying out of these obligations that transforms one from the it-status of early childhood, marked by an absence of moral function, into the person status of later years, marked by a widened maturity of ethical sense—an ethical sense without which personhood is conceived as eluding one.[6]

Generally, the adult member of either the Bantu or Yoruba communities, as it is the case in other African ethnic nationalities, is expected to discharge certain duties and observe certain moral dictates to be considered a person.[7] According to K. A. Opoku,

The end of morality in the religious heritage of Africa is social harmony and peace. Membership in the family, clan and community is based, not on individual rights, but on obligation, which extends through time. For although personal individuality is not denied, it is one's membership which is emphasized. For man is never considered alone, and to be a true human being means to belong to a community—Life is when you are together, alone you are an animal.[8]

Generally, it could be said that the precolonial Bantu and Yoruba communities were clear examples of a complex mix of interdependent and interwoven individual and communal socio-economic African polities. They are communal but not communist. Both the Bantu and the Yoruba have an archetype of what Desmond Tutu has described as the African communal worldview of humanity. For example, Ubuntu and Omoluwabi are paradoxically a universal ethical system applicable to running a cohesive and harmonious social order in any human society. Overall, today's universal relevance and significance of the respective Bantu and Yoruba Ubuntu and Omoluwabi has been encapsulated in Desmond Tutu's asserted morale of the African worldview of humanism: "*Ubuntu* teaches us that our worth is intrinsic to who we are. ... In our African worldview, the greatest good is communal harmony."[9] Tutu, the Nobel Peace Prize winner, has explained the African perspective and worldview of humanism. In his most controversial book, *God Is Not a Christian*, he talks about the nature of human community and the African concept of "*ubuntu.*"[10]

Tutu says,
In our African *weltanschauung*, our worldview, we have something called *ubuntu*. In Xhosa, we say, "Umntu ngumtu ngabantu." This expression is very difficult to render in English, but we could translate it by saying, "A person is a

person through other person."[11] We need other human beings for us to learn how to be human, for none of us comes fully formed into the world. In other words, 'we legitimize our own existence through our recognition of others.' ... In indigenous African society, *ubuntu* was coveted more than anything else, more than wealth as measured in cattle and the extent of one's land. Without this quality a prosperous man, even though he might have been a chief, was regarded as someone deserving of pity and even contempt. It was seen as what ultimately distinguished people from animals—the quality of being human and so also humane.[12]

In explaining the fundamental and practical aspect of *ubuntu*, Augustine Shutte states that "[a]t the centre of *UBUNTU* is the idea that *umuntu ngumuntu ngabantu*, persons depend on persons to be persons. This is our hidden secret."[13] The interdependency of the individual on her community is rightly expressed by Bernard Matolino who stated that,

> It can be deduced that a person attains her wholeness through other people. ... The individual does not only rely on her standing and relations with her community when faced with questions of her identity. She also relies on her community when faced with problems that may appear insurmountable. When faced with difficulties she can count on her community availing the necessary help. The community readily helps her, even when at times she has not asked for that help or is even unaware that she is in need of that help.[14]

Thus, John Mbiti noted that, "Whatever happens to the individual happens to the whole group, and whatever happens to the whole group happens to the individual. The individual can only say: 'I am because we are; and since we are therefore I am.' This is a cardinal point in the understanding of the African view of man."[15] The concrete expression of the ethic of *ubuntu* lies in the manner in which a person practically lives out her life. Thus, according to Bernard Matolino, it is not sufficient for one to have bonds of oneness with her community. She ought to have a certain moral worth that is recognized by her fellows as befitting her social standing. It is in executing the duties that she becomes a person. Given the interdependency of the individuals and their community, Bernard Matolino concluded that,

> there is an inseparable existence between the individual and her community. They do not exist side by side but together as one and for each other. ... The individual together with her fellow community members are strongly tied together by bonds of togetherness that permeate all the facets of her existence. This bond that ties all these individuals together in such a thoroughgoing and fundamental manner is the ethic of ubuntu. ... *Umuntu*, then, is an individual who has shown herself to be sufficiently integrated with the other so as to be one with her community.[16]

Among the Yoruba, the equivalent word for *Ubuntu* is *Omoluwabi*—a paragon of good character. Thus, Osun, one of the states in the core Yoruba kingdoms, has adopted *Ipinle Omoluwabi* (i.e., the state of people with good character); hence, the language of politics is infused with the concept of Omoluwabi suggesting that the modern Nigerian state could be governed on the basis of the ethical Omoluwabi principles in the same manner that Desmond Tutu had advocated the "Ubuntu" principles for running the affairs of the post-apartheid South African communities. They (Ubuntu and Omoluwabi precepts) at the same time project the unique peculiarities of the primordial African communal but not communist social ethics.

THE ROOTS OF CORRUPTION,[17] NEPOTISM, AND ANTI-BUREAUCRATIC BEHAVIORS

While reflecting on the problems with Nigeria, Chinua Achebe rhetorically asked, "*Where did rain start beating us?*" If African social ethics puts so much premium on probity, integrity, and social responsibility as germane to one's personhood and social standing, how then could one explain the pervasive corruption and nepotism across the spheres of life in Africa? There are five prominent roots for the incidence of corruption, nepotism, and anti-bureaucratic behaviors in the contemporary African nation-states. Ironically, the answer lies first in the interwoven, interdependent, and an integrated relationship between one's personhood and their community. In other words, if corruption simply implies using public goods to one's benefit, a communal social responsibility in which an individual's interest is intricately tied to the overall interest of the host community not only blurs the line between private and public but becomes problematic. Thus, a state governor in Nigeria could not understand anything morally wrong or bureaucratically unacceptable in having "*government money in government house!*"

The second root of systemic corruption, nepotism, and anti-bureaucratic behaviors could be traced to Willie Lynch's professed enduring programmed method for a perpetual enslavement of the black people. Lynch was a British slave owner in the West Indies. He was invited to the colony of Virginia in 1772 to teach his methods to slave owners there. In his infamous speech on the bank of the James River in the colony of Virginia in 1772, he spelled out his methods. I reproduced his speech at length herewith—with all the emphasis as in the original text—not only because of its prophetic relevance to a perceptive understanding of the impoverished state of the African nation-state but because of how the European colonizers and the postcolonial African leaders had in multifarious ways adopted Lynch's methods for the perpetual institutionalization of corruption, nepotism, and anti-bureaucratic behaviors in today's African nation-states.

> I have experimented with some of the newest, and still the oldest, methods for control of slaves. Ancient Rome would envy us if my program is implemented. As our boat sailed south on the James River, named for our illustrious King, whose version of the Bible we cherish, I saw enough to know that your problem is not unique. ... In my bag here, **I HAVE A FOOL PROOF METHOD FOR CONTROLLING YOUR BLACK SLAVES**. I guarantee every one of you that, if installed correctly, **IT WILL CONTROL THE SLAVES FOR AT**

LEAST THREE HUNDRED YEARS. My method is simple. Any member of your family or your overseer can use it. **I HAVE OUTLINED A NUMBER OF DIFFERENCES AMONG THE SLAVES; AND I TAKE THESE DIFFERENCES AND MAKE THEM BIGGER. I USE FEAR, DISTRUST AND ENVY FOR CONTROL PURPOSES**. These methods have worked on my modest plantation in the West Indies and it will work throughout the South. Take this simple little list of differences and think about them. On top of my list is "AGE," but it's there only because it starts with an "a." The second is "COLOR" or shade. There is **INTELLIGENCE, SIZE, SEX, SIZES OF PLANTATIONS, STATUS** on plantations, **ATTITUDE** of owners, whether the slaves live in the valley, on a hill, East, West, North, South, have fine hair, coarse hair, or is tall or short. Now that you have a list of differences, I shall give you an outline of action, but before that, I shall assure you that **DISTRUST IS STRONGER THAN TRUST AND ENVY STRONGER THAN ADULATION, RESPECT OR ADMIRATION**. The Black slaves after receiving this indoctrination shall carry on and will become self-refueling and self-generating for **HUNDREDS** of years, maybe **THOUSANDS**. Don't forget, you must pitch the **OLD** black male vs. the **YOUNG** black male, and the **YOUNG** black male against the **OLD** black male. You must use the **DARK** skin slaves vs. the **LIGHT** skin slaves, and the **LIGHT** skin slaves vs. the **DARK** skin slaves. You must use the **FEMALE** vs. the **MALE**, and the **MALE** vs. the **FEMALE**. You must also have white servants and overseers [who] distrust all Blacks. But it is **NECESSARY THAT YOUR SLAVES TRUST AND DEPEND ON US. THEY MUST LOVE, RESPECT AND TRUST ONLY US**. Gentlemen, these kits are your keys to control. Use them. Have your wives and children use them, never miss an opportunity. **IF USED INTENSELY FOR ONE YEAR, THE SLAVES THEMSELVES WILL REMAIN PERPETUALLY DISTRUSTFUL**.[18]

At the time of writing this chapter, in February 2019, it had been 247 years since Willie Lynch prophesized the guarantee of the efficacy of his methods for the enslavement of the black people for at least 300 years. With only 53 years to his seemingly unattainable eternity of 300 years, there is no sign that the black people would have broken the yoke of his enslavement program! In the nineteenth and twentieth centuries, the Europeans adopted, improvised, and applied variants of Lynch's methods as "divide-and-rule," racial segregation and polarization, "apartheid," and civilizing Christian evangelism for the imperial exploitation and colonization of Africa.

Paradoxically, the African postcolonial leadership and followership have deployed the heritage of racial, colonial, and imperial political culture of denigration of the African people for the exploitation and governance of their own people. They have also instituted the prototypes of the second-class colonial education policies, and sadly they continued to perceive their people and public goods simply as the European colonial officers, slave dealers, and the imperial governments, and companies viewed Africans as beasts that must as horses "*be broken*," and their human and natural resources as "*spoils of conquest*." As Lynch predicted, the indoctrinated Africans with colonial mentality are now refueling and regenerating the perpetual enslavement of themselves. The challenge for the post-independent African nation-states is how to *re-indoctrinate* both the African leadership and followership to break the spell and the intractable vicious circle of the Lynch's enslavement program from "self-refueling and self-generating for hundreds of years, maybe THOUSANDS."[19]

The third root factor of nepotism is not only a rider or a corollary to the intricacies between the private and communal social responsibilities in Africa but the byproduct of communal investment in the education and professional training of the few educated elites who took over the reins of power after independence. For example, many African states became independent with few qualified educated elites to run the affairs of the newly independent states.[20] Thus, in response to colonial racial policy of denying the Africans the most required access to professional courses such as medicine, law, accountancy, and engineering, many ethnic unions and families sponsored their *"sons-of-the-soil,"* that is, their brilliant boys, abroad to study in Europe and the Americas. Naturally it is not only a morally binding social responsibility for such beneficiaries to return home to help their own people but such ethnic groups and families expected the beneficiaries of such communal ventures to return home and give back their quota to development. For such communities, the concept of nepotism is akin to the original root of brotherhood, *being one's brothers' keeper* or the old saying, that, *one good turn deserves another*.[21]

The fourth factor for corruption and nepotism was the ruptures for the transfer of powers from colonial rulers to the Africans. Bureaucratic organizations often flourish with clearly defined, that's, written operational rules and guidelines for recruitment, advancement within the hierarchies, discipline, or sanctions for demeanors, and for compensation. Many African nation-states were ill-prepared and were not adequately well-staffed for a competent and efficient takeover after the Second World War. The transition time was short, and the process for independence was traumatic. For example, the French government moved out of their African colonies either abruptly overnight as was the case of Guinea in 1958 or after a prolonged period of civil unrest as was the case with Algeria. The British departure from Kenya, Zimbabwe, Namibia, and South Africa was not peaceful as well. Thus, the few educated African nationalists who emerged from the hitherto warring ethnic nationalities of the pre-1884 Berlin Conference for the indiscriminate partition of Africa did not have shared values and political ideology for ethical governance. They inherited ruptured economies and divided nations being dividends of the colonial policies of "divide-and-rule" and "the-north-south" dual political and socio-economic developmental disparities as evidenced in Sudan, Sierra Leone, the Congo, and Nigeria. They assumed power after the violent struggles for flag independence without a unifying leadership or a shared agenda for socio-economic development. Hence, they continue to institutionalize unbureaucratic behaviors and principles such as the Nigerian constitutional provision for federal character or a quota system for allocation of public offices—an antithesis of bureaucratic merit-recruitment—backed up with a constitutional commission for enforcement, presumably to redress the inherited inequities of the colonial and imperial political and socio-economic developments.

The fifth root of corruption and nepotism is that Africans have not developed a patriotic sense of citizenship. Unfortunately, because religion and ethnicity are unifying force for group action that transcend socio-economic class, politicians have traded on religion and ethnicity for mobilization and political legitimacy even for rationalization of corruption, nepotism, and unbureaucratic behaviors.

The Interface of the Primordial Social Ethics and the Contemporary Nation-States

In practice, just as individual rights and freedoms drive the practice of either parliamentary or presidential democracies in Europe and the Americas, so does the principle of Omoluwabi cut across the everyday material and spiritual lives of the rank and file of the Yoruba. The primordial Yoruba nation-state evolved seemingly simple cultural beliefs and values but sophisticated and complex political systems and democratic institutions for governance. Household members and groups, village members, and the town members have clearly defined functions and duties—unwritten morally binding traditions as in Great Britain though, but just as it is the case with the classic Weberian modern bureaucratic organizations. There are also rules binding on all the members of the community. The unwritten constitution also provides for due process for the succession of leadership positions.

As a way of life, Omoluwabi manifests in the Yoruba holistic worldview of cooperation between heaven and earth, and consequently in their beliefs in the cooperation between the dead ancestors and the living, in the responsibilities of the deities in the public and private affairs of the people (especially in the cause and effects and in the fair and just dispensation of justice not from the fallible and imperfect earthly rulers but from the Oba Orun [the king of heaven]), in reincarnation, and in the continuity of life. These sets of beliefs and values work together for the smooth running of the Yoruba primordial political systems.

The political culture of the Yoruba unwritten constitutional monarchy, hierarchy, deference to age (indeed, [*alagba/ogboni*] the rule of elders in which children are to be seen and not heard), and a seemingly male chauvinism is complex and deceptive. To a stranger, the system is autocratic and elitist. But in practice, it is democratic and indeed more plebiscite, "classless," and republican than aristocratic. The king *is* and operates solely as the "king-in-council" (of chiefs and elders), a variant form of "the-first-among-the-equals" premiership of the Westminster in the United Kingdom. Democratic institutions for the rule of law are built-in to check any abuse of power and to reward for compliance to the norms and mores. No member of the Yoruba household, village, or town leadership has absolute power, even to veto without due regard to precedent and the will of the people. While the *Ifa* oracle may choose a slave to become king, the political systems also allow the kingmakers to dethrone the king. The king, too, has the powers to sanction the chiefs. No citizen is above the law or untouchable within the constitutional authorities of the Yoruba nation-state. In today's "do-or-die politics," it is commonplace to make nostalgic reference to the good old days of a strict adherence to democratic values and due process for succession as a king would either voluntarily commit suicide or walk away from his kingdom once he had been disowned and become unacceptable to his people.[22]

Paradox of the Oral African Governance and the Weberian Bureaucratic Principles

Overtime, the pervasive incidence of corruption and nepotism in Africa demonstrates the cultural void in passing the African social ethics to the younger generations. The modern African nation-states have not imbued a commensurate faith in the nemesis potency of both the contemporary "Gods of Christianity and Islam" as they had in their ancestral primordial pantheon gods, and hence a degenerating morality and values. For example, a Yoruba Christian or Muslim would be more comfortable to lie under oath with either the Holy Bible or the Holy Qur'an than to make a false declaration with the invocation of the retributory powers of *Ṣàngó*, *Ògún*, or any of other Yoruba pantheon gods. Obviously, the most powerful instrument for enforcement of social ethics among the Yoruba is *ibúra*—taking an oath. Hardly will any Yoruba take an oath with his/her *orí*—inner head/destiny—unless s/he is totally truthful and honest. When a Yoruba invokes his/her life, the life of his/her children, or the spirits of the ancestors or the gods, especially the god of iron (*Ògún*) or the god of thunder and fire (*Ṣàngó*), or the god of smallpox (*Ṣànpọ̀nná*), such a person is unequivocal in convincing others that s/he is innocent or speaking the truth and nothing but the truth.

Because both Ubuntu and Omoluwabi precepts constitute shared internalized personal and statutory communal values and beliefs, they, on the one hand, transcend the faceless bureaucratic ideological preoccupation and focus on either the Russian-Chino communist or the Euro-American capitalist determinant principles for either the state or the price allocation of socio-economic resources and means of production and the bureaucratic political institutions for distribution of commonwealth and political power and authority on the other. They operationally transcend the Darwin's principle of survival of the fittest either in the free enterprise market or in the exploit of the Marxian class struggle between the proletariat and bourgeoisies in the labor market. In the dispensation of justice, African social ethics also focuses on reconciliatory justice and rehabilitation of the offenders as against the Anglo-Saxon retributory justice. Hence, among the Yoruba, the moral yardstick to measure who weighs up to a *person* is conceptually coded in *Ìwà*—upright character and integrity.

Ìwà as ethics is the unwritten constitution for the everyday running of both the public and private affairs of the Yoruba nation. At home, workplace, and in any relationship, even in routine greetings, there are codes of behavior for everyone.²³

Consequently, to reinforce compliance to social norms and values, the Yoruba have names for describing all ethical behaviors: *Olóòótọ́*—the truthful; *Olódodo*—the upright or one with integrity; *Onírẹ̀lẹ̀*—the humble or modest; *Ọmọ ọkọ*—the legitimate son; *Ọlọgbọ́n*—the wise one; *Olófin tótó*—the one who follows the rules to the letter; *Ẹni tí ó mọ́ àá-tií-gbọ́*—the one who would not do anything secretly that s/he would be ashamed if disclosed in public; and *Ọmọlúwàbí*—the one of high integrity and probity or the paragon of all ethical behaviors. There are also names for all unethical behaviors: *Onírọ́* or *Ọ̀pùrọ́*—the liar; *Jàǹdùkú* or *Ìpáǹle*—the hooligan or hoodlum; *Olè*—thief or rogue; *Aláìnítìjú* or *Kò mọ àá-tií-gbọ́*—the one who knows no shame; and *Ọ mọ àlè*—the bastard. Because ethical behaviors create harmony and peace, the Yoruba would say, *Ilé tí ó tòrò, a jẹ́pé ọmọ àlè ibẹ̀ ni kò tíì dàgbà*—when there is peace in a home, it means the bastard child in the family is still young! But in Yoruba culture, *Ìwà* is more than ethics—moral principle or codes of conduct. Thus, the Yoruba will say: *Ìwà l'ẹ̀sìn*—Ìwà is *the* religion; *Ìwà l'ẹwà*—Ìwà is *the yardstick* to measure the beauty or character of a person; *Ìwà niyì ọmọ ènìyàn*—Ìwà portrays the probity and dignity of a person; *Ìwà l'ọba àwúre*—Ìwà is the greatest secret of generating wealth or making a fortune; *Èéfín ni ìwà*—in life, *ìwà* is as a smoke that goes along with the smoker; and *Ìwà níí báni dé sàréè*—in death, *ìwà* follows us into the grave and lives after us.²⁴

Realities and Dilemmas of Corruption, Nepotism, and Anti-Bureaucratic Behaviors

There are endless lists of complaints about bureaucracies, and most dictionaries are uncharitable to bureaucracy. Carol H. Weiss has identified two themes that dominate the public and scholarly literature from the lavish array of complaints about government bureaucracies.²⁵ One has to do with the ineffectiveness and inefficiency of bureaucracy and dwells on a series of interlocking malfunctions, including rigidity, red tape, and the tyranny of the petty functionary brandishing the rule book, popularly known in Nigeria as the General Orders.²⁶ At the operating level, public agencies are viewed as staffed by the lazy and the incompetent, otherwise described by the 1974 Udoji Public Service Review Commission in Nigeria as the deadwood, people too concerned with their own rights and prerogatives to care about the people whom they are supposed to serve.²⁷ In the upper echelons, the inefficiency arguments center on rigid and stereotypical thinking. Bureaucrats are creatures of routine. They resist innovation and they reject new information and new perspectives. The popular image of civil servants in Africa is that of inaccessible and amateurish staff; in Nigeria specifically, they are, for example, described as either *not on seat* or *gone to toilet*.

The second theme of contemporary criticism is that government agencies are unaccountable to the public or its elected or (more appropriately in Africa) self-appointed military representatives and the emerging retired military officers in civilian garbs. In terms of their number and ubiquity, bureaucrats have become a law unto themselves, employing their continuity of tenure, inside knowledge of the ropes, and monopoly of expertise to shape the operation of enacted policies and to influence the initiation of new legislation to suit their own interests. Bribes and salary awards, assault through a purge and draconic actions, politicization, and other administrative reforms and reorganizations are among the common African governments' reactions to their bureaucracies. These bureaucracies face a spectrum of criticisms from all sectors, including populists, Marxists, neo-Marxists, pluralists, and libertarians who advocate applied public choice. While the hegemony of the market-led public service seems to reign supreme, a major lesson from the post-communist Eastern European countries is that policies intended to control the African bureaucracies seem to overlook not only the constraints facing the bureaucrats but the intrinsic nature of bureaucratic organization. These constraints include technical incapacity (limited computerization and professionalism), lack of ideological agreement on what government should do or should not do, and the divisive forces of ethnicity, religion, and regional imbalance in socio-economic and political development.[28]

There are two misconceptions about African bureaucrats and bureaucracies. First is the naive assumption that the apparent weakness of all sections of the state implies the hegemony of the bureaucracy in the policymaking process. Bureaucracy is only a part of the weak states.[29] The second misconception is the overlooked nature of large organizations. For an understanding of the nature of bureaucratic organizations, we found Robert Michels' classic bureaucratic organization theory instructive and appropriate. Ironically, while revolutions attempt to overthrow existing hierarchies, Michels' famous iron law of oligarchy states, "It is an organization which gives birth to the domination of the elected over the electors, of the mandatories over the mandators, of the delegates over the delegators. Who says organization says oligarchy."[30] In *Political Parties*, Robert Michels argued that the malfunctioning of existing democracy was not primarily a phenomenon that resulted from low-level social and economic development, inadequate education, or capitalist control of the opinion-forming media, and other power resources but rather was characteristic of any complex system for the running of human society. Oligarchy, the control of a society or an organization by those at the top, is an intrinsic part of bureaucracy or large-scale organizations.[31] Michels noted that the price of increased bureaucracy is the concentration of power at the top and the lessening of influence by rank and file members. Large organizations give their officers a near-monopoly of power. The leaders possess many resources that give them an almost insurmountable advantage over members who try to change policies. Among their assets are:

1. superior knowledge (e.g., they are privy to much information which can be used to secure assent for their program);
2. control over the formal means of communication with the membership (e.g., they dominate the organization press, and as full-time salaried officials, they may travel from place to place presenting their case at the organization's expense, and their position enables them to command audience); and
3. skill in the art of politics (e.g., they are far more adept than nonprofessionals in making speeches, writing articles, and organizing group activities).[32]

These occupational skills inherent to the leader's role are power assets that are further strengthened by what Michels called the "incompetence of the masses. Modern man, according to him, is faced with an irresolvable dilemma: he cannot have large institutions such as a nation states, trade unions, political parties, or churches, without turning over effective power to the few who are at the summit of these institutions."[33] Drawing on Robert Michels' thesis, therefore, rather than the class and power analysis, perhaps, a more appropriate and plausible explanation for the operational features of the African bureaucracies is that all large organizations tend to develop a bureaucratic structure, that is, a system of rational (predictable) organization, hierarchically organized.

The universal lesson of the African governments' reactions to the bureaucracy highlights the irony and the dilemma of attempts to make bureaucracy work[34] or to improve public management.[35] In a similar assessment of the American political system, Susan S. Fainstein and Norman I. Fainstein stated that, overall, governmental bureaucracies are accountable either to politicians within the democratic principle (after all the politicians are heads of, and responsible for what goes or doesn't go on in, their agencies) or to the corporate interests of capitalists in practice. While bureaucratic accountability, like bureaucratic performance, does indeed constitute a universal problem of governance, the real problem of the state system is not accountable bureaucracies but the group to which the bureaus are routinely accountable. The Fainsteins concluded that the problem lies not so much in bureaucracy itself, as in the political economy of capitalism.[36] They asserted accordingly that,

> The capitalist public choice solution, as distinct from socialist anarchism, gives no protection to those social groups who lack market power. It is Social Darwinism in new clothes. ... The market, however, does present a decisional mode that avoids the intrusion of a communal body, whether bureaucratic or democratic into every collective choice. The challenge for a socialist political theory is to incorporate arenas of market freedom into a system governed overall by communal and egalitarian principles, controlled by the votes of citizens rather than the dollars of owners and investors.[37]

Fainsteins' conclusion is, however, myopically American and British biased, if not naive, given the performance of the bureaucracies in the Japanese, German, and French capitalist economies and the level of accountability to the public by the Japanese and Swedish bureaucracies. The dilemma is how to strike a balance between bureaucratic efficiency and effectiveness on the one hand and administrative responsiveness and accountability on the other.

AFRICAN SOCIAL ETHICS IN TODAY'S GLOBAL WORLDVIEW OF GOOD GOVERNANCE

Contemporary African leaders have a dilemma and conflicting issues with the colonial and post-independence political systems. On the one hand, they cherish the historical-social ethics of the primordial African political systems and they would like to promote and create a place for it within the modern nation-state political systems. On the other hand, however, the historical political systems were workable within the small communities of individuals of a common primordial ancestry with shared cultural values and beliefs. While most of the African historical political systems are adaptable with the modern political economies and government practices, the historical political systems are, in reality, somehow anachronistic and problematic in today's world for five main reasons:

1. most African ethnic nationalities have embraced either Islam or Christianity, both religions are overtly incongruent with the African deities, for example the Yoruba deities (Ògún, Sàngó, Osun, Obatala, etc.);
2. the African ethnic nationalities, as nation-states, are now each a subsumed part of the conglomerations of ethnic nationalities—all with different cultural values and beliefs—that resulted from the European indiscriminate partition and colonization of Africa;
3. the multiethnic and socio-economic polarized modern African nation-states are also now a part of the global village with a new worldview of what is acceptable good practice for governance;
4. the emerging postcolonial African nation-states do not have the basic prerequisite homogeneity of ethnic shared cultural values and beliefs for nation-building and political cohesion. Economic migration, interethnic and interreligious marriages, Western education and Western mentalities, evangelical and fundamental orthodoxies, among other diverse worldviews have infiltrated into the hitherto collective and communal unifying social ethics and political culture of the primordial African ethnic nations; and
5. perhaps the greatest threat to the historical African social ethics and political systems is that the modern Africans are acculturating and bringing up their children with the enslaved colonial mindset and mentality that denigrate the indigenous African languages, values, beliefs, and even racially and imperially reinforce and promote inferiority complex, bigotry, and ethnic cleansing.

African humanism and social ethics recognize the interdependency of the socio-economic and political duties, obligations, and responsibilities of the individual and the community, respectively. For example, Ubuntu and Omoluwabi are rather more holistic than the Western form of democracy because they both look beyond the basic protection of individuals' rights and their property but also guarantee the equality of access to the economic, social, and political resources of power, what Nimi Wariboko has codified as the five "spiritual and moral energies behind the human flourishing and civilization."[38] For example, among the Yoruba, the proper socializing education of the child is the responsibility of all the adults in the community; land belongs to the community, and occupation is by apprenticeship from childhood; and decisions are often by consultation, negotiation, and consensus. More importantly, however, there is hardly any cheaper and more effective means of ensuring social responsibility and the enforcement of law and order than the clearly defined Ubuntu and Omoluwabi's precepts of moral duties and obligations for the individuals and their communities. They both demand no less self-discipline, self-control, and a strict sense of responsibility and integrity than the ongoing global worldview on corruption and graft. The relevance of the Ubuntu principle for the Truth and Reconciliation Commission in South Africa and also in the resolution of the over twenty years of violent dispute in Northern Ireland are signals to the prospective use of the Ubuntu and Omoluwabi principles for national and international conflict resolution, for restoration of probity and accountability in public affairs, and for good governance in the African continent.

Conclusion: Is Decolonization, Reorientation, Privatization, and Computerization the Way Forward?

There are two strands to decolonization of the African nation-states. The first strand, which was the easier one, was the nationalist fight for political independence. The second strand is decolonization in all its ramifications, including the restoration of African dignity and identity, the recovery of African philosophy, and the reconstruction of African social and political culture and institutions. As it has been difficult to root out institutional racism and racial prejudice in Europe and the Americas, because institutionalized colonialism and the internalized colonial mentality are systemic, it has been more difficult and rather intractable to decolonize the African independent colonial territories. Colonial subjects have been systematically and institutionally dehumanized, disorientated, and their human identity, dignity, and self-image have been eroded. Reversing this process of dehumanization would require a long-term structural social engineering and a reinvention of cultural values, tastes, fashion, and beliefs. In the postcolonial era, in order to address the social issues of ignorance, superstition, and disease, African nationalists had initiated and implemented education and health programs that were considered impossible for the first sixty years of colonial occupation.

But social ethics is about the activation of the individual's *conscience* and the discerning ability and capability to choose rightly what Nimi Wariboko has coded as "truth, beauty, justice, love, hope, and the eschatological New Creation."[39] Thus, to wipe out the African belief in the superiority of a foreigner, especially a white person, to their fellow Africans, and the superior quality of a foreign good over the homemade products, remains a big challenge. Even after over sixty years of independence, the few privileged and affluent African parents prefer to send their children abroad for education or to the privately owned international schools with white presence, including expatriate head teachers and heads of subject departments, thereby inadvertently perpetuating Lynch's "self-fueling and self-generating" subjugation of African social ethics to foreign values and beliefs. The desire for foreign qualifications has created a situation in which private-school owners employ commercial window dressing and showcase foreign educational toys and facilities to advertise their foreign-oriented schools.

The Fulani emirates, the Yoruba kingdoms, and the Igbo villages, among other hundreds of African ethnic nationalities, were administered with incredible ethical, political and judicial systems. Many Greek philosophers were noted to have trained in Egypt. The advent of the information age had put African nation-states on the same leveled playing field with the rest of the world. Unlike the old precolonial era, when African oral social ethics were forgotten easily, considered as nonexistent, or as inferior to the written Euro-Arabic cultures because there were no records of the African accomplishments and philosophical pronouncements, the nexus of today's global internet connection, media, and cable television technology is now bridging the gap between the European and the African civilizations.

The good news is that the postcolonial attitudes of Africans to public goods are quite much different from their attitudes to the privately owned properties. Yes, there is a prevalence of corruption and anti-bureaucratic behaviors in Africa. However, it has not choked the private sector as it has liquidated public enterprises and created collapsed and failed African governments. Private enterprises continue to flourish comparatively to public ventures, and hence, a case for privatization[40] and computerization of African public goods and services. With an appropriate attention to decolonization and reorientation of colonial mentality, and an appropriate privatization and computerization of ownership, production, and distribution of public goods and services, there is a window of opportunity that African nation-states could address and overcome the issues of corruption, nepotism, and anti-bureaucratic behaviors.

NOTES

1. For reviews of cases of corruption, see, for instance, Daniel Egiegba Agbiboa. "Between Corruption and Development: The Political Economy of State Robbery in Nigeria." In *Journal of Business Ethics*, vol. 108, no. 3 (July 2012), 325–345; Benjamin A. Olken and Rohini Pande. "Corruption in Developing Countries." In *Annual Review of Economics*, vol. 4 (2012), 479–509; Jon S. T. Quah. "Governance and Corruption: Exploring the Connection." In *American Journal of Chinese Studies*, vol. 16, no. 2 (October 2009), 119–135; Vishnu Bhagwan. "Corruption and Governance." In *The Indian Journal of Political Science*, vol. 68, no. 4 (October–December 2007), 727–738; K. Balachndrudu. "Understanding Political Corruption." In *The Indian Journal of Political Science*, vol. 67, no. 4 (October–December 2006), 809–816.
2. For reviews of the effects of corruption and the multifarious anticorruption initiatives, see, for example, Andrei Shleifer and Robert W. Vishny. "Corruption." In *The Quarterly Journal of Economics*, vol. 108, no. 3 (August 1993), 599–617; Leslie Benton, Jeffrey Clark, Mikhail Reider-Gordon and Anne Takher. "Anti-Corruption." *The International Lawyer*, vol. 45, no. 1, International Legal Development in Review: 2010 (Spring 2011), 345–364; John Mukum Mbaku. "Bureaucratic Corruption in Africa: The Futility of Cleanups." In *Cato the Journal*, vol. 16, no. 1 (Spring/Summer 1996); Eric C. C. Chang and Yun-han Chu. "Corruption and Trust: Exceptionalism in Asian Democracies?" In *The Journal of Politics*, vol. 68, no. 2 (May 2006), 259–271; Amaechi D. Okonkwo. "Gender and Corruption in Nigerian Politics." In *African Sociological Review/Revue Africaine de Sociologie*, vol. 20, no. 1 (2016), 111–136; Joseph R. A. Ayee. "Corruption and the Future of the Public Service in Africa." In *Verfassung und Recht in Ubersee/Law and Politics in Africa, Asia and Latin America*, vol. 35, no. 1 (1. Quartal 2002), 6–22; Julio Bacio-Terracino. "Linking Corruption and Human Rights." In *Proceedings of the Annual Meeting (American Society of International Law)*, vol. 104, International Law in a Time of Change (2010), 243–246; O. P. Dwivedi and Dele Olowu. "Bureaucratic Morality: An Introduction." In *International Political Science Review/La Morale bureaucratique* (July 1988), 163–165; Peter T. Leeson and Russell S. Sobel. "Weathering Corruption." In *The Journal of Law & Economics*, vol. 51, no. 4 (November 2008) 667–681; Bryan W. Husted and Instituto Tecnologico y de Estodios. In *Journal of International Business Studies*, vol. 30, no. 2 (2nd Qtr., 1999), 339–359; Femi Omotoso. "Public-Service Ethics and Accountability for Effective Service Delivery in Nigeria." In *Africa Today*, vol. 60, no. 3 (Spring 2014), 119–139; Economic and Political Weekly. "The Anti-Corruption Crusade." In *Economic and Political Weekly*, vol. 46, no. 34 (August 20–26, 2011), 7–8; Samuel Paul. "Fighting Corruption." In *Economic and Political Weekly*, vol. 46, no. 35 (August 27 – September 2, 2011), 17–19; Olakunle O. Olagoke. "The Extra-Territorial Scope of the Anti-Corruption Legislation in Nigeria." In *The International Lawyer*, vol. 38, no. 1 (Spring 2004), 71–88; Letitia Lawson. "The Politics of Anti-Corruption Reform in Africa." In *The Journal of Modern African Studies*, vol. 37, no. 1 (March 2009), 73–100; Naved Ahmad. "Corruption and Competition in Bureaucracy: A Cross-Country Analysis." In *Pakistan Economic and Social Review*, vol. 42, no. 1/2 (2004), 61–86; Leo V. Ryan. "Combating Corruption: The 21st-Century

Ethical Challenge." In Business Ethics Quarterly, vol. 10, no. 1, Globalization and the Ethics of Business (Jan., 2000), 331–338; Richard D. White, Jr. "Consanguinity by Degrees: Inconsistent Efforts to Restrict Nepotism in State Government." In *State & Local Government Review*, vol. 32, no. 2 (Spring 2000), 108–120.

3. For reviews and critiques of the theories of causes of corruption, see, for instance, Mlada Bukovansky. "The Hollowness of Anti-Corruption Discourse." In *Review of International Political Economy*, vol. 13, no. 2 (May 2006), 181–209; Fabio Mendez and Facundo Sepulveda. "What Do We Talk About When We Talk About Corruption." In *Journal of Law, Economics, & Organization*, vol. 26, no. 3 (December 2010), 493–514; Gjalt De Graaf. "Cause of Corruption: Towards a Contextual Theory of Corruption." In *Public Administration Quarterly*, vol. 31, no. 1/2 (Spring 2007), 39–86; Ghulam Shabbir and Mumtaz Anwar. "Determinants of Corruption in Developing Countries." In *The Pakistan Development Review*, vol. 46, no. 4 (Winter 2007), 751–764; and Bruce L. Benson. "Understanding Bureaucratic Behavior: Implications from the Public Choice Literature." Paper prepared for "KERI's International Symposium on the Market Economy" held on August 28–29, 1995; A. Cooper Drury, Jonathan Krieckhaus and Michael Luszig. "Corruption, Democracy, and Economic Growth." In *International Political Science Review/Revue internationale de science politique*, vol. 27, no. 2 (April 2006), 121–136; Wale Adebanwi and Ebenezer Obadare. "When Corruption Fights Back: Democracy and Elite Interest in Nigeria's Anti-Corruption War." In *The Journal of Modern African Studies*, vol. 49, no. 2 (June 2011), 185–213; A. F. Robertson. "Misunderstanding Corruption." In *Anthropology Today*, vol. 22, no. 2 (April 2006), 8–11; and Andrew I. Cohen, ed. *Philosophy and Public Policy*. London: Rowan & Littlefield International, 2018; and for a review of systemic corruption: What is it? What are its effects? See Gerald E. Caiden and Naomi J. Caiden. "Administrative Corruption." In *Public Administration Review*, vol. 37, no. 3 (May–June 1977), 301–309.

4. For a groundbreaking, bold, and refreshing perceptive pathway to social ethics, see Nimi Wariboko, *The Principle of Excellence: A Framework for Social Ethics*. Lanham: Lexington Books, A division of Rowan & Littlefield Publishers, Inc., 2009.

5. For a review of African humanism and ethics, see Bola Dauda, "African Humanism and Ethics: The Case of Ubuntu and Omoluwabi." In *Palgrave Handbook of African Philosophy*, 475–492, edited by Adeshina Afolayan and Toyin Falola, New York: Palgrave Macmillan, 2018.

6. Ifeanyi A. Menkiti. "Person and Community in African Traditional Thought." In *African Philosophy: An Introduction*, 176, edited by R.A. Wright. Lanham: University Press of America, 1984.

7. For the African concept of a person, see Didier Njirayamanda Kaphagawani. "African Conceptions of a Person: A Critical Survey." In *A Companion of African Philosophy*, 332–342, edited by Kwasi Wiredu. London: Blackwell Publishing Ltd., 2004.

8. K. A. Opoku. "Black Civilization and Religion." Paper presented at FESTAC 1977, quoted in Paul Bock, "Exploring African Morality," 463.

9. Desmond Mpilo Tutu. *God Is Not a Christian: Speaking Truth in Times of Crisis*. London: Rider Books, 2011, 24.

10. Tutu. *God Is Not a Christian*, 21–24.
11. Ibid., 21.
12. Ibid., 21–22.
13. A. Shutte. *Ubuntu: An Ethic for a New South Africa*. Pietermaritzburg: Cluster Publications, 2001, 3.
14. Bernard Matolino. "*Abantu* and Their Ethic in the Face of AIDS." In *African Philosophy and the Future Africa*, 71–81, edited by Gerald Walmsley. (Washington, D.C.: The Council for Research Values and Philosophy, 2011).
15. John S. Mbiti. *African Religions and Philosophies*. New York: Anchor Books, 1970: 141.
16. Matolino. "*Abantu* and Their Ethic in the Face of AIDS," 74.
17. See, for example, Robert L. Tignor. "Political Corruption in Nigeria before Independence." In *The Journal of Modern African Studies*, vol. 31, no. 2 (June 1993), 175–202; Moses E. Ochonu. "Corruption and Political Culture in Africa: History, Meaning, and the Problem of Naming." In *The Law and Development Review* vol. 4, no. 3, Article 3 (2011), 26–58; S. O. Osoba. "Corruption in Nigeria: Historical Perspectives." In *Review of African Political Economy*, vol. 23, no. 69 (September 1996), 371–386.
18. Culled from "Willie Lynch Letter: The Making of a Slave" by FINALCALL. COM NEWS on May 22, 2009.
19. Ibid.
20. For a comprehensive review of the colonial education in Nigeria, see David B. Abernethy, *The Political Dilemma of Popular Education: An African Case*. Stanford, CA: Stanford University Press, 1969; and Toyin Falola and Bola Dauda, *Decolonizing Nigeria (1945–1960): Power, Politics, and Personalities*. Austin, Texas: Pan African University Press, 2017.
21. For a review of the root and meaning of nepotism, see Paul W. Sherman, "The Meaning of Nepotism" in *The American Naturalist*, vol. 116, no. 4 (Oct., 1980), pp. 604–606.
22. Dauda, "African Humanism and Ethics: The Case of Ubuntu and Omoluwabi," 475–492.
23. Ibid.
24. Ibid.
25. Carol H. Weiss, "Efforts at Bureaucratic Reform: What Have We Learned?" In *Making Bureaucracies Work*, 7–27, edited by Carol H. Weiss and Allen H. Barton (Beverly Hills California and London: Sage Publications, Inc., 1979, 1980), 7–27.
26. On April 1, 1974, the Federal Government of Nigeria replaced the colonial and independence civil service codes called General Orders, Gazette Notices, Circulars, and so on published prior to April 1, 1974, with *Federal Government Civil Service Rules (Revised to 1st April, 1974)* (Lagos: Federal Government Printer, Federal Ministry of Information, 1974). For guidelines on financial operations, see *Federation of Nigeria: Revised Financial Instructions, 1962* (Lagos: The Federal Ministry of Information, Printing Division, 1962). All regional and later state governments have their versions of the Civil Service Rules and Financial Instructions.
27. See Chapter 2, "Cultural and Environmental Factors Which Affect the Public Service" in *Main Report of the (Udoji) Public Service Review Commission,*

Federal Government of Nigeria (Lagos: Federal Government Printer, 1974), pp. 3–6.
28. Christian P. Potholm, *Four African Political Systems.* Englewood Cliffs, New Jersey: Prentice-Hall Inc., 1970; and R. A. Joseph. *Democracy and Prebendal Politics in Nigeria: The Rise and Fall of the Second Republic.* Cambridge: Cambridge University Press, 1987.
29. Bola Dauda, "Taking Democracy Seriously: Democracy-Bureaucracy Relations." In *Democracy and Socialism in Africa*, 53–69, edited by Robin Cohen and Harry Goulbourne. Boulder, San Francisco, Oxford: Westview Press, 1991. See also Goran Hyden. *No Shortcuts to Progress: African Development Administration: The Kenyan Experience.* London: Heinemann Educational Books, 1983.
30. Robert Michels (Translated by Eden and Cedar Paul, introduction by Seymour Martin Lipset. *Political Parties: A Sociological Study of Oligarchical Tendencies of Modern Democracy.* New York: The Free Press, first published 1911 in French, 1962, 15.
31. Ibid., 15.
32. Ibid., 16.
33. Ibid., 16.
34. Carol H. Weiss and Allen H. Barton, ed. *Making Bureaucracies Work.* Beverly Hills, California and London: Sage Publications, 1980; and Thomas R. Dye, and Harmon Zeigler. *The Irony of Democracy: An Uncommon Introduction to Politics.* Belmont, California: Words Worth Publishing Co., 1970.
35. Les Metcalfe and Sue Richards. *Improving Public Management.* London: Sage Publications, 1990).
36. Susan S. Fainstein, and Norman I. Fainstein. "The Political Economy of America Bureaucracy." In *Making Bureaucracy Work*, 291, edited by Carol H. Weiss, and Allen H. Barton. London: Sage Publications, 1980.
37. Ibid., 294.
38. Wariboko, *The Principle of Excellence*, 135–161.
39. Ibid.
40. For a case of privatization and private ownership of public goods and services for the control of corruption, see, for example, Tomas Otahal. "Mises, Hayek and Corruption." In *Journal of Business Ethics*, vol. 119, no. 3 (February 2014), 399–404.

Bibliography

Abernethy, David B. 1969. *The Political Dilemma of Popular Education: An African Case.* Stanford: Stanford University Press.
Adebanwi, Wale, and Ebenezer Obadare. 2011. When Corruption Fights Back: Democracy and Elite Interest in Nigeria's Anti-Corruption War. *The Journal of Modern African Studies* 49 (2): 185–213.
Agbiboa, Daniel Egiegba. 2012. Between Corruption and Development: The Political Economy of State Robbery in Nigeria. *Journal of Business Ethics* 108 (3): 325–345.
Ahmad, Naved. 2004. Corruption and Competition in Bureaucracy: A Cross-Country Analysis. *Pakistan Economic and Social Review* 42 (1/2): 61–86.
Ayee, Joseph R.A. 2002. Corruption and the Future of the Public Service in Africa. *Verfassung und Recht in Ubersee/Law and Politics in Africa, Asia and Latin America* 35 (1): 6–22. 1 Quartal.

Bacio-Terracino, Julio. 2010. Linking Corruption and Human Rights. *Proceedings of the Annual Meeting (American Society of International Law)* 104: 243–246. International Law in a Time of Change.
Balachndrudu, K. 2006. Understanding Political Corruption. *The Indian Journal of Political Science* 67 (4): 809–816.
Benjamin, A., and Rohini Pande. 2012. Corruption in Developing Countries. *Annual Review of Economics* 4: 479–509.
Bruce L. Benson. 1995. Understanding Bureaucratic Behavior: Implications from the Public Choice Literature. Paper Prepared for "KERI's International Symposium on the Market Economy" held on August 28–29.
Benton, Leslie, Jeffrey Clark, Mikhail Reider-Gordon, and Anne Takher. 2011. Anti-Corruption. *The International Lawyer* 45 (1): 345–364. International Legal Development in Review: 2010.
Bhagwan, Vishnu. 2007. Corruption and Governance. *The Indian Journal of Political Science* 68 (4): 727–738.
Bukovansky, Mlada. 2006. The Hollowness of Anti-Corruption Discourse. *Review of International Political Economy* 13 (2): 181–209.
Caiden, Gerald E., and Naomi J. Caiden. 1977. Administrative Corruption. *Public Administration Review* 37 (3): 301–309.
Chang, Eric C.C., and Yun-han Chu. 2006. Corruption and Trust: Exceptionalism in Asian Democracies? *The Journal of Politics* 68 (2): 259–271.
Cohen, Andrew I., ed. 2018. *Philosophy and Public Policy*. London: Rowan & Littlefield International.
Dauda, Bola. 1991. Taking Democracy Seriously: Democracy-Bureaucracy Relations. In *Democracy and Socialism in Africa, 53–69*, ed. Robin Cohen and Harry Goulbourne. Boulder/San Francisco/Oxford: Westview Press.
———. 2018. African Humanism and Ethics: The Case of Ubuntu and Omoluwabi. In *Palgrave Handbook of African Philosophy, 475–492*, ed. Adeshina Afolayan and Toyin Falola. New York: Palgrave Macmillan.
De Graaf, Gjalt. 2007. Cause of Corruption: Towards a Contextual Theory of Corruption. *Public Administration Quarterly* 31 (1/2): 39–86.
Drury, A. Cooper, Jonathan Krieckhaus, and Michael Luszig. 2006. Corruption, Democracy, and Economic Growth. *International Political Science Review/Revue International de science politique* 27 (2): 121–136.
Dwivedi, O.P., and Dele Olowu. 1988. Bureaucratic Morality: An Introduction. In *International Political Science Review/La Morale Bureaucratique*, 163–165.
Economic and Political Weekly. 2011. The Anti-Corruption Crusade. *Economic and Political Weekly* 46 (34): 7–8.
Falola, Toyin, and Bola Dauda. 2017. *Decolonizing Nigeria (1945–1960): Power, Politics, and Personalities*. Austin: Pan African University Press.
Husted, Bryan W., and Instituto Tecnologico y de Estodios. 1999. Wealth, Culture, and Corruption. *Journal of International Business Studies* 30 (2): 339–359. 2nd Qtr.
Hyden, Goran. 1983. *No Shortcuts to Progress: African Development Administration: The Kenyan Experience*. London: Heinemann Educational Books.
Joseph, R.A. 1987. *Democracy and Prebendal Politics in Nigeria: The Rise and Fall of the Second Republic*. Cambridge: Cambridge University Press.
Kaphagawani, Didier Njirayamanda. 2004. African Conceptions of a Person: A Critical Survey. In *A Companion of African Philosophy, 332–342*, ed. Kwasi Wiredu. London: Blackwell Publishing Ltd.

Lawson, Letitia. 2009. The Politics of Anti-Corruption Reform in Africa. *The Journal of Modern African Studies* 37 (1): 73–100.
Leeson, Peter T., and Russell S. Sobel. 2008. Weathering Corruption. *The Journal of Law & Economics* 51 (4): 667–681.
Lynch, Willie. 2009. Culled from "Willie Lynch Letter: The Making of a Slave" by FINALCALL.COM NEWS on May 22.
Matolino, Bernard. 2011. *Abantu* and Their Ethic in the Face of AIDS. In *African Philosophy and the Future Africa, 71–81*, ed. Gerald Walmsley. Washington, DC: The Council for Research Values and Philosophy.
Mbaku, John Mukum. 1996. Bureaucratic Corruption in Africa: The Futility of Cleanups. *Cato the Journal* 16 (1): 99.
Mbiti, John S. 1970. *African Religions and Philosophies*. New York: Anchor Books.
Mendez, Fabio, and Facundo Sepulveda. 2010. What Do we Talk About When we Talk About Corruption. *Journal of Law, Economics, & Organization* 26 (3): 493–514.
Menkiti, Ifeanyi A. 1984. Person and Community in African Traditional Thought. In *African Philosophy: An Introduction, 176*, ed. R.A. Wright. Lanham: University Press of America.
Michels, Robert. 1962. *Political Parties: A Sociological Study of Oligarchical Tendencies of Modern Democracy*. Translated by Eden and Cedar Paul, Introduction by Seymour Martin Lipset. New York: The Free Press, First Published 1911 in French.
Ochonu, Moses E. 2011. Corruption and Political Culture in Africa: History, Meaning, and the Problem of Naming. *The Law and Development Review* 4 (3): 26–58. Article 3.
Okonkwo, Amaechi D. 2016. Gender and Corruption in Nigerian Politics. *African Sociological Review/Revue Africaine de Sociologie* 20 (1): 111–136.
Olagoke, Olakunle O. 2004. The Extra-Territorial Scope of the Anti-Corruption Legislation in Nigeria. *The International Lawyer* 38 (1): 71–88.
Olken, Benjamin A., and Rohini Pande. 2012. Corruption in Developing Countries. *Annual Review of Economics* 4: 479–509.
Omotoso, Femi. 2014. Public-Service Ethics and Accountability for Effective Service Delivery in Nigeria. *Africa Today* 60 (3): 119–139.
Opoku, K.A. Black Civilization and Religion. Paper Presented at FESTAC 1977, Quoted in Paul Bock, "Exploring African Morality," 463.
Osoba, S.O. 1996. Corruption in Nigeria: Historical Perspectives. *Review of African Political Economy* 23 (69): 371–386.
Otahal, Tomas. 2014. Mises, Hayek and Corruption. *Journal of Business Ethics* 119 (3): 399–404.
Paul, Samuel. 2011. Fighting Corruption. *Economic and Political Weekly* 46 (35): 17–19.
Potholm, Christian P. 1970. *Four African Political Systems*. Englewood Cliffs: Prentice-Hall Inc.
Quah, Jon S.T. 2009. Governance and Corruption: Exploring the Connection. *American Journal of Chinese Studies* 16 (2): 119–135.
Ryan, Leo V., and V. Leo. 2000. Combating Corruption: The 21st-Century Ethical Challenge. *Business Ethics Quarterly* 10 (1): 331–338. Globalization and the Ethics of Business.
Shabbir, Ghulam, and Mumtaz Anwar. 2007. Determinants of Corruption in Developing Countries. *The Pakistan Development Review* 46 (4): 751–764.
Sherman, Paul W. 1980. The Meaning of Nepotism. *The American Naturalist* 116 (4): 604–606.

Shleifer, Andrei, and Robert W. Vishny. 1993. Corruption. *The Quarterly Journal of Economics* 108 (3): 599–617.
Shutte, A. 2001. *Ubuntu: An Ethic for a New South Africa*. Pietermaritzburg: Cluster Publications.
Tignor, Robert L. 1993. Political Corruption in Nigeria before Independence. *The Journal of Modern African Studies* 31 (2): 175–202.
Tutu, Desmond Mpilo. 2011. *God Is Not a Christian: Speaking Truth in Times of Crisis*. London: Rider Books.
Wariboko, Nimi. 2009. *The Principle of Excellence: A Framework for Social Ethics*. Lanham: Lexington Books, A division of Rowan & Littlefield Publishers, Inc..
Weiss, Carol H. 1979/1980. Efforts at Bureaucratic Reform: What Have We Learned? In *Making Bureaucracies Work*, ed. Carol H. Weiss and Allen H. Barton. Beverly Hills California/London: Sage Publications, Inc.
White, Richard D., Jr. 2000. Consanguinity by Degrees: Inconsistent Efforts to Restrict Nepotism in State Government. *State & Local Government Review* 32 (2): 108–120.

CHAPTER 20

The Bretton Woods Institutions and Economic Development in Africa

Sunday Olaoluwa Dada

Introduction

Over the years, the Bretton Woods Institutions have been objects of diverse attacks and criticisms because they have been seen as major impediments to economic development in African countries, especially those of South of Sahara and other Third World countries such as Peru, Chile and Brazil. In a letter to the editor of *Economic and Political Weekly* in 1994, which marked the 50th anniversary of the founding of the Bretton Woods Institutions, the Women for a Just and Healthy Planet acknowledged that, in the name of development which they saw as "the extension of capitalist markets to all corners of the world and all areas of production,"[1] these institutions have "in the 1970s lent money to Third World countries; in the 1980s, the manipulation of interest rates led to growing indebtedness and increased control of Third World domestic economies and policies."[2] Focusing their attention on Third World countries, the association noted that due to the adventure of these institutions and the indebtedness of Third World countries, African countries inclusively transferred $50 billion annually to the North. This massive yearly transfer caused, according to them, "the disintegration of Third World economies and societies; the destruction of third world peoples; the degradation of local and global environments; dictatorship, militarism, and violence against women; forced migration producing millions of refugees."[3] The Association, therefore, requested for the assistance of the editor "in mobilising support for actions demonstrating against the international financial institutions and commercial banks."[4] The recog-

S. O. Dada (✉)
Department of Philosophy, Ekiti State University, Ado-Ekiti, Nigeria

© The Author(s) 2020
N. Wariboko, T. Falola (eds.), *The Palgrave Handbook of African Social Ethics*, https://doi.org/10.1007/978-3-030-36490-8_20

nition and mobilisation for action by this organisation is part of the effort to critique the relationship of the Bretton Woods Institutions with Africa.

There is no doubt about the fact that African economies are a part of the economy of the world, but it has to be noted that the original plan of these global institutions does not factor in African economies, which have become the focus of their activities, except in the ideological sense. The Bretton Woods Institutions today have become part of the agenda of the North to dominate the South. There are researches showing the performances of African economies before the domination of Africa by these institutions by forcing their economic policies on African countries. The question we have to answer is what is the justification for the adventure of these institutions in Africa? Is it that they are so interested in the economic development of African economies or they are just out to use them to further their mercantilist and neo-liberal and neo-colonial ideologies?

This chapter is divided into three sections. In the first section, we shall trace the creation and evolution of these institutions. This will help us to understand and evaluate their nature and purposes. In this section, we shall also examine the unexpressed ideological agenda of these institutions and how the US uses them to further its political and economic objectives. Since the Reagan administration in the 1980s, the US has aimed to convince the world of the truth of neo-liberal free-market ideology. The second section is an analysis of economic development in Africa. In this section, we shall examine the development challenges of Africa and the reasons why it has not broken through economically. In the last section, the chapter examines how the economic policies of the Bretton Woods Institution have negatively impacted African economies. We shall conclude the chapter by looking at the way forward by looking at the adjustments Africa and these institutions would have to make to further economic development in African countries.

THE BRETTON WOODS INSTITUTIONS

In July 1944, the United Nations (UN) Monetary and Financial Commission Conference was held at the Mount Washington Hotel in Bretton Woods, New Hampshire. This conference, according to Acheson, Chant and Prachowny, "was to be the most important conference on international financial arrangement since the London Conference of 1933."[5] It was at this conference that the document that was hoped would shape international economic relations during the post-war period was drawn up. World War II was just being concluded and the major problems of the time were the reconstruction of the war-ravaged areas of Europe, the elimination of the debilitating effects of balance of North American balance-of-payments surpluses and European deficits, and the prevention of another global economic depression that could precipitate another world war.

The Bretton Woods conference can be regarded as a direct product of the World War II disaster and the Great Depression that preceded it, which could be traced to the collapse of the international economic system after 1919. After World War II's devastating effects on most countries, nations wanted to return to the pre-war financial security as soon as possible. This led to unnecessary protectionism and competitive devaluations. Every country strived to devalue its way out of economic crisis. The purpose of the devaluation was to make their exports cheaper than those of rival nations, thereby increasing the competitiveness of their export and consequently provoke export-led growth. This was done to reduce balance-of-payment deficit. This "beggar thy neighbor" economic strategy was successful in whatever country as long as it was able to devalue its currency faster and more strongly than other nations. Though this policy had a way of stimulating economic growth through export, it harmed and stifled the growth potential of trading partners. The resultant effect was "mass unemployment, bankruptcy of enterprises, the failing of credit institutions, as well as hyper inflation in the countries concerned."[6] For instance, as McKinnon reports, when Britain gave up its fixed gold parity in September 1931, the pound became devalued falling by 25% from $4.86 to $3.40. This had effects on other countries including the US. According to McKinnon:

> This depreciation made the U.S. dollar less competitive with exports turning down, and in 1933, President Franklin Roosevelt virtually demonetized gold for domestic transacting while forcing the dollar to depreciate sharply in terms of gold even though the U.S. had a trade surplus. This left the remaining gold bloc countries in Europe—France, Germany and a raft of smaller ones—hopelessly overvalued and facing capital flight. In 1936, the remaining gold bloc countries gave up and depreciated, but not before they suffered a precipitate drop in exports and industrial production. Whence the odium associated with "beggar-thy-neighbor" devaluations.[7]

The unprecedented economic calamity of this period seemed to have necessitated and provided the ideal platform for the community of nations to come together and work out a plan to create an international financial institution that was to control exchange rates and take care of the economic problems of the international community. This was championed by the victorious allies in the war led by the US and Britain. Following this, in June 1944, the then US President Franklin Roosevelt invited delegations from allied nations to participate in discussions that would lead to international cooperation and the establishment of these institutions whose sole focus would be economic development. The discussions were to pave the way for the conference that was to take place in July the same year.

At the July 1944 conference, delegates from 44 countries met at Bretton Woods, New Hampshire, and agreed to create two new supranational economic institutions, that is, the International Monetary Fund and the International Bank for Reconstruction and Development which later became World Bank and signed an agreement to that effect which is known as the "Bretton Woods Agreements." The agreements were so named because the conference in which the agreements were signed was held at Bretton Woods. Besides, they also agreed to implement a system of fixed exchange rates with the US dollar as the base currency. The Bretton Woods Agreement was remarkable for two important reasons. Firstly, they represented the first experiment in global rulemaking and institution-building in terms of post-war monetary and financial relations. Secondly, the agreement was a decisive step in reopening of the world economy after the incidence of each country trying to protect its economy, which led to a negative impact on the economies of trading neighbour countries. The two institutions have also since been referred to as Bretton Woods Institutions. Both would be referred to in this chapter as the Fund and the Bank respectively.

The logic behind their creation was stability in international monetary affairs and the facilitation of the expansion of world trade. The institutions were to facilitate the expansion and balanced growth of international trade and also enable and foster the investment of capital for productive purposes.[8] The Fund was to be the guardian of a new system of international monetary cooperation, held up by stable exchange rates and a multilateral system of payments. The Bank, on the other hand, was to facilitate international investment to raise productivity, the standard of living and conditions of labour in all member countries. The countries that participated in the conference promised that they would maintain fixed currency exchange rates to facilitate a greater volume of international trade. In the new international monetary order occasioned by the birth of the Fund and the Bank, the gold which used to be the common anchor for exchange rates was dethroned in favour of the US dollar. However, the US that later became the centre of the Bretton Woods Institutions operations was free to determine its monetary policy and price level objectives. In contrast to this, however, other countries "had to subordinate, at least in part, their domestic monetary policies to maintain their dollar exchange rate parities." Further to this, delegations from the Unites States, Great Britain, China and the Soviet Union met between August and October 1944 and deliberated on a draft agreement for a United Nations Charter at a conference held in Washington, D.C.

The institutions were the dreams of economists on either side of the Atlantic; the UK was represented by John Maynard Keynes while the US was represented by Harry Dexter White. Underpinning their visions were "domestic debates about how to structure the post-war economy"[9] and, more importantly, how to get the US and British business elites back to power. They, therefore, needed international institutions that would promote capitalist tendencies and policies. There is no doubting the fact the agreement at the conference was a negotiation between the US and Britain. This is not to say that other countries represented do not have inputs, but the discussion and negotiations were majorly between the US and Britain.

Two proposals were made regarding the post-war economic arrangement. These proposals were discussed at the Bretton Woods conference. The first was the Britain proposal which was championed by Keynes. The proposal was for the creation of a financial agency to which all states would delegate their monetary powers. The agency would operate at a supranational level and would be "an automatic clearing union to which all countries would contribute and in which no currency had a special place."[10] As noted, the agency was proposed to operate at the supranational level and transfer of money to countries that have a balance-of-payment deficit would be virtually automatic. It was also proposed that no conditions would be attached to aid. It was also proposed that in the case of balance-of-payment imbalances, both the creditor and debtor nations should carry the burden of adjustment by changing their policies. Countries with payment surpluses should increase their import from the deficit countries to create foreign trade equilibrium.

The second proposal which was American was championed by White. This proposal also asked for the creation of a financial agency, but that would be under the control of the US and from which it "would derive considerable benefit."[11] This second proposal would use the US dollar as the core of monetary operations and transfer of money to borrowing countries would be discretionary with conditions attached, which would be exclusively determined by agency and "although formal authority would be delegated to the new institution, discretionary powers would permit the United States to influence the exercise of that power."[12]

It is no news that it was the American-White proposal that was accepted. The reason seems to be that the US emerged from the war as a hegemon with great political, industrial and economic strength than any other country and was in a position to wield this power. The US today continues to wield this power in international trade and politics. It is reasonable to aver that if the Britain-Keynes proposal had been adopted, the impoverished African countries would have been better off than they are today; this is because of the proposed adjustments on the part of the creditor and debtor nations. The American/White proposal gave the Bretton Woods Institutions undue power over African economies that have become heavily dependent on them since the 1980s. This, to my mind, has led to undue exploitation and, consequently, underdevelopment. Because of this dependent status, African leaders were unable to make autonomous decisions concerning the direction of the growth of their national economies.

Woods identifies some distinctive forces that influence the operational dynamics of the Bretton Woods Institutions. These forces which are three in number, according to him, "shape what the institutions do and determine how effective they do it."[13] This seems to show that the institutions are not independent in their operations as they claimed to be. This might mean that there may be some ideological parameters that are at the substructure of these institutions that are not their own making. The first force identified by Woods is what he calls "powerful governments." He rightly reports that "the political preferences of the United States and other industrialised countries provide a strong bottom line or outer structural constraints within which the IMF and World Bank work."[14] In his opinion:

> It is easy to see the U.S. influence in the institutions. They were created within the United States mainly by that country and that is where they are headquartered. In general, their policies have reflected U.S. economic and strategic interests, particularly in opening up markets in all parts of the world.[15]

So, as it were, the institutions become like a US-aiding institutions that are used to finagle other countries, especially the underdeveloped, so that they can control their economies and promote their selfish economic and political interests. Let us focus on the US influence on these institutions a little.

The US emerged out of the World Wars with great industrial power and wealth and thus became a world power that wanted to wield her influence on other nations. It found the Bretton Woods Institutions as useful instruments in this direction. Robert Wade explains that, on the one hand, the US:

> wishes to control these organizations so that they promote US foreign policy objectives. Therefore, it has to ensure that people are appointed at the top of the organizations who will reliably explain to the world why all benefit from free markets in the long run and why alternative institutional arrangements are not viable; or at least it has to ensure that people in prominent positions within them who say contrary things can be silenced or got rid of. On the other hand, the US needs to structure and operate within the organizations in a way that maintains the organizations' appearance of acting according to rules decided by the collective of member governments rather than according to discretionary US judgments. If not, the organizations lose the legitimacy of multilateralism and are less likely to achieve US objectives.[16]

In this sense, the US took a hegemonic position by trying to convince other members of the institution that it was acting in their interests, but it was acting in its interests and trying to subjugate other members, especially those of the developing countries. Consider the World Bank which, Wade contends, the US found as a "useful instrument for projecting its influence in developing countries."[17] The Bank is a source of fund and technical support to be offered to those that are deemed fit by the US. It is the US that chooses the president of the Bank who has to be a US citizen. Apart from this, it has the largest share of votes in the Bank which is 17%; hence, it has veto power on some constitutional issues. Wade also notes that the US "makes the single biggest contribution to IDA, the Bank's soft-loan affiliate dedicated to lending to the poorest countries."[18] It is no wonder then that it is the US thinking about the roles of government and market that set the conceptual substructure of the Bank's thinking.

Woods also says that the workings of the Bretton Woods Institutions are influenced by "professional economists whose labours are in turn shaped by a particular institutional environment."[19] These economists collect, analyse and interpret data in a professional way. They advise borrowing countries on how to utilise their loans and benefit from an integrated global economy. They also offer technical assistance to these countries. Part of their work is to provide road maps for policymakers who contemplate a change in the global economy. The problem, however, is that these professional economists are not free to operate independently. It is for this reason that Woods remarks that "policy is shaped by other forces. Often Fund and Bank prescriptions are based neither on clear evidence nor on pure expert analysis or predictions. Instead, they reflect bureaucrats trying to square political pressures and institutional constraints."[20]

The third force rocking these institutions is the relationship they have with countries that borrow from them. There seems to me then to be some kind of deliberate politics on the powerful countries behind these institutions to make members as permanent clients. This would explain their relationship with countries in Africa where their policies have made those countries worse off and tied to them, making the institutions to feed fat on them. Since they have the power to lend, impose tough conditionality, monitor and stop lending, they have become powerful in relation to these client-countries to the extent that they can be pervasive and sometimes coercive. Due to this influence, powerful industrialised nations that have strong voting power in these institutions marginalise the client-nations and pursue certain economic policies in those countries. Dasgupta remarks that "At present, the G-7 countries (the US, the UK, France, Germany, Canada, Italy and Japan) account for roughly half the voting power and virtually control the Organisation. Based on an informal arrangement, from which the less developed countries are excluded, the presidentship of the World Bank and the post of managing director are rotated between the United States and Europe."[21]

It should be noted, however, that in most African countries, the Bretton Woods Institutions find accomplices that facilitate the promulgation and enforcement of their policies, bearing in mind that most of the time, these policies have no beneficial effect on their countries other than to trigger unemployment, hike in price and aggravate poverty. There is no doubt that these accomplices who are government officials gain from acquiescing with their policies, but this is a symptom of selfishness on their part. It is like selling the economic prosperity of their countries for "a morsel of bread." This tendency made them refuse to subject the institutions' economic proposals to debate and critical scrutiny and has led to the uncritical appropriation of donors' economic policies. What is not clear is why the forces behind this institution are so much interested in African countries. Deep thinking will, however, reveal that they have purely economic and political interest, which dated back to the pre-colonial era. We are aware of the historical distortions that were produced about Africa by the West.[22] The stories that were the product of the West's encounter with Africa were deliberately produced, narratives upon which the conquering and domination of Africa was built. Such distortions and misrepresentations have not only permeated history, politics and international relations but have infiltrated every sector of Africa's interaction with the West, especially Western economic and financial institutions. For now, let us look a little more into these institutions and their operations.

International Monetary Fund (IMF) and the World Bank

In this section, we shall take a look at the Fund and the Bank, paying attention to their purposes of membership, quotas and voting right and operational dynamics. The Fund, in the perspective of Vreeland, can be regarded as "an international credit union with access to a pool of resources provided by the subscription of its member countries."[23] The original purpose of the Fund was to "monitor and help maintain pegged but adjustable exchange rates, primarily between industrialized countries of Western Europe and the United States."[24] The Fund was necessitated by the failure of the gold standard, which imposed too much austerity measure of the countries with balance-of-payment deficit as it forced them to cut down on domestic expenditure that consequently slowed down economic growth and led to an astronomical increase in unemployment. It was the attempt by the governments of deficit countries to avoid the economic severity of maintaining the gold standard that led to the beggar-thy-neighbour economic tactics that were mentioned earlier.

At the formation of the Fund in 1944, as mentioned earlier, it was the White/American plan that had the day. The White/American plan proposed a contribution of $5 billion stabilisation fund from which countries facing balance-of-payment deficits could purchase foreign exchange. However, contribution to this fund totalled $8.8 billion, $2.75 billion of which came from the US.[25] As Vreeland notes, this fund was insufficient to stabilise the economies and exchange rates of Europe after World War II. Instead of allowing the fund to expand and accept contributions from member countries, the US took it upon itself to directly assist with the Marshall Plan with a fund totalling $13 billion. This, I think, was a deliberate plan on the part of the US to increase its power and influence in the Fund more than the Fund would like to allow.

The World Bank like its twin, the Fund, is an intergovernmental pillar supporting the structure of the world's economic and financial order. However, unlike the Fund that is mandated to deal with ensuring stable international monetary system and to make sure that there is stable exchange rates and also to assist member countries in financing balance-of-trade needs, the Bank is a development institution that was established to "channel investment into projects within countries in need of reconstruction and development."[26] It focuses on the long run with an orientation towards the supply side of the member countries' economies; the Bank promotes long-term economic development and poverty reduction in member countries by providing fund and technical support to help them reform particular sector or execute specific projects. To do this, the Bank would raise money in the capital markets and lend it to members at market rates. It borrows money from the US, Japan, Germany Switzerland and the Organization of the Petroleum Exporting Countries (OPEC).[27] The main focus of the Bank is to "help the poorest people and the poorest countries,"[28] and through its five institutions, use the financial resources and extensive experience at its disposal to help developing countries to reduce poverty, increase economic growth and improve the quality of life. The Bank tries to fulfil its aims by supporting the creation of a favourable climate of investment and by empowering poor people.

The Fund is driven by ideology. A component of this ideology is universality. What this means, according to the Officer, is that it is "receptive to universal membership."[29] The Fund accepts membership from any part of the world as long as the country seeking membership can satisfy three criteria, that is, "the applicant country, it must control its external relations, and it must be both able to fulfil the obligations of IMF members."[30] Members' directory at the institution's website reveals that the Fund's membership has increased from 44 at inception to 189. This is practically all the countries in the world as only six countries of the world are not members. North Korea, Cuba and so on are not members for ideological reasons even though the Fund does not deny membership on ideological grounds. It is important to note that membership of the Fund is a prerequisite to joining the World Bank, which is an important source of development aid for small and developing economies. The Fund is attractive to both large and industrialised economies and small ones. For the large ones, it allows them to preserve and extend their influence over the Fund and consequently the small, developing economies.

To become a member of the Bank and have the ability to borrow from it, a country has to be a member of the Fund. Currently, the Bank has 189 member countries, which are categorised according to the size of their economies—some are categorised as low income, some as middle income and others as high income. Low- and middle-income countries are sometimes referred to as developing countries—countries in Africa South of Sahara fall into this category. It has to be noted that the fact that African countries are lumped into the same category does not imply that the economies experience similar development or performance or that they require the same kind of treatment the way they use the same kind of macroeconomic prescription to solve their varying economic problems.

Calderisi Robert, a one-time manager of the World Bank, African region, describes the Bank as a financial cooperative that is owned by member countries.[31] Marshall explains that this is not in the legal sense since the Bank's articles of Agreement does not explicitly say so. What the term conveys is the spirit and aspiration of its governance. According to Marshall, the Bank aims to:

> act for the common good, to seek solutions that are beneficial to the collective, and to avoid controversies that divide or pit members one against one another. An important feature of the World Bank is that the voting shares are weighted by economic strength, and thus the governance structure is not designed to be democratic. This sets the World Bank apart from the rest of the UN system. Although wealthier countries clearly exercise greater power than lower-income countries, the organization strives to operate cooperatively, seeking consensus where possible.[32]

In what follows, I focus more on the Fund. The reason is that when we consider the operational pattern, quotas and voting and conditionalities, both work in similar manners.

According to the articles of Agreement of the Fund,[33] its mandate includes the promotion of monetary cooperation among member nations through an institution which provides the machinery for consultation and collaboration on international monetary problems. This is based on the belief that leaving individual nations to pursue monetary policies without cooperation with other nations can lead to a global financial crisis and economic meltdown. Specified as part of its mandate also is the facilitation of the expansion and balanced growth of international trade and to, in consonance, contribute to the promotion and maintenance of high-level employment and the generation of real income, thereby furthering economic development. The Fund was also established to promote foreign exchange stability, maintain orderly exchange arrangement among member countries and avoid competitive exchange devaluation of the interwar period. The Fund is also mandated to assist in the establishment of a multilateral system of payment with respect to current transactions between members and in the elimination of foreign exchange restrictions that debilitate the growth of world trade. It is also expected to give confidence to members by making the general resources of the Fund temporarily available to members under adequate safeguards, thereby providing them with an opportunity to correct maladjustments in their balance of payments without resorting to measures that could hamper national or international prosperity. Finally, it is expected to shorten the duration and lessen the degree of disequilibrium in the international balances of payment of member.[34]

What the mandate of the Fund reveals is that the institution is empowered to have oversight of the global economy and to make sure that it functions in an orderly manner. To facilitate this, the Fund carries out a lot of activities. One of these is the surveillance of the economic policies of member countries. To be a member of the Fund, a country has to agree to pursue economic policies that are consistent with the objectives of the fund. There is no doubting the fact that the global economy is getting more integrated by the day and the economic policies of one country can have a great impact on the economies of other countries of the world. The Fund is thereby empowered to oversee and monitor each country to identify potential risks to global economic stability and recommend appropriate policy adjustments which will facilitate economic growth and promote financial and economic stability. The surveillance is done at two levels, that is, bilateral which focuses on individual countries and multilateral which focuses on the global economy. At the bilateral level, The Fund's state visits member countries annually to engage governments and central bank official about risks to domestic and global stability. According to Reedik, "the consultations focus of exchange rates, fiscal and monetary policy, the balance of payments and external debt problems and evaluation of the impact of economic policy steps on external balance and on other countries, as well as analysing the vulnerability of member countries to external influences."[35] They also hold talks with other stakeholders such as the legislature and representatives from the business community, labour unions and so on. This is to come up with factual report and evaluations of each country's economic policies, situation, outlook and prospects.[36]

In addition to the above, the Fund also finance temporary balance-of-payment needs by lending to member countries that have a balance-of-payment problem to provide a temporary respite and enable countries to put in place corrective policy measures and avoid a disorderly adjustment of the external imbalance. If a member country is to get a facility from the fund, it must have a balance-of-payment need. In other words, the country's balance of payment must be in deficit.[37] The purpose of the Fund's resources is to correct balance-of-payment disequilibrium and to help countries seeking the resources in their efforts to "rebuild international reserves, stabilize their currencies, continue paying for imports, and restore conditions for economic growth while undertaking policies to correct underlying problems."[38]

According to the IMF, the balance of payments is a

> statistical statement that systematically summarizes, for a specific period, the economic transactions of an economy with the rest of the world. Transactions, for the most part between residents and nonresidents, consist of those involving goods, services, and income; those involving financial claims on, and liabilities to, the rest of the world; and those (such as gifts) classified as transfers, which involve offsetting entries to balance—in an accounting sense—one-sided transactions."[39]

It is this accounting system that tells whether a country saves enough to pay for its imports and reveals whether the country produces enough to pay for its growth. In an accounting sense, the balance of payments must always balance, since it is a systematic record of all economic transactions between residents of one country and residents of other countries, presented in the form of double-entry bookkeeping. A balance-of-payments need exists when there is trade imbalance between import and export.[40] When a country's import is more than export that country is said to have a balance-of-payment deficit. Three factors could be responsible for this. The first is economic. Economic factors such as changes in the economy, changes in exchange rates or inflation/deflation could affect the relationship between import and export. Over time, when there is a progressive loss of key export market, high and rising import dependency, increase in foreign debt and currency overvaluation which makes the export of the country expensive, there is bound to be a balance-of-payment deficit. Also, as Vreeland explains, a country's reliance on the exportation of one primary good for generating foreign exchange may lead to a balance-of-payment need if the price of that product drops in the international market. He writes:

> The lower price may be so severe that the country cannot generate enough foreign exchange through its exports to maintain its imports. A large balance of payments deficit may ensue, along with a drop in the country's foreign reserves. The country's government may turn to the IMF to help get through this economic shock.[41]

Bad economic policies could also result in balance-of-payment needs. This occurs when, for instance, the government engages in spending that outpaces tax revenue. If this public expenditure is wasteful or does not generate corresponding growth in the economy, the government may not be able to pay for the service on its foreign debt.[42]

The second factor is social. Social factors such as changes in tastes and preferences due to demonstration effect, population growth rate and rate of urbanisation can also lead to trade imbalance. The third is political. This may include political instability in a country, war or changes in diplomatic policy. At the centre of the activities of the Fund is the provision of financial resource from the Fund's pool and the development of a framework to adjust the imbalance. It is this that forms the core of the Fund's dealing with developing countries, especially those of Africa South of Sahara.

Another reason that is cited as a reason for balance-of-payment problems which necessitates running to the Fund for resources is past participation in borrowing from the Fund. Vreeland quoted Graham Bird as saying that "as long as Fund-backed programs fail to effectively encourage economic growth as a top priority, many developing countries will remain Fund recidivists"[43] in Vreeland's opinion:

> Indeed, statistical work that distinguishes between the probability of entering into IMF programs from the probability of continuing IMF programs reveals that economic factors predict entering far better than they predict continuing. There seems to be something about past participation that causes countries to return and continue participation.[44]

Thinking along the same line, Dasgupta writes that:

> One perennial problem with IMF or World Bank assistance is that once dependence on those begins it seldom ends. One programme is followed by another and loanees, in particular, low-income countries, find it difficult to disengage themselves from those funding bodies. Counting of figures show that 21 countries had support for 14 years or more, and Mexico has continuously been on the agenda, one programme succeeding another, from the beginning of structural adjustment in 1980. There is, thus, strong evidence that IMF policies do not allow a country to graduate away from their reliance on these organisations. All these despite the idea incorporated in the Articles of Agreement of IMF that such assistance would be temporary and the funds would be revolving.[45]

What explains the above is that the Fund seems to play deliberate politics of keeping borrowers perpetually tied to it. Most of the time, the policies which the Fund uses as conditions for lending usually do not bring the desired economic growth in developing countries. What the policies do is to make the countries keep borrowing and keep them tied to the apron of the Fund. This keeps the Fund relevant(?) and making a huge profit from the borrowing of less developed countries.

Access to the Fund's resources is based on quotas and conditions. Quota refers to the capital subscription, which is a preset amount of currency that each member country contributes to the financial pool of the Fund.[46] Vreeland explains that the quota is neither a donation nor a grant, and neither is it paid annually. It is rather some amount of money held as a deposit at the fund and earns interest for the contributing country like a bank deposit. It is in this sense that the bank can be regarded as "a great international credit union with all of the countries of the world as members."[47] The quota of each member country is determined by its economic size, which is determined by the national income, the volume of current account transactions, official reserves and the amount of lending to the Fund.[48] What this shows is that developed and large industrial economies would have a larger quota than the less developed countries. As Officer has shown, less developed countries are not prone to criticise the quota system in terms of members' subscription because the quota system is based on the ability to pay which is, as noted, measured by the size of the economy.

While there may be no contestation with the quota system vis-à-vis subscription, there is another controversial side, that is, the linking of the quota with voting power. What this means is that the governance structure of the Fund is linked to each country's quota. The more a country's quota, the more its voting power and the more influence it has in the Fund. For a very long time now, the fundamental division in the Fund has been between "advanced economy 'creditors' and developing country 'borrowers'."[49] The advanced economy creditor-countries such as US, Britain and Japan are the ones who provide the bulk of the money the Fund uses for its operations and loans. This is because of their large quotas. It is interesting to note that though these creditor-countries provide the bulk of the Fund's resources, they do not make use of the Fund's lending facilities. At the other end, the contributions of developing countries to the Fund are minute compared to the creditor-countries. However, they are the ones who make use of a greater percentage of the Fund's resources. This makes the borrower-countries susceptible to the whims and caprices of the rich countries that govern the Fund. This has led to a conflict of interest to the extent that the developed industrial economies that make up the creditors marginalise and mortgage the interest of the borrowers. The reason is that, in any decision-making, the Fund's article of Agreement makes room for voting—mostly by a simple majority and some by 85% supermajorities.[50] It is pertinent to remark that both the creditors and the borrower depend heavily on the Fund, the less developed borrower-countries for resources to fund their economy and correct their balance-of-payment needs and the advanced creditor-countries to expand their influence on the borrower-countries economically and also politically.

Each member country is given a basic vote of 250 votes plus one additional vote for every 100,000 Special Drawing Right (SDR) contributed as its quota. SDR, that is, Special Drawing Right, is fictitious money, which represents the Fund's unit of account and was developed and introduced in 1969 as a reserve currency and is linked to a basket of currencies comprising US dollar, euro, pound sterling and Japanese Yen. Members pay 25% of the quotas in SDR, while the remaining 75% is paid in individual member's national currencies. So while Palau's quota accounts for only 0.001% of total contributions, it controls 0.01% of the votes. The US quota is 17.40% of total contributions, but it controls 17.08% of the votes which, according to Vreeland, is "enough to give the US veto power over decisions requiring an 85 per cent majority, such as quotas—hence influence—at the Fund."[51]

When one examines the quota system and its connection with voting power, one notices some level of deliberate politics of oppression. The practice of giving each country the same basic votes of 250 seems to depict the Fund's commitment to equality among nations, but this is not so. By the time attention is shifted to the votes based on financial contributions, one sees no such commitment. The reason is that the basic votes allotted to countries are quantitatively insignificant to votes based on quotas. This makes the Fund's decision-making quite dissimilar to that of the United Nations (UN). Commenting on the voting system and its lack of consideration for equality, Officer writes:

> In rejecting the "one country, one vote" system, the IMF violates the sovereign equality of states and fosters attitudes of resentment and alienation among countries with less voting power. Because such countries (with a few exceptions) are LDCs, the conflict between industrial countries and LDCs—admittedly present in any international organization—is exacerbated.[52]

At this juncture, let us shift attention to access to loans that are based on conditionality. For a country to access loans, the Fund imposes certain constraints in the form of policy guidelines and adjustments which are monitored from time to time. Conditionality is defined by Dreher as "the practice of giving financial assistance contingent on the implementation of specific policies."[53] For Fritz-Krockow and Ramlogan, it refers "to policies and actions that a borrowing member agrees to carry out as a condition for the use of IMF resources";[54] while for Tenney and Humphreys, "conditionality is the body of policies and procedures governing a member's use of the Fund's resources in support of adjustment policies that will enable the member to overcome its balance of payments problem in a manner that is not unnecessarily destructive of national or international prosperity and also enable the member to repay the Fund over the medium term."[55] It specifies policies, performance criteria and standards that borrowing countries must satisfy to receive resources from the Fund. It is believed that the prospect of receiving aid from the Fund during financial crisis tends to lower the incentive of the government to avoid bad economic policies that brought about the crisis. To avoid this moral hazard, certain strings are attached to the loans. The purpose of conditionality, on the one hand, is to ensure assistance to members to resolve their balance-of-payments crisis in a manner that is consistent with the IMF's articles. On the other hand, it establishes adequate safeguards for the temporary use of the IMF's resources. The Article of Agreements of the Fund provides that

20 THE BRETTON WOODS INSTITUTIONS AND ECONOMIC DEVELOPMENT... 353

The Fund shall adopt policies on the use of its general resources including policies on stand-by or similar arrangements, and may adopt special policies for special balance of payments problems, that will assist members to solve their balance of payments problems in a manner consistent with the provisions of this Agreement and that will establish adequate safeguards for the temporary use of the general resources of the Fund.[56]

In the perspective of the Fund, loan repayment would be at risk if there are no conditions, and without this, the revolving character of the Fund's resources cannot be guaranteed.

While the majority of the Fund's loans are based on certain conditionalities, there are portions of the loans that are not conditioned. If a country requests for a loan of or less than 25% of its quota, the loan is provided without conditions. The reason is that the 25% of each country's quota which is paid in hard currency is termed reserved tranche that is part of the country's owned reserve as distinct from the borrower's reserves provided by the Fund's other facilities. Drawings from this tranche are considered unique and attract to no condition and no interests are paid on it since it is not treated as a loan.[57] However, the borrowing country must be committed to making reasonable efforts to correct its balance-of-payment problem even though there are not explicit conditionalities.

There is another level of loan which is granted condition-free or at minimal conditions. This happens when the loan is needed because of the balance of payment that results from bad luck and not directly as a result of bad economic policies. This is known as Compensatory Financing Facility.[58] Vreeland provided the examples of Tanzania and Nigeria that got this loan in 1974 and 1982 respectively. He writes:

> Take, for example, Tanzania in 1974. With the rise in world oil prices, this fuel-importing country entered into a balance of payments crisis. President Julius Nyerere borrowed from the IMF exactly 25 per cent of Tanzania's quota and subsequently obtained two consecutive loans from the unconditioned Oil Facility. In sum, Nyerere obtained loans of nearly 50 per cent of Tanzania's quota (about 20 million SDR) and avoided conditionality. He did this both because he opposed the policy conditions that the IMF proposed were necessary for Tanzania, and because he opposed what he saw as an international organization infringing upon national sovereignty. As another example, consider Nigeria in 1982. With the drop in world oil prices, this oil-exporting country entered into a balance of payments crisis and turned to the IMF. President Alhaji Shehu Shagari withdrew a loan of 25 per cent of his country's quota, followed by an Oil Facility loan. Shagari also entered into negotiations for a conditioned IMF arrangement, but could not agree to the appropriate policy conditions. In particular, the IMF insisted that the national currency, the naira, be devalued, but the Nigerian president could not take this step—he faced elections and devaluation was politically risky.[59]

Vreeland noted however that Tanzania and Nigeria and nearly all other developing countries have bowed to the Fund's conditionality. This is because, most of the time, less developed countries require the "upper credit tranche," which is 75% of their quota. This is known as the Extended Fund Facility. This type of loan involves high conditionality, which is justified on the account that the Fund has to secure its resources because the Fund's money is revolving and has to be paid and on the ground that the countries must ensure the correction of balance-of-payment problems.

In earlier years of the operation of the Fund, conditionalities were few and not rigorously pursued as it is today. Then, conditionality focused primarily on macroeconomic policies involving monetary, fiscal, exchange rate, social security system and pricing policies, among others. They were concerned with macroeconomic management and operated from the demand side of the economy. However, this has changed with the growth in membership of developing countries. Attention now focuses, in addition, on economic infrastructure, privatisation, institution-building and opening up of the economy for foreign completion. It is in this area that Saner and Guilherme think that the Fund oversteps its area of expertise and "arrogates to itself the right to engage in much broader reforms including trade liberalization, pricing and marketing, labour market reorganization and generic institutional or regulatory changes."[60] For instance, the Fund compels borrowing countries to undertake unilateral commitments towards liberalisation within the World Trade Organization (WTO), which impinges on these countries' sovereignty and rights to pursue their economic interests. It is in these areas that the Fund tampers with the economy of the borrowing countries to make deep-seated changes that aggravate poverty in these countries in the name of trying to provide an adequate safeguard for the Fund's resources. In this direction, the Fund suggests that the borrowing country is unwilling to accept, whereas what the *Guidelines on Conditionality* stipulate is that the Fund will respect the principle of national "Ownership and capacity to implement programs."[61] The Guideline states that:

> National ownership of sound economic and financial policies and an adequate administrative capacity are crucial for successful implementation of Fund-supported programs. In responding to members' requests to use Fund resources and in setting program-related conditions, the Fund will be guided by the principle that the member has primary responsibility for the selection, design, and implementation of its economic and financial policies. The Fund will encourage members to seek to broaden and deepen the base of support for sound policies to enhance the likelihood of successful implementation.[62]

The fact is that regard is not given to the socio-economic and political conditions in these borrowing countries. There can be no one-size-fits-all economic approach to all less development countries suffering from economic problems.

Economic Development in Africa

It is pertinent to note that a good understanding of the concept of economic development is important. This is for two reasons: so that it is not confused with related concepts and so that we can assess whether the Bretton Woods Institutions are actually in pursuit of economic development in Africa. Economic development is a major part of the development agenda. Every nation that pursues development pursues economic development because where there is economic development, there will be transformation in unprecedented dimensions in the lives of the people and the countries in general.

Let me make some clarification on the relationship between economic growth and economic development. Though these are similar concepts and some tend to use them interchangeably, they are not the same. Economic growth is all about increase in the gross domestic product (GDP) of a particular country, that is making the economy bigger within a period. The GDP is calculated as the sum of all economic activities in a nation over a specific period. It relates to the net value of all the products and services that an economy produces over an accounting period, which is usually a year.[63] Economic development, on the other hand, is defined by the World Bank as "a sustainable increase in living standards including material consumption, education, health, and environmental protection."[64] Economic development, as Nafziger rightly contends is "economic growth accompanied by changes in output distribution and economic structure."[65] These changes, according to him, may include improvement in material well-being of the poor in the nation; a decline in agriculture's share in the gross national product (GNP) and a corresponding increase in the GNP share of industry and services; an increase in the education and skills of the labour force; and substantial technical advances originating within the country. What this shows is that growth is enough when we deal with economic development. For instance, oil-exporting countries such as Nigeria experienced sharp increases in national income during the oil boom of the 1970s but were without any significant change in the structure of the economy. Sen provides an example of how African Americans in the US despite higher per capita income have lower life expectancy than the Chinese average person or inhabitants of the Indian state of Kerala.[66] This is not to say that economic growth is no important; in fact, it is a necessary requirement but it is not sufficient. The reason is that an increase in a nation's income may not translate into development if there is a corresponding increase in the nation's population. In this sense, there is an increase in the GDP but there is no increase in per capita income. Sometimes also, there may be an increase in per capita income but no corresponding increase in the standard of living of the nation. This happens when the wealth of the nation is concentrated in the hand of a few rich people. One can say that the size of an economy says little about the welfare of the country in terms of income among the population or the composition of outputs such as education and health care. What we can infer from this is that economic growth is wider in scope than economic growth as it deals with economic, social and institutional mechanisms at both private and public levels that are necessary to bring about rapid and large-scale improvement in the living standard of the people.

> In short, economic growth is only a very partial measure of the development of a country and is only a means to an end rather than an end in itself. On a more positive note, GDP and GNP/GNI still provide a snapshot of economies and a useful starting point for analysing and comparing the health of economies throughout the world. For this reason, organisations such as the World.[67]

Economic development is the process by which people are lifted from poverty and their basic need satisfied. It is defined in terms of poverty eradication, literacy, access to quality health that reduces child mortality rate and increases life expectancy. It is thinking along this line of thought that Kindleberger and Herrick write that economic development "includes improvement in welfare, especially for persons with the lowest incomes, the eradication of poverty with its correlates of illiteracy, disease and early death".[68] Following this, Seers thinks that when we talk about development, we should not limit our consideration to economic growth and changes in economic structures. We should rather focus on whether there is a decrease in poverty and malnutrition, a decline in income inequality and improvement in employment situation. He writes:

> The questions to ask about a country's economic development are therefore: What has been happening to poverty, unemployment and inequality; if all three of these have declined from high levels, then beyond doubt this has been a period of development for the country concerned. If one or two of these central problems have been growing worse, especially if all three have, it would be strange to call the result 'development' even if per capita income doubled.[69]

It is in the inclusion of non-economic indicator to the concept of economic development that stimulates scholars like Amartya Sen to focus on human development rather than economic development. Sen argued that this discourse on development should focus on the concept of freedom.[70] He sees development as a multidimensional concept involving the process of expansion of substantive freedoms. For him, economic growth, technological advance and political change are all to be judged in the light of their contributions to the expansion of human freedoms, which include freedom from famine and malnutrition, freedom from poverty, access to health care and freedom from premature mortality.

According to a report of the United Nations, Africa as a continent "is still grappling with the problem of hunger and poverty, and unemployment and inequality have increased over the past decade".[71] Poverty rates in sub-Saharan Africa have increased despite a decade of relatively high growth.

THE ROLE OF BRETTON WOODS INSTITUTIONS IN THE (UNDER) DEVELOPMENT OF AFRICAN ECONOMIES

According to Adedeji, the Bretton Woods Institutions have been deeply involved with African economies pretty well before independence. He cited the instance of the Bank being invited in 1953 to be part of the development plan for Nigeria.[72] In the demonstration of the bias of these institution and lack of readiness to be involved in African economies for the right reasons, Adedeji notes that "while it [the Bank] not think then that investment in universal primary education in Africa was wise, it backed rather heavily large-scale infrastructural facilities such as highways and hydro dams. And while it provided some resources in support of industrialisation, it was more favourably inclined towards financing agricultural production for export."[73] So, from the beginning of their involvement with Africa, there has been a tendency to perpetuate the economic status quo and interested only in exploiting Africa—a tendency that started from the colonial period and is being furthered in new dimensions. Africans fell prey to these hegemonic institutions because of the external dependence that was inherited from the colonial and post-colonial periods. They became the "sole designers and overseers of economic policies that would command their support and the sole judges of which programmes were right and acceptable,"[74] maybe because we differed to them too much because of the advancements in their economies or because we do not have the theoretical wherewithal or the resources to do so. There is no doubting the fact that they became important, if not the most important, determinants of what happens or does not happen regarding the economic development of Africa South of Sahara to the extent that "virtually every external support to any African country, including debt rescheduling and relief, became dependent on the award of a certificated of good behaviour from these institutions such an award was and is dependent upon adherence to SAP and their conditionalities."[75] This greatly affects independent decision-making and national macroeconomic management. Consequently, this undermines African ownership of its development process.

The role of the Bretton Woods Institutions in African economies has been the integration of these economies into the US-dominated and multinational corporations-driven global capitalist system in which market forces are considered supreme(?) and raw material producers are subordinated to industrial product producers. This integration has led to the subjugation and marginalisation of African economies. Through these institutions, African economies have been forced to open to Western penetration and this has led to increased export of primary goods to wealthy countries. For this reason, the Fund and the Bank have, over the years, become major impediments to the economic development of African countries. They play a vital role in the formulation of policies and offering technical advice in their commitment to improving economic development and eradication of poverty. However, rather than further economic development, the institutions' policy recommendation has contributed to undermining and underdeveloping African economies.

Let me start with the structural adjustment programme (SAP), which has been regarded as the worst economic policy imposed on African countries by the Bretton Woods Institutions because of the negative effect it had on the African economies. During the 1980s sub-Saharan African countries became heavily dependent on Bretton Woods Institutions. Before this time, African economies had been performing well with an annual growth rate of 5.7%. This trend was reversed in the mid-1970s. Heidhues and Obare write:

> However, in the early 1970s, the growth engine in African countries began to slow down and by the mid-1970s, economic performance was lagging behind that of other parts of the developing world. This performance was reflected in poor growth of the productive sectors, a declining level and efficiency of investment, waning exports, mounting debt, deteriorating social conditions, and the increasing erosion of institutional capacity. These developments led to high budget and balance of payments deficits and significant public debt. ... By 1980, output was declining. By the end of the 1980s, Sub-Saharan African countries were facing fundamental problems: high rates of population growth, low levels of investment and saving, inefficient use of resources, weak institutions and human capacity, and a general decline in income and living standards.[76]

This was consequent upon the rise in the price of oil, the raising of US interest rates which was occasioned by the coming to power of monetarist regime of President Ronald Regan. This accentuated debt burden and led to a contraction in the global economy with a reverberating effect on Africa. All of these accompanied by what Woods calls "deep domestic weakness and poorly aimed interventions by Cold War rival, former colonial powers and aid donors"[77] and drought and civil wars aggravated the economic condition in the African continent. By the 1990s, growth in Africa had declined to 3.5%. Around this time the Bretton Woods twins began a widespread debate on what kind of economic reform would revamp the African economy and consequently became technical advisors and source of conditional funds for Africa.

The first recommendation which is part of the conditionality for aids was the African governments were required to undertake stabilisation policies by reducing budget deficit to stem inflation. The Fund's stabilisation programmes involve a standard set of policies aimed at reducing current account deficits. The programmes require internal adjustment through monetary contraction by reducing government's budget deficit. This necessitates a reduction in the wage bill, price subsidies and government support for social programmes such as health and education. Stabilisation also includes a contraction of the money supply and fiscal austerity measures aimed at reducing "excessive demand" in the domestic economy; demands for strict anti-inflationary monetary policy, privatisation of public enterprises, trade liberalisation and dismantling of foreign exchange controls; and more flexible labour markets reducing the size of the public sector.

The stabilisation policies were, according to The Structural Adjustment Participatory Review International Network (SAPRIN), "designed to generate savings and foreign exchange with which to bring countries' internal and external accounts into balance and facilitate repayment of foreign creditors."[78] Nonetheless, the resultant effect which called for the labelling of the stabilisation programmes as wrong-headed fiscal prescription was unemployment and reduction in the real income of worker—as we know that subsidy cuts reduce real income by a sudden increase in basic goods such as food, fuel, transportation, healthcare and education. When food, fuel and transport costs mounted with the removal of government subsidisations, street riots and protests exploded in several African countries. This led the Bank to step in with funds that were conditioned on longer-term, structural and institutional changes that had a less immediate impact than the austerity measures required by the Fund.

The literature shows that the stabilisation programmes worked, but only in the short-term, and what is needed for development is what can produce a long-term effect on the economy. As Wood shows, the short-term effect was evident in the Zambian experience during the 1970s. However, the Fund soon realised that the stabilisation policy did not enhance the country's capacity to repay loans. As Woods notes, even though the stabilisation policy worked by cutting down deficit by 50% in Zambia, it led to political backlash and soaring debt and as Boughton reported Zambia was no longer able to pay the Fund's money in a timely fashion.[79] From this experience, the Fund thought there was a need for a deeper and stronger policy measure to deal with the situation. It was this that led to the structural adjustment programme. This policy was necessitated by the interest of these institutions in the repayment of their fund rather than interest in the elevation of the countries involved out of economic mess. What the Zambian experience showed was that some underlying factors are external, which are needed to be addressed but which these institutions seemed to be blinded.

SAP can, therefore, be regarded as a policy response to the economic crisis in Africa. The policy was introduced in Africa in the 1980s and continued to operate until the 1990s, and even till now the policy is still being implemented in new dimensions. During the period of its explicit operation, the Fund and the Bank worked closely together with the Fund handling and setting macroeconomic development and policy agenda and the Bank providing structural adjustment lending.[80] The adjustment was to "bring less developed country imports in line with their dwindling foreign exchange earnings from exports and whatever little they could get from outside the world in the form of assistance."[81] As Dasgupta rightly remarks, structural adjustment was not initially meant for developing countries but for the restructuring of Organisation for Economic Co-operation and Development (OECD) countries and the most developed countries of the world and when it was shifted to be operationalised in the developing world, "adjustment got priority over other policy objectives such as poverty alleviation and redistribution."[82]

Structural adjustment programmes of the Bank and the Fund have been used by these institutions to create conditions that benefit Western government and corporations. These programme policies require governments to reduce public expenditure, raise interests, privatise state enterprises, increase exports and reduce barriers to trade investments such as tariffs and import duties. The purpose of these measures was the supposed generation of export-led growth that would attract foreign direct investments and foreign earnings that could be used to reduce debt and poverty.

The earlier dealings of the Bretton Woods Institutions, especially the Bank with Africa, show that it was involved in project lending. This kind of lending was instituted by the Bank in 1960 to target specific aspects of the African economies.[83] It was a deviation from the approach taken in the 1950s in which the focus was infrastructural development such as roads and railway projects, telecommunications and electricity generation. Project lending, however, focused on productive areas, such as industry and agriculture, and socio-economic areas such as education and health. Thus, as Lyakurwa rightly notes:

> The emphasis of the development strategies was therefore changed to focus more on investments that could directly affect the well-being of the masses of poor people in developing countries by making them more productive and by integrating them as active partners in the development process. Host countries initiated projects, but the Bank assessed the feasibility of the projects. The Bank's major justification for project lending stemmed from the emphasis on capital investment given in the literature on economic development in the 1940s, 1950s and 1960s, which implied that the rate of economic growth was considered as a function of the rate of growth of the capital stock.[84]

It is good to note that most of these projects failed because of the over-involvement of the Bank officials who were not familiar with the local terrains of the countries in which the projects were executed.

At the beginning of the 1980s, the Bank seemed to shift from project lending to programme- or policy-based lending. Although the Bank's conditionality is somewhat different from that of the Fund, the Bank like the Fund began to make some of its loans conditional upon the pursuit of a stipulated programme of policies.[85] From this period, the Bank began to base its loan on longer-term rather than the original short-term concerns.

What I think is responsible for this shift is the shift in ideology. Before 1980, the Bank's policies were based on supporting state-led development in African countries. Greater percentage of its financial assistance was targeted and utilised to help governments of African countries and other developing nations to construct solid infrastructures and facilities to drive development and serve the citizens of their countries. This was compatible with the Keynesian development model of that period which the Bank recognised as the most important engine for growth and development of the economy.

The policy change, from state-led development approach to the market-led approach at the beginning of the 1980s, came when Prime Minister Margaret Thatcher and President Reagan explained and advocated for the free-market ideology in the US and the UK during their time in office. This policy change was based on the neo-liberal ideology and The Fund and the Bank became the instruments that were used to enforce this ideology in developing African countries even though they were not ripe for it.

The neo-liberal ideology upon which the Bank and the Fund's SAPs are based is an ideology, economic model, a mode of governance and a policy package that is rooted in the classical liberal ideal of the self-regulating market. As an economic paradigm neo-liberalism supports a free-market mechanism with the state voluntarily reducing its role in the economy and performing functions that relate to defending the territorial integrity of the state, maintenance of law and order, crime prevention, human rights guaranteeing and protection, promotion of human capital formation and putting in place safe environment for those involved in business operations to accomplish their negotiations and trade deals in order to enhance healthy competition and bring progress to the market. The whole idea about neo-liberalism is that market mechanism should be allowed to direct the fate of human beings. The economy should dictate its rule to society, and not the other way around. Central doctrine of neo-liberalism is the notion of competition-competition between nations, regions, firms and of course between individuals without any interference of the government.

SAPs involve the basic element of neo-liberalism as a public policy package, namely liberalisation, privatisation and deregulation. Liberalisation refers to the removal of government interference in financial and capital markets and of all barriers to trade. The one that concerns us much here is trade liberalisation. This has to do with removing all barriers to trade at both the national and global levels allowing multinational companies to have a free day in any country whatsoever. This, it is supposed, would enhance a country's income by forcing resources to move from a less productive to more productive uses. But what happens under the Fund's and the Bank's SAP, as Stiglitz contends, is that resources are moved from low productivity to zero productivity and so does not enrich the nation. Under SAPs' trade liberalisation, jobs are destroyed as inefficient industries close down due to pressure from international competition. The ideology of these institutions is that more jobs will be created to replace the old one, but this did not take place in African countries because as Stiglitz argues, "It takes capital and entrepreneurship to create new firms and jobs, and in developing countries there is often a shortage of the latter, due to lack of education, and the former, due to lack of bank financing."[86] However, as Osabu-Kle argues, Bretton Woods Institutions were fully aware that "Africa is devoid of a bourgeois class of entrepreneurs, embark upon preaching privatization, which is essentially a means for strategically compelling African countries to invite the participation of international business from the West in joint ventures or surrender complete ownership of the means of production within their borders to the bourgeoisie located in the West."[87] There is a political agenda to this, namely economically weaken African economies for political and economic domination.

Privatisation as an element of the SAPs policy package involves the belief that the government has no business running steel companies or transportation companies and so on. In other words, the government has no business doing business. In consonance with this thought "whatever public sector economic activities are in operation should be closed down, or phased out or trimmed, or passed on to the private sector."[88] This may be intended to bring about competition, to take the government out of the position of having ownership of businesses and to remove those politicians who are involved in fraud and dishonest practices in the management of the resources, finance, income and expenditure of the country's economy. However, most of these government-owned businesses were purchased by foreign companies, leading to more impoverishment of the African economies. For instance, Ghana used to be self-sufficient in rice, but after the Bank insisted that subsidies had to stop and markets had to open for foreign investments, American rice took over the market until it became the staple for Ghanaians.

In 1991, Zimbabwe signed the SAPs agreement with the Fund for a loan of $484 million loan. This was intended to jump-start the economy that had stagnated for some time. According to Ismi "the IMF's SAP for Zimbabwe required reducing trade tariffs and import duties, eliminating foreign currency controls, removing protections for the manufacturing sector, deregulating the labour market, lowering the minimum wage, ending employment security, cutting the fiscal deficit, reducing the tax rate and deregulating financial markets."[89] This brought about closing down of companies, leading to a high rate of unemployment and poverty.

As noted earlier, one of the effects of the Bretton Woods Institutions' involvement with African economies is the integration of African economies into the global economies. This, nonetheless, has produced growth but has not resulted in economic development as a greater percentage of the African populace is still left in poverty. The reason is that the economic benefits of the growth are transferred to the developed world. Ismi writes:

> Between 1984 and 1990, Third World countries under SAPs transferred $178 billion to Western commercial banks. So enormous was the capital drain from the South that Morris Miller, a Canadian former World Bank director remarked: "Not since the conquistadors plundered Latin America has the world experienced such a flow in the direction we see today." By severely restricting government spending in favour of debt repayment, the loan terms of the Bank and the IMF eviscerated the Third World state leaving in its wake spiralling poverty and hunger fueled by slashed food subsidies and decimated health and education sectors. Growth stagnated and debt doubled to over $1.5 trillion by the end of the 1980s,

doubling again to $3 trillion by the end of the 1990s.19 As U.N. Secretary-General Javier Perez de Cuellar noted in 1991: "The various plans of structural adjustment—which undermine the middle classes; impoverish wage earners; close doors that had begun to open to the basic rights of education, food, housing, medical care; and also disastrously affect employment—often plunge societies, especially young people, into despair."[90]

One wonders then whether these institutions are interested in economic development in Africa. What then is the way forward?

Conclusion: The Way Forward

It is congruent with the earlier analysis to see the Bretton Woods Institutions as overseers of African economy—a position which they have badly managed over the years. One of the reasons for the mismanagement of this position is the unwillingness of the Fund and the Bank to rethink their strategies and the refusal of the leaders of African countries to think for themselves. When we look at the impact of the SAPs on Latin America, one would realise that the effect was increased poverty and mounting debt. By 1997, close to half of the region's population had become poor. The effect on Peru was the same as "the IMF pushed four million people into extreme poverty, almost halved real wages and cut those with 'adequate employment'."[91] Given this, the Bretton Woods macroeconomic recommendations became like a deliberate attack on African economies to make them repay their loan and continue to serve the interests of the US and other industrialised nations, which is "the maximization of profit and its repatriation to the metropoles."[92] Their dealing with Africa had and has continued to be driven by ideology. But when ideology conflicts with evidence and reality, I think it is wrong-headed to continue with the ideology. But this is what these twin institutions have been doing. Good economic policies have the power to change lives, but when an economic policy begins to have adverse and counterproductive effects on the people, it needs to be rethought. By failing to allow desirable government intervention, which is based on the myth that the market is efficient for the allocation of resources, the institutions make life difficult for the people of Africa. The issue is that they prescribe policies without consideration for the local contexts that they are less familiar with and without consideration for the effect it would have on the people, especially the majority of the people who live in the informal sector.

There is the need to let African countries have voices in the running of their economies. For the institutions, once there are prescriptions, alternative voices and alternative ideas are not sought. In this age of rationalisation, I think it is dehumanising not to allow critical debate on issues that bother on the welfare of the people. For me, such an attitude is not only dehumanising for me but also undemocratic. One wonders why the unworkable ideas of these institutions continue uncriticised among the people in power in these institutions, and when they are queried by the developing countries, they often cannot pursue their positions for the fear of being blacklisted by them and losing funding. I think that the institutions should review their voting strategy to give more voice to the countries that these economic policies affect directly, noting that these institutions would have lost relevance if not for the patronage of developing countries. When we examine the voting structure of the two institutions, one would realise that there is a politics of deliberate marginalisation of the less developed countries. The institutions can adjust in this area by learning from the one-country-one-vote system of the UN, and so review their undemocratic governmentality. Apart from this, both the Bank and the Fund need to adjust their conditionalities so that African countries and other developing nations would regain the authority to govern their economies since national economic policies are usually prepared and foisted on countries desiring loans.

African leaders also need a revolutionary attitude towards the Bretton Woods Institutions. These can be facilitated by revisiting the *Lagos Plan of Action* which Osabu-Kle described as "the embodiment of African attempts to resist neocolonialism and to own their economic recovery."[93] This represented a concerted effort on the part of Africa to propose an alternative development strategy to free Africans from the claws of Western domination.

Notes

1. Women for a Just and Healthy Planet, "Action Against Bretton Woods," *Economic and Political Weekly*, 29.27 (1994): 1618.
2. Ibid.
3. Ibid.
4. Ibid.
5. A. L. Keith Acheson, John F Chant, and Martin F. J. Prachowny, "Introduction," in A. L. Keith Acheson, John F. Chant and Martin F. J. Prachowny, Ed., *Bretton Woods Revisited* (Toronto: University of Toronto Press, 1972).
6. Sabine Dammasch, *The System of Bretton Woods: A Lesson from History*, Retrieved on 12 July 2018 from http://www.hiddenmysteries.org/money/policy/b-woods.pdf
7. Ronald I. McKinnon, Beggar-Thy-Neighbor Interest Rate Policies, Stanford University (2010) Retrieved on 17 September 2018 from http://citeseer.ist.psu.edu/viewdoc/download?doi=10.1.1.364.5619&rep=rep1&type=pdf
8. Ngaire Woods, *The Globalizers: The IMF, The World Bank and Their Borrowers* (London: Cornell University Press, 2006), 20.
9. Ngaire Woods, *The Globalizers: The IMF, The World Bank and their Borrowers* (London: Cornell University Press, 2006), 21.
10. Ngaire Woods, *The Globalizers: The IMF, The World Bank and their Borrowers*, 16.
11. Ibid.
12. Ibid.
13. Ibid., 3.
14. Ibid., 4.
15. Ibid., 15.

16. Robert Hunter Wade, "US Hegemony and the World Bank: The Fight over People and Ideas," *Review of International Political Economy*, 9. (2002): 201–229.
17. Ibid., 203.
18. Ibid.
19. Ngaire Woods, *The Globalizers: The IMF, The World Bank and their Borrowers*, 4.
20. Ibid.
21. Biplab Dasgupta, "SAP: Issues and Conditionalities: A Global Review," *Economic and Political Weekly*, 32.20/21 (1997): 1092.
22. See Horman Chitonge, *Economic Growth and Development in Africa Understanding Trends and Prospects* (New York: Routledge, 2015).
23. James Raymond Vreeland, *The International Monetary Fund: Politics of Conditional Lending* (New York: Routledge, 2007), 1.
24. Ibid.
25. Ibid., 8.
26. Ngaire Woods, *The Globalizers: The IMF, The World Bank and their Borrowers*, 7.
27. Michael Hodd, "Africa, the IMF and the World Bank," *African Affairs*, 86.344 (1987): 333.
28. World Bank, *Guide to the World Bank*, (Washington, DC: World Bank 2007).
29. Lawrence H. Officer, "The International Monetary Fund," *Proceedings of the Academy of Political Science*, 37. 4 (1990): 28.
30. Ibid.
31. Robert Calderisi, The World Bank and Africa, *Transformation*, 17.4 (2000).
32. Katherine Marshall, *The World Bank: From Reconstruction to Development to Equity*, (New York: Routledge, 2008): 3.
33. International Monetary Fund, *Articles of Agreement*. (Washington, DC: International Monetary Fund 2016).
34. Bernhard Fritz-Krockow and Parmeshwar Ramlogan, eds, *International Monetary Fund Handbook: Its Functions, Policies, and Operations* (Washington, DC: International Monetary Fund, 2007).
35. Reet Reedik, "International Monetary Fund and Economic Policy Surveillance," *Kroon & Economy*, 1 (2002): 44.
36. See John Williamson, "Economic Theory and International Monetary Fund Policies," *Carnegie-Rochester Conference Series on Public Policy*, 13 (1980): 255–278 and Reet Reedik, "International Monetary Fund and Economic Policy Surveillance," *Kroon & Economy*, 1 (2002): 44.
37. Lawrence H. Officer, "The International Monetary Fund," *Proceedings of the Academy of Political Science*, 37. 4 (1990).
38. International Monetary Fund, "IMF Lending," *Fact Sheet* (2017).
39. International Monetary Fund, *Balance of Payment Statistics* (Washington, DC: International Monetary Fund, 2003): xxi.
40. Sarah Tenney and Norman K. Humphreys, *Historical Dictionary of the International Monetary Fund* (3rd ed. Toronto: The Scarecrow Press, Inc. 2011).
41. James Raymond Vreeland, *The International Monetary Fund: Politics of Conditional Lending* (New York: Routledge, 2007), 51.
42. Ibid.
43. Ibid., 55.
44. Ibid., 57.

45. Biplab Dasgupta, "SAP: Issues and Conditionalities: A Global Review," *Economic and Political Weekly*, 32.20/21 (1997): 1097.
46. James Raymond Vreeland, *The International Monetary Fund: Politics of Conditional Lending* (New York: Routledge, 2007).
47. Ibid., 13.
48. See Vreeland, Ibid and officer, Opcit.
49. Brock Blomberg and J. Lawrence Broz, (2007) The Political Economy of IMF Voting Power and Quotas. Retrieved on 26 November 2018 from http://pages.ucsd.edu/~jlbroz/PEimf_blomerg_br0z_IPED.pdf
50. James Raymond Vreeland, *The International Monetary Fund: Politics of Conditional Lending* (New York: Routledge, 2007): 12.
51. Ibid., 15.
52. Officer, Opcit., 30.
53. Axel Dreher, "IMF Conditionality: Theory and Evidence," *Public Choice*, 141.1/2 (2009): 233.
54. Fritz-Krockow and Ramlogan, *International Monetary Fund Handbook: Its Functions, Policies, and Operations*. Washington, DC: International Monetary Fund, 25.
55. Sarah Tenney, and Norman K. Humphreys, *Historical Dictionary of the International Monetary Fund* (3rd Edition. Toronto: The Scarecrow Press, Inc., 2011), 95.
56. International Monetary Fund, *Articles of Agreement* (Washington, DC: International Monetary Fund 2016), 8.
57. Dasgupta, "SAP: Issues and Conditionalities: A Global Review," 1095.
58. Officer, "The International Monetary Fund," Vreeland, *The International Monetary Fund: Politics of Conditional Lending*.
59. Vreeland, *The International Monetary Fund: Politics of Conditional Lending*, 26–27.
60. Raymond Saner, and Ricardo Guilherme, "IMF Conditionalities for the Least Developed Countries" *G-24 Policy Brief, 19* (2008): 1.
61. International Monetary Fund (IMF), "Guidelines on Conditionality" 2002: 2 Retrieved from http://www.imf.org/External/np/pdr/cond/2002/eng/guid/092302.htm
62. Ibid.
63. A. P. Thirlwall, 'Development as Economic Growth' V. Desai, and R.B. Potter, eds, *The Companion to Development Studies* (2nd ed. New York: Oxford, 2008).
64. World Bank *The Challenge of Development. World Development Report* (Washington, DC: International Bank for Reconstruction and Development, 1991): 31.
65. E. Wayne Nafziger, *Economic Development* (Cambridge: Cambridge University Press, 2006): 15.
66. Amartya Sen, *Development as Freedom* (New York: Anchor Books, 1999).
67. Sylvia Chant and Cathy McIlwaine, *Geographies of Development* (London: University of London Press, 2008), 20.
68. Charles P. Kindleberger and Bruce Herrick, *Economic Development* (New York: McGraw-Hill, 1977), 1.
69. Seers, Dudley, The Meaning of Development. *Institute of Development Studies Communication series* No. 4 (1969).
70. Amartya Sen, *Development as Freedom*, (New York: A. Knopf, 1999).
71. United Nations, *Economic Development in Africa Report 2014: Catalysing Investment for Transformative Growth in Africa*, (Geneva: United Nations, 2014), 3.

72. Adebayo Adedeji, "An African Perspective on Bretton Woods," In Richard Jolly Mahbub ul Haq, Paul Streeten and Khadija Haq, Eds, *The UN and the Bretton Woods Institutions: New Challenges for the Twenty-First Century*. (London: Macmillan Press Ltd., 1995), 60.
73. Ibid., 61–62.
74. Ibid., 62–63.
75. Ibid., 63.
76. Franz Heidhues and Gideon Obare, (2011) "Lessons from Structural Adjustment Programmes and their Effects in Africa," *Quarterly Journal of International Agriculture*, 50. 1: 56.
77. Woods, *The Globalizers*, 141.
78. SAPRIN *Structural Adjustment: The Sapri Report: The Policy Roots of Economic Crisis, Poverty and Inequality* (New York: Zed Books, 2004), 2.
79. Wood, *The Globalizers*; James M. Boughton, *Silent Revolution: The International Monetary Fund, 1979–1989* (Washington, DC: International Monetary Fund, 2001).
80. Franz Heidhues, and Gideon Obare, "Lessons from Structural Adjustment Programmes and their Effects in Africa," *Quarterly Journal of International Agriculture*, 50. 1: 55–64, 2011.
81. Dasgupta, "SAP: Issues and Conditionalities: A Global Review," 1094.
82. Ibid.
83. William Lyakurwa, "Sub-Saharan African Countries' Development Strategies: The Role of The Bretton Woods Institutions," In Jan Joost Teunissen and Age Akkerman (Eds) *Helping the Poor? The IMF and Low-Income Countries* (FONDAD: The Hague, 2005).
84. Ibid., 157.
85. Graham Bird, Sisters in Economic Development: The Bretton Woods Institutions and Developing Countries. *Journal of International Development*, 5.1 (1993), 9.
86. Joseph E. Stiglitz, *Globalization and Its Discontents*. (New York: W. W. Norton & Company, Inc., 2002), 59.
87. Daniel Tetteh Osabu-Kle, "Politics of One-side Adjustment in Africa," *Journal of Black Studies*, 30.4 (2000): 524.
88. Dasgupta, "SAP – Issues and Conditionalities: A Global Review," 1097.
89. Asad Ismi, *Impoverishing a Continent: The World Bank and the IMF in Africa* Canadian Centre for Policy Alternatives (2004), 14 Retrieved on 10 October 2018 from http://www.halifaxinitiative.org/updir/ImpoverishingAContinent.pdf
90. Ibid., 9.
91. Ibid.
92. Osabu-Kle, "Politics of One-side Adjustment in Africa," 522.
93. Osabu-Kle, "Politics of One-side Adjustment in Africa," 525.

Bibliography

Acheson, A., L. Keith, John F. Chant, and Martin F.J. Prachowny. 1972. Introduction. In *Bretton Woods Revisited*, ed. A.L. Keith Acheson, John F. Chant, and Martin F.J. Prachowny. Toronto: University of Toronto Press.

Adedeji, Adebayo. 1995. An African Perspective on Bretton Woods. In *The UN and the Bretton Woods Institutions: New Challenges for the Twenty-First Century*, ed. Mahbub ul Haq, Richard Jolly, Paul Streeten, and Khadija Haq. London: Macmillan Press Ltd.

———. 1999. Structural Adjustment Policies in Africa. *International Social Science Journal* 51(162): 521–528.
Bird, Graham. 1993. Sisters in Economic Development: The Bretton Woods Institutions and Developing Countries. *Journal of International Development* 5 (1): 1–25.
Blomberg, Brock, and J. Lawrence. Broz. 2013. *The Political Economy of IMF Voting Power and Quotas*. Retrieved on 26 November 2018 from http://pages.ucsd.edu/~jlbroz/PEimf_blomerg_br0z_IPED.pdf
Boughton, James M. 2001. *Silent Revolution: The International Monetary Fund, 1979–1989*. Washington, DC: International Monetary Fund.
Calderisi, Robert. 2000. The World Bank and Africa. *Transformation* 17 (4): 132–135.
Chant, Sylvia, and Cathy McIlwaine. 2008. *Geographies of Development*. London: University of London Press.
Dammasch, Sabine. n.d. *The System of Bretton Woods: A Lesson from History*. Retrieved on 12 July 2018 from http://www.hiddenmysteries.org/money/policy/b-woods.pdf
Dasgupta, Biplab. 1997. SAP: Issues and Conditionalities: A Global Review. *Economic and Political Weekly* 32 (20/21): 1091–1095+1097–1104.
Fritz-Krockow, Bernhard, and Parmeshwar Ramlogan, eds. 2007. *International Monetary Fund Handbook: Its Functions, Policies, and Operations*. Washington, DC: International Monetary Fund.
Harrod, Roy. 1972. Problems Perceived in the International System. In *Bretton Woods Revisited*, ed. A.L. Keith Acheson, John F. Chant, and F.J. Martin. Prachowny Toronto: University of Toronto Press.
Heidhues, Franz, and Gideon Obare. 2011. Lessons from Structural Adjustment Programmes and their Effects in Africa. *Quarterly Journal of International Agriculture* 50 (1): 55–64.
Hodd, Michael. 1987. Africa, the IMF and the World Bank. *African Affairs* 86 (344): 331–342.
International Monetary Fund. 2016. *Articles of Agreement*. Washington, DC: International Monetary Fund.
Ismi, Asad. 2004. Impoverishing a Continent: The World Bank and the IMF in Africa. Canadian Centre for Policy Alternatives. Retrieved on 10 October 2018 from http://www.halifaxinitiative.org/updir/ImpoverishingAContinent.pdf
Kindleberger, Charles P., and Bruce Herrick. 1977. *Economic Development*. New York: McGraw-Hill.
Lyakurwa, William. 2005. Sub-Saharan African Countries' Development Strategies: The Role of the Bretton Woods Institutions. In *Helping the Poor? The IMF and Low-Income Countries*, ed. Jan Joost Teunissen and Age Akkerman. The Hague: FONDAD.
Marshall, Katherine. 2008. *The World Bank: From Reconstruction to Development to Equity*. New York: Routledge.
McKinnon, Ronald I. 2010. *Beggar-Thy-Neighbor Interest Rate Policies*. Stanford University. Retrieved on 17 September 2018 from http://citeseer.ist.psu.edu/viewdoc/download?doi=10.1.1.364.5619&rep=rep1&type=pdf
Nafziger, E. Wayne. 2006. *Economic Development*. Cambridge: Cambridge University Press.
Officer, Lawrence H. 1990. The International Monetary Fund. *Proceedings of the Academy of Political Science* 37 (4): 28–36.
Osabu-Kle, Daniel Tetteh. 2000. Politics of One-Side Adjustment in Africa. *Journal of Black Studies* 30 (4): 515–533.

Reedik, Reet. 2002. International Monetary Fund and Economic Policy Surveillance. *Kroon & Economy.* 1: 43–49.
Saner, Raymond, and Ricardo Guilherme. 2008. IMF Conditionalities for the Least Developed Countries. *G-24 Policy Brief 19.* Retrieved on 17 September 2018 from https://www.g24.org/wp-content/uploads/2016/01/G24-Policy-Brief-19.pdf
SAPRIN. 2004. *Structural Adjustment: The Sapri Report the Policy Roots of Economic Crisis, Poverty and Inequality.* New York: Zed Books.
Seers, Dudley. 1969. The Meaning of Development. *Institute of Development Studies Communication Series,* No. 44: 1–28. Retrieved on 10 August 2018 from https://www.ids.ac.uk/files/dmfile/themeaningofdevelopment.pdf
Sen, Amartya. 1999. *Development as Freedom.* New York: Anchor Books.
———. 1999. *Development as Freedom.* New York: A. Knopf.
Steger, Manfred B., and Ravi K. Roy. 2010. *Neoliberalism: A Very Short Introduction.* Oxford: Oxford University Press.
Stiglitz, Joseph E. 2002. *Globalization and its Discontents.* New York: W. W. Norton & Company, Inc..
Tenney, Sarah, and Norman K. Humphreys. 2011. *Historical Dictionary of the International Monetary Fund.* 3rd ed. Toronto: The Scarecrow Press, Inc..
Thirlwall, A.P. 2008. Development as Economic Growth. In *The Companion to Development Studies,* ed. V. Desai and R.B. Potter, 2nd ed. New York: Oxford.
Todaro, Michael P., and Stephen C. Smith. 2012. *Economic Development.* 11th ed. Massachusetts: Pearson Education, Inc..
United Nations. 2014. *Economic Development in Africa Report 2014: Catalysing Investment for Transformative Growth in Africa.* Geneva: United Nations.
Vreeland, James Raymond. 2007. *The International Monetary Fund: Politics of Conditional Lending.* New York: Routledge.
Wade, Robert Hunter. 2002. US Hegemony and the World Bank: The Fight Over People and Ideas. *Review of International Political Economy* 9 (2): 201–229.
Williamson, John. 1980. Economic "Theory and International Monetary Fund Policies". *Carnegie-Rochester Conference Series on Public Policy* 13: 255–278.
Women for a Just and Healthy Planet. 1618. Action Against Bretton Woods. *Economic and Political Weekly* 27 (1994): 29.
Woods, Ngaire. 2006. *The Globalizers: the IMF, the World Bank and Their Borrowers.* London: Cornell University Press.
World Bank. 1991. *The Challenge of Development. World Development Report.* Washington, DC: International Bank for Reconstruction and Development.
———. 2007. *Guide to the World Bank.* Washington, DC: World Bank.

CHAPTER 21

The Ethics of State Capture: Dangote and the Nigerian State

Saheedat Adetayo

Introduction

State capture came to the fore as a phenomenal discourse in state politics and economies during the period of political transition of a large number of states in Central and Eastern Europe from communism to democracy and the liberal market system.[1] The experiences of these European states also mirrored those of the African states just transitioning out of colonialism with a fundamental baggage of a state and its apparatuses that became factored into the colonial and postcolonial production processes. With the African experience of the state as a means of production, the idea of state capture has therefore been in existence long before it became resuscitated most recently as a significant political term for understanding the relationship between the state and its officials and private individuals or firms. It received its most recent adumbration by the World Bank in the year 2000 to refer to the situation in transitional countries that previously belonged to the Soviet Union. In the course of transiting, these states devised and adopted a variety of strategies, which resulted in some differences in the political and economical trajectories of each state. This period, however, saw to the emergence of different forms of corruption as a global threat. One of these forms of corruption is what Hellman, Jones and Kaufmann identified as "state capture".

State capture, one of the most pervasive forms of corruption, refers to a situation whereby "companies, institutions or powerful individuals use corruption such as the buying of laws, amendments, decrees or sentences, as well as illegal contributions to political parties and candidates, to influence and shape a country's policy, legal environment and economy to their own interests".[2] State

S. Adetayo (✉)
University of Ibadan, Ibadan, Nigeria

capture gained more topicality in political discourse in March 2016 with the incidence of the illegal business relations between Jacob Zuma, the then President of South Africa, and the Gupta family. With this South African incidence, state capture has arrived as a significant political concept in the global political, business and scholarly community.

This chapter not only discusses the theoretical and practical features of state capture but also attempts to interrogate its analytical utility within the Nigerian political context. The chapter is structured into three parts. The first part is a conceptual clarification of the subject matter. This part examines a number of definitions and analyses of the concept "state capture" according to different political theorists, economists and ethicists. It also analyses state capture as a global phenomenon with special attention to capitalist and transitional societies. The second part explores the specific incidence of state capture in South Africa, and the possible insights that this might yield. The third part then interrogates the application of this concept in the Nigerian context by querying the relationship between the foremost capitalist in the state, Alhaji Aliko Dangote, and the Nigerian government and public officials. This chapter concludes that there exists a kind of state capture in Nigeria and it also draws on the ethical implications of state capturing to the Nigerian state.

State Capture: Definitions and Conceptualisations

The abuse and misappropriation of state allocations and resources is not a new phenomenon in governance. The emergence of state capture on the global political landscape appears to be one out of the several manifestations corruption has taken in global politics. State capture refers to a situation in which an identifiable group of interests—leaders of a political party or members of a particular social group—secure control over the government and the public administration in such a way that their dominance is secure and unlikely to be challenged in the foreseeable future.[3] This implies that the state's autonomous right to enact laws and regulations is conceded by the public officials to a minute number of people in the state in such a way that it ceases to function well on a broad social level. The state ceases to perform its broad social function because it has been narrowed to the interest of a particular set of private individuals.

In the immediate post-independence period, African Marxists were particularly engaged with understanding of the nature of the African state and its colonial legacies. They were concerned with the analysis of the emergence of the state and its apparatuses from the dynamics that motivated the colonial state structure, as well as with the postcolonial logic of the postcolonial African state. One of the immediate issues that burst the euphoria of independence for most African states was the unravelling of the political legacy of colonialism. The statist orientation of Africa's colonial experience ensured that the absolutely powerful but arbitrary colonial state wielded enormous powers over the means of production in the colonies. It was this legacy—the identity of the

African state as the means of production—that necessitated the concern of African Marxists. Claude Ake particularly traced the trajectory that led from the absolutism and arbitrariness of the colonial state to the emergence of the postcolonial African state on the foundation of the effectiveness of political power as the weapon of governance and instrument of accumulation. According to him, the political power sought by the African nationalist elites was at a great cost:

> They created not only strong divisions within their own ranks but strong antipathies and exclusivity in society. As always, the exclusivity of the competing political formations increased the premium on Political power and the intensity of political competition. Political intensity was further reinforced by the tendency to use state power for accumulation. This practice was associated with the weak material base of the new political leaders, who had been economically marginalized by the discriminatory economic policies of the colonial regime. Even when they came to power, they had little experience of entrepreneurial activity and little or no capital. Invariably they were obliged to explore the one leverage they had: control of state power to strengthen their material base.[4]

This nature of the postcolonial African state, as well as the weak material base of the national elite, led to an increasing statist appropriation of the economy. It opened up a vista of possibilities on how state power could facilitate the accumulative tendencies of the political elite. This understanding of the state as the means of production facilitates an early understanding of what state capture means.

In the year 2000, a set of researchers at the World Bank used the term "state capture" to refer to the efforts by business groups—firms or corporations—to determine or shape the "basic rules of the game", that is, the laws and regulations that might have an impact on their operations—investment codes, for example.[5] This perspective introduces businessmen, large-scale entrepreneurs, investors and capitalists into the list of possible state captors (or capturers) who form dalliance with state officers in order to influence laws and regulations in favour of their private concerns. It should be noted, however, that state capturing is not merely about private individuals persuading officials to circumvent or not to apply the laws that govern their operations and businesses. It is also basically more about the formulation of rules than breaking of them. In this sense, the capturer (entrepreneurs, institutions and powerful individuals) forms an alliance with public officials in order to influence the formulation of the rules that govern the undertakings of its competitors such that the capturer benefits immensely from a protected domain in which its operations are exempted over a long time from these rules.[6]

State capture can appear in different forms, can operate at different levels, can be conducted at different levels of government and can involve different private individuals or companies; hence, there are ways in which state capture can be distinguished.[7] State capture can be described based on the type of institution that is being captured, that is, whether the legislature, judiciary, executive, regulatory agencies, public works departments or ministries. Although all types of institutions are susceptible to capturing, more often than not, it is the political decision-making institutions that are more susceptible, that is, the legislature and the executive.[8] State capture can also be distinguished based on the types of captors. The different types of captors (or capturers) include private organisations, political elites, prominent officials or interest groups.[9]

A third type of distinction has to do with the depth of the capture, either the capturing of a single organisation or government department, or the capture of all organisations or government departments.[10] The former is regarded as *local capture* while the latter is regarded as *global capture*. Local capture occurs when "only some public and private organisations enter into a capture relationship with their 'islands' which are relatively autonomous", while global capture occurs when the "captured organisations are linked to each other and a national level elite controls them".[11]

Mtimka identifies a fourth type of state capture which he refers to as the systemic and predatory types of capturing. *Systemic capture* refers to the "impact institutions have on a state's internal and external sovereignty, thereby preventing it from pursuing policies of its choice other than those beneficial to powerful interests or sectors". *Predatory state capture* occurs when individuals or small groups "hold specific political figures to ransom" and bully them for personal gain.[12] A fifth distinction can be drawn from Innes' characterisation of state capture into two types: the party state capture and the corporate state capture. *Party state capture* refers to the re-politicisation of the state by political parties to achieve political monopoly. *Corporate party capture*, on the other hand, refers to the exertion of power by private individuals to undermine legitimate canals of political influence mainly for private advantage.[13] State capture can also be distinguished based on the frequency of the incidence of capturing. A state could be captured by occasional nonconformity to the rules in order to profit private interests and public officials. This is referred to as *occasional state capture*. The *partial state capture* occurs when "there are averages of corrupt contracts and activities but this is not the norm and the state is in the main focused on achieving its developmental objectives". A fully captured state is "when high levels of corruption directed at the dominant private interest represents the norm and the developmental agenda is subordinated to corrupt exchanges".[14]

In conceptualising what state capture implies, ideologies founded on the notions of state, economy and politics also play significant roles. Neoliberalism, for instance, conceives state capture as an incidence that occurs basically because "policymakers are inherently corrupt and as such, they use state power for rent allocation and patronage". For neoliberals, rent allocation and patronage facilitates state capture by militating against an efficient allocation of savings and investments. And by so doing, they hamper economic development.[15] On the other hand, Marxists believe that the state is perpetually under capture because it is always under the control of a dominant group, class or coalition whose interests the state is meant to serve.[16]

Neo-institutional economics, however, presents a contrary view. This perspective sees the intervention of the state institutions in market transaction as a necessary condition for addressing market failure. State capture, therefore, occurs when the state institutions are weak or not independent enough to enact rules and laws, or, as the African experience has shown, when the ruling elites reject the capitalist rationality while deploying state power to facilitate the appropriation of wealth. For the neo-institutional economists, a strong state with minimal government authority, and that is able to enforce property and contractual rights or a developmental state with an independent professional bureaucracy, is the ideal state.[17] It is, however, worthy of note that the notions of state capture tendered by the neoliberals and neo-institutional economists did not take into consideration the private sector actors, that is, the capitalists, the entrepreneurs, the firms and companies. These set of people are critical to our understanding of what state capture is.

There are some features that are peculiar to state capture and are pointers to the fact that a state has been captured. Fundamentally, the motive for state capture is to subvert public interest by distorting laws, policies, regulations and decrees to achieve undue advantage or private gain.[18] It is not only about the implementation of rules and laws. Rather, it also seeks the distortion of the formulation of regulations that will be fair to all in the state. Secondly, the main targets of capture are usually the formal state establishments which perform significant roles in the formation of laws, regulations, decrees and policies. These institutions include the parliament, the judiciary, the legislature and other regulatory bodies. Thirdly, state captors are, more often than not, individuals and corporations in the private sector such as business persons, plutocrats, firms and groups. Lastly, the occurrence of state capture is archetypally in the context of transitional or post-conflict countries, although not limited to these countries.

State Capture: Occurrences in Global Economies and States

> The flaw of the Czech, Slovak, Latvian and Bulgarian systems compared to those of Poland, Hungary, Estonia, Slovenia and Lithuania was that they came into their transitions semi-formed in terms of political competition. In contrast to the higher performing cases, their legacies of relatively weak dissident oppositions and hence hard-line communist parties had prevented the emergence of reformed ex-communist social democratic parties to play the disciplining of strong opponents.[19]

Although the literature is scarce with regard to the occurrence of state capture in non-transitional countries, there are some pointers to the fact that state capture did occur in developed countries. One significant and most obvious demonstration of this comes with the large lobby and special interest groups, from the National Rifle Association (NRA) to the Republican Jewish Coalition (RJC), that not only exert enormous influence on the American legislature but essentially captured the policy-making dynamics of the United States. The close ties between private businesses and the government of these developed countries are suggestive of some ulterior economic interests. The hastiness and largeness of privatisation of public corporations also make room for the major politicians in each local space to forge connections with foreign investors to enable them acquire personal stakes.[20] This is especially so, for instance, with the neoliberalisation of economies in the African context.

In Singapore, there are some researches that show evidences of the capture of policies and regulations by the elite and powerful business owners. The research conducted by the Tax Justice Network shows that the financial services sector of the country exercises a strong influence on the policy- and law-making processes in the country.[21] In South Korea, there exist some controversial relationships between the politicians and private businesses. Aside the fact that these private conglomerates have a high control and influence over the regulations made by the state, records show that they are also beneficiaries of the government bailouts on different occasions.[22]

In European countries, the existence of state capture is often debated in the contexts of the obscure lobbying practices and politicians' dependence on the donations from private finances to support their election campaigns.[23] In the Americas, researches show that multinational corporations have become exceedingly powerful and have been employing various means such as lobbying, the revolving door and campaign financing to exert control over the rules governing their operations, as well as over the allocation of public resources in several sectors.[24] There are also reports by the Financial Crisis Inquiry Commission indicating that the financial industry in the state played a major role in weakening regulatory constraints on institutions, markets and products.[25]

STATE CAPTURE: THE SOUTH AFRICAN CONTEXT

Media outbursts in March 2016 led to the probing of the relationship between the South African President Jacob Zuma and the wealthy, Indian-born, South African business moguls known as the Gupta family by the public and political analysts. The media reports alleged that the relationship between the President and the Gupta family has evolved into a "state capture". The Gupta family was accused of wielding undue influence over the presidency and the entire state machineries. The accusation holds that the Gupta brothers were colluding with Zuma in the removal and appointment of government ministers, as well as the directors of state-owned enterprises (SOEs), and leveraging on their relationship with Zuma to get preferential treatment in state contracts, access to state-provided finance and in the award of business licences. The Gupta brothers, whose business empire spans from computer equipment and media to mining, aviation and technology, arrived in South Africa from India shortly before the first non-racial democratic elections in 1994.

In October 2016, a report was published by the Public Protector calling for the

> investigation into the complaints of alleged improper and unethical conduct by the president and other state functionaries relating to alleged improper relationships and involvement of the Gupta family in the removal and appointment of ministers and directors of State Owned Entities (SOEs) resulting in improper and possibly corrupt award of state contracts and benefits to the Gupta family's business.[26]

The call for the investigation sprang from the complaints lodged against the president by Father S. Mayebe on behalf of the Dominican Order, on 18 March 2016 (the first complainant); Mr Mmusi Maimane, the Leader of the Democratic Alliance and Leader of the Opposition in parliament, on 18 March 2016 (the second complainant); and a member of the public, whose name was withheld, on 22 April 2016 (the third complainant). In summary, the three complainants requested for investigations into

> (a) the veracity of allegations that the Deputy Minister of Finance Mr Jonas and Ms Mentor (presumably as chairpersons of the Portfolio Committee of Public Enterprises) were offered cabinet positions by the Gupta family; (b) whether the appointment of Mr Van Rooyen to Minister of Finance was known by the Gupta family beforehand; (c) media allegations that two Gupta aligned senior advisors were appointed into the National Treasury, alongside Mr Van Rooyen, without proper procedure; and (d) all business dealings of the Gupta family with government departments and SOEs to determine whether there were irregularities, undue enrichment, corruptions and undue influence in the awarding of contracts, mining licenses, government advertising in the New Age newspaper, and any other government services.[27]

Since Zuma was the head of the South African government, his relationship with the Guptas and the concurrent undue influences the latter wielded on the administration led political, business and scholarly communities to consider it as a case of state capture. Before the media outbursts and the petitions, the Guptas first entered the consciousness of South Africans in 2010 when they allegedly became involved in a "dubious potential iron-ore mining deal". With this deal, the Guptas, with the help of the government, acquired parts of the mining rights to an iron ore mine. Concurrently, their intimacy with some government ministers like Malusi Gigaba and Naledi Pandor came into the open.[28] The Guptas and the Zumas reportedly met for the first time in 2003 and the alliance was concretised with the employment of Zuma's wife, Bongi Ngema-Zuma, as the communications officer, and the appointment of his daughter and son, Duduzile and Duduzane, as directors of a number of Gupta companies at different times.[29] The employment and appointment should not have been an issue but for the open and blatant recommendation that Zuma gave the Guptas on his trip to India in 2010. Kalim Rajab, an occasional public commentator, noted that Zuma explicitly made it clear to potential investors that "the most suitable of channelling [their investments] would be through the Gupta family".[30] This outright show of support for these private business moguls and the several allegations against the Zuma-Gupta alliance made it more essential for the Public Protector to probe into this case and establish the veracity of the reports.

Despite the outcry and the call for Zuma to step down, it is worth mentioning that some persons within the ruling party, the African National Congress (ANC), defended him and supported his relationship with the Gupta family. Amongst these were the national leaderships of the African National Congress Youth League (ANCYL) and the African National Congress Women's League (ANCWL).[31] In defence of the Gupta-Zuma alliance, there is the view that the relationship was deliberately blown out of proportion by the local and international media. It was argued that the Guptas do not share any form of patriotism with the local and dominant Western-based media companies; hence, the reason for the exaggeration of the case. In 2016, the *Black Opinion* asserted that the recent exaggerated negative reporting about the corrupt activities of the Gupta family is less motivated by the desire to arrest corruption, but much driven by business jealousy of the White-owned companies and their Western-based international partners.

Characteristically, the post-apartheid South African economy was dominated by the emerging Black elites, Whites and their Euro-American partners. These elites established new companies that took over the South African markets. Therefore, it was in the best interests of these traditional business corporates of the South African economic landscape to criminalise, demonise and undermine the entrepreneurial efforts of their competitors.[32] Another reason presented for the overhyping of the Gupta-Zuma alliance is the outright preferential treatment to its Brazil, Russia, India, China and South Africa (BRICS) allies in trade matters, compared to traditional trading partners such as the United States and the European Union.[33] Defenders of the Gupta-Zuma alliance argued that the obvious reorientation of Pretoria's foreign policy from the West in favour of countries from the East is a development that cannot be overlooked by the Euro-American business moguls and their local allies.[34] It is from this backdrop that it was argued that these Western countries may be using local and international media to discredit the South African government and the Gupta business moguls (of Eastern origin) in order to prepare the grounds for a change of administration.[35] However, while Shai emphatically argues that the Guptas are not completely free of the allegation of state capture, he nonetheless contends that the Zuma-Gupta alliance was demonised and blown out of proportion by local and international media which, he claims, may be serving the interests of the traditional Western-owned businesses.[36]

This position was defended by some Black Consciousness movements, notably the Black First Land First (BLF) movement founded by Andile Mngxitama.

In defending this argument, Mngxitama, who believes strongly that "White monopoly capitalism renders the black majority powerless", posited that the Gupta-Zuma alliance was a deliberate

> strategy to look more towards the East. ... He is involved in what I call a "parallel power praxis", which is essentially about abandoning the state and its pro-white structures, which are enforced by constitutional principles to ensure white power, irrespective of who has the majority in Parliament. Zuma seems to be running a parallel system to the modern pro-white liberal state. The ruling party, having failed to transform the colonial state, is abandoning it and finding ways to circumvent it through parallel processes. Mbeki's presidency was about being good at running the inherited apartheid state and we got no meaningful result from it. Zuma's presidency is about creating a parallel power to this state and the jury is out on its impact. As the main part of the "parallel power structure", the Guptas by all accounts have been beating white capital at its own game. The labyrinth of business networks and deals that seem to be facilitated or funded by the state frustrates the interests of white capital.[37]

He stresses further that the call for the Guptas to leave South Africa and for Zuma to step down is

> dangerous as it involves the demagogic mobilisation of anti-Indian stereotypes and feeds into xenophobic tropes to organise the most backward sentiments in society and deflect attention from the real source of South African problem, which is white capital created from colonialism and apartheid.[38]

The South African case constitutes the most prominent of the African experience with the idea of state capture. But there have also been some instances in some other African states. In 1992, the Nigerian media reported the alliance between the then military head of state General Sani Abacha and Gilbert Chagoury, the head of the wealthy Lebanese Chagoury Group, with immense business concerns in Nigeria. The Lebanese were involved in various sectors of the Nigerian economy, from telecommunication and energy to the hospitality business and trade. Specifically, Gilbert Chagoury owned many business concerns in Nigeria, and particularly received strategic oil franchises and development deals from the Abacha regime. The relationship between Abacha and Chagoury came to light in 1998 when the Swiss Judiciary convicted the latter of money laundering charges. Chagoury was penalised with a fine of US $600,000 and asked to return US $65 million to Nigeria. With Aliko Dangote, the issue of the relationship between the state and private individuals becomes even more critical.

Dangote and the Nigerian State

Aliko Dangote, the owner of the largest African-owned conglomerate in Africa, was listed as the number one billionaire in Africa and the 136th in the world by *Forbes* in 2019. Earlier in 2018, Dangote was listed as the 66th most powerful person in the world.[39] This is the profile of the Nigerian-born chief executive officer (CEO) of the Dangote Group whose net worth as of July 2019 is pegged at US $9.8 billion.[40] Aside being born in a wealthy business-inclined family, Dangote's entrepreneurial skills have helped in no little way in making him the richest man in Africa. While writing on the versatility of the Dangote Group, Simon Allison, the cross-continental journalist, asserts that

> the Dangote group has substantial shares in just about every sector of the Nigerian economy. It makes salt, sugar, rice, pasta, flour and fruit juices; it supplies steel, cement and packaging; it buys and sells property, and holds a 3G communication licence; it manages ports; it operates a 5,000-truck-strong haulage fleet. If you can think of it, the Dangote group is probably doing it, and making plenty of money in the process.[41]

Moses Ochonu, while analysing the paradoxical nature of the Dangote's entrepreneurial ingenuity, stresses that

> Most of Dangote's investments reflect the spirit of Afrocapitalism and entrepreneurial pan-Nigerianism that I fully endorse. He raises most of the capital for his projects from Nigerian and African financial sources. An Afrocapitalist and pan-Nigerian investment model disavows Euro-America as the only source of large investment capital. It departs from the dominant narrative of "attracting" Foreign Direct Investment (FDI), a euphemism for letting expatriate investors flex their financial muscle to dictate the terms of investment on the continent. This model leverages Africa's own resources and funds to make investments by outsiders supplementary, and marginal outcomes. Africa needs more indigenous entrepreneurs, big and small, and such business innovators, regardless of which country they are based, should see Africa as their business habitat and field of play—this is the spirit of Afrocapitalism.[42]

However, the paradox that Ochonu hints at derives from situating the Dangote Group's entrepreneurial creativity and ingenuity within a larger perspective of economic and national dynamics in Africa and especially Nigeria. While it is incontrovertible that Dangote represents the essence of Afrocapitalism in its willingness to make Africa the very epicentre of its business dealings, and while it is also the case that the group enjoys what Ochonu calls "an economy of emotional commitment" which brings African investors like the Dangote Group into some critical partnerships with African states in their bids to resolve the African economic impasse, there should be no masking of the fact that this economy of emotional commitment opens the way for some penumbral economic dynamics that borders on unethical financial and economic dealings.

For Ochonu, however we see Dangote's business ingenuity and possible patriotic business culture, there is no denying that some level of patronage and "corrupt entanglements" must be involved. Dangote has been accused repeatedly by business critics, economists and political analysts of using his influence with successive governments to ban imports by his competitors, pushing port authorities to halt rivals' shipments and using sharp price drops to put them out of business.[43] In substantiating these accusations, it pays to take a retrospective look into the relationship between Dangote and the Nigerian government since the inception of her democracy. Quite curiously, Dangote admits of his friendship with several recent presidents of Nigeria, though he denies receiving any favour from them.

Olusegun Obasanjo came in as the democratically elected president of Nigeria in 1999 as an end to the years of kleptocratic military regimes. But in the run-up for a second term, Obasanjo had a fallout with his deputy, Atiku Abubakar, who doubles as the party's money man, over the latter's attempt to succeed him as the president after the first term. Obasanjo was thus left with no other option than to seek financial support from some other money bags through other fundraising techniques. Then, Dangote the multibillionaire came to mind. In the words of the former Governor of Kaduna State, Nasir El-Rufai:

> Obasanjo had to resort to making money from other sources and that was how Aliko Dangote came into prominence in the government. For 1999 to 2003, nobody heard of Dangote having anything to do with the federal government in any significant way.[44]

Thus, Obasanjo's quest for financial support paved the way for Dangote's entrance into the political landscape of Nigeria. Obasanjo, in paying back this favour, granted

> a series of import duty waivers and subsidies to the businessman as the latter expended his investment repertoire into cement production. Under Obasanjo, Dangote's quest to buy up poorly performing competitors such as Benue Cement was made easy by a friendly government peopled by allies in power. The businessman's desire to establish a virtual monopoly in the cement sector became a reality under that government. His competitors, such as Ibeto Cement, which lacked access to power languished and hibernated under the weight of competitive edge granted Dangote by subsidies, waivers and cheap acquisitions facilitated by his friends in government.[45]

While the Dangote Group covers a wide range of industries, the bulk of its profits come from its cement business which, of course, derives from lack of competition, monopoly and monopsony that the group enjoys. It is noteworthy that Nigeria already had a reasonably vibrant cement sector before Dangote plunged in and established a virtual monopoly in a short period. The Dangote Group therefore enjoys unfair advantages and governmental favours that are not open to its other competitors which give way to the liquidation of these other companies. Thus, whilst leveraging on this well-cemented relationship which he sustained despite the change of administration, Dangote successfully built his business empire. He sustains this relationship by lavishing money on the People's Democratic Party (PDP) which was the ruling party for sixteen consecutive years. The more unfortunate fact about Dangote's business strategy is that he does not just undermine his competitors, he also controls supply and as such determines prices which in no little way hurts the customers, the citizens of the African countries, whose economies he is purportedly promoting through indigenous investments.

> In June 2016, the World Bank published a report examining the impact and costs of lack of competition in a number of industries in Africa. They found that African cement prices averaged $9.57 per 50kg compared to $3.25 globally. Put another way, Africans paid 183% more than people around the world for the same product. The report also highlights how the Nigerian government had been phasing out import licenses for cement beginning in 2012 when Dangote ramped up cement production in Nigeria as well as the Central Bank of Nigeria banning the use of foreign exchange for cement imports.[46]

It would have been rightly assumed that a company that enjoys 183% gains above other global cement producers will be charged an even-handed tax rate to excuse its excess profits. On the contrary, however, as exploitative as Dangote Cement prices are, the company still enjoys an almost irrelevant tax rate. Feyi Fawehinmi spells it out as follows:

> Between 2010 and 2015 when Dangote cement earned around 1 trillion naira ($6 billion) in profits, it paid only 12 billion naira ($72 million) in taxes—a tax rate of just over 1%. It has done this through a particularly aggressive interpretation of a Nigerian investment incentive known as "Pioneer Status". … However, the law was described as "most abused in certain quarters" by Deloitte. No one has taken greater advantage than Dangote Cement. It has claimed pioneer status multiple times on the same plants by applying for a new exemption each time it extends the plant.[47]

Thus, the business magnate enjoys unfettered waivers, subsidies, monopoly, monopsony, price control, high profits, insignificant tax rate and preferential foreign exchange allocation. It was assumed that the change of administration and, subsequently, the ruling party from the PDP to the All Progressives Congress (APC) in May 2015 will effect a change in the relationship between Dangote and the government and its consequent impact on policy-making. This optimism has however not been justified by the evidence. Barely three months into the Buhari-led administration, the Vice President, Prof. Yemi Osinbajo, led a government delegation to Zambia for the commissioning of a Dangote Cement plant. Like the PDP-led administration, the Buhari/APC administration soon got entangled in this web of a questionable relationship with Dangote when the latter began his refinery-building project. The refinery project, of course, appears to be a good, timely and strategic investment particularly for a country that is in dire need of economic revitalisation and growth and with years of record of persistent fuel scarcity. However, the secrecy built into the deals, including the dynamics of government waivers, foreign exchange allocation, subsidies and so on, are indications that Dangote has concretised his business legacy with the new administration.

On 23 July 2019, the Governor of the Central Bank of Nigeria (CBN), Godwin Emefiele, disclosed the federal government's consideration on the banning of the importation of milk on the basis that it can be produced in the country to grow the economy.[48] He stated that the focus of this consideration remains forex savings, job creation and investments in local milk production.[49] This consideration, according to him, is because the amount of dollars spent on importing milk annually, if injected into the society, will boost the economy. This, of course, is a laudable effort. This step would have been taken as a people-oriented and economic developmental strategy but for the fact that the next day after this declaration by the CBN governor, Dangote announced his intent to go into dairy farming in order to ensure food security, to cut importation costs and to create jobs. Whilst it cannot be established yet that Dangote intends another state-capturing movement through the creation of a milk industry, the spontaneity of his declaration of intention sequel to the announcement by the CBN governor remains questionable and has generated a number of reactions, in the social media space, by Nigerians who believe that the declaration of interest by Dangote is another mean by which the Nigerian government will further feather Dangote's nest through the ban on the importation of milk.

It would seem inescapable, therefore, that Dangote, his business group and business model, is a very terrible demonstration of what has been called "patrimonial monopoly capitalism" in Nigeria. It participates in the continuum of corrupt practices because it easily amounts to a manipulation of the state's financial wealth in ways that favour a few private individuals.[50] In ethical terms, patrimonial monopoly capitalism confers an unfair advantage on wealthy business concerns over others without such questionable access to government funding and protection.

However, is this analysis sufficient to inscribe Dangote's business model as a specie of state capture? But one way to arrive at a suitable answer is to understand the nature of the firm in Africa. Wariboko (2004) suggests three specific understandings of the African firm that speak fundamentally to how it operates vis-à-vis the African state. The first has to do with the relationship between the firm and its owner. The link between the two is mediated by the kinship dynamics in Africa that ensures that the firm is entrenched within a communal framework of families and relatives. This immediately puts the owner of the firm in a delicate position where he or she has to walk a tight rope between the necessity of profit making and that of meeting the obligations to the family. For Wariboko, "One way African managers handle this conflict is by demarcating their value domain to emphasize one norm over the other at a particular moment in time, allowing decisions to fall somewhere in between the two ends. Indeed, management is a virtuoso balancing act between these two opposing forces."[51] The second contextual understanding of the African firm has to do with its capacity to deploy coercive power in the pursuit of its objectives and in the repression of opposition. In this regard, the African firm functions as a state "in the sense of its control of coercive forces and the provision of public goods".[52] The third understanding of the African firm derives from its real relationship with political power and the apparatuses of state. For Wariboko,

> Anyone who is familiar with doing business in Africa will easily agree that it is risky and dangerous to do business without the patronage of the state. This is because not only is the power of the state absolute and arbitrary, but the government often controls a large portion of the society's surplus as well. In this kind of an environment, economic success and personal security and welfare depend on access to state power.[53]

This automatically transforms corruption into a useful management practice that allows the private enterprises and individuals to deploy state resources for private concerns. Wariboko argues that corruption results from the

> limited development of productive forces and commodity exchange, as well as the behavior of African capitalists. Corruption is particularly linked to the limited commodification of the continent's economy, which makes the appropriation of surplus by non-formally equal exchange possible, and the limited autonomy of the state. When exchange and appropriation of surplus in a capitalist society is not done by the market, through the mediation of commodity exchange, surplus has to be appropriated by political power, at the point of making political decisions to collect for the state to transfer resources to it.[54]

From this contextual analysis of the African firm, we immediately come to the fundamental background from which to view Dangote's relationship with the Nigerian state. It would seem therefore that it is but a short step from this explanation and the understanding of what state capture means. Contrary to the earlier argument for Dangote's Afrocapitalist credentials, there is no doubt that his access to special import licences, preferential tax rates, laws to ban certain imports, special access to foreign exchange, supreme access to politicians, the state apparatuses like the Central Bank of Nigeria and price gauging all represent the irrefutable demonstration of state capture.

Even if the idea of Afrocapitalism provides an argument for the capacity of the African firm to engender internal economic development, justification for its fundamental utility would still have to rest on the question of the extent to which Dangote's business strategy has benefitted the Nigerian state. This immediately raises the idea of corporate social responsibility. But here again, we come short against the conceptual and contextual nature of the African firm. The idea of the public or of the social has meanings that have been inflected by contextual peculiarity in Africa. Peter Ekeh's idea of the two publics in Africa demonstrates that the concept of the public is split between the primordial loyalty and civic imperatives.[55] The answer to this question therefore hangs on specific empirical data. One of such would derive from, first, the extent to which the Dangote's employment framework has undermined Nigeria's unemployment statistics; and second, the extent to which Dangote's industrial practice has affected Nigeria's infrastructural development. There is no doubt however that Dangote's business culture crosses the legal line, and violates ethical imperatives, at several points.

Conclusion

This chapter examines the concept of state capture, its occurrences in global economies, the South African occurrence and the business strategies of Nigeria's Aliko Dangote. With his well-cemented relationship with the government of Nigeria, Aliko Dangote has been able to influence public actors in the making, modification and implementation of government policies. Recall that while conceptualising the term "state capture", we spelt out its different types and ways of manifestation. Whilst there may be subtle nuances between the South African Gupta-Zuma alliance and the Nigerian incidence by the Dangote-Federal Government of Nigeria friendship, there is no doubt that both incidences manifest terrible unethical business dynamics. Yet, while the Gupta-Zuma alliance has been dubbed as an instance of state capture, and has received more media, scholarly and legal attention—both local and international—the Dangote-Nigerian government alliance is more amenable to a deeper understanding of how the nature of the African state and the African firm makes the idea of state capture an almost inevitable means by which firms like the Dangote Group could survive such hostile business environments represented in various places in postcolonial Africa.

Notes

1. Hellman, J., Jones, G., and Kaufmann, D. 2000. Seize the state, seize the day: state capture, corruption and influence in transition. *The World Bank*.
2. Maira Martini. 2014. "State capture: an overview". *Transparency International*. Retrieved from tihelpdesk@transparency.org. on 13 June 2019. P1
3. Edwards, D. 2017. "Corruption and state capture under two regimes in Guyana". Working paper at the University of West Indies, Cave Hill, Barbados.
4. Claude Ake. 1996. *Democracy and Development in Africa*, Washington, D. C.: Brookings Institution, 5–6.
5. Lodge T. "State capture; conceptual clarifications". In Meirotti M. and Masterson G. (Eds.). 2018. *State capture in Africa*. South Africa: EISA.

6. Rijkers, B., Freund, C., and Nucifora, A. 2014. All in the family: state capture in Tunisia. *World Bank Policy Research Working Paper* 6810.
7. Dassah, M. O. 2018. "Theoretical analysis of state capture and its manifestation as a governance problem in South Africa", *The Journal of Transdisciplinary Research in Southern Africa* 14(1), a473, P 4. Available at https://doi.org/10.4102/td.v14i1.473.
8. Richter, S. 2016. "The 'Untouchables': state capture in post-conflict countries". Retrieved from http://www.afk-web.de/fileadmin/afk-web.de/data/zentral/dokumente/AFK-Kolluquium_2016/Paper_AFK_Solveig_Richter.pdf. P 8.
9. Dassah, M. O. 2018. "Theoretical analysis of state capture and its manifestation as a governance problem in South Africa". P 4.
10. Fazekas, M. and Toth, I. J. 2014. "From corruption to state capture: A new analytical framework with empirical applications from Hungary". Working Paper Series: CRCB-WP2014:01, Corruption Research Center. *Budapest and Government Transparency Institute, Budapest*. P3.
11. Fazekas and Toth, 2014. "From corruption to state capture: A new analytical framework with empirical applications from Hungary". P3–5.
12. Mtimka, O. 2016. Why state capture is a regressive step for any society. *The Conversation*. Retrieved 15 June 2019 from https://theconversation.com/why-state-capture-is-a-regressive-step-for-any-soceity-56837.
13. Innes, A. 2013. The political economy of state capture in Central Europe. JCMS: Journal of Common Market Studies 52(1), 88–104. ISSN 0021-9886. https://doi.org/10.1111/cms.12079. P 1.
14. ANC Today. (2016, May). Is South Africa a "captured state"? The anatomy of a "captured state". *ANC Today*. Retrieved from http://anctoday.org.za/south-africa-captured-state-anatomy-captured-state/.
15. Robinson and Hadiz. 2004. *Reorganizing power in Indonesia: the politics in and of market*. London: Routledge. P 4.
16. Srouji, S. 2005. Capturing the state: A political economy of Lebanon's public debt crisis 1992–2004. A research paper presented at the Institute of Social Studies, The Hague, Netherlands. P 16.
17. Srouji. 2005. Capturing the state: A political economy of Lebanon's public debt crisis 1992–2004. P 15.
18. Dassah, M. O. 2018. "Theoretical analysis of state capture and its manifestation as a governance problem in South Africa". P 5.
19. Innes. 2014. The political economy of state capture in Central Europe.
20. Harrison, G. 1999. Corruption as "boundary politics": The state, democratization and Mozambique's unstable liberalization. *Third World Quarterly*. 20(3). P 543.
21. Tax Justice Network. 2013. *Financial Secrecy Index*. Singapore. Retrieved from http://www.financialsecrecyindex.com/PDF/Singapore.pdf. Accessed on 10 July 2019.
22. Maira Martini. 2014. "State capture: an overview". Retrieved from www.transparency.org/whatwedo/answer/state_capture_an_overview. Accessed on 10 July 2019. P 3.
23. Transparency International. Corruption perceptions index. *Transparency International*. 2012. Retrieved from https://www.transparency.org/whatwedo/pub/corruption_percepions_index_2012.
24. Monks. 2012. *The corporate capture of the United States*. The Harvard school of law forum on corporate governance and financial regulation. Retrieved from

https://blogs.law.harvard.edi/corpgov/2012/01/05/the-corporate-capture-of-the-united-states/. Accessed on 10 July 2019.
25. Financial Crisis Inquiry Commission. 2011. *The Financial Crisis Inquiry Report*. Retrieved from http://fcic-static.law.stanford.edu/403B563C-52B2-4F9F-9231-73913C299762/FinalDownload/Downloadid-A3CD6E735DFFDF9F942B20CAFF41FA25/403B563C-52B2-4F9F-9231-73913C299762/cdn_media/fcic-reports/fcic_final_report_full.pdf.
26. Public Protector. 2016. *State of Capture*. Report No 6 of 2016/2017. Retrieved from http://saflii.org/images/329756472-State-of-Capture.pdf. P 4.
27. Public Protector. 2016. *State of Capture*. P6.
28. Desai Ashwin and Goolam Vahed. 2017. *The Guptas, the Public Protector's report and capital accumulation in South Africa*. Retrieved 24 June 2019 from https://doi.org/10.29086/2519-5476/2017/v24nla3. P 31.
29. Desai Ashwin and Goolam Vahed. 2017. *The Guptas, the Public Protector's report and capital accumulation in South Africa*. P 32.
30. Kalim Rajab, "Message to Cabinet: It is NOT just a wedding," *Daily Maverick*, 6 May 2013. https://www.dailymaverick.co.za/opinionista/2013-05-06-message-to-cabinet-it-is-not-just-a-wedding/
31. Msomi, S. 2016. "Rumbles of opposition but Zuma appears to be safe for now". *Sunday times*, 20 March.
32. Mbeki, M., and Mbeki, N. 2016. *A manifesto for social change: How to save South Africa*, Johannesburg: Picador Africa.
33. Black Opinion. 2016. It's a coup and you don't know it! *Black Opinion*. 12 April.
34. Shai, K. B. 2017. "South African state capture: a symbiotic affair between business and state going bad (?)", *Insight on Africa*, 9 (1). Sage publications. P 69. Available at https://doi.org/10.1177/0975087816674584. Accessed on 10 July 2019.
35. Shai, K. B. 2016. An Afrocentric critique of the United States of America's foreign policy towards Africa: the case studies of Ghana and Tanzania, 1990–2014. Unpublished PhD thesis. Sovenga: University of Limpopo.
36. Shai, K. B. 2017. South African state capture: a symbiotic affair between business and state going bad (?).
37. Mngxitama, A. 2016. "Guptas are just red herring", *Sunday independent*. 14 February 2016. Available at http://www.iol.co.za/sundayindependent/guptas-are-just-red-herring-1984163. Accessed on 10 July 2019.
38. Mngxitama, A. 2016. "Guptas are just red herring".
39. *Forbes Magazine*. Available at https://www.forbes.com/profile/aliko-dangote/#164eecd022fc. Accessed on 29 July 2019.
40. *Forbes Magazine*. Available at https://www.forbes.com/profile/aliko-dangote/#164eecd022fc. Accessed on 29 July 2019.
41. Allison, S. An in-depth look at how Africa's richest man made his fortune. *How We Made It In Africa: Africa Business Insight*. (2014, June). Retrieved from https://www.howwemadeitinafrica.com/an-in-depth-look-at-how-africas-richest-man-made-his-fortune/40460/. Accessed on 9 July 2019.
42. Ochonu, M. "The Dangote paradox". *Sahara Reporters* (2016, March). Retrieved from http://saharareporters.com/2016/03/25/dangote-paradox-moses-e-ochonu. Accessed on 29 July 2019.

43. Cocks, T. Special report: In Nigeria, a concrete get-rich scheme. *Reuters* (2012, September). https://www.reuters.com/article/us-nigeria-dangote/special-report-in-nigeria-a-concrete-get-rich-scheme-idUSBRE88913U20120911. Accessed on 29 July 2019.
44. El-Rufai, N. 2013. *The accidental public servant*. Safari Books. P170.
45. Ochonu, M. The Dangote paradox. *Sahara Reporters*. (2016, March). Retrieved from http://saharareporters.com/2016/03/25/dangote-paradox-moses-e-ochonu. Accessed on 29 July 2019.
46. Fawehinmi, F. "Africa's richest man has a built-in advantage with Nigeria's government", *Quartz Africa*. (2017, October). Retrieved from https://qz.com/africa/1098137/africas-richest-man-has-a-built-in-advantage-with-nigerias-government/. Accessed on 30 July 2019.
47. Fawehinmi, F (2017, October). Africa's richest man has a built-in advantage with Nigeria's government.
48. Vanguard. FG to put restrictions on milk importation. *Vanguard*. (2019, July). Retrieved from https://www.vanguardngr.com/2019/07/fg-to-put-restrictions-on-milk-importation/. Accessed on 30 July 2019.
49. Olasupo, A. CBN reacts to criticisms of forex policy on milk. *The Guardian* (2019, July). Retrieved from https://guardian.ng/nwes/nigeria/cbn-reacts-to-criticisms-of-forex-policy-on-milk/. Accessed on 30 July 2019.
50. Ochonu, "The Dangote Paradox".
51. Nimi Wariboko, 2004. "A Critical Review of the Firm in Africa," *Journal of International Business and Law*, Vol. 3, No. 1, 117.
52. Nimi Wariboko, 2004. "A Critical Review of the Firm in Africa," 121.
53. Nimi Wariboko, 2004. "A Critical Review of the Firm in Africa".
54. Nimi Wariboko, 2004. "A Critical Review of the Firm in Africa," 122.
55. Peter Ekeh, 1975. "Colonialism and the Two Publics in Africa: A Theoretical Statement," *Comparative Studies in Society and History*, 17, 1: 91–121.

PART IV

Culture (Creativity, and Forms of Organizing Creativity, Muses)

CHAPTER 22

Religion, Media and Ethics in Africa

Anthony Okeregbe

INTRODUCTION

Contemporary studies have shown that religion plays a very major role in the lives and experiences of many Africans. So entrenched are religion and religious sentiments that every facet of the African life is construed as the operation of vital forces connecting human beings and nature to the workings of some supreme and ultimate being. From birth to death, in work and play, and in everyday conversation, the nuances of religion are habitually expressed; for in the African's religious experiences the truth about his place in the universe, the principles guiding his interaction with nature and his fellow humans are culturally unveiled in a ritual of mutual interpenetration of vital forces.[1] Riding on the submissions of the likes of Idowu, Magesa, Mbiti and Achebe, who in their writings have expressed this intrinsic religiosity of their respective African societies, Kunhiyop concludes that "Africans are incurably religious and religion permeates all aspects of life."[2]

As religious as Africans are claimed to be, their social life reflects a complex paradox that may be attributed to apparent fragmented social ontology. While the African metaphysical worldviews opened their doors to the religious domination of other peoples, the same accommodating spirit ceased to exist when the foreign religions took root and superimposed themselves on the cultures of the African continent. Anyanwu's frank elaboration on this phenomenon is reflected by the assertion that: "What we find in Africa is the mortal competition by foreign Gods and ideologies for the African soul."[3] And true to expectations: "The results of this phenomenon are chaos, tyranny, anarchy, organized conspiracy and base assassinations which pave the way for foreign interventions."[4]

A. Okeregbe (✉)
University of Lagos, Lagos, Nigeria

Like the search applicable to religious experiences, the media (newspapers, radio, television and lately the social media), as a fact-gathering social institution, seeks truth aimed at providing citizens with flow of information they need to be free and self-governing.[5] This information is called news. At the centre of this information flow are the citizens, to whom news is targeted. For this information to be edifying, it should not only inform, educate and entertain, it must also be true. While journalistic practice owes its loyalty, first to the citizens, it assists government in the development of culture, social integration and good governance. In the multilateral and polyvalent African society, media practice often presents a moral dilemma because while media practitioners or journalists are unanimous on the truth-telling aspect of their profession, they seem confused about the meaning of truth. And so, the moral choice to accomplish this task is left to the conscience of the practitioner.

Both religious experience and media practice are functionally connected by the fact that each of them seeks truth. While religion seeks truth about humankind's acclaimed relationship with a supreme being called God, the media seeks truth about human's relationship with fellow beings. And in this truth-seeking relationship human beings integrate themselves in God and nature towards proper harmonious and progressive coexistence, even as human beings through the media promote self-governance for peace. However, to carry out such lofty aspirations, certain fundamental principles of otherness need to be established as guides. It is in this regard that this chapter intends to examine a fundamental problem of religion in Africa, namely that of intolerance, and also the question of information flow about Africa and her people. These twin challenges of contemporary African life are so pervasive that they demand social ethical analysis. This chapter attempts to discuss socio-ethical issues arising from the religion and media problematic from a purely existential-phenomenological standpoint.

ON THE TRUTH-SEEKING TASK OF RELIGION AND THE MEDIA

One of the greatest expressions of man's empowered status in the scheme of existence lies in his ability to seek to know. To seek to know is a fundamental characteristic and a natural inclination of man that pushes him towards a search for truth concerning his world, his being and the relationship between both. While some claim this ability arises out of "awareness instinct," the inclination to seek knowledge is what differentiates man from other inferior beings, since this endeavour transcends the horizons of sense perception to the innermost recess of his being to bring about action. Such a pursuit may be for its own sake, for self-transcendence, self-enlightenment and may have a social function. Augustine of Hippo, who provided a theological theory of the nature of religion, argued that the idea of religion is rooted in a hollowness and vacuum that humans want to fill. He posits further that man's natural search for God is an endeavour to fill the emptiness that comes from meaninglessness in existence.[6]

However, while he or she chooses to fill the vacuum or address the meaninglessness in existence, they need a transcendent other to which they direct their fears, expectations, hopes and aspirations. The personal actions, motivations and social relations pertaining to a culturally determined relationship with this transcendent other is what religious experience is all about. Thus, religious experience can be summarized according to four basic structures: the self and the other, social forms and expression, objective intention and the mystical aspect. As an encounter between the self and the other, it can be described in terms of three epistemic elements: first, the personal concerns, attitudes, feelings and ideas of the experiencer (subject); second, the object of experience, that is, the religious object disclosed in the experience or the reality to which the experience is said to refer; and third, the social form that arises from the fact that the experience can be shared—that is, can be expressed in language or symbolic form.[7] This latter element justifies religion as a social fact—a situation which led Emile Durkheim to define religion from a sociological dimension.[8] It is in this social expression of religion that the instrumentalization of religion becomes apparent. Here, both the positive, edifying and spiritually transforming values of religion and the negative, challenging and evil aspects of religion are manifested.

Contemporary Africa is afflicted by many religious challenges such as the proliferation of sects, the dissonance between religious knowledge and practices, the problem of syncretism and religious intolerance. But the most explosive and socially impactful of these challenges is religious intolerance. With a history dating back to the colonial period, religious upheavals tended to have been part of the social evolution of modern Africa. However, while religiously mixed countries like Senegal, Ghana, Tanzania and the likes have been able to maintain an appreciable level of religious tolerance, in countries like Nigeria, Egypt and Central African Republic, conflicts arising from religious intolerance have taken a crisis proportion that has become inimical to national development. The case of Boko Haram's Islamic revivalism, with its attendant infernal consequences, has been so protracted and dangerously politicized that the menace has ignited a subregional crisis affecting no fewer than four countries: Cameroun, Chad, Niger Republic and Nigeria.[9]

Just as religious experience, the craving for news happens to be one way of expressing this natural inclination of seeking to know. We might get a better grasp of this when we examine what news entails. What is news? "News," according to Kovach and Rosenstiel, "is that part of communication that keeps us informed of the changing events, issues and characters in the world outside."[10] News, as the name implies, is a piece of information that is new. It is the knowledge of the new, the unknown, the unfamiliar, the outside. Among its characteristics is a correspondence with reality. In other words, it must be factual, verifiable and should not be mere speculation or a figment of the reporter's imagination. Another characteristic of news is the fact that it is a report. Being a report it is a relay or an account of what is witnessed and an event that is seen, heard or said. Consequently, more than mere customary, quotidian contact with reality, the epistemic status of news has an element of novelty and freshness in it. It is this freshness and satisfaction of awareness instinct that make news a craving.

News-craving, as an expression of this natural inclination, has never been so greatly felt as in this age of globalization, wherein technology and cultural gap-bridging have made the world and its constituents objects of greater curiosity. In this age of complex interactions and opening horizons of experiences, news-craving becomes all the more necessary for survival. The reason for this, as Kovach and Rosenstiel tell us, is that people "need to know what is going on over the next hill, to be aware of events beyond their direct experience." This is because "knowledge of the unknown gives them security, allows them to plan and negotiate their lives. Exchanging this information becomes the basis for creating community, making human connections."[11]

At the forefront of the management of news are journalists, who with broadcasters and publishers are called the press. Journalists are basically reporters. They report news of events, set agenda for commentaries about issues and elicit reaction (feedback) from the masses who are consumers of news. They do this by employing the most sophisticated equipment—radio transmitters, television, satellites and daily publications—that can transmit information to a great number of people, with great speed and at the same time; hence, the name mass media. The press, therefore, by its sheer adaptability, fluidity and frequency can provide detailed reports of an event, comment on news reports, set an agenda and help the reader or the listener or viewer interpret opinions and news reports. In this way, it becomes a most effective means of stimulating the intellect and forming opinions.

Religious Intolerance as a Socio-ethical Problem

While the damning nature and the exponential increase in the spate of religious violence in many fragile spots in Africa, especially in Nigeria, have been objects of intellectual discourse and academic research works in recent years, the input of profound philosophical scholarship into such research works has been virtually far-flung. However, one bold attempt in the philosophical contribution was that of Campbell Shittu Momoh. In a series of essays published in his *The Funeral of Democracy* (1993) and in the four volumes on religious and ethnic tolerance titled *Nigerian Studies in Religious and Ethnic Tolerance* (1988), Momoh builds the intellectual framework of his principles of tolerance on a didactic approach to philosophy. In order to address the problem of religious tolerance in Nigeria, and by extension Africa, Momoh proposes an epistemic openness to a conference of ideas, which he claims would enlighten the populace on the doctrines and practices of the many belief systems. He calls this principle "Naretology"; and by this he means "the doctrine that any civilized or cultured man in the modern world ought to know the basic tenets of major religious and ethnic worldviews."[12]

Unah, in his collection of essays, *Essays in Philosophy* (1995), gives a Parmenidean metaphysical insight into religious intolerance. He posits via a

Parmenidean interpretation that, while the truth about a religion may be one, changeless and unidirectional, the understanding of this "true Reality" depends on the metaphysical temperament put up by an adherent. Because an adherent exhausts all his energies to present his views and sentiments as the objective reality which must be accepted by all and sundry, he is blind to all others, that is, he refuses to understand all other varied positions. Therefore, understanding as "metaphysical thinking often culminates in a conceptual freezing of experience ... because a metaphysical thinker usually mistakes an aspect or a principle of Being with which he is familiar for Being itself or the totality of Being."[13]

Consequently, owing to his metaphysical fixedness, an adherent begins to orientate the contents and ingredients of his beliefs according to the directions of his metaphysical currents. Not only does he see things only in the light of his religion, he begins to regard his own understanding as the right and only way. He forecloses his mind not only to antagonistic positions but also to positions that would facilitate adequate understanding of his own position. Little wonder then Unah elsewhere posits that "the narrower a metaphysician's position, the sharper his perspective," and "the sharper a metaphysician's perspective, the greater the scandal that is perpetrated against other aspects of reality not accommodated by his system."[14] It is because of this kind of religious fixedness that the early Romans had to persecute early Christians; that factions exist in Christianity; that Anne Askew had to be burnt on a stake in the sixteenth century for denying transubstantiation; that Hindus and Muslims had to fight in India and that the full implementation of *Sharia* law in some parts of northern Nigeria resulted in wanton abuse of human rights and dangerous political powerplay.

And so, in the attempt by many religionists to institutionalize that fixedness, there arises a lack of understanding concerning the nature of God, misunderstood relationship between religion and the socio-political realm of human interaction, as seen the *Sharia* crisis in Nigeria, and misinterpretation of secularism and religious authority. We shall briefly expose how they induce religious intolerance.

On the Deity

Although not all religions are theistic, religions such as Islam, Christianity and Judaism which trace their origin to a deity,[15] find a common ground in their different conceptions of God, in that they conceive God or this deity anthropomorphically.[16] Apart from this perception of God, revealed religions (Judaism, Christianity and Islam) are so called because they claim to have been founded by divine revelation, while their scriptures are claimed to be inspired. On the other hand, natural religions make no such claims, for their practices and tenets are founded in the culture from which the religion sprang.

The God of religion, Omoregbe posits, is one conceived in the image and likeness of man. He is as emotional as human beings, displaying all the characteristics human beings possess. God, in this sense, is only a higher degree of *Homo sapiens*.[17] He is equally a being of contradictory attributes. While God is a spiritual being, He possesses all the perceptual faculties for sense experience. While He is almighty, He is delimited by the human attributes he possesses. He is all-good, yet moral evil exists in the world. In all these attributes,[18] "there is an intrinsic contradiction in the very concept of the God of religion." It is the unavoidable presence of such intrinsic contradiction that gives logical weight to the Feuerbachian notion that God is a mental creation of man, a necessary transcendent of his imagination.

Owing to this anthropomorphism, different religions and different religious sects witness schisms and splinterings, and such other disagreements resulting from conflicting positions on doctrines and practices. That God is said to have a son—Jesus Christ—is a doctrine that separates Christianity from Islam and Judaism. Even among adherents of the Christian religion, the status of Christ in salvation history is still a matter of dispute. Even after the equiprimordial divinity and humanity of Christ had been resolved in both the Councils of Nicaea in 325 AD and Constantinople in 381 AD,[19] some adherents of Christianity still contest Christ's "equidivinity" with God. As many Christian sects inch towards doctrinal dissension, the Catholic Church, positioning itself as the "Via Veritas" of Christendom, maintains a sort of religious eclecticism that seems to be beyond the comprehension of other Christian denominations, especially emerging sects.

On the Social Point in Religion

Apart from this, there is the conflict concerning the social dimension of religion. This conflict raises questions as to whether or not religion is a force of social change, and also whether contemporary African societies are reflective of the effect of secularization on them. To say that secularization prevails in a society, or that a society is secular, is to view it as "having no particular religions affinities." In other words, it supposes that religion does not as a matter of civil policies have any affinity to social institutional life.

Following Larry Shiner's six dimensions or perspectives for examining secularism in a society, Michael Hill outlines the various meanings of secularism as follows[20]:

- The first meaning is that which specifies "the decline of religion." Secularization in this sense suggests a religionless society arrived at through what Bryan Wilson calls a "process whereby religious thinking, practice and institutions lose social significance."[21]
- The second meaning is identified as "a shift from other-worldly to 'this-worldly' orientations; within religious groups themselves."
- The third use of the term refers to the disengagement of society from religion or the attempt at making a "differentiation" between religious ideas and institutions from others of the social structure. In this case,

instead of religion being a source of legitimization for the whole society, it becomes a matter of private choice of interested participants.
- The fourth meaning "refers to the transposition of beliefs and activities that were once thought of as having a divine point of reference to activities that have an entirely 'secular' content." Here we have in mind the "surrogate religiosity" and "functional equivalents" found in those who are adherents or socially committed to such ideas as Humanism, Fascism, Communism, Marxism, etc.
- The fifth meaning suggests that "the world is gradually deprived of its sacral character, so that man increasingly discards magical images of his natural environment and comes more and more to regard it as incapable of empirical scientific manipulations."
- The sixth definition refers to a "change from a 'sacred' to a 'secular' society."

The contentious issue now is whether, based on the above-mentioned senses of secularization, the contemporary African society is a secularized one. Those who posit that the African society is a secularized one, invite us to examine our socio-economic structures in order to tease out the indices of secularization. Contemporary African society they submit is in a state of decadent paralysis, resulting from dilapidating social systems and the lack of response to such human conditions as (1) the perpetual uncertainty of social security for the masses and (2) the ubiquitous maladies that afflict public administration. This societal state brings about two broad divisions as far as religious dispositions are concerned. There is the religious attitude of the westernized, or the sophisticated and the religious attitude of the rural and low classed. Under this division, Ferdinand Tonnies' social classification into *Gemeinschaft* and *Gessellschaft* comes to mind.[22] Because of the social cohesion, the fused bonds of communal spirit interpenetrating the fibres of the community life, rural people and the low classed in society tend to derive existential meaning and social relevance from religion. The sense of religion perceptible from this system was what Emile Durkheim had in mind when he defined religion as a "unified system of beliefs and practices relative to sacred things ... beliefs and practices, which unite into a single moral community."[23] In this system we find the primaeval elements of religion.

On the other hand, in a *Gessellschaft*, religion is seen as a mere openness to the sacred. Here, religion is impersonal or private. It is cut off from the ordinary public life. It lacks the complete elements that validate a religion. On this level, the religiosity presents in or propagated by a *Gessellschaft* parade only elementary theological knowledge and superficial commitment to practices related to sacred things. If our interpretation is right, the *Gessellschaft* view seems to be what was in the mind of Otite and Ogionwo when they define religion as merely "a cultural institution" and "a means, an instrument for the satisfaction of needs."[24]

From these two views of religion, we can examine signs of secularization in the contemporary African society. Secularization could be seen from the point of view of the political structure or from the response to economic currents.

Prominent among the urbanized is the tendency to view religion as a means for political aggrandizement. Religion, owing to its volatility, is used to propagate sectionalism, division, rivalry and vantage positions. Hence, the whole commotion surrounding Sharia and the Organisation of Islamic Cooperation (OIC) are political issues "baptized" by religious sentiments.[25] Could it not be secularization when the Christian Association of Nigeria (CAN) had to take the government to court over matters concerning pilgrimages? While beneficial and socially rewarding religious duties are neglected in a society rooted in moral decay, the affluent and their ignoble acolytes struggle to take a glimpse of the Holy Lands for frivolous recognition and titles. Meanwhile, the wretched masses are denied the social benefits derivable from authentic religious duties. Such a portrayal of religion suggests a secularistic tendency that falls into the third of the six meanings of secularism explored above by Shiner, namely a "disengagement of society (social systems) from religion."

Another sign of secularization is seen in the economic sphere. This is demonstrated by the commercialization of religion. In this sense, there tends to be a removal of the divine character and also the absence of organized religious groups. As a result, religion is seen only as a means of livelihood. There is also another sign of secularism, which is found inside some sects themselves. It is that kind of secularization that stems out of the purges of economic situation. It is down to earth. It is the kind of secularism that tends to say that "You cannot serve God with an empty stomach." It tears out of its system, the dependence on the suprasensible and all corresponding "empty talks" about the unknown. It is a demythologization of platonic ideologies in religion. It is a tendency that shifts to the fact of life. These signs of secularization are typical of "prosperity Christianity" as practised by churches such as Living Faith Inc., aka Winners Chapel, and defunct churches such as Zoe Ministry and Bethel Ministry, amongst others.

Yet there remains another sign of secularization in the African society. This is the perspective, which tends to view religion like other social institutions, say politics, or the economy. From this angle, rituals like baptism, funeral services and weddings in churches and mosques are compared to political activities like voting and campaigning, and economic activities like buying and selling, importation and so on. Thus, religion becomes an ordinary social fulfilment, while its rites and rituals are "functional equivalents" of the activities of other social institutions. This is secularization of the fourth variant as espoused by Shiner and Hill (supra).

Even in the traditional African religion signs of secularization have been talked about. This may be well understood when one reads the words of Obierika in Chinua Achebe's *Things Fall Apart*.

> The Whiteman came peacefully and quietly with his religion. We're amused at his foolishness and allowed him to stay. Now he has won our brothers and our clan can no longer act as one again. He has put a knife on the thing that held us together and we have fallen apart.[26]

To some sociologists, secularization came to existence when the Whiteman "put a knife" on the thing that held us together. So, the very nature of propagated Christian faith was itself a sign of secularization within the African context. On this Bryan Wilson suggests:

> Many Christian commentators ... explicitly or implicitly, equate secularization with dechristianization. Their emotional involvement is often such that they go to considerable lengths to show that past ages were by no means religious. But paganism was usually more, rather than less, religious than Christianity. ... In so far as Christian discipline eventually reduced these motley manifestations of religious consciousness, Christianity itself must be seen as a secularizing agency, as Max Weber long ago suggested.[27]

From this sociological excursion, it seems clear that the African society manifests germs of secularization, even while a great majority of its peoples find moral and spiritual attachment with the primordial elements of religion such as magic, superstition, mysteries and divinities. However, what seems to be made evident by secularization is the dynamic symbiosis between religion and society: society nourishes religion, while religion is a catalyst for social dynamics. Whereas secularization demonstrates the former, the catalytic instrumentation of religion is experienced in its function as a force of social change.

There are so many reasons why religion is a force of social change. One of these is its authoritarian epistemology and its demands of fideism (obedience by faith). Since most religious tendencies point towards a suprasensible and superhuman being as its source, human beings tend to harken to religious injunctions to carry out a social function, for in the laws of God, or this superhuman dictator, believers tend to find an authentic value and maintain absolute reverence. Religion is also a force of change because its ability to ascribe meaning to such metaphysical evils as suffering and pain, and explain mysteries of the universe, is a source of motivation for, and mobilization of, the hoi-polloi who form a considerably large number of the populace in a given society. Thus, as a force of social change, religion subverts the status quo because it can mobilize people adequately while using divine pronouncements as a motivating force for action.[28] A typical social change of this sort was experienced in the sixteenth century at The Reformation. Apart from effecting a doctrinal redress in Christendom, it became one of the facilitators of modern democratic government as well as the rise of Nationalism.

In the not too recent times in Latin America, religion has been able to effect a form of social change that can be termed as one of "discordant harmony" in that there exists a warped blend of theology and Marxist methodology to form a radical religious doctrine for social mobilization. In this way, rather than vindicating the Marxian dictum that religion is the opiate of the people, there is an upturn of the elements of Marxian teachings to present religion as a stumbling block to the oppressive, exploitative and predatory tendencies of corrupt leader of the society. All these are apart from the fact that religion, through its elements of morals and dogma, effect social control by creating a sense of sin.

While many have thought that Islam and some traditional religions seem to be inhibitive to social change, a burgeoning trend in Africa, exemplified by the introduction of the *Sharia* legal system into the penal code of some states in Nigeria, seems to have debunked that claim. Now *Sharia* is becoming a contentious issue on religious tolerance.

On Sharia Law

As interpreted by Islamic scholars, Islam should govern all of life as directed by the Quranic injunction because Islamists view their religion as the centre of human life, while God is the ultimate decider of existence. The concept of God is captured by the reference to Him as "the fosterer of a thing in such a manner as to make it attain one condition after another until it reaches its goal of completion" (Shekoni 1988: 8). To regulate worship and ritual duties, judicial and political life and the Islamic religionist claims, *Sharia* has been handed on to him by God for such purpose.

According to the online *Encyclopaedia of the Orient*, Sharia should not be viewed as a mere legal device comparable to, say, law as in English Law, Canon Law and so on. The encyclopaedia states that "Sharia extends beyond law." It defines Sharia as "the totality of religious, political, social domestic (and) private life. Sharia is primarily meant for all Muslims."[29] On its epistemic authority, the encyclopaedia goes further: "Sharia is not something the intelligence of man can prove wrong, it is only to be accepted by humans: Sharia is based on the will of God."[30] Today, in some African countries, Sharia has become a most important socio-political issue in national discourse. Since 2000, local authorities in Nigeria's Zamfara imposed Sharia law and by 2002 it has spread to 12 states of the north.[31] Its political relevance as well as the seeming overestimation of its encompassing influence in socio-economic and political life by fundamentalists and adherents has fanned the embers of people's self-preservation instincts with sanguinary and infernal destruction. The result of this instrumentalization of Sharia is the emergence of insurgent groups such as Boko Haram in Nigeria, Chad, Cameroon and Niger.

INAUTHENTIC REPORTAGE AS SOCIO-ETHICAL ISSUE IN MEDIA PRACTICE

Throughout history, media practice has experienced a chequered metamorphosis that had been dictated by social evolution. Despite its chequered functional history and invasive political influence, historians and theorists of journalism are unanimous on the primary purpose of journalism. According to the American Society of Newspaper Editors, the goal of journalism is "to serve the general welfare by informing the people." John Paul II, in a declaration to journalists in 2000, viewed this service as a sacred duty. Speaking to the journalists at that occasion, he stated that it is owing to the sacred nature of their work that journalism should be "carried out in the knowledge that the powerful means of communication have been entrusted to you for the good of all."[32]

The above assertions substantiate the finding of developmental psychologists from Harvard University, Stanford University and University of Chicago, who, in a study of over a hundred journalists on what they considered the most distinguishing feature of their profession, conclude that: "New professionals at every level ... express an adamant allegiance to a set of core standards that are striking in their commonality and in their linkage to the public information mission."[33] This in turn gives credence to the assumption that the primary purpose of journalism is "to provide citizens with the information they need to be free and self-governing."[34] Thus the first loyalty of journalism is to citizens.

To provide the kind of information that will make the citizens free and self-governing, journalists must get the facts right. To get the facts right, they must report or tell the truth. In other words, a journalist's first obligation is to the truth. However, for the journalist, this may not be the case because news concerns the real world and, owing to the varied perspectives, beclouded by stereotypes and personal idiosyncrasies, from which journalists view events, journalists have never been "very clear about what they mean by truthfulness."

Besides, unlike many established professions, which have definite guidelines and rules regulating their practice, journalism does not have laws, regulations or professional code of conduct. This is the reason anybody can be a journalist; some theorists view it as "an act of character" or a passion. Others view it as a vocation rather than a profession like law or medicine. In many newsrooms in Nigeria, there are more non-journalism and non-Mass Communication graduates as reporters, editors and broadcasters, than those whose education should prepare them for journalism. Owing to this absence of an established regulation, "a heavy burden rests on the ethics and judgment of the individual journalist and the individual organisation where he or she works." In other words, the prerogative of ethical reporting rests on the moral compass of the journalist as dictated by his personal conscience.

Because there exists a tension between what journalists consider as loyalty to citizens and what is passed on to citizens as the truth, the press often finds itself neck-deep in harrowing challenges. Among these challenges are the following: the difficulty in passing on complete truth without error. Because news is what fresh and new, journalist must select from a mass of material that they judge to be of concern to their audience. Hence, they do not report the whole truth. In extreme cases of misinformation or disinformation, journalism could also become a weapon of mass deception and war. Nowhere is this more prevalent as in the social media, where the anonymous nature of communication practice has led to irresponsibility. The social media is replete with instances of despicable practice of irreverent presentation of issues, the use of brash, uncouth and abusive language to describe people and pass remarks about a person's private life and preferences, and outright condemnation and demonization of people's ethnic group, religion, tribe and sex, without prior adequate research carried out. That all these are done anonymously has made the social media a perfect recipe for war and continuous violence.

Moreover, since news must be immediate and often times comprehensible, journalists must rely on commentaries from competent and informed sources. However, many whose opinions are trustworthy and reliable do not often make hasty comments. So, because journalists are "impelled to demand quick comments, the initiative often passes to men who are less responsible and less well-informed."[35] Since journalists must keep the public informed as soon as the news has got fresh and hot, the competitive nature of the industry makes them sacrifice accuracy for speed. Furthermore, news comes in bits and pieces, and piecing them together speedily may well lead to an unbalanced or distorted idea of the whole picture it passes to the audience. Coupled with this, they also have to catch attention of their audience without the risk of a sensationalism that may distort news. Often times a true state of affairs is difficult to get especially if truth hurts the other party. So journalists risk their life, sacrifice their dignity and are prone to attack of all sorts in their search for truth. All these challenges lead to what Paul Johnson, an America veteran journalist, has outlined as the seven deadly sins of the media. These sins are distortion, worship of false images, theft of privacy, murder of character, exploitation of sex, poisoning of the minds of children and abuse of power.[36] To these one adds the desire for or expectation of gratification.

Ethical Evaluation

From the analyses so far, the socio-ethical focus of both religious experience and media practice centre around three main issues, namely the dignity of the human person, truthfulness or authentic presentation and representation of state of affairs, and social responsibility.

Concerning the issue of dignity of the human person, every religious experience is unique to individuals and to a given people. In other words, for us to address the problem of intolerance and by that fact be tolerant of other people's religion, we must respect the intentional experience of that person or group of people. The subject of a religious experience is the sole mental construct of the one who has had such an experience. Whatever revelation, whatever mystical encounter and whatever relationship the experiencer has with the otherworldly, has validity and meaning to him who expresses who he has experienced. No one has the right to assert that whatever a religionist has experienced is false. As Anyanwu, again remarks: "God manifests Himself through the cultural lenses of the people which include their thought process, language, imagination, and assumptions about reality."[37] In every religious expression, what an experiencer intends to do is to construct in human language whatever he has experienced. In attempting this mental construction, he brings to bear that part of his faculty known as the imagination in order to create a picture of what he has experienced and to thereby formulate precepts, and other principles he deems necessary and relevant to social order. If this is the case, a hermeneutical rendition of this context would reveal to us

> that, every revelation, every mental construction is a product of imaginative construction, and that man who receives revelation, or who experiences something is the most authoritative person to explain what he receives or experiences.[38]

When we cognize the fact that every mental construct, of which religious experience is a part, is peculiar to the individual, then we are able to understand that we do not have the right and cannot mentally construct for somebody what he has experienced himself. We can only, as Stein says, empathize with him since we cannot permeate into his personal realm of value-formations, just as we cannot feel the sensation of pain when he is flogged. Being aware of this fact, "we learn to let things be, to let things manifest themselves properly without preconceptions."[39]

Just as in religious experience, respect for the dignity of the human person is a requisite ethical principle for wholesome and socially healthy media practice. To evaluate this position, we may ask: how can journalism promote peace? What steps could be taken by journalists to seek truth and refuse to be bought over? If the media practitioner is to understand how he must work for peace, he has to reflect on the issues of salience so far delineated, namely the journalist's loyalty to citizens, the journalist's obligation to truth and the journalist and his conscience. If the first loyalty of the journalist is to citizens, then a proper understanding of the citizens, their value and their place in nature would enhance the journalist's job of promoting peace. Having a proper understanding of citizens demands that we recognize the fundamental equality of persons in the scheme of things. Citizens are persons, they are not things. Thus, a deeper reflection on personhood opens up a new vista of understanding about the human person. It teaches us that persons are not objects, and objects are not persons. It teaches that the ontological difference between persons and things lies in the intrinsic value of the former. Man is not just a bundle of emotions and passions to be exploited, he is also, as philosophical anthropologists have argued, one who has an autonomy of being, a distinct inviolability and that which makes him or her a unique and an irreplaceable individual in nature.[40]

For those who believe in God, this value is even enhanced by the belief that man is created in the image and likeness of God. For this reason the human person is a being worthy of respect and a being who should not be used or abused or cannon fodder for mundane pursuit and self-aggrandizement. This understanding of the human person would enable the journalist to possess a more contemplative and sober outlook at the target of their new reports—persons. It would enable him to see persons not as mere consumers of products. It would also enable the journalist to regard the people they report, not as mere objects, but also as beings like himself/herself with whom he/she can relate. In this way, journalist would be less inclined to be salacious, invade privacy, murder character, exploit sex and poison the mind of children.

With regard to truthfulness and authentic presentation and representation of state of affairs, man's existentiality imposes a limit about what he or she can know, either about God or about his or her fellow humans. Our existentiality is revealed in the limitation posed by our language in reference to God, for human language "operates within a cognitive system which is reflective and is most concerned with the objectification of predicates."[41] Our concept of God's eternity is limited by our existence, and His omniscience is limited by our own science and nescience, forcing us to conceive of a superior mind or power beyond human conceivability. Given the limitations posed by our existentiality, can any religion claim to understand God better than any other? Like the blind men of Hindustan who reduced the elephant to only the part their tactile faculties could take them, "God possesses several qualities, a group of which can form the doctrine of particular groups. There are therefore many ways in which God can be understood. None of them would be absolutely wrong, none represents the total truth."[42]

And since "None of the world religions has the legitimate right of regarding itself as the final arbiter in terms of which every other religion must be assessed or condemned,"[43] we are led to embrace the principles of Mitsein (Being-with and Bearing-with) and intersubjectivity, according to which religions can accommodate one another.

To the media practitioner also, fostering a culture of peace requires openness to, and deep reflection about, the information he or she gathers and disseminates. It is this deep reflection and careful self-examination that hones whatever values the journalist brings to bear on his profession. Being open to the benefits of deep reflection, it would enable a journalist to understand when and where prejudices and stereotypes are the prejudgemental cues for his reports, and when biases are motivations for setting an agenda. In situations where journalists need informed opinions from commentators and analysts, this deep thinking would enable him sift the incendiary comments of charlatans from the personality-enhancing and love-building messages of true opinion leaders. When this loving circumspection is combined with a mindset of critical reflection, the journalists, especially editors, would know when an opinion tender is fanning sensationalism by making sentimental and fallacious statements.

It follows from the earlier analysis that when one has respect for the dignity of the human person and has sufficient control of his or her freedom by expressing the true state of affairs, he or she is likely to be socially responsible. Social responsibility here suggests a recognition, sense and enthusiasm for integral spirituality. At the religious level it is the mutual respect and reciprocity that arise from recognition of one's limitation and the recognition and acceptance of the freedom of the other. In practice it entails the following: just as I accept my religious faith to be true on an absolute scale, I should expect followers of various religions to consider their own beliefs to be true. Just as I exercise my freedom in the acceptance of religious belief that are different from mine, I should expect others to exercise their freedom likewise by holding religious beliefs which are different from mine. Holding beliefs which are different from mine might even include the exercise of their freedom to change their religious beliefs. It may include the freedom to practice their religious faith within reasonable limits. If I allow the other to practice his religion, which he holds to be true just as I hold mine to be true, I will not discriminate in employment, accommodate and other social setting on religious grounds. It would also mean trying to accommodate their religious needs.

For the media practitioner, social responsibility would entail a practice consistent with the aspirations of the common good. A media practitioner who desires to carry out his or her duties with peace in mind should be motivated by the common good. The journalist or media practitioner, by his or her sacred duty of informing people, is a minister of value leadership. He or she should inform people not with the intention of objectifying them or making them instruments of his or her partisanship, but with the supreme purpose of making them as best as they can be. Such a practitioner needs to understand that information is power; power that can be used for good or for ill. Being a leader of values, a journalist should realize that, like every position of leadership, their profession is one of service; he or she is merely a servant of the people. Leadership as service is not a position of abuse of power; it is not an adventure in ego-tripping. Leadership is sacrifice; it requires an excellence of character that must kill the ego. It demands constant reflection that would make the practitioner ask: "Am I putting my interest above the interest of the people in my reporting?" "Is my reporting and agenda-setting such that will augur for peace and justice such that they promote the welfare of the people?" "Or am I just reporting for reporting sake?" Answers to these questions require the clarity of a Certain Conscience rather than a confused, lax or doubting conscience. It calls for a conscience with moral confidence; one whose judgement of an act is without their fear of the opposite being true. It calls for a conscience that will habitually see the truth and tell it, but it will do that with a sense of responsibility. By virtue of this sense of responsibility, a journalist with this kind of conscience would not be afraid to lead, for it would be courageous to show the way and be courageous to admit error, whenever they occur. A journalistic practice that embodies all this will seldom be hamstrung to promote an ethics of fair-mindedness and peace.

Notes

1. E. A. Ruch and K. C. Anyanwu, *African Philosophy: An Introduction to the Main Philosophical Trends in Contemporary Africa* (Rome: Catholic Book Agency, 1981), 370–372.
2. Samuel Waje Kunhiyop, *African Christian Ethics* (Nairobi: Hippo Books, 2008), 15.
3. Ruch and Anyanwu, *op. cit.*, 370.
4. Ibid.

5. Bill Kovach and Tom Rosenstiel, *Elements of Journalism: What Newspeople Should Know and What the Public Should Expect* (New York: Crown Publishers, 2001), 17.
6. Joseph Omoregbe, *A Philosophical Look at Religion* (Lagos: Joja Educational Research and Publishers Ltd., 1996), 14.
7. *Encyclopaedia Britannica*, 15th Edition, s.v. "Religious Experience".
8. Emile Durkheim. *The Elementary Forms of Religious Life* (London: George Allen and Unwin Ltd. 1915), 47. Durkheim defines religion as "a unified system of belief and practices relative to sacred things ... beliefs and practices which unite into a single moral community ...".
9. Abimbola Adesoji, "The Boko Haram Uprising and Islamic Revivalism in Nigeria". *Africa Spectrum*. 2/2010. Cited in *Wikipedia*, s.v. "Boko Haram". Available at: https://en.wikipedia.org/wiki/Boko_Haram. Accessed on 5 May 2019.
10. Kovach and Rosenstiel, op. cit., 21.
11. Ibid.
12. C. S. Momoh, *The Funeral of Democracy* (Lagos: African Philosophy Projects Publications, 1993), 110.
13. Jim Unah, *Essays In Philosophy* (Lagos: Panaf Publishers, 1995), 29.
14. Jim Unah, "The Philosophical Basis for Religious Tolerance and Peace Co-existence" in *Nigerian Studies in Religious Tolerance*. Vol. 4. C.S. Momoh, Eyeribe Onuoha, Tijani El-Miskin (eds.) (Lagos: Centre for Black and African Art and Civilization (CBAAC)/ National Association for Religious and Ethnic Tolerance (NARETO, 1989)), 285.
15. I. O. Alao, "The Supreme God In Christianity" in *Nigerian Studies In Religious Tolerance* Vol. 1, C. S. Momoh, M. S. Zahradeen and S. O. Abogunrin (eds.).(Lagos: Centre for Black and African Art and Civilization (CBAAC)/ National Association for Religious and Ethnic Tolerance (NARETO), 1988), 109.
16. Omoregbe, op. cit., 30.
17. Ibid., 31.
18. Ibid., 31.
19. Harry Boer, *A Short History of the Early Church*. (Ibadan: Daystar Press, 1976), 108 f.
20. Michael Hill, *A Sociology of Religion* (London: Heinemann Publishers, 1973), 228–251; Larry Shiner, "Toward a Theory of Secularization" *Journal of Religion* Vol. XLV:4.1965, 279–295.
21. Bryan Wilson, *Religion in Secular Society* (London: Wairs, 1966), 14.
22. Ferdinard Tonnies, *Gemeinschaft Und Gessellschaft (Community and Association)*, Charles P. Loomis (transl) (London: Routledge, 1887, 1955).
23. Emile Durkheim, *The Elementary Forms of Religious Life* (London. George Allen and Unwin, 1915), 47.
24. Onigu Otite and William Ogionwo, *An Introduction to Sociological Studies* (Ibadan: Heinemann Educational Books, 1985), 151.
25. In the mid-1980s, the then Military head of state Gen. Ibrahim Babangida, influenced by the rising power of certain Islamic countries in the Organization of Petroleum Exporting Countries (OPEC), signed Nigeria on as an observer member of the Organisation of the Islamic Cooperation (OIC). Besides the economic gains accruable to members of the OIC, some of the conditions for full membership of this body entailed the amenability of member countries to practise the Sharia.

26. Chinua Achebe, *Things Fall Apart*, African Writers Series (Ibadan: Heinemann Educational Books, 1962), 121.
27. Bryan Wilson, *Religion in Sociological Perspective* (Oxford: Oxford University Press, 1982), n. 150.
28. J. Perry and E. Perry, *The Social Web* (San Francisco: Cornfield Press, 1976), 430–432.
29. *Encyclopaedia of the Orient*, s.v. "Sharia" 1996.
30. Ibid.
31. Adesoji, op. cit. cited in *Wikipedia*.
32. John Paul II Papal Message to editors and media practitioners on World Communication Day, 2000.
33. Kovach and Rosenstiel, op. cit., 20.
34. Ibid., 17.
35. Vatican II Document, *Communio et Progressio* s. 38.
36. Paul Johnson, "The Media and Truth: Is there a Moral Duty?" in *Annual Editions: Media* 97/98 (Connecticut: Dushkin/McGraw-Hill, 1997), 103–4.
37. Ruch and Anyanwu, op. cit., 174.
38. Unah, 1989, op. cit., 289.
39. Ibid.
40. Battista Mondin, *Philosophical Anthropology* Cizdyn Myroslaw (transl.) (Rome: Urbaniana University Press, 1985), 257.
41. J. A. I. Bewaji, "Human Knowledge and the Existence of God" *Nigerian Studies in Religious Tolerance*. Vol. 4. C.S. Momoh, Eyeribe Onuoha, Tijani El-Miskin (eds.) (Lagos: Centre for Black and African Art and Civilization (CBAAC)/National Association for Religious and Ethnic Tolerance (NARETO, 1989)), 252.
42. Sophie Oluwole, "My God, Your God and the Clash" *Nigerian Studies in Religious Tolerance*. Vol. 4. C.S. Momoh, Eyeribe Onuoha, Tijani El-Miskin (eds.) (Lagos: Centre for Black and African Art and Civilization (CBAAC)/National Association for Religious and Ethnic Tolerance (NARETO, 1989)), 274.
43. Ibid., 275.

BIBLIOGRAPHY

Achebe, Chinua. 1962. *Things Fall Apart. African Writers Series.* Ibadan: Heinemann Educational Books.

Adesoji, Abimbola. 2010. The Boko Haram Uprising and Islamic Revivalism in Nigeria. *Africa Spectrum.* 2/2010. Cited in *Wikipedia*, s.v. "Boko Haram". Available at: https://en.wikipedia.org/wiki/Boko_Haram. Accessed 5 May 2019.

Alao, I.O. 1988. The Supreme God in Christianity. In *Nigerian Studies in Religious Tolerance*, ed. C.S. Momoh, M.S. Zahradeen, and S.O. Abogunrin, vol. 1, 109–117. Lagos: Centre for Black and African Art and Civilization (CBAAC)/National Association for Religious and Ethnic Tolerance (NARETO).

Bewaji, J.A.I. 1989. Human Knowledge and the Existence of God. In *Nigerian Studies in Religious Tolerance*, ed. C.S. Momoh, Eyeribe Onuoha, and Tijani El-Miskin, vol. 4, 243–270. Lagos: Centre for Black and African Art and Civilization (CBAAC)/National Association for Religious and Ethnic Tolerance (NARETO.

Boer, Harry. 1976. *A Short History of the Early Church*. Ibadan: Daystar Press.
Durkheim, Emile. 1915. *The Elementary Forms of Religious Life*. London: George Allen and Unwin.
Encyclopaedia Britannica. 1991. s.v. "Religious Experience". 15th ed. Chicago: Encyclopaedia Britannica.
Encyclopaedia of the Orient. 1996. s.v. "Shari'a" Tore Kjeilen. Available at: http.icias.com/e.o/sharia.htm. Retrieved 17 Dec 2008.
Flannery, Austin, ed. 1988. *Vatican Council II: The Conciliar and Postconciliar Documents*. Dublin: Dominican Publications.
Hill, Michael. 1973. *A Sociology of Religion*. London: Heinemann Publishers.
John Paul II. 2000. *Message of the Holy Father John Paul II for the 34th World Communications Day*. Vatican City, Rome: Libreria Editrice Vaticana.
Johnson, Paul. 1997. The Media and Truth: Is There a Moral Duty? In *Annual Editions: Media 97/98*. Connecticut: Dushkin/McGraw-Hill.
Kovach, Bill, and Tom Rosenstiel. 2001. *Elements of Journalism: What Newspeople Should Know and What the Public Should Expect*. New York: Crown Publishers.
Kunhiyop, Samuel Waje. 2008. *African Christian Ethics*. Nairobi: Hippo Books.
Momoh, C.S. 1993. *The Funeral of Democracy*. Lagos: African Philosophy Projects Publications.
Mondin, Battista. 1985. *Philosophical Anthropology*. Cizdyn Myroslaw (transl.). Rome: Urbaniana University Press.
Oluwole, Sophie. 1989. My God, Your God and the Clash. In *Nigerian Studies in Religious Tolerance*, ed. C.S. Momoh, Eyeribe Onuoha, and Tijani El-Miskin, vol. 4, 271–280. Lagos: Centre for Black and African Art and Civilization (CBAAC)/National Association for Religious and Ethnic Tolerance (NARETO.
Omoregbe, Joseph. 1996. *A Philosophical Look at Religion*. Lagos: Joja Educational Research and Publishers.
Otite, Onigu, and William Ogionwo. 1985. *An Introduction to Sociological Studies*. Ibadan: Heinemann Educational Books.
Perry, J., and E. Perry. 1976. *The Social Web*. San Francisco: Cornfield Press.
Ruch, E.A., and K.C. Anyanwu. 1981. *African Philosophy: An Introduction to the Main Philosophical Trends in Contemporary Africa*. Rome: Catholic Book Agency.
Shekoni, T.A. 1988. The Supreme Being: Allah in Islam. In *Nigerian Studies in Religious Tolerance*, ed. C.S. Momoh, M.S. Zahradeen, and S.O. Abogunrin, vol. 1, 8–28. Lagos: Centre for Black and African Art and Civilization (CBAAC)/National Association for Religious and Ethnic Tolerance (NARETO).
Shiner, Larry. 1965. Toward a Theory of Secularization. *Journal of Religion* XLV: 4.
Tonnies, Ferdinand. 1887, 1955. *Gemeinschaft Und Gessellschaft* (*Community and Association*). Charles P. Loomis (transl.). London: Routledge.
Unah, Jim. 1989. The Philosophical Basis for Religious Tolerance and Peace Co-existence. In *Nigerian Studies in Religious Tolerance*, ed. C.S. Momoh, Eyeribe Onuoha, and Tijani El-Miskin, vol. 4, 282–292. Lagos: Centre for Black and African Art and Civilization (CBAAC)/National Association for Religious and Ethnic Tolerance (NARETO).
———. 1995. *Essays in Philosophy*. Lagos: Panaf Publishers.
Vatican II Document. *Communio et Progressio* s. 38.
Wilson, Bryan. 1966. *Religion in Secular Society*. London: Wairs.
———. 1982. *Religion in Sociological Perspective*. Oxford: Oxford University Press.

CHAPTER 23

Ethical Benchmarks in Life and Art of Fela Anikulapo-Kuti

Sanya Osha

Fela Anikulapo-Kuti was a pioneer in many respects in the fields of music, social activism and ideology. And during his extraordinary lifetime, life and art were constantly marked by extreme polarities that reveal much about his uncommonly uncompromising temperament. Randy Weston, the distinguished Afrocentric jazz artist, had called him "one of the most courageous individuals" he had ever met, an immediately noticeable trait that colored both Anikulapo-Kuti's public and private conduct throughout the course of his incredibly eventful life.

Assessing Anikulapo-Kuti's ethical conduct and principles would lead us through an unlikely route in the sense that he published no comprehensive work in the area that he might have recommended to his numerous acolytes and admirers. However, he published a political magazine during the 1970s at the height of his powers (as a musical and political force) as he criss-crossed various Nigerian university campuses instructing students on the multiple ills of colonialism, post- and neocolonial anomie, pan-Africanism and other related matters.

Nonetheless, these diverse lectures have never been published in a concise volume. We are therefore left to analyze his various ideas and principles on Africanity, political deliberation and social activism, pan-Africanism and African spirituality and the manner in which they informed his ethical conduct without much writing to go by. In addition, he had a specific approach to music composition that might be said to amount to an ethic. It might not be helpful to develop a precise chronology as to how specific ethical principles might have shaped the course of his life because human existence, as we know, is often unpredictable and the multiple turns of Anikulapo-Kuti's life were particularly

S. Osha (✉)
Tshwane University of Technology, Pretoria, South Africa

tumultuous. What we observe during the stressful and traumatic periods of his life were an undying commitment to the principles of social justice, personal and collective freedom and unflinching opposition to military dictatorship even at moments when it seemed most injudicious. These characteristics obviously demonstrated him to be an uncommonly bold and principled activist.

Born in the Yoruba city of Abeokuta in 1938, his mother had consulted a *babalawo*, a soothsayer, which in the Yoruba language translates as "the father of secrets", who promptly predicted: "the child will be stubborn, impetuous, unbridled ... his path will be strewn with pitfalls, turbulence and violence ... his wives will be numerous ... he will live in poverty alongside beggars and thieves. His friends will be fugitives ... and he will be branded an outlaw. For he will flout laws, go counter to the taboos of men and the god of the *oyinbo*. And he will perish by their hand."[1] During his formative years, his parents, Funmilayo (nee Thomas) and Reverend I. O. Ransome-Kuti, were particularly stringent in enforcing a regime of discipline that involved corporal punishment in seeking to nullify the *babalawo*'s predictions.

However, the *babalawo*'s prognosis turned out to be deadly accurate. Anikulapo-Kuti eventually pursued his path of destiny to chilling effect. Even more importantly, the *babalawo*'s prediction regarding veering "counter to the taboos of men and the god of the *oyinbo*" appears to carry more ideological and discursive weight than it seems.

Indeed it appears that beginning from his mother's womb, Anikulapo-Kuti was a fully fledged Afrocentric visionary who duly rejected the foreign name conferred upon him by a German missionary, so the story goes. A son had been born to the Ransome-Kuti family in 1935 but died just three weeks later. Anikulapo-Kuti is described as an *Abiku*, a child who keeps dying and continues to be reborn to the eternal torment of his/her parents. By Anikulapo-Kuti's account, he passed away in his earlier incarnation as Hildegart because the name signified a gross violation of the wishes of his Yoruba ancestors.

The black race, as we know, had been subjected to all forms of oppression, humiliation and injustice beginning with various forms of slavery. It eventually became Anikulapo-Kuti's implacable mission to highlight and challenge these Eurocentric histories of oppression. As such, Anikulapo-Kuti's existential and ideological vision gradually acquired an Afrocentric cast that pitted it overwhelmingly against a Eurocentric appropriation of the world. In his view, Afrocentric constructs of the world should not be unduly vilified but instead had to be construed as being just and life-affirming.

As his ideological conditioning deepened, he was to perceive the world in somewhat crude and stark terms. Apart from the deliberate Afrocentricization of his ideological consciousness, the issue of personal aesthetics, music composition and lifestyle, in short almost everything, became duly radicalized to include distinctly Africanized elements.[2] There was indeed an evident moral contest at work in which whiteness was equated with evil while blackness signified goodness. Anikulapo-Kuti often drove this elemental conceptual comportment to extremes and also landed into confusing, vulnerable as well as glaringly dangerous situations as a result.

For instance, Anikulapo-Kuti inordinately valorized traditional African mores—sometimes to the detriment of otherwise innovative alien cultural practices—and this often proved to be conflictual in terms of praxis. Within traditional—and mostly rural—African settings, authoritarianism was widely entrenched and gerontocracy was the norm. But these characteristics were not respected by him in everyday life unless he was the sole beneficiary of the power and status symbols they usually conferred. Throughout his life, he displayed a constant anti-authoritarian streak that repeatedly led to his being severely clubbed, jailed and dispossessed. Nonetheless this anti-authoritarian element was often directed at the Nigerian military authorities and was in political terms appropriate, even exemplary, if also foolhardy. The main point being as Anikulapo-Kuti pitted an Afrocentric construct of the world against a hegemonic Eurocentric dispensation, arresting subtleties and telling contradictions and paradoxes arose blurring the lines between both mutually opposed constructs.

* * *

As from the early 1970s, Anikulapo-Kuti built a commune comprising multiple lovers, a revolving gallery of musicians and band members as well as assorted runaways, hangers-on and denizens of the streets. His compound was located in the Ojuelegba area of Surulere, Lagos, and became a notorious haven for transients of all sorts even though the original idea had been to build an inclusive commune based on traditional African values of mutuality, reciprocity and social cohesion. But Lagos, the city in which he was resident, was rapidly urbanizing and this meant the presence of Kalakuta (the famed commune's name) within the head-spinning potpourri that is Lagos, became, from a managerial and an authoritative perspective, both an eyesore and an anomaly because it simply defied most strictures of urban control and management. In the modern urban context, the preferred family unit is nucleated in form and nature and the recommended lifestyle is regular and fairly predictable in order to enhance the pace and processes of production and capital expansion. However, Anikulapo-Kuti and his motley crew existed like a band of uncontrollable transients, carousing excessively, creating a racket at every opportunity and undermining the authorities at every turn. The fact that he maintained an open-door policy meant that teenagers often sought refuge in his compound against the wishes of aggrieved parents and this led to violent clashes with the police force.

Ideologically speaking, Anikulapo-Kuti had sought to (re)create a communalized extended family context at the materialistic heart of a transitional postcolonial metropolis and wound up establishing an entity far more complex than he had anticipated. Lagos, as an intractable metropolis, is continually evolving, ingesting and expelling an almost infinite variety of beings, products and elements according to the vagaries of capital as well as the shifting pressures of sociopolitical geography and cultural ecology.[3] Perhaps the anonymity, fluidity and hybridity offered by Lagos afforded Anikulapo-Kuti and the varied members of his commune that opportunity to ignore, and at most times, even, subvert social mores and expectations. Over and above these tumultuous social dynamics, there was perhaps an even deeper contestation involving the often foundational tradition/modernity problematic at play.[4] This problematic, which has been explored employing a multiplicity of philosophical approaches, usually poses the questions.[5] When is tradition salutary and when is it not? In addition, the same query is addressed to modernity. How are the gray zones in-between negotiated without a debilitating loss of identity(ies)?

By most accounts, tradition, according to Anikulapo-Kuti, ought to be the ideal because it supposedly embodies an unalloyed African past, while modernity could be crudely associated with an intrusive, and therefore, deleterious Eurocentricism. But as it ought to be clear by now, the dichotomy between the variants of Afrocentricity and Eurocentricism, in different stages of historical development, is not always as decisive as most purists would have us believe.[6] For instance, African American jazz, or perhaps more succinctly, jazz, is a twentieth-century form of music characterized by improvisatory dexterity according to African performance ethics and precepts that are an inversion of, and a marked contrast to, Eurocentric conventions of music. Jazz naturally appealed to Anikulapo-Kuti because of its numerous African elements; nonetheless he went on to broaden his entire approach to music composition by immersing himself in West African drumming techniques and traditions.

* * *

Anikulapo-Kuti's life, art and ethical principles are no doubt inflected by an Afrocentric tenor and orientation. In addition, his personal sense of aesthetics attempts to embody this general orientation. The same can be said of his central precepts of music composition, which seek to appropriate indigenous African modes of music-making. Molefi Kete Asante asserts that:

> in Afrocentricity, the opening consciousness is assumed to be an awareness of the off-centredness of Africans as a result of alien military, cultural, and social intrusions that have dislocated African people, basically taking Africans off of their own physical and spiritual terms. This consciousness is characterized by an appreciation of the "Afrocentric posture" or a sense of "Afrocentric narratology" in the face of loss-ness and lost-ness leading to disorientation. Some Afrocentrists have regarded Western philosophies as contrary and often antagonistic to the proper understanding of African narratives; they are mainly distant and simply concerned with non-African realities.[7]

Asante's[8] definition of the Afrocentric project obviously relates to many aspects of Anikulapo-Kuti's life and ethical principles. For instance, the adoption of the world religions of Islam and Christianity is considered an index of lost-ness by African peoples and Anikulapo-Kuti (who incidentally dropped the family of Ransome-Kuti as an Afrocentric repudiation of Eurocentric otherness) has declaimed this tendency in hit songs such as "Shuffering and Shmiling" (1976) and "Coffin for Head of State" (1978). In compositions such as "Yellow Fever" (1976), he decries the widespread usage of skin-lightening treatments and potions by black women, which again, in his view, can be regarded as a (mis)appropriation of antithetical conceptions of Western beauty.

Another noteworthy point regarding Anikulapo-Kuti's ethical principles is the belief that strict injunctions needed to be adhered to in African procedures of music-making. Just as the act of libation, music ought to be informative in a fundamental way; it had to serve as a medium connecting the deliberations of the living together with the world of departed ancestors, in other words, the sentient living and the dematerialized dead.

And then on another level, given the deplorable neocolonial entrapment of most African societies, music had to assume a thoroughly political calling in directing persistent questions at the bastions of oppressive power. In pursuing this objective of collective liberation, music had to be employed, in Anikulapo-Kuti's words, as "a weapon"; otherwise it stood to serve as an act of mere vanity intended for the perpetuation of an odious and therefore disagreeable status quo.

But what is so remarkable about Anikulapo-Kuti's struggle against neocolonial subjugation and cultural erasure was the irrepressible confidence, strength of character and unfaltering resilience with which he confronted his formidable adversaries. Obviously, the nagging sense of loss-ness and lost-ness that confronts African peoples and the black race in general is defined by multiple variables pertaining to the length and nature of the colonial relationship, the extent of cultural subjugation and erasure and the retention and/or loss of indigenous languages and institutions, being some of the most prominent amongst them.[9]

It is clear that Anikulapo-Kuti did not confront the postcolonial sense of loss from a position of subservience or inferiority. Instead, he seemed to confront his existential dilemmas with an almost jarring sense of completeness and indomitableness which his shortsighted detractors viewed as unbridled arrogance. Rather than withdraw into the maw of postcolonial shame and cultural and epistemic reticence, he tirelessly projected a voice that served the dispossessed while at the same time railing against the transgressions of the miscreants of power.

* * *

Amid the flurry of eulogistic tomes and myriad, probably jaundiced personal accounts of ardent "felasophers", it is necessary to seek out competent interpreters of Anikulapo-Kuti's work who are also able to separate what is important and what is not worth expending too much time upon. As such one should allude to books such as Trevor Schoonmaker's *Black President: The Art and*

Legacy of Fela Anikulapo-Kuti (2003) and also his edited volume, *Fela: From West Africa to West Broadway* (2003). Tejumola Olaniyan's *Arrest the Music* (2004) is also deserving of mention just as Carlos Moore's *Fela! This Bitch of a Life* (2010). The tomes just mentioned do much more to separate the man from the myth without ignoring to place his music in its proper perspective.

Several undiscerning critics and admirers end up adding more wool to the Fela myth rather than illuminating his life and achievements as an artist. By any standard, as already mentioned, Anikulapo-Kuti's life was truly remarkable in terms of how he was able to create a fresh musical idiom and also the political struggles he waged. But in focusing primarily on his perennial conflicts with the Nigerian political establishment and not his invention of Afrobeat, the obfuscating mythology beclouds the line separating fact from fiction.

There is often a strident effort to present Anikulapo-Kuti as an atavistic ethnocentrist. But in the end, the Anikulapo-Kuti appeal has taken on a universal dimension in which observers are able to draw parallels between his life and those of Jean-Jacques Rousseau, Leonidas of Sparta and Che Guevara. However, Anikulapo-Kuti's espousal of a form of Egyptology and African spirituality toward the end of his life contradicts the underlying universalism of his musical vision. In fact, many non-Africans find a large dose of his eclectic spirituality quite alienating. Initially, it was not Anikulapo-Kuti's intention to create divisions among his audiences.

In 1958, he had traveled to London to study music at the Trinity College of Music where he moonlighted digesting the jazz of John Coltrane and Miles Davis. Back home in Nigeria, highlife was the dominant form of music with E. T. Mensah, Cardinal Rex Lawson and Victor Olaiya as its main proponents. Anikulapo-Kuti's early bands, the jazz quintet and Koola Lobitos, would not play straight highlife and so it took a while for audiences to latch on.[10] He turned to his mother who gave perceptive advice; he had to play something his audiences could understand. Tony Allen, a key figure in the evolution of Afrobeat, then took on a more visible role in incorporating indigenous Yoruba rhythms into a highly potent mix of highlife, jazz and funk. At this moment, Anikulapo-Kuti found his voice and the necessary musicians such as Lekan Animashaun to support him. Before then, a major experience that led to his moment of aesthetic self-discovery was a trip to the United States in the late 1960s. There, he met Sandra Isidore, an African American anthropology student who convincingly steered him to the philosophy of black consciousness and who turned him to ideologues of blackness and racial empowerment such as Malcolm X and the Black Panthers.

So two factors combined to form his essential palette: a philosophy of blackness and a carefully selected assortment of musical ingredients that could bear his ideological message. Having accomplished this distinctive creative self, the conservative Nigerian social and political classes began to take notice. It was not long before his numerous arrests and harassments by law enforcement agencies commenced. He and his entourages were frequently beaten and hurled into detention culminating in the sacking of his commune, Kalakuta, in

1977. During his particular assault, his aged mother, a noted feminist and political activist, was thrown out of a first-floor window. She died of her injuries a year later. His singers and dancers were raped and mutilated and Kuti himself was almost clubbed to death. In the decade after the burning of Kalakuta, his global fame grew as he concentrated on entertaining and educating the regular devotees who visited his shrine weekly.

True, Anikulapo-Kuti upheld pan-African views until the end of his life in 1997, but what is often forgotten in books written by insufficiently critical acolytes is that the journey that led to the discovery of his singular musical vision is often more interesting than the unduly repetitive mouthing off of secondhand ethnocentric beliefs. What makes Anikulapo-Kuti truly remarkable, we must never forget, is his music.

The more voluble fans of Anikulapo-Kuti—and they are numerous—on the other hand, tend to be more taken in by the paraphernalia of showmanship which does very little to explain the greatness of the art form. Also absent in the analyses of many inadequately critical admirers are the key moments and experiences—such as his introduction to the thought and activities of the Black Panthers in the United States and his rediscovery of his indigenous Yoruba music roots—in Anikulapo-Kuti's life that eventually made him the kind of artist he was. Fortunately, as mentioned earlier, there are quite a number of works on Anikulapo-Kuti that hit the mark in grappling with complex components of his art. Ultimately, there are also more accomplished efforts—such as the broadway musical—that throw useful light of the power of the Anikulapo-Kuti mythology while not undermining the powerful appeal of the mesmeric fusion of diverse sonic elements.

* * *

The question of Anikulapo-Kuti's status as an exemplar or purist of Yoruba music is quite problematic. True enough, Anikulapo-Kuti's music employs facets of indigenous Yoruba drumming to lend Afrobeat—the genre he largely created—its inimitable cadences, textures and character. But as noted, the form also draws generously from African American jazz and funk which ultimately inflect it with an unmistakable cosmopolitanism as opposed to the self-contained cultural microcosms of say *juju*, *sakara*, *fuji* or *apala*. Indeed, it can be argued that it is this distinctive cosmopolitanism that primarily accounts for his current popularity as a veritable icon of world music.

Coupled with this is that his iconoclasm which rather than reinforce traditional Yoruba cultural values departs from them and this is why it can be argued that Anikulapo-Kuti can be rather problematic as an unflinching beacon of Yoruba music in the narrow understanding of the term. However, this is the point which the ethnomusicologist, Bode Omojola, does not explore in great detail in his otherwise magisterial book *Yoruba Music in the Twentieth Century: Identity, Agency, and Performance Practice* (2012).

Also, Anikulapo-Kuti alienated the political and military establishments through constant verbal abuse and direct confrontation. Arguably, his approach could not have led to the transformation of decayed and malfunctioning sociopolitical order due to its often unduly confrontational manner. Instead, Anikulapo-Kuti's methods could only have courted violent reappraisals in the way they did. Inherent in indigenous Yoruba culture are powerful resources of satire, conceit, doublespeak and chameleonic invective which could be deployed for subversive political activity, but Anikulapo-Kuti chose to ignore them and instead adopted what may in many instances be regarded as the rights-based conception of Western democracy and traditions of social activism.

Anikulapo-Kuti may also have been a staunch pan-Africanist, but he appeared to be a less faithful adherent of Yoruba culture. So it is sometimes difficult to think of him as a worthy proponent of it. First of all, from the early 1970s onward, he used Yoruba language only sparingly in his increasingly complex compositions and opted instead for Nigerian/West African pidgin. However, the Yoruba language is probably the most suitable medium in which to explore and imbibe the rich cultural lore, history, mores and various traditions of the Yoruba, his ethnicity. True, Anikulapo-Kuti's singing was largely informed by the call-and-response format of age-old African traditions of song, but there are other equally powerful characteristics that Anikulapo-Kuti failed to explore fully or even at all such as indigenous Yoruba chanting, aphorisms, proverbs, incantations, the *oriki* (praise songs) and the general construction of community through artistic consensus-building. Anikulapo-Kuti's approach to consensus-building was marked by strident individualism and eccentricity and was also selective in favor of the socioeconomic dropouts and cultural renegades that converged around him often to his enormous detriment.

Pidgin, Anikulapo-Kuti's chosen medium of expression, is also not the best site to search for the richness of Yoruba culture as it is arguably a product of the odious colonialism Anikulapo-Kuti denounced. While pidgin serves as a dialect of linguistic resistance to European colonization, it can also be regarded as a direct reflection of it; a vulgarization of European languages—primarily English and Portuguese—and Nigerian languages through a continual reconfiguration of colonized linguistic subjectivity. The speaker of pidgin thus becomes a new subject of both modernity and colonialism while at the same time grappling for treasured fragments of a supposedly unalloyed precolonial heritage.

Tropes of hybridity, mimesis and reinvention are what mediate the consciousness of the speaker of pidgin, so, rather than a return to one's nostalgic cultural roots, what can be accomplished is a new subjectivity that draws more from the new rather than the old. And perhaps without fully understanding the gravity of his language choice, Anikulapo-Kuti was departing from an authentic African ethos in which linguistic resistance coupled with personal idiosyncrasy led to the creation of a new subjectivity that would always be difficult to replicate due to its pronounced iconoclasm.

Both Christopher Waterman[11] and Omojola use the terms "bourgeois" and "radical" to describe Anikulapo-Kuti, but both descriptions unexpectedly ring true. However, it is sometimes difficult to imagine him being purely "bourgeois" as he consistently articulated the interests, experiences and aspirations of the downtrodden, the caveat being that his charismatic heroism also stood him apart. His radicalism, on the other hand, is quite self-explanatory as it evidently stems from his trenchant sociopolitical critique.

* * *

It has been quite a while since Fela Anikulapo-Kuti passed but his memory would be kept alive as long as there are music lovers, and as long as people value the virtues of the perennial outsider, the avant-garde artist and the political rebel. As noted, once he returned to his native Nigeria after his brief spell in civil rights era Los Angeles, he was ready to meld all different cultural influences into a potent brew of radical politics, hypnotic beats (drawn, as mentioned earlier, from a mix of James Brown's funk, West African highlife grooves and indigenous trance music) and West African spirituality.

As his fame spread, he rapidly became a thorn in the flesh of corrupt military administrations of Nigeria. He was further radicalized by their gross incompetence, lack of foresight and criminal brutality. But these very "sins", or rather omissions, were precisely what defined his oppositional ideology, his irrepressible resolve to undermine questionable authority and its culpable agents. Anikulapo-Kuti was not merely an enemy of the state; he was also an adversary of the bourgeois values that partly produced him being the scion of a prominent educator and a courageous feminist. He spat in the face of middle-class good sense at every given opportunity that it became impossible for his original social class to appreciate his musical genius. What it saw instead was a betrayal of the class, a gadfly who needed to be taught a severe lesson.

Within the context of myopic politics, Anikulapo-Kuti was seen a social irritant. He undoubtedly did all he could to offend the social class of his parents. He also incurred the wrath of all manner of powerful political figures in the country such as Olusegun Obasanjo, Shehu Yar'Adua, Moshood Abiola and the redoubtable duo of General Sani Abacha and Major General Musa Bamaiyi who had paraded him at the tail end of his life, worn out, handcuffed, disheveled and HIV/AIDS-stricken before television cameras. And so he paid dearly for his unremitting irreverence. As mentioned earlier, his house was stormed by armed guards and razed to the ground. After a bizarre court battle, Fela emerged from the tragic ordeal with yet another masterpiece of music and protest, "Unknown Soldier", in which he castigated the military and civilian authorities that ordered the wanton violation of his human rights.

As mentioned earlier, Anikulapo-Kuti was not only an opponent of the Nigerian state and African dictatorships generally. He was also at war with society. He was at war with any known conventional way of doing things. He later turned his back on the institution of marriage which he saw as an artificial imposition on natural human relations. He maintained an open house and anyone could literally walk off the streets and become part of his fluid extended family. Of course different kinds of lost souls, social deviants, hardened criminals and neighborhood thugs took advantage of his openness in engaging in acts of criminality. Under-aged girls ran away from home attracted by the intoxicating sense of freedom, rebellion and adventure that came with his personality. For society's intractable dropouts he had a powerful messianic appeal, which many of his followers did not completely understand because no one could really say who drove him or how he had concocted his unique brew of Africanity, dissent, showmanship and musical vision. They were in part seduced by the jumbo-sized marijuana joints he smoked incessantly for his private pleasure and perhaps also as a slap on the face of society for its idiocies and hypocrisy. Anikulapo-Kuti represented vindication and success for the irreverent rebel and unrepentant renegade.

But what we must also understand is that it is only Africa that could have produced Anikulapo-Kuti. The virulence of his form of dissent could never have festered in Europe or North America. It is certain that the brew he was able to concoct would have been squashed in those regions. He probably would have been administered unsuited courses of electroshock convulsive therapy to correct his waywardness just as the great African American jazz artist Bud Powell had endured. Another great African American jazz musician, Charlie Parker, narrowly escaped electroshock treatment only through the sympathetic intervention of his wife, Chan, who did not want his creative abilities impaired as had happened with Powell. However, there is a distinct difference between Anikulapo-Kuti and these giants of American jazz. Anikulapo-Kuti was a redoubtable sociopolitical critic who made the Nigerian political establishment extremely uncomfortable, whereas these jazz artists revolutionized the American music industry through their artistic innovations and countercultural lifestyles without really confronting the mainstream political establishment in a manner that could ultimately be deemed threatening.

Indeed Anikulapo-Kuti might have ended up being institutionalized as a paranoid schizophrenic had he chosen to emigrate. Every establishment of normalization would have clamped down on him. He would have plied numerous "corrective" kinds of medication to douse his raging inner fire and keep him silent. It should not be a surprise that in spite of the torture, imprisonment and injustices Anikulapo-Kuti suffered in the hands of various Nigerian governments, he refused to emigrate. He remained firmly on Nigerian soil even when he found so much that annoyed and disgusted him. Where else could he be allowed to nurture countercultural communities that thrived beyond the confines of law? Which other society could tolerate his coterie of outlaws who sought to undermine constituted authorities at every turn? Anikulapo-Kuti could only have forged his identity in a hesitant and transitory postcolonial milieu such as Nigeria where everything was up for grabs.

Merle Haggard, the American country music maverick, complained that America has become so sanitized that it was now illegal to smoke a cigarette in a pool room. The spots of New York that produced rebellious punk rock have since been cleared out and gentrified. It is impossible to see Anikulapo-Kuti thriving in such a clinical ambience. Anikulapo-Kuti could only have functioned on the margins of society, and no matter how progressive a society could be, he could never have found a place within the mainstream. There is something really deep seated about his outsiderness and searing sense of opposition to all forms of normality or received convention.

But in Africa, in Nigeria in particular, in spite of some cultural and institutional constraints, he was able to bloom like a strange wildflower. His strangeness was what in turn made him a uniquely developed individual such that nothing about him—ideology, personality, music and dress sense—seemed normal. He often called himself "*abami eda*", meaning "the weird one" when in jest or when he was holding court amid throngs of loyal acolytes. But we are not to be deceived. He truly meant it.

Anikulapo-Kuti never tired of claiming he was an unapologetic Afrocentrist. His Afrocentricity was often carried to almost preposterous levels and several instances bear this out. For a number of years, he was overwhelmingly influenced by Kwaku Adalai, better known as Professor Hindu, a Ghanaian spiritualist and traditional healer upon whom Anikulapo-Kuti would entrust his worldly and spiritual affairs against his own better judgment. As he fell completely under Professor Hindu's spell, Kalakuta Republic became plagued with superstition, bigotry and paranoia and what had been its once laissez-faire atmosphere rapidly evaporated.

Paranoia, widespread suspicion and fear became dominant within the household and it is something of a mystery how Anikulapo-Kuti was able to remain creative and productive. During the unfortunate period when Anikulapo-Kuti was under Professor Hindu's influence, he never took any decision without consulting with the spiritualist. Of course his more rational friends and associates believed he was experiencing severe psychological difficulties that required urgent medical attention, but Anikulapo-Kuti dismissed all entreaties to embark on that route.

Another instance in which Anikulapo-Kuti's Afrocentricity proved problematic was in 1991 when he expressed his opposition to the use of condoms at the height of the HIV/AIDS pandemic. He even went on to compose a song, "Condom, Scaliwag and Scatter", which Carlos Moore calls "the most reckless song of his entire career" (Moore, p. 321).[12]

In arriving at his notion of Afrocentricity, Anikulapo-Kuti drew a sizeable part of his ideological armature from the ideas of Kwame Nkrumah, a formidable advocate of pan-Africanism on African shores. According to Nkrumah, pan-Africanism entailed the complete liberation of the continent from the yoke of colonialism. It also included a socialist form of social organization and development.[13] In turn, Nkrumah's pan-Africanism is immensely indebted to the work of W. E. B. Dubois, the great American sociologist.

In essence, Nkrumah's conception of pan-Africanism sought to confront the oppression of European subjugation of African peoples, on the one hand, and the urgent challenges of decolonization, on the other. As such, the project of decolonization is a thoroughly modernist enterprise, intimately entwined in the greater nation-building objective. If Nkrumah's pan-Africanism bore strong hints of socialism and copious elements of modernism, it displayed very few connections with Anikulapo-Kuti's understanding of "tradition" or, more precisely, African traditional culture. This was perhaps because the nation-building project is entirely modernist in its teleology.

In contrast, Anikulapo-Kuti espoused notions of tradition that were often antithetical to Nigerian/West African modernities. For instance, his adoption of Orisha spirituality collided with broad swaths of Nigerian Pentecostalism which has been on the ascendant for several decades. A certain public perception of charismatic Pentecostalism is associated with the spread and entrenchment of modernity and the gospel of late capitalism while the recourse to traditional spirituality evidently denotes an anachronism and possibly even, a relapse into outright heathen barbarity or demonology. Anikulapo-Kuti's promotion of Orisha was bound to lead to social ostracism, but he could not be bothered and instead seemed to wear his ostracism as a mark of distinction.

In addition, Anikulapo-Kuti adopted a form of pan-Africanism that was communalistic rather than socialist in the manner of Nkrumah or Sekou Toure of Guinea. Hence, his pan-Africanism was arguably folklorist rather than intellectualized in the fashion of say, Julius Nyerere of Tanzania. It stemmed as such from what he drew from at the deeply instinctual level rather than what had been developed through systematic theorizing. He did not seem unduly traumatized by the sense of lost-ness occasioned by Eurocentric domination most probably because he had flourished in a cultural environment that managed to retain a significant proportion of its indigenous heritage which he explored and employed in singularly inventive and, also, spectacularly self-empowering ways.

NOTES

1. Carlos Moore 2010, p. 32.
2. Osha 2013, 2016, 2017.
3. Whiteman 2012.
4. Wiredu 1980, 1983, 1993, 1994, 1996; Wiredu and Gyekye 1992.
5. Appiah 1992; Davidson 1959; de Buck 1935; Hountondji 1983, 1987, 1996, 2002.
6. Asante 1977; Cameron 1961; Cronon 1955; Cummings 1986; Diop 1974; Fanon 1967; Fanon 1963.
7. Asante 2017, p. 231.
8. Asante 1987.
9. Asante 1987, 2017.
10. Collins 1992; Palmberg and Kirkegaard 2002.
11. Waterman 2002.
12. Moore 2010, p. 321.
13. Nabudere 1980, 1994, 1997, 2002, 2003, 2004, 2006, 2007.

Bibliography

Appiah, Anthony K. 1992. *In My Father's House: Africa in the Philosophy of Culture.* New York: Oxford University Press.
Asante, S.K.B. 1977. *Pan-African Protest: West Africa and the Italo-Ethiopian Crisis 1934–1941.* London: Longman.
Asante, Kete Molefi. 1987. *The Afrocentric Idea.* Philadelphia: Temple University Press.
———. 2017. The Philosophy of Afrocentricity. In *The Palgrave Handbook of African Philosophy*, ed. Adeshina Afolayan and Toyin Falola. New York: Palgrave Macmillan.
Bascom, W. 1980. *Sixteen Cowries: Yoruba Divination from Africa to the New World.* Bloomington: Indiana University Press.
Bernal, Martin Gardiner. 2001. In *Black Athena Writes Back: Martin Bernal Responds to His Critics*, ed. D. Chioni Moore. Durham/London: Duke University Press.
Cameron, James. 1961. *The African Revolution.* London: Thames & Hudson.
Collins, John. 1992. *West African Pop Roots.* Philadelphia: Temple University Press.
Cronon, D.E. 1955. *Black Moses: The Story of Marcus Garvey and the Universal Negro Improvement Association.* Wisconsin: University of Wisconsin Press.
Cummings, Robert. 1986. Africa Between the Ages. *African Studies Review* 29 (3): 1–26.
Davidson, Basil. 1959. *Old Africa Rediscovered.* London: Gollancz.
de Buck, A. 1935–1961. *The Egyptian Coffin Texts.* Vol. 7. Chicago: Oriental Institute.
Diop, Cheikh Anta. 1974. *The African Origin of Civilization: Myth or Reality?* Trans. M. Cook. Westport: Lawrence Hill.
Durkheim, E., and M. Mauss. 1970. Primitive Classification. 2. Translated with an introduction by R. Needham. London: Cohen & West.
Fanon, Frantz. 1963. *The Wretched of the Earth.* London: Penguin.
———. 1967 *Black Skin, White Masks.* Trans. C. Van Markmann. New York: Grove Press.
Hountondji, Paulin J. 1983. Distances. *Ibadan Journal of Humanistic Studies* 3: 135–146.
———. 1987. What Philosophy Can Do. *QUEST: An International African Journal of Philosophy* 1 (2): 19.
———. 1996. *African Philosophy: Myth and Reality.* Bloomington: Indiana University Press.
———. 2002. *The Struggle for Meaning: Reflections on Philosophy, Culture and Democracy in Africa.* Athens: Ohio University Center for International Studies.
Moore, Carlos. 2010. *This Bitch of a Life.* Abuja: Cassava Republic Press.
Nabudere, D.W. 1980. *Imperialism and Revolution in Uganda.* London: Onyx Press.
———. 1994. The African Challenge. *Alternatives: Global, Local, Political* 19 (2 (Spring)): 163–171.
———. 1997. Beyond Modernization and Development, Or, Why the Poor Reject Development. *Geografista Annaler: Series B, Human Geography* 79 (4): 203–215.
———. 2002. *How New Information Technologies Can Be Used for Learning in Pastoral Communities in Africa.* Porto Alegre: World Social Summit. http://tinyurl.com/pjaq2ko.
———. 2003. Conflict over Mineral Wealth: Understanding the Second Invasion of the DRC. In *The War Economy in the Democratic Republic of Congo*, ed. S. Naidoo. Braamfontein: Institute of Global Dialogue.
———. 2004. Traditional and Modern Political Systems in Contemporary Governance in Africa. *Journal of African Elections* 3 (1): 13–41.

———. 2006. Towards an Afrokology of Knowledge Production and African Regeneration. *International Journal of African Renaissance Studies* 1 (1): 7–32.

———. 2007. Cheikh Anta Diop: The Social Sciences, Humanities, Physical and Natural Sciences, and Transdisciplinarity. *International Journal of African Renaissance Studies* 2 (1): 6–34.

Olaniyan, Tejumola. 2001. The Cosmopolitan Nativist: Fela Anikulapo-Kuti and the Antimonies of Postcolonial Modernity. *Research in African Literatures* 32 (2): 76–89.

———. 2004. *Arrest the Music! Fela and His Rebel Art and Politics*. Bloomington: Indiana University Press.

Omojola, Bode. 2012. *Yoruba Music in the Twentieth Century: Identity, Agency, and Performance Practice*. New York: University of Rochester Press.

Osha, Sanya. 2013. Fela Anikulapo-Kuti: Musician or Ideologue. *Africa Review of Books/Revue Africaine des Livres* 9 (1): 14–15.

———. 2016. Anikulapo-Kuti, Fela. In *Encyclopedia of the Yoruba*, ed. Toyin Falola and Akintunde Akinyemi. Bloomington: Indiana University Press.

———. 2017. Music for the Gods. *Africa Review of Books/Revue Africaine des Livres* 13 (1): 7–8.

Palmberg, Mai, and Annemette Kirkegaard, eds. 2002. *Playing with Identities in Contemporary Music in Africa*. Uppsala: Nordiska Afrikainstitutet.

Schoonmaker, Trevor. 2003a. *The Art and Legacy of Fela Anikulapo-Kuti*. New York: New Museum of Contemporary Art.

———. 2003b. *Fela: From West Africa to West Broadway*. New York/Basingstoke: Palgrave Macmillan.

Waterman, Christopher. 2002. Big Man, Black President, Masked One: Models of the Celebrity Self in Yoruba Popular Music. In *Playing with Identities in Contemporary Music in Africa*, ed. Mai Palmberg and Annemette Kirkegaard. Uppsala: Nordiska Afrikainstitutet.

Whiteman, Kaye. 2012. *Lagos: A Cultural and Historical Companion*. Oxford: Signal Books.

Wiredu, K. 1980. *Philosophy and an African Culture*. Cambridge/New York: Cambridge University Press.

———. 1983. The Akan Concept of Mind. *Ibadan Journal of Humanistic Studies* 3: 113–134.

———. 1993. Canons of Conceptualisation. *The Monist* 76 (4 (October)): 450–476.

———. 1994. Towards Decolonizing African Philosophy and Religion. *African Studies Quarterly* 1 (4). http://tinyurl.com/onm6kuy.

———. 1996. *Cultural Universals and Particulars: An African Perspective*. Bloomington: Indiana University Press.

Wiredu, K., and K. Gyekye. 1992. *Persons and Community*. Washington, DC: The Council for Research in Values and Philosophy.

CHAPTER 24

Ethical Thought of Kwasi Wiredu and Kwame Gyekye II

George Kotei Neequaye

INTRODUCTION

Wiredu and Gyekye both stress that the function of ethics in the Akan society is to bring harmony, stability, prosperity, welfare, unity and solidarity. Good in Akan society, in their opinion, is synonymous to the welfare of the community. For the Akan, therefore, what is morally good is that which brings human well-being. Evil (*bone*), on the other hand, is that which destroys the welfare and harmony of the community. They emphasized that in the African social life, ethics of responsibility, which is the care and concern for the needs of others in the community, is paramount. Concerning the source of morality, they both agree that in Akan social morality the will of God is logically unqualified in determining the good, and as such has nothing to do with Akan social morality. The motivation for doing the good is, therefore, not because of God even though God is known to be impeccably good. Consequently, for the Akan, morality is devoid of religion since there is nothing like an institutional religion in Akan culture. Thus, they demystified morality by dissociating it from any supernaturalistic sources and gave it a humanistic character. But I argue that insofar as it is unanimously believed by Africans that the Supreme Being is the creator of human beings and the universe, and also that He is believed to be morally impeccable, then Africans, and for that matter Akans, logically derive their innate religious inclinations from God. Admittedly, society plays a role in the origination of morality, but it may be erroneous, as far as I am concerned, to ground the origin of morality only on society and simply affirm, like they did, that religion is not the source of morality. I argue, therefore, that morality is contingent upon religion.

G. K. Neequaye (✉)
Trinity Theological Seminary, Legon, Ghana

Kwame Gyekye's Akan Ethics

Philosophy as a raison d'être of morality

Kwame Gyekye is a product of the University of Ghana and Harvard University in the USA where he did his Ph.D. with a thesis on the Graeco-Arabic philosophy. He is a prominent African philosopher and has written extensively on African philosophy.

At the heart of Gyekye's conception of ethics is his interpretation of philosophy. Gyekye defines philosophy in the Akan language as *onyansafo* (wise person), which according to him refers to someone who

> reflects, imagines, intuits, and then condenses these reflections, imaginings, and intuitions in proverbs. The *onyansafo* is able to speculate about human experience. Probing aspects of human experience and the external world, he or she may pose questions about the fundamental principles that underlie human life. ... The wise person of the Akan community is essentially a speculative philosopher.[1]

According to Gyekye, *nyansa* or *adwen (mental faculty)*, which by nature is linked to one's *sunsum* (spirit), is a priori and not a posteriori. In other words, *nyansa*, our thinking faculty, the source of wisdom, is an inborn mental faculty that is imputed at birth and not acquired by experience. *Nyansa* is, therefore, the thinking faculty of a person. Gyekye further opines that "thought (adwen) in the narrow sense is in Akan philosophy an activity of the sunsum."[2] *Sunsum* is, therefore, the source of a person's personality and character.[3] Since *sunsum* ultimately derives from Onyame, the Supreme Being who is the creator of the universe and the source of all being, it follows logically that *nyansa* also ultimately derives from the Supreme Being, the Great Spirit.[4] But when the Akan refers to a person as *nyansafo*, it means one who is capable of using his/her *nyansa* to analyze and digest issues to come out with wise decisions for life. It is, therefore, the one who is genuinely called a *nyansafo* in the Akan language who can be said to be a philosopher. Consequently, it is not everybody or every elder in the society who can be called *nyansafo* in the true sense of the word. Everyone has *nyansa*, which is a function of the inborn *sunsum*, but not everyone can be referred to as *nyansafo*; *nyansafo* is, therefore, a posteriori, not a priori like *nyansa*. In other words, whereas *nyansafo* is acquired by experience, *nyansa* is innate. So, by inference, the *Philosopher King* of Plato is the *nyansafo* in the Akan experience. Like Plato, it is the *Nyansafo*, the *Philosopher King*, who has the ability to rule society since by virtue of the knowledge he/she has acquired, he/she is closer to God, the source of all goodness, and, subsequently, he/she has the mental and moral capabilities to lead society. Philosophy, *nyansa*, is thus the source of Akan ethical thought.[5] The one who is able to analyze problems to come out with solutions is a *nyansafo*, the philosopher. Gyekye puts it succinctly this way:

The Akan philosopher aims at comprehensive understanding of the world and human life and conduct. He or she attempts a description of not only how things are, but also how human beings ought to live and what their values ought to be—hence the existence of many proverbs relative to morality. The wise person of the Akan community is essentially a speculative philosopher.[6]

On that account, philosophy is a function or a raison d'être of morality. According to Gyekye, the *nyansafo* is the one who can analyze problems of society and, in consequence, comes out with philosophies of life and policies that govern society.[7] Philosophy is, therefore, not meant to be an academic exercise, but a fountain from which policies, proverbs, morality and wisdom derive.

On the question of how the Akan defines *ethics*, he is of the view that since the Akan defines bad or good actions pragmatically, the state of one's character (*suban*) is paramount in determining the rightness or wrongness of an action. The character then appears to be the most important determinant of morality. Gyekye further surmises that the Akan word *suban* defines the word *ethics*. According to him, if *ethics* is "the science of character" as defined by W. D. Ross, then ethics in the Akan language could be translated as "*suban ho nimdee* or *suban ho adwendwen*," which is a literal translation of *ethics* as a reflection on morality. In other words, ethics is a study of morality.

It is imperative to draw a logical conclusion from the views of Gyekye above that if *sunsum* ultimately derives from the Supreme Being, the Highest Spirit,[8] and *nyansa* is a derivative of *sunsum*, then moralizing (not morality), which is a function of *nyansa*, also derives from the Supreme Being. He puts it this way: "sunsum, the active aspect of the soul, plays a role in character formation, that moral attributes are ascribed to the sunsum, and that like the superego of Freud it constitutes the moral dimension of personality."

Gyekye outlines two types of morality in the Akan context: one that refers to the rules and regulations of a community and the other as the empirical commitment to such rules and regulations. The one who observes the latter, he is referred to as the moral person. Thus, to be regarded as a moral person in the Akan society, one must know the rules and regulations of that community and put them into practice. If one only knows the moral prescriptions but does not practice them, then such a person is not a moral person. Consequently, knowing the moral mind of the Akan community and putting it into practice forms the core of Akan ethics. That led Gyekye to distinguish between *morality$_1$*, which, according to him, refers to "moral beliefs, norms, rules, principles, ideals," and *morality$_2$*, which he explicates as "patterns of behavior, that is, attitudes or responses to moral norms, rules, etc.; moral practice or commitment."[9] Where he refers to both, he merely writes *morality*. According to him, *morality$_1$* is formulated to counter humanity's selfishness or self-aggrandizement.[10]

He then went on to address the issue as to whether religion is the source of morality or it merely influences morality. This is the way he puts it:

> In Akan thought goodness is not defined by reference to religious beliefs or supernatural beings. What is morally good is not that which is commanded by God or any spiritual being; what is right is not that which is pleasing to a spiritual being or in accordance with the will of such being.[11]

Thus, Gyekye demystified morality by dissociating it from any supernaturalistic sources and gave it a humanistic character. He argues that in Akan moral thought, the sole reason for morality$_1$ and morality$_2$ are for the welfare or well-being of the community. He argues that "Within the framework of Akan social and humanistic ethics, what is morally good is generally that which promotes social welfare, solidarity, and harmony in human relationships." In other words, the function of morality in the Akan society is to bring stability, harmony, peace and prosperity in the community. He further notes that the motivating factor for observing rules and regulations in a given society is not only for a harmonious relationship but also to serve the interest of others and at times at the cost of one's interest. He is of the opinion that "a certain minimum of altruism is absolutely essential to the moral motivation."[12] He affirms that altruism is universal in all human societies, even though he agrees that not all individuals are known to have been altruistic. He, however, observes that different peoples and individuals have a different understanding of morality for various reasons. Some of the distinctive features, he notes, are the particular cultural context within which one finds himself/herself; the contingencies of space, time and clime in a particular society; and the way the community sees the relationship between male and female, pleasure and pain, life and work and so on.[13] It means that normative principles are relative to a particular society.

Good in Akan society, in the opinion of Gyekye, is synonymous to the welfare of the community. For the Akan, "What is morally good is that which brings about—or is supposed, expected, or known to bring about—human well-being."[14] He outlined the good in Akan thought to include "kindness, compassion, generosity, hospitality, faithfulness, truthfulness, concern for others, and the action that brings peace, justice, dignity, respect, and happiness" and bad habits to include, "backbiting, selfishness, lying, stealing, adultery, rape, incest, murder, and suicide."[15] That means that evil (*bone*) is defined by Akan society as that which destroys the welfare and harmony of the community. Gyekye emphasized that in the African social life, ethics of responsibility, which is the care and concern for the needs of others in the community, is paramount.[16] Gyekye further notes that Akans normally will practice the good, not because he/she wants to please any supernatural being or afraid that he/she will be sanctioned by any supernatural being, but simply because he/she wants to avoid disgrace for one's self or the family name. Gyekye puts it this way: "The fear or thought of shame, of disgrace, or loss of social esteem and opportunity, and so on, constitutes a real influence on moral conduct, and as such can be regarded as a kind of sanction, if an obscure one."[17]

Gyekye indicates that there are two types of evil: bone and *musuo* (*okyiwade*—something hateful). Bone is the ordinary type of evil, which includes "theft, lying, backbiting, and so on," while *musuo*, a moral taboo, refers to serious evils like "murder, sexual intercourse with a woman impregnated by another man, suicide, incest, words of abuse against the chief, and stealing from among the properties of a deity."[18] Even though acts of *musuo* are punishable by the gods and ancestors, Gyekye still insists that "the acts classified as moral taboos were so regarded simply because of the gravity of their consequences for human society, not because those acts were hateful to any supernatural beings."[19] Subsequently, morality does not originate from religion, even though the practice of morality may be related to religion.[20] The reasons he gives for his position, first, is that the Akan religion is not a revealed religion like Christianity or Islam or Judaism. According to him, in revealed religion, divine truth is transmitted to a founder, who in turn teaches it to others, which is not the case in indigenous African religion.[21] Second, the Akan knows God to have characteristics like "good, compassionate, merciful, just, benevolent, comforting, and so on" and therefore ascribe goodness to God, not because He is the source of morality.[22] Third, from Akan thought, God approves of the good because it is good, not that it is good because it is coming from God.[23] Fourth, because Akans give much respect to the opinions of elders, kin and heads of the various clans, their opinions ultimately become the morality of the community.[24]

AKAN ETHICS AS ENCAPSULATED BY KWASI WIREDU

Kwasi Wiredu is also a Ghanaian and a product of the University of Ghana, completing in 1958. He did his B Phil. at the University College, Oxford, in 1960, graduating with a thesis entitled "Knowledge, Truth and Reason." He is a world-renowned scholar in African philosophy. He has written volumes on African philosophy.

Like Gyekye, Wiredu also stresses that African morality is of humanistic classification and, as such, it is a social morality. He avers that "What is good in general is what promotes human interests,"[25] affirming the Akan saying that *onipa na ohia* (meaning, it is a human being who has value). According to him, o(hia) means that which is needed and at the same time has value. *Ohia*, therefore, means that humanity is of prime importance in communalism. Furthermore, for the Akan, two things characterize what is regarded as moral: first, the motive must be right and, second, the rational, the objective aspect of morality, must be acceptable.[26] Wiredu, like Gyekye, observes that the context within which the African child learns his/her morality is the home, especially from parents and kinsmen, and the process continues for the rest of a person's life.[27] Like Gyekye, Wiredu also argues that as far as the Akan social morality is concerned, the will of God is logically unqualified in determining the good, and as such has nothing to do with Akan social morality.[28] The motivation for doing the good is, therefore, not because of God, even though God is known to be impeccably good. Consequently, for the Akan, morality is devoid of religion since there is nothing like an institutional religion in Akan culture.[29] In his own words, he puts it this way, "Another significant contrast with other religions, particularly certain influential forms of Christianity, is that although God is held to be all-good, morality is not defined in Akan thought in terms of the will of God, but rather in terms of human interests."[30]

Comparing the customs of the West and Akan societies, Wiredu made it clear that in this era of globalization and industrialization, Western customs seem to be erasing African customs fast and that individualism seems to be replacing community in African communalism. According to him, Africans in large cities are the most vulnerable because they are bombarded with the customs of the West in such a way that the care system that is prevalent in communalism seems to be eroding. This also has an effect on morality in Africa as the individual's contribution to the running of the society is declining. Urbanization even makes the situation worse as many people who move from the rural areas to the urban areas are deprived of the moral teachings, care, mutual aid, responsibility and solidarity that characterize communalism. In spite of urbanization and globalization, it is my opinion that support for families and the extended family system still linger on. This is because whether in urban areas or abroad, solidarity among Africans and support for their relatives continue. This is what has been described as the *we-feeling* in communalism—this means that the well-being of a member of the extended family system is linked to the well-being of another member of the extended family in the community. As I mentioned elsewhere, its maxim could run this way: *Because you are well, I am well; because you are satisfied, I am satisfied; and because you are clothed, I am clothed*. Léopold Senghor's description of *ubuntu* is appropriate here: "I feel the other, I dance the other, and therefore I am."[31] So, in the midst of globalization and industrialization, most Africans still feel obligated to support their families and relatives. Thus, the we-feeling continues pragmatically even if in a weak form.[32]

The rationale for the moral rule, according to him, is illustrated in the Akan art in which a crocodile is depicted as having one stomach and two heads in conflict with each other. The moral lesson here is that even though human beings have common desires, we also have conflicting desires, but when we come to realize that we are living with a common cause—the welfare of the same community, represented by the stomach of the crocodile—then morality serves as a guiding principle for the harmonious relationship in a community. Interdependency of persons is, therefore, of prime importance in the Akan community. For him, "A rule of conduct is not a moral rule unless its non-existence or reversal would bring about the collapse of human community."[33] Morality is, therefore, what holds the human community together, for "Any society without a modicum of morality must collapse,"[34] Wiredu stressed. The moral imperative of responsibility among the Akan, therefore, agrees with the golden rule: "Do not do to others what you would not that they do to you"— *Nea wo yonko de ye wo a erenye wo de no mfa nye no*. This principle agrees with the Akan social practice where the community takes turns to clear each other's farm during the farming seasons. Anyone who refuses to partake of this exercise is considered a useless person (*onipa hunu*), and he/she is likely to be ostracized from the community.[35] When someone is bereaved, it is morally imperative for the bereaved family to be helped materially and financially by the community to give a fitting burial to the loved one. This practice takes a cyclical turn in the community. A person's central rights and obligations are, however, focused on the mother's side as the Akan practice a matrilineal system of inheritance. In general, each member of the community is expected to play his/her role of providing support for members of the community, especially those who are less privileged.

In summary, both Gyekye and Wiredu agree that morality is at the center of the African community, and that without morality, there is bound to be chaos in the community. Religion, for them, is not the source of morality. Morality is the result of socialization and has nothing to do with God.

CRITICISM OF GYEKYE AND WIREDU'S AKAN ETHICS

Gyekye has a point in his conclusion that the source of morality is the society and not from religion, but it is interesting to note that when he was refuting Mbiti's assertion that Africans have only a two-dimensional time, he appealed to an Akan culture that affirms that when you are born on a particular day, it affects the way you behave, which to me defeats his argument that morality comes from society and not from God. He observes that among the Akans, those born on a particular day of the week have some inherent moral characteristics. For example, those born on a Monday are said to be suppliant, humble and calm. Those born on Tuesdays are said to be compassionate, and those born on Sundays are said to be protectors and so on.[36] If that is the case, it logically follows that if the values above solely come from the teachings of the society, the moral characteristics will not be assigned to days people were born. The characteristics the elders of the community assigned to the day on which people were born were as a result of many years of observation of the behavior pattern of people born on those days. If that is the case, it follows logically that if the values above solely come from the teachings of the society, the moral characteristics won't be assigned to days people were born. It is therefore not correct to affirm that "Akan moral thought assumes a person's original nature to be morally neutral."[37] If Africans, and for that matter, Akans, believe that humans were from the Supreme Being, and those born on certain days have certain moral traits, then it follows that the Supreme Being might have given these personal moral traits at birth.

Furthermore, contrary to the view of Gyekye that the source of morality is the community, I believe that insofar as Africans unanimously believed that God is the creator of human beings and the universe, and also that God is believed to be morally impeccable, then Africans, and for that matter Akans, logically derive their religious inclinations from God. For me, it is the innate ability to distinguish between right and wrong that enables the Akan or humanity to determine the rules and regulations (morality$_1$) in the community.

Admittedly, society plays a role in the origination of morality, but it may be erroneous, as far as I am concerned, to ground the origin of morality only on society and simply affirm that morality has a relationship with religion.[38] For me, therefore, the metaethical ground for morality is contingent upon religion.

According to Wiredu, the question as to whether a young person could have sex before marriage is not an issue in the Akan community. There are no written or oral rules regarding sex before marriage as it is stipulated, for instance, in the Christian religion. The only injunction placed on the man or woman with regard to sex is a taboo against having sex in the bush. When that happens, the goddess of the land, Asase Yaa, is likely to inflict punishment on such recalcitrant members of the community, and that punishment is likely to affect their whole family or the community at large. According to Wiredu, taboos were designed not because the elders want to prevent sex before marriage, but to prevent women from being sexually abused in the bush. With regard to the moral aspect of taboos, he states that "First, in view of the humanistic conception of morals in Akan thinking, any conception of badness defined in terms of taboo falls outside the pale of morality in the strict sense."[39] Then, on the same page, he states that "It is arguable that the taboos are a pedagogical expedient designed by our sages of old to concentrate ordinary minds on the path of desirable behavior."[40] So, in one moment he defines Akan taboos to fall "outside the pale of morality," and yet in another statement, he affirms that taboos are "designed by our sages of old to concentrate ordinary minds on the path of desirable behavior." If "desirable behavior" is not morality, then what is it? Much as I agree with some of Wiredu's line of thinking, I believe certain moral injunctions were put in place in the Akan society, as well as almost all Ghanaian communities, to prevent sexual promiscuity in the communities. The prohibition against having sex in the bush is a moral injunction and one of the ways by which premarital sex and pregnancy outside marriage are prevented in the community. Even though rape may be included in the reasons, it may not be the main reason. The elders knew that the bush is the most convenient place for sex to take place in a village setting. To prevent sex from happening in the bush, therefore, is a deterrent against premarital sex and teenage pregnancy. Another deterrent for the youth to indulge in premarital sex is that if one impregnates a woman before marriage, it is regarded as a disgrace to the woman's family. Consequently, the family of the woman virtually dumps her in the man's parents' home, or the man is made to pay a fine by the elders and, also, made to take care of the lady until she gives birth. The other alternative is for the man to deny that the pregnancy is his. When that happens, the disgrace is even worse as the woman will give birth to a child that will be improperly named, since the child will not have a father to name him/her.[41] These cultural practices and others are put in place especially for the youth to think twice before engaging in premarital sex. Gyekye puts it this way:

> But there are compelling reasons in traditional African society why marriage should precede the bearing of children. The primary reason is that a growing

child whose parents are not married may lack the social standing or respect normally accorded to children of married couples. Such a child may occasionally suffer ridicule from peers or even relatives within the lineage who may have knowledge of his or her background. This treatment may affect the mental health or emotional stability of the growing child.[42]

So, there are serious social implications for the parents, the woman and the child to be born if a woman gives birth outside marriage. Even with the inception of globalization and industrialization, no parent is happy to see their children engage in sex before marriage. Furthermore, chiefs, parents and elders in the community will consider it disrespectful to find any youth of the community engaging in sexual activities. Sex is reserved for marriage whether it is in an African community or a Christian community. Premarital sex is, therefore, not an accepted norm in the Ghanaian community as portrayed by Wiredu.

Contrary to the argument of Wiredu,[43] the fact that the "traditional knocking" has taken place does not mean that the couple has been given the license to have sex. When one performs the cultural "knocking," and even decides to live together and have children, it is clear in the minds of the community that they are not married, and should the man die, the woman is not allowed to perform the traditional widowhood rites as they are deemed not to be married. "Knocking" is the first step of the marriage process when you let the parents of the woman know that "you want to marry their daughter"; it is not the consummation of the marriage. There is a constant reminder from the members of the family and friends for the couple to go ahead and complete the process of marriage that they have initiated. Among the Ga community in Ghana, you hear people say to such couples: "Mɛɛbei nyɛbaabote gbala shihile mli" (meaning, "when are you going to enter into marriage?").

According to Wiredu, among the Akan, one vital element, which he calls the *life principle*, comes from God, the creator. Moreover, it is this *life principle* which points to the fact that all human beings are from the same source and, therefore, are one universal family: "Literally: all human beings are the children of God; none is the child of the earth,"[44] he stressed. If that is the case, and if God is believed by almost all Africans to be impeccably moral and all human beings come from Him, I wonder why Wiredu also thinks that God has nothing to do with the morality of the Akan and ultimately the African. He believes that the Akan or the human person is made up of three elements: the life principle or "a speck of the divine substance," the blood principle from the mother and the charisma principle from the father. If we have "a speck of the divine substance" in us then it follows that we also have a bit of God's character in us. Busia expressed it this way:

> A man's kra is a life force, 'the small bit of the Creator that lives in every person's body.' ... As the Supreme Being gives you a *kra*, so he gives your child his *kra*.' A child receives two spiritual gifts, a *sunsum* and a *kra*. A father transmits his *sunsum* to the child; this is what moulds the child's personality and disposition.[45]

If a bit of the Supreme Being is in us, it is logical to conclude that the root of our moral awareness stems from God; we are morality conscious because we have an innate moral "speck" or "life force" from God. That is why we are able to make moral laws in the first place. The innate moral character from God is, therefore, the foundation of our ethical behavior. It is the human inner craving for goodness which leads them to formulate morality for the well-being of their communities.

Moreover, like Wiredu earlier, Gyekye makes the argument that since the Akan religion is not a revealed religion, and for that reason, the Akan do not have a direct relationship with God, God does not give them rules and regulations. For him, "If moral habits were thought to be acquired by nature or through birth, it would be senseless to pursue moral instruction."[46] However, it is imperative to note that we can know right and wrong and in consequence give moral instructions to our children because of our inner sense of morality. God created the Akan, and for that matter human beings, and He implanted in them the ability to determine what is right and wrong. The rules and regulations that we make for ourselves are therefore contingent upon how God created us in the first place. Regarding morality, our minds are not *tabula rasa* (empty slate) when we were born as the empiricists believe. We are born with an inborn ability to determine what is right and wrong.

Additionally, like Wiredu, Gyekye also argues from Akan thought that God approves of the good because it is good, not that it is good because it is coming from God. He puts it this way: "It follows from what has been said that to the question asked by Socrates (in Plato's *Euthyphro*) whether something is good because God approves of it or whether God approves of it because it is good, the response of the Akan moral thinker would be that God approves of the good because it is good."[47] This argument makes the creature (the Akan) God, and God the creature. In other words, if God created the Akan, they cannot determine what is right for God, who is known to be intrinsically good. Therefore, God knows what is right already before He created the Akan and other human beings and gave them the ability to differentiate right from evil. Religion is, therefore, the source of morality.

I am not alone in my argument that morality develops from a divine source and ultimately affects the formulation of morality in the African communalism. One of the African scholars who advocates that morality comes from God is Bishop Peter Sarpong, an Akan and a Roman Catholic theologian. In his discussion on the ethics of the Akans, Sarpong notes that "Some people, before they are born into the world, are supposed to have their course of life well-laid out for them by God. Others enter the world with their own 'plans.' Neither the divinely-imposed Fate (Nkrabea) nor the self-determined Destiny (Hyɛbrɛ) is avoidable except through very extraordinary magico-religious means."[48] That, for the Akan, explains why some people are by nature "kindhearted, affable, gentle, hospitable, respectable, while others are wicked, ungentlemanly, dishonest, and generally prone to evil."[49] Even though this belief in the double destiny has its logical problems, it infers that the source of morality is God. Sarpong admits that the Akan people also create their laws, but so that wicked people do not take advantage of the slowness of God to punish wickedness.[50] Joshua Kudadjie, a Ghanaian moral philosopher, like Sarpong, believes that there are other sources of morality apart from religion that account for morality in a community.[51] One of the socio-religious advocates, Bénézet Büjo, a Roman Catholic moral philosopher, asserts that the source of African morality is not exclusively anthropocentric, as postulated by Western authors but also includes the "invisible community," who is God, the ancestors and even the unborn.[52] The reason why it appears that the source of African ethics is from the community is that Africans, according to him, do not speak very much about God, but rather speak about human beings. That is because they believe that "one who pays heed to the dignity of the human person also pleases God, and that one who acts against the human person offends precisely this God."[53]

For me, therefore, even though Africans formulate moral laws for their communities, they can do so because of the innate knowledge of right and wrong implanted in them by the Supreme Being.

NOTES

1. Kwame Gyekye, *An Essay on African Philosophical Thought: The Akan conceptual scheme* (New York: Cambridge University Press, 1987), 64.
2. Gyekye, *An Essay on African Philosophical Thought*, 87.
3. Gyekye, *An Essay on African Philosophical Thought*, 90.
4. Gyekye, *An Essay on African Philosophical Thought*, 73.
5. It is not surprising that Gyekye will equate *Nyansafo*, a wise person, to philosophy since ethics is, by nature, a branch of philosophy.
6. Gyekye, *An Essay on African Philosophical Thought*, 64.
7. Gyekye, *An Essay on African Philosophical Thought*, 66.
8. Gyekye, *An Essay on African Philosophical Thought*, 73.
9. Gyekye, *An Essay on African Philosophical Thought*, 131.
10. Gyekye, *An Essay on African Philosophical Thought*, 140.
11. Gyekye, *An Essay on African Philosophical Thought*, 131.
12. Gyekye, Kwame, Person and Community in African thought, in Coetzee, P H & Roux, A P (eds.), *Philosophy from Africa: A text with readings,* 2nd ed. (Oxford: Oxford University Press, 2002), 287.
13. Gyekye, *Person and Community in Africa*, 287.
14. Gyekye, Kwame, *African Cultural Values: An Introduction* (Philadelphia, PA/Accra: Sankofa Publishing Company, 1996), 57.
15. Gyekye, *African Cultural Values*, 58, 68.
16. Gyekye, *African Cultural Values*, 70.
17. Gyekye, *An Essay on African Philosophical Thought*, 141.
18. Gyekye, *An Essay on African Philosophical Thought*, 134.
19. Gyekye, *An Essay on African Philosophical Thought*, 135.
20. Gyekye, *An Essay on African Philosophical Thought*, 141.

21. Gyekye, *An Essay on African Philosophical Thought*, 135–136.
22. Gyekye, *An Essay on African Philosophical Thought*, 137.
23. Gyekye, *An Essay on African Philosophical Thought*, 138.
24. Gyekye, *An Essay on African Philosophical Thought*, 139.
25. Gyekye, Kwame and Wiredu, Kwasi (eds.), Person and Community: *Ghanaian Philosophical Studies* (Washington: The Council for Research in Values and Philosophy, 1992), 194.
26. Gyekye and Wiredu, *Person and Community*, 64.
27. Gyekye, Kwame, *Person and Community in African thought*, 288.
28. Gyekye & Wiredu, *Person and Community*, 194.
29. Gyekye & Wiredu, *Person and Community*, 194.
30. Kwasi Wiredu, On Decolonizing African Religions, in *The African Philosophy Reader*, P. H. Coetzee and A. P. J. Roux, eds. (South Africa: International Thomson Publishing Southern Africa, Pty, Ltd., 1998), 192.
31. Munyaradzi Felix Murove (ed.), *African ethics: An anthology of comparative and applied ethics* (South Africa: University of KwaZulu Natal, 2009), 101.
32. Kwasi Wiredu, *Cultural Universals and Particulars: An African Perspective* (Bloomington and Indianapolis: Indiana University Press, 1996), 77.
33. Wiredu, *Cultural Universals and Particulars*, 73.
34. Gyekye & Wiredu, *Person and Community*, 193.
35. Gyekye & Wiredu, *Person and Community*, 201–202.
36. Gyekye, *An Essay on African Philosophical Thought*, 172.
37. Gyekye, *An Essay on African Philosophical Thought*, 151.
38. Gyekye, Kwame, *African Cultural Values*, 57.
39. Wiredu, *Cultural Universals and Particulars*, 75.
40. Wiredu, *Cultural Universals and Particulars*, 75.
41. Even though in a matrilineal culture the child inherits on the mother's side, marriage is still very important in an African community.
42. Gyekye, *African Cultural Values*, 77.
43. Wiredu, *Cultural Universals and Particulars*, 63.
44. Kwasi Wiredu, *Person and Community in Africa*, 289, 313.
45. Kofi A. Busia, The Ashanti, in Daryll Forde, *African Worlds: Studies in the Cosmological Ideas and Social Values of African Peoples* (London: Oxford University Press, 1968), 197.
46. Kwame Gyekye, *An Essay on African Philosophical Thought*, 150.
47. Kwame Gyekye, *An Essay on African Philosophical Thought*, 138.
48. Peter Sarpong, Aspects of Akan ethics, *The Ghana Bulletin of Theology* 1972, 4(3), 42.
49. Peter Sarpong, Aspects of Akan ethics, *The Ghana Bulletin of Theology* 1972, 4(3), 42.
50. Peter Sarpong, Aspects of Akan ethics, *The Ghana Bulletin of Theology* 1972, 4(3), 43.
51. Joshua N. Kudadjie, Does religion determine morality in African Society? A viewpoint, *Ghana Bulletin of Theology* 1973: 4, 47.
52. Benezet Bujo, *Foundations of an African ethics: Beyond the universal claims of Western morality* (New York: Crossroads Publishers, 2001), 1.
53. Benezet Bujo, *Foundations of an African ethics*, 2.

Bibliography

Bujo, B. 2001. *Foundations of an African Ethics: Beyond the Universal Claims of Western Morality*. New York: Crossroads Publishers.

Busia, K.A. 1968. The Ashanti. In *African Worlds: Studies in the Cosmological Ideas and Social Values of African Peoples*, ed. Daryll Forde. London: Oxford University Press.

Gyekye, K. 1987. *An Essay on African Philosophical Thought: The Akan Conceptual Scheme*. New York: Cambridge University Press.

———. 1996. *African Cultural Values: An Introduction*. Philadelphia/Accra: Sankofa Publishing Company.

———. 2002. Person and Community in African Thought. In *Philosophy from Africa: A Text with Readings*, ed. P.H. Coetzee and A.P. Roux, 2nd ed. Oxford: Oxford University Press.

Gyekye, Kwame, and Kwasi Wiredu, eds. 1992. *Person and Community: Ghanaian Philosophical Studies*. Washington: The Council for Research in Values and Philosophy.

Kudadjie, J.N. 1973. Does Religion Determine Morality in African Society? A Viewpoint. *Ghana Bulletin of Theology* 4: 30–49.

Murove, M.F., ed. 2009. *African Ethics: An Anthology of Comparative and Applied Ethics*. Scottsville: University of Kwazulu-Natal Press.

Sarpong, P.K. 1972. Aspects of Akan Ethics. *Ghana Bulletin of Theology* 4 (3): 40–54.

Wiredu, K. 1996. *Cultural Universals and Particulars: An African Perspective*. Bloomington/Indianapolis: Indiana University Press.

———. 1998. On Decolonizing African Religions. In *The African Philosophy Reader*, ed. P.H. Coetzee and A.P.J. Roux. Johannesburg: International Thomson Publishing Southern Africa.

CHAPTER 25

Ethical Thought of Paulin Hountondji

George Kotei Neequaye

INTRODUCTION

According to Hountondji, African Philosophy must aim at developing science and technology using African source materials for the progress of African societies and solving some of the myriads of problems facing the continent through analytical philosophy. The aim of his discourses was, therefore, to emphasize the fact that as long as Western anthropologists and African scholars continue to satisfy Westerner readers in their ethnophilosophy, and in so far as they dabble in mediocre and uncritical philosophy, they are indulging in intellectual sophistry and moral irresponsibility. According to him, the intellectual, moral responsibility he demands from African ethnophilosophers is not the policing type where one is accountable in a civil or legal sense, but a moral responsibility where one is accountable to oneself, making sure that readers are not misled in one's presentation of his/her philosophical ideas. He is of the opinion that the sources of African Philosophy are hard to authenticate, and therefore the so-called African Philosophy can best be described as myth. Hountondji further calls for collaboration and unity among all sectors of African Studies in African universities—African sociology and anthropology, African history, African politics, African linguistics and so on—to bring about development in Africa. For him, all sectors of our studies in our universities need each other if ever scientific development can take place in Africa as in Europe and America. According to him, when philosophy is done correctly, it draws conclusions that add to knowledge and the issues so discussed and analysed ultimately benefit the emancipation of society. He, therefore, argues that African Philosophy is not present but in the future. However, the question is, "how can this endogenous knowledge be used for the benefit of Africans if Hountondji has questioned the

G. K. Neequaye (✉)
Trinity Theological Seminary, Legon, Ghana

authenticity of the sources used by African intellectuals and declares them as myth and unverifiable?" If African endogenous knowledge is a myth and, therefore, unverifiable, how can we get authentic African traditional materials for the development and progress of Africa? We conclude that if progress can be made with African development through philosophy, then we need the authentic philosophical research works of all the ethnophilosophers, including new knowledge on African culture and traditions, as well as knowledge from sources outside Africa to further our African Philosophy, with the aim to develop Africa through philosophy.

Correctness in African Scholarship as Intellectual Moral Responsibility

Hountondji's French education from the beginning to the end accounts for his choice of scientific approach to philosophy and therefore his condemnation of what is called African Philosophy. From his primary through secondary school to university, he encountered French Philosophers like Husserl, Ricoeur, Derrida and Althusser who favoured a scientific approach to philosophy than any other philosophical approaches. Because he had been trained to be rigorous, critical and analytical in his educational development, especially in the area of philosophy, he dismisses what has been categorized as African Philosophy currently parading in the academic world as not philosophical enough. Philosophers singing the same song with him are Kwasi Wiredu,[1] Robin Horton[2] and Bodunrin,[3] among others.

Philosophy, according to Hountondji, is a serious business. Philosophy is not about scratching the surface of facts, it is not a descriptive activity but a search for wisdom in which deep reflection is required in order to come out with how the totality of reality works. He agrees that philosophy is an arduous enterprise, one in which the truth is almost impossible to unravel. Nevertheless, every philosopher must search for the truth, even if it is highly inaccessible, and be morally responsible for the knowledge so produced. Even though it is the search for the truth or facts, he also agreed with the relativists that truth might vary from place to place. However, whether or not truth varies from place to place, every person doing philosophy must be held accountable for the intellectual, ethical validity and the verifiability of the truth so propounded. Philosophy, he rightly surmised, is a logical activity and therefore must be exercised in flawless coherency. Philosophy is not a dogmatic enterprise but the search for truth that is bound to change as new revelations are unravelled. The philosopher must, therefore, be ready to change his/her mind to embrace a new idea that has been discovered which throws light on his/her philosophy or that which completely changes his/her philosophy.

It is the moral responsibility of the one philosophizing to prove beyond doubt the authenticity of their sources but also to endeavour to give a very detailed description of the fact being investigated and be able to put the knowledge so acquired to good use. Hountondji is of the view that "One of the basic demands of philosophy as usually understood is the demand for rational proof, the need for demonstration and theoretical justification."[4] The key phrases in this quotation are "demand for rational proof," "the need for demonstration" and "theoretical justification." Those phrases, for him, are the core of the philosophical enterprise. However, accompanying this digging for the truth is also an ethical responsibility. Every philosopher must be held morally responsible for the truth or otherwise of his/her premises and conclusions. "Conversely, human responsibility is not just about actions, it also extends to the realm of thought. It includes both moral and intellectual responsibility. We are accountable for our statements as much as we are for our deeds,"[5] he stressed. According to him, the intellectual, moral responsibility he demands from African ethnophilosophers is not the policing type where one is accountable in a civil or legal sense, but a moral responsibility where one is answerable to oneself, making sure that readers are not misled in one's presentation of his/her philosophical ideas. In other words, everyone is morally and intellectually responsible for the academic work he/she produces for consumption. For him, every thought must be traced back to its parent who must be held accountable for his/her elaboration. Hountondji's ethics can, therefore, be described as intellectual, moral responsibility. What, then, did he describe in the intellectual world as intellectual, moral irresponsibility? We shall endeavour in the next section to outline his argument and follow it up with a counter-argument in the subsequent sections as to whether he is justified in his critical analysis of the writings of the scholars he referred to as ethnophilosophers.

Philosophy and Oral Tradition

How can oral literature be accounted for in philosophy? It is an accepted fact that oral literature precedes written literature? What is passed on from father to son and the next generation is what has been preserved as the oral traditions of the people. According to Hountondji, it is true that oral literature is vital in philosophical reflections, but oral traditions are not philosophies until they are recorded as written literature and analysed. As far as Hountondji is concerned, in its oral form, knowledge tends to be dogmatic because the same idea is held on and passed on from generation to generation without subjecting the oral tradition to scrutiny. It is when recorded that it opens itself to critical analysis by the community whose traditions they are.[6] Because the mind is preoccupied with preserving the oral tradition, there is no room to criticize the knowledge so transmitted. However, once the oral knowledge is committed into writing, it frees the mind to do a critical investigation of the material so recorded.[7] Critically thinking through the material so recorded gives room for new knowledge to be acquired for the expansion of the already existing knowledge. Even though philosophy is possible in an oral form, nonetheless, philosophy, for Hountondji, is born out of an analysis of existing material. For example, Socrates' ideas were able to enter into the history of Greece and live on till today because his disciples took the time to write them down as they attempt to do a critical investigation of his thoughts. According to Hountondji, "The absence of transcription certainly does not intrinsically devalue a philosophical discourse, but it prevents it from integrating itself into a collective theoretical tradition and from taking its place in history as a reference point capable of orienting future discussion."[8] In its oral form, it is likely to lose its original chain of argument and be confined to a specific time and place.[9] He surmises that the proverbs, folklore, moral tales, aphorisms and the like are not in themselves philosophy but are the results of critical thinking lost with time. It is, therefore, the work of current philosophers to question those ideas until the reasons for their formulations are disentangled for the benefit of Africa and the world at large.[10]

The Myth and Reality of African Philosophy

Hountondji's criticism of African Philosophy and what he subsequently describes as ethnophilosophy is an argument against the intellectual mediocrity in philosophical enquiry, a scratching of the surface in the ethnic traditions and worldviews of the African people, the failure to discuss the real issues that will bring about the scientific and technological development of Africa using their own cultural resources and therefore a renunciation of intellectual moral responsibility. Consequently, ethnophilosophy, according to Hountondji, falls short of the nature of philosophy. It aims at providing the philosophy of an ethnic group and their worldviews but only describes the social cohesion and interactions of the people without giving a detailed explanation of the issues involved and the proof of the authenticity of the sources of information. He concluded, therefore, that "most of these scholars are not really doing philosophy but ethno-philosophy: they were writing a special chapter of ethnology aimed at studying the systems of thought of those societies usually studied by ethnology—however such societies are defined or characterized."[11] It is, therefore, not philosophy, but cultural anthropology.[12]

He bemoans the flippant use of oral sources without any means of checking the genuineness of the sources. In that light, ethnophilosophy, which according to Hountondji is an invention of the West, outlines a worldview of the African people without an object of research.[13] The sources of ethnophilosophy are, therefore, suspect "Because it has to account for an imaginary unanimity, to interpret a text which nowhere exists and has to be constantly reinvented, it is a science without an object, a 'crazed language'[14] accountable to nothing, a discourse that has no referent, so that its falsity can never be demonstrated."[15] In that vein, it is challenging to ascertain who is right when two African scholars argue against each other on a subject matter since what they are arguing about never existed anywhere except in their imagination. For instance, when Tempels, a European, informs us that for the Bantu, being has everything to do with power and Kagamé, an African, refutes that assertion, it is tough to judge who is right and who is not since there is no way of validating their sources of information. That is the sense in which African Philosophy is a myth. "It is a smokescreen behind which each author is able to manipulate his own philosophical views," he averred.

He agreed that African Philosophy exists, but he argues against what is peddling around intellectual circles as "African Philosophy."[16] He gives exception to African Philosophers like the Cameroonians Eboussi-Boulaga, Towa and N'joh-Mouelle, the Ghanaian Wiredu, and the Kenyan Odera and to himself.[17] Even though he sympathizes with the Ghanaian Anton Wilhelm Amo for growing up in Germany and therefore had a mainly Western audience to interact with, he also had his share of criticism for producing philosophies meant for Western readers.

He addressed the problem of the myth and reality of African Philosophy in his classic book entitled "African Philosophy: Myth and Reality." For him, philosophy is a serious academic exercise and therefore must not be taken lightly. He argues that the corpus of philosophy can only be described in the first person singular, and not in the third person. In other words, philosophy does not describe the worldview of a group of people, thus referring to their ideas as "They think so and so," "They say so and so," as often done by ethnologists and cultural anthropologists, including African writers themselves, but a philosopher owns the subject matter, making it its own, giving details of what the subject matter is, analysing the issues and going further to synthesize the philosophical enquiry by giving proof of sources and using the knowledge so obtained about a particular group of people to solve the problems that the philosopher set out to tackle. African Philosophy, as we now understand it, is therefore descriptive and not a subject matter well articulated and engaged with by the writers of the subject. He stressed that "African philosophy, like any other philosophy, cannot possibly be a collective world-view. It can exist as a philosophy only in the form of a confrontation between individual thoughts, a discussion, a debate."[18] It is, therefore, qualified to be called ethnophilosophy, meaning the description of an ethnic group, or metaphilosophy, meaning a reflection on an existing philosophical affirmation. For him, African Philosophy as we have it now has no philosophical depth, no engagement with the issues so researched, a refusal to grapple with the issues involved and therefore does not qualify to be called philosophy. For instance, Dominique Zahan, a French anthropologist, alluded to an African tradition on ancestorship in his book entitled "African religion, spirituality and thought" that when Ghezo, the King of Abomey in the Benin Republic died, several of his wives agreed to be sacrificed to continue to be his wife in the ancestral world. According to Hountondji, when such a story is presented to the Western world, it sanctions their opinion that Africans are savages, and this is what ethnophilosophy does to Africa. Hountondji wants such material to be handled differently: to find out why such a tradition is practised, whether the women agreed under compulsion or because of the cultural demands on them or not, how did such a tradition originate and what criticisms are there against such a tradition.[19] In other words, Africans need to question their cultures from within instead of allowing the Western world to do the questioning for them. By so doing, philosophy will serve its purpose in Africa. In like manner, witches have been allotted powers to kill or to destroy, and the ascription so accepted without really engaging with the subject matter to give a critical analysis of whether or not they indeed have the powers they are believed to have, and if they have those powers, how those powers were acquired. But best of all, how can those powers be channelled into good use for the benefit of society. However, in addition to their own culture, the African public wants to know what is happening elsewhere and how that knowledge can affect their society positively. He argues more succinctly this way:

> As for the African public, what it wants most is to be widely informed about what is going on elsewhere, about current scientific problems in other countries and continents, out of curiosity in the first place (a legitimate curiosity), but also in order to confront those problems with its own preoccupations, to reformulate them freely in its own terms and thus to steep them in the melting-pot of African science.[20]

Moreover, to what extent can we verify the authenticity of the worldviews so described. Is it enough to say, for instance, that "I am an African and therefore I know what I am talking about," or should we go further than that to investigate the sources? In other words, how can we be sure that what the writers are writing about Africans are true or not? How far back can we go to ascertain the truth or otherwise of the stories about Africans? This situation is what Hountondji refers to as the "myth of African Philosophy." What, on the other hand, Hountondji describes as African Philosophy is this—a true search for meaning, proof of sources, analysis of the data and how the data so analysed could be used for the benefit of society. That is the sense in which Hountondji believes the phrase "African Philosophy" exists in "reality" and not "a myth." For him, African Philosophy should be described as African Philosophical literature.[21] He stressed that

> Attention had to shift from the supposedly collective, anonymous discourse of the group to the endless debate between individual thinkers speaking on their own behalf. ... Hiding behind one's society is an easy, too easy way to dismiss one's own responsibility. Inviting complete immersion of the individual into the group may sound a revolutionary discourse.[22]

He further reiterated that Africa could be liberated from its scientific and developmental slumber if it is made to recover its "self-confidence and self-realization." That can only be realized if individuals are respected for who they are. When individuals are recognized and the discussions taken to their doorsteps, it opens the floodgates for a stronger ability for the community to think collectively for itself and, therefore, leads to a shared intellectual responsibility and progress.

A Defensive Philosophy

Furthermore, one of the intellectual moral irresponsibility that Hountondji refers to is the efforts by African writers to elucidate ethnophilosophy for the benefit of Western readers. He is of the view that most of the writings of the African writers like Leopold Senghor, Kwame Nkrumah, Alexis Kagamé, John Mbiti, Kwame Gyekye, John Idowu and the rest are meant to prove a point to Western anthropologists, ethnologists and the general Western readers that Africa has a rich culture and religious heritage.[23] Hountondji describes such attitude towards the West as cultural nationalism, which "seeks to justify all inherited practices including the most unjustifiable."[24] However, all that these discourses prove is a warped worldview of Africans, and the knowledge so generated does not affect the scientific, technological and economic plights of Africa as a whole.[25] Ethnophilosophy, or cultural anthropology, according to Hountondji, excludes the people being discussed and therefore does not affect them in any way at all. It happens because most journals and books produced about Africa are in libraries outside Africa and read mainly by non-African readers.[26] He puts it this way, "To put it bluntly, each African scholar has been participation so far in a vertical discussion with his/her counterparts from the North rather than developing horizontal discussion with other African scholars."[27]

According to him, when philosophy is done properly, it draws conclusions that add to knowledge and the issues so discussed and analysed ultimately benefit the emancipation of society. He articulated it more precisely this way:

> We need to invent today an African way of doing African studies. We need a critical reappropriation of our endogenous traditions of wisdom, knowledge and know-how, not for any kind of display or exhibition to the external world, nor for the purpose of narcissistic and passéistic self-contemplation, but first and foremost, to make us better prepared to face the challenges of our time.[28]

He further argues that for scientific and technological progress to be achieved in this world, efforts should be made to see how Western medicine and African medicine could be harnessed together for the common good of society. African knowledge systems should no more be left in the periphery but must be seriously researched in order for the world of science and technology to benefit immensely from the rich cultural heritage of Africa. That is the place in which African Philosophers and scientists could be brought together to produce African Philosophies that will marry with Western science and technology for new developments to be unearthed for the benefit of not only Africans but the world at large. "We need to invent together a new world order of science and technology, a new world intellectual order, to allow equal sharing of the existing heritage and equal participation in its development,"[29] Hountondji stressed. He advises that African Philosophy is inseparable from African science and that African scholars must endeavour to use African source materials like herbal and other healing medicines for the development of science and the acquisition of scientific knowledge for scientific and technological progress.[30]

Consequently, like Wiredu,[31] he insists that African Philosophy "is before us, not behind us, and must be created today by decisive action."[32] That can only be done if Third World intellectuals and African Philosophers can refrain from self-justification and create an internal debate that will look critically at all the traditional practices of the African people with the aim to develop new philosophies for the future development of Africa.[33] Hountondji further calls for collaboration and unity among all sectors of African Studies in African universities to bring about development in Africa. For him, all sectors of our studies in our universities need each other if ever scientific development can take place in Africa as in Europe and America.[34]

INVESTIGATION OF THE ETHICS OF PAULIN HOUNTONDJI

First, by his training and association, Hountondji has by choice been initiated into Western imperial intellectualism, which he finds very difficult to break away from. He, therefore, thinks and does philosophy in the context of Western philosophy, which he sees as the ideal philosophy. In this wise, he seems to have been trapped in the same prison from which he purports to be liberating other African writers.[35]

Second, Hountondji is right to insist that philosophy is scientific and must be done in a more critical and analytical way, but for me, rather than condemning African ethnophilosophy as not philosophical enough or unscientific, it is best for him to carefully study the existing African Philosophy to decipher from them the common ideas to draw new African Philosophies from. This duty, for me, is an intellectual, moral responsibility incumbent on Hountondji and all African Philosophers to pursue, instead of, as Gyekye put it, "throwing the baby with the dirty bath water away." If the whole of Mbiti's book entitled, *African Religions and Philosophy* is not philosophical but descriptive, then what is a reflective activity or a search for wisdom, which philosophy represents? If philosophy is a search for wisdom, then the proverbs in African culture are true philosophy. It is imperative that Hountondji learns to appreciate African Philosophy and not look down on the intellectual capabilities of African Philosophers, thus dabbling in the same accusation that he levelled against the African Philosophers—doing philosophy to please the Europeans. If at all, he must see the genuine philosophical works of the ethnophilosophers as alternative forms of philosophy within another culture and tradition. Mohammed Al-Mawabi's advice concurs with my argument here: "In order to successfully navigate through life, we need to appreciate nuance, understand complexity and embrace flexibility."[36] That, for me, is the intellectual, moral discipline Hountondji lacks. Anthony Agwuele accused him of being an essentialist because "He emphasizes the essential properties of philosophy but maintains a very very distressing silence on the non-essential features or differences of philosophy."[37] It is also imperative that in addition to African source materials,

materials from other traditions and cultures outside Africa should be explored and indigenized into African Philosophy.[38]

Third, in his intellectual enquiry, Hountondji sees Europe as possessing superior scientific philosophical approach and therefore represents a mirror for Africa and the rest of the world. However, who determines who owns absolute truth? Is there an absolute truth? What is knowledge and what is an opinion? Has European philosophy the absolute truth and the rest of the world only an opinion? Even though he agrees that philosophy is not a dogmatic activity and that knowledge changes all the time into new ones, he gave a general impression that European philosophy, especially the Greek philosophy, are doing philosophy right and African writers have got it wrong.

Nevertheless, who defines what is the truth? Are we not discovering new things about life that shatters the supposed absolute truths all the time? For instance, before the time of Romanticism[39] in the late eighteenth century, the work of William Shakespeare was scorned by the academic critics, describing his writings as academic indiscipline because he did not follow the concepts of drama writing by the ancient Romans and Greeks. According to Paul Brians, Emeritus Professor of the Washington State University, the accepted way of writing drama at the time of the European Enlightenment in the eighteenth century was as follows:

> A good play should not mix comedy with tragedy, not proliferate plots and subplots, not ramble through a wide variety of settings or drag out its story over months or years of dramatic time. ... A proper serious drama should always be divided neatly into five acts.[40]

However, Shakespeare's plays flouted all those supposed absolute rules. His plays "simply flowed from one scene to the next, with no attention paid to the academic rules of dramatic architecture (the act divisions we are familiar with today were imposed on his plays by editors after his death)."[41] At the birth of Romanticism in the late eighteenth century, the accepted norms before and during the European Enlightenment were overturned by the Romantics in favour of works by the uncultivated popular who were reckoned to have the imagination that was capable of bettering that of the educated composers and court poets. During the Romantic period, there was recognition and a huge collection of, for instance, folklore and popular art in Germany and England by Jakob and Wilhelm Grimm and Johann Gottfried von Herder respectively.[42] Against all odds, the work of Shakespeare was accepted as a standard form of drama and literature worldwide, and his works were converted into textbooks for many educational institutions around the world. In the light of these nuances in philosophy, I wonder why Hountondji is still flirting with absolutism. He has no intellectual, moral responsibility to impose what he sees as the ideal philosophical style and truth in Europe upon Africa and the rest of the world. For Imo, such a way of thinking continues to immortalize African cultural traditions as "primitives" and "clan societies."[43] At one point, he says that philosophy is not a system but history and that there is no absolutism in philosophy. Then, at another point, he contradicts himself by arguing that European philosophy is the universal philosophy which Africa must look up to in her development of philosophy.[44] Who says that the world should follow the philosophical style of the West and the East? Can't African Philosophers develop their form of experiential philosophy within the context of their culture and tradition? The reason why philosophy is difficult to define is that people define it in the context of their own experience, language and culture. For instance, phenomenological philosophers define philosophy in the context of "lived experience"; linguistic philosophers define philosophy in the context of the etymological analysis of language; and Islamic philosophy defines philosophy in the context of the religious experience of Prophet Mohammed. Gyekye rightly debunks Hountondji's argument that there is a unique model of philosophy and argues that rather than recognizing one philosophy as a criteria for all philosophies, every reflective cultural activity must be seen as valid philosophical discourse since "philosophy of some kind is involved in the thought and action of every people and constitutes the intellectual sheet anchor of their life in its totality."[45] Even though Gyekye sees philosophy as universal, he did not elucidate it in the context of the meaning Hountondji gives to it. For Gyekye, the universality of philosophy hinges on the fact that every culture is constantly philosophizing and asking questions on human life, conduct and experience, which transcend cultures.[46] He rightly observed that "answers to philosophical questions provided by thinkers from different cultures may differ in quality, sophistication, and persuasiveness."[47] It is within this context that he concludes that there is a philosophical wing of every culture and tradition. Philosophy is a reflective activity and seeks after the truth. If, therefore, the works of Mbiti, Idowu and Gyekye, which seek to untangle the truth about African culture and traditions, are not philosophical, then what else is philosophy? When Plato developed the allegory of the Cave to elucidate his philosophy of the two worlds, and Aristotle uncovered the Uncaused Cause to explain why things change in this world, were they not dabbling in philosophical myth? What was so philosophical about their findings that are different from most of the works of the ethnophilosophers? How are those stories different from the African creation of stories and the reflections on the Supreme Being among the Yoruba by Idowu?

Fourth, since African Philosophers started writing on ethnic philosophy, there have been a lot of philosophical discussions and arguments among them on the true nature of African culture and tradition. For instance, there was a debate between Mbiti and Gyekye on whether African time looks into the future or not.[48] Mbiti describes the African concept of time as a two-dimensional phenomenon. According to him, whereas the Western linear concept of time involves an indefinite past, a present time and an infinite future, the African concept of time only dwells on the long past (Zamani) and the present (Sasa). According to him, Zamani and the Sasa, which are Swahili words, overlap. Concerning the future, he is of the view that African concept of time does not go beyond two years; Africans are mainly interested in seasons within the year, and they name the seasons according to the agricultural, cattle or farming year. Whereas in the West "time is a commodity which must be utilized, sold and bought," in traditional Africa, "time has to be created or produced."[49] Gyekye refutes his assertion by arguing that the fact that in two East African languages, Gikuyu and Kikamba, time is limited to Zamani and Sasa does not mean that it is the same for all Africa. He insists, by drawing from the language, proverbs, folklore, dirges and maxims of the Akan people that time in Akan thought is akin to the Western linear concept of past, present and future. According to him, the Akan word *bere* (time) expresses both the abstract and concrete concept of time. The Akan proverb, "Time is like a bird: if you do not catch it and it flies, you do not see it again," the maxim "Time changes" (*bere di adannan*), the saying "wo bedi hen (daakye)," that is "You will be a king (in the future),"—to mention a few—all point to the fact that the Akan has a concept of time that points to the past, the present, as well as the future.[50] If this discussion between Mbiti and Gyekye above is not philosophical, then I wonder how Hountondji understands philosophy. Gyekye's response to Hountondji's critical work on ethnophilosophy and Hountondji's indirect reply in his lecture at the Central Division Meeting of the American Philosophical Association at Chicago in April 1996 is another classic example of a philosophical dialogue between Gyekye and Hountondji. So, Hountondji's assertion that there is no discussion among ethnophilosophers is misleading. Even when rational discussions are going on among African scholars, Hountondji still criticizes those debates as giving a clear indication that there is no unanimity among Africans concerning ethnophilosophy, which, to him, puts a question mark on the authenticity of the sources of ethnophilosophy.[51] So, at one point, he criticizes African Philosophers as not doing critical work enough, and at the same time criticizes them when they engage in doing a critique of each other's works in order to come out with the truth about African belief systems.

Fifth, our elders did a lot of deep reflections to land on most of the African traditions and culture. For example, deep reflections went into the formulation of African taboos. Taboos in Polynesian language mean "forbidden." According to Osei:

> Within its historical context taboo was a sacred term for a set of cultic or religious prohibitions instituted by traditional religious authorities as instruments for moral motivation, guidance, and objectivity for protecting the sanctity of their shrines and the well-being of their worshipping communities. The term is also applicable to any sort of social prohibition imposed by the leadership of a community regarding certain times, places, actions, events, and people etc. especially, but not exclusively, for religious reasons for the well-being of the society.[52]

Thus, taboos are mainly formulated by the elders or religious leaders to check actions that are inimical to the unity and peaceful coexistence of the people in the community. For instance, Among the Akan and Ewe, the taboo against incest was specially formulated to prevent, firstly, blood mixing, which over time they realized that it breeds abnormal births, genetic diseases and congenital disabilities in their community. In this context, this incest taboo is called medical taboo.[53] Secondly, incest also tends to cause disunity within families, thus threatening the very existence of the community. Thirdly, incest is abominable to the gods and ancestors and as such may call for punishment from them.[54] So, a lot of deep reflections go into most of the African traditions and culture.

Sixth, unlike Greek or British or German philosophy, which generally deals with individual thinkers, African Philosophy is known to be a corporate philosophy without reference to individual thinkers. Gyekye rightly argues that before any African thought systems become an accepted culture, it originates from individual wise men and ultimately becomes a collective philosophy of the people. He, therefore, concludes that it is a misnomer to regard African Philosophy as a "collective" philosophy. It seems to me that African Philosophy is a "collective" philosophy because of the nature of communalism. In much the same way that land, for instance, is owned by the community or family at large, so are the culture and traditions of the people. It is, therefore, not surprising that the philosophy of the people is a collective or owned philosophy. So, when we talk about Akan philosophy, we are referring to the philosophy of the group as a whole, a communalistic philosophy and not an individualistic philosophy like British philosophy. As more people begin to live in cities and are influenced by Western way of life and individualism, we may come to a time when we will begin to talk about Gyekye philosophy, or Mbiti philosophy, or Idowu philosophy and so on. However, as it stands now, African Philosophy is owned by the whole community even though the initial thought may have been put forward by an individual member of the community.

Seventh, if, as he contends, African Philosophy is in the future and the current sources of African Philosophy are mythical and unverifiable, then where are we going to get the raw materials upon which his supposed critical work could be generated among African scholars? One cannot build a critical African Philosophy ex nihilo. Our sages tell us that in order to project into the future, one needs the experiences of the past and present. Gyekye argues that rather than talk about African Philosophy in the future, we should talk about *traditional African Philosophy*, out of which we can do the critical and analytical work to come out with a *modern African Philosophy*.[55] It is essential that African Philosophers should draw from the past to feed the experiences of today in order to aid the formulations of future philosophies. For me, African Philosophers, like Mbiti, Idowu, Gyekye, Wiredu, Menkiti and so on, must be commended for producing detailed research on African Philosophy based on African culture and traditions that can be used as springboards for further philosophical discussions.

In the light of the above discussions, Hountondji may have to revise his criticism of African Philosophy and credit some of the writers with good intellectual, moral responsibility in the light of the earlier discussions.

NOTES

1. Kwasi Wiredu, *Philosophy and an African Culture* (Cambridge: Cambridge University Press, 1980), 36.
2. Robin Horton, Traditional Thought and the Emerging of African Philosophy Department: A Comment on the current Debate, *Second Order, An African Journal of Philosophy*, Vol. VI, No. 1, January 1977, 64–80, in Gyekye, *African Philosophical Thought*, 3.
3. P. O. Bodunrin, The Question of African Philosophy, *Philosophy* Vol. LVI, 1981, 169.
4. Fulbright 50th Anniversary Distinguished Lecture. Proceedings and Addresses of the *APA*, 70:2, 77.
5. *Fulbright 50th Anniversary Distinguished Lecture*, 79.
6. Pauline Hountondji, *African Philosophy, myth and reality*. Translated by Henri Evans with the collaboration of Jonathan Rée (Bloomington: Indiana University Press, 1983), 103.
7. Pauline Hountondji, *African Philosophy*, 103.
8. Pauline Hountondji, *African Philosophy*, 106.
9. Pauline Hountondji, *African Philosophy*, 105.
10. Pauline Hountondji, *African Philosophy*, 105.
11. Paulin Hountondji, Knowledge of Africa, knowledge by Africans: Two Perspectives on African Studies, *RCCS Annual Review*, 1, 2009, 124.
12. Paul Hountondji, *Dialogue with Lansana Keita: Reflections on African Development* – www.codesria.org/IMG/pdf/5-3.pdf
13. Quest Vol. XIV, No. 1–2, 2000, 7.
14. This is a phrase he borrowed from Zaïrois V. Y. Mudimbe from his book L'Autre Face du royaume. Une introduction à la critique des langages en folie (Lausanne: L'Age d'homme 1973).
15. Pauline Hountondji, *African Philosophy*, 62.
16. Pauline Hountondji, *African Philosophy*, 69, 101.
17. Pauline Hountondji, *African Philosophy*, 105.
18. Pauline Hountondji, *African Philosophy*, 53.
19. Paulin Hountondji, Tradition, Hindrance or Inspiration. *Quest* Vol. XIV, No. 1–2, 2000: 6.
20. Paulin Hountondji, *African Philosophy*, 54.
21. Paulin Hountondji, *African Philosophy*, 101.
22. *Fulbright 50th Anniversary Distinguished Lecture*, 84.
23. *Quest* Vol. XIV, No. 1–2, 2000, 6. Also see Pauline Hountondji, *African Philosophy*, 50.
24. *Quest* Vol. XIV, No. 1–2, 6.
25. Pauline Hountondji, *African Philosophy*, 67.
26. Paulin J. Hountondji, On the universality of science technology, *Open Access Repository*, Hamburg, 1986, 387.
27. Paulin Hountondji, *Knowledge of Africa, knowledge by Africans*, 128.
28. *Fulbright 50th Anniversary Distinguished Lecture*, 86.
29. *Fulbright 50th Anniversary Distinguished Lecture*, 87.
30. *Fulbright 50th Anniversary Distinguished Lecture*, 86.
31. Kwasi Wiredu, *Philosophy and an African Culture* (Cambridge: Cambridge University Press, 1980), 36.

32. Paulin Hountondji, *African Philosophy*, 53.
33. Quest Vol. XIV, No. 1–2, 2000, 7.
34. Paulin Hountondji, Knowledge of Africa, knowledge by Africans: Two Perspectives on African Studies, *RCCS Annual Review*, 1, 2009, 121.
35. Compare Samuel O. Imbo, An Introduction to African Philosophy, (Maryland: Rowman & Littlefield Publishers, Inc., 1998), 22, 86, 88.
36. http://brewminate.com/the-danger-of-absolute-thinking-is-absolutely-clear/. Mohammed Al-Mawabi is a PhD Candidate in Psychology at the Reading University, England.
37. Anthony O. Agwuele, *Rorty's Deconstruction of Philosophy and the Challenge of African Philosophy* (Frankfurt am Main: Peter Lang GmbH, 2009), 19.
38. Kwame Gyekye, An Essay on African Philosophical Thought, 42–43.
39. It is important to note here that Romanticism also had its excesses.
40. Paulin Hountondji, *African Philosophy*, 69–70.
41. http://brewminate.com/origins-and-growth-of-romanticism-the-early-modern-movement-of-the-bourgeoisie/
42. http://brewminate.com/origins-and-growth-of-romanticism-the-early-modern-movement-of-the-bourgeoisie/
43. Samuel O. Imbo, *An Introduction to African Philosophy*, 21.
44. Kwame Gyekye, *An Essay on African Philosophical Thought*, 71–73.
45. Kwame Gyekye, *An Essay on African Philosophical Thought*, 9.
46. Kwame Gyekye, *An Essay on African Philosophical Thought*, 9.
47. Kwame Gyekye, *An Essay on African Philosophical Thought*, 10.
48. Kwame Gyekye, *An Essay on African Philosophical Thought*, 169–177.
49. John Mbiti, *African religions and philosophy*, 2nd ed. (Oxford: Heinemann, 1999), 19.
50. Kwame Gyekye, *An Essay on African philosophical Thought*, 169–177.
51. Paulin Hountondji, *Knowledge of Africa, knowledge by Africans*, 125.
52. Joseph Osei, The value of African taboos for biodiversity and sustainable development. *Journal of Sustainable Development in Africa* 8 (3), 2006, 42–61.
53. Joseph Osei, *The value of African taboos*, 7.
54. Joseph Osei, *The value of African taboos*, 5.
55. Kwame Gyekye, African Philosophical Thought, 11.

Bibliography

Agwuele, A.O. 2009. *Rorty's Deconstruction of Philosophy and the Challenge of African Philosophy*. Frankfurt am Main: Peter Lang GmbH.

Bodunrin, P.O. 1981. The Question of African Philosophy. 56 (216): 161–179.

Gyekye, Kwame. 1987. *An Essay on African Philosophical Thought. The Akan Conceptual Scheme*. New York/Cambridge: Cambridge University Press.

Horton, R. 1977. Traditional Thought and the Emerging of African Philosophy Department: A Comment on the Current Debate. *Second Order, An African Journal of Philosophy* VI (1): 64–80.

Hountondji, P. 1983. *African Philosophy, Myth and Reality*. Translated by Henri Evans with the Collaboration of Jonathan Rée. Bloomington: Indiana University Press.

———. 1986. *On the Universality of Science Technology*, 387. Hamburg: Open Access Repository.

———. 2000. Tradition, Hindrance or Inspiration. *Quest* XIV (1–2): 6.
———. 2009. Knowledge of Africa, Knowledge by Africans: Two Perspectives on African Studies. *RCCS Annual Review* 1: 124.
———. (1996, November). 50th Anniversary Fulbright Lecture. *Proceedings and Addresses of the APA* 70 (2): 77–92.
———. *Dialogue with Lansana. Keita: Reflections on African Development.* www.codesria.org/IMG/pdf/5-3.pdf
Imbo, S.O. 1998. *An Introduction to African Philosophy.* Maryland: Rowman & Littlefield.
Mbiti, J. 1999. *African Religions and Philosophy.* 2nd ed. Oxford: Heinemann.
Osei, J. 2006. The Value of African Taboos for Biodiversity and Sustainable Development. *Journal of Sustainable Development in Africa* 8 (3): 42–61.
Wiredu, K. 1980. *Philosophy and an African Culture.* Cambridge: Cambridge University Press.

Websites

http://brewminate.com/origins-and-growth-of-romanticism-the-early-modern-movement-of-the-bourgeoisie/
http://brewminate.com/the-danger-of-absolute-thinking-is-absolutely-clear/.
Mohammed Al-Mawabi is a PhD Candidate in Psychology at the Reading University, England.

CHAPTER 26

Strangers and Patriots: Anthony Kwame Appiah and the Ethics of Identity

Adeshina Afolayan

INTRODUCTION: IDENTITY POLITICS ON THE RAMPAGE

Identity politics has become a serious and significant feature of today's world. We can move from Donald Trump to Viktor Orban, and we are still talking about the same nationalist impulse that is sweeping across the world, from Finland to South Africa. Brexit is the loudest nationalist rumbling so far that has caught the attention of the world. It represents the yearning of Marie Le Pen (France), Matteo Salvini (Italy), the Vox Party (Spain), Sebastian Kurz and the People's Party (Austria), Jair Messias Bolsonaro (Brazil), and many more across the world. All these conservative parties and right-wing nationalists are all united in their anti-immigration agitations and the mystique of a pure nation. However, identity politics is not always a mild perception of strangers and immigrants. On the one side, we have seen European countries that turned back refugees and immigrants who often go to great and dangerous extent, like crossing the churning Mediterranean or the vastly hostile Sahara Desert, to get from their oppressive countries to North America and Europe. But while Donald Trump insists on building a wall, "Fortress Europe" is locked up with the stentorian advice for migrants to return home.

On the other hand, we see a more tragic side of identity politics at play in the xenophobic attacks that have made South Africa a very bad example of relationship with strangers. Since 1984, South Africa became a choice place for migrations for Africans, from Mozambicans to Nigerians. This occasioned some series of attacks on foreigners which increased especially with the achievement of black majority rule in 1994. Between 2000 and 2015, there was an increase in xenophobic attacks that followed on the economic hardship

A. Afolayan (✉)
University of Ibadan, Ibadan, Nigeria

© The Author(s) 2020
N. Wariboko, T. Falola (eds.), *The Palgrave Handbook of African Social Ethics*, https://doi.org/10.1007/978-3-030-36490-8_26

witnessed by black South Africans and the failure of the African National Congress (ANC) to make good on the promise of a postapartheid South Africa of economic and political freedom. A 2018 Pew Research demonstrated that xenophobia has become entrenched in the South Africans' perception of immigrants to their country. While 34% of those polled believed that immigrants have the capacity to make South Africa great through their talents and contributions, 62% were of the opinion that immigrants are a burden on social benefits which belong legally to South Africans. And while 33% accepted that immigrants could not be blamed for the rising spates of crimes in South Africa than other groups including South Africans themselves, 61% pointed accusing fingers at immigrants as being solely the cause of crimes. And thus, it is easy to see how this kind of statistics could translate into the rampaging side of identity politics for South Africans.

The paradoxical reality, however, is that to the extent that identity politics has been ferocious, to that same extent it has constituted itself into an emancipatory framework for disenfranchised groups, minorities and social movements. Thus, identity-based movements and intellectual activists

> who self-consciously invoked the concept of identity in their struggles for social justice held at least the following two beliefs: (1) that identities are often resources of knowledge especially relevant for social change, and that; (2) oppressed groups need to be at the forefront of their own liberation. In viewing their politics as "identity politics," activists involved in these movements were trying to sum up—and deepen—the lessons they had learned from the oppressed. (Alcoff and Mohanty 2006: 2)

From religious fundamentalism to ethnic/cultural/racial identity, and from sexuality politics to environmentalism, identity politics has gained global currency, and it gestures at a sense of the self or the subject that is originary, essentialist, unified and exclusionary. This essentialist idea of identity signals a "stable core of the self, unfolding from beginning to end through all the vicissitudes of history without change; the bit of the self which remains always-already 'the same,' identical to itself across time" (Hall 1996: 3). The irreducibility of the concept of identity, according to Stuart Hall, derives from "its centrality to the question of agency and politics" (1996: 2).

However, the successes of the identity-based movements have not prevented the barrage of criticisms that has attended identity politics. From the political and theoretical perspectives, opponents have railed against the capacity of identity politics to project difference and undermine solidarity. For them, "racial categories are specious ways to categorize human beings, that gender differences are overblown, that sexuality should be thought of as a practice rather than an identity, and that disability itself is often the product of social arrangements rather than a natural kind" (Alcoff and Mohanty 2006: 3). The ideas of identity and identity politics have therefore been the subject of deconstructive critique that seeks to undermine their totalizing and essentialist features by putting them "under erasure." This implies that as long as these concepts remain in their present essentialist forms, they cannot be "good to think with" (Hall 1996: 1). But, deconstructing concepts like identity do not take away their irreducibility. For Hall,

> since they have not been superseded dialectically, and there are no other, entirely different concepts with which to replace them, there is nothing to do but to continue to think with them—albeit now in their detotalized or deconstructed forms, and no longer operating within the paradigm in which they were originally generated. … The line which cancels them, paradoxically, permits them to go on being read. (ibid.)

Anthony Kwame Appiah is a strident critic of identity as an essentialist concept. His critique is unique because it deploys an ethical methodology that enables us to deconstruct identity in multiple ways. In this chapter, we outline Appiah's ethical and theoretical reactions to cosmopolitanism and nationalism as identity forms, and how both could be complicated to give us better understanding of the modes of being of the self, and of subjectivity, in a global world.

NATIONALISM AND THE COSMOPOLITAN IMAGINATION

The major objective of cosmopolitanism is to force a rethinking of the boundary of the self. The major instigator of this reassessment of the nature of the self are the emerging global forces and flows that are energetically transforming every dimension of human experience, from the technological to the cultural. Thus, in thinking about the environment and territorial borders, and about citizenship and community, we are compelled to engage with the trajectory of interdependence that reconstitutes inhabitants of various parts of the world as participants in a common humanity. Gerald Delanty argues that globalization's normative significance consists in its birthing of a new imagination that opens up new ways of seeing the world "in terms of its immanent possibilities for self-transformation and which can be realized only by taking the cosmopolitan perspective of the Other as well as global principles of justice" (Delanty 2009: 3).

Cosmopolitanism as a social theory is founded on the diminishing significance of the nation-state as a category for understanding our territorially bounded social reality. In other words, beyond the limitation imposed on the understanding of the self and its relationship with the non-self, cosmopolitanism enables us to "theorize the transformation of subjectivity in terms of relations of the self, Other and world" (Delanty 2009: 6). Thus, the cosmopolitan imagination "entails a view of society as an ongoing process of self-constitution" (ibid.: 73). This self-constitution is a framework of social struggles that remains essentially incomplete in its narration. The self-constitution of the society is actually a process of self-problematization that invites deep interaction through fundamental openness. This is what Delanty calls "world disclosure":

an open process by which the social world is made intelligible; it should be seen as the expression of new ideas, the opening of spaces of discourse, identifying possibilities for translation and the construction of the social world. ... [I]t can be related to such virtues as irony (emotional distance from one's own history and culture), reflexivity (the recognition that all perspectives are culturally conditioned and contingent), scepticism towards the grand narratives of modern ideologies, care for other cultures and an acceptance of cultural hybridization, an ecumenical commitment to dialogue with other cultures, especially religious ones, and nomadism, as a condition of never being fully at home in cultural categories or geopolitical boundaries. (ibid.: 78)

The origin of cosmopolitanism is often traced to many ancient cultures and religious promptings that all attempted to unite humanity under one banner. From the ancient Greeks to the Abrahamic religions, there has always been a cosmopolitan imagination founded on love and peace among humans. But the most popular intellectual source of cosmopolitanism derives from the Greek *kosmopolités*, and it came from a statement uttered by Diogenes the Cynic who saw himself as a "citizen of the world." Diogenes meant this declaration to be a repudiation of his national attachment to his local Sinope, and it has since served as a template for a cosmopolitan rejection of "local forms of belonging" (ibid.: 20). Diogenes's significant declaration represents first an individual projection of freedom, and second a moral consciousness that embraces all the frameworks of belonging that transcend locality to those that reach toward a collective humanity. Even though Diogenes's cosmopolitan rascality was a mere individualistic reaction against conventional restriction, it contributes a significant critical item to the cosmopolitan imagination:

the Cynics did change irreversibly the view that the polis was the exclusive measure of political community. It is important to consider that the Cynics were challenging the relatively closed world of the classical Greek polis where the highest ideal was civic devotion to the political community. This was a republican order that had no place for cosmopolitan values since the republic was an internally ordered community that distinguished sharply between citizens and non-citizens. It was this distinction between an inside and an outside that cosmopolitanism challenged. (ibid.: 20)

The Cynic's challenge to the understanding of the polis is further enlarged in the Stoic's envisioning of the cosmos as the new polis. And it is this pull-push effect between the cosmos and the polis that constitutes the contemporary debate between the cosmopolitans and the nationalists. And there is no doubt at all about the moral and political allure of cosmopolitanism when compared to the tragic horrors of nationalism, from Hitler to the multiple genocides from Bosnia to Rwanda. Yet, global statistics reveals that the cosmopolitan imagination does not seem to have taken hold in the minds of those who live the realities of locality, of regional affinities, of nationalist values and finally of territorial identities. Thus:

The hypothesis of the rise of cosmopolitanism, understood as the feeling of being citizens of the world, in the age of globalization is not supported by the evidence. Only 15 percent of the people surveyed feel close to their continent or to the world as their primary identity. Furthermore, only 2 percent are pure cosmopolitans; that is, those who indicate exclusively a continental/world identity. Some 38 percent of those surveyed consider the nation to be their primary source of territorial identity, but the most widely diffused primary territorial identity is local/regional; that is, chosen in the first place by 47 percent of the people surveyed. In the younger generations there is a higher proportion of those who feel citizens of the world, up to 21 percent for the youngest cohort. But even for this age group, 44 percent of those interviewed chose their region or locality as their primary territorial identity. ... Pure localists/regionalists, that is those who identify only with their locality or region, represent about 20 percent of the people interviewed, a figure ten times greater than the pure cosmopolitans. There is, however, a trend toward increasing cosmopolitanism among the younger, more educated, and more affluent groups of the population, but this trend is overwhelmed by the persistence of localities, regions, and, to a lesser extent, nations, as the primary sources of territorial identity in the minds of most people, and particularly of those left out of the benefits of globalization. (Castells 2010: 335)

This surely is a dated statistics, and current realities may push the perception this way or that. Yet, the political realities in Europe, North America, Asia and Africa speak to the currency of the nationalist imagination everywhere.

Nationalism, as an ideological impulse, feeds well into the progressive vision of achieving social justice for those that have been maligned within national, regional or global sociopolitical arrangements that undermined the epistemic and political significance of identity, to quote one of the questions that motivated The Future of Minority Studies Research Project (FMS). Even though minority cultures and identities often project their political claims through the epistemic prism of relevant subjective experience, they believe that such subjective experiences constitute valid objective knowledge about shared social experience and reality (Alcoff and Mohanty 2006: 5). The real social significance of identity-based knowledge becomes evident in the dilemma that Seyla Benhabib sees between law and ethics, sovereignty and hospitality, universal human rights and particular cultural or national identities, or between cosmopolitan norms and democratic self-determination. This is how Post constructs the dilemma: "If the universalism of our ethics ultimately derives from commitments to the transcendent and equal dignity of all persons, the particularism of our law ultimately derives from the well-guarded borders of our states. We face two difficulties in attempting to imagine law that does not root itself in the circumscribed polis of a state" (2006: 2). Benhabib puts it in more specific form regarding the challenge of cosmopolitan norms:

> Although the evolution of cosmopolitan norms of justice is a tremendous development, the relationship between the spread of cosmopolitan norms and democratic self-determination is fraught, both theoretically and politically. How can

the will of democratic majorities be reconciled with norms of cosmopolitan justice? How can legal norms and standards, which originate outside the will of democratic legislatures, become binding on them? (2006: 17)

Benhabib notes the rise of what she calls the "international human rights regime": "a set of interrelated and overlapping global and regional regimes that encompass human rights treaties as well as customary international law or international soft law" (ibid.: 27). This regime serves as one of the foundations of the emerging cosmopolitan norms. Yet, as she argues, the laws and treaties are negotiated through the sovereign framework of the nation-state which then becomes "both sublated and reinforced in its authority" (ibid.: 31). This points at a central contradiction in the relationship between cosmopolitan norms and the sovereignty of nation-states:

> although territorially bounded states are increasingly subject to international norms, states themselves are the principal signatories as well as enforcers of the multiple human rights treaties and conventions through which international norms spread. ... Throughout the international system, as long as territorially bounded states are recognized as the sole legitimate units of negotiation and representation, a tension, and at times even a fatal contradiction, is palpable: the modern state system is caught between *sovereignty* and *hospitality*, between the prerogative to choose to be a party to cosmopolitan norms and human rights treaties, and the obligation to extend recognition of these human rights to all. (ibid.)

Constructing the contradiction this way occludes a different kind of contradiction. This is that between the national identity which the nation-state carries as a particular kind of political community and the multiple local identities that make such a community their home and live within it in perpetual conflict. This is because being French or Akan or Yoruba or Zulu—and even being a woman, gay, Muslim and physically challenged—is an identity trope that sometimes stands in agonistic relationship with the larger political community and its own unique identity. The hospitality that is central to cosmopolitan norms—that demands that all humans have rights that transcends sovereign borders—is often denied to national and non-national identities within particular sovereign territories. Thus, the attempt by the nation-state as a particular political community to order the identity of the multiple identities within its bounded territory often leads to several and severe contestations that threaten the nation-state and invokes cosmopolitan norms.

While scholars, like Benhabib, construct the cosmopolitan-nationalist discourse in terms of a contradiction between sovereignty and hospitality, others—from Homi Bhabha to Roland Robertson—see it in terms of a complementary relationship between cosmopolitanism and nationalism. Bhabha's concept of *narration*, for instance, demonstrates the negotiated dynamics that defines the identity of the nations and of national identities. More importantly, nations and national identities are also constituted by the transgressions of the others into a hybrid entity. The narratives of hybridity and multivocality at the heart of the nation transform it into a cosmopolitan category itself. Ulrich Beck's "cosmopolitan vision" however insists that cosmopolitanism must be contrasted to nationalism. For Beck, the human condition has become irretrievably cosmopolitan. Cosmopolitanism is no longer just a beautiful idea but a definite reality in "an era of reflexive modernity, in which national borders and differences are dissolving and must be renegotiated in accordance with the logic of a 'politics of politics'" (Beck 2006: 2).

The cosmopolitan world therefore requires, Beck insists, a "cosmopolitan outlook"—or methodological cosmopolitanism—contrasted to a "national outlook"—or methodological nationalism. The national outlook necessarily opposes the fundamental transformation of social reality that the cosmopolitan outlook promises. Beck's argument for the necessity of an irretrievably cosmopolitan world outlook is challenged by a consistent transformation of the politics of states, especially in Europe, North America, Asia and even Africa, into a nationalist, far-right ideological mold that signals a congealing of the national outlook rather than its dissipation. This is an irrefutable empirical point. Appiah does not make much of such an empirical claim. In fact, whatever the trajectory of global and national politics, it is one thing to make an empirical and methodological claim like Beck, and it is a different thing entirely to make a moral one.

How does Anthony Appiah and his cosmopolitan argument feature in this wide array of discourses on the relationship between the cosmopolitan and the national? Appiah brings to bear on the discourse of identity politics in its current theoretical form a deep sense of the ethical rather than the methodological as the starting point for our reflection on what it means to be cosmopolitan.

The Ambivalent Contours of Cosmopolitanism

In a most recent article in *Foreign Affairs* titled "The Importance of Elsewhere: In Defence of Cosmopolitanism," Appiah deftly and elegantly lays out the case for an understanding of cosmopolitanism that, for him and unlike other scholars, does not stand conceptually and theoretically exclusionary to the nationalist ethos and outlook. Appiah summarizes his argument:

> The cosmopolitan task, in fact, is to be able to focus on both far and near. Cosmopolitanism is an expansive act of the moral imagination. It sees human beings as shaping their lives within nesting memberships: a family, a neighborhood, a plurality of overlapping identity groups, spiraling out to encompass all humanity. It asks us to be many things, because we are many things. (2019)

His takeoff point is with Diogenes's rendering of the cosmopolitan creed, and how a conceptual unraveling of that declaration—"I am a citizen of the world"—could enable us get a grip on what cosmopolitanism means as a deep moral vision that represents how we ought to live in a global world. Appiah's understanding of cosmopolitanism commences from the need to come to terms with the paradox that lies within Diogenes's deployment of cosmopolitanism. Diogenes, the Greek iconoclast of sort, deliberately referred to himself as *kosmopolités*, and probably with some intent at deliberate conceptual mischievousness. Yet, Appiah argues, there is something fundamentally misleading about conceiving identity in this cosmopolitan sense of "a citizen of the world."

The paradox built into *kosmopolités* is very simple but fundamental:

> a *polités* was a free adult male citizen of a polis, one of the self-governing Greek towns in southeastern Europe and Asia Minor, and the *kosmos* was, well, the whole of the universe. It would have been obvious to any of Diogenes' contemporaries that you couldn't belong to the universe in the same way as you belonged to a town such as Athens, which had some 30,000 free male adult citizens in his day (and a total population of perhaps 100,000). It was a contradiction in terms as obvious as the one in "global village," a phrase coined by the media theorist Marshall McLuhan a little more than half a century ago. Village equals small; globe equals enormous. Cosmopolitanism takes something small and familiar and projects it onto a whole world of strangers. (Appiah 2019)

And yet, Appiah insists, something is significantly wrong with this projection of identity to a global level, despite the popularity of this vision as the underlying basis of what has come to be regarded as cosmopolitanism. And this is because the notion of identity ought not to be taken as a kind of weighing of the global and the local in some form of contrarian assessment. This is because, according to Appiah, the many things that matter to us, matter to us at different levels of identity commitments. And this is in addition to the fact that so many of the things that now matter to us no longer have political borders which appeal to our patriotic emotion. The challenge however is to find a way of squaring the moral appeal of patriotism with the moral demands of cosmopolitanism.

Appiah advocates what has come to be called patriotic cosmopolitanism or cosmopolitan nationalism. This is an attempt to "root" cosmopolitanism and make it more alive to people's multiple affiliations and entanglements, rather than the very concept scholars have bandied about because of its allure. Here, cosmopolitanism recognizes and embraces difference and the Other. So, cosmopolitan nationalism entails the argument, first, that it is a wrong interpretation that sees cosmopolitanism and patriotism as contraries and mutually exclusive. The literature on identity is rife with this exclusionary reading. And yet the history of the cosmopolitan idea belies it. At its core is a universalism which demands that every human being somewhere and anywhere matters. This universalism softens the excessive claims that have been made on behalf of both cosmopolitanism and nationalism. Both are emasculated by the imperative of reacting to and relating with the demands of the other. For Appiah:

> Managing multiple citizenships is something everyone has to do: if people can harbor allegiances to a city and a country, whose interests can diverge, why should it be baffling to speak of an allegiance to the wider world? My father, Joe Appiah,

was an independence leader of Ghana and titled his autobiography *The Autobiography of an African Patriot*; he saw no inconsistency in telling his children, in the letter he left for us when he died, that we should remember always that we were citizens of the world. (2019)

However, this universalism is not impartial, contrary to the expectations of the wooly cosmopolitan who thinks that "if everybody matters, they must matter equally" (ibid.). Unfortunately, the fact that everybody matters does not necessarily imply that we must owe to everyone the same moral obligation. In other words, it is not uncosmopolitan, argues Appiah, to be partial to some locality or my family. It is not morally arbitrary, within the rooted cosmopolitanism, for me as a Nigerian to favor my nephew rather than an unknown Briton or Ghanaian. "I can recognize the legitimate moral interests of your family, while still paying special attention to mine. It's not that my family matters more than yours; it's that it matters more to me" (ibid.).

The second point is that most national imaginings usually incorporate cosmopolitan ideas and norms. In fact, the argument is that the idea of the nation is already cosmopolitan in its hybridity—the nation's attempt to incorporate the Others and alterity in continuous negotiations:

> Nations are built upon narratives which are incomplete and perspectival; they are stories that people tell about their collective existence and in them the past is constantly redefined. This is more true today than ever when marginal groups are coming to play a greater role in defining national identity: women, migrants, indigenous peoples etc. are less outside the nation than within it. (Delanty 2009: 74)

This is the tolerant dimension of cosmopolitanism, according to Appiah. Tolerance exposes the flexibility which cosmopolitans must contend with: what we have read into nationalism itself. The cosmopolitan imaginations allow for the participation of all nations and localities in the conversation of humankind.

Appiah's cosmopolitanism is firmly rooted in a deep and complex philosophical tradition dating from Stoicism through Romanticism and German philosophy (from Schiller and Fichte to Hegel) and down to W. E. B. du Bois and his radical philosophical reflections on and imaginings of race. In *Lines of Descent: W. E. B. Du Bois and the Emergence of Identity*, Appiah traces the intellectual trajectory of du Bois's fascination with and integration into the identity discourse that was flowering within German philosophy and in Germany. One can immediately understand Appiah's fascination with du Bois: here is a black intellectual whose very life signifies the very struggles of the self to define itself against the multiple currents of identity tropes that beckon. And in his own case, the self was forced, against its own will, into a racial context that instigated a double consciousness which in turn facilitated the emergence of the "souls of the black folk"—the Negro and the American, "two souls, two thoughts, two unreconciled strivings; two warring ideals in one dark body, whose dogged strength alone keeps it from being torn asunder" (du Bois 2007: xiii).

Du Bois's sojourn in Germany was therefore a life-defining period for him. He became immersed in the intense debate and the shifting intellectual dynamics between the cosmopolitan and the uncosmopolitan currents. This period unraveled how the "the autobiography of a race concept"—as du Bois referred to himself—would be significantly influenced in his attempt to come to terms with the identities warring in his being. He was particularly influenced by Herder's brilliant intertwining of a concept of nation as a *volksgeist* and as being an active member in the communion of a common humanity. Herder's cultural cosmopolitanism invested du Bois's. Indeed, the relationship, the compatibility, between cosmopolitanism and nationalism was taken for granted in much of nineteenth-century European thought. So, one dimension of du Bois's intellectual gain from his Germany sojourn is the rejection of nationalism as the appropriate avenue for coming to terms with his racial agonies. For Appiah:

> He had no use for a nationalism that made claims only upon its own nationals; this was a nationalism of already established might. He had to make claims upon humanity. Nationalists before the ascendancy of the nation-state recognized that the demand for national rights made sense as a moral demand only if it was claimed equally for all nations. The strategy of the argument is one that Kant made familiar. My dignity cannot matter because it is mine; it has to matter because it is dignity. And if it is dignity that matters, then your dignity matters to. So, too, *mutatis mutandis,* for nationality. In Du Bois's view, the Negro legitimately had a higher degree of concern for his own kind, but this view was framed within the recognition both that they had obligations to people of other races and that they would gain greatly from conversation across the races. (2014: 53–54)

The second dimension of du Bois's intellectual gain is however even more fundamental to Appiah's argument for moral cosmopolitanism. This has to do with the place of the soul in du Bois's intellectual engagement with racism and the identity of the Negro. With the idea of striving which he got from German philosophy, and the connotation of the soul as "Geist," du Bois was able to formulate his "two-souls thesis" as an understanding of the Negro's plight in the racially charged context of the United States. Thus, when he talked about the "two souls" warring in irreconcilable strivings within "one dark body," du Bois introduced a problematic: How is it possible to have more than one soul? Appiah provides an answer deriving from du Bois's Herderian understanding of the *volksgeist*:

> We can think of the soul here not as an individual's unique possession, but rather as something she shares with the folk to which she belongs: think of it, that is, as a Volksgeist. Think of each Volksgeist, too, as striving to realize itself against a resisting not-I. Then a person who belongs to more than one people could share in two souls, each defined, in part, by its striving against a world that contains other souls. Furthermore, as Du Bois requires, a person who had both a Negro

and an American soul could participate in the intellectual and cultural—the geistige—life of both, and thus see herself through both a Negro and an American lens. Because the two visions are at odds, this person would, indeed, have two warring ideals contending within a single body. In describing this putative affliction, Du Bois was, in effect, rejecting the notion that each of us could participate in only one Volksgeist; an individual person could be, in part, the product of the souls of the various folks to which she belonged. (2014: 58–59)

In the attempt to reconcile the Negro and the American souls striving to achieve a "better and truer self," du Bois was at pain to insist that the striving was not meant to sublate one soul in the other; "In this merging he wishes neither of the older selves to be lost. He would not Africanize America, or America has too much to teach the world and Africa. He would not bleach his Negro soul in a flood of white Americanism, for he knows that Negro blood has a message for the world. He simply wishes to make it possible for a man to be both a Negro and an American" (du Bois 2007: 9). The critical takeaway from this interrogation of du Bois's rendering of racial striving is simple: an individual cannot be meaningfully characterized as having one soul or identity but disparate souls. This implies, according to Appiah, taking the soul not as an individual ontological category, "but rather as something she shares with the folk to which she belongs: think of it, that is, as a Volksgeist. Think of each Volksgeist, too, as striving to realize itself against a resisting not-I. Then a person who belongs to more than one people could share in two souls, each defined, in part, by its striving against a world that contains other souls" (Appiah 2014: 58–59).

Appiah's Ethics of Identity

Appiah's understanding of identity stands at the interstice of the ontological nature of the self, the idea of individuality and the ethics of relationship with others. In other words, it stretches as a continuum from individuality to sociability to an ethical vision of relational identity. Appiah rejects what he calls the authenticity and existentialist visions of individuality. The authenticity vision, which assumes the existence of a *true* self that is either realized or compromised circumstances, is wrong because it negates the place of creativity in the construction of the self. The existentialist vision, which supposed that there is no template or essence of the self anywhere except what we create for ourselves, is wrong because it supposed that everything about the self is constructed (2005: 17). The individuality of the self already presupposes a construction out of the social: "We come into the world 'mewling and puking in the nurse's arms' (as Shakespeare so genially put it), capable of human individuality but only if we have the chance to develop it in interaction with others. An identity is always articulated through concepts (and practices) made available to you by religion, society, school, and state, mediated by family, peers, friends" (ibid.: 20). And the sociability of our identities is further reinforced and consolidated through the narratives that bind the stories of our being with those of others. The individual self makes sense of itself through a narrativized structure of existence.

How then does this nuanced understanding of our collective self-making "fit into our broader moral projects?" At the first level, according to Appiah, identity enables us to maneuver our way through the many morally permissible options about values and the valuable lives available for humans to pick from: "One thing identity provides is another source of value, one that helps us make our way among those options. To adopt an identity, to make it mine, is to see it as structuring my way through life" (ibid.: 24). Identity internalizes many values which enable those who own that identity to relate with others who also share in it. Thus:

> There are thus various ways that identity might be a source of value, rather than being something that realizes other values. First, if an identity is yours, it may determine certain acts of solidarity as valuable, or be an internal part of the specification of your satisfactions and enjoyments, or motivate and give meaning to acts of supererogatory kindness. Indeed, the presence of an identity concept in the specification of my aim—as helping a fellow bearer of some identity—may be part of what explains why I have the aim at all. Someone may gain satisfaction from giving money to the Red Cross after a hurricane in Florida as an act of solidarity with other Cuban Americans. Here the fact of the shared identity is part of why he or she has the aim. By the same token, a shared identity may give certain acts or achievements a value for me they would not otherwise have had. When a Ghanaian team wins the African Cup of Nations in soccer, that is of value to me by virtue of my identity as a Ghanaian. If I were a Catholic, a wedding in a Catholic church might be of value to me in a special way because I was a Catholic. (ibid.: 25)

When this identity dynamics, especially about solidarity, is then calibrated in terms of the loyalty we owe to one another—to those who participate in the same identity trope we hold—morality becomes a significant issue to address.

As we have noted earlier, today's world is bifurcated between the cosmopolitan and the nationalist. Nationalism takes the issue of solidarity stemming from national membership very seriously. Nationalism—as solidarity with members of the same nation or nation-state—runs on exclusionary logic. It draws a very tight line between citizens and noncitizens and between patriots and political strangers. This raises the critical question of how we ought to deal with the moral status of these strangers. For Appiah, that this question has not been taken very seriously is a significant omission for cosmopolitan theorists. In other words, if, according to Appiah, the history of the world is a multiple trajectories of movements and migrations that brings contexts and localities into complex and complicated relationships, then "wherever you live, the matter of outsiders isn't a sociopolitical anomaly—a small, messy chore, like cleaning out the attic, to be dealt with when we have a spare hour or two. No island, you could say, is an island" (ibid.: 219). Cosmopolitanism therefore deeply challenges the partiality for membership, as different from non-membership, that reinforces the nationalist framework. For Appiah, this distinction demands a fundamental justification especially if ethical individualism—that persons rather than peoples are the basic unit of morality—is taken as the ethical standard. Thus, if all persons possess equal moral worth, then there is no moral justification for preferring one person over another—no matter the person's identity group.

Yet, it will be unfortunate to think that the cosmopolitan challenge to partiality implies the abjuration of local loyalties. Cosmopolitanism does not instantiate abstract impartiality that shields the self from loyalties to nation, gender, locality, religion and sexuality. Appiah's "wishy washy version of cosmopolitanism" seeks to balance between universalism and diversitarianism: "A tenable cosmopolitanism, in the first instance, must take seriously the value of human life, and the value of particular human lives, the lives people have made for themselves, within the communities that help lend significance to those lives. This prescription captures the challenge. A cosmopolitanism with prospects must reconcile a kind of universalism with the legitimacy of at least some forms of partiality" (ibid.: 222–223). So, if all humans everywhere have equal worth, what justifies or makes it obligatory for giving those who share some certain identities with me—gay, women, Nigerians, Africans—some form of preferences over others, without at the same time lowering their worth by reason of their non-participation in my identity trope?

Appiah argues that to get the best of this question, we need to shift the discourse away from the issue of moral equality which, as a concept for distributive justice, constitutes "a fit with particularist goods":

> *My friend Mary* is not simply an instantiation of the general good represented by *friendship*; she's not like one first-class stamp on a roll of first-class stamps. Second, I maintained that equality wasn't what morality demanded of us as individuals; it denotes a regulative ideal for political, not personal, conduct. We go wrong when we conflate personal and political ideals, and, in particular, when we assume that, because there are connections between the two, they are the same. (ibid.: 230)

And this brings us to an enunciation of the idea of obligation, of special obligations, that we owe those who share the same identities with us, and that justifies our being partial to them out of all humanity. Appiah adopts a distinction between morality and ethics as a means of understanding the special obligations that underline the cosmopolitan patriot's requirement of partiality. This enables him to delineate not only the space that explains partiality or special obligations but also what makes partiality most valuable for humans.

The distinction between ethics and morality, borrowed from Ronald Dworkin and Avishai Margalit, separates between the sphere of identity that relates us to strangers who are humans like us, and that which relates us to those who share identity traits with us. For Appiah, this distinction between the ethical and the moral corresponds to the "'thick' relations—which invoke a community founded in a shared past or 'collective memory'—and 'thin' relations, which we have with strangers, and which are stipulatively entailed by a shared humanity" (ibid.: 230). Ethics, in this sense, enables us to figure out what it means for us to live well, and this is founded on those historical circumstances, social practices and materials that contribute to the forging of our identities, the identities that are equally grounded in larger "collective narratives, but not exhausted by them" (ibid.). The sphere of the ethical therefore stipulates the dynamics of identity—who we are as ethical selves—as determined within the thick relations of belonging or encumbrances in specific moral communities. However, moral concerns are those that make me a person and connect me with other persons in the universal space. Morality in this sense does not require special obligations. All humans matter equally no matter their identity.

Appiah's further point is important: these two realms of the universal-moral and the particular-ethical cannot be separated because they constitute two normative registers or projects that require constant negotiation. This is to say that there is no way moral obligations to persons qua persons could always have the upper hand against ethical obligations. And furthermore, for Appiah, opting out of both types of obligation is never an option. Thus, while moral obligation is universal and is not modulated by the "vagaries of our motivations," ethical obligations are "motivationally sensitive" in that they require special responsibilities to wife, uncles, nieces, friends and so on. In fact, Appiah argues:

> the most powerful defense of partiality is the simplest: for human beings, relationships are an important good—I would be inclined to say they were objectively valuable—and many (noninstrumental) relationships … require partiality. These relationships are constituted, in part, by the sense of special caring between those involved, and couldn't exist "unless they are seen as providing reasons for unequal treatment." The pronoun "my" *is* magical, and we'd be inclined to view someone wholly unsusceptible to its magic as a monster, or, possibly, a utilitarian. (ibid.: 236)

But then, such a defense of thick relationship only constitutes a necessary but not sufficient condition for national identities, according to Appiah. Contiguous partiality is one thing, and partiality to those who inhabit the same national space with us but are too remote for special obligations of the contiguous type is another. A Ghanaian living in Kumasi is expected, through some mediating institutions and national symbols, to share an identity with another Ghanaian living in Accra. Yet, according to Appiah, while the "partiality of the nationalist may be thicker than water, … it is thinner than blood" (ibid.: 238).

One reason for the weakness of national partiality is that it is not thick enough; indeed, it seeks to abridge thicker allegiances, for instance, to one's *ethnie* or even family. And this same charge is legitimate against the cosmopolitans who urge another abstract identity claim on behalf of a shared humanity.

THE STARK REALITIES OF EVERYWHERE

There are several critical points of objections that could attend Appiah's understanding of cosmopolitan patriotism. The most fundamental, I suspect, is his understanding of liberal humanism, and the liberal metaphysics of the individual, as the best basis for understanding cosmopolitanism. Appiah is unabashedly a Millian in that he wholeheartedly supports J. S. Mill's version of liberalism and its grounding of autonomy as the most fundamental value that unites individuals as persons universally. In other words, the choices that individual autonomy make possible could only be assessed within the constraints of the universal-moral imperatives, rather than particularist frameworks of ethical concerns. Thus, it is this liberal individualism that makes possible Appiah's distinction between the moral and the ethical and the basis for fashioning his idea of rooted cosmopolitanism. According to Lennon, this distinction gives Appiah the advantage of "apparently respecting difference without the authority of his liberal individualism being called into question" (2006: 542). Yet, liberal individualism speaks about making sense of one's life and prospects in ways that could not be empirically universalized.

This raises two points of critique. The first is that cosmopolitanism projects an elite lifestyle that is only available to a small segment of the population in mostly liberal and industrialized states of the world. Cosmopolitan sensibility, that is, comes from much travels and cross-cultural and transnational experiences facilitated by affluent lifestyles that suggest some capitalist and high-culture opportunities which instigate class inequalities. This is the global reality of what Craig Calhoun calls "actually existing cosmopolitanism" that conjoins the real nature of capitalist expansion with the unfolding and tough inequality that it creates everywhere. For Calhoun, cosmopolitan ideals mask "sharp inequalities to the extent that even neoliberal corporate leaders and organizations find it convenient to deploy cosmopolitan rhetoric" (2002: 871). For Nigel Harris, global capitalism rides piggyback on cosmopolitan values and networks. According to him, there is now an emergent class of the "cosmopolitan bourgeoisie"—"the class of 'businessmen' (to use an anachronistic term for want of a better one) who created and sustained this system has normally been cosmopolitan, composed of networks of people of different ethnic, cultural, linguistic and religious origins, threading their way between the murderous rivalries of the territorial rulers" (2003: 15). This cosmopolitan capitalism contributes largely to what Calhoun calls the "class consciousness of the frequent travelers" who rides on the inequality created by capitalism to achieve a cosmopolitan sensibility. One other way to put this thought is: how does a poor person become cosmopolitan when the global institutions that make for that orientation are already skewed against such a person?

It seems to take little reflection to move from the capitalist orientation of actually existing cosmopolitanism to the projection of liberal humanism as a dangerous ideological hub for the fetishization of a Eurocentric worldview. Chike Jeffers raises a critical question about the relationship between cosmopolitanism and world integration. If cosmopolitanism aspires to the integration of the world into one single community, especially through the facilities and technologies of interactions and interconnectivity, then we need to be concerned about the how of the integration:

> The strength and plausibility of cosmopolitan ideals, then, are tied to concurrent levels of world integration. It matters, however, from a moral standpoint, *how the world gets integrated*—that is, whether the new relationships created by the increased interaction of the world's people are egalitarian in character, or whether they are examples of *asymmetrical integration*, privileging one side while disadvantaging the other. Attention to this matter is not, I would argue, inherent in cosmopolitanism and, as a result, it becomes possible for cosmopolitan dreams to be tainted by their acceptance of oppressive forms of world integration as a means to their realization. (2013: 497)

Asymmetrical integration comes with the ideological territory within which the Eurocentric worldview roams omnipotently through the channel made possible by European imperialism and colonialist *mission civilisatrice*. Indeed, and contrary to Appiah's spirited attempt to undermine what he called uniformitarian universalism or support an "antiuniversalist cosmopolitanism," we must always return to the baggage of liberal humanism and its racist Eurocentric legacy. How do we arrive at an "overarching love of humanity" through a liberal humanism tainted by a disdain for a significant portion of that humanity?

Within the context of Appiah's "wishy washy cosmopolitanism," there is a space for the cosmopolitan and the nationalist to co-exist. But Appiah's liberal humanism only allows for the nationalist or localist to exist as persons claiming individual human rights. The question however is whether the cosmopolitan tolerance can still hold if group rights or collective identities are asserted. This question becomes so fundamental when it is noted that significant segments of humanity define themselves in terms of race, ethnicity, language and religion, and the issue of global and social justice rears its head as a significant feature of the global reality. This is an important issue because groups of all kinds—from ethnic to national to gender groups—are important and even critical features of our social reality. Why then does the great institutional and intellectual dynamics of liberalism, like John Rawls and the Constitution of the Unites States, for instance, relate to groups from the basis of their individuality as persons, wondered Nathan Glazer, among other identity theorists. Liberalism is decidedly "colorblind in a society where color and national origin are key realities determining in some measure the fate of the individuals of any group" (Glazer 1995: 125). Yet, in countries like Canada and India, for example, we have alternative legal and constitutional frameworks that protect individuals not on the basis of their being persons but based on their group affiliations. This approach, contrary to the American liberal approach, inscribed a language "that specifically guarantees the rights of groups, by name, that specifically reserves for groups a certain proportion of posts in government, in the civil services, in the universities, in business. This kind of approach to group rights is clearly just as compatible with a regime committed to human rights as the approach that focuses only on the individual" (ibid.: 126).

It is this group language that Appiah's liberal humanism attempts to suppress. In Bhikhu Parekh's words, group and collective identities, especially of the national type, become significant for its members because

> It provides a home, a place they can call their own, and whose membership of it generally cannot be taken away from them. They grow up and are educated within it, and are deeply shaped by its values and ethos. Being territorially bounded, the political community also creates a structured space that gives intensity and depth to their relations with each other, and forges common bonds. Their personal and collective security is also bound up with it, and creates the ties of common interest. Its laws shape and leave an imprint on all aspects of their lives, including marriage, sexuality, structure of the family, property, career, and formal and informal relations with each other. They pay its taxes, receive its welfare benefits, fight in its wars, travel abroad carrying its passport and enjoying its protection, and identify themselves to, and are in turn identified by, others as its members. (2008: 56–57)

Yet, national identity, as wonderful as it is, presents a paradox—it unites and divides. As a significant understanding of humanity, it makes it possible to achieve an inclusive perception of who we are as humans while also simultaneously providing an exclusivist othering that essentially fragments diversity along ethnic, linguistic, cultural and religious bases. One can then see the fundamental reason why Appiah insists on a liberal individualist framework for understanding national identity in terms of citizens. Most interpretations of cosmopolitanism, that is, understand the concepts as an essentially individual expression of selfhood: how individuals as persons discover themselves in meandering through complex multiples of localities and cultures. Yet one wonders whether citizenship is sufficient to fulfill the longing for collective identity. In the rest of this section, I will briefly outline two understandings of the cosmopolitan subject that react against each other in response to the idea of collective identity as a mode of being in the world.

The first is Irene Skovgaard-Smith and Flemming Poulfelt's discussion of transnational professionals working in multinational companies (especially in Amsterdam), and their framing of identity formation as "non-nationals." For them, this identity formation involves "downplaying national affiliations and cultural differences while also marking national identity categories and 'cultural features' to maintain the difference they collectively embrace. This however does not imply openness to all otherness" (2018: 129). Here, collective identity, which cosmopolitans seem to disdain, is contrasted to national identity which a cosmopolitan like Appiah interprets as an individual phenomenon. While this identity strategy "neutralizes" national affiliations and cultural differences in a demonstration of openness, Skovgaard-Smith and Poulfelt insist that this "does not imply openness to and embrace of all manifestations and performances of cultural difference. It equally involves boundary drawing to establish who does *not* belong and what the 'non-nationals' define themselves vis-à-vis, namely national (mono)culture and parochialism" (ibid.: 130). Indeed, in this sense, these transnational professionals construct a cosmopolitan identity trope that is as cultural and collective as the national identity that includes and excludes. For instance, the authors consider the role that stereotypes play as a strategy of differentiation that is relevant but benign:

> Stereotypes are not really considered valid, but still used to construct both the internal difference that is embraced as we saw earlier and also the external difference that is excluded. The latter involves differentiation in relation to those who are not bringing off the expected performance of cosmopolitan openness, flexibility, neutralization and, as hinted at here, also liberalist political views associated with cosmopolitanism as a civic ideology. The Others are those who fit the stereotype and the "narrow-minded" who cannot "cope with people from different cultural backgrounds." These Others can include for instance "traditional expats." (ibid.: 136)

For Vince Marotta, the concept of the cosmopolitan stranger in itself delineates a midpoint between the cosmopolitan and the patriot in a struggle for the space of identity formation. The figure of the stranger is already an established concept in the sociological imagination. The advantage of the concept derives from the fact that since humanity must necessarily be parceled into identity segments that make the "us"-"them" distinction inevitable, we need an analytic term to take care of the segments categorized as the Others—the stranger becomes someone who is neither a friend nor an enemy: a figure that sometimes reinforces and sometimes undermines the binary framework and prefigures (re)conciliation and instability. They represent the ambivalent in-betweenness that unsettles and hybridizes the identity equation. The hybridized stranger possesses certain epistemological dynamics—some sort of subjective objectivity—that allows for a critical intervention in the worldviews of the host or the margin identity. For Marotta:

> The belief that strangers perceive the host's practices, customs and values from a less subjective perspective than the host allows them to critically reflect on those practices, customs and values. As a consequence of this experience strangers are also able to reevaluate and reflect upon their own group's traditions and worldview. Their exposure to the otherness of the host self allows them to reassess their "home" culture as less stable and fixed. What was once given is now contingent. This intellectual mobility provides strangers with the ability to transcend conventional and "situated" knowledge and, by implication, the in-between, third position permits strangers to see things more clearly than, or differently from, those who occupy opposing cultural perspectives. (2010: 109)

With this epistemological stance, we arrive at the idea of the stranger as a cosmopolitan who facilitates cross-cultural encounters and engagements. The cosmopolitan stranger demonstrates the cosmopolitan virtue of openness to difference and pluralism, and the dialogic imagination. But then, we are forced to the realization that the cosmopolitan stranger is a really strange being, with a stranger mode of being in the world that is too good to be real! On empirical grounds, for instance, if such a cosmopolitan stranger were to exist, Marotta asks,

> to what extent are they able to juggle the various demands placed upon them? How can these social actors combine the care and respect for others, with the skepticism of grand narratives, with the detachment from locality, with the accommodation of hybridization and with a universal commitment to cross-cultural dialogue? If such a personality does exist, [it] has not clearly demonstrated how these individuals can effectively accommodate the tensions and complexities arising from these demands. (ibid.: 116)

The utopian and idealistic basis of cosmopolitanism is counterpoised to the reality of cultural encounters in the global world, even at the level of transnational professionalism demonstrated by Skovgaard-Smith and Poulfelt above. The cosmopolitan hope, and even the claim of steady cosmopolitanization of the world, is consistently undermined by the brute realities of the material conditions of the real world. How, for instance, does the epistemic stance of "subjective objectivity" work in the attempt to achieve a dialogic imagination and an openness to the other? As we saw in the preceding argument for the non-nationality of the transnational professionals, their supposedly cosmopolitan temperament is actually a template for the construction of difference and differentiation. No cosmopolitan subject or stranger has the capacity to achieve a free-floating epistemic standpoint that will not automatically collapse into another standpoint with its own unique exclusionary prejudices.

Conclusion

This chapter is concerned with unpacking Kwame Anthony Appiah's understanding of cosmopolitanism as a viewpoint that accommodates localism and patriotism. Appiah's cosmopolitanism is grounded on an ethical framework that foregrounds the idea of identity on the liberal humanist's understanding of a person as an individual bearer of rights. This leads him to an understanding of collective identity, especially of the national type, as a trope that can only be understood in terms of the persons occupying those national spaces. Yet this understanding of cosmopolitan patriotism and the ethics underlying it must, despite Appiah's brilliant and spirited arguments in its favor, come short vis-à-vis the ungainly reputations of liberal humanism and its uncosmopolitan relations with other perspectives and worldviews across the globe, as well as the material realities of those who are meant to assume the cosmopolitan stance. Identity politics as positioning holds more potent meanings for those cut in the cross fires of global inequalities than the promise of the ethics of openness and the dialogic imagination.

Bibliography

Alcoff, Linda Martin, and Satya P. Mohanty. 2006. Reconsidering Identity Politics: An Introduction. In *Identity Politics Reconsidered*, ed. Linda Martin Alcoff, Michael Hames-Garcia, Satya P. Mohanty, and Paula M.L. Moya, 1–9. New York: Palgrave Macmillan.

Appiah, Kwame Anthony. 2005. *The Ethics of Identity*. Princeton: Princeton University Press.

———. 2014. *Lines of Descent: W.E.B Du Bois and the Emergence of Identity*. Cambridge, MA: Harvard University Press.

———. 2019. The Importance of Elsewhere: In Defence of Cosmopolitanism. *Foreign Affairs*, March/April issue. https://www.foreignaffairs.com/articles/2019-02-12/importance-elsewhere

Beck, Ulrich. 2006. *Cosmopolitan Vision*. Trans. Ciaran Cronin. Cambridge: Polity Press.

Benhabib, Seyla. 2006. The Philosophical Foundations of Cosmopolitan Norms. In *Seyla Benhabib, Another Cosmopolitanism*, 13–44. Oxford: Oxford University Press.

Calhoun, Craig. 2002. Class Consciousness of Frequent Travelers: Toward a Critique of Actually Existing Cosmopolitanism. *South Atlantic Quarterly* 101 (4 (Fall)): 869–897.

Castells, Manuel. 2010. *The Power of Identity*. 2nd ed. Malden: Wiley-Blackwell.

Delanty, Gerard. 2009. *The Cosmopolitan Imagination: The Renewal of Critical Social Theory*. Cambridge: Cambridge University Press.

Du Bois, W.E.B. 2007. *The Souls of Black Folk*. Oxford: Oxford University Press.

Glazer, Nathan. 1995. Individual Rights Against Group Rights. In *The Rights of Minority Cultures*, ed. Will Kymlicka, 123–138. Oxford: Oxford University Press.

Hall, Stuart. 1996. Introduction: Who Needs 'Identity'? In *Questions of Cultural Identity*, ed. Stuart Hall and Paul du Gay, 1–17. London: Sage Publications.

Harris, Nigel. 2003. *The Return of Cosmopolitan Capital: Globalisation, the State and War*. London: I.B. Tauris.

Jeffers, Chike. 2013. Appiah's Cosmopolitanism. *The Southern Journal of Philosophy* 51 (4. (December): 488–510.

Lennon, Kathleen. 2006. Review of Kwame Anthony Appiah's *The Ethics of Identity*. *Philosophy* 81 (317 (July)): 539–542.

Marotta, Vince P. 2010. Cosmopolitan Stranger. In *Questioning Cosmopolitanism*, ed. Stan Van Hooft and Wim Vandekerckhove, 105–120. Dordrecht: Springer.

Parekh, Bhikhu. 2008. *A New Politics of Identity: Political Principles for an Interdependent World*. Hampshire: Palgrave Macmillan.

Post, Robert. 2006. Introduction. In *Another Cosmopolitanism*, ed. Seyla Benhabib, 1–9. Oxford: Oxford University Press.

Skovgaard-Smith, Irene, and Flemming Poulfelt. 2018. Imagining 'Non-Nationality': Cosmopolitanism as a Source of Identity and Belonging. *Human Relations* 71 (2. (February): 129–154.

CHAPTER 27

Ritual Archives

Toyin Falola

By ritual archives, I mean the conglomeration of words as well as texts, ideas, symbols, shrines, images, performances, and indeed objects that document as well as speak to those religious experiences and practices that allow us to understand the African world through various bodies of philosophies, literatures, languages, histories, and much more. By implication, ritual archives are huge, unbounded in scale and scope, storing tremendous amounts of data on both natural and supernatural agents, ancestors, gods, good and bad witches, life, death, festivals, and the interactions between the spiritual realms and earth-based human beings. To a large extent, ritual archives constitute and shape knowledge about the visible and invisible world (or what I refer to as the "non-world"), coupled with forces that breathe and are breathless, as well as secular and non-secular, with destinies, and within cities, kingships, medicine, environment, and sciences and technologies. Above all, they contain shelves on sacrifices and shrines, names, places, incantations, invocations, and the entire cosmos of all the deities and their living subjects among human and nonhuman species.

I am deploying the term "archives" in relation to rituals as a means of challenging the conventions of Western archives, namely, what is deemed worthy of preservation and organization as data, whether or not it is interpreted at any given moment. My intervention is not to restrict archives inside the location of the library or university or museum. I am also seeking to apply the techniques and resources of academic archives to rituals so that there can be greater preservation and valuation. Furthermore, I add the metaphorical and mystical sense of "archive" as well, one that does not exclusively require residence in the academy. I am insisting that we must never lose sight of that dimension of archive that is never (fully) collected but retains power and agency in invisible ways. I offer a provocative exploration of the category of "archive" itself,

T. Falola (✉)
Department of History, University of Texas, Austin, TX, USA

coupled of course with the revolutionary insistence on expanding our understanding of it through an elevation of the significance of ritual as a name for a large component of cultural meaning-making. How do we contend with the destruction of archives via various forms of violence? Can we even clarify with certainty what can and cannot be reclaimed?

In varied ways, a countless number of sages, priests, devotees, and practitioners created oral and visual libraries, which are linked to ritual complexes and secular palaces. Subsequently, cultural knowledge has extended from the deep past to our present day. It is through their knowledge that histories and traditions were constituted, while identities were formed, and philosophy as we know it emerged. Although learned people were part of the community, they were there as ordinary members, while others constituted the leadership. Today, without specific names, we label the originators of knowledge collectively as the "past" and as "traditions," which go a long way to create for humankind access to the past. In the process, the traditions in ritual archives provide some templates for the future; the contents of the archives become the philosophy, literature, and history; their interpretations become manifested in our present as part of our engagement with heritage and modernity.

Just as in poems, ritual dances, sacred drums, and ritual textiles, components of the archives can be isolated, but they can also be combined into a body of interlocking ideas and philosophy in the context of the broad terrain of ancestral knowledge. Whether aggregated or disaggregated, ritual archives fully encode memory and remembrance in various ways and forms. Moreover, ritual archives store most of our indigenous production, memories, legacies, and even the histories of our lives and ancestors. Ritual archives lead us into the reinvention of the cosmos that we inhabit, different from but not useless to what modern science does.[1]

While postulating that there is a coloniality of archives (i.e., archives resulting from the colonial encounter) built on the template of Western knowledge, I can further deduce that it has served us—in our colonial and postcolonial world—in a number of ways. However, it has not only proven to be severely limited in terms of both intellectual possibilities and scope, but it is also an agency of control that frames our subjectivities and objectivities and, indeed, how we can pursue them. The colonial archive has been imposed and given prominence over the ancestral ritual archive, leading to the erasure and degradation of indigenous perspectives and local talents that Ki-Zerbo once called the *endogenius*. In fact, nothing reveals the shallowness of the colonial archive more than the very timeframe its contents are able to cover. Be it in the national archives of Nigeria or Ghana in West Africa, or in the East African nation of Kenya, the restored records, if at all constituted as expected, speak to no more than 65 years. Contributions in those colonial archives are crowded within the colonial time era and, after decolonization, many of them have been left to their own devices as postcolonial leaders struggle to make themselves leaders for life or icons. And as to the time before, only the long nineteenth century has had a few interpreters.

Regarding the postcolonial era, its archivable knowledge has basically been confined to the media. While humankind struggles for sheer economic, political, and cultural survival, histories of centuries between the Stone Age and the eighteenth century have been either left to rot or are easily ignored, and, in the process, lost for posterity for the most part. This loss is a function of lost archives and sadly, there is disregard for those archives that can still be reclaimed, as in the case of ritual archives. The contention that the past was unrecoverable became a mythical thought or assertion that many people came to accept, simply because of how it was packaged by the coloniality of knowledge, which unfortunately incapacitated the possibility of the use and transformation of our collective memories. The very incapacitation of ritual archives is by itself an example of what prevails as epistemic violence.

The foregoing two archives, competing but not necessarily complementary, have created a knowledge divide: the colonial one that is aligned to power—both external and internal—and the ritual that is aligned with marginality. As we peruse great works of such historians as Trinidad and Tobago-born Eric Eustace Williams of *Capitalism & Slavery* fame; A. Adu-Boahen of Ghana and his famous *Topics in West African History*; and the Nigerian historian J. F. Ade-Ajayi, ritual feeds the colonial as raw materials, by and large, existing permanently in its shadows and dominance, sometimes in the mode that Ghana's Kwame Nkrumah and other socialist thinkers have referred to as neocolonialism and neo-imperialism. Indeed, the archives of coloniality privilege methodologies that go a long way toward advancing the projects of European concepts and legacies, to say nothing of economic and political interests. Ritual archives, on the other hand, deal with ancestral legacies and indigenous concepts and epistemologies. History, as defined in the colonial archives, is different from *itàn* as defined in the Yorùbá ritual archives. While *itàn*, based on ritual archives, is assessed within the realm of folklore or mythologies in the academy, analyses of colonial archives are assessed in the categories of originality and validity in the same academy.

In the Western conception of historical knowledge, *itàn* lacks validity, while academic history is imbued with it; *itàn* is unreliable but "history" is; *itàn* is not accessible and transparent while "history" is. Yet, *itàn* entails and binds both historical and hagiographic knowledge in ways the Western conception of knowledge does not. As an assessment of Western education, a new elite successfully acquires new forms of knowledge for mobility, de-rationalizing the pre-Western but grudgingly absorbing indigenous worldviews while distancing themselves from the previous keepers of established indigenous knowledge. A mytho-historical knowledge system or a hagio-historical epistemology has been ruptured, replaced by a "formal" Western system invested with colonizing values of progress and modernity.

At this juncture, the larger part of the remaining portion of this chapter, first and foremost, touches on a few of the contents of ritual archives and their meanings. Toward that end, whether I invoke either oral or written literature, ritual performances, whether physical representation of gods and goddesses, it is a fact that these enter the realm of routine expressions of spirituality, proverbs, songs, and poetry, all of which generate meanings of religious and secular significance. Second, and more importantly, I utilize the opportunity to frame some dimensions of the epistemological and ideological significance of these archives, which is in fact a body of knowledge on a wide range of issues, including but not limited to cultural cognition, ideas and idea formation, semiotics, and education. Finally, the tail end of the chapter suggests transformational strategies in according a critical place for ritual archives and their transition from individualized to public spaces.

The goal here is certainly to endeavor to revalidate ritual archives in Western-derived academies; to involve indigenous practitioners in research and knowledge dissemination; and to formulate evaluation mechanisms to authenticate indigenous knowledge and those who communicate them using data-driven and emic standards. At all levels of the educational system, indigenous ways of knowing, along with the knowledge and researchers of those accumulated knowledge, must be fully blended with the Western academy. Ritual archives tell us that we must review and question our externally derived approaches and the limitations of the methodologies we deploy. Western-derived disciplines (such as Religious Studies, History, and Philosophy as subjects of the Humanities) have carefully fragmented ritual archives, but it is time for all those disciplines to combine to provide an understanding of the centers of indigenous epistemologies, to unify their ontologies, and convert them to theories that will be treated as universal. To take an example of how ritual archives can work, if Ifalogy (studies of Yorùbá divination system) had been created as a discipline and department 50 years ago, it could have enabled hundreds of scholars to learn and work across disciplines, and they probably would have decoded its epistemology by now and used it to create other forms of knowledge. They would have uncovered hidden dimensions of the Yorùbá *endogenius*, which has sustained and guided the people since their genesis.

As scholars dealing with Africa, questions must be posed as to how each of us understands and applies indigenous knowledge, which border on values and cultures in our research and teaching. Should we ground the analyses and understanding of our fields solely in Western-derived epistemologies? My answer is a categorical "No," which means that the preeminent alternative we have is to "return to the source," to use a phrase made memorable by the title of Amilcar Cabral's treatise.[2] Indeed, while we study practitioners and others who create archives for us, the others have not studied us, and sadly we have not studied ourselves either. I, therefore, put scholars in conversation with ritual archives in order to highlight the voices that are often unheard and delegitimated in academic spaces, pointing to the contents of ritual archives as a source of multiple epistemological as well as methodological, political, and cultural messaging.

Furthermore, I also seek to interrogate broader academic concerns, arguing against the constant re-centering of universalism, reproducing colonial domination, and allowing the empowerment of alternative voices. An understanding of ritual archives is an important process for the edification of Africa in terms of the constitution of knowledge and the socio-historical process by which identities are created, practiced, transformed, dominated, and, to a large extent, destroyed.

PART ONE: TEXTS AND MATERIALITY AS RITUAL OBJECTS

Gods and goddesses generate around them a wide range of paraphernalia of texts and sounds, visible and invisible symbols, and objects and signs. Orality, in itself, is extensive, comprising parables, proverbs, tales, allegories, and dilemma stories. Drums and musical compositions go with venerations, along with sacrifices, and practitioners and priests with insignias and dress. Rituals and ritual speech connect with kingship and indigenous power systems, as Andrew Apter demonstrates in his book on "how an indigenous hermeneutics of power is put into ritual practice."[3] Similar connections can also be made with social control. Invocations have to be made. Offerings, comprising food, are identified with specific deities, as in boiled yams and snails for Òrìṣàńlá.[4] A god and the definitive markers go with its divination methods, dress, dances, oral literature, rituals, drama, and music.[5]

Take Ògún, for instance, and the god leads you to *ìjálá* chants, to *ìrèmòjé* on death rites, to dancing, to folklore and literature, and to body paintings and decorations.[6] Ọṣun and Yemoja combined land with water, humans with fish and crocodiles, and fertility with productivity, adding to the storehouse of knowledge on women and gender.[7] A few books have demonstrated the richness of ritual archives in studying women and gender.[8] Furthermore, the oral tradition on women and gender is so expansive that only a small amount of folklore and poems have actually been collected on them.[9] All the gods created folders upon folders of materials in individual rites in their compounds, while rituals at their shrines were dedicated to each god and the huge annual festivals that cemented relationships at the city level. Kingship becomes connected with the festivals, adding to ritual archives the limitless amount of information on and around palaces.

As we rework the complexities around the deities to modern disciplines, we disaggregate the ritual archives into many component units as literature, music, drama, psychology, anthropology, and many more. Experts work around each component, so that a scholar can study Ifá in various departments—Philosophy, Music, Drama, Literature, Linguistics, Religious Studies, Government, Sociology, Art, Anthropology, and History. In each of the disciplines, Ifá may become disconnected from the multilayered and intricately connected indigenous epistemology that produces it in favor of the concerns of the disciplines framed from other epistemologies external to the indigenous. In this regard, Ifá has been disembodied and fragmented. The questions posed can become "external" to its own organic makeup, for example, whether Ifá is a philosophy or religion. Are incantations magical texts or creative literary texts? If Ifá verses are originally recited orally, what happens when they become printed texts? Do the printed texts, when read, become as effective as divination? Texts, as in the case of *ẹsẹ Ifá* chants, taken out of *odù Ifá*, are entry points to the understanding of history, philosophy, and literature grounded in the epistemologies of cosmology and mythology. But the cosmology and mythology cannot operate without forms of rationality, as they need to explain other issues such as medicine, politics, and critical appreciation.

Conversation on a broader framing of Ifá, to take an example, has begun. In a 2016 exchange on two popular listservs that I moderate, a scientist makes the linkage with one kind of rationality:

> the Yoruba divination protocol is embodied in 256 odu (= 2 to the power 8 chapters) of the Sacred Ifa Oracle. Ifa teaches correct character forms for all human and humane situations, simultaneously with the mathematics of the binomial probability distribution and its extrapolations to both the Poisson and normal distributions. Neither Christianity nor Islam has based its spiritual doctrine on any logical reality as embedded in probability. Au contraire, each of these foreign religions is based on the certainty of heaven, hell, and a God whose main occupation is to wait to put you in one or the other.[10]

Other contributors responded to the assertion, especially the indomitable Toyin Adepoju, who laid out the metaphysical and mathematical components of Ifá. And to move the discussion forward, anthropologist Babatunde Emmanuel decided to pose additional questions:

Since you see it as a possible mathematical system, may I posit the following suggestions:

1. How does a religious matrix based on revelation and symbolic classification transform into an empirically validatable and refutable source of knowledge that will not depend on dogma and persecution to justify and corroborate its views as valid?
2. Since mathematics is the language of science because it is logic in symbols, in order to make anything scientific, it must be mathematically replicatable, refutable, and verifiable. When will Yoruba Renaissance occur that will move claims of Ifa from the realm of belief to the realm of fact?
3. I am fascinated by your mapping. When and what can we do to move Yoruba metaphysics to the point when it can provide mathematical knowledge for the laws of gravity?[11]

Archeologist-cum-historian Akin Ogundiran gave an immediate answer:

1. Ifa is not based on revelation. It is based on learning, and its processes and outcomes can be replicated. My own field research has proven this in multiple places, over several years. Moreover, the intellectual communities from which Ifa developed are not based on dogma. This is a point that a number of us argued in a book that I co-edited *Materialities of*

Ritual in the Black Atlantic (Indiana University Press, 2014). The Niger-Congo worldview (10,000 + years old) that provides the context for Ifa is not based on dogma. It is based on openness of thought, critique, and experimentation.
2. Ifa is a corpus of different categories of knowledge, not just religion. It is also a body of knowledge on history, philosophy, and so on. Over the past few days, I have been in email correspondence with scholars in the fields of mathematics and computer science (Toyin Adepoju was part of the exchanges). Computer scientists, such as Dr. Tunde Adegbola, are doing fascinating work that shows that "the scientific basis of Ifa is the same with the subject of simulation in Operations Research" (Adegbola). What is important in the methodology that Adegbola is using is that he is also doing ethnographic field research in order to systematically collect the data needed for his systems analysis work. As far back as the 1990s, Oba Pichardo and his Lukumi collaborators in Miami (Florida) were able to write computer codes that allowed them to conduct computer-based Ifa divination. It was a preliminary work when I saw it around 2007. It is possible that they have expanded the work since then.
3. A number of scholars from different fields have started to answer these questions. What their studies are telling us is that one cannot stand outside a tradition or a system of knowledge to make declarations about that knowledge. Emmanuel Kant, for example, cannot be the path to the understanding of Ifa. For one must learn Ifa from the Babalawo and/or the Iyanifa in order to know what Ifa entails or not. Wariboko stated, Ifa offers a rich fodder for theorizing a diverse range of ontological issues. These areas will continue to be relevant. However, the area of systems and mathematical analysis offer a very fascinating path of inquiry. This effort should involve the collaboration of traditional academics, scientists, and practitioners.[12]

There are other forms of rationality in relation to data processing and interpretation, as in the distinctions between *Ifá pípè* (chants), *Ifá títè* (signature and printing), *Ifá rírán* (insight), *Ifá kíkà* (reading), and *ìtumọ̀ odù* (interpretations of divinations and texts). All these are specialized branches with their own logic.

Space does not permit the elaboration of the depth and breadth of the archives or the density of each genre with its own hydra-headed fragments and hundreds of individual constructions and presentations. Instead, I would like to take some organic matters and objects such as *ewúro*, kolanuts, cowries, photographs, textiles, paintings, and sculptures as items of religious relevance and texts that can be cumulated into rich archives that speak to many issues, secular and religious. I would argue that the data the objects embody have not been put to commensurate interpretive use and are yet to be fully converted as entries in an epistemology.

I base my examples mainly on Yorùbá objects that also reach Cuba, Brazil, the United States, and other areas to form part of the ritual archives in Afro-Atlantic religions. On the African side, spirituality and materiality are united, as in the use of sculpture to represent the deities. Similarly, spirituality and materiality became united in the African Diaspora. Converting Catholic saints to Yorùbá gods and goddesses, Yorùbá divinities were represented by statuettes and lithographs as worshippers danced before Catholic altars. Bow and arrow symbolize the Òrìṣà Ochosi in Bahia, Brazil. Objects of various kinds—plants, images, water, food, and so on—are integral to Santeria and Candomblé. In the religious complex of the Afro-Atlantic world, prominent Yorùbá gods and goddesses including Èṣù, Ṣàngó, Yemoja, Ògún, Obàtálá, Òsanyìn, and Òṣun, all with extensive material cultures, cumulate into and populate the ritual archives.

Objects speak and communicate without words. The objects supply narratives, encourage the creativity of storytelling, and they facilitate performance. Indeed, in the use of such objects as Egúngún costumes, clothed ritual trees, wood carvings, metal sculpture (e.g., jewelry, bells, staffs), cowries, and kolanuts, ritual specialists become ritual performers. As performers manipulate the objects, songs and stories may follow, presented as ritual performances before an audience that participates.

Objects encode the characters of the being they represent, even telling us if they are hot or cool-headed, calm or volatile. Colors are denotative, as in red for being aggressive and quick-tempered and white for being calm. In contrast is a binary epistemology that leads to a series of long conversations on human behavior and interpersonal relationships in society. The extensive poetry around Ifá does work with words, in relation to objects, yielding both methodologies and epistemologies in the realm of the mytho-historical and institutions that lead us to modes of knowing and forms of knowledge.

Most certainly, objects have been treated more as museum pieces, with short descriptions to describe them, rather than as archival items. Yet, such objects actually fit into the description of an archive as a place to keep historical records, although the collection of such objects may defy categorization. Kolanuts and *orógbó* are historical records. The location of an archive may be characterized as an archive itself: the grove of a ritual tree is such a place, where the tree and its location constitute a library. Documents in an archive are treated as primary sources. So also should many ritual objects be treated as such as they communicate messages that can be used to reconstruct the past and understand various ideas about the world.

Above all, objects open a wide door to a large body of mythologies, stories, legends, and many sayings, short and long. The categories are many. Some are like written records, created for a specific meaning that is communicated from one person to another, or from one generation to another. Such objects may be connected with signs, as in the *àrokò* among the Yorùbá.[13] In this example, the number of cowries in relation to words and other objects formulate a code that, when decoded, generates a text and an interpretation. Ritual communications were not uncommon, from Osanyin's messages to the interpretations of dreams and divinations.

Like archives, some objects are permanent records. *Ojú-oórì* (the cemetery) is one such example, as it is a ground of memory. So also are sacred groves that provide data on the past of an enduring nature. These data touch upon culture, history, and sociology. *Ojú-oórì* is dead silent, but it speaks to spirits and celestial bodies, generating conversations on life and death. The "cemetery" stays still but not the stories of those who visit looking for ghosts or body parts for money rituals, with wandering souls, constantly traveling between heaven and earth policing the space. Not far away from the cemetery are the spirits of *iwin*, *ògán*, *ẹbọra*, and *egbére*. Humans and fairies are united in ways of knowing that need their secularization in academic programs, as some students engage with the belief that witches are with them in their classrooms, thus leading them to the generation of non-Western ideas. Some students actually carry on them protective charms and rituals, while reading Western books on science.

Ritual objects supply texts on the environment and open us to multiple worlds of charms, magic, and medicine. The song, *ewúro làgbà igi, igi gbogbo bòwò fẹ́wúro*, is based on sound observation of its multi-various uses for curing diseases. *Ewúro* (better known as bitter leaf) is part of the species known as *Vernonia amygdalina*. It is not just useful for food but for its medicinal properties, from its connections with diabetes to the reduction of headaches and fever associated with acquired immunodeficiency syndrome (AIDS) as well. The Brazilian species of *ewúro*, known as "necroton," has multiple uses as anti-inflammatory, antithermal, and antibacterial. Plants are part of our knowledge system. Such plants as *ewúro* entangle our world with those of nonhumans. In this entanglement, facts and fiction become merged into both complex and simple ideas. *Ayé* (the world) and *Ọ̀run* (invisible world) are united by these objects, in various ways. Kolanuts may invoke the power of ancestors to bless the living, but it has always been a major trade item for centuries that united long-distance traders, facilitating the creation of trading colonies as well as the spread of languages. Ritual objects supply ideas on prayers and philosophy. Kolanut, for instance, has tremendous symbolic power, associated with peace, conflict mediation, and life sustenance. Kolanut generates a limitless number of prayers around rites of passage, politics, and social order. In non-secular spaces, kolanut generates a tremendous amount of data on perceptions of self and of the other, and it can be used to affirm convictions and affections.

Images in sculpture and paintings are abundant, but their connections with historical writings need to be strengthened. They tend to be used more as book covers than as elaborate texts within the books. Yet, images are philosophical expressions connected with thought and life. Located in museums, we tend to see and appreciate them, not necessarily engage in dialogue with them. However, images represent mentalities, power, and strength. Images can be used to generate image theories and create extensive narratives on cultures, transcultures, and intercultures. They supply critical issues on hybridity. To carve an object is about the representation of self, history, identity, and much more. One image of Èṣù tells us about social and cultural issues, portrayal of multiple and ambivalent ideas, representations of hybridity, discourse on difference, perception, semiotics, and religion. Multiple specializations can emerge around image theory, image critical methodologies, image anthropology, image and culture, image philosophy, perceptions and seeing, listening, silences, and image styling. An image moves you toward the spiritual and religious. But there is an aesthetic idea living within it, allowing for texts on cultures, forms, and styles. While gazing without talking, you create the text, saying something, creating what Nietzsche calls an "army of metaphors." It generates a wide range of imaginations and thought systems.

An Èṣù image, like the ambiguity of Èṣù itself, cannot be read in an interpretive singularity. The image has ideas within itself and ideas outside of itself. Seeing the image is to see force and strength, power, epistemic responses that connect back to language, and metaphysical perceptions. The image is about the body, in its physical and nonphysical realms. An element in the body gestures to sexuality and yet another to the sanctions of transgressions. The politics of images lead us to the pregnancy of culture ready to give birth to social issues. In its external, outward look, you move to the realm of beauty, visual effects, conversation on everyday practices, languages and word creation, forceful inscriptions of perception, and experience onto our consciousness. Look further, and the Èṣù image unfolds more dimensions around performance, and other bodies of knowledge open up, some kinesthetic and others synesthetic. The thought that you express to yourself and to others moves you back to the Èṣù image. Its force becomes a part of you. Whether you hate or like Èṣù, the image is activated. In the process, you must generate text around the image, expressing your religiosity, philosophy, and opinions. Èṣù has entered your mental system, active in your conversation with yourself and others. Your thought is a text, on the physical world, on the afterlife, on mythologies, on religions, and more. An artistic production becomes a body of knowledge at various levels—political, cultural, and social. The Èṣù image transfers you to the understanding of culture and society; what is left of the past; and how the past is reformed, deformed, transmogrified, ordered, and reordered. The past may even be disappearing and that image affirms it.

What originally appears as a small wooden object opens up a vastness of knowledge, its edges become borderless and its existence acquires a force. We are no longer dealing with the aesthetic of difference, as in looking at objects in the British Museum in London and looking at Èṣù in the National Museum, Aléṣinlóyé at Ìbàdàn or the Èṣù in the Heritage Museum of the University of Ìbàdàn. We are forced to move into the orbits of knowledge in which all component parts of the body become signifiers as *ojú* Èṣù becomes different from *etí* Èṣù, *okó* Èṣù, *ògo* Èṣù, and *inú* Èṣù. Each unit is semiautonomous but aggregated to *gbogbo ara* Èṣù in another layer of meaning. Add Èṣù *pípè*: yet another meaning. Like your own *orí* (always erroneously translated as the "head"), that of Èṣù is also the zone of intelligence and emotions. All his calculations and miscalculations reside here. You can see *orí* Èṣù, with *ògo* Èṣù, as fronting multiple ideas. Attributes, then, derive from *ojú* Èṣù, *eti* Èṣù, and *imú* Èṣù, all connected with personal foibles and destiny. You must trigger your own wisdom and strength to deal with *orí* Èṣù, and as you do, your own *orí* begins to break down into a series of components as that of *ọgbọ́n* (wisdom) or *òmùgọ̀* (foolishness). You draw in your "bowel," to rely on *ọgbọ́n inú*. Your eyes must work well, to recall your inner essence as in *ojú inú*, and on your perceptions, *ojú ọ̀nà*. Should you be confused, look for an *ẹnu àgbà* (elder's wisdom) for guidance. And following the conversation, your *inú* ("stomach") becomes the point of validation as in *inú ẹ bàjẹ́* (you are sad), *inú ẹ dùn* (you are happy), and *inú ẹ bu* (you are damn stupid).

The Èṣù image, coupled with all other objects as well as all texts, and the entire ritual archives lead us to the indigenous intellectuals and their epistemologies. Combined, they deal with the invisible realities of knowledge, as in witchcraft. But they complicate the visible ones, as in all forms of epistemologies.

Part Two: Indigeneity and Indigenous Epistemologies

The identification process of the ritual archives may be characterized as the beginning of a larger project: the understanding of indigenous thought systems; and the insertion of the entire range of vernacular epistemologies into formal educational institutions. To ignore the ritual archives is to undermine the origins of African epistemologies, as well as the historical circumstances of our location in modernist projects. Civilizations are many and different, and so too are their historical experiences and trajectories. To cite Puebla:

> Each society has its own rhythm, pattern, obstacles, problems, solutions, wars, and social memories....we need to find our place in the struggle between dominators and dominated, right and left, past and future, core and peripheries, and superior and inferior perspectives.[14]

Intellectual projects have emerged around the issues of domination. A series of anticolonial writings emerged around the subaltern epistemology of giving voice to the marginalized and peripheries of empire.[15] A wide range of ideas under the rubric of postcolonial studies has spoken to hybridity, a way to speak to commonalities and aggregate many of our experiences.[16] A wide range of cultural theories has spoken to our divisions, varying knowledge and values, invented traditions, and the disconnection between the conquered and the conquerors. While those in the African academy have adopted many of these great epistemological insights, we have not fully imprinted ourselves upon them by drawing from our own heritage and cultural resources.

The continent of the dominated and the oppressed, but it keeps drawing more and more from the theories and ideas of those who oppressed and dominated it. Colonization cannot be divorced from domination, as both were built upon the history of slavery and racism. The insertion of Africa into the modern world and the texts produced by Africans are entangled with notions of race and domination: the core ideas that foreground them revolve around exploitation, domination, and conflicts. Many of the subjects we inherit are shaped by those core ideas. Indeed, modernity is entangled with coloniality. Our task is not to reject modernity but to disentangle it from race and domination. Ritual archives offer us the possibilities of creating knowledge that can become integrated into the process of that disentanglement.

Together, capitalism and coloniality have imposed a knowledge divide. The core represents the center of power, where universal ideas are generated. The peripheries are colonies where internally generated ideas are categorized as "local." The status of researchers in both worlds is not the same, and the relevances of their research outcomes are equally unequal. The researchers at the core produce methods and theories, and those in the periphery consume and apply them. It is as if this core-periphery divide will remain with us:

> Core is producing theory and methods, and peripheries are consuming and reproducing it. We can think about the postcolonial, decolonizing, and Indigenous knowledge systems discussion as a kind of rebellion against such distribution. Global coloniality is marginalizing and even suppressing the knowledge and culture of subaltern groups; it seems like this oppression will never end.[17]

One way to break this divide is actually to turn to ritual archives to create alternative pathways: decolonizing paradigms based on indigenous knowledge systems. Just as we live in different parts of the world, we can also engage in different ways of thinking.

Categories of analysis, like words in texts, are not always neutral. *Ìwà* in Yorùbá does not necessarily translate into "character" in English. The breakdown of *ìwà* and "character" are contextualized within specific cultures. A gentleman in England is not necessarily expected to be generous as is the *ìwà* associated with his equivalent in Yorùbá. *Ìwà* is linked to a broader category of *omolúwàbí*, which deals with virtues and morality,[18] and linked with aesthetics, as in the saying, *ìwà lẹwà* ("character is beauty").[19] A Christian in New York may not mean the same as a Christian in Ìbàdàn where witches and àbíkú roam the streets, where *àwọn ayé* (narrowly translated into English as enemies) are everywhere, including in his bedroom. The *òtá* to the Christian in New York is so far inferior to the *òtá* at Ìbàdàn: the one in the former does not have the wings to fly to the 16th floor of an apartment building while ours at Ìbàdàn can turn into thin air! The *òtá* in New York may be identifiable by name and occupation, but look at ours as compiled by Akintunde Oyetade below:

> *òtá ilé* (enemy in the household or enemy within)
> *òtá òde* (enemy from the outside or enemy without)
> *òtá idílé* (enemy in the family or the lineage)
> *òtá ibi-iṣẹ́* (enemy at the place of work)
> *òtá òrun-ò-gbẹbọ* (enemy believed to be from heaven, who cannot be appeased or placated by offerings or sacrifices)
> *òtá ikòkò tàbí òtá ibábá* (secret or hidden enemy)
> *òtá alọrẹ́* (persistent enemy)

There are more:

> *a-bínú-kú-ẹni* (one who is angry with someone and wishes death for him)
> *elénìní* (bitter enemy)
> *a-mọni-ṣeni* (one who knows someone well and does evil to him)
> *a-fàì-mọni-ṣeni* (one who does not know someone too well but still does evil to him)
> *a-ṣeni-bani-dárò* (one who, after doing evil to someone, commiserates with him)
> *a-fojú-fẹ́ni-máfọkàn-fẹ́ni* (one who appears to love someone to his face but who does not love him from the heart)
> *a-fẹ́-a-jẹ-má-fẹ́-á-yó* (one who wants someone to eat but does not want him to eat his fill)
> *ojú-la-rí-ọ̀rẹ́-ò-dẹ́nú* (one who appears superficially to be a friend but is not)
> *a-ṣekú-pani* (one who plans another one's death)
> *a-pani-má-yọdà* (one who kills without drawing a sword)
> *a-dáni-lóró-tíí-fagbára-kóni* (one who acts callously to someone and thereby toughens his attitude to life).[20]

To take yet another example: *owe* in Yorùbá, which becomes translated into English as proverbs. Oyekan Owomoyela has not only pointed to significant differences but warned that the equivalences can be misleading. This is why it is a fact that words can designate different meanings in different cultures. While as a scholar, he sees some similarities in aphorisms, apothegms, and Wellerisms, Owomoyela is quick to note: "But ferreting out Yorùbá correspondences to the English subgenres, although a useful comparative exercise, has little relevance to understanding the Yorùbá concept and usage of *òwe*, which do not exactly coincide with those of the English proverb."[21] A number of English proverbs will not count as proverbs among the Yorùbá, while "some verbal forms that come under the general rubric of *òwe* in Yorùbá do not have equivalents in the English proverb corpus."[22] There are other differences around aesthetics, humor, speech forms, uses, and even the rich and creative *orin òwe* (proverb songs). Owomoyela is, indeed, very convincing in his argument on critical epistemological differences, while over 5000 proverbs in his book themselves should be incorporated into ritual archives.

All the examples lead us to non-Western meanings, ideas of the cosmos, and alternate philosophies. The binary between *ọ̀run* (inhabited by deities, spirits, and ancestors) and *ayé* (the world inhabited by humans) generates different meanings from other epistemologies. In *ayé* are the humans and the deadly reality of *ọmọ aráyé*, which may include witches and sorcerers. Invisible ladders link *ọ̀run* with *ayé*, and the Orunmila mediates both spaces. Men and women must engage with *ọ̀run* and *ayé* as they deal with birth, life, destiny, and death. Then the bodies of men and women are structured and defined not just in their anatomical senses but also according to the binary of the *ara*, the physical parts such as legs and arms, and in the destiny of *orí*, and the metaphysical vital force of *èmí*, a consciousness with autonomous behavior since it can do things not told by *ara*: *èmí* can leave the body to roam the spiritual planes or the invisible other worlds.

Jose Gaos, the Mexican-Spaniard philosopher, coined the phrase the "imperialism of categories," which refers to how his Latin American colleagues use external methods, concepts, and theories, warning them that they are headed in a wrong direction if they don't change or adapt them. Gaos accuses them of committing the mistake of universalizing "the local knowledge" of "great" Anglo-American authors.[23] Here is the way Gaos links "global theories" to specific localities:

> Max Weber analyses and describes the bureaucrat of the "old continent"; Joseph Schumpeter focuses on the innovative European, but mainly British capitalist; Jürgen Habermas directs his attention to the industrialized First World society, in particular to the German society; and Pierre Bourdieu studies mainly the French socio-cultural and socio-political condition.[24]

Without any exaggeration, I can postulate at this juncture that African scholarship fits into Gaos' criticisms. Rather than always borrowing, we need to convert our own categories into theories of knowledge. Philosophies must emerge from them to multiply the origins and scopes of knowledge. Indigenous languages and education are needed to make it possible. To fall on the use of ritual archives, we must delink knowledge from European-based education and literacy. In other words, we must reject the claim that failure to use European languages is by itself a failure to acquire knowledge. Be it Hausa or Ajami, languages can be used to create large bodies of knowledge.

The decolonization project of the post-Second World War (WWII) period recognized the need for scholarship connected with nation-building. In decolonizing the various curricula, the pioneer scholars embarked upon the worthy project of indigenizing scholarship, which brought a lot of achievements. The pioneers went to school in the West, and the majority among them actually accepted Western values and various aspects of lifestyles. They understood and worked with Western methods, concepts, and approaches that were never abandoned, even if occasionally questioned. In seeking decolonization, economic freedom, as well as peace and justice, their main contribution related to the application of those Western concepts, approaches, and theories to the African condition, that is, a process of adaptation. Some attempts were made to indigenize received ideas but not always successfully. It was difficult for the nationalist pioneers to break their linkages with the West. The efforts and struggles were directed at imitation: the creation of Western archives and educational institutions. While they recognized the relevance of oral texts and traditions, these were weakly integrated into the knowledge systems. Indeed, there are many works that explain oral traditions but only a handful of books and essays based on them.[25] The keepers of those traditions were approached as inferiors. Certainly, in ways that are difficult not to condemn, there were no attempts to create a pact of reciprocity between Western-trained scholars and indigenous generators of knowledge: the scholars took the data they needed to generate their writings, which were circulated only among their colleagues.

Yet, without developing indigenous knowledge, the epistemic linkage between Africa and the colonized geopolitics of epistemology will not go away. Without an aggressive decolonization of knowledge, ancestral knowledge will never find its deserved pride of place. Indigenous knowledge creates the pathways to the creation of multiple universalisms, what I have characterized elsewhere as pluriversalism. Without ritual archives, there will be no pluriversalism.

Part Three: Ritual Archives and Pluriversalism

The connection between global power and global knowledge is clear-cut. Global knowledge translates into domination by Anglo-American methodologies, concepts, and legacies. Western experiences shape what we label as universalism. To challenge this domination, we have to accept a new intellectual order: pluriversalism. As to the domineering impact of universalism, many scholars have spoken, pointing to how local ideas derived from Western experiences are projected as global.[26] The globalization of African epistemologies and methodologies, derived in part from ritual archives, will elevate African-derived knowledge, acknowledge indigenous knowledge, and challenge the domination of Anglo-American scholarship. African scholars should not always be consuming the theories and methods produced by others.

Scholarship in a global context operates in zones of power and marginality. Scholars and texts are not equal, just as nations are not equal. This inequality affects the production and consumption of knowledge. Within nations, humans are treated unequally, and so too are the narratives they produce. If Christianity and Islam are treated as superior, so too will they treat African ritual archives as inferior. Global and international inequalities are reflected in the domination of people, places, races, classes, genders, and the ideas associated with them and what they produce.

Once a global social order is constructed, it is supported by an unequal epistemological order in which those above its power hierarchies lay claim to universalism and consign others to parochialism. In the case of Africans and the African Diaspora, in relation to their archives, the template of "modernity" imposed on their being and historical processes has involved "otherizing" based on ignorance, as explained in the following assertion:

> because the only way of knowing was to eliminate, subordinate, and/or oppress our differences from the Other....the narrative of modernity needs the notion of "primitives" to create the spatial colonial difference and define the identities of supposed superior and inferior human beings. Colonization was based on such terrible assumptions, and the effects of such narratives have been substantial, leading to different ways of producing societies and creating knowledge. Colonization was based on such terrible assumptions, and the effects of such narratives have been substantial, leading to different ways of producing societies and creating knowledge. Coloniality of power also had and still has influence in the ways science is organized and institutionalized in each society.[27]

Power shapes knowledge, which is obviously not neutral and free of context. Even our own stories around the tortoise and spider are not devoid of interest and agenda. Many of these stories are not power-free, as they are shaped by patriarchy. Stories around why women were not kings at Ilé-Ifẹ̀ or Ọ̀yọ́ are ultimately shaped by the patriarchy and politics of kingship. So too is global knowledge and how it is circulated through the instrumentalities of advanced technologies. Just as culture grounds our patriarchal stories, so too does culture ground what we accept to be universal knowledge. Cultural differences embedded in ritual archives are sufficient to make bold claims that knowledge is heterogeneous, that epistemologies are neither uniform nor homogenous, and that thought systems should not move in the direction of the West to Africa but also the other way round.

It is one's culture that foregrounds ritual archives, which gives it the requisite power, autonomy, and agency. They are the resources we need to point to the limitations of both globalized knowledge and globalized methodology; indeed, to argue that the association of globality with applicability is an exaggeration and even to question their originality. Epistemological perspectives derived from ritual archives will be both original and unique. The use of ritual archives is one major way to recover the past in ways that decolonize Western-based academic spaces and Western-derived knowledge systems. Knowledge operates within geopolitics, or what some call the "global academy." On the one hand, it is not difficult to track what is owed to Western scholarship as scholars invoke such works, as in cultural and postcolonial studies where such names as Foucault are mentioned. It is also easier to track theoretical *silsilas* (genealogies), as in semiotics, structuralism, formalism, and the like.

What we are unable to track is the recourse to our own organic epistemologies. In this regard, scholarship exhibits no less than four limitations. First, the overall encounter with local knowledge is weak and limited in the sense that we relate to them as "sources" not to validate the local but to engage with the global and, most importantly, to assert our "perspectives" while accepting the externally derived paradigms and ways of knowing. For instance, in the use of oral traditions and chronicles for historical reconstruction, the ways of writing history, according to Western convention, are not questioned, but the presumption is that Western notions of the archives can be complemented. Second, we create epistemological hierarchies, sometimes even following the Darwinist racial categorization of the nineteenth century: Western, Islamic, Orientals (Indian, Japanese, Malays, Chinese, etc.), and African, with African at the very bottom. By this claim, I am referring to the sources of the ideas we extend to our scholarship. It is even in minority intellectual spaces that Islamic epistemologies and methodologies are worked into our intellectual universe. Third, it is unclear as to the extent that we interrogate the historical contexts of the theories we deploy and how they often emerge from historical circumstances and events different from ours. Most concepts and theories are grounded in specific historical circumstances that produce them. Fourth, scholarship shifts so rapidly that the way we erect canons and lock them as unquestionable is misleading. Indeed, the caution not to question established scholars in Africa is itself a drawback to intellectual growth. Serious questioning could have provoked different epistemological choices.

Part Four: Encounters with Public Spaces

Whether as texts, objects, or symbols, ritual archives have faced serious dangers, ranging from extinction, ridicule, marginalization, and erasure. The first problem is that of intellectual inequality. All externally derived knowledge systems—Islamic and Western—are seen to be superior to them. The inability to create permanent written texts with specialists linked to formal systems of knowledge, as in the case of the Western-derived academies, creates a drawback. The social context of knowledge production is crucial, and this is a second source of trouble: African scholars who produce knowledge for Africa seek globalized knowledge instead of fully embracing ancestral epistemologies and then linking them to that which they seek.

It is important, at this crucial point, to reiterate that a three-prong recovery mission is needed: (1) validating of serious empirical work; (2) generating a series of dialogues between empirical data and multiple theories; and (3) using ritual archives to create distinctive theories. Rather than always taking theories from other knowledge systems, we should use ritual archives to generate theories for others to use. Doing history, philosophy, and theory without basing them on our own unique data and experience is equivalent to talking about a forest without trees.

The generators and creators of these archives are equally undermined. There have been systematic and deliberate attempts to destroy what they create and to silence their voices. Where they operate as their own archivists to take the knowledge to public spaces, they have knowledge but lack power. In cases where they are drawn into university spaces, as the case of Babaláwo in the Institute of African Studies at the then University of Ifẹ̀, Nigeria, they recorded their data on equipment that did not stand the test of time and was unable to withstand rapid technological changes. The recorded voices are subsequently discarded and never put to use. Those who study ritual archives, outside of university-based jobs with permanent remunerations, lack respect.

Indeed, the broad terrain of ritual archivists and indigenous researchers is usually embattled. Drawing on data from various places, a collection of their voices in *Indigenous Pathways into Social Research*[28] has reached depressing conclusions:

> Indigenous peoples experience inequalities that push them to the edge of society, make them unwell, and often result in premature death. While many non-Indigenous people are committed to eliminating these disparities, the voices of Indigenous peoples themselves need to be heard loudly and clearly in terms of their own accounts of their histories, their present-day needs and priorities, and their aspirations and dreams for their future. The involvement of Indigenous people in research and evaluation is an important part of enabling this to happen.[29]

While the focus of Mertens, Cram and Chilisa's book is on Indigenous researchers drawn from the United States, Mexico, Canada, Panama, Vanuatu, New Zealand, Botswana, Australia, South Africa, Japan, Papua New Guinea, Cameroon, and Spain, there are parallels with respect to the marginalization of practitioners of Ògún and Ṣàngó in West Africa, poets and singers among the Zulu, and carvers of religious items in Cameroon. While the book implies white researchers in its use of the category of "nonindigenous," I would like to include fellow Africans, notably researchers whose intellectual orientation and disengagement from indigenous epistemologies fit into that paradigm. In the various personal testimonies in the book, other similarities emerge: indigenous researchers are poor; they "venture out into the world from a place of family poverty"; access to educational opportunities is limited for them; and they have limited access to formal sector occupations.

It is important to point out that our entire research and academic orientation must be modified or changed toward active partnership and collaboration with indigenous researchers and practitioners. In Africa, the complaint is always about Western domination of discourse and intellectual production. However, within Africa itself, forms of internal colonization or balkanization of ideas exist, whereby those with formal education in the Western-derived academies exercise near-supreme power as the "baptized" elite. This power subordinates others and operates on three faulty premises. The first premise is that university-based scholars are the researchers, and those outside of it are the suppliers of raw materials. This dichotomy is actually false. The indigenous way of knowing is a form of research, as difficult as what we do. Nobody creates songs, dance, poems, and stories without one form of research or another. Words have to be created; bands have to be arranged, and performances have to be fashioned and refashioned. The point cannot be made that an *ijálá* chanter or an Ọbàtálá priestess does not carry out research to do their work. They are essentially methodologists as well as researchers. They evaluate inherited knowledge and create the tools and networks to repackage and present what is vital and useful.

The second relates to what I see as the outcome of research. The assumption that the research generated within universities is the most important is misleading. Indeed, indigenous researchers connect with their organic communities more directly, with locales feeding the constitution of knowledge and the ways of knowing. Local values and indigenous traditions shape their data and knowledge. Indeed, they are social agents in ways that academically trained scholars lack the full capacity to become. As active social agents, they ultimately contribute to the transformation of the spaces they occupy. This leads me to the third point: the assumption that the power of social agency inheres in academic scholars, which while true to a point, is actually exaggerated. Social agency lies in number, the ability to mobilize that number, and how that mobilization connects with broader goals and agenda that resonate with communities. Communities have the capacity to transform themselves far more than scholars can transform them. As social agents, the texts and objects they produce have immediate utilitarian values—they exist in societies and not on shelves in scholars' homes.

Thus, we have to rethink how we produce knowledge as well as the connections we make. Permit me to sue for maximum civility, so that our privileges must not be deemed an inalienable right to the point of arrogance and the breakdown of bridges. We have to encourage indigenous practitioners to be part of our larger academic community, by not just studying what they produce but by creating a dialogue of respect, and returning back to the community our own products for their use and validation. Diversity of knowledge is crucial to the need to ground our experiences and formulate collaborative strategies to elevate the disciplines and society itself.

A befitting query is "Who are we anyway?" After all, we write about the sociology of knowledge not necessarily by building on indigenous inheritances but by appropriating indigenous voices into chaotic global discourses. We write about the sociology of social movements without joining the working class to protest injustice. We write about gods and goddesses while not joining in their worship except as observers. Indeed, Christians actually have little respect for them. We even write about peasants, traders, and daily lives of the ordinary people while using those writings as steps in the academic ladder. We draw on the data of the traders and market women but leave them behind as we become professors while they remain in their slums. Let me invoke the words of César A. Cisneros Puebla, a scholar-activist, who queried our beings as scholars:

> But a sociology of our own practices as researchers, as scientists, as persons of blood and flesh is still pending. We don't really know too much about ourselves as researchers, and/or as human beings, and how we came to be what we are. In some ways, the personal pathways of becoming a researcher, scientist, activist, or practitioner of any discipline are mysterious and hidden.[30]

Measures to evaluate what academic researchers do and the impact of their work on development and their role as social agents have not been undertaken. Indeed, in many instances, we actually do not know. Indeed, we lack a body of work on why Africans take to the academy as a profession, what ethics guide their research, and what responsibilities they owe to the larger society. New bodies of work must review the wide range of our activities and the social responsibility of scholars since the 1940s, and see through our internal self-assessments, and beyond the propagandist claims in Inaugural Lectures for the validity of our disciplines. The criteria for assessing the relevance of disciplines have not been created.

After taking several intellectual liberties, let me close with five practical issues that are achievable as a starting point before we deal with complicated epistemologies and academic reorganization. First, ritual archives have to be located, and communities should be encouraged to compile and update catalogues. Ritual archives already exist in many private spaces as well as some public institutions. There are hundreds of associations and collectives with extensive libraries that have to be promoted and organized. It has become urgent to preserve various aspects of ritual archives and to collect and circulate the limitless ideas around them. The easiest and most obvious is for researchers to follow the traditional path of data collections through interviews and recordings. Thus far, those materials reside in the private hands of many collectors, including the oral interviews that I have also done over a 40-year period. What now needs to be done is to convert thousands of notes in private hands to public data banks in multiple locations where they can be accessible to as many people as possible. While the preservation of what individuals collect resides in private hands and are good for individual research agendas, they do create limitations to sharing and enabling far-reaching interpretive options.

Second, a vigorous effort must be made to encourage autobiographies, autoethnographies, and religious ethnographies—coupled with the creation of rich data banks by the practitioners of various practices, religious and secular. These stories will be many, so many that they have no limits. They can be composed as written texts for circulation or as stories recorded in audio and video. Autobiographies, autoethnographies, and religious ethnographies ensure the survival of individual and collective experiences and practices that we can relate to in place and time. The abundant evidence will form a rich archive that can become public and serve to capture specific ages, and analyze society and religion on less generalized terms.

Third, digital archives can be established to organize, preserve, and share the texts. Such a project will not be one-time, or even a unified, effort. A digital archive will be accessible at a global scale. The voices of our people should not be discarded; the knowledge of our people should not be abandoned. Wisdom does not lie only in the West; it exists in the East, North, and South.

Fourth, attention should be paid to the ongoing research and legal frameworks in South Africa on Indigenous Knowledge Systems (IKS) that cover research, pedagogy, and funding.[31] It links IKS to the overall agenda of the country:

> The intention of this Funding instrument is to promote and support research to deepen our understanding of Indigenous Knowledge Systems and its role in community life. Although both applied and basic (i.e., epistemological studies) research is encouraged, the Indigenous Knowledge Funding instrument focuses on experimental research which will lead to technology transfer and patents (i.e. innovation and entrepreneurship). Clear evidence of active participation and equal ownership of IKS practitioners and communities in all research activities is a crucial feature of this instrument. So is appropriately acknowledging those who contributed intellectually (i.e., knowledge holders/practitioners) as more than just mere subjects or informants. The IKS Funding instrument scope covers the following:
>
> - IKS and Bioeconomy (African traditional medicine, food security, technology, nutraceuticals, health and beauty, and cosmetics);
> - IKS Epistemology (Ubuntu and cosmology, taxonomies, pedagogies and methodologies);
> - IKS and Climate Change (Environmental Management);
> - Women and IKS based technology innovations;
> - IKS and Energy (Alternative and clean sources);

- IKS Practices of Khoi, Nama, Griqua and San communities; and/or
- Novel and creative thinking that will shift the boundaries of IKS knowledge production and that address national priorities in South Africa.

The ultimate aim of the IKS instrument is to contribute to sustainable economic development of not only South Africa, but the African region as a whole. The IKS instrument achieves this goal through knowledge development and human capacity development.[32]

Fifth, I am calling for the reconfiguration of the disciplines. The colonial structure of the old and the very new universities has not created hospitable place and role for ritual archives. Would institutions allow a Ph.D. dissertation to be written with ritual archives, not just data but as epistemologies? I can understand opposition to this in American and European universities where hegemony maintenance is crucial but what about Nigeria or Brazil? Some professors have to take up this challenge and begin a set of innovations. Would the African academy nurture dissertations in African episteme? Would the institutions fund research on ritual archives? Practical steps have to follow conceptual innovations. If we continue to conduct fieldwork, who does the coordination and the archiving? We need to ask other pertinent questions: In the age of science and technology, cyber age, and so on, what would indigenous knowledge production in the African world ultimately translate to? Would it generate ideas for jobs? Would they connect to technological innovations? All these must be part of the rethinking process.

There is the question of administrative power and resources. We understand that university administration, department directions, and research agendas are often aligned with the state and its perceived political interests and the common sense epistemological frameworks that underwrite them. The question for the African academy is the extent to which research agendas can be independent of hegemonic purposes or even in conflict with them. There is, of course, the history of Marxist and anti-colonial, nationalist frameworks, but these have given way, in the postcolonial period, to the exigencies of professional survival and institutional budget crises based on neoliberalism.

I am arguing that there is room for maneuver in redefining research agendas without directly confronting the hegemonic forces that govern institutional resources and professional advancement. If so, the balance must be delicate, keeping in mind that not all young scholars would have the political maturity to pursue research agendas without making explicit the confrontation, which can devastate an individual career and even dismantle a department. One way of framing the issue is the extent to which African academics are operating with epiphenomenal Euro-American epistemologies based on internalized racism as a legacy of colonialism against the extent to which they operate within those frameworks as a way of aligning themselves with the realities of global and state power, within which they seek professional survival and alignment. Ultimately, and this is not something that must happen in every instance, we must take seriously the conflict between the academic researcher and the subaltern (organic) intellectual—their visions and horizons of social transformation and communal health are different. While there can be skepticism and cynicism about the power of knowledge projects in the context of violence and corruption, I will continue to insist that we must look to other forms of knowledge.

One hope, in my judgment, is generational. I recognize the perceived need for each generation to establish career and financial security. So, is it the job of the current generation of scholars to support new archives for the next, or will the revitalization of ritual archives depend on the revolutionary zeal of the next? We can see the contradictions involved for those who first disavow their own traditions in the hopes of entering a golden space of Western respectability, legitimacy, and prosperity, who are subsequently disillusioned and then perhaps seek out the resources and meaning-making from their natal communities and ancestors. But, are there not those of the next generation of academics who do not first disavow their embeddedness in a communal, ritual world before entering the academy? These are the young warrior princes and princesses who will bring the strength and brilliance of their traditions and rituals to create a hybrid, vibrant life within the academy as researchers and teachers. I would argue that this latter case should represent pathway of a new generation of Africans to the academy.

I will be the first to recognize the large difference between asking the current generation of academics to shift their research agendas (to include ritual archives, for example) against making room for newer voices that are reimagining their cosmologies to integrate and give new flame to their traditions. This is why indigenous publishing projects are so essential as they can refuse the limits of Western epistemologies. Rather than trying to persuade a unified audience to do something completely new, maybe we should continue to give examples with vivid details of the power of the ritual world and those who are narrating it. In this case, the persuasion is twofold: (1) to give hope and inspiration to the younger generation of academics that they need not abandon and that they should urgently reclaim their communal traditions as they develop their research agendas and academic identities; (2) to ask the older generation of academics, those in leadership and administrative positions, to create space for what has previously been foreclosed. The latter must be concerned with money and institutional politics, but their ability to mobilize will be enabled by the legitimacy and visibility that indigenous publishing houses are giving to new voices.

The theoretical implications of my ideas around ritual archives are complex; the uses to which ritual archives can be put are equally complex and the outcomes will be revolutionary. African languages will flourish in the process, the archives will expand, and African-language intellectuals will multiply in number. African forms of knowing will become the core of humanistic scholarship in its practical and contemplative manner. Perhaps, the discovery of new core areas will reorganize and relabel the disciplines; revalorize imaginative forms of knowing; and see value in ritual practices, performances, ceremonies, observations, crafts, skills, and agriculture. Alphabetical technologies will grow, further encouraging new creative projects, interpretations, and translations.

Perhaps, respect for indigenous religions, preference for the use of African languages, recognition for all forms of oral texts, and attention to translation will unleash an intellectual revolution. Perhaps, legitimacy will be accorded to indigenous epistemologies, and we will reduce our energy in borrowings and adaptations. Perhaps, the "traditional" intellectuals will stop abusing and marginalizing the organic intellectuals. Perhaps, we will preserve and refound/rediscover/recover our precolonial knowledge, collective memories, and genealogies. Perhaps, we will put a break to the path toward the cultural void that we are now treading. Perhaps, we will overcome identity and religious ambiguities. Perhaps, we will stop the extirpators of indigenous cultures hiding under the masks of modernization. Perhaps, extirpating religious priests will have their powers curbed. Perhaps, new exemplars of knowledge will replace or be added to those whose knowledge is based on Western models. Maybe a new order of indigenous knowledge system will emerge as a new intellectual order, and the emergent exemplars will find answers to the hegemonic projects of universalism and resist the organizers of dominating knowledge systems.

"A person who carries a basket of eggs on his head must walk with measured steps." In the final analysis, perhaps we as practitioners, operating in the Western academies, will ultimately become the "traditional intellectuals," whose power and legitimacy will be challenged and superseded by the ideas of the "organic intellectuals," whose power and legitimacy will be based on epistemologies derived from ritual archives, as well as intellectual rationality built around cultural legitimacy. Organic intellectuals may rethink our modernity and subsequently create alternative development paradigms for the benefit of all and sundry, indeed for the commonwealth. We cannot continue to carry baskets of eggs on our heads and be walking in haste. We must continue to write, read, and be awakeners at home and abroad as the Murid master Ajami poet, Muusaa Ka (1889–1963), enjoins us to do:

> If there were no writer, our paths would fade away
> If there were no reader, our knowledge would vanish
> If there were no awakener, our people would be in slumber
> And they would never be awake until they are ruined

Notes

1. On the differences between these inventions, although not drawing from the African data, see Aveni (2002).
2. Cabral (1973). In passing, permit me to add briefly that the Guinea-Bissau nationalist hero (Cabral) is known for his radical assertions, as he told Pan-Africans, at the huge Guinean funeral rites for the late President Kwame Nkrumah of Ghana, that the indomitable Pan-Africanist liberator of Ghana died from a cancer of betrayal but not the disease itself; soon after, he suffered his own unfortunate fate. He was a good creator of varieties of archives!
3. Apter (1992: blurb).

4. On individual characteristics of the deities, see, for instance, Elebuibon (1998).
5. See, for instance, Simpson (1980).
6. See various chapters in Barnes, ed. (1997).
7. Murphy and Sanford, eds. (2001).
8. See, for instance, Matory (1994).
9. Barber (1991).
10. Adeboye in Yoruba Affairs, https://groups.google.com/forum/#!topic/yorubaaffairs/lO_hfvu_4j0
11. Ibid.
12. Ibid.; https://groups.google.com/forum/#!topic/usaafricadialogue/zMbz01Cbyvo
13. Doris (2011).
14. Cisneros-Puebla (2015: 396).
15. See, for instance, Spivak (1995).
16. Bhabha (1994).
17. Cisneros-Puebla (2015: 397).
18. On Omoluabi, see Ogundeji and Akangbe, eds. (2009).
19. See Hallen (2000).
20. Oyetade (2004).
21. Owomoyela (2005: 3).
22. Ibid.
23. Quoted in Maerk (2009: 186).
24. Ibid.
25. Biobaku, ed. (1973).
26. Among others, see Samuel P. Huntington (1996).
27. Cisneros-Puebla (2015: 396).
28. Mertens, Cram, and Chilisa, eds. (2013).
29. Ibid., 9.
30. Ibid., 395.
31. http://www.nrf.ac.za/sites/default/files/documents/IKS%20Guide%202015.pdf
32. Ibid.

Bibliography

Abimbola, Wande. 1976. *Ifa: An Exposition of Ifa Literary Corpus*. Ibadan: Oxford University Press.

Adesanya, Aderonke Adesola. 2012. *Carving Wood, Making History: The Fakeye Family, Modernity and Yoruba Woodcarving*. Trenton: Africa World Press.

Apter, Andrew. 1992. *Black Critics and Kings: The Hermeneutics of Power in Yoruba Society*. Chicago: The University of Chicago Press.

Aveni, Anthony. 2002. *Conversing with the Planets: How Science and Myth Invented the Cosmos*. Boulder: University Press of Colorado.

Barber, Karin. 1991. *I Could Speak Until Tomorrow: Oriki, Women and the Past in a Yoruba Town*. Washington, DC: Smithsonian.

Barnes, Sandra, ed. 1997. *Africa's Ogun: Old World and New*. Bloomington: Indiana University Press.

Bhabha, Homi. 1994. *The Location of Culture*. London: Routledge.

Biobaku, S.O., ed. 1973. *Sources of Yoruba History.* Oxford: Oxford University Press.
Cabral, Amilcar. 1973. In *Return to the Source: Selected Speeches by Amilcar Cabral*, ed. Africa Information Service. New York/London: Monthly Review Press.
Cisneros-Puebla, César A. 2015. The Onward Journey. In *Indigenous Pathways into Social Research: Voices of a New Generation*, ed. Donna M. Mertens, Fiona Cram, and Bagele Chilisa. Walnut Creek: Left Coast Press.
Doris, David T. 2011. *Vigilant Things: On Thieves, Yoruba Anti-Aesthetics, and the Strange Fates of Ordinary Objects in Nigeria.* Seattle: University of Washington Press.
Elebuibon, Ifayemi. 1998. *The Adventures of Obatala.* Lynwood: Ara Ifa.
Fadipe, N.A. (1970). *The Sociology of the Yoruba.* Edited with an Introduction Francis Olu Okediji and Oladejo O. Okediji. Ibadan: Ibadan University Press.
Hallen, Barry. 2000. *The Good, the Bad and the Beautiful: Discourse About Values in Yoruba Culture.* Bloomington: Indiana University Press.
Hucks, Tracey E. 2012. *Yoruba Traditions and African American Religious Nationalism.* Albuquerque: University of New Mexico Press.
Huntington, Samuel P. 1996. The West: Unique, Not Universal. *Foreign Affairs* 6: 28–46.
Idowu, E. Bolaji. 1962. *Olodumare: God in Yoruba Belief.* London: Longman.
Maerk, J. 2009. Overcoming Cover-Science in Latin American Social Sciences and Humanities—An Intervention. In *Power and Justice in International Relations: Interdisciplinary Approaches to Global Challenges: Essays in Honor of Hans Köchler*, ed. M.-L. Frick and A. Oberprantacher, 185–192. Farnham: Ashgate Publishing.
Matory, J. Lorand. 1994. *Sex and the Empire That Is No More: Gender and the Politics of Metaphor in Oyo Yoruba Religion.* Minneapolis: University of Minnesota Press.
Mertens, Donna M., Fiona Cram, and Bagele Chilisa, eds. 2013. *Indigenous Pathways into Social Research: Voices of a New Generation.* London/New York: Routledge.
Murphy, Joseph M., and Mei-Mei Sanford, eds. 2001. *Osun Across the Waters: A Yoruba Goddess in Africa and the Americas.* Bloomington: Indiana University Press.
Ogundeji, Adedotun, and Adeniyi Akangbe, eds. 2009. *Omoluabi: Its Concept and Education in Yoruba Land.* Ibadan: Ibadan Cultural Studies Group.
Ojo, G.J.A. 1966. *Yoruba Culture.* London: University of London Press.
Owomoyela, Oyekan. 2005. *Yoruba Proverbs.* Lincoln/London: University of Nebraska Press.
Oyetade, B. Akintude. 2004. The Enemy in the Belief System. In *Understanding Yoruba Life and Culture*, ed. Nike S. Lawal, Matthew N.O. Sadiku, and P. Ade Dopamu. Trenton: Africa World Press.
Simpson, George E. 1980. *Yoruba Religion and Medicine in Ibadan.* Ibadan: Ibadan University Press.
Spivak, Gayatri C. 1995. Can the Subaltern Speak? In *Post-Colonial Studies Reader*, ed. B. Ashcroft, G. Griffiths, and H. Tiffen, 24–28. London: Routledge.

PART V

Religion (Comprehensive Worldview)

CHAPTER 28

The Role of Religious Practitioners in Sustaining Social Morality

Obaji Agbiji and Emem O. Agbiji

INTRODUCTION

Poverty and corruption have become critical issues that pose huge challenges to the sociopolitical and economic transformation of African countries.[1] Scholars and international development agencies continue to argue that concerted efforts by African governments and international agencies such as the World Bank to address poverty in Africa will continue to fail unless the menace of corruption is eradicated or at least greatly curtailed.[2] Whilst in some countries poverty exists as a result of scarcity of resources, in some such as Nigeria, South Africa and Zimbabwe, mismanagement and looting of resources by public officials is the cause of poverty.[3] "There is, for example, a consensus among development experts that, granted proper management of resources, some countries in Africa, such as Nigeria, the Democratic Republic of Congo and a good number of others, given the abundance of their human and natural resources, ought not" to be counted among the poorest countries in the World.[4] Regrettably, these countries are today rated amongst the poorest in the world. These countries are also heavily indebted and saddled with many social problems such as poverty, hunger, disease, illiteracy and social turmoil. The theft and mismanagement of billions of dollars of public funds in Africa by African leaders is unique in the way that the thieves get away without being held to account for their crime.[5] But the spate of corruption in African countries is not only blamed on political and economic leadership. Religious leaders have also been accused by scholars and social commentators to be

O. Agbiji (✉) • E. O. Agbiji
Research Institute for Theology and Religion, University of South Africa (UNISA), Pretoria, South Africa

© The Author(s) 2020
N. Wariboko, T. Falola (eds.), *The Palgrave Handbook of African Social Ethics*, https://doi.org/10.1007/978-3-030-36490-8_28

contributing to the moral challenges of African societies by their failure to reprimand persons of questionable character and by their direct involvement in immoral and corrupt practices.[6]

Whilst international and local organisations such as Transparency International (TI), Human Rights Watch (HRW), Economic and Financial Crimes Commission (EFCC) of Nigeria and the Office of the Public Protector in South Africa have made attempts to expose the corrupt practices of public officials and to ensure accountability in countries in Africa, much still remains to be done.[7] In our view, a successful implementation of the notion of probity and accountability in African societies aimed at sustaining social morality could achieve a better impact if civil society organisations such as religious institutions (the church in particular) become more active partners with governments and international organisations. Despite the indictment of some African Christian religious leaders for their negative contribution to moral problems, some religious leaders and indeed the Christian community have made contributions in sustaining social morality in Africa.[8] However, it is our opinion that there is still much scope for the church's moral engagement.

This chapter is informed by Frederick Bird's theories of moral accountability and moral responsibility[9] within the discipline of the sociology of religion. "Moral accountability is defined as the individual awareness that a person is expected to act in keeping with moral expectations. These moral expectations may include social rules and laws, religious sanctions, routine interpersonal demands, role expectations, personal standards of excellence, and internally held notions about what significant others expect".[10] Moral accountability also involves an awareness of the relationship or discrepancy between a person's actual activities and these moral expectations, between action and intention and between ego and ego ideal. This sense of moral accountability may be accompanied by feelings of personal satisfaction or dissatisfaction, of justification or guilt.[11] Unlike moral accountability which has to do with an individual's moral awareness in relation to self and the significant other, moral responsibility involves not merely awareness but also the personal avowing of obligations in relation to oneself and others and the acknowledging of one's answerability for their realisation. In line with this view, moral responsibility involves choice, decision and action, not merely awareness.[12]

Beginning with the introductory discussion, this chapter proceeds from the assumption that morality and ethics are cornerstones for an authentic engagement of religious communities in response to poverty and other forms of social injustice such as corruption in any society. This area of specialisation attributed to religious communities is not only viewed by religious communities themselves, but it is also a sphere which has been allocated to religious communities by socio-economic and political institutions.[13] Based on this demand on religion, a response has become inevitable from ecclesiastical communities, in the sense of providing a relevant perspective that could assist in dealing with the crisis of poverty and corruption. Probity and accountability are social constructs that could be employed by religious communities to initiate and sustain social morality in African societies in the light of the enormous crisis of corruption and poverty on the continent. The definition of religion is generally agreed upon by scholars of religion: it comprises beliefs, practices and rituals that are related to the sacred, to God, to the mystical or to the supernatural.[14] Religion has rules about conduct that guide life within a social group, and it is often organised and practised in a community, instead of being an individual or personal affair.[15] Our reference to religion will basically relate to the Christian faith and African Traditional Religion (ATR).

Informed by this understanding, we will first deal with the notions of probity, accountability, social morality and the problem of moral consensus in a modest way. We will thereafter argue why African societies are in dire need of building social morality and the imperative of that endeavour now more than ever. We will discuss the role of religion (the Christian Faith in particular) in fostering moral accountability in society before going on to explore how the role of religion (Christian Faith) could move beyond the domain of moral accountability to the realm of fostering moral responsibility in society.

Probity, Accountability, Social Morality and the Challenge of Moral Consensus

Whilst probity relates to being law-abiding and not engaging in criminal activities,[16] accountability involves being answerable for decisions or actions, often to prevent the misuse of power and other forms of inappropriate behaviour. Access to relevant and timely information is an essential characteristic of accountability. Accountability is basically about who is accountable to whom and for what? It requires stewardship and acting in the public interest, openness in account giving, whereby those in power are held accountable in public for their acts and omissions, decisions, policies and expenditures.[17] Accountability fosters probity and transparency in society. Social morality connotes beliefs or ideas of a society about what is right or wrong and about how people should behave. Social morality evolves as a result of the concern of human society about its organisation, the quality of people's lives in relation to what is right or wrong conduct. Right conduct which fosters social morality includes contentment, justice, honesty, fidelity to one's duty, generosity, altruism or consideration of the interest of other people. Wrong conducts which hamper social morality include avarice, greed, stealing, embezzlement of public funds, bribery, exploitation, cheating, manipulation, lying and falsehood.[18] Public morality refers to the moral behaviour of public officials and public institutions while private morality is the moral behaviour of individual citizens.[19] Both concepts are subsumed in social morality which connotes beliefs or ideas of a society about what is right or wrong and about how people should behave in private and public life.

Of particular note to the discussion on probity, accountability and social morality is the contribution of Paulus Zulu to the discussion on social morality in the South African context, in his work *A Nation in Crisis: An Appeal for*

Morality.[20] The main purpose of Zulu's work was "to address how the public, the elite and officials have translated and internalised the values of responsibility, accountability and transparency", as these values constitute the core values in the allocation and distribution of resources in a society.[21] Zulu's focus was in respect of "the moral behaviour of public institutions and public officials" not "the private morality of the general citizenry".[22] His interest in the morality of public institutions and public officials is based on his argument that while the general citizenry acts for itself and there are sufficient institutional and legal mechanisms to address issues of private morality, South African legal institutions appear to be less capable of handling the moral transgressions of public officials and public institutions.

However, Zulu goes further to acknowledge that the moral problem in South Africa is "pervasive, ranging from a callous disregard for life, a tendency towards rape and theft in ordinary citizens, to bribery, fraud and corruption by petty officials through to the elite and corporates".[23] In line with the notion of the pervasive presence of corruption in South Africa, J. M. Vorster has argued that "in spite of the emphasis in the South African Constitution on a high standard of professional ethics in Public Administration, the South African society continues to stagger under an immense wave of corruption in both the private and public sectors".[24] Whilst Zulu's focus on the morality of public institutions and public officials is tenable and his argument on the difficulty of holding public institutions and public officials accountable in South Africa, (although we believe this happens also in many African countries) can hardly be faulted, we argue that the public morality expected from public institutions and public officials is dependent on the private morality of each citizen. Vorster appears to subscribe to this view but deals with the matter of morality as it relates to the South African context from a purely Christian moral angle, suggesting that the church's role is to create a moral awareness. Yet, Zulu and Vorster make an important point on the moral challenges that abound in South Africa, and in our view, the problem affects many African countries regarding private and public morality, which are all contributing negatively to social progress in Africa.

But one may ask: what are the relations between the region of the ethical and the sphere of morality, and how are the concepts of probity and accountability related to them? As already pointed out at the beginning of this section, probity relates to being law-abiding and not engaging in criminal activities. Accountability involves being answerable for decisions or actions, often to prevent the misuse of power and other forms of inappropriate behaviour, while social morality connotes beliefs or ideas of a society about what is right or wrong and about how people should behave. Thus, social morality provides the basis from where society derives ethics.[25] Probity and accountability depend on ethics and social morality as they are both informed and sustained by the demands of social morality and ethics. Whereas the complexity of these notions and the big debate on what is moral or ethical in modern societies should be acknowledged, these notions or concepts are a condition for the existence of any form of social organisation and of any human community that certain expectations of behaviour on the part of its members should be regularly fulfilled.[26]

Yet, the question still remains if there is a possibility of applying a body of universal ethical or moral principles or sets of rules for the entire African continent that will govern public and private morality of individuals and institutions and on which bases sanctions can be meted out? An acceptable way of dealing with this problem is in terms of the idea of rules or principles governing human behaviour which apply universally within a community or class. This class should be thought of as a definite social group (Africans) or the sum of rational human species in Africa and the African diaspora. A good beginning point is the idea of minimal conception of morality and ethics.[27] However varied and complex as the national, cultural and religious differences may be in the world, "they all concern human beings and nowadays in particular through modern systems of communication, above all radio and television but also telephones and the internet, these human beings experience themselves increasingly as a community of destiny on our spaceship earth" which a mistake in biological or technological issues could threaten human existence in the entire universe.[28] The question then arises whether there cannot, should not, be a minimum of values, criteria and attitudes that are common to all human beings not just in Africa but also beyond—a minimal ethical or moral consensus. The answer to this question is that there can be, and should be, a minimum moral consensus in the world and in Africa in particular.[29] Such minimal morality can, for instance, be found in what is called the golden rule which has a commonality in all the great religions in the world, rendered in the Christian faith as "Whatever you want people to do to you, do also to them" (Luke 6:31).[30] We are well aware of the arguments for and against the validity and universality of the golden rule for especially an irrational being including the fanatic and rapist. The golden rule applies as a minimal and universal morality, but in addition to it, natural law can also apply as a complement. We posit again that the moral order holds as sacrosanct the fact that "one must do good and avoid evil". In line with this view, the International Theological Commission has therefore argued that there are three great sets of natural dynamisms that are at work in the human person. The first set of natural dynamisms, which is in "common with all substances, comprises essentially the inclination to preserve and to develop one's own existence. The second, which is in common with all living things, comprises the inclination to reproduce, in order to perpetuate the species. The third, which is proper to the human person as a rational being, comprises the inclination to know the truth about God and to live in society".[31] It is from these inclinations that "the first precepts of the natural law, known naturally, can be formulated". It further posits that such "precepts remain very general, but they form the first substratum that is at the foundation of all further reflections on the good to be practiced and on the evil to be avoided".[32]

On the basis then of our argument for a minimal morality that could serve as a beginning point for Africans across the continent in the sense of transiting from moral awareness (moral accountability) to living out the moral obligation with regard to self and the other (moral responsibility), as a beginning point in the moral regeneration project, we will now focus on the imperative of social morality in African societies and will alongside endeavour to respond to the question of the common grounds through which minimal standards of morality can be derived from for the African continent in addition to the demands of the golden rule and natural law which could arguably be encapsulated in the demands of the concept of social morality.

THE IMPERATIVE OF SOCIAL MORALITY IN AFRICAN SOCIETIES

A discussion on the concept of social morality in African society calls to question among other possible questions what commonalities exist within the African continent that could pave the way for a common moral compass? What are African indigenous concepts that relate to social morality and to what extent are those concepts still informing the morality of Africans, given the diverse races and ethnicities that now comprise Africa[33] and the impact of the forces of globalisation? Can those indigenous concepts still assist Africans to navigate the moral terrain? Why is a moral standard such an imperative to contemporary African society?

In spite of myriads of subcultures, sub-Saharan Africa constitutes a specific cultural context. As such there are common denominators and cultural signifiers that underscore shared identity and denote the deep-level assumptions and allegiances that format the different cultural ingredients and provide larger meaning to the existence of Africans.[34] In South Africa, and in many other African countries, morality has been shaped by the colonial experience, as well as an internal indigenous African ethos "tempered by Judeo-Christian and Greco-Roman traditions".[35] Islam has also contributed to the shaping of morality in African countries where it has a strong presence.[36] According to John Mbiti, religion permeates all departments of life to such an extent that it is not easy or possible to isolate it.[37] In African traditional life, the individual is immersed in religious participation that starts before birth and continues after death.[38]

Religion as a shared cultural identity among Africans is indeed fundamental for Africans, since human beings live in a religious universe. Both the universe and practically all human activities in it are seen and experienced from a religious perspective. This religious worldview informs the philosophical understanding of African myths, customs, culture, traditions, beliefs, morals, actions and social relationships.[39] This same worldview also accounts for the religiosity of the African in political and socio-economic life.[40] That Africans resort to religion unconsciously shows how deeply a religious consciousness is ingrained in an African person, whether he or she is at home or in the diaspora.[41] Graveling has pertinently argued that culture is not static and discrete but rather fluid and dynamic, with customs and traditions being continually adapted according to new circumstances and ethnic groups intermingling and sharing cultural values and practices. Thus, in the postmodern era, it is increasingly becoming difficult to talk of an "authentic" African, Western, or even British, Yoruba or Olulumo culture.⁴² The fluid nature of culture explains why there exist a lot of similarities among African countries and should ease the often imagined tensions in cultural diversity among the various races and religious traditions in Africa and the impact of globalisation on the continent as impediments to social transformation.

Unfortunately, the similarities among Africans also include the high level of poverty, unaccountable leadership and corruption in private and public life of persons and in public institutions.⁴³ Using two African countries, Nigeria and South Africa, for example, we briefly discuss the level of corruption at different levels of society. We begin with the Nigerian account. Corruption is so pervasive in Nigeria that it has turned public service for many into a kind of criminal enterprise. Graft has fuelled political violence, denied millions of Nigerians access to even the most basic health and education services and reinforced police abuses and other widespread patterns of human rights violations,⁴⁴ despite the attempts of anti-corruption agencies to tackle the problem. One such agency is the Economic and Financial Crimes Commission.

Essentially, the EFCC is a law enforcement agency that was established in 2003. According to the Economic and Financial Crimes Commission (Establishment) Act, 2003, the agency is the designated Financial Intelligence Unit (FIU) in Nigeria charged with the responsibility of co-coordinating the various institutions fighting money laundering and enforcement of all laws dealing with economic and financial crimes. The commission exists to investigate all financial crimes including advance fee fraud, money laundering, counterfeiting, illegal charge transfers, market fraud, fraudulent encashment of negotiable instruments, credit card fraud and similar offences. Its powers also include the adoption of measures to identify, freeze, confiscate or seize proceeds derived from terrorist activities and economic and financial crime-related offences. Accordingly, the commission has used provisions in the Act, establishing it to apprehend some corrupt politicians and to investigate reported cases of economic and financial crimes, with a view to identifying individuals, corporate bodies or groups involved, and determine the extent of financial loss and such other losses by government, private individuals or organisations.⁴⁵

Since its inception, the EFCC has arraigned 30 nationally prominent political figures on corruption charges and has recovered US$11 billion through its efforts. But many of the corruption cases against the political elite have made little progress in the courts: there have been only four convictions to date and those convicted have faced relatively little or no prison time.⁴⁶ Former EFCC chairman Nuhu Ribadu has estimated that between independence and the end of military rule in 1999, more than US$380 billion was lost to graft and mismanagement. Endemic corruption has continued since then.⁴⁷

Within the South African context, Zulu has decried "the moral behaviour of public institutions and public officials" in the post-apartheid era while also acknowledging that the moral problem in South Africa is "pervasive, ranging from a callous disregard for life, a tendency towards rape and theft in ordinary citizens, to bribery, fraud and corruption by petty officials through to the elite and corporates".⁴⁸ In respect of corrupt public officials, the case that has continued to attract media, public and parliamentary discourse is the Nkandla security upgrade of the home of the immediate past president of the Republic of South Africa, Jacob Zuma.[49] According to the findings of the Public Protector, "the implementation of the Nkandla Project leaves one with the impression of excessive and unconscionable 'Rolls Royce' security constituting an island in a sea of poverty and paucity of public infrastructure. This cannot be accepted as conscionable in any state and certainly not in a state where section 195 and 237 of the Constitution promise to put people first and where the Batho Pele White Paper undertakes to transform the state from the insular apartheid state to one that is people centred and puts people first".[50]

The cost of the Nkandla project is conservatively estimated at about US$17 million.[51] The expenditure constitutes opulence at a grand scale, and President Zuma and his immediate family members also improperly benefitted from the measures implemented in the name of security which include non-security comforts such as the Visitors' Centre, the swimming pool, amphitheatre, cattle kraal with culvert, chicken run and the private medical clinic at the family's doorstep. The public protector further argued that such acts and omissions that allowed this to happen constitute unlawful and improper conduct and maladministration on the part of the president and all persons that were involved.[52] Unfortunately, the cost of the project was at the detriment of the masses that the president was expected to be accountable to as funds were reallocated from the Inner City Regeneration and the Dolomite Risk Management Programmes of the Department of Public Works (DPW), and as a result, proper demand management and planning service delivery programmes of the DPW were negatively affected.[53] In her findings, the public protector notes: "It is my considered view that the President, as the head of South Africa Incorporated, was wearing two hats, that of the ultimate guardian of the resources of the people of South Africa and that of being a beneficiary of public privileges of some of the guardians of public power and state resources, but failed to discharge his responsibilities in terms of the latter".[54] The public protector makes an important point that relates to the arguments of this chapter which stresses the fact that public morality of public officials and institutions is dependent on the private morality of citizens, when she reasoned that the president was wearing two caps, one as a guardian of the South Africa resources and the other as a beneficiary. In our view, this way of viewing the president represents the official and the personal roles of the president, which are all to be carried out by the same person. No matter the situation, the responsibility for moral choice rests with the individuals who also make institutional decisions.[55]

In line with this view, we argue that moral accountability which has to do with an individual's moral awareness in relation to self and the significant other is indispensable in the journey towards attaining minimal acceptable standards of private and public morality. However, the journey does not stop there. It must continue towards moral responsibility which involves not merely awareness but also the personal avowing of obligations in relation to oneself and others and the acknowledging of one's answerability for their realisation.

In line with this view, moral responsibility involves choice and decision, not merely awareness.⁵⁶ As a matter of fact, the wearing of more than one cap as was previously referred to by the public protector in her Nkandla report does not only relate to the president of South Africa, but it also relates to all Africans who engage in various walks of life. Whatever cap is worn at any time, the person wearing the cap remains the same person and his or her moral standard remains the same, as has been shaped in the person's private life. "Moral behaviour involves more than simply the decisions and choices persons make about specific problems; it also includes the kinds of persons they are (their character and virtues), the kind of beliefs they hold and the way they organise their resources and energies to form a coherent life plan".⁵⁷ But given the fact that African societies are urgently in need of a moral compass that can inform private and public morality, are there African indigenous views that can inform morality in contemporary Africa?

In South Africa, Nigeria and many other postcolonial African countries, public morality rests on three distinct but interrelated roots which have shaped the moral fibre of these societies and influence private and public morality. These roots which can also be "termed philosophical traditions include traditional African philosophies, including Ubuntu, as the spirit that regulates social relations, and western moral philosophies from the Judeo-Christian and Greco-Roman traditions".⁵⁸ Ogbu Kalu has also argued that the impact of Western culture on Africa has altered and reconfigured African morality with "ambiguous morality and value system".⁵⁹ This impact has given rise to "three publics where this morality and value system functions namely: primal, external and emergent public that is neither fowl nor fish".⁶⁰ Somewhere else these three publics have been dubbed "the indigenous worldview, emergent culture, and Western alternatives".⁶¹ Some Africans such as Nigerians refer to it as the "Whiteman's world", where the person is beyond the purview of traditional sanctions. "The development of urban contexts created the ambiguous space for people who neither internalised Western values nor kept faith with the traditional. It has been argued that the indiscipline and corruption among the political elite could be explained by the gap". This has led Kalu to suggest that "A politician who robbed the state could still dance to the big drum in the village as a warrior who has forayed out into the Whiteman's world and returned with a piece of the national cake for his people".⁶² Kalu further argues that "the battering of traditional models of social control and yet inability to install a viable Western alternative has many implications"⁶³ for African societies, one of which is the problem of corruption in private and public life.

The traditional concept of morality, accountability, responsibility, duties and obligations is rooted in ancestry and kinship community.⁶⁴ Personal motives and external or objective considerations in morality and ethics are subordinated to the kinship community. One lives in traditional society in terms of one's ancestors and community of blood relations, not for one's self or objective principle. The primary loyalty, affinity and obligations are to be given to this group above all else. Patriotism and loyalty to the state and stranger becomes a problem because primary responsibility and accountability are to the kinship community.[65] What this means is that despite the concept of Ubuntu, as the spirit that regulates social relations, "what is right and wrong can only be committed against a member of their own ethnic group, race or tribe, but not against a stranger or an outsider". Based on this understanding, "an outsider has no rights or protection and anything done to him has no moral or ethical value".[66] Traditional African morality can be summarised as being communalistic, anthropocentric pragmatist and utilitarian, tribalistic and this-worldly.[67] Traditional African morality and institutions can no longer be relied upon as a primary and singular moral compass for African societies.[68]

Yet, corruption in the various sectors of African societies has been identified by scholars, economists and political analysts as a key contributing factor to the perennial challenge of poverty and social injustice in Africa. The need to address the problem of corruption beyond the confines of the courts of law and law enforcement agencies has therefore become imperative for the sustenance of social morality and at the same time the development of viable sociopolitical, economic and religious institutions.[69] Moral principles constitute the foundation on which society is built. A continual deviation from right moral behaviour by members of society will inevitably lead to the destruction of society. If everyone in society were to continuously violate right moral principles, there would be no society.[70] The level of well-being or ill-being and social harmony or disharmony of any society is proportionate to the level of the cultivation of right or wrong morality amongst fellow members of society. The concepts of moral accountability and moral responsibility must guide the development of social morality in Africa. It is also on the basis of these concepts that probity and accountability will flourish amongst African societies. But given the privileged position of religion and the Christian faith in particular, in the mediation of morality in society can the church in Africa play a vital role in charting a moral compass for the continent?

The Church in Africa as a Custodian and Transmitter of Social Morality

African traditional religion and institutions and various civil society groups have in their own right contributed to the shaping of moral behaviour amongst African societies, and their roles in the moral rehabilitation project will always be valuable.[71] However, it has become doubtful that traditional African moral standards drawn from African traditional religion and institutions can adequately inform the moral demands of African society both as a singular source of morality and moral compass for private and public morality. Just as traditional African institutions can no longer be relied upon as a primary and singular moral compass for African societies in the postmodern era due to their deficiencies, political and economic institutions cannot also adequately serve as the providers of the moral standard for society.[72] This is partly so because a number of economic and political policies/legislations that have been instituted in some African countries and elsewhere have been morally deficient. For example, some of the excesses in financial policies and management of financial institutions, which were also backed up by government legislations in the 1990s and 2000s, eventually led to the global financial crisis in 2008. Even though these regulations were morally dubious, they were legal.[73] Significant changes to the regulatory environment which were supported by financial institutions and governments resulted in the denigration of effective oversight and the elevation of short-term profit over integrity.[74]

Whilst courts of law and law enforcement agencies are also doing their part to curb corruption among individuals, public officials and institutions, the process of moral formation and revival goes beyond the capacity of legal and law enforcement institutions.[75] The fear that the law evokes to curb corruption and other vices in society is not peculiar to the law and its institutions; religious institutions are also known to evoke similar fears that could be used to curb moral decadence in society.[76] Moral formation and regeneration is the domain of religious institutions such as churches, mosques,[77] synagogues and others. Religion (the Christian faith in particular) is central to the lives and values of most people in developing countries thereby also playing an important role in shaping development programmes.[78]

Religion, the Christian faith in particular, has been seen as "a custodian of morals and an agent for promotion of moral conduct".[79] The majority of the world's Christians are now Africans,[80] both at home and in the diaspora. African Christians should therefore take the lead not only in theological discourses but also in developing ethical and moral standards that will enable the faithful to live responsibly and such that they can foster social transformation in Africa. The role of the Christian faith through both its leadership and faithful in the moral project is unique, crucial and inevitable. The fact that some quarters of the church have in some instances failed does not invalidate the important role the Christian community can fulfil in the sustenance of social morality in Africa. The communiqué of the joint conference of the World Bank and Council of Anglican Provinces in Africa (CAPA) held in Nairobi on 10 March 2000 has well captured the role of the church in Africa when it stated the following:

> The Church brings its ability to influence constructively, based on its numbers, its position as the moral conscience of nations, its closeness to the poor, and its own accountability to God. The churches take spiritual issues seriously and see development as more than a secular process. Therefore, the Church seeks to hold forth humane and spiritual values to underpin social, political, and economic development. These values have kept the churches close to the poor in ways in which international development institutions and many government agencies are not.[81]

But despite the acclaimed role of the church in Africa, the multiracial, multicultural and multireligious nature of present-day African societies coupled with the ongoing impact of globalisation on the contingency of morality raises important questions as to what could constitute an authentic moral standard to which African societies can subscribe to. Such an acceptable moral standard should also cater for the socio-religious, political and economic engagement of the African in such a manner that he/she, the community and her institutions can relate adequately to the global community.

Unlike the ethical motives of traditional African societies, political and economic institutions, Christian morality and ethical standards are neither limited to one's kinship community of blood relations nor for the purpose of profit. The Christian faith is founded on divine revelation, and its ethos is ultimately rooted in a personal responsibility towards God, the commitment to build the common good through personal responsibility and a relation of trust with other persons. This approach to existence in relation to self, God and other human beings which is also typical of the monotheistic religions (Christianity, Judaism and Islam) gives a sound and stable basis to the search for the common good and connects it to some non-negotiable principles that, being rooted in divine revelation, transcend socio-economic consensus and political expediency.[82]

The scope of Christian moral duty and responsibility embraces and caters for the whole of humanity. The church has served as a custodian of morality in Africa from colonial and missionary times. The church's moral initiatives include stoppage of killing of twin babies and extrajudicial killings including trial by ordeal. She strengthened indigenous patriarchy to curb female migration and/or sexual autonomy and the promotion of Christian marriage to control sexual promiscuity in some African societies such as Belgian Africa (the Democratic Republic of Congo, Rwanda), South Africa and Nigeria. Religious institutions such as churches and mosques have served as custodians of morality in society through their sacred writings such as the Holy Bible and Q'uran from where moral teachings have been drawn for the faith community and the larger society.[83] Important to the navigation of the moral terrain is the development in the lives of members of the Christian faith community "the mind that was in Christ Jesus" through the "persistent study of the New Testament" and the imbibing of the teachings of Christ on "the principles of the love of God and love of the neighbour".[84] Thus, the teachings of Christ premised on the golden rule, complemented by natural law and the principle of love for God and the neighbour could satisfy the basic requirements of social morality, namely contentment, justice, honesty, fidelity to one's duty, generosity, altruism or consideration of the interest of other people. These concepts could find a grounding among the varied religious traditions, communities and private and public institutions in Africa and elsewhere. But the question still remains as to what means the church could engage persons and institutions to foster probity and accountability towards the attainment of social morality.

Sustaining Probity and Accountability in African Societies: Reimagining the Role of the Church in Mediating Social Morality

There is a specificity in Christian moral behaviour based on an inseparable intimate connection with Christian religious convictions. Christians believe their moral values are an inseparable part of the meaning of the faith they confess.[85] In line with this view, moral behaviour is shaped by "stories and metaphors through which we learn to intend the variety of our existence. Metaphors and stories suggest how we should see and describe the world – that is how we should 'look-on' our selves, others, and the world – in ways that rules taken in themselves do not".[86] These stories and metaphors shape character and combine to give a design or unity to the variety of things we must and must not do in our lives.[87] Although there may be great areas of agreement, it cannot be assumed that moral behaviour for Christians is the same in all aspects as for other persons.[88]

The specific contribution of Christianity and Judaism towards the enhancement of secular ethos consists in bringing existing social norms into relationship with God. By so doing, these religions exposed the deepest meaning of morality by making it an important place of encounter between God (as the ultimate being unto whom human beings/institutions are accountable) and the human person/institutions.[89] The church must therefore take its most important place in society to practice, proclaim and demand for probity and accountability through its leaders and the faithful, but also from the larger society, based on its moral frame of reference shaped by the stories and metaphors revealed in the Scriptures of the Old and New Testament and the ethical teachings of Christ, all of which constitutes basic or minimal and higher moral demands.[90] As the "image of the ideal society, the church is challenged by the Gospel to witness against all ideologies of self-interest" of individuals, institutions and nations.[91] The church must expose and protest the idolatry of nations, institutions and persons.[92] In line with its anticipated role in society and in order to be able to initiate and sustain probity and accountability through moral accountability and responsibility, religious institutions such as churches can no longer stick to traditional ways through which social morality was taught and practised in the past such as family circles, educational institutions, catechism, preaching and teaching in church services. Whilst the old ways can be maintained and some reformed, new ways should be evolved and sustained.

A key area that could be termed "a challenge and an opportunity" to the church's reimagined role in fostering social morality is the advancement of technology with particular reference to cyberspaces. Technology changes everything around us on a daily basis, and these changes caused by technology have positive and negative dimensions. It changes the homes we live in, cars we drive and work we do for good, but our technological society has also changed our morality, making it difficult to grapple with some moral challenges.[93] As a result of technological advancement, online spaces are constantly changing, creating new and unfamiliar environments. For example, rules regarding privacy and property are not always applicable. Internet users have a certain anonymity which makes it difficult to know identifiable information or to pinpoint harassment. There is an element of remoteness from feedback or harm with distance technology, with the absence of face-to-face communication and physical presence. The anonymity of electronic communications like e-mail and message-board posts means that it is difficult to locate and punish misbehaviour. This makes it difficult for our society to regulate behaviour that is illegal. For example, threats of violence towards others may not ever lead to legal action because authorities cannot easily determine the identity of the offender or even the offender's location. As a result, even if we still have the same moral values as before, "some of the rules and laws that accompany these values will need to be reshaped otherwise, we risk eroding those underlying values".[94]

The church's role in the moral regeneration project in Africa must take into serious consideration the enormous opportunity that technology is providing but must also at the same time acknowledge the challenge of keeping pace with the ever-changing terrain of cyberspaces in selling her "moral product". We suggest that the church must deliberately move out of the comfort zone of ecclesial sanctuaries to cyberspaces by engaging in that world in creative ways. The purpose of the engagement of the church in the cyberworld is to infiltrate that world with the gospel and its moral demands. The cyberworld is a community with its own people, language, tools, products and interests. The use of electronic gadgets such as cell phones, television, computers and so on and social networks such as Facebook, Twitter, Skype, WhatsApp, WeChat, Viber, Instagram, Pinterest and many more constitutes tools and spaces of the cyberworld. Their products cover blogs, reality shows, music, film, creative art, gaming, chat rooms, fashion and many more. Engaging the youths in this project is inevitable. Such youths must themselves be aware of the stories and metaphors of the Christian faith in other to be morally accountable. They must also have resolved to be morally responsible and therefore demonstrated such responsibility in their private lives. Such youths and other persons that get involved in the project must be supported by churches to fulfil this moral project in society.

Alongside the technological engagement of the moral project, the church must take advantage of her enormous growth rate in Africa with particular reference to her teaming audience in worship centres and other places of fellowship to mediate moral values in all spheres of society. Sound biblical teaching through sermons, bible study, cell groups and personal/family devotions by well-trained Christian religious leaders and the faithful and a concomitant demand of accountability in sound moral living in private and the public will always remain relevant to the very existence of the church and her social role in African societies. Religious leaders must set the example of accountability in managing the affairs of their religious communities in all areas of their private and public life. Of special importance is their sexual lives and financial management. The structures of accountability must be clearly spelt out in all Christian denominations and fellowships. Accountability ante must not be seen as a legal requirement; it should first be viewed from the perspectives of moral responsibility and an exemplary conduct which paves the way for integrity and the well-being of religious communities and the larger society.

The church's prophetic role in society which places enormous responsibility on religious leaders and the faithful to call persons and institutions to account for their actions and inactions before human beings and God must be reignited wherever the church exists. The fulfilment of this role requires the church to use all possible avenues to accomplish the role. Fulfilling this role on the part of the church requires that the church must be well informed about the constitution of the country and policies of governments and cooperate with institutions of the countries where she exists and the unacceptable social conditions of their communities. In carrying out this role, the church must be objective and well informed. Informed members of the church in the various fields of expertise such as public policy and management, economics, political governance and so on could constitute enormous resource to the statements and public utterances of religious leaders and churches. Integral to its prophetic role in society is the engagement of the church in advocacy, lobbying of legislative bills, rallies and mass protests against immoral and corrupt practices of persons and institutions.

Moral education in schools and moral awareness campaigns could also be of enormous benefit in the moral regeneration project in Africa. In this regard, two types of approaches to moral education in schools (nursery, primary and secondary) could be useful: relatively autonomous and complementary approaches.[95] The first approaches should aim to teach the learner to experience, think and act in a critical manner with regard to concrete current social problems. Reference could also be made to how Jesus dealt with similar or related issues. The second approach will be to invite the learner to examine Jesus' conduct and personality, those of his disciples and early Christians and those of the Old Testament prophets. Particular attention should be given to Jesus' values and preferences and those of early Christian figures. This approach to moral education could as well be addressed to adults in the moral campaign. The focus in both approaches is to play down on the demand for moral uprightness based on fear of God's punishment but on the responsible conduct of rational beings and their responsible conduct in society. The moral campaigns carried out by churches in society should be such that they can develop a moral consciousness and responsibility among the citizenry based on responsible conduct and each individual's contribution to the well-being of society. This approach to morality could be more useful than that based on the fear of punishment from God or legal authorities. The church's moral engagement in society must be carried out bearing in mind the demands of social morality, namely contentment, justice, honesty, fidelity to one's duty, generosity and consideration of the interest of other people. Focusing on the minimal demands of morality which can be clearly outlined makes room for seeking to see them manifest and provides a basis for evaluation on how well or not the project is doing.

Yet, it is pretentious to conclude this chapter without acknowledging that a realistic analysis of the human society in Africa and elsewhere "reveals a constant and seemingly irreconcilable conflict between the needs of society and the imperatives of a sensitive conscience".[96] This conflict exists as a result of the double focus of the moral life which on the one hand focuses on the inner life of the individual on the basis of achieving unselfishness as the highest ideal while on the other hand focuses on society for the attainment of the highest ideal which is justice. To harmonise the two moral perspectives, it is pertinent to appreciate the fact that "the highest moral insights and achievements of the individual conscience are both relevant and necessary to the life of society". The most perfect justice cannot be established if the moral imagination of the individual does not seek to comprehend the needs and interests of his fellows. In addition "justice could degenerate into something that is less than justice if it is not brought under the control of moral goodwill".[97] The difficulty in engaging in the moral debate and the historical baggage of the church's moral failures in society are also acknowledged.

Conclusion

From the outset in this chapter, Frederick Bird's theories of moral accountability and moral responsibility were engaged to enter the discourse on the quest for probity and accountability in African societies towards the realisation of social morality. We have portrayed a very positive tilt to the role of religion with particular reference to the Christian faith in the moral transformation of African societies, the historical antecedents of the church's negative moral profile notwithstanding. This, for us, is a tentative engagement in the very complex debate on morality in society with special reference to African societies. It is important however to caution that whilst the relevance, transcendence and universality of the Christian ethical standard and its engagement as a moral compass for society has been emphasised, the universality and persistence of sin both on the part of the Christian and non-Christian who engages in the moral regeneration project and the beneficiaries of the project must be acknowledged. The Christian must therefore seek to be controlled by the Christian faith and ethics in the motives that prompt him to make his decisions. He/she must be guided by humility in being self-critical in making social decisions. More so, all engagements must be kept under the criticism of Christian love. Above all, authentic moral engagement in social morality must be guided in determining the goals which represent the purpose of God in our time.[98]

Notes

1. Christopher Kolade, "Corruption in Africa: Causes, Effects, and Counter-Measures," in *Faith in Development: Partnership between the World Bank and the Churches of Africa*, ed. Deryke Belshaw, Robert Calderisi and Chris Sugden (Oxford: Regnum, 2001), 82.

2. Jan Marino Ramirez, "Peace and Development in Africa," *International Journal on World Peace* XXII 3 (2005), 55, 56.
3. Paul D. Ocheje, "Refocusing International Law on the Quest for Accountability in Africa: The Case Against the 'Other' Impunity," *Leiden Journal of International Law* 15 (2002):750. B. J. Van der Walt, *Understanding and rebuilding Africa: From Desperation Today Towards Expectation for Tomorrow* (Potchefstroom: Institute for Contemporary Christianity in Africa, 2003), 42–46.
4. Ocheje, "Refocusing International Law on the Quest for Accountability in Africa: The Case Against the 'Other' Impunity," 750–752. Greg Mills, *Why Africa is poor and what Africans can do about it* (Johannesburg: Penguin Books, 2010), 4–8.
5. Ocheje, "Refocusing International Law on the Quest for Accountability in Africa: The Case Against the 'Other' Impunity," 750. Mills, *Why Africa is poor and what Africans can do about it*, 180–184.
6. Jacob Olupona, "Forward," in *Creativity and Change*, ed. D. O. Ogungbile and A. E. Akinade (Lagos: Malthouse Press, 2010), xiv. Jacob Kehinde Ayantayo, "Prosperity Gospel and Social Morality: A Critique," in *Creativity and Change*, ed. D. O. Ogungbile and A. E. Akinade (Lagos: Malthouse Press, 2010), 211–212.
7. Transparency International, 'Corruption Perception Index, 2013' http://www.ey.com/Publication/vwLUAssets/EY-Transparency-International-Corruption-Perceptions-Index-2013/$FILE/EY-Transparency-International-Corruption-Perceptions-Index-2013.pdf. (25 June 2015). Human Rights Watch, 'Corruption on Trial? The Record of Nigeria's Economic and Financial Crimes Commission' *2011 Human Rights Watch*, http://www.hrw.org/sites/default/files/reports/nigeria0811WebPostR.pdf. (25 June 2015). Economic and Financial Crimes Commission (EFCC) 2015, *EFCCALERT! Economic and Financial Crimes Commission*, 4 1, https://efccnigeria.org/efcc/images/EFCC_Alert.pdf. (25 June 2015). Thuli Madonsela, 'Statement by Public Protector', 19 March 2014, http://www.publicprotector.org/media_gallery/2014/Nkandla%20Statement%20by%20Public%20Protector%2019%20March%202014.pdf. (25 June 2015). Emeka Emmanuel Okafor, "Combating High-Profile Corruption in Transitional Societies: Overview of Experiences from Some African Countries," *Anthropologist*, 11 2 (2009).
8. Olupona, "Forward," in *Creativity and Change*, xiv, xv.
9. Federick Bird, "The Pursuit of Innocence: New Religious Movements and Moral Accountability," *Sociological Analysis*, 40 4 (1979), 335, 336.
10. Ibid., 335.
11. Ibid., 336.
12. Ibid.
13. The International Bank for Reconstruction and Development/The World Bank, "Millennium Challenges for Development and Faith Institutions 2003," http://siteresources.worldbank.org/EXTDEVDIALOGUE/Resources/Millenium_Challenges.pdf (10 June 2019), ix. World Bank/CAPA, "Common Ground and Common Concerns: Communiqué of the CAPA–World Bank Conference," in *Faith in Development: Partnership between the World Bank and the Churches of Africa*, ed. Deryke Belshaw, Robert Calderisi and Chris Sugden

(Oxford: Regnum, 2001), 8, 9. Also campare Kolade, "Corruption in Africa: Causes, Effects, and Counter-Measures," 86.
14. Harold G. Koenig, "Research on Religion, Spirituality, and Mental Health: A Review." *Canadian Journal of Psychiatry* 54 5 (2009), 284.
15. John S Mbiti, *African Religions and Philosophy* 2nd ed. (Oxford: Heinemann, 1999), 15.
16. A. W. Siegman, "On Religion and Probity", *Religious Education*, 57 2 (1962), 132.
17. Wayne Cameron, "Public accountability: Effectiveness, equity, ethics," *Australian Journal of Public Administration* 63 4 (2004), 59.
18. Ayantayo, "Prosperity Gospel and Social Morality: A Critique," 202.
19. Paulus Zulu, *A nation in crisis: An appeal for morality* (Cape Town: Tafelberg, 2013), 23.
20. Ibid.
21. Ibid., 22.
22. Ibid., 23.
23. Ibid.
24. J. M. Vorster, "Managing Corruption in South Africa: The Ethical Responsibility of Churches," *Scriptura* (2012), 133.
25. Peter Frederick Strawson, "Social Morality and Individual Ideal," *Philosophy*, 36, 136 (1961), 5.
26. Ibid.
27. Ibid., 5–8.
28. Hans Kung, *A Global Ethic for Global Politics and Economics* (London: SCM Press, 1997), 94.
29. Ibid.
30. Ibid., 98.
31. International Theological Commission, "In Search of a Universal Ethic: A New Look at the Natural Law," http://www.vatican.va/roman_curia/congregations/cfaith/cti_documents/rc_con_cfaith_doc_20090520_legge-naturale_en.html (10 June 2019).
32. Ibid.
33. It is now a well-known fact that besides the varied ethnicities in sub-Sahara Africa, we now have European and Asian Africans. A good example is White South Africans who have dual nationalities and some who have no other nationality but South Africa. We have Asian-Africans also in the same context.
34. Ogbu U. Kalu, "African Protestant Theology," in *Religions in Africa: Conflicts, Politics and Social Ethics, The Collected Essays of Ogbu Uke Kalu Vol 3*, ed. Wilhelmina Kalu, Nimi Wariboko and Toyin Falola (Trenton: Africa World Press, 2010), 4. R. M. Green, "Religion and Morality in the African Traditional Setting", *Journal of Religion in Africa*, XIV 1 (1983), 6.
35. Zulu, *A nation in crisis: An appeal for morality*, 22, 23.
36. Obaji M Agbiji and Ignatius Swart, "Historical Sources of Christian Religious Leadership Ideology: Implications and Challenges for Social Transformation in Post-military Nigeria," *Studia Historiae Ecclesiasticae* XXXIX 1 (2013), 225, 226.
37. Mbiti, *African Religions and Philosophy*, 1.
38. Ibid.
39. Ibid., 15.
40. Ogbu U Kalu, "Faith and Politics in Africa: Emergent Political Theology of Engagement in Nigeria," in *Religions in Africa: Conflicts, Politics and Social*

Ethics, *The Collected Essays of Ogbu Uke Kalu Vol 3*, ed. Wilhelmina Kalu, Nimi Wariboko and Toyin Falola (Trenton: Africa World Press, 2010), 11–15.
41. Ezra Chitando, Afe Adogame and Bolaji Bateye, "Introduction: African Traditions in the Study of Religion in Africa: Contending with Gender, the Vitality of Indigenous Religions, and Diaspora," in *African Traditions in the Study of Religion, Diaspora and Gendered Societies*, ed. Afe Adogame, Ezra Chitando and Bolaji Bateye, B. (Farnham: Ashgate, 2013), 5–7.
42. Elizabeth Graveling, "Marshalling the Powers: The Challenge of Everyday Religion for Development," in *Development and Politics from Below: Exploring Religious Spaces in the African State*, ed. B. Bompani and M. Frahm-Arp (London: Palgrave, 2010), 200, 201.
43. Zulu, *A nation in crisis: An appeal for morality*, 22, 23. Okafor, "Combating High-Profile Corruption in Transitional Societies: Overview of Experiences from Some African Countries," 117.
44. Human Rights Watch, "Corruption on Trial?", 1.
45. E. Oladesu, A. Avwode and L Salaudeen, "EFCC: Ten years after." *Nigeria Intel.* http://wwwnigeriaintel.com/2013/09/18/efcc-ten-years-after/ (25 June 2015), 1, 2.
46. Human Rights Watch, "Corruption on Trial?", 1.
47. Ibid., 6.
48. Zulu, *A nation in crisis: An appeal for morality*, 23.
49. Madonsela, "Statement by Public Protector", 5, 438.
50. Ibid., 426.
51. Ibid., 4.
52. Ibid., 430, 431.
53. Ibid., 426.
54. Ibid., 439.
55. Zulu, *A nation in crisis: An appeal for morality*, 43.
56. Bird, "The Pursuit of Innocence: New Religious Movements and Moral Accountability," 336.
57. Iddo Tavory, "The Question of Moral Action: A Formalist Position," *Sociological Theory*, 29 4 (2011), 277, 278.
58. Zulu, *A nation in crisis: An appeal for morality*, 43. C. U. Manus, "The Nigerian Schools: Towards National Morality," *Religious Education* 79 2 (1984), 216, 217.
59. Kalu, "Faith and Politics in Africa: Emergent Political Theology of Engagement in Nigeria," 13, 14. Ogbu U. Kalu, "Poverty and Its Alleviation in Colonial Nigeria," in *Religions in Africa: Conflicts, Politics and Social Ethics, The Collected Essays of Ogbu Uke Kalu Vol 3*, ed. Wilhelmina Kalu, Nimi Wariboko and Toyin Falola (Trenton: Africa World Press, 2010), 180.
60. Kalu, "Faith and Politics in Africa: Emergent Political Theology of Engagement in Nigeria," 15.
61. Kalu, "Poverty and Its Alleviation in Colonial Nigeria," 181.
62. Kalu, "Faith and Politics in Africa: Emergent Political Theology of Engagement in Nigeria," 14.
63. Ibid.
64. Yusufu Turaki, *Christianity and African Gods: A Method in Theology* (Potchefstroom: University of Potchefstroom, 1999), 140.

65. Turaki, *Christianity and African Gods: A Method in Theology*, 140. Van der Walt, *Understanding and Rebuilding Africa: From Desperation Today Towards Expectation for Tomorrow*, 224.
66. Turaki, 68; Van der Walt, 223.
67. Van der Walt, 220. Laurenti Magesa, "Theology of Democracy," in *Democracy and Reconciliation: A Challenge for African Christianity*, Laurenti Magesa and Zablon Nthamburi eds. (Nairobi: Acton Publishers, 1999), 124, 125.
68. Turaki, *Christianity and African Gods: A Method in Theology*, 122.
69. EFCC, *EFCCALERT! Economic and Financial Crimes Commission*, 7.
70. Ayantayo, "Prosperity Gospel and Social Morality: A Critique," 202.
71. Silvio Ferrari, "Religion and the development of civil society," *International Journal for Religious Freedom* 4 2 (2011), 29–36. Funso Afolayan, 1994. "Civil Society, Popular Culture and the Crisis of Democratic Transitions in Nigeria, 1960–1993," *Wits History Workshop Papers* http://hdl.handle.net/10539/7493 (1994), 12–16.
72. Turaki, *Christianity and African Gods: A Method in Theology*, 122.
73. Justin O'Brien, "Ethics, Probity, and the Changing Governance of Wall Street: Cure or Remission?," *Public Integrity*, 7 1 (2004–2005), 44.
74. Ibid.
75. EFCC, *EFCCALERT! Economic and Financial Crimes Commission*, 7. Zulu, *A nation in crisis: An appeal for morality*, 22.
76. E. Patey, *For the Common Good: Morals Public and Private* (Oxford: A. R. Mowbray, 1988), 18.
77. EFCC, *EFCCALERT! Economic and Financial Crimes Commission*, 7.
78. Graveling, "Marshalling the Powers: The Challenge of Everyday Religion for Development," 198.
79. Zablon Nthamburi, "Theology and Politics in Africa," in *Democracy and Reconciliation: A Challenge for African Christianity*, Laurenti Magesa and Zeblon Nthamburi eds. (Nairobi: Acton Publishers, 1999), 143. Zulu, *A nation in crisis: An appeal for morality*, 43.
80. Andrew F. Walls, "World Christianity, theological education and scholarship," *Transformation*. 28 4 (2011), 237.
81. World Bank/CAPA, "Common Ground and Common Concerns: Communiqué of the CAPA – World Bank Conference," 8, 9.
82. Ferrari, "Religion and the development of civil society," 32.
83. EFCC, "*EFCCALERT! Economic and Financial Crimes Commission*," 7.
84. Patey, *For the Common Good: Morals Public and Private*, 20.
85. Stanley Hauerwas, "The Self as Story: Religion and Morality from the Agent's Perspective," *Journal of Religious Ethics*, 1 (1973), 74.
86. Ibid.
87. Ibid., 76.
88. Ibid.
89. Chris Ukachukwu Manus, "The Nigerian Schools: Towards National Morality," *Religious Education* 79 2 (1984), 216.
90. Hauerwas, "The Self as Story: Religion and Morality from the Agent's Perspective," 74–76. Manus, "The Nigerian Schools: Towards National Morality," 216.
91. Nthamburi, "Theology and Politics in Africa," 144.
92. Ibid.

93. IGI Global, "Tech and Ethics: The Decline of Morality in the Digital Age," 2013, http://www.igi-global.com/newsroom/archive/tech-ethics-Adecline-morality-digital/1501/ (7 July 2015).
94. Stan Mack, "The Effects of Technology on Moral Development," http://www.ehow.com/list_5898835_effects-technology-moral-development.html. (7 July 2015).
95. Manus, "The Nigerian Schools: Towards National Morality," 220.
96. Reinhold Niebuhr, "The Conflict Between Individual and Social Morality," in *Social Christianity: A Reader*, J. Atherton ed. (London: SPCK, 1994), 199.
97. Ibid., 199, 200.
98. John C. Bennett, "Christian Ethics and Social Policy," in *Social Christianity: A Reader*, J. Atherton ed. (London: SPCK, 1994) 240–249.

Bibliography

Afolayan, F. 1994. Civil Society, Popular Culture and the Crisis of Democratic Transitions in Nigeria, 1960–1993. Wits History Workshop Papers. http://hdl.handle.net/10539/7493.

Agbiji, O.M., and I. Swart. 2013. Historical Sources of Christian Religious Leadership Ideology: Implications and Challenges for Social Transformation in Post-military Nigeria. *Studia Historiae Ecclesiasticae* XXXIX (1): 221–246.

Ayantayo, J.K. 2010. Prosperity Gospel and Social Morality: A Critique. In *Creativity and Change*, ed. D.O. Ogungbile and A.E. Akinade, 201–216. Lagos: Malthouse Press.

Bennett, J.C. 1994. Christian Ethics and Social Policy. In *Social Christianity: A Reader*, ed. J. Atherton, 225–254. London: SPCK.

Bird, F. 1979. The Pursuit of Innocence: New Religious Movements and Moral Accountability. *Sociological Analysis* 40 (4): 355–346.

Cameron, W. 2004. Public Accountability: Effectiveness, Equity, Ethics. *Australian Journal of Public Administration* 63 (4): 59–67.

Chitando, E., A. Adogame, and B. Bateye. 2013. Introduction: African Traditions in the Study of Religion in Africa: Contending with Gender, the Vitality of Indigenous Religions, and Diaspora. In *African Traditions in the Study of Religion, Diaspora and Gendered Societies*, ed. A. Adogame, E. Chitando, and B. Bateye, 1–12. Farnham: Ashgate.

Economic and Financial Crimes Commission (EFCC). 2015. *EFCCALERT! Economic and Financial Crimes Commission* 4 (1). Available: https://efccnigeria.org/efcc/images/EFCC_Alert.pdf. Accessed 25 June 2015

Ferrari, S. 2011. Religion and the Development of Civil Society. *International Journal for Religious Freedom* 4 (2): 29–36.

Graveling, E. 2010. Marshalling the Powers: The Challenge of Everyday Religion for Development. In *Development and Politics from Below: Exploring Religious Spaces in the African State*, ed. B. Bompani and M. Frahm-Arp, 197–217. London: Palgrave.

Green, R.M. 1983. Religion and Morality in the African Traditional Setting. *Journal of Religion in Africa* XIV (1): 1–23.

Hauerwas, S. 1973. The Self as Story: Religion and Morality from the Agent's Perspective. *Journal of Religious Ethics* 1: 73–85.

Human Rights Watch (HRW). 2011. Corruption on Trial? The Record of Nigeria's Economic and Financial Crimes Commission. *Human Rights Watch*. Available: http://www.hrw.org/sites/default/files/reports/nigeria0811WebPostR.pdf. Accessed 25 June 2015.

IGI Global. 2013. Tech and Ethics: The Decline of Morality in the Digital Age. Available: http://www.igi-global.com/newsroom/archive/tech-ethics-Adecline-morality-digital/1501/. Accessed 7 July 2015.

International Theological Commission. 2009. In Search of a Universal Ethic: A New look at the Natural Law. Available: http://www.vatican.va/roman_curia/congregations/cfaith/cti_documents/rc_con_cfaith_doc_20090520_legge-naturale_en.html. Accessed 10 June 2019.

Kalu, O.U. 2010a. African Protestant Theology. In *Religions in Africa: Conflicts, Politics and Social Ethics*, The Collected Essays of Ogbu Uke Kalu, ed. W. Kalu, N. Wariboko, and T. Falola, vol. 3, 3–10. Trenton: Africa World Press.

———. 2010b. Faith and Politics in Africa: Emergent Political Theology of Engagement in Nigeria. In *Religions in Africa: Conflicts, Politics and Social Ethics*, The Collected Essays of Ogbu Uke Kalu, ed. W. Kalu, N. Wariboko, and T. Falola, vol. 3, 11–30. Trenton: Africa World Press.

———. 2010c. Poverty and Its Alleviation in Colonial Nigeria. In *Religions in Africa: Conflicts, Politics and Social Ethics*, The Collected Essays of Ogbu Uke Kalu, ed. W. Kalu, N. Wariboko, and T. Falola, vol. 3, 179–200. Trenton: Africa World Press.

Koenig, H.G. 2009. Research on Religion, Spirituality, and Mental Health: A Review. *Canadian Journal of Psychiatry* 54 (5): 283–291.

Kolade, C. 2001. Corruption in Africa: Causes, Effects, and Counter-Measures. In *Faith in Development: Partnership Between the World Bank and the Churches of Africa*, ed. D. Belshaw, R. Calderisi, and C. Sugden, 79–87. Oxford: Regnum.

Kung, H. 1997. *A Global Ethic for Global Politics and Economics*. London: SCM Press.

Mack, S. 2013. The Effects of Technology on Moral Development. Available: http://www.ehow.com/list_5898835_effects-technology-moral-development.html. Accessed 7 July 2015.

Madonsela, T. 2013–2014. Secure in Comfort: Report on an Investigation into Allegations of Impropriety and Unethical Conduct Relating to the Installation and Implementation of Security Measure by the Department of Public Works at and in Respect of the Private Residence of President Jacob Zuma at Nkandla in the KwaZulu-Natal Province. Report No: 25 of 2013/14. Available: http://www.publicprotector.org/library%5Cinvestigation_report%5C201314%5CFinal%20Report%2019%20March%202014%20.pdf. Accessed 25 June 2015.

———. 2014. Statement by Public Protector Adv. Thuli Madonsela During a Media Briefing to Release the Report on an Investigation into Allegations of Impropriety and Unethical Conduct Relating to the Installation and Implementation of Security Measure by the Department of Public Works at and in Respect of the Private Residence of President Jacob Zuma at Nkandla in the KwaZulu-Natal. Available: http://www.publicprotector.org/media_gallery/2014/Nkandla%20Statement%20by%20Public%20Protector%2019%20March%202014.pdf. Accessed 25 June 2015.

Magesa, L. 1999. Theology of Democracy. In *Democracy and Reconciliation: A Challenge for African Christianity*, ed. L. Magesa and Z. Nthamburi, 117–134. Nairobi: Acton Publishers.

Manus, C.U. 1984. The Nigerian Schools: Towards National Morality. *Religious Education* 79 (2): 212–228.

Mbiti, J.S. 1999. *African Religions and Philosophy.* 2nd ed. Oxford: Heinemann.

Mills, G. 2010. *Why Africa Is Poor and What Africans Can Do About It.* Johannesburg: Penguin Books.

Niebuhr, R. 1994. The Conflict Between Individual and Social Morality. In *Social Christianity: A Reader*, ed. J. Atherton, 197–224. London: SPCK.

Nthamburi, Z. 1999. Theology and Politics in Africa. In *Democracy and Reconciliation: A Challenge for African Christianity*, ed. L. Magesa and Z. Nthamburi, 135–162. Nairobi: Acton Publishers.

O'Brien, J. 2004–2005. Ethics, Probity, and the Changing Governance of Wall Street: Cure or Remission? *Public Integrity* 7 (1): 43–56.

Ocheje, P.D. 2002. Refocusing International Law on the Quest for Accountability in Africa: The Case Against the "Other" Impunity. *Leiden Journal of International Law.* 15: 749–779.

Okafor, E.E. 2009. Combating High-Profile Corruption in Transitional Societies: Overview of Experiences from Some African Countries. *Anthropologist* 11 (2): 117–127.

Oladesu, E., A. Avwode, and L. Salaudeen. 2013. EFCC: Ten Years After. *Nigeria Intel.* Available: http://wwwnigeriaintel.com/2013/09/18/efcc-ten-years-after/. Accessed 25 June 2015.

Olupona, J. 2010. Forward. In *Creativity and Change*, ed. D.O. Ogungbile and A.E. Akinade, XI–XV. Lagos: Malthouse Press.

Patey, E. 1988. *For the Common Good: Morals Public and Private.* Oxford: A. R. Mowbray.

Ramirez, J.M. 2005. Peace and Development in Africa. *International Journal on World Peace* XXII (3): 51–73.

Siegman, A.W. 2006/1962. On Religion and Probity. *Religious Education* 57 (2): 132–160.

Tavory, I. 2011. The Question of Moral Action: A Formalist Position. *Sociological Theory* 29 (4): 272–293.

The International Bank for Reconstruction and Development/The World Bank. 2003. Millennium Challenges for Development and Faith Institutions.

Transparency International Report. 2014. Transparency International Corruption Perception Index, 2013. Available: http://www.ey.com/Publication/vwLUAssets/EY-Transparency-International-Corruption-Perceptions-Index-2013/$FILE/EY-Transparency-International-Corruption-Perceptions-Index-2013.pdf. Accessed 25 June 2015.

Turaki, Y. 1999. *Christianity and African Gods: A Method in Theology.* Potchefstroom: University of Potchefstroom.

Van der Walt, B.J. 2003. *Understanding and Rebuilding Africa: From Desperation Today Towards Expectation for Tomorrow.* Potchefstroom: Institute for Contemporary Christianity in Africa.

Vorster, J.M. 2012. Managing Corruption in South Africa: The Ethical Responsibility of Churches. *Scriptura* 109: 133–147.

Walls, A.F. 2011. World Christianity, Theological Education and Scholarship. *Transformation* 28 (4): 235–240.

World Bank/CAPA. 2001. Common Ground and Common Concerns: Communiqué of the CAPA–World Bank Conference. In *Faith in Development: Partnership between the World Bank and the Churches of Africa*, ed. D. Belshaw, R. Calderisi, and C. Sugden, 7–16. Oxford: Regnum.

Zulu, P. 2013. *A Nation in Crisis: An Appeal for Morality.* Cape Town: Tafelberg.

CHAPTER 29

Religion and Social Justice in Africa

Patrick Kofi Amissah

Introduction

There is a diversity of conception of social justice in Africa. This is due to the continent's heterogenous historical, traditional, political and religious experiences. Also, since Africa is not a homogeneous people, her religious and cultural practices vary. Again, Africa's current situation transcends any trajectory of her history, with the composite combination of all her experiences coming to bear on any subject, including social justice. From their origins of indigenous culture and religion, through their encounter with the slave trade, Christianity, colonization and Islam, the people of Africa have wrestled with different understandings and practices of religion, tradition, culture, politics and society, all of which have impacted on the current understanding and execution of social justice. It is therefore appropriate to approach the subject of religion and social justice in Africa from multiple angles. This chapter examines how social justice is perceived in Africa in relation to religious practices, including traditional religion and other non-indigenous religions such as Christianity. Scholars have focused on the positive view of religious and traditional social justice but neglected the challenges that cast a slur on the same. The chapter first explores two of three major approaches to social justice in Africa and continues to examine issues of social injustice that pose challenges to religion and social justice in twenty-first-century Africa.

At the background of this chapter is a field research on social justice in Ghana using interviews (including focus groups) and news materials from both the electronic and print media. The interview involved 77 Ghanaians from all walks of life, including heads of churches, academics and social commentators. The research identified three main views of social justice in Ghana.[1] First, the

P. K. Amissah (✉)
School of History, Archaeology and Religion, Cardiff University, Cardiff, UK

© The Author(s) 2020
N. Wariboko, T. Falola (eds.), *The Palgrave Handbook of African Social Ethics*, https://doi.org/10.1007/978-3-030-36490-8_29

traditio-cultural approach to social justice focuses on communal living and responsibility. Second, and closely related to the traditio-cultural view, social justice, from the religious point of view, is a divine responsibility for the welfare of members of the community. Finally, the socio-economic angle perceives social justice in the light of the equitable distribution of resources, human rights and equality and where political leadership, the judiciary and other state institutions are the custodians of social justice. Though these three perceptions of social justice can be identified separately, they are not necessarily independent of each other and the administration of social justice in Africa today is a composite of all three. Social justice in twenty-first-century Africa is, therefore, the recognition of the fact that each individual has a divine responsibility to use the resources and power at their disposal to enhance harmonious communal relationships, to ensure the well-being and fair treatment of all people and to empower the vulnerable to become self-sufficient and able to support the community. The selection of religious and traditio-cultural approaches to social justice for the purposes of this chapter is because both perspectives are rooted in the indigenous African way of life which hardly separated religion from culture and life in general. In *The Wiley-Blackwell Companion to Religion and Social Justice*, Robert M. Baum discusses religion and social Justice among the Diola[2] of Senegal, Gambia and Guinea-Bissau. In the same publication, Brigid M. Sackey and T. John Padwick deliberate on various social justice issues that have been impacted by religion in Africa. Also, Nimi Wariboko adequately explores the African concept of social justice in *The Depth and Destiny of Work: An African Theological Interpretation*.[3] These excellent works provide a platform for generalizing the conclusions on traditional and religious approaches to social justice in Ghana for a wider African context.

Religious Approach to Social Justice in Africa

A discussion on religion and social justice in Africa requires a survey of what religion is in the African context. Gerrie ter Haar has defined religion for the African as: 'a widespread belief in an invisible world, inhabited by spiritual forces or entities that are deemed to have effective powers over the material world'.[4] These spiritual forces include an ultimate power that is transcendent, generally referred to as the supreme being[5] but given a specific name in every African culture and language, such as *Onyankopon* among the Akan in Ghana, *Olorun* among the Yoruba in Nigeria and *Emitai*, among the Diola of Senegal, Gambia and Guinea-Bissau. In their daily living, regarding their occupation, community and leadership, Africans have a sense of this spiritual other who is supreme and in control of all affairs. This is coupled with the belief in spirits, smaller gods and ancestors who form part of the daily consciousness of every African community. How this belief translates to religious rituals and ceremonies differs from community to community.

African religious rituals and ceremonies differ from one community to another and, for that matter, scholars of African traditional religion have varied approaches to understanding religion in Africa. For instance, while it is generally accepted that there are many religious systems in Africa,[6] J. S. Mbiti underscores that these numerous religious practices are underlined by a singular philosophy,[7] for which reason both rites and ethics are used by the African to express religious experience.[8] This makes religion innate, inalienable and part of everyday life of the African,[9] providing 'answers to the stirring of the human spirit' and elaborating 'on the profundity of the experience of the divine-human encounter...'.[10]

The importance of religion in the execution of social justice in Africa lies in the fact that to the African, religion itself unifies the society. Following J. S. Krüger et al.'s emphasis on religion as unifying the African community, Beyers draws attention to the premium placed on the individual within the community in traditional African religion, expressed in the strong bonding that exists between people, their extended families, their clans or tribes, the ancestors, nature and God.[11] This bonding may extend to 'the mineral world'[12] and the 'coming generations'.[13] The far-reaching effects of this communal solidarity facilitated by a unifying religion give the African identity, and ensure continuity and interdependence among members of the community.[14] Laurenti Magesa points out that, for Africans, 'the universe is perceived as an organic whole' and that in African religion, 'humans maintain the bond between the visible and invisible spheres of the universe'.[15] Beyers asserts the interconnectivity of every sphere of life for the African and how religion becomes part of that interconnectivity, with no distinction between the physical and the spiritual. Here, religion expresses unity, celebrates unity and reveals reality.[16] Thus, since the African takes seriously the role of these spiritual beings in everyday life, their influence on the fortunes and stability of the community and their capacity to promote harmonious social relationships, African social justice must be understood against the backdrop of religion.[17]

Thus, with the role of religion in social justice in view, Africans perceive social justice in terms of a divine responsibility towards members of the community.[18] This perception stems from a composite consideration from both traditional religion and other non-indigenous religious movements. Here, while biblical teachings become the yardstick for social justice among Christians, practitioners of the traditional religion and those who hold indigenous beliefs 'in a supreme being who is all-powerful and who sees to ordering justice in the world'[19] also influence social justice. A Ghanaian proverb, which means 'when God makes a judgement on a dispute, no human being can alter it', could be claimed by all religions in such communities as the pillar for social justice. Thus, social justice in these Ghanaian and African communities is based on the supreme justice of God. In addition to its own indigenous understanding of the justice of God, the twenty-first-century African approach has also been influenced by the African encounter with the Bible and Christianity.

Every African community believes that when there is a harmonious relationship between the community, on the one hand, and their gods, ancestors and the supreme being, on the other hand, and among themselves, the community will prosper. Baum confirms that in Diola communities: 'Throughout the day, at the foundation of all social interaction is the quest for this harmonious relationship with Emitai, lesser spirits, the land, one's neighbours, and one's family'.[20] Also, Brigid M. Sackey writes that in most African communities, 'It is believed that the spiritual world rewards good human conduct with abundant rain, harvests, children, and general prosperity, and punishes adverse conduct with drought, famine, infertility, and misfortune'.[21] Thus, when the community fails to 'maintain harmonious relations with humans and other beings', according to T. John Padwick, blessings from the creator God will be blocked and numinous punishments will be executed by the spiritual world to the detriment of the welfare of the people, including sicknesses, loss of political power, unemployment and poverty.[22] To avert these disasters, each community and its leaders imposed taboos and prohibitions on many aspects of life to ensure proper conduct. To Sackey, this shows that 'the administration of justice was the duty of both spiritual entities (deities) and human entities (chiefs and family elders)'.[23] The role of deities in regulating social relationships and behaviour to ensure social justice is seen in the imposition of obligations by spirit shrines in African communities. When one violates such obligations, the spirit shrines afflict such wrongdoers with diseases, including leprosy, which could affect anyone in the family of the wrongdoer who benefited from the theft. The African also believed that ultimately, 'the Supreme Being judges the moral worth of individuals when they die and determines the nature of their afterlife'.[24]

James N. Amanze proposes four moral principles that permeate all African pursuit of social justice. The first is the sanctity of human life, expressed through the directive that no person can murder, torture, torment and wound another person. This affirms 'right to life, safety and free development...'. The second is the right to own property, expressed by 'the moral principle that no one has the right to rob or dispossess in any way another person of his or her property'. The third is truthfulness, which expresses itself through forbidding the telling of lies. The fourth is sexual purity, proscribing sexual promiscuity and expecting human sexuality to be 'expressed and fulfilled in a loving relationship in accordance with societal norms ...'.[25] These principles may sound modern, yet they have been embedded in the African consciousness of a fair society throughout the ages.

It should be noted that all the above ideals of social justice have been deformed and transformed through the different historical, economic, political and religious trajectories. Sackey points to the conflict that ensued as these traditional African social justice ideals came into contact with Christianity and colonialism.[26] An example is what Padwick refers to in Kenya, where 'the missionary encouragement of nuclear families and of an educated and upwardly mobile middle class...was regarded as destructive of communal values'. To fight this off, Kenyans demanded 'community building and the redistribution of surplus resources among the poor...'.[27] In the traditional religious spheres, people rose up to challenge the destruction of the African traditional and religious way of life that protected the welfare of the people through the harmonious community relationships. An example is what Baum calls 'prophetic visions of social justice', which emerged through the springing up of Diola traditional religious prophets who, in the twentieth and twenty-first centuries, stood up against colonial powers and the political agenda to destroy the traditional approach to social justice. These prophets introduced 'ethical critique of the colonial and postcolonial situation' and challenged the colonial political, agricultural, economic and social reforms as causes of drought and scarcity and sought to bring society back to practices that were sanctioned by the supreme being to maintain prosperity.[28]

Despite the challenges posed by foreign religious movements and the resistance they were met with, non-indigenous religions, notably Christianity and Islam, have firm roots and influence on the religious landscape of modern Africa. Twenty-first-century deliberations on religion and social justice in Africa can thus no longer be limited to the influence of African traditional religion and culture. They must take into consideration the influence of foreign traditions and religions that made their entrance into Africa before, during and after colonization. Throughout the ages, Africans who converted to or were born into Islam and Christianity have expressed these religions in their own unique African ways. It may therefore be right to assert that the overall execution of social justice in twenty-first-century Africa has a multifaceted religious influence.[29]

J. Kwabena Asamoah-Gyadu reiterates the duty felt by Christians in Africa to ensure fairness and justice, guarantee that people will have enough to eat, to secure justice for the poor and marginalized and to treat all persons with dignity. In addition to direct involvement in providing suitable material interventions in people's lives, the Church in Africa must 'use her prophetic voice to challenge conditions of systemic poverty caused by the abuse of power and misuse of resources that lead to social injustices'.[30] Through the provision of education, health care, personal economic development initiatives and advocacy against bad economic practices and political governance, and in favour of poverty alleviation programmes, most churches in Africa have sought to ensure social justice. Unfortunately, some Christian leaders abuse their authority, reduce the vulnerable among their flocks into objects of exploitation and behave as if they have access to the resources of their members. Asamoah-Gyadu also notes the unfortunate 'failures in love on the part of the church in certain parts of the continent' which resulted in 'the proverbial African traditional sense of community and care for neighbours' breaking down and church buildings becoming 'locations of ethnic cleansing instead of places of refuge and protection for those under attack'.[31] These and others raised in the 'Challenges' section make any talk of social justice from the religious point of view very difficult.

Traditio-Cultural Approach to Social Justice in Africa

What is described here as the traditio-cultural approach to social justice in Africa predates Africa's encounter with the slave trade, Christianity, colonization and Islam. It is the home-grown approach to the well-being of all African communities which suffered stigmatization, demonization and censure, through the ages, but which has survived and transcended these attacks. This approach to social justice is anchored on the traditional African belief in and practices of communal living, where privileges and responsibilities of belonging to a community are enshrined in the sharing of resources and burdens by all. Even in the modern globalized world where the individual is at the centre, the ethos of sharing resources as a community still thrives in most African societies.

Social justice in Africa is adequately summed up in Nimi Wariboko's description of justice among the Kalabari community: 'A man is considered just if the moral impact of his practical activities and his exercise of all other virtues contribute to the good of the community…'.[32] The other virtues which a socially just African needs to exercise include piety towards the community and respect for the environment. The rest are friendship and relationship building among members of the community, and forgiveness as a means of reconciliation to arrest the failures and betrayals that threaten the well-being of the community.[33] Wariboko agrees with Peter J. Paris that such a community-oriented social justice '…requires a basic structure of inclusive equality, wherein the well-being of all the community's members is assured'.[34] Thus, in the tradition and culture of the African, social justice is accessed through the community. The African person's life, identity, sustenance and well-being are expressed by his or her belongingness to a community. Wariboko underscores this when he writes: '…the Kalabari person cannot be understood apart from his or her relationship to the community'. To this end, a person is endued with capacities such as right to life, spirituality, education, practical wisdom and property ownership, to enable him or her to participate fully in the life of the community.[35]

My research in Ghana confirmed my childhood experience where children in what is called 'compound house'[36] in Ghana were given food to eat whether their parents were at home or not. This was because of the sharing culture and communal living. Baum demonstrates that meal sharing during feasts and sacrifices is one means by which Africans ensure social justice. This obligation to share the family bounty with neighbours is underpinned by the maxim: 'when one had no food, one's neighbour would provide'.[37] This communal sharing culture expresses the African traditional and cultural view of social justice in most indigenous African communities where families share their resources, including food, clothing and even land, among themselves. This guarantees that no one is left without adequate resources. Here, social justice is seen as 'a condition for the possibility of community living',[38] which is achieved when 'people in the society feel that there is a sense of belonging'.[39]

The traditional African approach to social justice places the responsibility on the 'larger family to take care of one another', beginning with the family, to the larger but homogeneous community that shared the same ancestry and cultural values.[40] The community elders and/or the traditional ruler stepped in[41] when matters of both justice and support went beyond the capability of the family and the homogeneous community. A Ghanaian proverb which means 'when the eye cries the nose is also affected' aptly emphasizes the interconnectivity in traditional African communal living. Thus, social justice for the community was expressed in shared responsibility for the survival of all members and in ensuring that everybody's needs, or problems, were everyone else's. Clearly, therefore, as Gyekye forcefully avers, though African tradition recognizes individuality and its worth, it focuses, individual actions and successes, on community interest.[42] For that matter, an individual who acquired wealth beyond his/her needs must be seen to fulfilling the social, moral and biological obligations of supporting those who did not acquire enough wealth.[43] In traditional African societies, as Asamoah-Gyadu rightly contends, 'a wealthy individual who does not pursue communal interests is considered a worthless person and such people are not even "beatified" as ancestors when they pass away'.[44] Julius Nyerere once argued that 'in African primal culture, nobody starved, either for food, or human dignity, because he lacked personal wealth; he could depend on the wealth possessed by the community of which he was a member'.[45] Strategically, African traditional societies ensure equity by debarring the sale of land for money. This is because the land 'enabled people to eke out a living…' and the ancestors who were custodians were 'keen to ensure that those with large swathes of it did not deny the poor access to land for economic survival'.[46] For most African communities, social justice concerns focus, among other things, on the 'expectations that people will be generous with their own goods and with their time, helping their neighbours and their community'.[47]

Traditio-cultural social justice in Africa is anchored on the spiritual and physical well-being of the people and the community. In Ghana, the Dangme[48] traditional vision of social justice, known as *kplɔkɔtɔ* (well-being), is achieved when, among other things, '…there is contentment and harmony, peace and progress; where no man is an island to himself, but each is part of the other, what affects one, affects all'.[49] Baum's explanation of the term *cashumaye*, the Diola expression closest to social justice, complements the above. *Cashumaye* means 'all things good, a correct relationship with the supreme being…, as a result of a peaceful and harmonious life'.[50] Julius Nyerere used the term ujamaa (familyhood and equality) to describe the concept of African social justice that emphasizes the building of a society where every member has equal rights and opportunities. Ujamaa further describes a community in which all lived in peace, where none suffered or imposed injustice, where no one was exploited and where the gradual increasing basic level of material welfare for everyone superseded any individual pursuit of luxury.[51] For Alyward Shorter, 'Social justice, in traditional Africa was…intended to contribute to social stability, and harmonious relationships'.[52] Brigid M. Sackey affirms this when she writes that 'Traditional African social justice seeks first and primarily the well-being of the larger community…'.[53] Amanze also writes that at its highest level, the systems that promote social justice in indigenous African communities have the potential of fostering peace, cohesion and unity because they are primarily built on the understanding that the 'happiness of one is the happiness of all'.[54] This collective sense of responsibility, reward and benefit, as Baum rightly asserts, underlies African concepts of social justice, where 'one is one's brother's keeper'.[55] The South African concept of 'ubuntu', which emphasizes humanity as a community that exists together and that acts towards each other in other to achieve the universal bond of sharing that connects all humanity, sits right at the centre of traditio-cultural social justice in Africa. Sackey rightly emphasizes the 'sense and practice of community as well as a readiness for reconciliation and friendship' embedded in 'ubuntu', promoting peace and stability in the community.[56] The traditional African believes in the 'we' rather than the 'I', such that replacing 'I' with 'we', means that even 'illness' could become 'wellness'. Thus, the African 'I am because we are' is the bedrock of social justice that ensures harmony in society and well-being of all its members. The focus on 'economic equality, gender complementarity, respect for the elderly, generosity, hard work, and cooperation'[57] makes African indigenous social justice attentive to community cohesion and harmony. Thus, the African cultural and/or traditional social justice is at odds with modern Western social justice, which, according to John Rawls, stressed the inviolability of each person, which even the welfare of society as a whole could not override.[58]

Relationship defines traditio-cultural and religious social justice among the people of Africa. Mercy Amba Oduyoye rightly underscores this when she writes: 'It is the quality of relationships rather than power or prestige that informs the daily encounter of the traditional African…'[59] Traditional African communities are interconnected, and people define their identity and survival in terms of their relationships with other people in the community. It is expected that members of the community will treat one another equally, especially those who are from different social statuses. To this end, the traditional African understanding of social justice focuses on how communities come together to settle disputes, restore broken relationships and mobilize resources to help the vulnerable. Restoring the waning communal life of African communities, therefore, could enhance social justice.

CHALLENGES

Many scholars, as discussed above, have emphasized the innumerable strengths of traditional social justice in Africa, such as forging cohesion, nurturing strong communities, protecting the vulnerable through sharing resources and preserving natural resources through the norms and taboos. However, not much has been done to highlight the difficulties that make it impossible to totally trust the traditional African community to ensure social justice. Patriarchy, poverty and gender inequalities are examples of practices and issues in twenty-first-century Africa that cast a slur on traditional and religious social justice.

First, most African communities are patriarchal and hierarchical, with the father figure being dominant and authoritative.[60] Children and women must know their place and not question the status quo. The Ghanaian adage which means 'an elderly person does not plead guilty in the presence of a young person' or 'a superior does not plead guilty in the presence of a subordinate' means that when the perpetrator of injustice is a person of authority, hardly will he/she face the consequence. This has resulted in many high-ranking members of the community suffering nothing for perpetrating injustice. Rape offences, for instance, are settled by the family in order to prevent shame. Again, traditional leaders are regarded sacral, and though they are supposed to serve their people, they lay claim to powers and privileges, which sometimes lead to them coveting other people's properties. This limits the extent to which the traditional and religious approaches to social justice can guarantee fairness for all, especially the vulnerable.

Second, poverty in Africa is a challenge to the traditional religious approach to social justice. In an indigenous African community, poverty is not social injustice, because family and friends support those trapped in poverty. In primal African communities, where poverty and affluence existed side by side,[61] material poverty was not a problem if one had significant relationships.[62] Among the Igbo of Nigeria, when one produces less than enough to exchange for what he/she needs, it is referred to as *ubiam*, which is material poverty. However, if a person cannot afford daily bread and lacks kinship support, relations, family network and social security, the situation is *ogbenye*, abject poverty.[63] This is similar to *assoukatene* (a person without cattle), among the Diola.[64] However, such a person could bounce back as long as there are family and friends to lend him a cow and other resources. Thus, in Africa, '…A person is not regarded as poor as long as the kinship system with its coterie of extended family remains functional'.[65] Again, contrary to the accusation that the poor in Africa are lazy, incompetent and apathetic, my personal encounter with people caught up in the vicious web of abject poverty in Ghana and other African countries proves that they are hard-working. They struggle in rural and urban communities, doing all kinds of menial jobs just to earn a living. They spend each day and night working, amassing all their skills, knowledge and abilities to ensure the survival of themselves and their dependents. Their abject poverty is surely not due to lack of diligence or ingenuity. They are pauperized by the unfair treatment and less deserving rewards for their effort. They are poor because their surpluses are taken away from them, for very little or nothing. For example, that coconut seller, who sleeps by his goods throughout the night, who struggles to bring his goods to the city but cannot generate an economic or living wage from his sale, is not sluggish, but hard-working. He is poor because the system is unjust. If the socio-economic system gives him his due, he will not be poor. The street hawkers and petty traders are all industrious people who have fallen victims to an unfair socio-economic scheme. The tragic reason why poverty has become a major social justice issue even in indigenous African communities, therefore, is the unrelenting occurrence of inequitable distribution of national resources and the inauspicious socio-economic environment, which have rendered most people poor beyond the capability of the community support network.[66] This socio-economic dysfunction renders ineffective the social network and support, which irrespective of the extent of individual lack of material wealth, could stem the tide of poverty in Africa.

The increasing pauperization of the human person and society in Africa, therefore, constitutes the biggest challenge to African traditional religious communities and other non-indigenous religious missions. Poverty significantly challenges Christian stewardship in Africa.[67] Poverty alleviation must thus be an integral part of the future of Christianity in Africa,[68] because the faith of most poor people in Africa is a strategy for survival, a sense of community and source of hope.[69] Thus, as the presence of Christianity continues to grow in Africa, the Church must place poverty alleviation and wealth creation on top of its agenda.[70] This demands that religious organizations, such as the Church, should reconfigure their role in social justice by going beyond handing out aid, to advocating for proper economic policies and effective social interventions that involve the poor themselves and to holding political leaders to account.

Another issue in Africa that has negative implications for religious and traditional social justice is gender insensitivity and inequality. This manifests in acts of social injustice against women and girls, such as female genital mutilation (FGM), shrine slavery and widowhood rites. In most African cultures, when a woman loses her husband, she is forced to undergo humiliating, oppressive and inhuman cultural practices and, in most cases, is left to fend for herself and her children without being allowed to inherit any of her late husband's estate.[71] Among the Gà, Akan, Ewe and other tribes in Ghana, a widow is confined and made to wear black clothes during a period of mourning. At dawn, she could be forced to bathe in a stream[72] or in the sea.[73] In some communities, the women in the family of the deceased mix other herbs with pepper and bathe the widow with it.[74] I fail to agree with George, I. K. Tasie's claim that 'widowhood rites in Africa were not primarily designed to de-womanize African womanhood or impoverish and oppress women...[but] intended for the overall good of the widow'.[75] Drawn from the experience of widowhood rites among the Isiokpo in the Niger Delta of Nigeria, Tasie explains the ordeals that African widows go through, deferring to the religious, superstitious and traditional benefits of warding off the spirit of the dead man from the widow.[76] However, using Uganda as an example, Leda Hasila Limann rightly demonstrates that 'the rights of widows in many African countries are constantly being abused through the practice of widowhood rites'.[77] Rose Korang-Okrah and Wendy Haight have shown that it is rather the widows' resilience and support from social networks that help them to bounce back[78] and that it is the widows themselves who survive by resisting oppression.[79] There is no doubt that the very community that, through its religious and cultural practices, must protect the widow is indulging in practices that deprive her of her human rights, dignity and self-esteem.

FGM is another unjust means by which women and girls are put through ordeals in Africa. According to the United Nations Children's Fund (UNICEF),[80] FGM still takes place in 29 countries worldwide, 24 of which are in Africa. FGM is an excruciating ordeal, resulting in permanent physical, psychological and physiological damages, with life-long suffering for its victims. Religious and traditional champions of FGM justify it as part of ancestral beliefs and rites, designed to preserve the woman's virginity by diminishing her sex drive and the consequent temptation to have sex before marriage. Yet, while FGM oppresses and dehumanizes women, it at the same time promotes male dominance and superiority. Oduyoye is therefore right that FGM is a response to the needs of men, which women are socialized to meet. To her, many mothers reluctantly but inevitably force their daughters to go through the ordeal of FGM because they live in a society where 'marriage and childbearing define women and where a woman would not be married without circumcision'.[81] Furthermore, the negative health impacts of FGM on its victims and the attendant medical complications are numerous, including: infections such as tetanus, human immunodeficiency virus (HIV) and hepatitis B, as unsterilized sharp instruments are used. Indeed, FGM negatively affects the dignity of women and violates their fundamental human rights. Instead of protecting the well-being of women and girls, these same cultures and religions are justifying discrimination against girls by practising FGM.

One more unjust practice in Africa that oppresses women is traditional shrine slavery that deprives victims of all their human rights and dignity. Known as *trokosi* (slave of the gods) among the Ewes in Ghana, Benin and Togo, it is an important part of the traditional religious justice system, whose custodian is the priest of the local shrine. When a crime (such as murder, rape, adultery and theft) is detected, the priest consults the gods, who will reveal the family and the person responsible for that crime. To atone for the crime, the family must provide a virgin girl to serve the gods at the shrine, without which an untold misfortune could befall the whole family or the whole community. E. K. Quashigah sees *trokosi* as unimaginable and dehumanizing slavery.[82] Asamoah-Gyadu's assertion that the practice of shrine slavery falters in maintaining fundamental human rights[83] is thus right. Here again, the very communal and collective living that is meant to secure the well-being of the people has become the means of endangering the lives of young virgins in the community.[84] In the attempt to restore and maintain harmonious community relationships, the powers of the gods are invoked to deter people from committing a crime. However, the abuse of the rights of the innocent virgin is social injustice.[85] Mercy Amba Oduyoye aptly acknowledges how African sociocultural norms such as widowhood rite, FGM and shrine slavery, '…demand submissive and subordinate behaviour of women', turn them into '…easy victims of violence' and predispose them to accept violence without challenge. Oduyoye writes: 'When I look at the model in which religion has cast women, the psychological binds of socioeconomic realities that hold us in place, our political powerlessness, and the daily diminution of our domestic influence by Western-type patriarchal norms, I call what I see injustice. No other word fits...'.[86]

Conclusion

The chapter has discussed the role religion, both traditional and non-indigenous, plays in social justice in Africa. Since religion is an integral part of the life of the people of Africa, the well-being of every African community is influenced by its traditional and religious practices. However, the African experience of religion has gone through various stages and challenges, including colonization and the influence of modern religious movements such as Christianity and Islam. It has thus been recommended that religion and social justice in twenty-first-century Africa must be viewed in the light of how African traditional religion and indigenous lifestyle ensure a harmonious relationship among the people, the supreme being and other territorial spirit beings and how they maintain the welfare of the community. However, they must acknowledge how these traditions and religions have been deformed and transformed through their encounter with Christianity and Islam during and after the colonial days. While Africa's traditions and religions aim at communal living, guided by morals and ethics that ensure fruitful relationships and support to the vulnerable, foreign religions, such as Christianity, also ensure social justice both through their teachings and provision of social amenities and support to communities. These and many other issues of religion and social justice in Africa have been highlighted in many scholarly works as sighted above. However, the negative effects of traditional and indigenous religious practices, such as FGM, widowhood rites and shrine slavery and the effects of poverty on achieving social justice need more research. Future scholarship must, thus, examine thoroughly how religion and social justice in both traditional and twenty-first-century Africa can be maximized to eliminate the spate of injustice that bedevils Africa today. It must also systematically explore the challenges of some traditional religion in Africa and the behaviour of other religious movements that inhibit the smooth execution of social justice.

Notes

1. See P. K. Amissah, *Justice and Righteousness in the Prophecy of Amos and their Relevance to Issues of Contemporary Social Justice in Ghana* (Online, London: King's College London, 2016), https://kclpure.kcl.ac.uk/portal/files/51215526/2016_Amissah_Patrick_Kofi_0848210_ethesis.pdf [Accessed 20 November 2018].
2. The Diola are a minority community in southern Senegal and Gambia and north-western Guinea-Bissau.

3. Nimi Wariboko, *The Depth and Destiny of Work: An African Theological Interpretation* (Trenton, Africa World Press, 2008).
4. G. ter Haar, *How God Became African: African Spirituality and Western Secular Thought* (Philadelphia, University of Pennsylvania Press, 2009), 1.
5. See K. Gyekye, *African Cultural Values: An Introduction* (Accra, Sankofa Publishing Company, 1996), 3.
6. L. Magesa, *African Religion: The Moral Tradition of Abundant Life* (Maryknoll, New York, 1997), 16; J. S. Mbiti, *African Religions and Philosophy*, Second Edition (London, Heinemann, 1989), 1.
7. Mbiti, *African Religions and Philosophy*, 2.
8. J. Beyers, 'What Is Religion? An African Understanding', *HTS Theological Studies 66.1* (2010), 1; T. Sundermeier, *Only Together Can We Live: The Humanity of Black African Religions* (Gütersloher Verlagshaus Gerd Mohn, Gütersloh, 1990).
9. See Gyekye, *African Cultural Values*, 3–5.
10. K. A. Opoku, 'African Traditional Religion: An Enduring Heritage', in J.K. Olupona & S.S. Nyang, eds. *Religious Plurality in Africa: Essays in Honour of J. S. Mbiti* (Berlin, Mouton de Gruyter, 1993), 67.
11. J. S. Krüger, *Along Edges: Religion in South Africa: Bushmen, Christian, Buddhist* (Pretoria, University of South Africa, 1995), 38; see Beyers, 'What Is Religion?', 5.
12. Sundermeier, *Only Together Can We Live*, 22.
13. S. A. Thorpe, *African Traditional Religions: An introduction* (Pretoria, University of South Africa, 1991), 120.
14. Beyers, 'What Is Religion?', 6.
15. Magesa, *African Religion*; Mbiti, *African Religions and Philosophy*, 52, 72.
16. Beyers, 'What Is Religion?', 6.
17. Beyers, 'What Is Religion?', 7.
18. Amissah, *Justice and Righteousness*, 124.
19. Amissah, *Justice and Righteousness*, 181.
20. R. M. Baum, 'Religion and Social Justice among the Diola of Senegal, Gambia, and Guinea-Bissau', in *The Wiley-Blackwell Companion to Religion and Social Justice*, ed. M. D. Palmer and S. M. Burgess (Chichester, Blackwell Publishing Limited, 2012), 350.
21. Brigid M. Sackey, 'Colonialism' in *The Wiley-Blackwell Companion to Religion and Social Justice*, ed. Michael D. Palmer and Stanley M. Burgess (Chichester, Blackwell Publishing Limited, 2012), 457.
22. T. John Padwick, 'Abundant Life or Abundant Poverty? The Challenge for African Christianity' in *The Wiley-Blackwell Companion to Religion and Social Justice*, ed. Michael D. Palmer and Stanley M. Burgess (Chichester, Blackwell Publishing Limited, 2012), 472.
23. Sackey, 'Colonialism', 457.
24. Baum, 'Religion and Social Justice', 352.
25. James N. Amanze, 'The Global Ethic And African Conceptions Of Social Justice, Law And Order: An Appraisal', *Boleswa* 4/3 (2017), 7–16 @ 9–10.
26. Sackey, 'Colonialism', 457.
27. T. John Padwick, 'Abundant Life or Abundant Poverty? The Challenge for African Christianity' in *The Wiley-Blackwell Companion to Religion and Social Justice*, ed. Michael D. Palmer and Stanley M. Burgess (Chichester, Blackwell Publishing Limited, 2012), 335–42.

28. Baum, 'Religion and Social Justice', 357–9.
29. See Mohammad Saeed Bahmanpour and Heiner Bielefeldt, *The Politics of Social Justice: Religion Versus Human Rights?* (2002), https://www.opendemocracy.net/democracy-europe_islam/article_689.jsp, accessed 31 October 2018.
30. J. Kwabena Asamoah-Gyadu 'Poverty, Wealth and Social Justice in Africa', *Religions* (2012), 56.
31. Asamoah-Gyadu 'Poverty', 59.
32. Wariboko, *The Depth and Destiny of Work*, 133.
33. Wariboko, *The Depth and Destiny of Work*, *132–133*.
34. Peter J. Paris, *The Spirituality of African Peoples* (Minneapolis, Minnesota, Fortress Press, 1994), 153.
35. Wariboko, *The Depth and Destiny of Work*, 132.
36. A compound house in Ghana is a shared house with a unique architecture that allows many nuclear families to live in one house, occupying different rooms but sharing common facilities and spaces other than bedrooms.
37. Baum, 'Religion and Social Justice', 355.
38. Interview, Ghana, 14 August 2014.
39. Interview, Ghana, 8 August 2013.
40. Interview, Ghana, 8 August 2013.
41. See Sackey, 'Colonialism', 457.
42. K. Gyekye, *The Unexamined Life: Philosophy and the African Experience* (Legon, Sankofa Publishing, 2004), 56.
43. Kofi Appiah-Kubi, 'The Akan Concept of Human Personality', in *Traditional Religion in West Africa*, ed., E. A. Adegbola (Accra, Asempa Publishers, 1983), 261; Magesa, *African Religion*, 2.
44. *Asamoah-Gyadu*, 'Poverty', 58.
45. See Ogbu U. Kalu, *Clio in a Sacred Garb: Essays on Christian Presence and African Responses 1900–2000* (Trenton, NJ, Africa World Press, 2008), 56.
46. *Asamoah-Gyadu* 'Poverty', 57.
47. Baum, 'Religion and Social Justice…', 351.
48. The Dangme people are part of a bigger ethnic group called Gà-Adagme in the Greater Accra and Eastern Regions of Ghana.
49. J. N. Kudadjie, *Moral Renewal in Ghana: Ideals, Realities, and Possibilities* (Accra, Asempa Publishers, 1995), 1.
50. Baum, 'Religion and Social Justice …', 350.
51. Julius K. Nyerere, *Ujamaa: Essays on Socialism* (London, Oxford University Press, 1968). See Sackey, 'Colonialism', 465.
52. Alyward Shorter, 'Concepts of Social Justice in Traditional Africa', *Pro Dialogo Bulletin* 12:32–51 (1977).
53. Sackey, *'Colonialism'*, 457.
54. Amanze, 'The Global Ethic', 15.
55. Baum, 'Religion and Social Justice…', 352.
56. Sackey, 'Colonialism', 457.
57. Baum, 'Religion and Social Justice…', 353.
58. John Rawls, *A Theory of Justice* (Cambridge, Massachusetts, The Belknap Press, 1971), 3.
59. M. A. Oduyoye, *Daughters of Anowa: African Women and Patriarchy* (Maryknoll, New York, Orbis Books, 1995a), 132.
60. Interview, Ghana, 12 February 2014.

61. John Iliffe, *The African Poor: A History* (Cambridge, Cambridge University Press, 1987).
62. Padwick, 'Abundant Life or Abundant Poverty?', 469–70.
63. Kalu, *Clio in a Sacred Garb*, 60–63.
64. Baum, 'Religion and Social Justice…', 354.
65. Kalu, *Clio in a Sacred Garb*, 60–63; see Engelbert Mveng, 'Impoverishment and Liberation: A Theological Approach for Africa and the Third World', in *Paths of African Theology*, ed. R. Gibellini (Maryknoll, NY Orbis Books, 1994), 144–165.
66. See Padwick, 'Abundant Life or Abundant Poverty?', 472. See also John De Coninck, 'Furthering an African Perspective on Social Justice: East Africa Social Justice Group', in *African Perspectives on Social Justice*, ed., Sarah Tangen, (Kampala, Friedrich-Ebert-Stiftung, 2013), 4.
67. Asamoah-Gyadu, 'Poverty', 59.
68. Kalu, *Clio in a Sacred Garb*, 58.
69. Deryke Belshaw, Robert Calderisi and Chris Sugden, *Faith in Development: Partnership Between the World Bank and the Churches of Africa* (Oxford, Regnum, 2001), 3.
70. Asamoah-Gyadu, 'Poverty', 56.
71. M. M. Tei-Ahontu, *Widowhood Rites in the Ga Traditional Area of Accra-Ghana: A Review of Traditional Practices Against Human Rights* (Norway: Norwegian University of Life Sciences, 2008), 39–57. Accessed 10 November 2018. http://www.umb.no/statisk/noragric/publications/master/2008_michael_martey_teianhontu.pdf
72. M. A. Oduyoye, 'Women and Ritual in Africa', in *The Will to Arise: Women, Tradition, and the Church in Africa*, eds. M. A. Oduyoye and M. R. Kanyoro (Maryknoll, New York: Orbis Books, 1995b), 15.
73. Tei-Ahontu, *Widowhood Rites in the Ga Traditional Area*, 42.
74. E. Ardayfio-Schandorf, *Violence Against Women: The Ghanaian Case*, presented at An Expert Group Meeting Organized by the UN Division for the Advancement of Women (Accra, Ghana: United Nations, 2005). See Tei-Ahontu, *Widowhood Rites in the Ga Traditional Area*, 57.
75. G. I. K. Tasie, 'African Widowhood Rites: A Bane or Boom for the African Woman', *International Journal of Humanities and Social Science* (2013), 155–162.
76. Tasie, 'African Widowhood Rites, *158–160*.
77. Leda Hasila Limann, *Widowhood Rites and the Rights of Women in Africa: The Ugandan Experience* (Kampala, Makerere University, 2003), 61.
78. Rose Korang-Okrah and Wendy Haight, 'Ghanaian (Akan) Women's Experiences of Widowhood and Property Rights Violations: An Ethnographic Inquiry', *Qualitative Social Work* (2014), 1–18.
79. Rose Korang-Okrah, *Risk and Resilience: Ghanaian (Akan) Widows and Property Rights* (Urbana, Illinois, University of Illinois, 2011), 1; Rose Korang-Okrah, *Widowhood and Resilience: Akan Widows Experiences of Challenges and Survival* (a paper presented at NACSW Convention, 2012).
80. UNICEF, *29 Countries, More than 125 Million Girls and Women*, https://www.google.co.uk/url?sa=t&rct=j&q=&esrc=s&source=web&cd=12&cad=rja&uact=8&ved=2ahUKEwjogY7l0sreAhWMKcAKHahSAGwQFjALegQIARAC&url=https%3A%2F%2Fwww.unicef.org%2Fspanish%2Fprotection%2Ffiles%2F00-

FMGC_infographiclow-res.pdf&usg=AOvVaw0tlaPhkRbNhp8hViNZROPX, accessed 10 November 2018.
81. Oduyoye, 'Women and Ritual in Africa', 165.
82. E. K. Quashigah, 'Religious Freedom and Vestal Virgins: The Trokosi Practice in Ghana', *JICL*, 10 (1998), 193–215, at 199.
83. J. K. Asamoah-Gyadu, 'Of "Sour Grapes" and "Children's Teeth": Inherited Guilt, Human Rights, and Processes of Restoration in Ghanaian Pentecostalism' in *Exchange*, 33 (2004), 334–53 at 346.
84. See J. Egbas, *Trokosi: How Girls Are Donated to Shrines as Sex Slaves in Ghana*, https://www.pulse.ng/news/local/how-girls-are-donated-to-shrines-as-sex-slaves-id8384101.html (2018), accessed 9 November 2018.
85. Amissah, *Justice and Righteousness*, 220.
86. M. A. Oduyoye, *Daughters of Anowa: African Women and Patriarchy* (Maryknoll, New York, Orbis Books, 1995a), 157.

Bibliography

Amanze, J.N. 2017. The Global Ethic and African Conceptions of Social Justice, Law and Order: An Appraisal. *Boleswa* 4 (3): 7–16.
Amissah, P. K. 2016. *Justice and Righteousness in the Prophecy of Amos and Their Relevance to Issues of Contemporary Social Justice in Ghana*. London: King's College London. https://kclpure.kcl.ac.uk/portal/files/51215526/2016_Amissah_Patrick_Kofi_0848210_ethesis.pdf. Accessed 20 Nov 2018.
Appiah-Kubi, K. 1983. The Akan Concept of Human Personality. In *Traditional Religion in West Africa*, ed. E.A. Adegbola. Accra: Asempa Publishers.
Ardayfio-Schandorf, E. 2005. *Violence Against Women: The Ghanaian Case, Presented at an Expert Group Meeting Organized by the UN Division for the Advancement of Women*. Accra: United Nations.
Asamoah-Gyadu, J.K. 2004. Of "Sour Grapes" and "Children's Teeth": Inherited Guilt, Human Rights, and Processes of Restoration in Ghanaian Pentecostalism. *Exchange* 33: 334–353.
———. 2012. Poverty, Wealth and Social Justice in Africa. *Religions* 2: 55–69.
Bahmanpour, M. S., and Bielefeldt, Heiner. 2002. *The Politics of Social Justice: Religion Versus Human Rights?* https://www.opendemocracy.net/democracy-europe_islam/article_689.jsp. Accessed 31 Oct 2018.
Baum, R.M. 2012. Religion and Social Justice Among the Diola of Senegal, Gambia, and Guinea-Bissau. In *The Wiley-Blackwell Companion to Religion and Social Justice*, ed. M.D. Palmer and S.M. Burgess, 350–360. Chichester: Blackwell Publishing.
Belshaw, D., R. Calderisi, and C. Sugden. 2001. *Faith in Development: Partnership Between the World Bank and the Churches of Africa*. Oxford: Regnum.
Beyers, J. 2010. What Is Religion? An African Understanding. *HTS Theological Studies* 66: 1.
De Coninck, J. 2013. Furthering an African Perspective on Social Justice: East Africa Social Justice Group. In *African Perspectives on Social Justice*, ed. Sarah Tangen, 4–11. Kampala: Friedrich-Ebert-Stiftung.
Egbas, J. *Trokosi*. 2018. *How Girls Are Donated to Shrines as Sex Slaves in Ghana*. https://www.pulse.ng/news/local/how-girls-are-donated-to-shrines-as-sex-slaves-id8384101.html. Accessed 9 Nov 2018.

Gyekye, K. 1996. *African Cultural Values: An Introduction*. Accra: Sankofa Publishing.
———. 2004. *The Unexamined Life: Philosophy and the African Experience*. Legon: Sankofa Publishing.
Iliffe, J. 1987. *The African Poor: A History*. Cambridge: Cambridge University Press.
Kalu, O.U. 2008. *Clio in a Sacred Garb: Essays on Christian Presence and African Responses 1900–2000*, 56. Trenton: Africa World Press.
Korang-Okrah, R. 2011. *Risk and Resilience: Ghanaian (Akan) Widows and Property Rights*, 1. Urbana: University of Illinois.
———. 2012. *Widowhood and Resilience: Akan Widows Experiences of Challenges and Survival*. A Paper Presented at NACSW Convention.
Korang-Okrah, R., and Wendy Haight. 2014. Ghanaian (Akan) Women's Experiences of Widowhood and Property Rights Violations: An Ethnographic Inquiry. *Qualitative Social Work*: 1–18.
Krüger, J.S. 1995. *Along Edges: Religion in South Africa: Bushmen, Christian, Buddhist*. Pretoria: University of South Africa.
Kudadjie, J.N. 1995. *Moral Renewal in Ghana: Ideals, Realities, and Possibilities*. Accra: Asempa Publishers.
Limann, L.H. 2003. *Widowhood Rites and the Rights of Women in Africa: The Ugandan Experience*. Kampala: Makerere University.
Magesa, L. 1997. *African Religion: The Moral Tradition of Abundant Life*. Maryknoll: Orbis Books.
Mbiti, J.S. 1989. *African Religions and Philosophy*. London: Heinemann.
Mveng, E. 1994. Impoverishment and Liberation: A Theological Approach for Africa and the Third World. In *Paths of African Theology*, ed. R. Gibellini, 144–165. Maryknoll: Orbis Books.
Nyerere, J.K. 1968. *Ujamaa: Essays on Socialism*. London: Oxford University Press.
Oduyoye, M.A. 1995a. *Daughters of Anowa: African Women and Patriarchy*, 132. Maryknoll: Orbis Books.
———. 1995b. Women and Ritual in Africa. In *The Will to Arise: Women, Tradition, and the Church in Africa*, ed. M.A. Oduyoye and M.R. Kanyoro, 9–24. Maryknoll: Orbis Books.
Opoku, K.A. 1993. African Traditional Religion: An Enduring Heritage. In *Religious Plurality in Africa: Essays in Honour of J. S. Mbiti*, ed. J.K. Olupona and S.S. Nyang, 67–82. Berlin: Mouton de Gruyter.
Padwick, T.J. 2012a. Abundant Life or Abundant Poverty? The Challenge for African Christianity. In *The Wiley-Blackwell Companion to Religion and Social Justice*, ed. Michael D. Palmer and Stanley M. Burgess, 472. Chichester: Blackwell Publishing.
———. 2012b. Abundant Life or Abundant Poverty? The Challenge for African Christianity. In *The Wiley-Blackwell Companion to Religion and Social Justice*, ed. Michael D. Palmer and Stanley M. Burgess, 335–342. Chichester: Blackwell Publishing.
Paris, P.J. 1994. *The Spirituality of African Peoples*. Minneapolis: Fortress Press.
Quashigah, E.K. 1998. Religious Freedom and Vestal Virgins: The Trokosi Practice in Ghana. *JICL* 10: 193–215.
Rawls, J.A. 1971. *Theory of Justice*. Cambridge, MA: The Belknap Press.
Sackey, B.M. 2012. Colonialism. In *The Wiley-Blackwell Companion to Religion and Social Justice*, ed. Michael D. Palmer and Stanley M. Burgess, 456–468. Chichester: Blackwell Publishing.

Shorter, A. 1977. Concepts of Social Justice in Traditional Africa. *Pro Dialogo Bulletin* 12: 32–51.

Sundermeier, T. 1990. *Only Together Can We Live: The Humanity of Black African Religions*. Gütersloh: Gütersloher Verlagshaus Gerd Mohn.

Tasie, G.I.K. 2013. African Widowhood Rites: A Bane or Boom for the African Woman. *International Journal of Humanities and Social Science* 3: 155–162.

Tei-Ahontu, M.M. 2008. *Widowhood Rites in the Ga Traditional Area of Accra-Ghana: A Review of Traditional Practices Against Human Rights*, 39–57. Norway: Norwegian University of Life Sciences. http://www.umb.no/statisk/noragric/publications/master/2008_michael_martey_teianhontu.pdf. Accessed 10 Nov 2018.

Ter Haar, G. 2009. *How God Became African: African Spirituality and Western Secular Thought*. Philadelphia: University of Pennsylvania Press.

Thorpe, S.A. 1991. *African Traditional Religions: An Introduction*. Pretoria: University of South Africa.

UNICEF. 2018. *29 Countries, More than 125 Million Girls and Women*. https://www.google.co.uk/url?sa=t&rct=j&q=&esrc=s&source=web&cd=12&cad=rja&uact=8&ved=2ahUKEwjogY7l0sreAhWMKcAKHahSAGwQFjALegQIARAC&url=https%3A%2F%2Fwww.unicef.org%2Fspanish%2Fprotection%2Ffiles%2F00-FMGC_infographiclow-res.pdf&usg=AOvVaw0tlaPhkRbNhp8hViNZROPX. Accessed 10 Nov 2018.

Wariboko, N. 2008. *The Depth and Destiny of Work: An African Theological Interpretation*. Trenton: Africa World Press.

CHAPTER 30

The Spirit Names the Child: Pentecostal Names and Trans-ethics

Abimbola A. Adelakun

My research took me to a church in Ibadan where I was to interview a pastor on the subject of prayer. To start off such sessions, I typically engage in small talk with interviewees before turning on the tape recorder so both of us would be at ease with each other. The pastor told me that he had just concluded a naming ceremony, and merely to keep the conversation going, I asked the name of the child. "Jesutunde," he responded. Jesutunde? I was taken aback by what seemed to me then a strange configuration of names. A name like "Tunde" catalogues the Yoruba/African belief in reincarnation or what might be described as metempsychosis. The name is typically prefixed by Baba (father) or "Ye-" (short for Yeye, mother), and it means that one's father or mother has returned again (to this world from the dead). Ironically, John Mbiti's popular study of African religions specifically used such names with "-tunde" suffix as examples of those ones that demonstrate African religious beliefs. Those beliefs are transposed into names, and they communicate religious values and ethics such as reincarnation and the cyclicality of movement between the worlds of the living and the dead.[1] So, how does a name like Jesutunde square with the Christian/Pentecostal belief in afterlife and does not accommodate the belief in the cyclicality of souls through reincarnation? Is "Jesutunde" an awkward consequence of an attempt to replace the ethical structures that uphold cultural belief in the supernatural by inserting the name and persona of Jesus into indigenous myths or is the name a reflection of a systematized nudge towards transcending those ethical structures?

A. A. Adelakun (✉)
African/African Diaspora Department, University of Texas, Austin, TX, USA

Belief in reincarnation in the traditional African world view is one of the most potent myths in the cultural repertoire. Unlike Christian mythology, they believe that "the posthumous survival of individuality is not for the purposes of a future resurrection of the righteous, a reanimation in the materialistic hereafter, but re-incarnation in a new body."[2] The new body being referred to here is that of a child and, following Wole Soyinka's delineation of the African cosmological imagination into the worlds of the living, the dead, and the unborn, shows the mutual correspondence between these three cosmological spaces.[3] Africans' belief in life after death is part of the reason the culture of ancestral worship and masquerade performances exist. This conviction in reincarnation is also articulated through naming practices. In the past, when a child was born, the parents consulted the diviner to know which ancestor might have "tun de," that is, which one might be making a return trip back into this world. This is where it gets clunky: to construe Jesus as an ancestor in a similar manner as the ones who depart the world of the ancestors to re-enter a child's body would be considered blasphemous. The foundation of Christianity was laid on the myth of the resurrection of Jesus and the eternal life he was imbued with as a result of his triumph over death. Construing him as one of many ancestors, making the rounds from one cosmos to the other, lessens his elevated status as an iconized member of the Trinity/Godhead in a universalized religion, and reduces him to one of the many ancestors in the world of the dead. So, I asked the pastor, by that name, are you suggesting that an already resurrected Jesus could enter into a woman to be reborn again like our Yoruba ancestors believed? Is that not a theological contradiction? No, the pastor shook his head and replied, "Not at all. That name was what the spirit chose for the child. We do not name our children by ourselves, *Emi ni o maa n so omo loruko.*" That is, "it is the *Spirit* that names the child." That last sentence, rendered in Yoruba language, got me thinking further about the spirit and the spirit's underlying political agenda in naming the child a superficially ideologically incoherent name like "Jesutunde"? What kind of identity construct is the spirit urging Pentecostals by giving their children a name that literally superimposes Jesus into a mythic space of African belief? Is the spirit making a radical rewrite of the mythic essence of names or generating the formation of new geographies of meaning through an evolution of a naming subculture? Or, is the spirit creating new religious myths through the substitution of the pantheon gods, ancestors, and their histories with that of Jesus?

In this chapter, I want to proceed to investigate the notion of the *spirit* and the onomastic politics of child naming among contemporary Pentecostal Christians beyond the obvious allusion the pastor makes to the Holy Spirit as the inspirational source of child naming. Various studies have construed the spirit as a stimulating force and demonstration of the eschatological outpouring of the divine into the ethical life of African Pentecostals. This transcendental dynamism meshes into the African social configurations and has raised the question of the possibility of Africans' conception of the Spirit as revelatory of a Christ personality that differs from the actual historical Jesus.[4] Outside

Christian theological studies, spirit relates to spiritism, the study of the phenomena that are suggestive of the links of the spiritual world with the immediate physical one humans inhabit.[5] *Spirit*, in scholarly studies, therefore has multiple thought strands and theoretical exegesis that have built vast estates of interdisciplinary knowledge. "Spirit" has a universal resonance as an incorporeal being, one that is not necessarily anchored to Judeo-Christian religious mythology but as transcendental energy or superhuman agent that can impinge upon or activate the human agency. In Hegelian terms, spirit has also meant human consciousness and the ways it unfolds; the principle or the underlying ethic that animates social consciousness and the spate of actions that ensue. In theological studies, spirit has also meant both the Holy Spirit or the pneumatic force that inspires people and prompts them to take creative action and, also, the immaterial beings that participate in activities on this material plane.[6] These differing notions of the spirit, I acknowledge, sometimes overlap in their engagement as forms of theoretical exegesis and exertions, and they are not cleanly separated as absolute categories. In the following sections, I briefly engage some of its fibrous roots as I walk through contemporary naming practices among Pentecostals.

To proceed in this inquiry of the spirit naming the child, I draw on Clifton Clarke's methodological proposal of the study of African Pentecostalism through an investigating mode he called "call-and-response."[7] According to Clarke, call-and-response is emblematic of African Pentecostalism because it denotes the historical exchanges that have come to characterize Pentecostalism. The "call," he notes, is the authoritative prompting of African Pentecostalism through the Bible as the received Word of God for theological practices; the history of the church delineated into epochs, and whose practices and legacies have framed contemporary Christianity; and also the religio-cultural context that gives African Pentecostalism its distinct flavour. On the other hand, "response" is Africans' reaction to these stimuli through their various performative activities and intense corporeal activity that form the lived theology of their Pentecostalism. Call-and-response is therefore the interaction of the many "transcendences" of Africa: histories—past and present; worlds—human and supernatural; and cultural belief systems—indigenous and appropriations, all of which jumble and are manifested through Pentecostal actions.

Clarke maintains that call-and-response is both dynamic and dialogical, an illustration of a social religious culture that is demonstrative, experiential, uncontainable, highly expressive, and which merges the seen and unseen worlds into a coherent whole. Indeed, call-and-response, as an African(ist) performance method has been deployed as a mode of critical engagement and theoretical exploration in multiple studies of African/Black/Diaspora oral/written performance traditions.[8] This procedural method of interactivity, improvisation, communality, and spontaneous exchange of call-and-response has been variously explored in African(ist) studies of ritual performance, literature, spirituals, and other artistic expressions that are based on orality. Apart from Black traditions, call-and-response has also been used as a critical paradigm in the study of engaged theatre with those studies dwelling on the potentials of the democratic feature of call-and-response to assemble people for social and political reasons.[9] One area where call-and-response remains unexplored, however, is the one where its antiphonal nature is virtually literal: names.

Names are given to be called and for the bearer to respond, except also that in this rather simple and dynamic exchange are dense packages of historical cadences, cultural impulses, and the ethical agenda of the name giver. The name bearer (who might also be the name bearer, as seen in instances of self-renaming) considers the outstretching of his/her social existence as a series of unfolding performance that responds to—or are impelled by—the name called at one's natural birth (or spiritual rebirth). Call-and-response, as metaphor for methodological inquiry, is thus well suited for an analysis of naming practices because names, by their very nature, involve a sketching out of past experiences, conjoined with acquired knowledge and embodied insights, and clobbered to respond to ongoing circumstances. They are implanted into the life of a child who will respond to the name throughout its lifetime. The name tradition, as a cultural universal, is thus considered an important determiner in how one would live his or her life "authentically."[10] The political economy of names is so crucial that it is only a "mad person" who does not care what she/he is called.[11] As Katja Guenther says:

> The act of naming is an act of power. Parents naming children, conquerors naming new lands, and organizations naming themselves all involve the assertion of authority and control. Names allow us to communicate through the development of shared meanings.[12]

In the mythical traditions of the Bible too, one of the clearest demonstrations that God had given man total power and dominion over His creation was the authority he gave Adam to name everything in creation, including the woman. According to the Bible, it was the name he gave them that they are called, a detail that shows that the significance of names goes beyond the invocative or the illocutionary force embedded in their meanings, it also registers the extradiegetic circumstances that determined the choice of the name.[13] Beyond all the political agenda that underlines names and naming practices, names are also given for their malleable qualities that make them fusiable into oral performances such as drumming, *oriki* chanting, and spiritual invocation.[14]

Names are as powerful as described because they evoke an idea, reflect the ecological structures that hold up terms of social relations, familial tensions, and human-divine relationships. Names also measure historical changes, register ethical progressions, and reflect cultural comprehensions of situations and the subsequent systematization. Names touch the "psychic substrates associated with superstition, ritual, irrational belief and primitive behavior."[15] They are an "open diary," in which people both store information about the social order as it is at the time of a child's birth and reinforce such data.[16] Panos Bardis describes names as an "idiom creating event" in human communities.[17]

The rites of naming itself form part of the social processes that reflect the realities and the values of the society—and by "reflect" I echo Bruno Latour to state that these names are not merely a mirror that reflect parallel social events, but that they are constitutive of the fabric that shapes the society.[18] This reality is also expressed in the proverb that says one considers the condition of one's house before one names a child.

In the next sections, I study the spirit and Pentecostal onomastics to argue that contemporary naming practices are a deliberative performative act of response to the call being made by history, the times we live in, and the shaping of their desired Africa through what Lee Edelman describes as "reproductive futurism" (i.e. the belief that all our political actions are motivated by the conviction that we are fighting on behalf of our children's future), all of which are being expressed through the ethos created by a network of multiple Pentecostal names.[19] The name given at birth—whether natural or spiritual—not only represents one's condition, it also shows how the name giver operationalizes the name to trigger the social relations that further speaks to such condition, demands a response, and creates a sequential interaction between the bearer, the society, and their circumstances.[20] Thus, the name imbued on the new life and the future it represents is an investment in the stability or maintenance or, even rarely, the disruption of the ethical balance. African Pentecostal naming practices are illuminative of contemporary myth-making and are a rich site to traipse how names signal the call-and-response of history and culture: the changes being made to language and social thought, the ideological imperatives that undergird the shift in reformulating language, Pentecostal self-making and remaking, the Pentecostal absorption of foreign encounters and subsequent creative inclinations, shifting class values, and the conditions of altering or producing new orthographies for local languages.[21]

African Naming Ethics: Of Histories, Culture, and Performance

A Yoruba proverb expresses the interactive nature of names with a saying that translates: because of people's propensity to run into trouble, everyone is given a name to individuate them. There is also another proverb that says that one's name divines one's life and the events that constitute it. The different ways onomastics are discursively treated in proverbs and folk tales index names as a kind of predictive force or symbolic charm that has power beyond the physical to activate the acts and scenes that form the chain of singular life experiences. Names are not an objectified label that floats above a person so called but are a codification of history and belief imposed on a person at birth so they could be recycled in demotic enactments. Like other religious-based performances such as sharing testimonies in church, names are "a socially situated use of speech that involves rules or norms for its appropriate expression."[22] Names are drawn from culture's repertoire as a performance of being and becoming—that is, what one is hoped to be in future and the string of life experiences that will make one be that expected persona that was determined at birth—that are interpellated by the power of the spoken word. Putting the name of Jesus in their names is thus an objectification of faith and testimony to their expressively living out Jesus' mythic power, glory, and history. The name is the "call" and the unfolding outcome of one's life is the "response."

Since that incident with the pastor at the child-naming ceremony, I have come across other (mostly) Pentecostal Christian names among both Yorubas and even non-Yorubas that have also been prefixed with "Jesu" or other similar iconic Christian symbols, and a lot of them can be—at least on the surface—contradictory of the world view that informs African naming culture. Names like Adajesus (where "Ada" in Igbo language means "first daughter") and Jesurinde (where the -rinde suffix means "to walk back home after a journey") appear as a rather tenuous reconciliation of differing world views. Such contradictions are, however, instructive because their semantic and linguistic outcomes also mark an ongoing historical formation of the interconnection of what has been disparate pieces of theological thoughts into the formation and consolidation of an essentialized African Pentecostal identity. As the example of Jesutunde (or its female variant, Jesuwande as substitute for Yewande) shows, Jesu—the Yoruba word for "Jesus"—prefacing names that symbolize African beliefs about post-life becomes a new aesthetic creation, a hybridization of different religious and cultural myths to shape a new or an emergent frame of references. Pentecostalism, like any other religious movement, absorbs existing forms to create new meanings that answer to questions being evolved by time. This observation has been registered in studies, engaging its features of global and local interfaces, transnationalism, transsubjectivity, and bricolage. While these approaches engage the cross-fertilization of religious subjectivities through the lenses of history and the sociocultural changes that inform and shape new experiences, this chapter is interested in exploring the names as an outworking of the different histories and cultural convergences that have folded into the embodied theology of Pentecostalism and which are being expressed through the trans-ethical formations that play out in "Jesu-" naming practices.

Samson Olanisebe has delineated the three epochs of naming practices in Africa and how the praxis of each has been inflected by Christianity. It the first phase, considerations such as family history, occupation, deity, or circumstances form the basis for the name selection. The earliest Christian converts began to choose Western and "Christian" names to separate themselves from their "heathen" brothers. At the second, that is, the "Ethiopianism phase," cultural nationalism and anti-colonial sentiment drove a number of Africans being socialized into Western/Christian culture to change their attitude to names. From the English/Biblical names, they began to choose names in local language to sound more "native." In the third phase, he shows that African Pentecostals are once again shedding their names of all cultural baggage of familial and historical affiliation, which are considered inimical to their well-being in the world and contrary to their identities as Pentecostals. This time, they are opting for fashioned names that reflect their Christian identity, shed them of all cultural baggage of familial and historical affiliation, which are considered inimical to their well-being in the world and contrary to their identities as Pentecostals.[23] Meanwhile, the people in each of these eras whose gesture towards creating new ethical traditions through the practices of child naming and self-renaming have patterned their agential inclinations according to the Bible narrations where human characters changed their names or chose a name to signify a new era in their social and spiritual relationships. While Olanisebe thinks the latest development of naming practices signals cultural erosions, especially when Pentecostals prefer biblical names that in themselves reflect the names of deities and idols in Ancient Hebrew history, I think the development of naming practices that draws from African history and culture prefixed with Jesus or similar symbols shows another stage in cultural beliefs.

The "Jesu-" names are not only an Africanization of Jesus, but they are also a making of an "African" identity because, in outlook, these names resonate within cultural contexts in a way "Christian" names might never do. They signal the desires of African Pentecostals, having accomplished so much cultural power, to be grounded in their identity as Africans. The offspring of people who have de-linked themselves from their ancestral idols by choosing so-called Western/Christian (or Biblical) names re-establish associations as an act of cultural affirmation and self-retrieval, but they do so within a born-again paradigm. Unlike the times when people combined a Western-derived or biblical first name with a surname in indigenous language, this naming template that fuses in Jesus into the histories coded into onomastic traditions also marks the "X" spot in the grounds of present time, indicating a response to the voice of the spirit calling on Africa and prompting a re-creation and reformulation of the ethical structures that govern public life. That is, apart from the current Pentecostal practice of also giving names allegorical like Vision, Wealth, Testimony, Hallelujah, Miracle, Faith, Glory, Dominion, Power, Blossom, Flourish, Bible, Anointing, Winner, and so on, names in local language that start with "Jesu" are a move towards African authentication. Apart from the historical function they perform, these names are also cultural artefactual texts and because they are practically hand-woven to meet the exigent demands of a new identity, they also signpost Pentecostal creativity.

While a variety of African Christian names are, in fact, a hybridization of identities fused into a coherent whole, the synchronization in name combinations like "Jesutunde" does not merely signal a bridging of disparate belief systems but an attempt to rejoin the African "past" Pentecostalism once enjoined its converts to break away from and might now be said to be making peace and reconciling with their history.[24] This so-called past is not static, and through its dynamism, it keeps catching up with the present culture. This "past" and the social rituals that are expressed through names are now being selectively corralled as means of authenticating their Christian ethical identity as they march towards the future. By choosing names in indigenous language and framing them with Jesus, African Pentecostals are rejoining their shed history, reclaiming their inheritance, and entering the territory they had previously ceded to embrace the promises of modernity Pentecostalism offered. The popularity of the Jesu names shows a grid of practices, an ethical formation but one which is being purposively drawn out as lived through the lives of their children. Contemporary Pentecostal naming patterns, whether dedicatory, allusive, praising, philosophical, metaphorical, assertive, commissive, prophetic, declarative, or descriptive, are all part of the building blocks of the society's order. Names, by their nature, are forms of praises, rewards, highlight, or allusion to certain symbolic references that are either mutually shared or which the party doing the naming hopes to impress on the social system. "Jesu" naming traditions can also be described as "mythic onomastics," a process that stimulates in the imagination, "the primordial functions of names as descriptors of human reality."[25] Thus, names are a creative site for people to perform certain ethics, and for Yoruba people, this is also easy because the malleability of their language means new categories of meaning are easily introduced from existing ones through the use of "prefix to roots, stems, or a given syntactic categories."[26]

To go on in the chapter, I elaborate on the notion of spirit and the praxis of Pentecostal onomastics by starting out with the analysis of the role of name as a particular kind of oratory in the creation and the maintenance of a society's ethical order. The next section therefore engages the notion of the ethical order as spirit and how these dynamics might play out in the context of an African social life. This section takes its illustration on names and the ways they form part of the skeletal system of the ethical order of the society from the African classic novel by Chinua Achebe, *Things Fall Apart*. After that section, I move on to a further conceptual exploration of naming practices by analysing Nimi Wariboko's conception of the spirit as an inherent principle that is both established and also always in the process of formulation. In this section, I engage how a social order, its founding spirit, and its orthodoxy can be reshaped to give way to a new "spirit." Finally, I go to the section where I analyse the Pentecostal names that I gathered during my ethnographic study to argue that the name patterns posit a trans-ethical shift in the African cultural life. Also, sequel to the era where similar patterns index a modernistic aspiration, these names are means of transcending particularities and bringing everything in the African social life to the obedience of Christ.

Names, Metaphysics, and the Balancing of an Ethical Order

My engagement of Hegel's notion of the ethical order is an application of its formulaic presentation of challenging social structures in the bid to study what the balance, disruption, and the renegotiation of human and divine law might look in a context where a character is weighed down by the burden of collective expectations. To illustrate this, I turn to the story of Ekwefi, one of the supporting characters in Achebe's classic, *Things Fall Apart*, who uses the politics of child naming to consciously conscientize the community on her traumatic fate. As said earlier, the names that people bear and the process of naming them are taken quite seriously. Some scholars have noted that the rites of naming a child separate a child from the world of the unborn where she/he sets out from and prefaces one's existence in the physical world with fellow humans. Thus, names are means of bracketing one's life between the worlds where unborn children come from and the worlds where they go when their time on this material plane is over. They anthropomorphize a quintessence and a prefiguration of a future they want to shape through the power of language; performative utterances that are bodied into a living human whose life is expected to unfurl the mythical essence encoded in the name. This section is such an engagement with *Things Fall Apart*. I should note that this text was particularly chosen for its essentialized representation of African life and because literary texts are one of the discursive spaces where an analysis of onomastics frequently occurs to develop an understanding of how names are used as a rhetorical strategy to pass a commentary to the reader in obvious and sublime manner.[27]

According to Chinua Achebe, one can measure how good life has been to an Igbo man through the names he gives to his children.[28] By that, Achebe suggests that names are an invocation of an idea, ideal, memory, prayer, beliefs and histories, autobiographical narrations, expression of individual and collective ethics, articulation of people's anxieties, desires, and prayers, linking of kinship ties, and description of the world as it is or as it should be.[29] As a rendering of speech that conveys not just personal emotions, names also describe how those who give the name contribute to the society's ethos and the structures of their symbolic universe through the performative quality of names. They call out to a society, the society responds, and the response also becomes a call, thus forming a cycle of dialogical engagement between a person and the society. Names are about the only thing we are given or which we acquire that are meant to be used by others and the economy of that use is expressed in the ways they are chosen for the politics they announce, the values they propagate, and the ethics—social and collective—that they curate. Names are a fiction, a product of imagination that is expressed in language, and like all fictions, they forth-tell, perform, and even control.

A subplot in *Things Fall Apart*, Ekwefi's story is the narration of a woman who is unable to fulfil her expected role of motherhood within the social structures of her village. She was plagued with what was known as "ogbanje" children—a rather malevolent set of supernatural beings who are literally born to die. Called "abiku" in Yoruba mythology too, these children's transversal journey from the chthonian realm to the world of the living are made through a near-endless rotations of life and death through the same woman. The abiku-ogbanje phenomenon in southern Nigeria has been a subject of critical exploration of the interface of folk beliefs and modern science and has also been applied as a metaphor for disjunctures in the rites of weaving cultural memories.[30] In the case of Ekwefi, she had borne ten children, and nine of them had died in infancy. According to Achebe:

As she buried one child after another her sorrow gave way to despair and grim resignation. The birth of her children, *which should be a woman's crowning glory*, became for Ekwefi mere physical agony devoid of promise. The naming ceremony after seven market weeks became an empty ritual. Her deepening despair found expression in the names she gave her children. One of them was a pathetic cry, Onwumbiko –'Death, I implore you.' But death took no notice; Onwumbiko died in his fifteenth month. The next child was a girl, Ozoemena – 'May it not happen again.' She died in her eleventh month, and two others after her. Ekwefi them became defiant and called her next child Onwuma – 'Death may please himself.' And he did.[31] (Emphasis mine)

There are two points to note from the world of Umuofia that Achebe describes: one, the society's ethical system is adjusted on clear definition of roles. The men occupy and dominate the public sphere, and this is illustrated by their mode of use of the village square space for associations and public gatherings that border on political and social issues. When women are part of the mix, it is mostly during festive periods or spectacular parades where their participation is relegated to the margins as audience and side commentators. Men are at the top of the hierarchical order, especially if they are rich, physically brave, older, or the three together.

Achebe, in 2008, reflecting on *Things Fall Apart* at its 50-year anniversary, mentioned that Igbo culture premises masculinity and makes a show of all of its trappings—power, strength, and success without giving its feminine side as much chance. This feminine side, however, is there but sublimated into the culture. It speaks with a gentle voice, with vocal cords so soft and so gentle that one has to "make a special effort to listen to hear it."[32] From his reflection, one might therefore conclude that one of the fears that haunted the Umuofia community, and which was viscerally expressed through the actions of the protagonist, Okonkwo, was feminization. Whereas Umuofia would manage the cataclysmic changes that challenged its idea of masculinity with relative prudence and strategic redefinition of its traditional ideals through a re-narrativization of the concept of bravery, Okonkwo's strong-headed wedding to the old ideals proved his tragic flaw—a point Joseph Slaughter makes in his allegorized re-reading of the "simple" tales women weave in their retracted spaces.[33] The narrative landscape of *Things Fall Apart* shows that there was a genuine reason to be wary of feminization. The book is littered with women's appearance on the social stage as subalterns: wives, daughters, mothers, public mothers,[34] ghosts of mothers, goddess and priestess, spectres, children, metaphors and metonyms, and overall, and ironically too, an underlying ethical principle that makes a rather idolatrous gesture towards the supremacy of motherhood. Overall, the women's participation in the Umuofia's ethical order is dependent on the varying dynamics of their domestic and nurturing roles. According to Achebe, a woman's crowning glory is the birth of children, and Ekwefi's failure to successfully sustain the lives of the children she produces has significant consequences for her and her relationship with the society.

This first assertion leads to the second one: in this context, the woman is relegated to the margins, and her worth in the overall social construct is based on her fulfilment of her biological destiny. The space where she exercises herself is mostly the domestic sphere and, consequently, the atomized agency against the inveighing power of the community that she can deploy is through naming her ogbanje children. The names she chooses are a self-reflexive act that cries to not only the metaphysical being responsible for her misery—death, that is—but she also addresses the instinctive ears of the community and the ethical substance that binds her as an individual with her community. In African cultures, it is not unusual to use a child's name to speak to the members of the community to challenge them to live up to collective interests, a trait that J.A. Sofola describes as a form of "moralistic activism."[35] A similar trend was observed by Susan Suzman in her study of changes to the Zulu personal naming practices, although she also noted that the trend is being altered by changes to the family unit such as urban culture and evolving family patterns.[36] Equally, it is noteworthy that Ekwefi's story is similar to that of another character in the Bible, Leah, who also named her children to make a commentary on her existential condition (see Genesis Chapter 29).

Since the ethics of Umuofia rests on the seeds of the family relationships and the larger interconnections of the individual to the society, a childless woman is twice disadvantaged. As a marginalized citizen, one means of appeal to the inhabitants of the ethical order for failing her role in spawning the offspring that will carry forward either the dynamics of the domestic sphere or the political power of the public one—through male and female children, respectively—is the vocalization of her desperation, trauma, agony, pain, and supplications to both the society and the unseen forces that mediate affairs between the various worlds. Her children's names become a moral and an oral performance, an appeal to the conscience of the community who see her suffering and also understand that her displacement in the order of things is beyond her control. As Achebe said in his reflections, in this society that Umuofia represents, material achievements are lauded (or "loud-ed") to the detriment of the subterranean voices from the margins where women occupy. Ekwefi's means of speaking up and cutting through the din of the celebration of material achievement is using child naming, a rhetorical strategy that is implicitly understood by all. As Chima Anyadike said of the politics of the rhetoric deployed through this gentle voice, "the sense of the rhetorical in use here is not so much that of the elaborate and fanciful as that of the effect and persuasive use of language."[37]

For Ekwefi, this weaponization of the politics of names and naming process is a means of sublimation of her failures of her womanly essence into the social order. She is not a threat to the survival of that order because the marriage/family structure is—among other contributing reasons, polygamous—but the order is a threat to her well-being as an individual because where she fails in her duty, her husband's co-wife succeeds. With the co-wife's celebration of multiple sons, Ekwefi's case drives her further on the scale of margins to the level of an unfortunate outlier. It is remarkable that despite the densely patriarchal nature of society she lives in, the practice of naming the ogbanje children was left to her. She uses the oral function of the names to speak to not only the metaphysical forces that have taken her children but also the physical human ears in the community who watch the drama of her life. Through those various names, she expresses her cycles of emotions to them—a mode of communal communication that uses the intangible and subconsciously understood semiotics to narrate the dynamics of fate. Such embodied oral gesture is a moral plea—a call—for them to understand her plight, and respond by bearing with her, giving her fate a chance, and letting her live without the jeers and shame that attend women who cannot fulfil their biological roles. The names represent Ekwefi's astute conceptualization of what is required of her, her failure to live up to it, and her self-conscious appeal to the custodians of the ethical order.

Making Spirit, Transcending Ethics

Since Max Weber's *The Protestant Ethic and the Spirit of Capitalism*, "spirit" has been an important frame of analysis in the study of the dimensional essences of social culture. In the spirit of Weber's study, "spirit" has been used to theorize the ethical structures that make up social cultures, anti-capitalism, neoliberalism, various forms of capitalism, and so on. Spirit has also been applied into the studies of disparate cultural formations and acts such as democracy, violence, mafia, economic behaviour, communalism, individualism, and even transcendentalism. Spirit, as it pertains to these studies, is the moral or ethical armature that defines these social practices, explains the dispositions that are imbibed in the historical processes of cultural formation, and also tracks how the embodiment of a social character provides the impetus for the continued reproduction of certain behaviours. Having described in the previous section how naming practices are important to the social and metaphysical balances of the ethical order, this section explores how those same onomastic acts are also an ideological means of unsettling the ethical order, restructuring its moral framework, and ultimately generating a new spirit through a subtle reconfiguration of what subsists. To go on in this section, I turn to Nimi Wariboko's theory of the spirit to analyse the philosophical means of creating the spirit and how the spirit nudges us towards the directions of collective habits.

Wariboko's theory of the spirit defines the "spirit" as is based on social interactions and human practices, and the emotional energy people generate by working in concert and fixatedly on a common goal. Even though the theory is fashioned from Pentecostal theology, Wariboko takes great pains to explain that this spirit does not have a transcendental dimension, neither does it mean the supernatural or creative pneumatic force to which Judeo-Christian mythology attribute the founding of the world. The spirit here is "the culmination to which all social practices are heading…a kind of *principle* that inheres in organized human activities."[38] While the spirit is contingent on social performances and the "mesh of orders and practices"[39] that unfold creative acts enacted as a collective, its emergence also relies on bodies. The materiality of bodies makes them the connective channel between the spiritual/metaphysical and the physical realm. Bodies, with their unique placements as the anchor point between the spiritual or the social can become spirit—a spirit—when a web of human agents assemble within a clearing to initiate actions that not only dictate a new collective ethic, but by the substance and consistency of their practices, also normalize them. Now, if Wariboko's conceptualization of the theory of the spirit sounds democratic and organic in its generation, it is because the facilitation of this spirit requires a gathering, collective will of assembled bodies, a clearing site, and their mutual sharing.

Wariboko also situates the theory of the spirit between two poles: the antecedent and the consequent natures. For the former, "bodies and minds, and the interconnections between them…are responsible for the site emerging…," while the consequent nature is the "spirit that arises in relation and in response to the dynamics of focused concentration and attunement of humans in the common."[40] Both the antecedent and consequent poles illustrate how the "spirit" might be generated when a mesh of "Jesu" names crop up among a generation of Pentecostals: they build an interconnective network of "Jesu" names that signal to each and every one with similar names and beliefs, and the call-and-response of those Jesu names among the bearers begin to shape the intangible and moral structures of a society. Bearing the name of Jesus becomes means of producing a referential access to both spiritual and social privileges, gradually turning the society into an emergent site where socio-ethical practices take on the Pentecostal *spirit* as its inherent principle. The reconfiguration of the society benefits Pentecostalism because its worship and ritual performances find a conducive and amenable site that helps towards making its practices normative. While, once again, the antecedent and consequent poles between which the spirit generation occurs seem horizontal in nature, there is also the *precedent* of history and the verticality of power relationships that prompts a community and sets in motion a sequence of cultural practices that will lead them to the point where their bodies and minds can coherently form an interconnection.

So, if the spirit is generated as the consequence of focused attunement of social practices and intersubjective relations among people, what are the factors that precede the formation of their subjectivity which they network? If we can agree that the process of the generation of spirit is not always egalitarian in conception and constituted from the bottom-up, what are those extraneous factors that galvanize the subjectivity of people and the spirit they can facilitate when they commune? In other words, what might be the *precedent* to the antecedent and consequent poles between which Wariboko situates the theory of spirit? To answer this question, I turn to history and what it documents about the efforts of Christian colonial missionaries in Africa to change the ethical character of their societies by urging their converts to change their names.

As names are also means through which we try to apprehend, subsume, control, and negotiate wider and abstractive social and ideological spaces, they became a target of those missionaries because they activate various intersubjective relations that irrupt the ethical configurations of a place. For example, colonial modernity used the inscriptive processes of identifying, labelling, and differentiation to rename people, either by giving them new "pronounceable" names to facilitate interaction with European missionaries or because they thought African names stemmed from their pagan heritage that had to be scrubbed off to make the conversion complete.[41] Their mode of urging those converts to a change of name was not always subtle, it was administered through the demonization of their ways, and/or by re-creating the African social site so that access to social services such as education, health, and class benefits are tied to religious conversion and conformity.[42] Those that renamed or chose to rename themselves after their Christian conversion were able to access "new possibilities, new attributes, new values, reshaping ideologies and creating new concepts of the self as well as the redefining the groups from which the self operates" through the "....complex nature of onomastic erasure and de-erasure and the resuscitation of dormant identities."[43]

As personal names also serve a psychic function to the African conception of the self, the self in relation to others, self-esteem, and self-autonomy,[44] the name-changing process amounted to more than a switch in label. The sonant practices of calling the converts by their "Christian" names and the responses their bearer made had far-reaching effects of also varying the ethics of their social cultures. The names became part of the politics of class inclusion and exclusion, and it helped in the constructions of the category of the enlightened Christian against the African heathen. The cultural process triggered by the missionary preceded the changes to the society's ethical structure and made possible—and continually too—the generation of a new religious spirit within the polity. The site that would emerge from the interconnected bodies and minds of those earlier Christians would become the norm, the spirit against which several social and religious relations interchange and conflicts would serially occur through history, and which contemporary Pentecostals are once again redefining through "Jesu" names.

"Christian first names" first became customary for Yoruba Christians (and Muslims) from the nineteenth century to the early twentieth century to signify their severance of ties with their paganistic origins and embrace of a modern culture.[45] In *The History of the Yorubas*, Samuel Johnson spoke extensively about this trend in local culture from a nativist perspective by complaining about the violence modern naming practices were doing to the creativity and epistemic content that are embedded into the culture. He worried about how modernity's preoccupation with arranging things into categories was violently disruptive of how Yoruba people understood naming and lineage tracing. As people adopt the arrangement pattern of first names, middle names, and surnames,[46] they were forcing their own culture into the narrow box of Western modernity's structuration of names and ending up with ridiculous results such as a married woman becoming Mrs Taiwo (a name given to a twin-born) but has no twin in her family and whose husband is not a twin either. Or, a name like "Babarimisa," typically given to a child that was born after the death of the father/patriarch, becomes a surname and transmitted across his generations even while the patriarch was yet alive! Johnson ended his disgust with the trend of civilization and its corruption of Yoruba naming practices with the hope that with education and further enlightenment, people would see that name like "Phillip Jones or Geoffrey Williams" were not more "Christian" than "Adewale or Ibiyemi."[47]

If Samuel Johnson could look back, he would have been amused about the different levels of change that Yoruba names have gone through since then and how education has not totally purged the attitude to change names to reflect social and religious status. Instead, the different epochs of Christianity have produced different attitudes to names—for example, the Aladura movement once triggered a pride in African names,[48] while Pentecostalism resulted in both symbolic and inventive indigenous names. Both developments have shown the integrations of different social and ethical strands and how much they have plumbed the depths of civic organizational structures, the internal divergences of the faith movement, the constituent of the social impulse of the society, and the "underside" of their oral and embodied theology.[49] People do not seem to take any more note of the patterning of their names after a Western style that demands that there be a listing of first, middle, and last names. Instead, social and modern infrastructural politics have adapted to accommodate these changes such that anyone who takes Samuel Johnson's concerns seriously to revert to the "old" ways as far as nomenclature is concerned will be the outlier who will find no space in contemporary society. The precedence of colonialism that triggered both the antecedent and consequent of spirit making gave us a new "call." The "response," through name-changing practice, continues to reproduce the social encounters and the ethical changes as seen in Pentecostal naming practices. In the next section, I give a list of names that are specific to Pentecostal practices and consider how they are part of the project of the formation of new ethics of identity and a re-creation of the cultural site and its values.

The Spirit of the Spirit

For this chapter, my field assistant and I collected over 200 names borne by people who identify as Pentecostals and sieved through them for trends and new directions in naming practices. While our name collections include allusive names like Gospel, Kingdom, Hallelujah, Success, Power, Miracle, Testimony, Dominion, Anointing, Anointed, Divine Heritage, Divine, Overcomer, Abundance, and Prosperity, in the final analysis we had to drop them for two reasons. One, we found that while those names are borne largely by Pentecostals, they are not exclusive to them. In fact, we found an agnostic who had named his children Vision and Power, and he stridently denied that his choice of name had anything to do with the Pentecostal movement. The second reason was that a section of Nigeria, specifically, the Niger Delta area, also has naming practices that are quite similar to those of Pentecostals even though their choice of names does not seem to have a direct correlation to the contemporary Pentecostal movement in Nigeria. Such names include Government, Goodluck, God's power, Chief, God's will, God's child, and so on. As a result, we narrowed our focus on names that loudly proclaim the Christian ethic as the imperative behind the choice, and those are the names that have "Jesu" attached to as either prefix, suffix, or part of the stem. Although a lot of the names collected were first names, we have a substantial number of them that are surnames that have been altered by the bearers. The following chart shows our effort to categorize the names, and because of various reasons of history that we shall explain later in the chapter, the four groups are not as hermetic as demarcated in the chart. Their meanings, origins, and what they attempt to subvert overlap.

A	B	C	D
Jesurinde	Jesutunmise, or Jesutunwase	Jesulayoayemi, or Jesulayomi	Jesutunde
Jesujimi	Olajesu	AgbaraJesu	Jesuwande
Jesugbemi	Jesujimi	Ayanfejesu	Jesujide
Jesugbohun(mi)	Jesufela	Okiki Jesu	Jesujimade
Jesudele	Jesujuwon	Jesutisomiji	Jesudurotimi
Jesuranti	Jesutosin	Jesuloba	Jesujide
Jesumoroti	Jesuwumi	Jesuloluwa	Jesugbeye
Jesugbamila	Jesujomiloju	Abajesurin	Jesudola
Jesutoyinbo	Jesusegun	Obajesu Obanijesu	Jesuwole
Abajesude	Jesulowo	Jesugboromiro	Jesulaja
Jesubunmi	Jesubukunmi	Jesudolapofunmi	Jesugboye
Jesuwale	Jesubukola	Jesudolamu	Jesujaguntolu
Jesugbero	Jokotijesu	Tijesu, or Tijesuni	
Jesutola	Jesusogo	Oreofejesu	
Jesuwole	Jesuwale	Ifejesu	
Jesukeyede	Jesugbolahan	Jesupamilerin	
Jesusina	Olajesu	Jesunipin	
Jesudele	Ifejesu	Jesunitemi	
Jesukoya	Akinjesu	Jesunifemi	
Jesukorede	Wurajesu	Jesuniye	
Jesudiran	Jesuwole	Jesunbo	
Jesudipe	Jesukemi	Jesunbowale	
Jesugboye	Jesusina	Jesudunsin	
Jesufunke	Jesudiran	Jesulolami	
Jesulabi	Jesufunke	Jesudowole	
Jesuloni(mi)	Jesulabi		
Jesugbamila	Jesuniyi		
Jesuniyi	Diekololajesu		
Jesulana	Jesulana		
Jesulola	Jesuseun		
Jesulere			
Jesulokun			
Jesulade			
Jesudairo			
Abajesude			

A. Names that are traditionally associated with deities and lineage gods such as the "Ifa" oracle (and prefixed with "Fa-"), Ogun, Osun, Sango, Oya, Esu, Ore, Orisaoko (prefixed as "So-" as in "Soyinka"), Obaluaye (prefixed as "Oba-" as in Obasanjo), Obatala, Orisha (prefixed as "Osha/Orisha-") but whose monikers have been substituted with Jesu. The names in these categories are both first names and surnames, but mostly the latter. Some of their bearers confirm their names have undergone the process of renaming after their born-again conversion or some other life-altering experiences. They claim various reasons for the change such as divine instructions received directly from God or their pastors/ spiritual leaders encouraging them to disengage from their lineage deities, extricate themselves from negative connections to histories of ancestral and "demonic" worship in their families, and also make a performative disconnection from ancestors whom they—the Pentecostals, that is—are supposed to be incarnates of. Some of the respondents, born to born-again parents, were named with "Jesu" right from their births. Ironically, while some of the bearers of these names have "Jesu" appended to their first names, their surnames still bear evidence of their familial links to Orishas. They said they have kept their surnames intact for various reasons, ranging from not wanting to sever nomenclatural links with family members who will read other meanings into such a move; those who cannot go through the hassle of name-changing and issuance of new documents; those who keep the name for the social capital the family name has accrued in the society; and those for whom surnames do not matter. An example of such combo is a name like Jesugbemi Fajemirokun.

B. Names that were originally associated with certain ideals such as "Ola" (wealth)…"ibi" (birth), and so on…*but which have been overridden by Jesus*. This category is rather expansive because some of the names that were modified or implanted with "Jesu" here are similar in construction with the names in category A. For instance, as there is "Falola," there is also "Omolola." For those in this category who renamed themselves or gave their children "Jesu" names, much of their reason stemmed from the jadedness of the traditional prefixes listed earlier. Traditionally, Yoruba Christians have always been inventive with the language when it comes to naming practices unlike their Muslim counterparts for whom (indigenized) Arabic names have largely served as "Muslim" names. Names such as "Oluwasegun" (God—i.e. the Christian one—triumphs) and "Oluwatobiloba" (God is great a king) are traditionally Yoruba Christian names; they are peculiar to Christian converts who carved such names as indigenous expression of their faith ethic. However, the "Jesu" angle is a more recent development and a culture that will be self-reproducing for many years. They are the generations of those who have grown up and given their children names with "Jesu" because, according to some of our respondents, prefixes like "Olu/wa," "Ola," and

"Omo" are jaded "nambiguous," and no longer distinguish them from Muslims or even nominal Christians.[50] Jesu, they say, has more edginess to its proclamation of their faith, and people know where you belong when they hear the name.
C. Names that are newly created by Pentecostals and do not seem to have any traditional precedent. These "Jesu" names simply seem showier and overtly partisan in appearance. They are also proclamative of Jesus and the gospel. Like one of our respondents told us, his father gave him the name "Jesutobi" purely by a divine instruction, which came at a time they were celebrating the birth of what his father thought would be his second and last child. These names, like Biblical names, are thought to be both definitive and distinguishing.[51]
D. Names that depict circumstances surrounding the birth of the child on which had been superimposed "Jesu," thus giving a different meaning to the names. In this category are names that were previously abiku names or depicted a situation around when a child was born but has now been usurped with "Jesu." For instance, a name like "Durotimi" (Stay with me) is a mother's plea to an abiku/ogbanje child not to die. Another example is Dairo (make this one stay), which is sometimes rendered as Fadairo, or Ogundairo. When these names are added with Jesu, they take on an entirely new meaning that overshadows their etymological origins as a plea to supernatural power to intercede in repeated cycles of child deaths. A name like "Jesudurotimi" now becomes "Jesus stays with me" while Jesudairo becomes "Jesus made this one stay." Also, in this category are names like "Otegbeye" (Conspiracy/strife becomes a thing of honour) and "Omolaja" (this child has come to reconcile warring factions) that become Jesugbeye and Jesulaja, respectively. Some of the respondents in this category claimed that the names had no link to how they were traditionally expressed, they just coined it because it suited them or suited their circumstances.

Overall, we made several conclusions from the pattern of names that have "Jesu" in them. One is their tendency towards monotheism, a development that erases the diversity of Orishas and lineage deities in Yoruba land. From the examples of names in category A where there were a number of references to Orishas such as Ogun, Oya, Osun, Oba, Sango, and Esu, what we now see is a replacement of these deities or a trans-valuation of their ethical essences recalibrated through a monistic and singularized notion of God and stylistically subsumed under the name of Jesus. On the one hand, their name construction invokes the idea or the belief that a transcendental force inheres in them and the capability of such a force is drawn out in their lives. On the other hand, those who bear such names also engage in a public act of self-deification. They apotheosize themselves but not merely as a miniaturized version of Jesus or the Christian God but also to conjure the myth in others that they share in his divinization, the transforming capabilities of his power and the glory, and, overall, derive the social and supernatural blessings that accrue from being named with the name of Jesus.

While some scholars that I have consulted in the course of this chapter consider the "Jesu" pattern an erasure of indigenous culture, particularly the ones that substitute the local gods with Jesus, Pentecostal onomastics is also the transcendence of the aspects of the structures of African ethics that are founded on names and naming traditions. In the world of the Yoruba people where different gods coexist, what we see is a widening of the pantheon of the gods to accommodate Jesus as one of their gods. Pentecostal Christians might disagree that Jesus is merely another god in a pantheon and, instead, argue that he is *the* God. However, because he takes the place that the gods have traditionally occupied in Yoruba names, Jesus too becomes another mythic figure born from the imagination of the spiritual. In the same vein, names that depict family professions and similar characteristics such as found in names such as "Ayan-" (for a family of drummers) or "Ode-" (for a family of hunters) or "Oje-" (for a family entrusted with egungun masquerade traditions) no longer feature in these patterns. The same development is true for the names that are called amutorunwa (literally names given from heaven but means names that have self-selected prior to birth such as the ones given to twins). In fact, as one of the respondents told me, her "Jesu" name is an amutorunwa name because the inspiration for the name came directly from "heaven above." In her conception, heaven has shifted from the Yoruba idea of where the gods of the pantheon, unborn children, and immaterial beings reside to the Christian one occupied by the Trinity—God the father, son, Holy Spirit, and other celestial beings.

Another observation is that there are no more names registering negativity, despair, rebellion, criticism, or even expressing disappointment using proverbial language. For instance, it was not uncommon for Yorubas to have names like "Fatanmi" (Ifa deceived me), "Matanmi" (Do not deceive me), "Ebisemiju" (The family offended me too much), and "Bekolari" (Things did not go as expected). Jesu names are either determinedly constructed as an act of prayer and which is constantly activated each time the child's name is mentioned, or they are descriptive of the joy of worshipping Jesus. None of the names we came across was critical of the Christian God/Jesus for whatever reasons as can be found in traditional indigenous names. The curious one, however, was the Fatoyinbo surname that was changed to Jesutoyinbo. While some arguments do arise on the meaning of Yoruba names and their recondite meanings lost to time, development of writing, and the tonality of language, Fatoyinbo is translatable to means "Ifa is equal to, or up to the level of the white man," a line of thinking that has been attributed to the kind of relationship "natives" had with the colonial officers. By implication, Jesutoyinbo means that Jesus is being equated to the white man! However, one defence of such choice by the name bearer is that the translation is less important than the banner of Jesus they bear alongside the name. Thus, the semantic content of the name is not so much in the meaning but in the politics of choice behind the selection.

Conclusion

This chapter was a quest to find out the agenda of the "spirit" in naming a child with the name of Jesus such as "Jesu-" names, a practice that is observed to be fast-growing among the Pentecostals of contemporary era. My preoccupation is to find the broader implications of such practices for African social ethics. To properly situate the study in theoretical and theological context, I have worked with the framework of "call-and-response" that was proposed by Clifton Clarke. The choice of call-and-response is based on many reasons, and one of them is its resonance with African performance traditions. In this chapter, I have found call-and-response a particularly useful methodology because its ouroboros cycle of responsiveness speaks to the Pentecostal practice of naming their children with Jesus names. As shown throughout the chapter, names are part of the ethical substrates and the incorporeal materials that form the character of a society and also a measure of a culture's progression through its historical impulses. By tending towards "Jesu" names, Pentecostals, empowered by the spirit who names their children through divine inspiration, nudges them towards transcending the ethical life and culture of their societies and fashioning the one where Jesus and all it represents becomes the norm. This transcendence, I must note, is not uncontended, neither is it a merely placid process of revising social ethics. What has made the challenge far muted and not evoke the ire people witness when their ethical space is being reconfigured is that names are primarily a personal possession before they are a community ownership. As such, individuals can give themselves or their children "Jesu" names in their bid to demonstrate their faith and cannot be defied by those who understand and oppose the underlying agenda behind these names and the traditions they signal.

Appendix

Jesulayoayemi: Jesus is the joy of my life
Jesutunde: Jesus has arrived again
Jesutunmise: Jesus has refurbished my lot
Jesurinde: Jesus has walked back (on foot) (to this world)
Ayanfejesu: the beloved of Jesus
Jesuseun: Thanks to Jesus
Jesuwande: Jesus has sought me out
Jesujide: Jesus has arisen/awoken to come (here)
Jesutunwase: Jesus has refurbished our lot
Jesufela: Jesus spreads wealth
Okiki jesu: The fame of Jesus
Jesugbemi: Jesus has benefitted me
Jesugbemi Fajemirokun
Jesugbohunmi: Jesus heard my voice
Jesudurotimi (abiku name): Jesus stayed with me

Jesudele: Jesus has arrived home
Jesuranti: Jesus remembers
Jesumoroti: Jesus is the one I stand with
Jesujide: Jesus has arisen and arrived
Jesugbamila: Jesus has delivered/saved me
Jesutosin: Jesus is worthy to be worshipped
Jesutoyinbo: Jesus is equivalent to the white man
Jesuwumi: I desire Jesus
Jesujomiloju: Jesus has surprised me
Jesutisomiji: Jesus has quickened me (or animated me)
Jesulowo: Jesus has honour
Jesuloba: Jesus is king
Jesuloluwa: Jesus is Lord
Abajesurin: The one who walks with Jesus
Abajesude: The one who arrives with Jesus
Obajesu: King Jesus
Obanijesu: Jesus is king
Jesubukunmi: Jesus adds to me
Jesubukola: Jesus adds to my wealth
Jokotijesu: Sit with Jesus
Jesusogo: Jesus has made (this) glorious
Jesuwale: Jesus has come home
Jesubunmi: Jesus has given me
Jesugboromiro: Jesus interceded on my behalf
Olajesu: The wealth of Jesus
Ifejesu: The love of Jesus
Akinjesu: Jesus' warrior/champion
Wurajesu: Jesus' gold
Jesuwole: Jesus has entered the house
Jesukemi: Jesus has blessed me
Jesusina: Jesus opens the way
Jesudele: Jesus has come home
Jesukoya: Jesus has rejected suffering (on my behalf)
Jesukorede: Jesus has brought goodness
Jesudiran: Jesus is multiplied across generations
Jesulaja: Jesus has settled the quarrel
Jesudipe: Jesus supplicated (on my behalf)
Jesugboye: Jesus has received honour
Jesufunke: Jesus gave me this one (child) to care for
Jesulabi: We gave birth to Jesus
Jesujaguntolu: Jesus fought the battle like the chief one
Jesulonimi: Jesus is the one that owns me
Tijesu(ni): (This child) belongs to Jesus
Ifejesu: The love of Jesus
Oreofejesu: The grace of Jesus

Jesupamilerin: Jesus made me laugh
Jesunipin: Jesus is my portion
Jesunitemi: Jesus is mine
Jesunifemi: Jesus is my love
Jesuniye: Jesus is life
Jesunbo: Jesus is coming
Jesunbowale: Jesus is coming home
Jesudunsin: Jesus is sweet/pleasant to serve
Jesulolami: Jesus is my joy
Jesuniyi: Jesus has honour
Jesulola: Jesus is wealth
Jesudowole: Jesus laid hands on (this one)
Jesulere: There is gain in Jesus
Jesulokun: Jesus is a vast ocean
Jesulade: Jesus is nobility
Jesudairo: Jesus holds this one down
Jesulana: Jesus paves the way
Abajesude: The one who arrives with Jesus

Notes

1. Mbiti, John S. *Introduction to African religion*. IL: Waveland Press, 2015: 28.
2. Olomola, Isola. "Contradictions in Yoruba folk beliefs concerning post-life existence: The ado example." *Journal des africanistes* 58, no. 1 (1988): 107–118.
3. Soyinka, Wole. *Death and the King's Horseman*. NY: WW Norton & Company, 2002: 7.
4. Ngong, David. "African Pentecostal Pneumatology." Clifton Clarke (Ed.) *Pentecostal Theology in Africa*. Pickwick Publications, Oregon: 2014. Kindle.
5. Vasconcelos, João. "Homeless spirits: Modern spiritualism, psychical research, and the anthropology of religion in the late nineteenth and early twentieth centuries." *On the margins of religion, edited by Frances Pine and João Pina-Cabral* (2008): 14.
6. Anderson, Allan Heaton. *Spirit-Filled World: Religious Dis/Continuity in African Pentecostalism*. Springer, 2018.
    Yong, Amos. "On Binding, and Loosing, the Spirits: Navigating and Engaging a Spirit-Filled World." In *Interdisciplinary and Religio-Cultural Discourses on a Spirit-Filled World*, pp. 1–12. Palgrave Macmillan, New York, 2013.
7. Clarke, Clifton. "Call and Response: Towards an African Pentecostal Theological Method." Clifton Clarke (Ed). "Pentecostal theology in Africa." OR: Pickwick Eugene, 2014.
8. Boan, Devon. "Call-and-Response: Parallel 'Slave Narrative' in August Wilson's The Piano Lesson." *African American Review* 32, no. 2 (1998): 263–271.
    Callahan, John F. *In the African-American grain: Call-and-response in twentieth-century black fiction*. University of Illinois Press, 2001.
    Crawford, Evans E. *The hum: Call and response in African American preaching*. Abingdon Press, 1995.
    Sale, Maggie. "Call and response as critical method: African-American oral traditions and Beloved." *African American Review* 26, no. 1 (1992): 41–50.

9. Cohen-Cruz, Jan. *Engaging performance: Theatre as call and response.* NY: Routledge, 2012.
10. Sarajlic, Eldar. "The Ethics and Politics of Child Naming." *Journal of Applied Philosophy* 35 (2018): 121–139.
11. Osundare, N. *African Literature and the Crisis of Post-Structuralist Theorising.* Ibadan: Options Book and Information Services, 1993: 3.
12. Guenther, Katja M. "The politics of names: rethinking the methodological and ethical significance of naming people, organizations, and places." *Qualitative Research* 9, no. 4 (2009): 411–421.
13. For a study of names and speech act, see Yost, Lauren. "The Speech Act of Naming in Context: A Linguistic Study of Naming in the Old Testament" (2018).
14. Finnegan, Ruth. *Oral literature in Africa.* Open Book Publishers, 2017: 471–473.
15. Kaplan, Justin, Anne Bernays, and Kaplan Educational Centers. *Language of Names: What We Call Ourselves and Why It Matters.* New York: Simon & Schuster, 1997: 16.
16. Akinnaso, F. Niyi. "The sociolinguistic basis of Yoruba personal names." *Anthropological Linguistics* 22, no. 7 (1980): 278–9.
17. Bardis, Panos D. "Social aspects of personal onomastics among the ancient Hebrews." *South African Journal of Sociology* 1972, no. 4 (1972): 14–22.
18. Latour, Bruno. "When things strike back: a possible contribution of 'science studies' to the social sciences." *The British journal of sociology* 51, no. 1 (2000): 113–114.
19. Edelman, Lee. *No future: Queer theory and the death drive.* Duke University Press, 2004.
20. Agyekum, Kofi. "The sociolinguistic of Akan personal names." *Nordic Journal of African Studies* 15, no. 2 (2006): 206–235.
21. Komori, Yuri. "Trends in Japanese first names in the twentieth century: A comparative study." *International Christian University Publications 3-A, Asian Cultural Studies* 28 (2002): 67–82.

   Makoni, Busi, Sinfree Makoni, and Pedzisai Mashiri. "Naming practices and language planning in Zimbabwe." *Current Issues in Language Planning* 8, no. 3 (2007): 437–467.
22. Kroll-Smith, J. Stephen. "The testimony as performance: The relationship of an expressive event to the belief system of a holiness sect." *Journal for the Scientific Study of Religion* (1980): 16–25.
23. Olanisebe, Samson O. "Elimination by substitution: the travesty of changing cultural names to biblical names by Pentecostals in southwestern Nigeria." *Ilorin Journal of Religious Studies* 7, no. 2 (2017): 107–124.
24. Meyer, Birgit. "'Make a complete break with the past.' Memory and Postcolonial Modernity in Ghanaian Pentecostalist Discourse." *Journal of Religion in Africa* 28, no. Fasc. 3 (1998): 316–349.
25. Compagnone, Vanessa, and Marcel Danesi. "Mythic and occultist naming strategies in Harry Potter." *Names* 60, no. 3 (2012): 133.
26. Orie, ọlanikẹ ọla. "Yoruba names and gender marking." *Anthropological linguistics* (2002): 115–142.
27. Ogbaa, Kalu. "Names and Naming in Chinua Aehebe's Novels." *Names* 28, no. 4 (1980): 267–289.

Wamitila, Kyallo Wadi. "What's in a name: Towards literary onomastics in Kiswahili literature." In *Swahili Forum VI*, pp. 35–44. 1999.
28. Achebe, Chinua. *Morning yet on creation day: Essays.* London: Heinemann, 1975.
29. Agyekum, Kofi. "The sociolinguistic of Akan personal names." *Nordic Journal of African Studies* 15, no. 2 (2006): 206–235.

Ogie, Ota. "Edo personal names and world view." *New perspectives in Edoid studies: Essays in honour of Ronald Peter Schaefer. Cape Town RSA: Centre for Advanced Studies of African Society, Book Series* 20 (2002).

Omoloso, Rahim Kajogbola. "A speech act analysis of selected Yoruba anthroponyms." *Dialectologia: revista electrònica* 15 (2015): 117–135.

Oseni, Z. I. "A guide to Muslim name, with special reference to Nigeria." (1981).

Oyěwùmí, Oyèrónkẹ́. *What gender is motherhood?: Changing Yoruba ideals of power, procreation, and identity in the age of modernity.* Springer, 2016.

Smith, Daniel Scott. "Child-naming practices, kinship ties, and change in family attitudes in Hingham, Massachusetts, 1641 to 1880." *Journal of Social History* 18, no. 4 (1985): 541–566.
30. Achebe, Christie C. "Literary Insights into the Ogbanje Phenomenon." *Journal of African Studies* 7, no. 1 (1980): 31.

Falola, Toyin. *A mouth sweeter than salt: An African memoir.* University of Michigan Press, 2005.

Ilechukwu, Sunday TC. "Ogbanje/abiku and cultural conceptualizations of psychopathology in Nigeria." *Mental Health, Religion and Culture* 10, no. 3 (2007): 239–255.

Ilechukwu, Sunny TC. "Ogbanje/abiku: a culture-bound construct of childhood and family psychopathology in West Africa: the ogbanje/abiku syndrome: a case study of an interface between a culture-bound concept and modern psychiatry." *Psychopathologie africaine* 23, no. 1 (1990): 19–60.

Maduka, Chidi T. "African religious beliefs in literary imagination: ogbanje and abiku in Chinua Achebe, JP Clark and Wole Soyinka." *The Journal of Commonwealth Literature* 22, no. 1 (1987): 17–30.

McCabe, Douglas. "Histories of Errancy: Oral Yoruba 'Àbíkú' Texts and Soyinka's 'Abiku'." *Research in African Literatures* (2002): 45–74.

Ogunyemi, Chikwenye Okonjo. "An Abiku-Ogbanje Atlas: A Pre-Text for Rereading Soyinka's 'Aké' and Morrison's 'Beloved.'" *African American Review* 36, no. 4 (2002): 663–678.
31. Achebe, Chinua. *Things Fall Apart.* HEP, New Hampshire, 1996: 54.
32. Achebe, Chinua. Cited in *Listening to the Gentle Voice; Rhetorical Strategies in Things Fall Apart.* Chima Anyadike and Kehinde A. Ayoola. Ibadan: HEBN Publishers Plc, 2012: 311–2.
33. Slaughter, Joseph R. "'A Mouth with Which to Tell the Story': Silence, Violence, and Speech in Chinua Achebe's Things Fall Apart." *Achebe's Things Fall Apart* (2009): 88.
34. Semley, Lorelle. "Public motherhood in West Africa as theory and practice." *Gender & History* 24, no. 3 (2012): 600–616.
35. Sofola, J. A. *African culture and the African personality: What makes an African person African.* African resources publ., 1978: 110–111.
36. Suzman, Susan M. "Names as pointers: Zulu personal naming practices." *Language in society* 23, no. 2 (1994): 253–272.

See also:

Chitando, Ezra. "Signs and portents? Theophoric names in Zimbabwe." *Word and World* 21, no. 2 (2001): 145.

Kadenge, Maxwell, Patricia Ruramisai Mabugu, Esther Chivero, and Rejoice Chiwara. "Anthroponyms of albinos among the Shona people of Zimbabwe." *Mediterranean Journal of Social Sciences* 5, no. 27 P3 (2014): 1230.

37. Anyadike, Chima. *Listening to the Gentle Voice; Rhetorical Strategies in Things Fall Apart*. Chima Anyadike and Kehinde A. Ayoola. Ibadan: HEBN Publishers Plc, 2012: 313.
38. Wariboko, Nimi. *Nigerian Pentecostalism*. NY: University of Rochester Press, 2014: 128 and 140.
39. Schatzki, Theodore R. *The site of the social: A philosophical account of the constitution of social life and change*. Penn State Press, 2002: 123.
40. Wariboko, *Nigerian Pentecostalism*, 125.
41. Oduyoye, Mercy A. *Hearing and knowing: Theological reflections on Christianity in Africa*. Wipf and Stock Publishers, 2009: 33.
42. Ajayi, JF Ade. *Christian missions in Nigeria, 1841–1891: The making of a new elite*. Longman, 1965.

    Ayandele, Emmanuel Ayankanmi. *The missionary impact on modern Nigeria, 1842–1914: A political and social analysis*. London Longmans, 1966.

    Taiwo, Olufemi. *How colonialism preempted modernity in Africa*. Indiana University Press, 2010.
43. Pfukwa, Charles, and Lawrie Barnes. "Negotiating identities in guerrilla war names in the Zimbabwean war of liberation." *African identities* 8, no. 3 (2010): 209–219.
44. Gilmore, David D. "Some notes on community nicknaming in Spain." *Man* (1982): 686–700.
45. Oyěwùmí, Oyèrónkẹ́. *What gender is motherhood?: Changing Yoruba ideals of power, procreation, and identity in the age of modernity*. Springer, 2016: 198.
46. Surnames, according to Yonge, is also a relatively modern invention even in Western cultures.

    Yonge, Charlotte Mary. *History of Christian names*. Macmillan and Co. mpany, 1884: 1.
47. Johnson, Samuel. *The history of the Yorubas: From the earliest times to the beginning of the British protectorate*. Cambridge University Press, 1966: 86–89.
48. Ayandele, Emmanuel Ayankanmi. *The missionary impact on modern Nigeria, 1842–1914: A political and social analysis*. London Longmans, 1966.
49. Chitando, Ezra. "Theology from the Underside: The case of African Christian names in Zimbabwe." *Journal of theology for Southern Africa* 101 (1998): 23.
50. Korta, Kepa, and John Perry. *Critical pragmatics: An inquiry into reference and communication*. Cambridge University Press, 2011: 74.
51. Botterweck, G. Johannes, Helmer Ringgren, and Heinz-Josef Fabry, eds. *Theological dictionary of the Old Testament*. Vol. 14. Wm. B. Eerdmans Publishing, 2004.

CHAPTER 31

African Environmental Ethics

Oluwatoyin Vincent Adepoju

Abolo and Temi walked to the forest which meant so much to Abolo. He had invited her there to show her why his love for the place was so great. It was an almost primaeval environment, a scene suggesting Chinua Achebe's evocation of the Igbo mythic context "morning yet on creation day",[1] water seeping from under the earth as a powerful river flow emerged from the density of the forest space. Suffusing the entire zone was a sense of majestic presence, amplified by the large trees and isolation of the location but not completely identifiable as emanating from it, so mysterious and yet palpable this presence was. The Ogba Forest in Benin City, where the Ogba River breaks ground for the first time after a long underground journey.

Temi: "Fantastic. How did you discover this place?"

Abolo: "That is the crux of what I would like to share with you."

Temi: "I have long been inspired by classical African views on the nature of the non-human environment, such as this one, and human relationship with it, as you demonstrate in relation to this place."

Abolo: "What inspires you about these views?"

Temi: "I am moved by their sensitivity to nature as something demonstrating its own intrinsic value, independent of humans, but which humans can learn from."

Abolo: "Really?"

Temi: "Yes. A major challenge I face in my exploration of this subject, however, is that I have not come across explanations of how these ideas could have been developed, thereby clarifying their originating logic and suggesting how one could educate oneself to identify with them, an understanding vital for adapting them within one's own context."[2]

O. V. Adepoju (✉)
Lagos, Nigeria

Abolo: "Hmm…it should be possible to speculate, in a critical manner, on how those ideas were developed and how to study them, adapting them to oneself. Such speculation could be complemented by exploring what is known on these histories and the adaptations of the ideas already developed."

Temi: "The focus then would be on process, education and adaptation?"[3]

Abolo: "Yes."

Temi: "That would be wonderful. It would unify a broad range of research in a coherent manner. How could one begin such an analytical and synthesizing effort?"

Abolo: "One could build it on an expansion of what is known about a group centred in such subjects, the Yoruba origin Ogboni esoteric order."[4]

Temi: "Sounds plausible. As Toyin Falola put it, 'reflections, fed by observations and insights anchored to previous knowledge, can initiate a new form of knowledge'."[5]

Abolo: "Exactly."

Temi: "What is Ogboni? Why do you see it as helpful in this context?"

Abolo: "Ogboni is a Yoruba origin esoteric order, a group of people united in their secret deliberations by their belief in Earth as universal mother."

Temi: "Interesting. Even if their discussions are largely concealed one can appreciate their veneration of Earth as an effort to make meaning of life in the world."

Abolo: "True. Life on Earth can be seen as brief and puzzling, at times requiring some reassurance to persist with."

Temi: "Absolutely. We find ourselves here without any known prior agreement of ours to come here, ignorant of any identity we might have had, any place we might have been before entry into the Earth, and where we shall go after that. Various answers are provided to these questions, none of definitive value or universally accepted."

Abolo: "A perplexing situation indeed."

Temi: "The human being grows in physical and mental powers, reaches a climax in both, though at different times, then descends in strength of those abilities, until they break down totally, leading to his leaving the Earth, his body interred in soil. A distressing prospect, a bird flying swiftly through a lighted room and out again into the dark, the dark of a cold, winter night, as Bede describes human life in his *Ecclesiastical History of the English People*."[6]

Abolo: "Magnificent image. Interestingly this sensitivity to transience is core to Ogboni thought. 'In the light of life being bracketed by the two great unknowns of birth and death, how should a person live?' is a question that drives their philosophy."

Temi: "True?"

Abolo: "Yes."

Temi: "How does their philosophy respond to this question?"

Abolo: "It responds by transposing the understanding of nature into the human realm. Ogboni is the product of a forest civilization, a world surrounded by forest, a society built by shaping space for humanity out of forest space, relating with the forest as a zone from which to win ground and livelihood as well as an immensity that inspires awe."

Temi: "Interesting."

Abolo: "Exploring the variety and wonder of the forest, its conglomeration of various forms of existence, the forest came to stand for 'the universe, inhabited by obscure forces to which the human being stands in a dynamic moral and spiritual relationship and with which his destiny is involved' as Abiola Irele sums up the vision of Ijala, Yoruba hunter's poetry."[7]

Temi: "An intriguing perspective."

Abolo: "Exploring the forest facilitates an appreciation of 'animal and plant life, of the essence and relationships of growing things and the insights they enable into the secrets of the universe', as Wole Soyinka crystallizes the same vision."[8]

Temi: "Superb. Particularly in an agrarian and hunting civilization as Yoruba societies were for a long time. But with the eventual development of high levels of urbanization, do such ideas have practical value?"

Abolo: "They do. The forest may be transposed in terms of the everyday world, the cosmos constituted by the office and the school, the crossing of traffic lights and the buying of food in the market, the movements in space and the navigations of the individual and social realities that constitute the modern world."

Temi: "A powerful imaginative leap. How would that work?"

Abolo: "Ayi Kwei Armah, adapting Ghanaian Akan thought in his novel *The Healers*, puts it this way, 'People walk through the forest. They see leaves, trees, insects, sometimes a small animal, perhaps a snake. They see many things. But they see little. They hear many forest sounds. But they hear little.'"[9]

"'In the universe', continues Damfo, the healer in that novel, 'there are so many signs. A few we understand, the way farmers know what clouds mean, and fishermen understand the stars. But most signs mean nothing to us because we aren't prepared to understand them.'"[10]

Temi: "Intriguing."

Abolo: "'He who would be a healer', a person who works to heal individuals and communities in the fragmentation that defines this world, Damfo asserts, 'must set great value on seeing truly, hearing truly, understanding truly, and acting truly',[11] so as to facilitate, in himself and others, an understanding of the authentic as different from the inauthentic self, the division between people and their essential selves being a primary source of personal and social chaos, Damfo surmises.

"'The healer's work concerns wholeness', he concludes. 'Those who learn to read the signs around them and to hear the language of the universe reach a kind of knowledge healers call the shadow. The shadow, because that kind of knowledge follows you everywhere.'"[12]

Temi: "A rich transposition."

Abolo: "Exactly. In this view, human life is a theatre of learning where the self is developed through interpreting its experiences as demonstrating the working out in the phenomenal world, in the psychological, social and material contexts of human life, of the metaphysical structure and dynamism of the cosmos."

Temi: "Wow. Strikingly expansive."

Abolo: "The human and non-human contexts of human life, this view holds, constitute semiotic structures, frameworks of learning. Through these frameworks, the individual is presented with challenges that facilitate their understanding of the network of individual and social environments through which their conceptions of themselves and the universe is constructed."

Temi: "Is this a purely theoretical understanding or one that could also be lived in practice?"

Abolo: "It's a guide to how to live. The individual may be guided by these ideas to work towards an understanding of self and cosmos that is self-consciously realized and accurate rather than derivative and illusory."

Temi: "An ambitious perspective. In what specific ways can these ideas be applied?"

Abolo: "To appreciate that, one could learn from Ahmadou Hampate Ba, on the classical culture of the Bambara and the Fulani :

> If an old teacher comes upon an ant-hill during a walk in the bush, this gives him an opportunity for dispensing various kinds of knowledge...Either he will speak of the creature itself, the laws governing its life and the class of being it belongs to, or he will give children a lesson in morality by showing them how community life depends on solidarity and forgetfulness of self, or again he may go on to higher things if he feels that his audience can attain to them.
>
> Thus any incident in life, any trivial happening, can always be developed in many ways, can lead to telling a myth, a tale, a legend. Every phenomenon one encounters can be traced back to the forces from which it issued and suggest the mysteries of the unity of life, which is entirely animated by Se, the primordial sacred Force, itself an aspect of God the Creator."[13]

Temi: "I can identify with that. The universe may thus be made meaningful rather than resigned to obscurity or to an order with no meaning beyond its self-perpetuation."

Abolo: "Exactly. Every phenomenon, concrete or abstract, every experience, may thus be seen as having a meaning as part of the developing story of existence, a story of which one is a part, a story which one is contributing to working out through one's life, a story the outcome of which is unknown, but which one can influence through how one lives."

Temi: "Wow. Are there specific ideational correlations with aspects of existence people could use in cultivating such a rich sensitivity to existence, any texts that can provide inspiration or more precise guidance?"

Abolo: "Of course. Visual and verbal texts, previously oral, now increasingly rendered in writing, as well as primarily written texts and art inspired by the classical examples, play this role."

Temi: "Interesting. How may these texts and art be found? In what contexts are they used?"

Abolo: "Various contexts. Divination literature. Hunters' literature. Praise poetry. Creation myths. Visual and performative arts. Classical and post-classical. These various genres, among others, actualize the following vivid description by Toyin Falola whom you referenced earlier:

> [Through] Orality [and other artistic forms, visual and performative, classical African culture] recognizes the organic relationship between the environment and human beings [developing] a strong understanding of everything around them, from insects to trees, and [call] upon the resources of the environment to organize [its] religions and rituals…sensing nature itself, and in doing so, using a language that draws heavily on all available objects and elements…working them into idioms, proverbs, and parables".[14]

Temi: "Can you give any examples of this scope of reference, from animals to plants to inanimate forms?"

Abolo: "Of course. Animals are central to the personalistic universe of the Yoruba origin Ifa literature, for example. Along with Yoruba Ijala and other genres of classical Yoruba poetry, this literature demonstrates actions and attitudes dramatizing ideas through animal imagery, such as the story of the squirrel who was advised by the Ifa oracle to avoid being talkative, disobeying which injunction led to disaster for his family."

Temi: "Interesting. Do the ideas associated with animals go beyond such folkloristic contexts?"

Abolo: "Of course. These intimate identifications with the animal world, running across Africa, North to South, West, Central and East, cover the entire gamut of hermeneutic possibilities, interpretations of phenomena in terms of broader contexts relating to the meaning of existence in general."

Temi: "Really?"

Abolo: "Of course. Evans-Pritchard also makes a remarkable summation on conceptions of relationships between birds, spirit and God in his work on the Nuer of the Nile valley:

> God is Spirit, which, like wind and air, is invisible and ubiquitous. But though God is not these things he is in them in the sense that he reveals himself through them….he is in the sky, falls in the rain, shines in the sun and moon, and blows in the wind. These divine manifestations are to be understood as modes of God and not as his essence, which is Spirit.
>
> God being above, everything above is associated with him….Some birds also are spoken about by Nuer as gaat kwoth, especially those which fly high and seem, to us as well as to Nuer, to belong to heaven rather than to earth and therefore to be children of light and symbols of the divine."[15]

Temi: "Striking. The abstract is thus made vivid through the immediacy and vitality of the concrete. What about depictions of plants?"

Abolo: "Examples of response to plants range from verbal celebrations of such obvious attributes as the majesty of the iroko tree to the mystical beauty of fonio in the thought of the Bambara, the Dogon and the Balanta Kanja, the latter as described by Owen Burnham:

> The importance of plants for humanity began when fonio, the smallest seed, fell to the earth and spread the consciousness of the creator to all. To the Bambara and Dogon peoples of Mali the value of fonio is immense. It is at once both the smallest and the greatest. In fonio we hear the echoes of the past, and sitting in a field of these fragile plants, listening to the wind, it is truly possible to understand the spirituality of plants. Fonio 'is all the wisdoms' for the Balanta Kanja people. It is the embodiment of the creative spirit, the giver of life, the gentleness of being, the entwined fragility of life and death, for it is a weak, easily broken plant, yet strong enough to bend in the wind without breaking."[16]

Temi: "Sublime ideas. Beautiful in conception and expression."

Abolo: "Another striking picture along similar lines is John Mbiti's summation on the image of rain in classical African spiritualities:

> rain is seen as the eternal and mystical link between past, present and future generations. It is one of the most concrete and endless rhythms of nature; as it came, it comes and it will come...a deeply religious rhythm...the manifestation of the eternal, in the here and now."[17]

Temi: "Marvellous. Are there ethical implications to these ideas? Have they influenced people's conduct in relation to the cosmos, to nature, to each other?"

Abolo "I would think so. The Yoruba concept of 'farabale', circumspection in relating with situations, may be understood as responding to the sensitivity to the unknown individual power of various elements in nature, their own distinctive expression of ase, the cosmic force that enables being and becoming, agency and creativity.[18]

The Yoruba deity Eshu, understood as distinctively present in each person and mediating between forms of being, may be seen as dramatizing these varied possibilities.[19] Being so small, he cannot look into the cooking pot, yet is so tall his head hits the roof, he throws a stone today and hits a bird yesterday, he sits on the skin of an ant."[20]

Temi: "Searingly powerful images. I can see the links these images of paradoxical qualities suggest, the convergence of the miniscule and the large in nature, all demonstrating their unique majesty."

Abolo: "Exactly. 'Fun iwa ni oniwa', 'grant to each existent its own unique existence, its own distinctive mode of being', the Yoruba expression goes.[21] Mazisi Kunene presents a similar conception in classical Zulu thought:

> the ultimate authority that emanates from the Creator ensures a fulfillment for each species in accordance with its own overall cosmic purpose [a] purpose [that] cannot be grasped or defined [a purpose known only by the Creator, the Creator

being also unknowable, there being no] absolute truth, only a working hypothesis...several truths converging to express a variation of the ultimate truth [even as an ideal of knowledge in that culture is the unity of the particular and the universal, of the 'precision and the cosmic minds' in the human being, leading to the erasure of] the boundaries between the past and the present, the living and dead, the physical and the non-physical [creating] the power to conceptualize the totality of life at once [akin to] the chameleon's all round vision."[22]

Temi: "Wonderful. Do these ideas have any relevance to the question of whether or not classical African thought can be seen as a generally unified whole, demonstrating cultural peculiarities in the expression of largely correlative perspectives?"

Abolo: "They do. John Mbiti's *African Religions and Philosophy* is both pioneering and summative in mapping these regularities. Negritude, with some modifications, is also rich in these metaphysical summations, although such unifying pictures, as that which I am developing here, are best understood as individual constructs rather than existing givens."[23]

Temi: "How would you sum up these consistencies?"

Abolo: "In relation to the character of classical African thought as an earth-centred spirituality, the best summation I know of comes from Awo Falokun Fatunmbi on the Yoruba origin Ifa philosophy, an idea that applies not only to classical African thought but to world views outside the Manichean, Judeo-Christian paradigm:

...the fabric which binds the universe together. The threads of this fabric are the multi-leveled layers of consciousness which Ifa teaches exist in all things on all levels of being. Ifa teaches that it is the ability of forces of nature to communicate with each other, and the ability of humans to communicate with forces in nature that gives the world a sense of spiritual unity."[24]

Temi: "Wow. Consciousness in all things?"

Abolo: "Yes. Olabiyi Babalola Yai presents this idea with particular force in his description of ori, a central concept in the understanding of consciousness in Yoruba cosmology:

Ori is essence, attribute, and quintessence...the uniqueness of persons, animals, and things, their inner eye and ear, their sharpest point and their most alert guide as they navigate through this world and the one beyond."[25]

Temi: "A very bold perspective. I wonder how such views are developed."

Abolo: "Most likely from experience. A life lived close to nature in which what would be considered anomalous in other contexts would be more readily appreciated."

Temi: "I wonder if such animistic perspectives emerged through slow accumulation and diffusion or through the impact of particularly perceptive individuals in various locations."

Abolo: "I suspect it's a combination of both factors, enabling animism occur in a good number of cultures beyond Africa."

Temi: "Perhaps the animistic mentality is a primordial development of humanity, emerging through humanity's intimacy with nature across the ages."

Abolo: "That perspective agrees with the facts available to us. I also find striking the extension of the already bold idea of individual consciousness in diverse phenomena, animate and inanimate, to the idea of a force pervading existence, enabling consciousness and creative capacity. The most eloquent expression known to me of this idea, recurring in various forms in various African cosmologies and beyond, is by Chinua Achebe on Igbo thought:

> The Igbo world is an arena for the interplay of forces. It is a dynamic world of movement and of flux. Igbo art, reflecting this world view, is never tranquil but mobile and active, even aggressive. Ike, energy, is the essence of all things, human, spiritual, animate and inanimate.
>
> Everything has its own unique energy which must be acknowledged and given its due. 'Ike di na awaja na awaja' is a common formulation of this idea: 'Power runs in many channels.' [The complement of that saying] 'Onye na nkie, onye na nkie'—literally, 'Everyone and his own'—is a social expression of the same notion often employed as a convenient formula for saluting en masse an assembly too large for individual greetings."[26]

Temi: "A potent concept, compellingly stated. Do you know of any imagistic expressions of a pervasive, consciousness enabling force of the kind referenced by Achebe, expressions that facilitate understanding of such abstractions?"

Abolo: "There is a remarkable one by Susanne Wenger, inspired by her experience of Nigeria's Oshun forest in relation to her immersion in Yoruba cosmology, not so much testifying to the idea of a cosmic force but witnessing to unity between the human self, elemental nature, the animal world and the divine, within the ambit of eternity:

> Here I am, one with the water; I think and feel like the river, my blood flows like the river, to the rhythm of its waves, otherwise the trees and the animals wouldn't be such allies.
>
> I am here *in* the trees, *in* the river, in my creative phase not only when I am here physically, but forever—even when I happen to be travelling—hidden beyond time and suffering, in the Spiritual Entities, which, because they are Real in many ways, present ever new features.
>
> I feel sheltered with them—in them—because I am so very fond of trees and running water—and all the gods of the world are trees and animals long, long before they entrust their sacrosanct magnificence to a human figure."[27]

Temi: "Fantastic. It would be wonderful if methods could be developed for the critical examination of these ideas, and even for the pursuit of the experiences that enable such insights, such methods as ratiocinative logic, imaginative exploration and experiential engagement."

Abolo: "I expect similar methods already exist for exploring their experiential possibilities, but these methods might not be well known, being limited to adepts either unable to record them in writing on account of literacy issues or who are not willing to, since the knowledge is an intimate bond shared by groups of initiates.

A moving example of the effects of exposure to such a technique is John McCall's account of the psychological effects of his initiation into the esoteric guild of Igbo dibia:

> I became lost in contemplation of the vast star-studded sky above me. Though the wine, the herbs, the songs, and the ritual had left me feeling euphoric, I couldn't say I felt any awakening abilities in the form of telepathic powers or occult vision. I certainly hadn't had any great mysteries revealed to me or received interpretations of esoteric signs as I had during my Ekpe secret society initiation. Yet I felt an exhilaration that seemed to blossom from a source more profound than mere intoxication.
>
> As I leaned back, taking in the vastness of the night sky…I recalled…myriad… uncanny events I had experienced since my arrival in Ohafia that had been chipping away at the ontological foundations of my rational assumptions about reality. It was not that these phenomena inspired a 'belief' in the certainty of some sort of "'Ohafia worldview.' Rather, my frame of mind was one of an enhanced uncertainty, and I realized that it was this uncertainty itself that was in some sense liberating".
>
> The knowledge of the dibia takes for granted that human experience is not reducible to known and predictable facts. And in this the traditional doctor displays a wisdom deeper than that of the positivist social scientist.
>
> The knowledge of dibia resides not in formal 'laws' but in a continual reading of the shifting and negotiable relations between things. I could not expect instantly to gain these abstruse abilities. After all, the ceremony hadn't transformed me into a dibia, it had only given me the right to continue learning and to develop myself into a dibia if I was able to master the skills and knowledge required. Still, a kind of new vision had in fact been realized in the course of my initiation. I had glimpsed another order of knowledge."[28]

Temi: "It would be wonderful if such methods could be accessible to those uninitiated in the traditional sense."

Abolo: "One approach to such democratization of knowledge would be that of enthusiasts constructing the relevant learning systems themselves, building on available knowledge."

Temi: "That is how modern Western magic and its Pagan, nature centred components have developed."[29]

Abolo: "Exactly. A promising ideational structure for organizing such explorations into a system is Germaine Dieterlen's account of initiation among the Peul pastoral Fulani, a branch of a people spread across various African regions and nations, an account which may be understood as integrating much of what we have discussed in terms of a sequence of human development."[30]

Temi: "Interesting. Can such a sequence be adapted for use outside its traditional contexts?"

Abolo: "I expect it can."

Temi: "What drew you to this developmental sequence in particular, as different, for example, from Marcel Griaule's account of the growth of the human person in terms of the being of Nommo, the primordial personality in Dogon cosmology?"[31]

Abolo: "I see the Fulani progression, being an initiatory system, as lending itself better to adaptation and as particularly rich in its ideas, ideas readily transposable to a context different from the original."

Temi: "What is at the core of those ideas?"

Abolo: "Spatial orientation, elemental identification, confronting existential challenges and a culminating invocation of ultimate reality."

Temi: "Is there any summative statement of this expansive vision, something memorable, that subsumes these ideas, facilitating the deduction of these ideations from perhaps a few striking images?"

Abolo: "There is. A creation story which unifies ideas of nature/human convergences, opening with, 'In the beginning, there was a huge drop of milk'."[32]

Temi: "Interesting. Visualizing ultimate generative power in terms of their primary means of sustenance, a means deriving from a creature that is intimate to their lives, the cow."

Abolo: "Well put. The story continues in terms of a progression bringing the fundamental elements into being in unity with humanity, 'Then Doondari came and he created the stone/Then the stone created iron;/And iron created fire;/ And fire created water;/And water created air./ Then Doondari descended the second time./ And he took the five elements and he shaped them into man'."

Temi: "Magnificent. How is this story developed in terms of an initiatory sequence?"

Abolo: "From the world view represented by this story a method is constructed for generating integrations between discrete units in their environment with increasingly larger units, using a prominent aspect of the environment as a template for the broadest generalizations, thereby arriving at an integrated conception of the cosmos."

Temi: "Ingenious. Is any aspect of the environment emphasized by the Fulani development of this method?"

Abolo: "Cattle. The Fulani relationship with their cattle, regarded as kinsmen rather than property or wealth, inspires them to interpret their cattle and their qualities in terms of the most expansive symbolism, from the terrestrial to the cosmic."[33]

Temi: "Magnificent. Any particular aspects of the cattle?"

Abolo: "The various patterns of the coats of cattle. These patterns are elaborated in terms of a symbolic scheme in which they serve as templates for integrating a broad range of conceptions on the nature of the universe, from the material and non-material constitution of the human person to the metaphysical structure and dynamism of the cosmos."

Temi: "Most ingenious. How are these conjunctions developed?"

Abolo: "The various patterns of the coats of cattle are each aligned to one of the four directions of space, one of the four elements and a part of the human body and developed in terms of temporal associations eventuating in the cycle of the year and 'the spiritual beings who intervene after each other in the march of the Universe…above all of whom is God, Gueno, the immortal, omniscient and omnipresent', beings who instruct the candidate in cultivating understanding of the elemental constituents of existence, their essence penetrating and being penetrated by the initiate in the context of 'a series of tests… struggle[s] he must wage with himself, with the help of God, in order to progress'. After the untying of the 'knots' of knowledge representing this spatiotemporal and spiritual unity, 'he invokes God, Doundari [another name for Gueno] the master of creation', bringing his initiation to a climax."[34]

Temi: "Magnificent. To what degree would adaptation of these ideas require assenting to the belief system underlying it?"

Abolo: "I think this initiatory structure can be employed by interpreting the ideas in symbolic rather than literal terms, leaving literal identification with its metaphysics open to any who may so wish, but extending its value beyond those who share such identification."

Temi: "Beyond the sublime example from Susanne Wenger you just gave, which can be seen as a climatic experiential stage of such nature/human identifications, do you know of any other demonstrations of experiential engagement with such ideas, such as the notion of penetrating and being penetrated by the essences of the elements?"

Abolo: "I do. One of my favourite examples is Wole Soyinka's imaginative identification with earth, water and fire in his almost two-year imprisonment in solitary confinement, invoking tree roots to assist him draw nourishment from earth, visualizing himself as plunging into 'pools of silence', there encountering empowering presences, 'bygone voyagers', facilitating his immersion in waters 'promising from far to slake immortal thirst',[35] a strategy of resistance empowered by his anointing his heart, 'within its flame I lay/Spent ashes of your hate'."[36]

Temi: "Amazing invocations. Would you describe such imaginative, rather than direct encounter with nature, as contributing to a process of penetrating and being penetrated by the elements?"

Abolo: "Of course. The significance of the elements extends from their materiality to their role as a part of the structure of the human body, as with water and air, and constitutive of human consciousness, since they shape the world we are aware of, a pervasive presence resonating in human imagination as an extension of human physical experience."

Temi: "Insightful. The experience of the great English Romantic poet William Wordsworth agrees with that view of yours in describing the 'animal spirits' of his childhood growing into the quietly profound reflections of older years, when those memories sustained him in the densely built habitations of cities, transporting him in imagination to sublime vistas."³⁷

Abolo: "Thanks for that Wordsworthian reference. I would hold, in line with Wordsworth's account in such a poem as 'Tintern Abbey', that penetrating and being penetrated by the elements, in the words of the Fulani initiation sequence, is equivalent to invoking the ultimate, the culmination of that sequence."

Temi: "Why?"

Abolo: "Because within the animistic universe of classical African cosmologies, the divine is expressed in nature. This expression may be given various names, but is ultimately recognized as participating in or as expressing the character of an ultimate creative power."

Temi: "Is this a definitive interpretation or a blend of your personal speculation and a slant in terms of which the scholarly evidence could be interpreted?"

Abolo: "It's a blend of my personal experience and my interpretation of the scholarship on the subject."

Temi: "How so?"

Abolo: "Through contemplating the beauty of trees in Benin City, a centre of nature spirituality, I came to these conclusions."

Temi: "Really? To what end?"

Abolo: "In an effort to pierce to the foundations of trees in the source of existence."

Temi: "Wow. What's the logic of that?"

Abolo: "The belief that every form of existence is rooted in the metaphysical source of being."

Temi: "How did you come across this idea?"

Abolo: "Through various cultures, but I was inspired to explore appreciation of the beauty of nature in pursuit of this goal by reading the Western magical theorist Dion Fortune who described inanimate nature as both demonstrating consciousness and as being capable of stimulating sensitivity to the source of existence."³⁸

Temi: "Intriguing. An animistic and mystical conception."

Abolo: "Yes. Apt summation."

Temi: "Why Benin as the place of exploration?"

Abolo: "I was living in Benin at the time and the place has an ancient culture of tree veneration, with sacred trees standing untouched in various locations in the busy city."

Temi: "Wow. So that motivated your exploration?"

Abolo: "Yes. Gradually, I began to notice an otherwise invisible and intangible field around certain trees, particularly those understood as sacred."

Temi: "Amazing. So you were participating in a form of intersubjectivity with those who had designated those trees as sacred in the first place, observing what they saw that led to that designation?"

Abolo: "Exactly. There was even one such tree I was convinced was self-conscious, so vibrant, so potent, was the energy field it emanated."

Temi: "Amazing."

Abolo: "I had stumbled on the reality of a universe of existence in nature, expressed by its purely material though often living being, but transcending the conventional understanding of that materiality as limited to its inanimate and non-sentient qualities."

Temi: "Wow."

Abolo: "The climatic point of this discovery was observation of a further level of wonder in the form of particular locations which exuded a presence corresponding to what I have learnt of the divine in the most exalted descriptions of that phenomenon from various spiritualities and philosophies."

Temi: "Truly? Can you describe this more precisely?"

Abolo: "A place where a river gushed out of the forest and where one could see it coming out of the ground, a zone described as where the river breaks ground for the first time after a long underground journey and therefore the home of a goddess, as described in the culture of the Benin people, such locations preserved free from human interference in respect for the sacred presence, the very place where we are seated right now."

Temi: "And you encountered that presence?"

Abolo: "It is palpable. It does not need faith to recognize. It is as definite as electricity, only subtle rather than physical. A radiance projecting a sense of absolute holiness. Suffusing the lofty trees in a sense of cathedral majesty. A profound stillness and inexplicable depth."

Temi: "Wow. Your description reminds me of the characterization of Rudolph Otto's concept of the numinous as 'an invisible but majestic presence that inspires both dread and fascination and constitutes the non-rational element of vital religion'."[39]

Abolo: "A most accurate depiction."

Temi: "Amazing. How do you explain the logic of how you came by this experience of yours?"

Abolo: "The best explanation I have got so far comes from a harmony of Yoruba and Igbo theories of perception, which suggest that phenomena are best appreciated as demonstrating an outer and an inner dimension, and that, dissimilar as they might be in their outer qualities, they demonstrate a degree of convergence in their inner natures at the level of ultimate identity."[40]

Temi: "In terms of ultimate identity are you referring to 'ori', the 'inner eye and ear' described by Yai?"

Abolo: "Yes."

Temi: "Through what means are these convergences perceived?"

Abolo: "Through the movement from 'oju lasan', 'the ordinary eye' or corporeal perception, to 'oju inu', the 'inward eye' or inward perception, as understood in Yoruba thought."[41]

Temi: "So, the mere fact of your admiring the beauty of those trees, trying to see through them to their invisible underlying reality, sensitized your eyes to a level of vision beyond the physical, enabling you to perceive those numinous qualities in nature?"

Abolo: "Yes."

Temi: "Could such an effect also be achieved by contemplating trees in any context, including trees in those urban centres designed in terms of sensitivity to nature?"

Abolo: "Possibly, but I suspect those trees and groves that accelerated the expansion of my perception in Benin are entities concentrating a peculiar form of energy, perhaps a kind related to the Yoruba concept of ase and the Igbo ike, a quality that led to their being designated as sacred."

Temi: "Interesting. Could the architects of Benin town planning who insisted on that policy of leaving sacred trees and groves inviolate have had in mind the effect they had on you, in the understanding that they would stimulate people who related with them?"

Abolo: "I doubt it. I don't get the impression the deeper aspects of their religious culture are so democratic. I suspect my experience was an unintended by-product of the character of those trees."

Temi: "Hmmmm...so one could describe Benin City at the time you engaged in these explorations as designed in strong biophilic terms, a design vision generating an experience of awephilia, to reference Nimi Wariboko's *The Charismatic City*?"[42]

Abolo: "Well put. Love of nature leading to a sense of awe at the glory, wonder and mystery of existence."

Temi: "Amazing. Does Benin cosmology take these ideas further?"

Abolo: "It does, in the complex of ideas built around the figure of Olokun, the intelligence of the world's waters, an aquatic presence that permeates the world in terms of the water pervasive in the atmosphere and in the human body, and as symbolized by the earth/water constitution of mud, an evocation of the interface between ultimate and terrestrial reality, between humanity and spirit, between time and eternity."[43]

Temi: "Another striking grounding of the abstract in the concrete. Are these ideas developed, in verbal, visual or performative terms or both?"

Abolo: "All three. The abstract visual expressions are particularly powerful. Norma Rosen, a Benin Olokun initiate, is particularly perceptive in reproducing the sensitive beauty of these symbols and explicating what they mean to those who create and use them.

The group of symbols Rosen discusses, out of the broad set, are known as igha-ede, used for demarcating the division and unification of space and time as pillars of existence, superb for unifying the ideas we have been discussing."[44]

Temi: "Is there a template for the use of these ideas?"

Abolo: "There is. A ritual template which one may adapt for uses outside the more complex traditional ritual context."

Temi: "Really? How?"

Abolo: "Igha-ede constitute approaches to time and space that could inform one's understanding of every spatial and temporal context as demonstrating the most immediately accessible aspect of a continuum that integrates matter and spirit, time and infinity, the human and the divine."

Temi: "Amazing. Any example of anyone who has applied such ideas in a manner enabling a more flexible context outside the traditional ritual frame?"

Abolo: "There is a magnificent example. That of Christopher Okigbo's poetic cycle *Labyrinths*, which, though built in an Igbo context, is an aspect of the same veneration of an intelligence of aquatic space in the Benin framework."[45]

Temi: "How does Okigbo develop this orientation?"

Abolo: "He does it in terms of an invocation of the goddess of his village stream, an invocation depicted as leading to a journey to the sources of existence and culminating in the bowels of the earth, where he unites with the goddess in her cavern, an intimate encounter with the goddess as the 'water spirit that nurtures all creation'."

Temi: "Wow. From goddess of a village stream to nurturer of cosmos."

Abolo: "Exactly. I describe that as a form of 'animistic mysticism', an effort to relate intimately with, even achieve union, with ultimate reality through the enablement provided by an animistic presence."

Temi: "Unusual kind of mysticism but logical."

Abolo: "Having summed up Okigbo's mystical journey from stream to underwater cavern, taking in various approaches to the significance of earth and water, air and fire, may we not be said to have covered a broad range of possibilities across Africa in terms of relationships with nature?"

Notes

1. Chinua Achebe, *Morning Yet on Creation Day* (New York: Anchor Press/Doubleday, 1975).
2. This summation is a response to three major recent summations of the field of African environmental ethics, Chinedu Stephen Ifeakor and Andrew Otteh's "African Environmental Ethics: A Non–Anthropocentric African Environmentalism. The Journey So Far" in *IGWEBUIKE: An African Journal of Arts and Humanities*, 3, no. 6 (September 2017): 67–97, Michael Onyebuchi Eze's "Humanitatis-Eco (Eco-Humanism): An African Environmental Theory" in *The Palgrave Handbook of African Philosophy*, ed. Adeshina Afolayan and Toyin Falola (New York: Palgrave Macmillan, 2017): 621–632, and Edwin Etieyibo's "Ubuntu and the Environment" in *The Palgrave Handbook of African Philosophy*. 2017: 633–657.
3. This conception of creative process may be understood in response to such accounts of non-Western and non-Asian philosophy of mind and of nature that present it as inadequately logical, such as the *Stanford Encyclopedia of Philosophy* essay on panpsychism, "the doctrine that mind is a fundamental feature of the world which exists throughout the universe" as defined by the encyclopedia at https://plato.stanford.edu/archives/win2012/entries/panpsychism/ Accessed 19 February 2019. The idea of adaptation is correlative with the school of thought that holds that it is vital to complement ecological theorizing with systematic ecological education, represented, for example, by the work of Michael Bonnett, who unfolds various aspects of this imperative in such texts as "Environmental Consciousness, Sustainability, and the Character of Philosophy

of Education" in *Studies in the Philosophy of Education* 36 (2017): 333–347, where he argues for the grounding of human existence in the environment, thereby placing "our relationship with nature at the heart of both human being and authentic education", as summed up in the abstract.

4. The richest summation on Ogboni known to me, particularly in relation to the esoteric group's adoration of Earth, is Babatunde Lawal's "À Yà Gbó, À Yà Tó: New Perspectives on Edan Ògbóni" in *African Arts*, 28, no. 1 (Winter, 1995): 36–49+98–100.
5. From a private group email communication.
6. The Venerable Bede's *Historia Ecclesiastica Gentis Anglorum*, AD 731, translated by Leo Sherley-Price as *Ecclesiastical History of the English People* (London: Penguin, 1990).
7. Abiola Irele, "Tradition and the Yoruba Writer: D.O. Fagunwa, Amos Tutuola and Wole Soyinka", in *The African Experience in Literature and Ideology* (London: Heinemann, 1981): 174–197.
8. Wole Soyinka, *Myth, Literature and the African World* (Cambridge: Cambridge UP, 1990): 28.
9. Ayi Kwei Armah, *The Healers* (London: Heinemann, 1979): 79.
10. Armah, *The Healers*, 80.
11. Armah, *The Healers*, 81.
12. Armah, *The Healers*, 82.
13. Ahmadou Hampate Ba, "The Living Tradition" in *UNESCO General History of Africa. Vol. 1: Methodology and African Prehistory*, ed. J. Ki Zerbo. (London: Heinemann, 1981): 166–203. 179.
14. Toyin Falola, *In Praise of Greatness: The Poetics of African Adulation* (Durham: Carolina Academic Press, 2019): 121.
15. E. E. Evans-Pritchard, *Nuer Religion* (Oxford: Oxford UP, 1956): 2.
16. Owen Burnham, *African Wisdom: A Practical and Inspirational Guide* (London: Judy Piatkus, 2000): 43–44.
17. John Mbiti, *African Religions and Philosophy* (London: Heinemann, 1976): 181.
18. As described by Henry John Drewal, John Pemberton, Rowland Abiodun and Allen Wardwell in *Yoruba: Nine Centuries of African Art and Thought* (New York: Harry N. Abrams, 1989): 16.
19. "If someone did not have his Esu in his body, he could not exist, he would not know that he is alive; therefore everybody must have his individual Esu" as stated by Juan Elbein and Deoscoredes Dos Santos in "Esu Bara: Principle of Individual Life in the Nago System" in *Colloque International sur la Notion de Personne en Afrique Noire*, quoted by Ayodele Ogundipe in "Retention and Survival of Yoruba Traditional Religion in the Diaspora: Esu in Brazil and Benin Republic" in *Ivie: Nigerian Journal of Arts and Culture*. 1. no. 3, 1986: 56–68. 62. Toyin Falola complements this, asserting Esu is "a constant traveller" "with the enormous capacity to know the truth and reveal it…" "ubiquitous and invisible, so much so that his 'temple' can also be within the individual self" in "Esu: The God Without Boundaries" from *Esu: Yoruba God of Power and the Imaginative Frontiers*, ed. Toyin Falola (Durham: Carolina Academic Press, 2013): 4.
20. From "Eshu, God of Fate" in Jack Mapanje and Landeg White, *Oral Poetry from Africa* (Harlow, Essex: Longman, 1984): 110.

21. Rowland Abiodun, "The Future of African Art Studies: An African Perspective" in *African Art Studies: The State of the Discipline* (Washington: The Smithsonian, 1987): 63–89. *Yoruba Art and Language: Seeking the African in African Art* (Cambridge: Cambridge UP, 2014): 245–283.253.
22. Mazisi Kunene, *Anthem of the Decades* (London: Heinemann, 1981) XXIII.
23. John Mbiti, *African Religions and Philosophy*. The richest expositions of Negritude known to me are by Abiola Irele, particularly his account of Negritude metaphysics in "What is Negritude" in *The African Experience in Literature and Ideology* (London: Heinemann, 1981): 67–88. His "The African Scholar" in *Transition*, No. 51 (1991): 56–69, takes further similar ideas in relation to classical Yoruba philosophy.
24. Awo Fa'lokun Fatunmbi, "Obatala: Ifa and the Chief of the Spirit of the White Cloth". 2. Scribd: https://www.scribd.com/document/47061087/OBATALA-Ifa-and-the-Chief-of-the-Spirit-of-the-White-Cloth-EDITED-AND-FORMATTED Accessed 2/22/2019.
25. Olabiyi Babalola Yai, Review *of Yoruba: Nine Centuries of African Art and Thought* by Henry John Drewal, John Pemberton, Rowland Abiodun and Allen Wardwell in *African Arts*, 25, no. 1 (Jan., 1992): 20+22+24+26+29.22.
26. Chinua Achebe, "The Igbo World and Its Art", in *African Philosophy: An Anthology*, ed. Emmanuel Chukwudi Eze (Oxford: Wiley-Blackwell, 1997): 435–437.
27. Rolf Brockmann and Gerd Hötter, *Adunni: A Portrait of Susanne Wenger* (München: Trickster Verlag, 1994). Back cover.
28. John McCall, "Making Peace with Agwu" in *Anthropology & Humanism* 18. 2 (December 1993): 56–66. 63-64.
29. As impressively described, among other texts, in Ronald Hutton's *Bringing Down the Moon: A History of Modern Pagan Witchcraft* (Oxford: Oxford UP, 1999).
30. Germaine Dieterlen, "Initiation among the Peul Pastoral Tribes" in *African Systems of Thought*. Preface by Meyer Fortes and Germaine Dieterlen (London: Oxford UP, 1966): 314–327.
31. Marcel Griaule, "The Dogon of the French Sudan" in *African Worlds: Studies in the Cosmological Ideas and Social Values of African Peoples*. Ed. Daryll Forde (London: Oxford UP, 1970): 83–110.
32. "The Fulani Creation Story" in *A Selection of African Poetry*, ed. K.E. Senanu and T.E. Vincent (Harlow, Essex: Longman, 1988): 24–25.
33. Dieterlen, 314–327.
34. Dieterlen, 314–327.
35. Wole Soyinka, *A Shuttle in the Crypt* (London: Rex Collings, 1972): 4.
36. Wole Soyinka, *A Shuttle in the Crypt*, 19.
37. William Wordsworth, "Tintern Abbey" in *The Oxford Anthology of English Literature* (New York: Oxford UP, 1973): 146–150.
38. Dion Fortune, *The Training and Work of an Initiate* (London: Aquarian, 1955) 65.
39. From Rudolph Otto's *The Idea of the Holy*, trans J. W. Harvey (New York: Oxford UP, 1923) as presented in *Webster's Third New International Dictionary of the English Language Unabridged. 1966.*
40. The concept of ori as understood in Yoruba philosophy and defined by Yai and of chi in Igbo thought as depicted by John Umeh in *After God Is Dibia: Igbo*

Cosmology, Divination and Sacred Science in Nigeria (London: Karnak House [1999]): 71–81.
41. As described by Babatunde Lawal for Yoruba philosophy in "Àwòrán: Representing the Self and Its Metaphysical Other in Yoruba Art" in The Art Bulletin, 83, no. 3. (Sep., 2001): 498–526. 516 and by John Umeh of Igbo thought in After God Is Dibia: Igbo Cosmology, Divination and Sacred Science in Nigeria (London: Karnak House [1999]): 71–81.
42. Nimi Wariboko, The Charismatic City and the Public Resurgence of Religion: A Pentecostal Social Ethics of Cosmopolitan Urban Life (New York: Palgrave, 2014).
43. Ideas evident in Paula Ben-Amos, "Symbolism in Olokun Mud Art" in African Arts, 6, no. 4 (Summer 1973): 28–31+95.30 and Ndubuisi Ezeluomba, "The Explanation of a Text with Reference to the Mud Sculptures of Benin" in Black Arts Quarterly, 33, vol. 12, Issue 1 (Winter 2007): 33–35. www.stanford.edu/group/CBPA/BAQWinter2007.pdf. Accessed 2/25/2019.
44. Norma Rosen, "Chalk Iconography in Olokun Worship" in African Arts, 22, no. 3 (May 1989): 44–53+88.
45. Christopher Okigbo, Labyrinths with Path of Thunder (London: Heinemann, 1971).

Bibliography

Abiodun, Rowland. 1987. The Future of African Art Studies: An African Perspective. In *African Art Studies: The State of the Discipline*, 63–89. Washington, DC: The Smithsonian.

———. 2014. *Yoruba Art and Language: Seeking the African in African Art*. Cambridge: Cambridge University Press.

Achebe, Chinua. 1975. *Morning Yet on Creation Day*. New York: Anchor Press/Doubleday.

———. 1997. The Igbo World and Its Art. In *African Philosophy: An Anthology*, ed. Emmanuel Chukwudi Eze, 435–437. Oxford: Wiley-Blackwell.

Armah, Ayi Kwei. 1979. *The Healers*. London: Heinemann.

Ba, Ahmadou Hampate. 1981. The Living Tradition. In *UNESCO General History of Africa. Vol. 1: Methodology and African Prehistory*, ed. J. Ki Zerbo, 166–203. London: Heinemann.

Ben-Amos, Paula. 1973. Symbolism in Olokun Mud Art. *African Arts* 6 (4): 28–31+95.

Bonnett, Michael. 2017. Environmental Consciousness, Sustainability, and the Character of Philosophy of Education. *Studies in the Philosophy of Education* 36: 333–347.

Brockmann, Rolf, and Gerd Hötter. 1994. *Adunni: A Portrait of Susanne Wenger*. München: Trickster Verlag.

Burnham, Owen. 2000. *African Wisdom: A Practical and Inspirational Guide*. London: Judy Piatkus.

Dieterlen, Germaine. 1966. Initiation Among the Peul Pastoral Tribes. In *African Systems of Thought*, Preface by Meyer Fortes and Germaine Dieterlen, 314–327. London: Oxford University Press.

Drewal, Henry John, John Pemberton, Rowland Abiodun, and Allen Wardwell. 1989. *Yoruba: Nine Centuries of African Art and Thought*. New York: Harry N. Abrams.

Elbein, Juan, and Deoscoredes Dos Santos. 1986. Esu Bara: Principle of Individual Life in the Nago System. In *Colloque International sur la Notion de Personne en Afrique Noire*, Quoted by Ayodele Ogundipe in "Retention and Survival of Yoruba Traditional Religion in the Diaspora: Esu in Brazil and Benin Republic" in *Ivie: Nigerian Journal of Arts and Culture* 1 (3): 56–68.

Etieyibo, Edwin. 2017. Ubuntu and the Environment. In *The Palgrave Handbook of African Philosophy*, 633–657. New York: Palgrave Macmillan.

Evans-Pritchard, E.E. 1956. *Nuer Religion*. Oxford: Oxford University Press.

Eze, Michael Onyebuchi. 2017. Humanitatis-Eco (Eco-Humanism): An African Environmental Theory. In *The Palgrave Handbook of African Philosophy*, ed. Adeshina Afolayan and Toyin Falola, 621–632. New York: Palgrave Macmillan.

Ezeluomba, Ndubuisi. 2007. The Explanation of a Text with Reference to the Mud Sculptures of Benin. *Black Arts Quarterly* 33, 12 (1): 33–35. www.stanford.edu/group/CBPA/BAQWinter2007.pdf. Accessed 25 Feb 2019.

Falola, Toyin. 2013. Esu: The God Without Boundaries. In *Esu: Yoruba God of Power and the Imaginative Frontiers*, ed. Toyin Falola. Durham: Carolina Academic Press.

———. 2019. *In Praise of Greatness: The Poetics of African Adulation*. Durham: Carolina Academic Press.

Fatunmbi, Awo Fa'lokun. Obatala: Ifa and the Chief of the Spirit of the White Cloth. 2. Scribd. https://www.scribd.com/document/47061087/OBATALA-Ifa-and-the-Chief-of-the-Spirit-of-the-White-Cloth-EDITED-AND-FORMATTED. Accessed 22 Feb 2019.

Fortune, Dion. 1955. *The Training and Work of an Initiate*. London: Aquarian.

Griaule, Marcel. 1970. The Dogon of the French Sudan. In *African Worlds: Studies in the Cosmological Ideas and Social Values of African Peoples*, ed. Daryll Forde, 83–110. London: Oxford University Press.

Hutton, Ronald. 1999. *Bringing Down the Moon: A History of Modern Pagan Witchcraft*. Oxford: Oxford University Press.

Ifeakor, Chinedu Stephen, and Andrew Otteh. 2017. African Environmental Ethics: A Non–Anthropocentric African Environmentalism. The Journey So Far. *IGWEBUIKE: An African Journal of Arts and Humanities* 3 (6): 67–97.

Irele, Abiola. 1981a. Tradition and the Yoruba Writer: D.O. Fagunwa, Amos Tutuola and Wole Soyinka. In *The African Experience in Literature and Ideology*, 174–197. London: Heinemann.

———. 1981b. What is Negritude. In *The African Experience in Literature and Ideology*, 67–88. London: Heinemann.

———. 1991. The African Scholar. *Transition* 51: 56–69.

Kunene, Mazisi. 1981. *Anthem of the Decades*. London: Heinemann.

Lawal, Babatunde. 1995. À Yà Gbó, À Yà Tó: New Perspectives on Edan Ògbóni. *African Arts* 28 (1): 36–49+98–100.

———. 2001. Àwòrán: Representing the Self and Its Metaphysical Other in Yoruba Art. *The Art Bulletin* 83 (3): 498–526.

Mapanje, Jack, and Landeg White. 1984. *Oral Poetry from Africa*. Harlow/Essex: Longman.

Mbiti, John. 1976. *African Religions and Philosophy*. London: Heinemann.

McCall, John. 1993. Making Peace with Agwu. *Anthropology & Humanism* 18 (2): 56–66.

Okigbo, Christopher. 1971. *Labyrinths with Path of Thunder*. London: Heinemann.

Otto, Rudolph. 1923. *The Idea of the Holy*. Trans. J.W. Harvey. New York: Oxford University Press.
"panpsychism" in *The Stanford Encyclopedia of Philosophy*. https://plato.stanford.edu/archives/win2012/entries/panpsychism/. Accessed 19 Feb 2019.
Rosen, Norma. 1989. Chalk Iconography in Olokun Worship. *African Arts* 22 (3): 44–53+88.
Senanu, K.E., and T.E. Vincent. 1988. *A Selection of African Poetry*. Harlow/Essex: Longman.
Soyinka, Wole. 1972. *A Shuttle in the Crypt*. London: Rex Collings.
———. 1990. *Myth, Literature and the African World*. Cambridge: Cambridge University Press.
The Venerable Bede. 1990. *Historia Ecclesiastica Gentis Anglorum*, AD 731. Trans. Leo Sherley-Price as *Ecclesiastical History of the English People*. London: Penguin.
Umeh, John. 1999. *After God Is Dibia: Igbo Cosmology, Divination and Sacred Science in Nigeria*. London: Karnak House.
Wariboko, Nimi. 2014. *The Charismatic City and the Public Resurgence of Religion: A Pentecostal Social Ethics of Cosmopolitan Urban Life*. New York: Palgrave.
Wordsworth, William. 1973. Tintern Abbey. In *The Oxford Anthology of English Literature*, 146–150. New York: Oxford University Press.
Yai, Olabiyi Babalola. 1992. Review *of Yoruba: Nine Centuries of African Art and Thought* by Henry John Drewal, John Pemberton, Rowland Abiodun and Allen Wardwell. *African Arts* 25 (1): 20+22+24+26+29.

CHAPTER 32

Ethical Thought of Archbishop Desmond Tutu: Ubuntu and Tutu's Moral Modeling as Transformation and Renewal

Sheila A. Otieno

My Humanity is bound up in yours, for we can only be human together.

African morality and value structures are of particular interest to scholars of global ethical systems and their transformations. Modeling an African social ethic, more specifically, has recently become an urgent concern for those doing research on the continent and numerous questions surrounding the nature of African thought, theory and classifications continue to be a primary driver for which present history can be benchmarked and via which emergent themes can be identified. For example, what does it even mean for a social ethic to be "African"?

While many African philosophers, sociologists and anthropologists have somehow found answers that define and describe socio-ethical nuances and materializations in the African context, plotting a discrete way of curating, crafting, modeling and reproducing moral imperatives from African value systems, while of the utmost contemporary importance, remains relatively underexplored. Privileging African social narratives, their history and their inherent indigenous hermeneutics has to become the premier mining methodology for social ethicists seeking to identify morality and moral presence in African societies. Thus, in order to make primary African voices and experiences, scholars must reevaluate the way we speak about the African identity and infuse it into how we relate with the narratives coming from the motherland. The relational

S. A. Otieno (✉)
Boston University's School of Theology, Boston, MA, USA

© The Author(s) 2020
N. Wariboko, T. Falola (eds.), *The Palgrave Handbook of African Social Ethics*, https://doi.org/10.1007/978-3-030-36490-8_32

aspects of African cultural heritages are therefore key to unlocking the potential of African value systems as embedded within the African worldsense.[1] The goal of social ethics, then, is to bring to the fore these cultural gradations that pontificate the formative aspects of the African value system and determine what distinguishes them from non-African ones. Additionally, African social ethics should lift up the unique moral strategies that are a cadence of holistic cultural interweaving and of moral story in African communities as keenly as they were deployed in the past, and as subtly as they are still operative today.

Another way one could educe (and perhaps mine) characteristic moral sensibilities from the African cultural milieu is through autobiographical memory. The efficacy of autobiographical narrative in invoking African moral systems that we might no longer have access to are, today, inculcated into contemporary understanding through the heroic retelling of history and through the lives of living heroes. As a culture that thrived on oral narrative, poetry, myth and song, mining Africanity from such sources, and from what we might call present history, would be appropriate. However, historicity and periodization proves insufficient as a textual tool without critical engagement and interception through social constructionism.[2] The work that we all must do as Africanist scholars is to call into question the ideologies that have sometimes bound up the value of phronesis as embedded into our moral reality.[3] By viewing African morality through the eyes of those we still consider as moral revolutionaries and exemplars, we can perhaps grasp the core of what triggers the renewal of morality and ethics in our societies. Hence, this chapter attempts to do just that, by acknowledging and emphasizing areas of our subject's life that indicate moral transformation and renewal.

I begin this exploration at the nexus of African phronesis and sagacity as a site for social construction, where morality can be recognized in cultures of the African continent from the efforts of the people.[4] African social ethics are therefore evident in deliberate attempts by Africans on the continent to work toward positive moral development. While the nature of these grounded implementations might be difficult to track and preserve in reality, we must assume that present history, that is, history that is currently happening, is a relevant source for both mining and recovery of lost pieces of identity and indicative of hybrid identities currently being formed. The life of Desmond Mpilo Tutu, therefore, serves as an effective backdrop for this conversation.

In this chapter, I argue that Tutu's life is itself performative of a kind of social ethic, embodying "sagacity," as deployed and enacted in the public space, as well as politically adjudicated by it as it encounters moral quandaries. Tutu, arguably one of the most prolific African revolutionaries of our time, is consequently an active and realistic text from which answers, on how the complexities between practical morality and political realism are navigated in the contemporary African reality, can be drawn. As I underscore in the narrative vignettes selected for this chapter, the Archbishop's rise from Anglican priest to freedom fighter was a turbulent one. However, in his continued role as champion for morality in South Africa, his past and present history solidifies his legacy as one of the more celebrated peacekeepers in the world.

When Tutu began his clerical duties in Johannesburg, he unwittingly took on one of the worlds' biggest moral crises to date: *apartheid*. As the first black African Anglican bishop of Cape Town in 1986, the subsequent events precipitated by President P. W. Botha's declaration of a nationwide state of emergency and the United Nations' advance against apartheid completely transformed Tutu's worldsense.[5] Indeed, Tutu might have been nurtured into this role by his surroundings, perhaps even prepared for the clergy by Huddleston, his foster parent in the ministry, but his role as moral revolutionary, I submit, was shaped by his embrace of personhood and his adherence to the Ubuntu philosophy activating it to face the realities of apartheid and aggressive military action in South Africa at the time.

Famously known as "the moral conscience of South Africa," Tutu still stands as an embodiment of ethical reform in a nation that has suffered several moral crises over the years. As moral exemplar for South Africa, a country he once dubbed "the rainbow" nation, his life models for us what an individual's input in moral community might look like. One could ask: of what consequence is "moral modeling" to the Africa we live in today?[6] What does it matter that one good man did good things? For the sake of this exploration, we must look beyond Tutu's individuality and consider how cumulative experiences propelled him onto the frontlines, impacted and perhaps even triggered and shaped the moral transformation of his community. For this reason, this reflection should not be perceived as a call to imitate Tutu's accomplishments. Instead, it should be received as a tracing of exemplary moral journeys, which sometimes have to self-convict, renovate and adjust to the public space in order to achieve moral transformation.

I wish I could shut up, but I can't, and I won't.

In 2005, Desmond Tutu was interviewed by American TV host Craig Ferguson. Sitting across from the talk show host, the somewhat diminutive man clasped his fingers together in a tent as he listened to questions posed to him. Dressed in a black suit, and a clerical shirt of the same color, the then Archbishop represented his vocation as a clergy person to a tee. His usual silver cross was not dangling from his neck, but if one closed their eyes, they could almost surface its image in their mind. His rimless spectacles rested accurately on his face, not shielding the dark eyes in his expressive face. He laughed out loud to what his host had said about him in the introduction, the corners of his eyes crinkling slightly with genuine mirth. His host spoke up:

> Was it surprising, Archbishop Tutu to hear all those things I said about you? Do you ever get used to it?

Craig Ferguson, known for his cheek, did not disappoint in his questioning of Tutu. The clergyman seated across from him replied softly to this in a slight South African accent:

> Well…it's like that story that is told about the woman and her son who went to her husband's funeral. Do you know it? [Craig answers "No."] The woman and her son go to the husband's funeral. And as they were reading the eulogy, she leans over to her son and whispers "I think we came to the wrong funeral."

The host's raucous laughter and that of his audience were punctuated by Tutu's own infectious giggle. Tutu's laughter is loud and full—just like one would imagine an African elder's laugh would be. Mischievous. It's a definitively South African laugh—one without pretense, one that revels in its sharing of merriment with others.[7]

In the interview, I have just mentioned, we could say that to his host, Tutu's indirect answer was perhaps a strategic deflection from his actual sentiments—that is, an escapist way of avoiding the question—but, in fact, was a definitive answer. To a native African, Tutu answered as any elder would. In oral narrative, by telling a story, and not in a deceptive manner, but, instead, embedding an answer within humor. Rather than declare his own modesty, he exemplified it. Through narrative, Tutu had circuitously shifted the attention of the audience and that of his interviewer from their captivation of him. He humanized himself, welcoming them into the space with a joke. The use of humor in this situation not only dissipated the seriousness of the interview but also mirrored the intensity of the man.

Tutu's actions during this interview may have communicated how he wanted to be (and perhaps preferred to be) portrayed by his host but, additionally, demonstrated a primary relational ethic he embraces. By diffusing the hierarchy between him and Ferguson, he asked to be seen not only as an Archbishop or as a global celebrity but as a person. And by reframing access into his own reality, Tutu rejected the narrative of global popular opinion and determined the lens through which he should be encountered. Seeing goes beyond the act of looking at or noticing something. To really "see" something is to take it into one's consciousness and embrace it in one's mind as something worth being engaged, acknowledged and considered. The Archbishop actively took control of the interview, demanding that both audience and host see *him* with more than just their eyes. This roundabout way of coming to this moment is what I perceive as enactments of sagacity. Perhaps, I could have read too much into the way the interview went. Possibly, Tutu's character is simply understated, and he took this opportunity to merely self-identify. Yet, I submit that taking Tutu's deflection at face value would be a simplistic understanding of how his subversion of self-aggrandizement and celebrity operates. Granted, I might be imposing the moniker "sage" onto one who might not willingly accept it. However, the title is an embodiment of Tutu both in character and in demeanor, and as verified by his accomplishments ramping up to the contemporary moment.

Definitions of the adjective "sage" portray one who holds this title or trait as "having, showing, or indicating profound wisdom."[8] The word from the Latin form *sapere*, that is, 'be wise,' inspired African philosopher Henry Odera

Oruka to defend philosophic sagacity in both *Four Trends in African Philosophy* (1978) and *Sagacity in African Philosophy* (1983), proposing that the critical reflective thought of sages differs fundamentally from that of ethnophilosophers, in that the latter is both individualist and primarily dialectical.[9] The account of African philosophical contributions as simply "folk philosophy" diminishes the quality of African thought as not sufficiently rigorous and philosophical. Oruka disagreed with this Western assessment of African philosophical thought, by clarifying philosophic sagacity as distinctive from cultural philosophy or mythos, which would produce what he referred to as "ordinary sages." Wise folks who specialize in the existing knowledge order and capable of both explaining and maintaining it fall into this category. A philosophic sage or a sage philosopher, on the other hand, "operates at a second order level, producing systems within a system and orders within an order."[10] This means they are able to operate within both the primary epistemology and through practical engagement with it, create substitutionary knowledge systems that can supersede it. Oruka addressed key aspects of how the African moral value system is activated, together with its inherent flexible nature, allowing for both addition and subtraction of moral compendia as needed. These systems, as aligned with the passage of time, also constitute phronetic applications of individual reasoning, as well as performative recreation and exchange of ethical norms and sources.

Hence, to name Tutu a philosophic sage would not be unfitting. At the time of his birth, South Africa was under the administration of colonial Dutch Prime Minister James Hertzog. Only whites and a few blacks in the Cape province were allowed to vote, and Hertzog planned to further limit, rather than expand, black South African political and economic rights.[11] Over the years, apartheid's insidiousness was most suffered by the black population of South Africa, inasmuch as it affected the whole nation. Its racial hierarchizations placed white people at the top of a very high totem pole, one which prioritized the Boers over and above all other racial groups. "It was into this rather harsh world that Desmond Mpilo Tutu arrived on October 7, 1931."[12] The moral reality in which Tutu grew up could only prepare him for a career either tending to the wounds of those in despair or in participating in revolts against the Boers and their policies. Eventually, he chose both.

Moreover, Tutu's sagacity did not happen suddenly. To follow Oruka's evolutionary sequence, it is quite possible that he was, at first, wise in the way that any person can be, as they accumulate knowledge and life experience. As a cultural philosopher, owing to his age at the time he became a bishop in 1985, even though he had quit teaching and begun participating in protests and activism work in 1957, entering Anglican ministry the year after. Some of the values he picked up from the home that his parents Zachariah and Aleatha had built may have contributed to this, but it must have been his grandmother, who had (first) imparted some of these cultural wisdoms in that small house in Klerksdorp, Transvaal province.[13] Sickly as a baby, autobiographers often mention that his father so feared he would not survive infancy, refusing to name him for the first few years of his childhood. When his condition stabilized, his grandmother named him *Mpilo*—meaning life, a central feature in African culture and religious tradition. By naming him "life," Tutu's grandmother sought to ward off the death that seemed to stalk him but perhaps also made him a force for life. His family, being inter-tribal by marriage, already identified themselves as "Africans" or "South Africans," embedding within Desmond a nonpartisan understanding of his existence; perhaps it is here that Tutu learned to be Ubuntu. By the time he returned to South Africa after receiving his Master of Theology degree from King's College in England, Tutu's sagacious voice had already been fully developed.

A person is a person because he recognizes others as persons.

Tutu told one of his stories of metanoia, to longtime NPR interviewer Krista Tippett in April 2010, when he spoke of the first time he realized the damage apartheid had done to South Africans. The Archbishop's dream for South Africa had always been one of transformation; as a South African, he had many small moments where he "had a glimpse of how South African society might be differently ordered."[14] Tutu revealed one of these formative moments in his own life that had brought him face to face with his blackness. With a humorous chuckle, Tutu recounts his personal story, highlighting deep self-awareness as follows:

> ...I think, I mean, that we have very gravely underestimated the damage that apartheid inflicted on all of us. You know, the damage to our psyches, the damage that has made—I mean, it shocked me. I went to Nigeria when I was working for the World Council of Churches, and I was due to fly to Jos. And so I go to Lagos airport and I get onto the plane and the two pilots in the cockpit are both black. And whee [sic], I just grew inches. You know, it was fantastic because we had been told that blacks can't do this.[15]

While on the journey, the plane's passengers (including Tutu) become terrified when it passed through very turbulent skies. He continues to Tippett:

> Do you know, I can't believe it but the first thought that came to my mind was, "Hey, there's no white men in that cockpit. Are those blacks going to be able to make it?" And of course, they obviously made it—here I am. But the thing is, I had not known that I was damaged to the extent of thinking that somehow actually what those white people who had kept drumming into us in South Africa about our being inferior, about our being incapable, it had lodged somewhere in me.[16]

Oral narratives and life experiences are often invoked as primary sources for moral wisdom in most African cultures. By sharing this story with Tippett, Tutu divulged an intimate and crucial moment in his own moral transformation history, while also exposing the insidious nature of the anti-blackness of apartheid. This kind of anti-blackness could turn the master's tools back on the subject to use upon herself, the master's absence notwithstanding. In this particular account, Tutu recalled both a realization and a recognition of his own woundedness that led him to understand something new and important about himself as the head of the Truth and Reconciliation Commission (TRC). He was not chosen only to serve as arbiter and judge, but he too was still recovering from a moral woundedness inflicted by apartheid that also required healing.

Kwame Anthony Appiah in *Honor Code: How Moral Revolutions Happen* posits that the subtle spark that begins moral revolutions is entrenched in human interaction. He posits that:

> ...Identity connects these moral revolutions with an aspect of our human psychology that was widely neglected by moral philosophers working in English for too long, though it has come into sharper focus in recent moral and political philosophy: and that is our human need for what Georg Wilhelm Friedrich Hegel called *Anerkennung*—recognition....We need others to recognize us as conscious beings and acknowledge that we recognize them.[17]

What Appiah wants us to understand is that ethics are situated within a context, and it is the contextual and the people within it that can overturn a moral order. As human connects with another human, all of a sudden an urgent need for humanity to be respected and accepted is brought to light. In Tutu's case, it was at the moment that Huddleston saw Aleatha that Tutu's life was transformed. A tiny ripple effect began that would change Desmond's life forever. As Appiah notes, there are certain moral revolutions that could be easily won. Clearly, morality, in this sense, is an important dimension of ethics; doing what one should for others is part of living well, and one of the distinctive features of the last few centuries has been a growing appreciation of the obligations each of us has to other people.[18]

Ubuntu's primary relational ethic is similar to Appiah's use of "recognition." To see the personhood, and subsequently the humanity, of another is to recognize the other as being worthy of one's acknowledgment of human decency. It is in symbolically "doffing one's hat" to another person walking across the street that one finds one's own humanity.[19] Tutu learned this aspect of humaneness quite early on in his career and carried it with him throughout his career. Like Nelson Mandela, he is a proponent of Ubuntu, even admitting in one of his monographs on forgiveness, that the Truth and Reconciliation Commission was ultimately a third way, in which amnesty functioned as "a central feature of the African *Weltanschauung*—what we know in our languages as *Ubuntu* in the Nguni group of languages, or *Botho*, in the Sotho languages."[20] Ubuntu, Tutu says, is very difficult to render into a Western language:

> It speaks of the very essence of being human. When we want to give high praise to someone we say "*Yu, u nobuntu*"; "Hey, so-and-so has Ubuntu." Then you are generous, you are hospitable, you are caring and compassionate. You share what you have. It is to say, "My humanity is caught up, is inextricably bound up, in yours." We belong in a bundle of life.[21]

Only a person who has *Ubuntu* can demonstrate it to another person. This guiding philosophy, as eloquently woven into Tutu's own personal ethic, contributed to his vision of social harmony and community as a prime good; a prime virtue if you will. As one can suppose, this "virtue" constitutes several actions that would also be considered virtuous, but it signifies even more than that. Being human is also belonging. In African conception, it is being a part of something greater than oneself—a community. It is this philosophy that served the Archbishop well in the transition to a post-apartheid South Africa. After the Nuremberg trials, South Africans still had to live together, even though their humanities had been essentially diminished and destroyed by apartheid's segregation laws and racial hatred. A new mandate for Tutu arose—to reconstitute the broken pieces of the rainbow nation through the quest for justice and forgiveness in the Truth and Reconciliation Commission.

Hope is being able to see that there is light despite all of the darkness.

Another aspect of Tutu's sagacity that is also particular to his ethics is his theological commitments to African Christianity.[22] Tutu's Christianity is a central and significant part of his worldsense.[23] As one of the illustrations in the opening chapter of the book *God is not Christian* phrases it, "nothing epitomizes Desmond Tutu's radicalism (using the word radical, as he likes to say, in the original sense of getting to the root of an issue) more than his views on the relationship of his faith to the faiths of others."[24] While interfaith tolerance has been a contiguous factor in Tutu's Christianity, I submit that perhaps it is not the most dominant, nor even the most congruent for Tutu. African religiosity not only presages the addition of other religious viewpoints and faith lenses, it also supports it. Hence, Tutu's adherence to the values of Ubuntu in this sense is bound to permeate his Christianity and inevitably results in an interfaith-focused tolerant Christianity. This is, of course, not to undermine Tutu's commitment to his faith and to the Anglican communion. His theological duties served him most generously in the formation and leadership of the Truth and Reconciliation Commission in South Africa.

The determining factor for Tutu remained that South African people could live together after all the atrocities they had committed against one another. Forgiveness became very fundamental for the TRC when it needed to define itself and decide what its work would be. Tutu's discourse on *ubuntu* is so proximate to the principle of *salus* in classical political reason that he even goes so far as to translate it as a *summum bonum*.[25] In truth, *Ubuntu* is **the** *summum bonum* for African communities, where the ultimate good is a search for oneness with one another and with community.[26] In a post-apartheid state reality, this was the primary goal, one which Tutu believed the TRC could not only access but encourage South Africans to pursue as an ultimate good that governed their relations with one another from Nuremberg onward. Confirming this, Tutu proposes in *No Freedom without Forgiveness* that "social harmony is for us, the *summum bonum* – the greatest good" and that "anything that subverts or undermines this sought-after good is to be avoided like the plague" if we are to exist together.

Similarly, Tutu's famous relationship with the Dalai Lama, sometimes playfully referred to as a "holy bromance," exhibits Tutu's genuine care for persons outside his community of influence's orbits.[27] Together, he and the Dalai Lama coauthored *The Book of Joy*, which outlines eight pillars of happy living (or flourishing). Thought can and should be given to how this ethic actually materializes in Tutu's context. Contrary to how communality often functions in African religiosity, the recent upsurge in intolerance and divisiveness between Christian denominations on the continent is a phenomenon that we are yet to fully understand. Nonetheless, Tutu's affiliation with the Anglican Communion and vocal morality has often put him at odds with both his faith and with Christians in Africa and around the world. The Archbishop's Christianity, however, had to take on a distinct voice in Tutu in a way it does not often manifest in church eldership and leadership. Its moral corrective lies in its approach to moral dilemmas and its haste to intervene in moments when it assumes that the religious order has failed and cannot be solely relied on anymore. In this vein, Tutu has often embraced the role of critical-insider within the Anglican Communion and in other organizations he is associated with.

In the wake of the recent sexual abuse scandals that embroiled the humanitarian aid giant—Oxfam—Tutu immediately distanced himself with his duties there. The scandal also prompted Tutu to speak out publicly for the first time about sexual misconduct by humanitarian agencies on the continent. The statement from his office affirmed that Tutu was "deeply disappointed by allegations of immorality and possible criminality involving humanitarian aid workers linked to the charity. He was also saddened by the impact of the allegations on the many thousands of good people who have supported Oxfam's righteous work."[28] Although the Archbishop has long abandoned public life, he has retained his status as moral voice in matters both local and global. This, I contend, is not indebted only to his Christianity but also to his sagacity. Key to this contention is Tutu's assertion that God does not belong only to Christians, a claim that he has made severally. In one of his more detailed theological arguments made during his 1992 lecture in memory of Catholic Archbishop of Cape Town, Stephen Naidoo, Tutu averred that "to claim God exclusively for Christians, is to make God too small and in a real sense is blasphemous. God is bigger than Christianity and cares for more than Christians only….God has been around since even before creation, and that is a very long time."[29]

Here, there also lies a shrewd pronouncement that Christianity is a latecomer to the religions game, one which, while not invalidated by its late entrance, should perhaps be humbler in its encounter of other religions. The abstention of othering is essential to Tutu's Christian identity, in that it considers the detriments caused by use and application of divisive rhetoric, and the comprehension that even the most righteous of religious morality can be "wrong" or "immoral" as has often been the case in the justification of colonialism and apartheid. Tutu has often utilized his Anglican identity with tact, strategy and, sometimes, politically exercised, as we shall see in the following paragraphs.

> *If you are neutral in situations of injustice, you have chosen the side of the oppressor. If an elephant has its foot on the tail of a mouse and you say that you are neutral, the mouse will not appreciate your neutrality.*

What has been surprising about Tutu's brand of moral sagacity is its deliberate willingness to speak out against atrocities and continually support efforts toward complete wholeness at certain times and opt out of such activist roles at others.[30] This particularly fascinates me, as a scholar of the processes involved in moral deliberation. When does one choose to activate their moral voice? Why and for which reasons would one openly exhibit their moral position? The answer to these questions, I think, is critical for the task of moral renewal. Since 1994, the Rainbow Nation has been at a moral crossroads, as a new form of difference has become a spark that frequently flares up violence and intolerance all over the country. The cries of *Makwerekwere* rose up in the voices of dissenting South Africans in the post-apartheid era and have often been deployed as a nationalist ideology, declaring people from other African nations as personae non gratae.[31] The term "Makwerekwere" slang derogatorily employed to refer to "other Africans" became a common xenophobic utterance during South Africa's post-apartheid reconstruction. In 2008, more than 60 people were killed in and around Johannesburg, Durban and on account of xenophobic attacks. During this time, Tutu condemned the xenophobic acts when he put out a statement through his foundation saying that the nation that had once "filled the world with hope [was] being reduced to a grubby shadow of itself." Recalling the reforms made by the TRC hearings, Tutu was surprised that the processes of national healing were set up as safeguards against such acts of violence and segregation in the country reoccurring, highlighting xenophobia's similarity to apartheid. Scholarly debates on the political exercise of virtue have often disagreed on who is more liable to benefit from social cohesion. Even more crucially, on whose responsibility it is to ensure that social cohesion is maintained. In cases like these, exceptionalism is sometimes intertwined into national narratives that call for social cohesion, without thought to how harmful the elevation of national pride can be on a nation's immigrants. This has been the case in other places, such as America and Brazil, where divisive rhetoric has quickly incited xenophobic attacks on immigrants and perceived non-indigenes. However, state governance issues are always a game of moral balancing between individual attributes and social conditions.

Such has also been the case with the growing South African nation-state. The reality of poverty and a widening economic gap in South Africa underscored the pressure of economic inequity in the young democratic nation. An influx of foreign immigrant and flexible immigration policies hurried to compensate for decades of black underrepresentation. Woefully, many of the new opportunities invited other black Africans seeking safe harbor in the now economically stable nation, needing their new businesses, prospects and skills. The stigmatization of the other, as inspired by South African social dissatisfaction, was one where black representation was no longer restricted to native South African blacks. A local news outlet summarized the crisis via the dissatisfaction of a South African man:

> They should go because we have no jobs. I'm a citizen and want to work for 150 rand a day but foreigners will do it for seventy Rand a day. In the kitchens and the factories, they are taking over our jobs. They bring cheap goods and we don't know where from. They leave their countries with a lot of skills and we have nothing. Our education is not good enough.[32]

Historically, struggle for power, prestige and survival intensifies as disparities between the competing groups escalate. In other words, as groups tend toward diminishing contrasts, especially when the means of survival are scarce, they exert greater competitive pressure on each other, tending toward ruthlessness.[33] While xenophobic attacks in South Africa became more visible after 2004, they had been bubbling under the social surface for a much longer time. By the time Tutu eventually spoke up against South Africa's phobogenic behavior, he did it in response to the worst of these attacks, which had happened in Durban from mid- to late 2015.[34] Collective global pressure had pushed South Africa's leaders to address the issue, criticizing many for either not doing enough, not saying enough or doing nothing at all. This was a particularly peculiar case for Tutu, whose moral trendsetting is often expected. Many rightly questioned why he had remained silent on the matter for so long, and worse, why it took compulsion from outside forces for his voice to be heard.

Inversely, in a matter where several African states and individuals have chosen social silence over moral transformation: the lesbian, gay, bisexual, transgender and Queer (LGBTQ+) debate, Tutu has been one of the more vocal clerics in Africa. Although South Africa had already legalized gay marriage in 1996, speaking publicly about homosexuality, especially around black South Africans, was just not done. Even after constitutional legalization, several LGBTQ+ people living in South Africa believed that despite provisions in the constitution, they remained largely unprotected from prejudice, bigotry and other hate crimes. Several gay rights groups and queer communities protested against killings across the nation and asserted that the government was not doing enough to protect the rights of LGBTQ+ citizens. The traditional and cultural divides that separated Africans around this issue came to a head for the African members of the Anglican Communion during the Lambeth Conference of 2008.

Hence, it was that in this, the latter part of his career, that Tutu was faced with a moral dilemma that forced his hand when it came to taking a definitive stand on LGBTQ+ issues. His moral position, at the time, placed him at loggerheads with African Anglicanism and the South African people—demanding that he offer his personal truth as a clarification for what was "right." Several conservative bishops, including some Africans, had vehemently disagreed with the consecration of American Episcopalianism's (US Branch of Anglicanism) first openly gay bishop, boycotting the conference altogether. For Anglicanism, this was a significant moment in history as traditions were challenged and cultures clashed. Tutu was one of the few African bishops, even then, who supported LGBTQ+ rights, later asserting his stance during a Free and Equal campaign in Cape Town stating: "I would refuse to go to a homophobic heaven. No, I would say sorry, I mean I would much rather go to the other place."[35] The Archbishop further said that he would not worship a homophobic God. Instantly, he became a champion for LGBTQ+ rights around the world.

At the end of 2015, when his daughter, Mpho Tutu van Furth, was suspended by the Anglican church and later expelled from her clerical position after marrying her long-term partner, Dutch Professor Marceline van Furth, Archbishop Tutu became even more vocal about LGBTQ+ issues. One cannot be certain if this was directly tied to his daughter's open declaration of her relationship, or because the backlash from South Africans had triggered a more active voice and role for the Archbishop, making it imperative for him to speak out. Whichever it was, with increasing cases of homophobic violence, Tutu visibly aligned himself with several international organizations, including Amnesty International, and turned his moral conscience outwards to condemn African countries like Uganda, Liberia, Nigeria and Tanzania for outlawing same-sex relationships and instituting other prohibitive laws against same-sex relations. Whether his daughter's recent marriage was a determining factor or not, there was a distinctive shift in Tutu's positioning of his moral voice. The question is not so much if Tutu's employment of sagacity in this case was effective but, instead, if it occasionally had to abjure engagement in moral transformation in issues that were not locally akin with his own moral stance. An inherent question in there for me is whether abjuration is itself a subversive moral act and therefore just as deliberately activated as participation would be.

> *Do your little bit of good where you are; it's those little bits of good put together that overwhelm the world.*

I cannot conclude this chapter without mentioning that the centrifugal nature of humaneness or humanity for the Ubuntu philosophy unquestionably configures its moral arc. Tutu's sagacity further establishes that an African social ethic is one that places personhood and humanity at the center but through the activation of individual moral deliberation processes, either engages or disengages moral issues, ensuring continuity of an invested moral goal. Thus, the ethos of communal preservation, of seeking signs of life, not only undergirds and encourages relationships that are able to sustain the ethos itself but spurs it toward revolution should the need arise. The life of Archbishop Tutu, thus, in this way, models the fashioning and restructuring of social order from a moral focal viewpoint, one which positions itself as a center around which all other value systems can operate. Cultural value systems, therefore, infuse social and moral orders determining the development of a nation's ethical narrative altogether. An African social ethic, therefore, must take seriously the influences of culture and regular social construction as a mitigating factor of moral crisis and repair for developing African nations and emerging citizens of African states.

Notes

1. Here, I refer to worldsense as conceived of and applied by Oyeronke Oyĕwùmí in her book *The Invention of Women: Making African Sense of Western Gender Discourses* (1997), instead of the more popular "worldview"—Oyĕwùmí eschews the Western impulse to prioritize sight over all other bodily senses, in view of the African multisensory way of being and knowing in the world.
2. Not to be confused with social constructivism. Social constructionism is a theory of knowledge and communication that examines the development of jointly constructed understandings of the world that form the basis for shared assumptions about reality. It centers on the idea that meaning is shared and developed in relationship and coordination with others rather than separately within each individual. (Leeds-Hurwitz 2010).
3. I use the word *phronesis* in its Aristotelian form to refer to the practical application of wisdom that activates goods/virtue in the moral space and therefore integrally tied to character (Nicomachean Ethics, Trans. Bartlett, R. C. and Collins, S. D.: 2012).
4. Unless otherwise stated, I refer to "African" nations, people, culture and contexts in general and give specific examples to support my claim in reference to Tutu and South Africa. In doing so, I do not intend to collapse all African nations into one monolithic entity or posit that all of these issues are encountered by all countries in Africa in the same way. However, I hint at some similarities in the way these problems appear on the continent in different ways in my prescriptions for African Social Ethics. In these moments, I use Africa as a descriptive term—to identify a continental coherence that I do not necessarily expand on in this chapter, which particularly attends to South Africa, where our main character is a citizen.
5. Allen, John. *Rabble-Rouser for Peace: The Authorized Biography of Desmond Tutu.* Free Press, 2006, p. 26.
6. I use the term moral modeling to refer to the ways in which an individual's experience and moral transformation might serve as an example to those who admire and respect them. This is not the same as Emmanuel Katongole's (2017) use of Sara Lawrence-Lightfoot and Jessica Hoffmann Davis's (1997) portraiture methodology. Portraiture, as used by both Katongole and Lightfoot, is a method of social science inquiry that blends art and science to capture the subtle nuances of human experience and social life. Moral modeling, on the other hand, simply refers to the modeling of morality or aspects of morality, whether virtuous or not within a community where the model is perceived as an authority.
7. This is a recounting of the infamous *Late Late Show with Craig Ferguson* interview held on 4 March 2009 and subsequently for which Ferguson won the Peabody award that same year. I accessed it from https://www.youtube.com/watch?v=12OlAe2Sfes&t=1171s
8. Ibid.
9. Oruka, H. O., *Trends in Contemporary African Philosophy,* Nairobi: Shirikon Publishers (1990) p. 17.

10. Oruka, H. O., *Sagacity in African Philosophy*, International Philosophical Quarterly, Vol. XXIII, No. 4, December 1983: p. 386.
11. Gish, S. D. Desmond Tutu: A Biography, Westport, CT: Greenwood Publishers (2004): p. 2.
12. Gish 2004. p. 3.
13. Ibid.
14. Ibid.
15. Transcript of Desmond Tutu Interview with Krista Tippett dated 29 April 2010—accessed from https://onbeing.org/programs/desmond-tutu-a-god-of-surprises/ on 17 June 2019.
16. Ibid.
17. Appiah, K. A. *The Honor Code: How Moral Revolutions Happen*: W. W. Norton, 2011. p. xiii.
18. Ibid., p. xiv.
19. Here, I am subtly referencing the famous story of Tutu's mentor doffing his hat to Tutu's mother even though he didn't know who she was.
20. Tutu, Desmond. *No Future Without Forgiveness*. Random House: New York, NY, 2012. p. 31
21. Ibid.
22. I specify "African" Christianity here in concert with Ogbu U. Kalu's portrayal of the African identity in Christianity on the continent in *African Christianity: An African Story* (2007), in which he posits a privileging of the patterns of African agency without neglecting the noble roles played by missionaries in bringing Christianity to Africa. The history of African Christianity in this volume tells the story of African Christianity as a distinct form of Christianity by identifying the major themes and plotlines of the African encounter and appropriation of the Gospel.
23. I preference Oyeronke Oyěwùmí's use of this term in *The Invention of Women: Making an African Sense of Western Gender Discourse* (1997) over the term worldview, eschewing the Western proclivity to privilege sight as the only sense engaged in encountering the world. Here and elsewhere in this chapter, I speak of this as Tutu's way of being in the world—which involves more than just perception and viewpoint, but it encompasses all aspects of personhood in its understanding of person and community vis-á-vis their interaction with the Divine and natural aspects of the world as well.
24. God is not a Christian p. 3.
25. Sitze, Adam. *The Impossible Machine: A Genealogy of South Africa's Truth and Reconciliation Commission*. University of Michigan Press, 2013. p. 245.
26. This is, in a sense, an imagining of a realization of Plato's idea of the *polis* and perhaps even Cicero's *salus publica* in his *De Legibus*, both of which translate to the ideal working community—one which allowed for both full presence of the citizen and full productivity of the state.
27. Informal noun referring to a close nonsexual friendship between men. Tutu and the Dalai Lama refer to themselves as "the spiritual brothers" and have often declared themselves as each other's best friend.
28. In the wake of the Oxfam Scandal, the statement from Tutu was reported by the *Times* of South Africa. As accessed from https://www.timeslive.co.za/news/south-africa/2018-02-15-tutu-quits-as-ambassador-for-oxfam-over-charitys-sex-scandal/ dated 021518; on 8 December 2018.
29. Tutu, Desmond. *God is not a Christian: And other provocations*. HarperCollins, 2011, p. 14.

30. Here, I augment the idea of sagacity by adding the descriptor "moral" to attest to Tutu's modeling role as an individual whose integrity and personality can be classified as heroic. I eschew using the phrase "moral hero" for obvious reasons—as this deliberately bucks against the connotations of sagacity. Moral heroism is primarily situational, suggesting that the individual is thrust into heroism once faced with a moral dilemma. However, a much larger conversation undergirds the perception that moral goods/virtues are acquired or collected from a storage of goods within society. As most African moral philosophy supports, "goods" are present within oneself and need only to be activated. Tutu would probably agree with this view, particularly as supported by his thesis in the book coauthored with his daughter, Mpho titled *Made for Good*ness (2010), where he compares theological natural law arguments with the principles of Ubuntu and argues that goodness is already within every human being.
31. K. Mathers and L. Landau, "Natives, tourists, and Makwerekwere: Ethical concerns with 'Proudly South African' tourism," Development Southern Africa, 24(3), 2007, pp. 523–537.
32. Smith, David, *Xenophobia in South Africa: "They beat my husband with sticks and took everything!"* in The Guardian Online dated 17 April 2015 accessed online at https://www.theguardian.com/world/2015/apr/17/xenophobia-south-africa-brothers-violence-foreigners on 9 December 2018.
33. Mario Matsinhe, David. *Africa's Fear of Itself: The Ideology of Makwerekwere in South Africa*. Third World Quarterly 32, no. 2 (2011): 295–313.
34. I have co-opted Matsinhe's nod to Frantz Fanon's phrase in *Black Skins, White Masks* (1952), where he characterized a cultural production of blackness created to induce fear in others (particularly white people) where the black "object" is one to be feared and cautioned against as determined by the white gaze. Here, blackness turns the gaze back upon itself—by resituating the phobia onto national ethnicity and ethnic boundaries. Matsinhe identifies this strange fear of other black people as being.
35. Accessed from BBC World News Online dated 26 July 2013. *Archbishop Tutu 'would not worship a homophobic God'* at https://www.bbc.com/news/world-africa-23464694 on 120918.

Bibliography

Allen, J. 2006. *Rabble-Rouser for Peace: The Authorized Biography of Desmond Tutu*. New York: Free Press.

Appiah, K.A. 2011. *The Honor Code: How Moral Revolutions Happen*. New York: W. W. Norton.

Aristotle, R.C. Bartlett, and S.D. Collins. 2012. *Aristotle's Nicomachean Ethics*. Chicago: University of Chicago Press.

Author Unknown. BBC World News Online Dated July 26, 2013. *Archbishop Tutu 'Would Not Worship a Homophobic God'*. https://www.bbc.com/news/world-africa-23464694. On 9 Dec 2018.

Battle, Michael. 1997. *Reconciliation: The Ubuntu Theology of Desmond Tutu*. Cleveland: Pilgrim Press.

Gish, Steven. 2004. *Desmond Tutu: A Biography*. Westport: Greenwood Publishing Group.

Kalu, Ogbu. 2013. *African Christianity: An African Story*. Pretoria: Dept. of Church History, University of Pretoria.

Katongole, Emmanuel. 2017. *Born from Lament: The Theology and Politics of Hope in Africa*. Grand Rapids: W. B. Eerdmans Publishing Company.
Lawrence-Lightfoot, Sara, and Jessica Hoffmann Davis. 1997. *The Art and Science of Portraiture*. 1st ed. San Francisco: Jossey-Bass.
Leeds-Hurwitz, Wendy, ed. 2010. *The Social History of Language and Social Interaction Research: People, Places, Ideas*. Cresskill: Hampton Press.
Matsinhe, David. 2009. Cleaning the Nation: Anti-African Patriotism and Xenophobia in South Africa. ProQuest Dissertations and Theses.
———. 2011. Africa's Fear of Itself: The Ideology of Makwerekwere in South Africa. *Third World Quarterly* 32 (2): 295–313.
Mathers, Kathryn, and Loren Landau. 2007. Natives, Tourists, and Makwerekwere: Ethical Concerns with 'Proudly South African' Tourism. *Development Southern Africa* 24 (3): 523–537.
Oruka, Henry Odera. 1985. Ideology and Truth. *Praxis International* 5 (1): 35–50.
———. 1990a. *Trends in Contemporary African Philosophy*. Nairobi: Shirikon Publishers.
———. 1990b. *Sage Philosophy: Indigenous Thinkers and Modern Debate on African Philosophy*. Vol. 4. Leiden: Brill.
Oruka, H. Odera, Anke Graness, and Kai Kresse. 1997. *Sagacious Reasoning: Henry Odera Oruka in Memoriam*. Frankfurt Am Main/New York: P. Lang.
Oyěwùmí, O. 1997. *The Invention of Women: Making an African Sense of Western Gender Discourses*. Minneapolis: University of Minnesota Press.
Savides, Matthew. 2018. Tutu Quits as Ambassador for Oxfam Over Charity's Sex Scandal. *Times Live, South Africa*, February 05.
Serequeberhan, Tsenay. The Hermeneutics of African Philosophy: Horizon and Discourse. New York: Routledge, 1994.
Sitze, Adam. 2013. *The Impossible Machine: A Genealogy of South Africa's Truth and Reconciliation Commission*. Michigan: University of Michigan Press.
Smith, David. Xenophobia in South Africa: "They Beat My Husband with Sticks and Took Everything!" in The Guardian Online Dated April 17, 2015. Accessed Online at https://www.theguardian.com/world/2015/apr/17/xenophobia-south-africa-brothers-violence-foreigners. On 9 Dec 2018.
Tutu, Desmond. 1994. *The Rainbow People of God: The Making of a Peaceful Revolution*. New York: Doubleday Books.
———. 1998. *Exploring Forgiveness*. Madison: University of Wisconsin Press.
———. 2003. *Truth and Reconciliation Commission of South Africa Report*. Cape Town: Commission.
———. 2007. *Believe: The Words and Inspiration of Desmond Tutu*. Boulder: Blue Mountain Arts.
———. 2009. *No Future Without Forgiveness*. New York: Image.
———. 2011. *God Is Not a Christian: And Other Provocations*. New York: HarperCollins.
Tutu, D., and M. Tutu. 2010. *Made for Goodness: And Why This Makes All the Difference*. New York: HarperCollins.

OTHERS

Late Late Show with Craig Ferguson Interview Held on March 4, 2009. Accessed from https://www.youtube.com/watch?v=12OlAe2Sfes&t=1171. On 10 Dec 2018.
Transcript of Desmond Tutu Interview with Krista Tippett Dated April 29, 2010. Accessed from https://onbeing.org/programs/desmond-tutu-a-god-of-surprises/. On 17 June 2019.

CHAPTER 33

"Reminders of What Once Was": The Ethics of Mercy Amba Oduyoye

Oluwatomisin Oredein

Mercy Amba Oduyoye

Mercy Amba Ewudziwa Oduyoye was born to Mercy Yaa Dakwaa Yamoah and Minister Charles Kwaw Yamoah on her grandfather's cocoa farm near Asamankese, Ghana, approximately 46 miles northwest of the current capital city of Accra, Ghana.[1] Her beginnings were humble, but her drive world-changing. Throughout her life, the practices of religious life would become a keen point of interest for this Christian Akan woman.[2] All three subsets of her identity would inflect her critical voice: what mark might a woman, an Akan woman, an Akan woman who also identifies as Christian have in the world of religious and social thought?

Over the past six decades, Oduyoye's voice has contributed critical ideas to Christian theology from an African woman's perspective, one cognizant of both matriarchal and patriarchal cultures, both postcolonial and neocolonial iterations of theological and ethical principles, and the plights of both African women and men. She purports a view and voice aware of the fullness of African culture, its positive and negative elements.

Her classic works and contributions such as *Daughters of Anowa, Beads and Strands, Hearing and Knowing, A Will to Rise,* and *Introducing African Women's Theology*, all illumine her commitment to the wellness of African women and the African community as a whole through theological narration and interrogation. She writes *for* African women in order to see their stories made public and visible, but she also writes to educate those who have benefited, consciously and unconsciously, from the silencing of African women—European men and women and African men.[3]

O. Oredein (✉)
Brite Divinity School, Fort Worth, TX, USA

© The Author(s) 2020
N. Wariboko, T. Falola (eds.), *The Palgrave Handbook of African Social Ethics*, https://doi.org/10.1007/978-3-030-36490-8_33

Unafraid to call out the challenges of being an African woman in the world, Oduyoye's intentions are threefold: (1) the uplift of African women's voices and concerns; (2) the education of the beneficiaries of such realities, all toward; (3) the total empowerment of African people. Her prophetic and corrective approaches to identifying the social, cultural, and religious ills in African and Western societies are not toward the punishment or denigration of another but toward the collective thriving of all continental Africans.

Her priorities are bound together: ensuring the thriving of African women ensures the thriving of African communities as a whole.[4] This furthers into ecological frames as well; once the world learns to treat its peoples well, it could learn to love all creation in a similar manner. Educating privileged persons can help educate the world toward right treatment of all of humanity, humanity connected to an ailing earth. Oduyoye's approach is holistic: the world can be made well if those who impact it understand themselves well within it. The moral frame with which people should live is learned through thoughtful discernment and right practice. How people see the world and all therein determine how they treat the world.

The Already Known

Oduyoye's aims, while respectable in their own right, only reach as far as her name. Many have heard of her, but many have not. A critical figure in the life of African theology, African women's vocality, and ethical thought, Oduyoye advocates for the overlooked through her life's work. Most prominently, she has provided countless gathering and publishing spaces in which African women's voices could be centered in religious conversation.

Loyal to the first general rule of the United Methodist Church "Do no harm," Oduyoye interrogates the places from which injurious social and cultural values come.[5] For Oduyoye, justice is the moral frame on which she grounds her arguments. Her ethics most noticeably illustrates this. They detail the stories she tries to tell.[6]

Oduyoye is chiefly known for her participation in African theological conversation. Categorizing her work as ethics, in part, may come as a surprise, given her lack of claiming a prescribed ethical discourse. Can an ethical position be claimed for her? Does Oduyoye, the theologian, *do* ethics?

The case can be made that she does in her own right. For Oduyoye, ethics is already present within theological reflection: "The African women's theological reflections intertwine theology, ethics, and spirituality. It therefore does not stop at theory but moves to commitment, advocacy, and a transforming praxis."[7] Oduyoye's theology *is* her ethic. The best that one can do, then, is place Oduyoye's work in conversation with particular ethical branches, but one must only do so understanding that ethical categorical distinctions are not a concern of Oduyoye. The content of the reflection, however, is of the utmost importance within both theological and ethical circles.

Depending on the moment and the interpretation of her work, she can be in the virtue ethics corner, the situation ethics group, the social ethics conversation, and so on. For the purposes of "choosing" and because of her focus on community and social implications of one's actions, I associate her work most closely with social ethics. But to be clear, her involvement in what ethics sounds like in an African register signals something akin to an intrinsic ideation, a commonly known reality that does not require the formal labeling—at least in the title of her work or categorical claims within which her voice has been heard.

Theology attentive to voice, to communal impact, to social practices, and their effect on the world and those in it comprise the mission of social ethics.[8] Though Oduyoye makes no formal claim on the discourse of ethics in or upon her work, her place in the conversation of ethics is a rightful and natural one. The turn to social ethics makes the most sense. Hers is an intrinsic African cultural ethos, articulated through an Akan Christian ethic that reveals the heart of a social ethic.

Oduyoye's ethical work is intrinsic to her theological voice, one reflective upon her identity and experience. Both her feminist and prophetic tongue ground her moral thought, thought rooted within her culture. Her voice ultimately argues and, subsequently, centers African ways of knowing, and ways of being, particularized cultural living and moving about in the world,[9] as ethically discoursed in itself.

The imprint of African culture onto African conceptions of morality is a key idea to hold on to. Language of a "return" might be helpful here. Through the moral tone of her work, Oduyoye's task is to remind African peoples of who they are, of how their foundational claims on life were articulated and should be reinstated in modernity. Her undertaking is not necessarily nostalgic, but about re-formation. Questions can be heard underneath her work. They ask: "What ethical ideas help comprise the foundations of African communal life?" and "How might women's focused commentary on the roots and foundations in this way express an African cultural ethic inherent to African ontological sensibilities?" They return us to praxis as the heart of cultural truth. Oduyoye's wonderings inquire about the helpful practices and ideologies of African cultural life that have been abandoned or replaced with notions of communal life countercultural to Africanness itself, especially through colonialism's imprints.[10]

Considering what morality means and what ethics comprises in this way mirrors African ways of knowing, or Africans' comparable means of living out social and cultural praxis. In the essence of Oduyoye's work, morality is not necessarily a subcategory of social, cultural, or even religious thought; rather, it is an ontological expression. It is how one is or is known in the world. It is placing a frame around how African communities already exist, already engage in their interaction and understanding of self and other. It cannot be parsed out or dissected as an element of social life or cultural life or religious life; it is all those things and more.

The convexity of African culture illumines and magnifies the ethical renderings already pre-existing within African culture. Thus, a formal conversation in, of, or about ethics is an exercise in further examining that which already should exist, that which already should be put into place and practice. Ethics is an external label for that which African culture already must assume into its movement in the world, whether on communal or global scales. Ethical thought within the African context is the corporal expression of lived community, sociality extended outward, and inquiry turned inward as it relates to such categories of living.[11]

Answering a Different Question

This chapter, then, explores how Mercy Amba Oduyoye, a Ghanaian intellectual, theological, social, and communal voice within and outside of the African continent, employs ethics from an African woman's standpoint as integral to expressing and examining African personhood/selfhood. The visibility of ethics as formal discourse within her work is not her concern; yet, it is her ethics that subversively comprises the *crux* of her discourse as a whole. Ethics is foundational to the groundbreaking ideas and work Oduyoye has given to her community and to the world because of its intrinsic nature. She does not need to formally name or discuss that which is inherent and elemental to what she illustrates: to be African is to practice a cultural ethos, a social ethic. Her work further shows that to be an African woman is to be committed to refine such practices.

What Oduyoye does as an African woman doing theology (and subsequently ethics) is alert us to that and those whom are invisible within such conceptions of Africanness. We should not ask what the formal category under which Oduyoye's ethics falls but rather what we can learn from the *points of difference* grounding Oduyoye's particular work and moral inquiries.

If Oduyoye is a leading voice in theological thought in Africa, have we considered that as a woman her ethics might vary from her male theological counterparts? Have we interrogated how so and why? As a feminist voice, where might her voice vary from Western feminist accounts? Are points of distinction enough to build a new line of inquiry for us? In other words, it would be most helpful to lift up the general line of inquiry around why her ethical framing is not found in typically cited discourses of which conceptually, or, at the bare minimum, nomenclatively—she is or *should* be a part—African social ethics, African Christian ethics, Christian ethics, feminist ethics, feminist theological ethics, and so on.

What is Oduyoye doing per se that attracts different questions surrounding her ethical objective and method? Is her approach—a cultured, gendered approach—a sound ethical approach? What can we learn from her contextual pointedness that would open up new trains of thought in the categories in which she is not normalized or frequently considered?

This chapter asks questions of Oduyoye's impact in light of where her voice and voices like hers *are not*. In two parts, I introduce and explore her relationship to the (complicated) discipline of ethics. The first part, "Understanding

Foundations" briefly snapshots Oduyoye's work and unpacks the framework of Christian ethics through which her work can be understood and framed. The second, "Ethics Intertwined" tangibly gestures toward how Oduyoye has crafted alternative ways of thinking about social, theological, and ethical landscapes in keeping to African conceptions of sociality. I conclude with "New Terrain," mapping out the positive effects of Oduyoye's ethical formulation. Granting Mercy Amba Oduyoye space within the African ethical canon and conversation is a welcomed gesture of making sacred and proving beneficial the marginalized voices that wholly contribute to philosophical and moral thought from the burgeoning continent.

Understanding Foundations

What Is Christian Ethics? The Role of Faith

Where or how Oduyoye might fit in the conversation of ethics first requires a common understanding of what comprises "ethics." I tend toward the following explanation: ethics is a process of recognizing the interconnection of facts, opinions, actions, ways of life, and circumstances and—given these factors—creating a right response through our choices.[12] Its windows are internal and external. The ethical decisions and choices one makes impact themselves and impact others.

Ethics is discerning process, a means by which one figures out what is right and wrong in a situation. Fundamentally, it is about the *process* of choice, the *path* by which one arrives as a decision. Determining factors such as faith and culture drive one's ethical compass.

Oduyoye's ethic is a Christian one. For Christians then, ethics holds a more particular meaning. The contours of faith precepts require Christian ethics to be framed around three things in particular: one's relationship to God, self, and others.[13]

How one does ethics as a Christian is about their process of choosing what is right, given their position in the world as a being created by God living in this world alongside other created beings. It is morality deeply infused with faith principles.

Christians' ethics should keep in mind what decisions do, where they go, and whom they impact. What is most critical to Christian forms of ethical thought centers around the figure of the faith, Jesus of Nazareth. A Christian ethical stance reflects on whether and how Jesus can be seen or understood in a positive light, given the moral actions or the decision-making of a Christian.

The foundation of the Christian moral life mirrors the qualities of social ethics. The importance of scripture as moral guide, the communal setting of church and ecclesial bodies, and the overarching heeding of wisdom gleaned from both sources also impact the ethical weight and influence of Christians in the world.

While one's Christian identity is deeply important in their practice of ethics, it is not the most powerful determinant of one's moral decision-making. Christian ethics has more to do with *who one is* culturally. One's cultural identity plays the greatest role in how one sees things and thus how they decide what to do or believe. Christianity, for many, is a faith practice into which one enters and with which a culture can be united, but it is not the cultural root from which one comes or is ethnically born. The case I am making is for considering ethical foundation as rooted within one's ethnic identity.[14] One's ethnic culture can contain particular ethical positions that may not necessarily come from one's *Christian* faith or identity. My aim is not to invalidate the cultural effects of Christianity but rather the opposite, to name the powerful claim that Christian values can have on peoples. Christianity is a formidable moral force, but it is also an identity that can be claimed. For many, ethnic culture is primary; the Christian faith can be joined.[15]

My argument is as such: Christianity did not invent ethical position or ethics. The notion of an ethical position, or ethics, most likely existed in some form among African peoples prior to the introduction of Christian values, especially those peoples colonized by Christians.

Recall that I define ethics as "the *process* of choice, the *path* by which one arrives as a decision." This neither assumes nor precludes a Christian position. It, instead, highlights the malleability of ethics as a cultural practice. Thus, one's moral identity can be separated from as well as enhanced by their Christian position.[16] As a Yoruba person, I can hold ideals inherent to the values of my people and ancestors who may or may not have come from Christian values—cultural taboos, for example, can inform the shape of my decision-making. Subsequently, through my claim of the Christian faith, this frame can be enhanced and built upon, but it does not mean that I did not have an ethical frame with which to begin. This culturally foundational ethic comes first; my choice to align it with, or subject it to, a Christian framing of such is secondary.[17]

To assume ethics as inherently or primarily Christian runs the danger of assuming modes of valuation and ethical importance as a practice absent within many African cultures and societies. To assume ethical values as primarily or solely Christian within even a *Christian* peoples' valuation of life assumes a lack of a positive and good moral foundation prior to said people's Christian conversion. Both positions reinvigorate the colonial and missionizing logic of colonial Christianity.

What is most important to avoid and be wary of is the implication that African peoples, even those who identify as culturally Christian, received the entirety of their moral compass from the Christian faith alone. Morality existed among African peoples before the colonial moment; it lived in their cultural baseline of living.

This inkling and trace of moral positioning from one's ethnic culture prior to Christian contact is that which I read Oduyoye gesturing toward, in part. Christianity has imparted harmful ideas and strengthened pre-existing questionable systems, such as patriarchy within African contexts. Thus, African

Christian ethics must wage the war of holding onto its best cultural practices and values, while drawing upon the rich values found in the Christian faith.

Identity as Moral Compass: Ethics as Christian, Ethics as Social

Doing ethics as a Christian is *primarily* tied to about one's culture. The tools one has to see life, to see people, and to see situations are first and foremost, cultural. In other words, how a Christian deciphers morally right actions has everything to do with who they are in this world in relation to who others are in this world. One is not born into this world a Christian. One is born into this world as belonging to ethnic cultures, however.

There is no such thing as a universal mode of "Christian ethics," but there *is* such a thing as Christians doing ethics. Most prominently within that idea of Christians doing ethics is the reality that one's identity impacts their Christian expression. This, in turn, impacts one's moral choices. To put it differently, who one is *is* just as important as their religious commitments. This is incredibly important to recognize.

A turn to Christian scripture would be helpful here. In the Old Testament text of Genesis 12, Abram, the father of the Hebrew faith who would then become the father of the Christian faith, was a Chaldean from Ur. He had a culture before he experienced his calling. God "called forth" a religious people from this man, a man who already had a culture. Abram brought his culture *into* his identity in God. Abram's story makes sense because of the cultural elements with which Africans can see themselves and connect.

God made something out of a man who already had certain details to his life. Abram's decision-making would be attuned to the details of who he was. We can glean the same truths: culture deeply impacts one's Christian ethics. Ethics with religious commitment also has cultural imprints.

Christians have contexts—social places and environments from which they come and in which they are formed—much of this formation being based on who one is and what relationship they have to people, people who are powerless, powerful, or somewhere in between. All Christians come from somewhere—and thus, their moral decision-making comes from those places, too. All have backgrounds that make up just as much of the story of their identity, or more, than their faith practices do.

People practice faith; people become Christian. But people are who they are before those realities take hold or, at least, are those things alongside exercising religious praxis. Christian's decisions do not only come from a pattern of faith per se but are a part of a lineage of thinking and carefully constructed patterns of thought, based on where one comes from, who one is, and how one has experienced this life.

I focus heavily on cultural influence and formation to expose the contradictory commitments of many found at the intersection of certain cultural ideas and Christian hermeneutics. For Oduyoye, conflict exists in the reality that a Christian church called to express love, justice, and total wellness encourages practices of subjugation toward certain persons within their communities—its women. She reminds us that "It is necessary to know the social location of the authors as well as the gender and other orientations from which they interpret experience."[18] One's value system can privilege their social location. Oduyoye's work keeps the truth of context in front of us. Contextual recognition informs one's ethics; thus, although what is behind a Christian's ethics is faith, most importantly is *the person*—their stories, experiences, the lessons that life has taught them, which all determine in the decisions one makes.

Context is critical to the mold of ethics for Christian persons. Christian ethics impacts social life; Christian ethics, if attentive to details such as marginalizing realities, can be an extension or form of social ethics. Social ethics holds the truths of ethics and the influence of Christian ethics, together. It relies on spiritual principles and ideas but is also contingent on context and narrative.[19] Social ethics is interdisciplinary not only in its categorical approaches but also in its presence.

It "increasingly incorporates resources from economic, environment, political, and social sciences, as well as other theological sciences," Catholic ethicist Mary Elsbernd, O.S.F., argues.[20] Social ethics, at its core, is broad and narrow; it inquires about social practices, religious understandings, narrative truths, and moral frameworks.

Given the porous bounds of what forms ethics can take, it is not far-fetched to think Oduyoye's Christian ethics as synonymous with social ethics; they are companions, siblings, related to the same end.

Ethics Intertwined, or African Sociality as an Ethic

Wholeness as Ethic

Humanity is interconnected, human interdependence a critical concept of African culture. Communal wholeness and wellness emerge through recognizing the multiplicity of persons/personhood. Community trumps individuality; the self knows itself because of the collective calls itself such. This bears different weight in various African contexts: within Yoruba-Nigerian culture it might be called "Alafia," meaning wellness/wholeness. In South Africa, it is commonly referred to as "Ubuntu" or "I am because we are."

Oduyoye employs a similar standpoint, but instead of being intercultural, her focus is intra-cultural. Her focus privileges gender as a lens through which to frame African social ethics. She asks: how might women and men within the *same* culture be attuned to its own conceptual wellness? For Oduyoye, the task is in sharing responsibility for the thriving of one's people, one's culture, and one's people's cultural values. She advocates for equal cultural consideration of women to men within African culture, especially West African contexts where such a possibility appears to remain impossible because of fractured practices of African culture. She, along with women from within patriarchal leaning or outright patriarchal cultures, calls out ill-conceived community practices and calls forth realities indigenous to the communal heart of said communities.[21] She is not issuing new cultural precepts but reminding people of those value systems that pre-existed colonial interruption and legacy. Oduyoye helps us parse culture from "pre-" toward "post-" and ultimately to "de-" colonial emphases.

Oduyoye does not bemoan the fate of the African peoples on the shoulders of its women alone. Her aim is the opposite—African women work toward the male inclusion in the liberation of the entire African community. Women's liberation, and liberation of the invisibilized within African culture as a whole, is not the task of women alone—egalitarianism in cultural, social, and religious form is a matter of cultural cooperation, the ethical feet on which communal convictions stand. The approach of African women in their theological and ethical positions is one "of relations, replacing hierarchies with mutuality."[22] The closest language Oduyoye offers is one of justice. Her reflections on dealing justly with African women from a Christian perspective are helpful here:

> Dealing justly with African women must begin with taking seriously women's questions and concerns about their status. Trivializing women's concerns...does far more harm than good. Women's voices should be listened to when they speak about the God-ordained dignity of every human person and the consequent need of each person of respect.[23]

To reiterate her ultimate aim, it is a means to return African cultural praxis to its true form, to its actual self—whether this reflects Christian values or not.[24] To engage and employ patriarchal beliefs and praxis rooted in colonial logic roots colonialism into the story and fabric of the African people in a troubling way, not one of imposition and force, but rather through a negligent hospitality, a menacing welcome of actions that privilege European culture over and against African culture, the interests of the individual over the interests of the collective.[25] This is the unique problem to which African women are forced to respond "at their own pace, from their own place."[26] According to Senegalese politician and academic, Awa Thíam, the African woman is "both an ornamental symbol and a maid-of-all-work."[27] For African women, oppression comes from all sides, including cultural distortions, colonial mentalities, and religious rationale.

While neocolonial comparisons are not Oduyoye's *primary* aim or task, it is a concern etched into the heart of her work. To adopt and adapt to the ethical measures of the colonial forces that stripped so much dignity and voice from African peoples in order to exercise internal power over and against one's own people *is* the Western patriarchal agenda, one to which African men should not attach themselves.[28]

Though patriarchal culture is not a new phenomenon in West African contexts, its joining colonial power and ideation is most unsettling. Oduyoye's voice serves as the echo with which men and women who practice "African counter-culturality" can hear themselves and return to their true pitch, for this countercultural identity distorts African value systems and cultural idioms.[29]

Mercy Amba Oduyoye is valuable for ethics within the African context as she reminds Africa what it sounds like. Oduyoye asks not only for a "return" of sorts but also for a restoration—can African culture live again within African culture? Can it live into itself? These questions sit beneath the surface of her work, waiting to see if they might have space in the imagination of West African generations so accustomed to colonial mentalities and rationales that they have forgotten themselves.

To be clear, for Oduyoye, a West African essential self is not influenced by additional and external cultures and structures—this would dismantle the narrative of West African intercultural connection and notions such as inculturation and syncretism. Colonialism introduced regional, economic, and racial polarizations that Africans did not exercise as normal until they injected themselves into the landscape of African social life.[30] The West African self, however, knows its core values, holds on to its cultural standards, and knows that the interior self of African personhood holds particular ideals and practices, practices and ideas unmoved by time and concepts (chronos or logos). African cultural idioms exceed external propagation; its centeredness is too rooted in its "isness," to invoke womanist logic around the conception of self, for it to be forgotten, to be un-practiced, to not be returned to the heart of African ethical and cultural practice in modernity. The African is first and foremost African in their actions, doings, and beliefs; anything outside of this core form of self is only an addition to that which, to those whom, have existed across and in spite of time.

Ethics as Gendered

Colonial interruptions are not the only obstacle against which Oduyoye has to resist. Gender makes its way into cultural and religious practices as a delimiting marker. Oduyoye alerts us to the fact that it, therefore, must be a critical component of any ethical conversation.

Can ethics be gendered? Is African social life under the influence of cultural assumptions and conceptions of gender indigenous to or foreign to African ways of knowing? These are questions attended by the presence of Oduyoye's voice in Christian theological discourse. She bores into these questions with rhetorical relish: can ethics *not* be gendered? What is a pure African cultural ethic? Does such a notion exist? Oduyoye's theological inquiries point us in a helpful direction.

Again, the point is not to find what ethical camp Oduyoye's work might fit, but to open up what ethics means in the collective imagination and parse out where her work hits on those points illumined by its broad definition. Ethics for an African Christian woman might have a different form than ethics for an African Christian man. Though their principles might be close in proximity, their mission as well as stating points vary enough for other discourses to exist in order to address these disparities. A parsed-out voice might signal inadequate attention given to an issue from a more mainline approach or it may signal the creative need to explore potential ideas in a different direction—Oduyoye's work does both.

The ambition of Oduyoye's work in centering African women's experiences is to remind African culture and community of whom it is comprised, who upholds elements of its existence. Women's existential realities open up their theological and ethical insight to exceed that which only a male perspective might offer. This is the gift of women's createdness; they differ from men in order for humanity to give the broadest vision possible of human and, further, created life.

African women hold a lens of cultural, social, and religious affairs because their place in the world and subsequently how they experience and see the world have been determined by cultural practices, social logics, and religious rationale. In *Daughters of Anowa*, Oduyoye demonstrates how all three factors directly correlate with the *problems* that African women currently face in religious praxis. From gendered origin stories and the concretizing of sexist cultural norms, Oduyoye outlines that the subordinate place of women in their cultures, societies, and religious frameworks has nothing to do with women's own doings, but it is an aftershock of beliefs and practices bent toward hierarchical recognition and power structures. Women's voices do not emerge from nothing but are the response crafted as a result of illegitimate consideration of community and the righteous cultural ideals.

Oduyoye's critical works, *Hearing and Knowing* utilizing a church historical approach and *Beads and Strands*, taking on an essay format around African cultural issues and its ties to injustice, specifically concerning gender, both hold similar messages. There is a turn within African culture that has resulted in the neglect of women's voices and ideas as pertinent contributors to the life of African social and ethical thought. This turn can be best described as one informed by colonial presence, but such ideology is only impressed into foundations already laid. Patriarchy as a colonial problem is not the focus of Oduyoye's work, but rather that to which it attaches itself.

African theology inattentive to the experiences and, subsequently, the social, cultural, and religious realities of its women is not suffering from colonial illness, but un-interrogated cultural ideologies. When African social and cultural practices do not recognize its women, it has adopted a mentality outside of itself. Oduyoye specifically comes from Akan culture rooted in matrilineal recognition and practice, but even with this framing, Akan men are not absent or insignificant figures. Akan women are honored as bearers of Akan identity and thus *recognized* as critical figures within the life of Akan agency. *Both men and women* are known by maternal ties. This does not assert men as secondary or insignificant, but as not the main persons through whom one's tribal identity is understood or primarily recognized. Historically, Akan men and women exercised a type of mutuality and equality when it came to communal affairs. Decision-making was a community activity.

Within some patriarchal cultures in West Africa, such as with the Yoruba of Nigeria, a culture into which Oduyoye married, the opposite is true. One is recognized primarily through their father's bloodline. While the patriarchal character of Yoruba culture has harsher restrictions concerning the influence of women within their respective social context, this much is clear, women have their own respective "places" within the patriarchy, the household being the most noticeable marker of a sphere of influence for Yoruba women. While the household is ultimately controlled by the male head of the house, the interior doings of the house are the direct result of the woman's decision-making. In Yoruba culture, the impetus is more for its women to create their *own* spaces of voice and authority. Even within patriarchal folds, women subversively work to speak, to influence the contours of their social life. Women carve out space for them to have a say.

Their having to do so is a point of illumination of Oduyoye's work. Why *must* women have to find spaces where they are heard? Why isn't social and communal life the space where all voices are heard and considered? What is the cultural ethos, the social ethic, that allows for women to craft their own spaces instead of having space readily available to them as it is to their male counterparts? What is behind women having to create that which is culturally "inherent" to men? Why is women's wellness not inherent to African culture? Oduyoye argues that examining the cultural practices of old reveals that women's wellness and full inclusion once was the cultural norm in various West African contexts.

One such point of examination is theological anthropology within both Akan cosmology and Christian study. This line of inquiry opens up possibilities to understand foundational ideas of parts of African life and African culture. For Oduyoye, Akan cosmology can aid in highlighting the original structured system of relationship between both divine-created beings and created beings to one another.

A Cosmic Ethos

Within Akan belief, the physical and spiritual worlds are interconnected as harmony between both is critical. Spiritual and secular life are considered together; they cannot be separated. Life in harmony with the living and with the spiritual beings of the cosmos serves as moral compass and ethical guide within Akan cultural life.[31] The cosmos impacts and directs created life.

It is important to note that all beings exist around the Supreme Being—no one creature, no being, is above the Supreme Being.[32] Akan culture incites relationship of mutual respect between beings—human beings, spiritual beings, the Creator God, as well as other created beings, non-animate and animate, operate with a mode of mutual recognition of the other.[33] Each being relies on the other. Thus, reliance on the Supreme Being as well as other beings is foundation to Akan conceptions of cosmic life.[34]

Akan origin stories serve as examples of the connectedness of beings, Supreme and created. In the popular creation story Ananse Kokroko[35] (God) who slams "Half and Half" to create one human out of two, it is known that not only God's rectifying a disharmonious situation is critical to the narrative[36] but also what comes into view is the diverse nature of being human. In this account, humans comprise two halves, two combined differences toward one whole human. Humanity is thus multiplicitous, not biologically hierarchized, but diverse in its being. Varied existence is the essence of personhood. The interweaving of difference comprises wholeness, whole humanness.

Oduyoye's Ethics in Sum

According to Akan wisdom all persons are created beings and thus desired by God.[37] God's desire expressed in this way is not something to be corrected through androcentric or patriarchal logics, theological or otherwise. Yet the reality of the divine nature present in all does not align with the treatment of women justified by theological rationale. Women are often placed on the periphery and made marginal.

Oduyoye argues, "in the present state of man/woman relationship, our culture-bound typologies condition not only the individual but also the whole community to believe that labels are decreed by God."[38] Traditional notions of gender have proved inadequate. It fails to realize the primacy of human relationality as determined by the divine. If this rationale holds and humanity understands itself in relation to the Supreme Being, or to a force outside of itself, then both females and males must be considered fully part of or equal determinants of the shape and function of a community and society.

The dismissal of women from the creative point of theological revelation, especially from an African standpoint, is no longer an option if African theology wants to hear and know its own fullness. To mishandle women's voices in African theological expression is to forgo its Africanness. On a practical level, the inclusion of all within the African community yields the fullest expression of African voice and viewpoint. Oduyoye's insistence, then, is toward what undergirds Akan (and African) ways of life: an African-centeredness that makes space for Africa's naming itself.

NEW TERRAIN

The African community is a living, breathing entity complete only in its best expression of itself. But it will not be well if it does not balance itself by eliminating marginalizing practices. Women cannot be socialized to inferior status but must be lifted up as equally important for the ultimate good of the entire community.[39] African women, kept away from influential conversations and spaces, have theological and ethical insight beneficial to African social collectives.

The cultural influence of Oduyoye's Christian ethics has everything to do with what shape her ethics and ethical voice takes in the world. Framing Christian ethics as done by persons with various histories, life experiences, and commitments in many ways illuminates Oduyoye's problem and mission. That to which she is responding is the result of individualized, ontological separations uncharacteristic of African common life. Thus, in many ways, in her reminding her community and the world of its omissions (in excluding the voices of African women), Oduyoye is helping African social and ethical praxis return to itself. Oduyoye's life mission, her ethical determination, is one toward seeing her culture and cultures like her own live into itself in its fullness. Her work and ethics are grounded in a sort of retrieval—a return to its intended form, culturally and cosmologically. Her Akan Christian ethics *is* social ethics foregrounding voices often unheard and perspectives under-shared.

One does not have to claim outright categories in order for their work to perform the work within it. Oduyoye's voice and work are a strong example of allowing one's just cultural values to serve as a right form of moral framing—a framing with the prospect of return, a framing with a vision for full inclusion.

Notes

1. Mercy Amba Oduyoye, *Beads and Strands: Reflections of an African Woman on Christianity in Africa* (Maryknoll: Orbis, 2004), xi, and Christina Landman, "Mercy Amba Ewudziwa Oduyoye: Mother of Our Stories," *Studia Historiae Ecclesiasticae* 33, no. 2, accessed November 1, 2015, http://www.christina-landman.co.za/mercy.htm
2. Oduyoye makes it clear that she is "writing in the context of Africa as a person with roots in the Christian church." Her primary context is Christian church, thus her theological and ethical reflections will have the Christian ecclesial context in mind as her primary audience (see Mercy Amba Oduyoye, "The Fire of Smoke" in *Daughters of Anowa: African Women and Patriarchy* [Maryknoll: Orbis Books, 1995], 5).
3. Mercy Amba Oduyoye, *African Women's Theology* (Sheffield, England: Sheffield Academic Press, 2001), 125. Oduyoye is clear about her African feminist approach. She asserts that "African women do not perceive their men as the enemy." She, instead, critiques patriarchal praxis detrimental to Africa's women. She challenges those caught in the crosshairs of harmful practices to find better and more just ways to be in society and the world.
4. Oduyoye pursues this mission cognizant of the various modes of African religious life. Though she is clear that she is speaking from a Christian perspective, Methodist to be specific, she is aware that the implications of Christian religious interpretation have an impact on how all Africans, Christian, and otherwise are treated in their respective contexts. (See Mercy Amba Oduyoye, "The Fire of Smoke" in *Daughters of Anowa: African Women and Patriarchy* [Maryknoll: Orbis Books, 1995], 5.).
5. https://www.umcdiscipleship.org/resources/first-do-no-harm
6. Mary Elsbernd, "Social Ethics." *Theological Studies*, 66, no. 1 (February 2005): 137–58. doi:https://doi.org/10.1177/004056390506600107, p. 139. Case studies are utilized as a key approach to examining the details of social ethics at work.
7. Mercy Amba Oduyoye, *African Women's Theology* (Sheffield, England: Sheffield Academic Press, 2001), 16.

8. Mary Elsbernd, "Social Ethics." *Theological Studies*, 66, no. 1 (February 2005): 137–58. doi:https://doi.org/10.1177/004056390506600107, 137.
9. "Ways of knowing" speaks to a cultural framing or inherent cultural epistemology gained from the practices, values, principles, and beliefs of one's particular community. "African ways of knowing" thus gestures toward these similar values across cultures and peoples, such as the critical value of the many (the community) toward the wellness of the one (individual), and so on.
10. Mercy Amba Oduyoye, *Daughters of Anowa: African Women and Patriarchy* (Maryknoll: Orbis Books, 1995), 159. Sexism is the main area in which African communal principles and values have been overthrown by colonial ideology. She comments on the problem of African communal imbalance across gender lines, "Unfortunately, a communal view of women's being, one which focuses on the community's well-being and coherence, often breeds a cultural sexism that rigidly positions a woman even though it leaves a man mobile." The life of its own that sexism has taken within African communal thriving is palpable and injurious for many African women.
11. Mary Elsbernd, "Social Ethics." *Theological Studies*, 66, no. 1 (February 2005): 137–58. doi: https://doi.org/10.1177/004056390506600107, 138. Elsbernd categorizes social ethics as containing literature cognizant of the relationship between context and ethics.
12. See Robin Lovin, "Choices" in *Christian Ethics: An Essential Guide* (Nashville: Abington Press, 2000) and Rowan Williams, "Making Moral Decisions" in Robin Gill, Ed. *The Cambridge Companion to Christian Ethics* (Cambridge: Cambridge University Press, 2012).
13. See Lisa Cahill, "The Bible and Christian Moral Practices" in Lisa Sowle Cahill and James F. Childress, Eds. *Christian Ethics: Problems and Prospects* (Cleveland: Pilgrim Press, 1996).
14. Christian identity can be considered a root *in addition to* and perhaps more determinant of one's initial form of identity in the world, their ethnic identity.
15. In a way, I am making an argument for closer recognition of the presence of something akin to an ethnicized ethic. This angle illumines what one's culture has taught them to prioritize about their life as well as another's. I am hoping to put a name to the factors and ideations that oftentimes override and come before a (proposed "identifiable" and sometimes singularized) notion of a Christian ethic.

    Though potentially controversial to organize ethical thought in this way, I am highlighting the notion of the order of Christianity's impact and incorporation into one's cultural identity. It is not that Christianity is not important, but that it may not have come "first" in one's moral formation. Various peoples hold values and morals, what can be deemed ethical positions, before the influx of colonial influence and the subsequent religious messages brought with them, many being that of the Christian persuasion.
16. Mercy Amba Oduyoye, *Beads and Strands: Reflections of an African Woman on Christianity in Africa* (Maryknoll: Orbis, 2004), 28. Oduyoye describes Africans as having similar roots and recognizing "the same divinity" and recognizing a source of a "one true God." What this clarifies is that certain social and religious ideas and practices existed before the categorization Christianity provided. It can later be classified as the God of Christian tradition or not.

17. To assert that every ethical decision I make comes from my Christian identity not directed by cultural and ethnic commitments is a tough sell. Though a difficult task to parse apart entirely, given the generational and personal infusion of Christianity with my cultural identity, to assume all decisions as made through something called my "Christian ethical position" alone instead of my *Nigerian-American* Christian ethics is false. The ethnic aspect of my identity is just as relevant, if not most relevant, to where and how Christianity determines my ethical lens.
18. Mercy Amba Oduyoye, *African Women's Theology* (Sheffield, England: Sheffield Academic Press, 2001), 18.
19. Mary Elsbernd, "Social Ethics." *Theological Studies*, 66, no. 1 (February 2005): 137–58. doi:https://doi.org/10.1177/004056390506600107, p. 140.
20. Ibid., 141.
21. Mercy Amba Oduyoye, *Daughters of Anowa: African Women and Patriarchy* (Maryknoll: Orbis Books, 1995), 159.
22. Mercy Amba Oduyoye, *African Women's Theology* (Sheffield, England: Sheffield Academic Press, 2001), 17, and Awa Thíam, "Feminism and Revolution (1978)" in *I Am Because We Are: Readings in Africana Philosophy* (Boston: University of Massachusetts Press, 2016), 115. Thíam articulates black African women's struggle as having two aspects, the second arguing for "the struggle for the recognition of and respect for the rights and duties of men and women of all races."
23. Mercy Amba Oduyoye, *Daughters of Anowa: African Women and Patriarchy* (Maryknoll: Orbis Books, 1995), 171.
24. Interestingly enough, Christian values are said to purport the same message of recognition of all and the full inclusion of the many.
25. Awa Thíam, "Feminism and Revolution (1978)" in *I Am Because We Are: Readings in Africana Philosophy* (Boston: University of Massachusetts Press, 2016), 115. Thíam argues that black African women suffer both the harmful effects of colonialism and the problematic actions of the men within their families and communities, "the colonized African male."
26. Mercy Amba Oduyoye, *African Women's Theology* (Sheffield, England: Sheffield Academic Press, 2001), 11.
27. Awa Thíam, "Feminism and Revolution (1978)" in *I Am Because We Are: Readings in Africana Philosophy* (Boston: University of Massachusetts Press, 2016), 115.
28. Mercy Amba Oduyoye, *African Women's Theology* (Sheffield, England: Sheffield Academic Press, 2001), 18. Oduyoye is clear to assert, "certainly not all of Africa is patriarchal, but the hegemony of the patriarchal mind-set strives to make it so...".
29. Mary Elsbernd, "Social Ethics." *Theological Studies*, 66, no. 1 (February 2005): 157–58. doi:https://doi.org/10.1177/004056390506600107, p. 157–158. Elsbernd questions whether personal and collective agency non-first-world persons requires the force of Western (and individualistic) influence that has asserted itself into these cultures.
30. Mercy Amba Oduyoye, *Daughters of Anowa: African Women and Patriarchy* (Maryknoll: Orbis Books, 1995), 2.

31. Samuel Awuah-Nyamekye, "Salvaging Nature: The Akan Religio-Cultural Perspective," *Worldviews: Global Religions, Culture, and Ecology*, 11/2008, Volume 13, Issue 3, 255, especially 255–256.
32. Ibid., 255.
33. Esther Acolatse, *For Freedom or Bondage?: A Critique of African Pastoral Practices* (Grand Rapids: Eerdmans, 2014), 61.
34. Samuel Awuah-Nyamekye, "Salvaging Nature: The Akan Religio-Cultural Perspective," *Worldviews: Global Religions, Culture, and Ecology*, 11/2008, Volume 13, Issue 3, 256.
35. Mercy Amba Oduyoye, *Hearing and Knowing: Theological Reflections on Christianity in Africa* (Eugene: Wipf & Stock, 1986), 91. Oduyoye notes that Ananse Kokroko is a linguistic means to avoid calling God by God's personal name, "Nyame," which can also be spelled, "Onyame." See also Samuel Awuah-Nyamekye, "Salvaging Nature: The Akan Religio-Cultural Perspective," *Worldviews: Global Religions, Culture, and Ecology*, 11/2008, Volume 13, Issue 3, 265, and Rose Mary Amenga-Etego, "Gender and Christian Spirituality in Africa: A Ghanaian Perspective," *Black Theology: An International Journal*, 11/2012, Volume 10, Issue 1, 21.
36. Mercy Amba Oduyoye, *Hearing and Knowing: Theological Reflections on Christianity in Africa* (Eugene: Wipf & Stock, 1986), 91.
37. Esther Acolatse, *For Freedom or Bondage?: A Critique of African Pastoral Practices* (Grand Rapids: Eerdmans, 2014), 69.
38. Mercy Amba Oduyoye, *Hearing and Knowing: Theological Reflections on Christianity in Africa* (Eugene: Wipf & Stock, 1986), 129.
39. Ibid.

Bibliography

Acolatse, Esther. 2014. *For Freedom or Bondage?: A Critique of African Pastoral Practices*. Grand Rapids: Eerdmans.

Amenga-Etego, Rose Mary. 2012. Gender and Christian Spirituality in Africa: A Ghanaian Perspective. *Black Theology: An International Journal* 10 (1): 21.

Awuah-Nyamekye, Samuel. 2008. Salvaging Nature: The Akan Religio-Cultural Perspective. *Worldviews: Global Religions, Culture, and Ecology* 13 (3): 251–282.

Cahill, Lisa Sowle, and James F. Childress, eds. 1996. *Christian Ethics: Problems and Prospects*. Cleveland: Pilgrim Press.

Elsbernd, Mary. 2005. Social Ethics. *Theological Studies* 66 (1): 137–158, 157–158. https://doi.org/10.1177/004056390506600107.

Gill, Robin, ed. 2012. *The Cambridge Companion to Christian Ethics*. Cambridge: Cambridge University Press.

Landman, Christina. Mercy Amba Ewudziwa Oduyoye: Mother of Our Stories. *Studia Historiae Ecclesiasticae* 33 (2). http://www.christina-landman.co.za/mercy.htm. Accessed 1 Nov 2015

Lovin, Robin. 2000. *Christian Ethics: An Essential Guide*. Nashville: Abington Press.

Oduyoye, Mercy Amba. 1986. *Hearing and Knowing: Theological Reflections on Christianity in Africa*. Eugene: Wipf & Stock.

———. 1995. *Daughters of Anowa: African Women and Patriarchy*. Maryknoll: Orbis Books.
———. 2001. *African Women's Theology*. Sheffield: Sheffield Academic Press.
———. 2004. *Beads and Strands: Reflections of an African Woman on Christianity in Africa*. Maryknoll: Orbis.
The United Methodist Church. Leadership Resources. https://www.umcdiscipleship.org/resources/first-do-no-harm. Accessed 16 Nov 2018

Index[1]

A

Aba, 238
Abacha, General Sani, 379, 417
Abacost, 218, 228n4
Abami eda, 419
Abiku, 560
Abiola, Moshood, 417
Absolutism, 445, 446
Abuses, 51, 52, 58
Accountability, 328–330, 502–506, 508–516
Achebe, Chinua, 118, 550–553, 569, 576
Adalai, Kwaku (Professor Hindu), 419
Ade-Ajayi, J. F., 475
Adepoju, Toyin, 478, 479
Adu-Boahen, A., 475
Africa, 1–5, 11–13, 15, 19, 22, 28, 34, 69–72, 82, 103–121, 203–213, 231–243, 339–364, 437, 438, 440–447
African Anglicanism, 599
African Christianity, 596
African cosmology, 169–171
African Diaspora, 480, 487
African economics, 340, 343, 357–363
African ethic of war, 220–222, 225–226
African firm, 383–385
African identity, 589, 602n22
Africanity, 409, 418
African National Congress (ANC), 378, 454
African National Congress Women's League (ANCWL), 378
African National Congress Youth League (ANCYL), 378
African ontology (AO), 94, 169–171, 301, 312
African Pentecostals, 544, 547–550
African personality, 287
African philosophy, 105, 168, 437, 438, 440–445, 448
African political ethics of neighbourliness (APEN), 167–182
African social ethic, 147, 149, 150, 154, 155, 158, 160
African Socialism, 258, 270, 272
African spirituality, 409, 414, 417
African Studies, 437, 444
African theology, 606, 615, 617
African traditional religion (ATR), 152, 299, 503
African woman, 605, 606, 608, 613
Afrifa, Col. A. A., 253
Afrobeat, 414, 415
Afrocapitalism, 380, 384
Afrocentricity, 412, 419
Agbo-ilé, 34

[1] Note: Page numbers followed by 'n' refer to notes.

624 INDEX

Agikuyu, 98, 99
Agonistic communitarianism, 147–161
Akan, 5, 106–109, 111, 113, 114,
    117–119, 122n13, 124n47, 186,
    194, 196–198, 247, 248, 250, 251,
    253, 254, 303, 304, 307, 423–433,
    605, 607, 615–618
Akan cosmology, 616
Akan ethics, 424–433
Akan philosophy, 448
Akoto, Bafour Osei, 249
Algeria, 284, 289
Algerian War of Independence, 284, 286
Allegory of the cave, 100
Allen, Amy, 28, 32, 40–44
Allen, Tony, 414
All Progressives Congress (APC), 382
Amanze, James N., 528, 531
Ambiguous Adventure, 259
American Episcopalianism, 600
Amo, Anton Wilhelm, 441
Ancestors/ancestorhood, 103, 106, 108,
    109, 114, 115, 119, 121, 137–139,
    142, 197, 198, 217–227, 301–305
Anglican Provinces in Africa
    (CAPA), 511
Angolan Civil War, 203, 206
Anikulapo-Kuti, Fela, 409–420
Anthropology, 437, 440, 443
Anthropomorphism, 396
Anti-neighbourliness, 167, 168, 171,
    181, 182
Apartheid, 591, 593–596, 598
Appiah, Kwame Anthony, 291, 453–471
Armah, Ayi Kwei, 571
Asante, 303
Ase, 574, 582
Ashimolowo, Matthew, 311
Assimilation policy, 266
Attachment theory, 13, 16–17
Augustine of Hippo, 392
Authoritarianism, 411
Autonomy, 129–132, 135, 136, 467

B
Baálé, 37
Baba, Alhaji Amadu, 252
Babalawo, 410, 479, 489

Bacon, Francis, 100
Balance of payment, 348, 349, 352,
    353, 358
Benhabib, Seyla, 457, 458
Bhabha, Homi, 458
Bird, Frederick, 502, 516
Bishop Gladys, 84
Black First Land First movement
    (BLF), 378
Blackness, 410, 414
Black Panther, 414, 415
Black Skin, White Masks, 285–287,
    289, 290
Blood principle, 108, 114
Bonded labor, 57
Bonsam, Kweku, 300
Born-again, 549, 559
Botha, P. W., 591
Botswana, 232, 234, 239–243
Botswana Democratic Party
    (BDP), 240–243
Botswana National Front (BNF), 240
Brazil, Russia, India, China and South
    Africa (BRICS), 378
Bretton Woods agencies, 231, 238
Bretton Woods Agreements, 341, 342
Bretton Woods institutions, 339–364
Britain, 206, 207, 209, 210, 232, 235,
    238, 239
British philosophy, 448
Brown, James, 417
Budget deficit, 358
Bureaucracy, 317, 326–329
Busia, Dr. Kofi Abrefa, 194, 249,
    250, 252
Büjo, Bénézet, 433

C
Call-and-response, 545–547, 555, 562
Camus, Albert, 149
Candomblé, 480
Capitalism, 149, 155, 290, 306, 328,
    484, 554
Care for Child Development
    (CCD), 13–15
Caregiver, 12–14, 16–18, 21–23
Cashumaye, 531
Cattle, 578, 579

Central Bank of Nigeria (CBN), 382–384
Césaire, Aimé, 258, 260–262
Chagoury, Gilbert, 379
Charisma principle, 108, 114
Charismatic, 61
Chatty Masangu wa Nkulu, 220
Child abuse, 20, 51
Child and childhood, 11–23, 52–54, 58
Child labor, 51, 52, 54–58, 64
Childrearing, 11–23
Children, 51–56, 62–63
Child Right, 57
Child witchcraft, 59, 61
Child work, 56
Christian Association of Nigeria (CAN), 398
Christian Council of Ghana, 190, 192
Christian ethics, 607–612, 617, 618
Christian faith, 503, 505, 510–512, 514, 516
Christianity, 11, 152, 158, 159, 187, 196, 197, 199n36, 269, 306–310, 312, 329, 395, 396, 398, 399, 427, 428, 512, 513, 525, 527–530, 534, 536, 544, 545, 548, 557, 596, 597
Church, 502, 504, 510–516
Citizen/citizenship, 148, 159, 167, 168, 170–172, 178–180, 232, 233, 288, 324, 392, 401, 403, 455, 460, 469, 503, 504, 507, 508
Civic/primordial realms, 159
Civic public, 233
Civilisation de l'universel (Civilization of the Universal), 267–272
Civilization, 257, 258, 260, 264, 267, 268, 570, 571
Civil society, 232
Civil society organisations, 502
Cockroach, 98, 100
"Coffin for Head of State," 413
"Cogito ergo sum," 94, 95
Cold War, 204–207, 211
Colonialism, 158, 159, 204–206, 210, 233, 285–287, 289, 317, 330, 371, 372, 379, 409, 416, 419, 493, 528, 597–598, 607, 613, 614, 620n25
Coloniality, 474, 475, 484, 487
Colonization, 257, 259, 261, 262, 267, 269, 270, 525, 529, 530, 536

Coltrane, John, 414
Common good, 5
Communal ethics, 129–142
Communalism, 4, 5, 95, 97–99, 103–105, 115, 117, 118, 129–133, 258, 261–265, 270, 271, 427, 428, 432, 448
Communism, 103
Communitarian/communitarianism, 4, 5, 95–97, 129, 147–161
Community, 11–23, 95–101, 103–106, 108–112, 114–121, 147–161, 220, 221, 223, 225, 226, 257, 259, 264–272, 319–321, 323, 324, 329, 330, 423–431, 433, 455, 456, 458, 465, 466, 468, 469, 526–536
 collectivist, 130
 constituted, 130
Community development, 232, 236, 238–242
Communotheism, 225
Conditionalities, 345, 348, 352–354, 357, 358, 360, 364
Conflict, 167–182
Consciencism, 187–196
Consciousness, 266, 574–576, 579, 580
Convention People's Party (CPP), 190, 192–194, 197, 249–252
Corporate party capture, 374
Corruption, 317–331, 371, 372, 374, 377, 378, 384, 501–504, 507, 509–511
Cosmopolitan imagination, 455–459, 461
Cosmopolitanism, 159, 415, 455–463, 467–471
Cosmopolitan nationalism, 460
Cosmopolitan stranger, 470, 471
Cosmos, 571, 572, 574, 578, 579, 583
Creativity, 2–5
Cultural practices, 51, 52
Culture, 11–14, 18–23, 28, 30, 103–106, 108, 113, 121, 299, 300, 303, 304, 307, 311, 416, 420, 438, 441–448, 544, 545, 547–550, 552–554, 556, 559, 561, 562, 605, 607–616, 618, 619n15, 620n29

D

Damas, Léon-Gontran, 258, 260
Dangote, Aliko, 371–385
Dangote groups, 380, 381, 385
Danquah, Joseph Boakye, 249, 252
Davis, Miles, 414
Death, 108
Debt, 348–350, 357–360, 362, 363
Decolonial/decoloniality, 283, 284, 287, 289, 290
Decolonization, 188, 231, 233–236, 238–243, 318, 330–331, 474, 486, 487
Democracy/democratic, 221, 319, 324, 325, 327, 328, 330, 371, 381
Democratic Alliance, 377
Democratic Republic of Congo, 217
Democratic Republic of Congo (former Zaire), 203, 207
Deontology, 134, 142
Derrida, Jacques, 290
Descartes, Rene, 94
Destiny, 113–115
Development, 339–364, 437, 438, 440, 443, 444, 446, 501, 509–512
Diallo, Samba, 259
Dictatorship, 410, 417
Difference, 454, 459, 460, 467, 469–471
Dignity, 96, 99–101, 129, 131–137, 141, 142, 284, 285, 287–292, 402–404
Diogenes the Cynic, 456
Diola, 526, 528, 529, 531, 533
Diversitarianism, 465
Divinities, 480
Divinization, 561
Divorce, 70–72
Dogon cosmology, 578
Dombo, S. D., 252
Domestic chores, 56
Domination, 40–44
Doondari, 578
Du Bois, W. E. B., 419, 461–463
Durkheim, Emile, 393, 397
Dworkin, Ronald, 465

E

Early childhood education, 21, 23
Earth, 569, 570, 573, 574, 579, 582, 583
Economic and Financial Crimes Commission (EFCC), 502, 507
Economic development, 339–364
Economic growth, 341, 346–350, 355, 356, 360
Economics, 2, 3, 299–312, 371, 373, 374, 378–380, 383, 384
Education, 12, 15, 21, 23, 38, 39, 355, 357–363, 475, 476, 486, 490
Egalitarianism, 156
Egyptology, 414
Ekeh, Peter, 233
Elite, 233–235, 239–241, 243
"Else-where"/"else-when," 4
Emi-arojinle (spirit of deep thinking), 176–177, 179
Emi-idariji/emi-iforiji (forgiveness spirit), 177, 179
Emi-irepo (relationship-bonding spirit), 178, 179
Émi suru (spirit of patience), 174
Empowerment, 41–44
Endogenius, 474, 476
Endogenous knowledge, 437, 438
Eniyan, 111, 117
Enlightenment, 445
Entrepreneur/entrepreneurial/entrepreneurship, 234, 236–238
Environment, 569, 572, 573, 578
Environmental ethics, 129, 140–142
Epistemology, 260–263, 265, 270, 272, 276n35, 475–480, 483–491, 493–495
Eros, 3
Eshu, 574
Essentialism, 29, 32
Èṣù, 480–483
Ethical, 51, 52, 54, 59, 62, 64
Ethics, 1–4, 129–142, 167–182, 203–213, 257–273, 299–312, 391–405, 423–426, 432, 433, 439, 444–448, 457, 463–466, 471, 502, 504, 505, 509, 516, 543, 545, 547–551, 553–559, 561, 562, 605–618

Ethics of identity, 453–471
Ethiopia, 205, 207, 311
Ethiopianism, 548
Ethnicity, 324, 327, 468
Ethnology, 440
Ethnophilosopher, 437–439, 444, 446, 447
Ethnophilosophy, 437, 440, 441, 443, 444, 447
Ethos, 1–6
Eurocentricism, 412
Evil, 423, 426, 427, 432, 433
Excellence, 212, 213, 310
Exceptionalism, 598
Existentialism, 105
Existentiality, 404
Extended family, 71
Extended Fund Facility, 354

F
Faith, 69–87, 548, 557, 559, 560, 562
Falola, Toyin, 570, 573
Family, 2, 3, 5, 69–80, 82, 83, 85–87, 89n30, 105–107, 114–116, 119, 131, 139, 426, 428–431
   consanguineal, 34–37
   extended, 27–44
   nuclear, 27–44
Family studies, 32, 33
Fanon, Frantz, 283–292
Father Divine, 253, 254
Female genital mutilation (FGM), 534–536
Feminine, 552
Feminism/femininity/feminist, 27–44, 72, 73, 607, 608, 618n3
Feminization, 552
First Festival of Negro Artists, 268
Folktales, 18–19
Foucault, Michel, 27, 28, 39–42
Foundation, 607, 609, 610, 615, 616
France, 258–261, 264, 266, 267, 269
Francophony, 268
Freedom, 149, 155, 285, 287–292, 356, 410, 418
Fundamentalism, 454

G
Ga, 106, 107, 111–114, 116, 118, 124n47
Gandhi, Mohandas, 286
Gaos, Jose, 486
Garvey, Marcus, 253, 254
Gbɔmɔtso, 112
Gboloma (togetherness), 157
Gemeinschaft, 397
Gender, 28, 30–32, 39, 41, 42, 69–71, 73–76, 612, 614, 615, 617
General Orders, 326, 334n26
Genocide, 98, 100
Geopolitics, 487, 488
German philosophy, 461, 462
Gessellschaft, 397
Ghana, 185–198, 525, 526, 530, 531, 533–535, 605
Ghana Christian Council, 252
Ghana Congress Party (GCP), 249
Ghana Young Pioneers (GYP), 190, 251
Gikuyu, 303
Global capture, 374
Globality, 488
Globalization, 12, 96, 159, 299, 300, 428, 431, 487
God, 103, 105–109, 111, 112, 115, 118–121, 137–139, 142, 224, 302, 304–309, 311, 312, 391, 392, 395, 396, 398–400, 402–404, 423, 424, 426–429, 431–433, 473, 475, 477, 478, 480, 491, 503, 505, 511–513, 515, 516, 573, 579
Goddesses, 475, 477, 480, 491
Gold Coast Ex-Servicemen's Union, 249
Gold Coast Muslim Association (GCMA), 190
Gold Coast Muslim Council (GCMC), 190
Good, 423, 425–427, 432
Gordon, Lewis, 283, 284, 286
Governance, 231–234, 236–243, 347, 351
Gowon, Yakubu, 210
Gupta family, 372, 376–378
Gyekye, Kwame, 5, 105, 118, 157, 423–433, 443, 444, 446–448

H

Hampate Ba, Ahmadou, 572
Haram, Boko, 393, 400
Harlem Renaissance, 260
Healthcare, 359
Hegel, 550
Herder, Gottfried, 462
Heritage, 474, 483
Hermeneutics, 300, 309–311, 611
Hertzog, James, 593
Heterosexual gospel, 77–80
Highlife, 414, 417
History, 474–479, 481, 483, 488, 489, 493
HIV/AIDS, 417, 419
Holy Spirit, 308–310
Homosexuality/homosexual, 28, 32–33
Hospitality, 457, 458
Hountondji, Paulin, 437–448
House of Chiefs, 240–242
Humanism, 105, 258, 262, 265–272, 289, 291, 292, 319, 330
Humanity, 263, 264, 268, 276n40, 284–288, 290–292, 606, 612, 615, 617
Human Rights Watch (HRW), 502
Hybridity, 412, 416, 459, 461
Hybridization, 548, 549

I

Identity/identities, 27, 95–97, 100, 101, 453–466, 468–471, 474, 477, 481, 487, 494, 495, 527, 530, 532, 544, 548, 549, 556, 557, 605, 607, 610–613, 615, 619n14, 619n15, 620n17
Identity politics, 453–455, 459, 471
Ideology, 187, 188, 190–192, 195, 196, 340, 347, 360, 361, 363
Ifa, 477, 478, 480, 573, 575
Ifalogy, 476
Igbo, 569, 576, 577, 581–583
Ijala, 571, 573
ìjálá chants, 477
Ike, 576, 582
Imperialism, 12, 317
Inculturation, 614
Independence, 203, 205, 206, 210, 211, 231–236, 239–242, 249, 250, 254
Indigenous, 474–477, 483–487, 489–491, 493–495
Indigenous knowledge systems (IKS), 484, 492, 493
Individual, 147–150, 152–161, 161n1, 162n16, 264–266
Individualism/individualistic, 4, 5, 38, 94, 95, 101, 147–149, 151, 153–158, 160, 161, 428
Individuality, 463, 468
Industrialization, 29, 46n42, 238, 428, 431
Infidelity, 73, 74, 79
Information and Communication Technology (ICT), 13, 21–23
Interdependence, 103, 121
International Bank for Reconstruction and Development, 341
International Monetary Fund (IMF), 341, 343, 346–354
International Theological Commission, 505
Intolerance, 392–400, 402
ìrèmòjé, 477
Isidore, Sandra, 414
Islam/Islamic, 12, 186–188, 190, 197, 329, 395, 396, 400, 506, 512, 525, 529, 530, 536
ìtàn, 475
I-Thou, 105, 117
I-Thou-Other, 105, 106
Ìwà (character), 174, 325, 326
Iwa-irele (humility of conduct), 175, 179
Iwa-pele (gentleness/moderation in conduct), 176, 179
Iwofa, 57

J

Jazz, 409, 412, 414, 415, 418
Jesus Christ, 306, 308, 312, 543, 544, 548–550, 555, 560–562
"Jesutunde," 543, 544, 548, 549
Johnson, Samuel, 556, 557
Journalist/journalism, 392, 394, 400–405
Judaism, 395, 396, 512, 513
Jus ad bellum, 220–223
Jus in bello, 221, 223

INDEX 629

Justice, 148–150, 152, 155, 157, 158, 204, 206, 209, 212, 286, 288–291, 503, 512, 515, 516, 606, 611, 613

K
Kagamé, Alexis, 440, 443
Kalabari, 107–111, 148, 149, 151–157, 162n5, 162n11, 162n15
Kalakuta Republic, 419
Kane, Cheikh Hamidou, 259, 260
Kantianism, 150
Kavula, 108
Kente, 194
Kenya, 69–87
Keynes, John Maynard, 342
Kgotla, 241, 242
Khama, Seretse, 239
King, Martin Luther Jr., 286
Kingship, 473, 477, 488
Kinship, 34–36, 233, 234, 238, 533, 551
Knowledge, 283, 437–439, 441–445, 473–484, 486–495, 570–572, 575, 577, 579
Kolanuts, 479–481
Kosmopolités, 456, 460
Kpləkotə (well-being), 531
Kudadjie, Joshua, 433

L
Lagos, 411, 412
Lagos Plan of Action, 364
Lama, Dalai, 597, 602n27
Land Use Degree/Land Use Act (1978), 237
Language, 27, 28, 46n52
Laramie, Alhaji Othman Larden, 252
Lawson, Cardinal Rex, 414
Leaders/leadership, 172, 179–181, 185–187, 194, 247–253, 322–324, 372, 373, 378, 405
Legends, 480
Levinas, Emmanuel, 290–292
LGBTQ+, 599, 600
Libation, 303, 304
Liberal humanism, 467–469, 471
Liberalism, 467, 468
Liberation, 413, 419, 613

Library, 473, 474, 480, 491
Libya Civil War, 203
Life principle, 107–111, 431
Lineage, 30, 34–37
Loan, 344, 351–354, 359, 360, 362–364
Lobitos, Koola, 414
Local capture, 374
Lotus-self, 159, 160
Love, 149–152, 154, 155, 158
Lynch, Willie, 321–323, 331

M
Machiavelli/Machiavellianism, 248, 254
Mai-Mai, 217–220, 222–227
Maimane, Mmusi, 377
Makwerekwere, 598
Malcolm X, 414
Mandela, Nelson, 269, 289, 595
"Man-the-hunter" theory, 31
Margalit, Avishai, 465
Marriage, 12, 19, 20, 29, 31, 34–37, 39, 42, 44, 45n28, 70–75, 77–79, 81–83, 85, 86, 116, 430, 431, 434n41
Masculine Christianity, 77–80, 86–87
Masculine/masculinity, 72–74, 77–80, 552
Mayebe, Father S., 377
Mbiti, John, 130, 138, 139, 443, 444, 446–448, 543, 574, 575
Meaning, 27, 28, 40, 93–101
Media, 391–405
Menkiti, Ifeanyi, 130, 135, 137
Mensah, E.T., 414
Meritism, 155
Michels, Robert, 327, 328
Mill, J. S., 467
Ministry of Repentance and Holiness (MRH), 84–85
Mngxitama, Andile, 378, 379
Modernity, 299, 300, 412, 416, 420, 474, 475, 484, 487, 495, 607, 614
Modernization, 11, 12, 20, 22, 71, 96, 187, 194, 251, 495
Momoh, Campbell Shittu, 394
Monistic pluralism (MP), 167–171, 173, 174, 178, 179, 181
Monogamy/monogamois, 33

Moral accountability, 502, 503, 505, 508, 510, 513, 516
Moral compass, 610–612, 616
Moral education, 515
Moralistic activism, 553
Morality, 105, 110, 112, 247, 285, 288, 291, 292, 423, 425–433, 464–466, 502–506, 508–510, 512, 513, 515, 516, 589, 590, 595, 597, 601n6, 607, 609, 610
Moral modeling, 589–601
Moral philosophy, 147, 160, 225
Moral responsibility, 437–440, 444, 445, 448, 502, 503, 506, 508–510, 515, 516
Mother Earth, 302–304
Motherhood, 70–73, 76
Mphahleles, Ezekiel, 258
Multivocality, 459
Museum, 473, 480, 481
Museveni, Yoweri, 204
Music, 409, 410, 412–415, 417–419
Muslim Association Party, 249
"My mother," 147–161
Mystical warfare, 222, 223, 225–227
Myth, 437, 438, 440–442, 446
Mythic onomastics, 550
Mythologies, 475, 478, 480, 482

N
Name, 543–562
Naming, 543–554, 556, 557, 559, 561, 562
Naretology, 394
Narration, 455, 458
Natasha, Lucy (Reverend), 83
National Association for the Education of Young Children (NAEYC), 14, 15
National identity, 457, 458, 461, 466, 469, 470
Nationalism, 273, 455–462, 464
Nationalities, 318, 319, 323, 329
National Liberation Movement (NLM), 249, 250
National Party of Nigeria (NPN), 236
Nation-building, 186, 248, 318, 329
Nationhood, 288
Nations, 186, 187, 192, 196, 247–249, 251

Nation-states, 231–235, 318, 321, 323–325, 329–331, 455, 458, 462, 464
Negritude, 257–262, 264, 266, 268, 272, 287, 575, 585n23
Negro, 258–265, 268, 270
Neighbourliness, 167–182
Neo-liberal/neoliberalism, 340, 361, 374, 554
Neo-patrimonialism, 231, 233
Nepotism, 317–331
News, 392–394, 401, 402
Nigeria, 232, 235–239, 243, 372, 379–383, 385
Nigeria-Biafra War, 215n30, 237
Nkandla project, 508
Nkrumah, Kwame, 185–198, 247–254, 257, 264, 266, 419, 420, 475, 495n2
Nkrumaism, 187, 188
Nnewi, 238
Non-violence, 285
North Atlantic Treaty Organization (NATO), 206
Northern People's Congress (NPC), 236
Northern People's Party, 249
Nyansa, 424, 425
Nyerere, Julius, 257, 264, 420, 531

O
Obasanjo, Olusegun, 381, 417
Obligation, 129, 130, 132–138, 141, 142
Obote, Milton, 203, 204
Occasional state capture, 374
Ochola-Adolwa, Linda (Pastor), 77, 85–86
Ochonu, Moses, 4
Oduyoye, Mercy Amba, 605–618
Office of the Public Protector, 502
Ogbanje, 551, 553, 554, 560
Ogboni, 570, 584n4
Ogundiran, Akin, 478
Ojigbani, Chris (Pastor), 80–83
Ojukwu, Emeka, 209
Ojú-oórì (the cemetery), 481
Okigbo, Christopher, 583
Okonkwo, 304, 305
Olaiya, Victor, 414

Oligarchy, 327
Olodumare, 173
Olokun, 582
Omo ilé, 34
Omoluabi, 175, 177
Omoluwabi, 318–321, 324, 325, 330, 484
Onitsha, 238
Onomastics, 544, 547, 549–551, 554, 556, 561
Ontological principle, 109
Ontology, 107, 109, 110, 138–141, 260–263, 265, 266, 270, 272
Onyansafo (wise person), 424
Openness, 455, 469–471
Oppression, 285–287
Orality, 477, 573
Oral tradition, 439–440
Organization, 323, 324, 327, 328
Organization of African Unity (OAU), 270
Òrìṣànlá, 477
Orisha, 420, 559, 560
Orógbó, 480
Oro-rere (good words), 175–176, 179
Orphée Noir, 258
Oruka, Henry Odera, 592–593
Orunmila, 485
Osagyefo, 193, 194
Ọ̀sun, 477, 480
Otabil, Mensa (Pastor), 310, 311
Other, 290, 291, 455, 460, 470
òwe, 485

P
Pan-Africanism, 267, 268, 409, 419, 420
Parenthood, 32, 33
Parent/parenting, 11–14, 17, 19, 20, 22, 28, 30, 32, 33, 35, 36
Parker, Charlie, 418
Partiality/impartiality, 465, 466
Partial state capture, 374
Party state capture, 374
Patriarchy/patriarchal, 69–87, 532, 605, 610, 612, 613, 615–617
Patriotism, 460, 467, 471
Patriots, 453–471
Pawning, 57

Peace, 168, 170, 174–178, 182, 392, 403–405
Pentecostal churches, 77, 82, 86
Pentecostalism/pentecostal, 77, 79, 81, 82, 86, 545, 548–550, 555, 557
Peonage, 57, 58
People's Democratic Party (PDP), 382
Perebo-kalakeibari, 155, 156
Performances, 473, 475, 480, 482, 490, 494, 544–550, 553–555, 562
Person, 93–101, 103–121, 125n78, 130, 131, 133, 135, 136, 141, 142, 148–153, 155, 157, 160
Personality, 108, 109, 112, 113, 115, 120, 121
Personhood, 94, 96, 103–121, 129–137, 141, 148, 158, 159, 292, 319, 321, 591, 595, 600, 602n23, 608, 612, 614, 617
Philosopher, 438–441, 446
Philosophic sagacity, 593
Philosophy, 1, 2, 4, 424, 425, 427, 437–448, 473, 474, 476–479, 481, 482, 485, 486, 489
Phronesis, 590
Pidgin, 416
Plato, 97, 99–101, 424, 432
Pluralism, 167–182, 189, 195, 196
Pluriversalism, 487–489
Poetry, 476, 480
Political ethics, 247–254, 257–273, 283–292
Political philosophy, 247
Political religion, 192, 196
Politics, 185–198, 232, 233, 236, 239–241, 243, 248, 251, 283, 284, 286, 288, 289, 292, 343, 345, 350, 352, 364, 371, 372, 374
Polity, 2, 3, 5
Polyandry, 33
Polygamy/polygamous, 33, 35, 36
Polygyny, 70, 72, 74
Positive Action, 192, 193
Postmodern/postmodernism, 27
Poverty, 55–58, 62, 345–347, 354, 356, 357, 360, 362, 363, 501–503, 507, 508, 510, 598
Powell, Bud, 418

Power, 27–29, 39–44, 247–253, 473, 475, 477, 478, 481, 482, 484, 487–490, 493–495
Praxis, 606, 607, 611, 613, 615, 618, 618n3
"Praying for husband," 69–87
Predatory state capture, 374
Pregnancy, 71–73
Premarital sex, 430, 431
Preventive Detention Act (PDA), 252
"Prière de Paix" (Prayer for Peace), 258
Primordial public, 233
Privatization, 318, 330–331, 354, 358, 361, 362
Probity, 502–506, 510, 512–516
Professionalism, 310
Progressive Pentecostalism, 308, 309
Prosperity gospel, 308–311
Proverbs, 38, 118, 119, 153, 154, 156, 476, 477, 485

R
Rabaka, Reiland, 258
Race, 28, 32, 42, 44, 461, 462, 468
Racism, 483, 493
Radical empathy, 289–292
Ransome-Kuti, Funmilayo, 410, 413
Ransome-Kuti, I.O. (Reverend), 410
Rationality, 478, 479, 495
Reality, 134, 137, 138, 140–142
Reason, 291
Re-incarnation, 543, 544
Relationality, 152–154, 156, 169, 170, 173–181, 225–226, 617
Religion, 3, 5, 28, 185–198, 205, 248, 251, 253, 299–312, 317, 324, 326, 327, 329, 391–405, 423, 425, 427–430, 432, 433, 502, 503, 505, 506, 510–513, 516, 525–536, 597
Religious experience, 391–393, 402, 403
Reproductive futurism, 547
Republic of Biafra, 210
Republic of China, 211
Research, 476, 478, 479, 484, 489–494
Resistance, 40–44
Resource theory, 42
Responsibility, 131–137, 141, 142, 290, 291, 321, 323, 324, 330

Revolution, 595, 600
Rights, 129–137, 142
Ritual archives, 473–495
Romanticism, 445, 461
Roosevelt, Franklin, 341
Rosevere, Reginald Richard (Bishop), 190, 251, 252

S
Sagacity, 590, 592, 593, 596–598, 600
Sakawa, 300
Santeria, 480
Sarpong, Bishop Peter, 432, 433
Sartre, Jean-Paul, 289, 291, 292
Scholarship, 486–488, 494
Science, 473, 474, 478, 481, 487
Secularism, 189, 395, 396, 398
Secularization, 396–399
Self, 160, 167, 169–178, 181, 182, 182n5, 285, 454, 455, 461, 463–465, 470, 556, 571, 572, 576
"Self-Government Now!," 249
Selfhood, 608
Self-making, 547
Senghor, Léopold Sédar, 103, 257–273
Serer, 264, 266–268, 271
Shadow concept, 109
Sharia, 395, 398, 400
"Shuffering and Shmiling," 413
Sikaduro, 300
Single/singlehood, 69–74, 76–87
Single women, 69–87
Sociability, 463
Social activism, 409, 416
Social change, 396, 399, 400
Social ethics, 1, 2, 4, 5, 147, 148, 150, 151, 317–321, 324–325, 329–331, 333n4, 589, 590, 600, 601
Socialism, 103
Sociality, 3, 4, 608, 609, 612–617
Socialization, 28, 29, 38, 39, 46n48
Social justice, 410, 525–536
Social media, 392, 401, 402
Social morality, 501–516
Social responsibility, 404, 405
Society, 231–243, 547, 550–557, 559, 562
Solidarity, 288–290, 423, 426, 428, 454, 464

INDEX 633

Songs, 476, 480, 481, 485, 490
South Africa, 372, 377, 379, 453, 454, 501, 502, 504, 506–509, 512, 590, 591, 593, 594, 596, 598, 599
Sovereignty, 457, 458
Soviet Union, 209, 211, 212
Soyinka, Wole, 258, 264, 269, 272, 273, 571, 579
Special Drawing Right (SDR), 351–353
Spirit, 299–312, 543–562
Spiritual and moral energies, 3
Spirituality, 220, 225, 226, 300, 306, 476, 480, 575, 580, 581, 606
Spiritual lifeworld, 220, 222
Stabilisation, 346, 358, 359
State, 231–243, 371–385, 457–459, 463, 467
State capture, 371–385
Statecraft, 247
State power, 373–375, 384
State-society relations, 232, 234, 236–239, 242
Statism, 231
Stoicism, 461
Stories, 477, 480, 481, 488, 490, 492
Storytelling, 11, 18, 20
Strangers, 453–471
Structural adjustment programme (SAP), 357–363
Subjectivity, 159, 455, 548, 555
Sudan, 203
Sunsum, 108, 109, 424, 425, 431
Superpower ethics, 208, 209
Superpowers, 203–213
Supreme Being, 106–109, 111–115, 119, 301, 302, 304, 423–425, 429, 431–433, 616, 617
Susuma, 112, 113
Syncretism, 393, 614
Systemic capture, 374
Systems of knowledge, 1

T
Taboos, 427, 430
Tabula rasa, 260, 262, 268, 270
Tamakloe, B. E. A., 249
Technology, 513, 514
Teme (soul), 109, 111, 157

Terror, 217, 219, 221
Te Whāriki practices, 21
Text, 473, 477–484, 486, 487, 489, 490, 492, 495
Theology, 605–608
Things Fall Apart, 118, 259, 304, 398, 550–552
Togoland Congress, 249
Tolerance, 468
Tombo (person), 157
Toure, Sekou, 261, 420
Toward the African Revolution, 287
Trade liberalization, 354
Traditions, 103, 104, 106, 121, 122n1, 124n72, 412, 416, 420, 438–441, 443–448, 474, 477, 479, 483, 486, 488, 490, 494, 525, 529–531, 536, 545, 546, 549, 550, 561, 562
Transparency International (TI), 502
Trans-religious, 186, 194, 200n48
Tribal Land Act (1968), 242
Trinity College of Music, 414
Trump, Donald, 453
Truth, 391, 392, 395, 401–405, 438, 439, 442, 445–447
Truthfulness, 401, 402, 404
Tutu, Desmond, 286, 319, 321, 589–601
"Two-souls thesis," 462

U
Ubuntu, 110, 111, 123n39, 131, 134, 135, 318–321, 325, 330, 428, 532, 589–601
Ujamaa, 131, 531
Umuntu, 110, 111
United Gold Coast Convention (UGCC), 194, 197, 249, 250
United Nations International Children's Emergency Fund (UNICEF), 13, 14, 23
United Nations Mission in Congo (MONUC), 219
United Nations Monetary and Financial Commission Conference, 340
United States of America, 206, 209, 211
Unity Party of Nigeria (UPN), 236
Universal human rights, 457

Universalism, 457, 460, 461, 465, 468, 476, 487, 495
University, 473, 489, 490, 493
"Unknown Soldier," 417
Urbanization, 71, 72, 428

V

Values, 11–14, 18–20, 22, 23, 456, 464, 465, 467, 469, 470
"A Verandah Boy's Creed," 193
Vernacular epistemologies, 483
Violence, 51, 54, 57, 58, 62, 64, 71, 72, 74–76, 79, 167, 169, 219–221, 227, 283–289, 292, 474, 475, 494
Vital force, 95, 107, 109, 110, 137, 225–227
Volksgeist, 462, 463

W

War, 203, 204, 206–213, 217–227
Warfare, 217–227
Wariboko, Nimi, 107–111, 115–117, 120, 212, 309–312, 330, 331, 526, 530, 550, 554, 555
Wenger, Susanne, 576, 579
Western academy, 476, 495
Weston, Randy, 409
White, Harry Dexter, 342, 343
Widowhood, 71
Williams, Eric Eustace, 475
Wilson Vwende wa Mutompa Kalunga, 220
Wiredu, Kwasi, 107–110, 117–119, 423–433, 438, 448
Witchcraft, 51, 59–62
Witchcraft accusations, 51, 52, 58–62, 64
"Woman-the-gatherer" theory, 31
Women, 605–607, 612, 613, 615–618
Wordsworth, William, 579, 580
World Health Organization (WHO), 22
World Trade Organization (WTO), 354
The Wretched of the Earth, 286, 287, 289

X

Xenophobia, 454

Y

Yai, Olabiyi Babalola, 575, 581
Yar'Adua, Shehu, 417
"Yellow Fever," 413
Yemoja, 477
Yoruba, 37–39, 44, 46n46, 46n52, 167–182, 318–320, 324, 325, 329, 330, 410, 414–416, 475, 476, 480, 484, 485, 543, 544, 547, 548, 550, 551, 556, 557, 559–561, 570, 571, 573–575, 581, 582, 610, 615, 616
Yoruba cosmology, 575, 576

Z

Zerosumness, 153, 157
Zulu, Paulus, 503, 504, 507
Zuma, Jacob, 372, 376–379, 508

Printed in the United States
by Baker & Taylor Publisher Services